THE PAPERS OF

WOODROW WILSON

VOLUME 40

NOVEMBER 20, 1916–JANUARY 23, 1917

SPONSORED BY THE WOODROW WILSON
FOUNDATION
AND PRINCETON UNIVERSITY

The Happy Warrior

THE PAPERS OF

WOODROW WILSON

ARTHUR S. LINK, *EDITOR*

DAVID W. HIRST, *SENIOR ASSOCIATE EDITOR*

JOHN E. LITTLE, *ASSOCIATE EDITOR*

FREDRICK AANDAHL, *ASSOCIATE EDITOR*

PHYLLIS MARCHAND AND MARGARET D. LINK,
EDITORIAL ASSISTANTS

Volume 40
November 20, 1916–January 23, 1917

PRINCETON, NEW JERSEY
PRINCETON UNIVERSITY PRESS
1982

Note to scholars: Princeton University Press
subscribes to the Resolution on Permissions of
the Association of American University Presses,
defining what we regard as "fair use" of copyrighted works. This Resolution, intended to encourage scholarly use of university press publications and to avoid unnecessary applications
for permission, is obtainable from the Press or
from the A.A.U.P. central office. Note, however,
that the scholarly apparatus, transcripts of
shorthand, and the texts of Wilson documents
as they appear in this volume are copyrighted,
and the usual rules about the use of copyrighted materials apply.

Publication of this book has been aided by a
grant from the National Historical Publications
and Records Commission.

Printed in the United States of America
by Princeton University Press
Princeton, New Jersey

INTRODUCTION

THE opening of this volume finds Wilson basking in the afterglow of his reelection and in the midst of preparations for what would be the most important initiative in his political career to this point—his independent mediation of the European war. As a preliminary step, he persuades the Federal Reserve Board to warn American bankers of the dangers of continuing to purchase renewable short-term Allied notes. Wilson's move threatens the very continuance of the Allied war effort because the British have virtually exhausted their dollar reserves; however, Wilson is simply putting the screws on the British and French in this reminder of his ability to force them to come to the peace table.

Wilson, on November 25, 1916, completes the first draft of a note which describes the terrors of the war and its threat to the fabric of civilization and invites the belligerents to a conference for a frank discussion of peace terms. Then two dramatic events stay Wilson's hand temporarily. One is the German government's deportation of thousands of Belgians for work in Germany, which sets off an international hue and cry and an outbreak of anti-German sentiment throughout the United States. The second is the dispatch from Berlin on December 12 of an invitation to the enemies of Germany to come to the peace table. This independent German move raises the danger that the Allies might think that Wilson is cooperating with the Germans if he sends his own peace note at some time in the near future.

But Wilson grasps the nettle danger and sends his own appeal to all the belligerents on December 18. Upon the insistent advice of House and Lansing, Wilson eliminates his suggestion of an early peace conference; however, his call for a frank avowal of peace terms and his statement that the United States might have to reexamine its own policies of neutrality in the light of the replies to his request is a clear warning that Wilson is determined to bring the war to an early end if possible.

The British and French are aghast at and infuriated by what they think is clear proof that Wilson is supporting the German demand for a peace conference at a time when the Germans hold most of the bargaining chips. Lansing sets out to allay their fears and to torpedo Wilson's move. The Secretary of State issues a statement to the press in which he says that the United States is drawing to "the verge of war" (by implication) on the Allied side. Privately, Lansing assures the British and French governments that Wilson is on their side. Moreover, in an apparent effort to tilt the balance in Germany in favor of the hardliners who are pressing for an all-out submarine campaign which will surely force the United States into the war, Lansing even suggests the specific terms to be embodied in the Allied reply to Wilson— terms which can be won only by a smashing defeat of Germany. House, too, rushes to assure the British and French that Wilson is simply paving the way for American entry into the war on their side. The Allies reply as Lansing had suggested; the Germans tell Wilson that they cannot divulge their terms, which are moderate, until a peace conference actually convenes.

Undaunted, Wilson makes plans to set in motion top-secret negotiations with Great Britain and Germany. Wilson also begins secret negotiations with the Swiss government looking toward Swiss-American cooperation for peace. All the while, he works on a state paper which will tell the world the kind of a peace settlement which the American people will be willing to support and help to enforce through a postwar league of peace. As this volume ends, Wilson embodies this statement in his "Peace without Victory" address to the Senate—and the world —on January 22, 1917.

Meanwhile, the sessions of the Mexican-American Joint High Commission grind on in futility on account of Carranza's refusal to sign any protocol for the protection of the Mexican-American border until the last American soldier has left Mexican soil. The Joint High Commission adjourns *sine die* on January 15, and Wilson begins a withdrawal of Pershing's force which is complete soon after this volume ends.

"VERBATIM ET LITERATIM"

In earlier volumes of this series, we have said something like the following: "All documents are reproduced *verbatim et literatim*, with typographical and spelling errors corrected in square brackets only when necessary for clarity and ease of reading." The following essay explains our textual methods and review procedures.

We have never printed and do not intend to print critical, or corrected, versions of documents. We print them exactly as they are, with a few exceptions which we always note. We never use the word *sic* except to denote the repetition of words in a document; in fact, we think that a succession of *sics* defaces a page.

We usually repair words in square brackets when letters are missing. As we have said, we also repair words in square brackets for clarity and ease of reading. Our general rule is to do this when we, ourselves, cannot read the word without stopping to determine its meaning. Jumbled words and names misspelled beyond recognition of course have to be repaired. We correct the misspelling of a name in the footnote identifying the person.

However, when an old man writes to Wilson saying that he is glad to hear that Wilson is "comming" to Newark, or a semiliterate farmer from Texas writes phonetically, we see no reason to correct spellings in square brackets when the words are perfectly understandable. We do not correct Wilson's misspellings unless they are unreadable, except to supply in square brackets letters missing in words. For example, for some reason he insisted upon spelling "belligerent" as "belligerant." Nothing would be gained by correcting "belligerant" in square brackets.

We think that it is very important for several reasons to follow the rule of *verbatim et literatim.* Most important, a document has its own integrity and power, particularly when it is not written in a perfect literary form. There is something very moving in seeing a Texas dirt farmer struggling to express his feelings in words, or a semiliterate former slave doing the same thing. Second, in Wilson's case it is crucially important to reproduce his errors in letters which he typed himself, since he always typed badly when he was in an agitated state. Third, since style is the essence of the person, we would never correct grammar or make tenses consistent, as one correspondent has urged us to do. Fourth, we think that it is obligatory to print typed documents *verbatim et literatim.* For example, we think that it is very important that we print exact transcripts of Charles L. Swem's copies of Wilson's letters. Swem made many mistakes (we correct them in footnotes from a reading of his shorthand books), and Wilson let them pass. We thus have to assume that Wilson did not read his letters before signing them, and this, we think, is a significant fact. Finally, printing typed letters and documents *verbatim et literatim* tells us a great deal about the educational level of the stenographic profession in the United States during Wilson's time.

We think that our series would be worthless if we produced unreliable texts, and we go to some effort to make certain that the texts are authentic.

Our typists are highly skilled and proofread their transcripts carefully as soon as they have typed them. The Editor sight proofreads documents once he has assembled a volume and is setting its annotation. The Editors who write the notes read through documents several times and are careful to check any anomalies.

Then, once the manuscript volume has been completed and all notes checked, the Editor and Senior Associate Editor orally proofread the documents against the copy. They read every comma, dash, and character. They note every absence of punctuation. They study every nearly illegible word in written documents.

Once this process of "establishing the text" is completed, the manuscript volume goes to our editor at Princeton University Press, who checks the volume carefully and sends it to the printing plant. The volume is set by linotype by a typographer who has been working on the Wilson volumes for years. The galley proofs go to the proofroom, where they are read orally against copy. And we must say that the proofreaders at the Press are extraordinarily skilled. Some years ago, before we found a way to ease their burden, they used to query every misspelled word, absence of punctuation, or other such anomalies. Now we write "O.K." above such words or spaces on the copy.

We read the galley proofs three times. Our copyeditor gives them a sight reading against the manuscript copy to look for remaining typographical errors and to make sure that no line has been dropped. The Editor and Senior Associate Editor sight read them against documents and copy. We then get the page proofs, which have been corrected at the Press. We check all the changes three times. In addition, we get *revised* pages and check them twice.

This is not the end. Our indexer of course reads the pages word by word. Before we return the pages to the Press, she comes in with a list of queries, all of which are answered by reference to the documents.

Our rule in the Wilson Papers is that our tolerance of error is zero. No system and no person can be perfect. We are sure that there are errors in our volumes. However, we believe that we have done everything humanly possible to avoid error; the chance is remote that what looks at first glance like a typographical error is indeed an error.

We here take note of the request of Katharine E. Brand to become a member emeritus of the Editorial Advisory Committee, and we acquiesce in her request with regret tempered by affectionate gratitude. Miss Brand was Ray Stannard Baker's research assistant while he wrote *The Life and Letters*. She then became Mrs. Wilson's literary adviser and curator of the Wilson Papers; afterward, she was head of the Recent Manuscripts Section in the Manuscript Division of the Library of Congress. She has been a member of the Editorial Advisory Committee since its formation and, over the years, she has been a faithful and loyal member whose advice and support have contributed greatly to the ongoing work of *The Papers of Woodrow Wilson*. We will continue to seek her advice and to enjoy her enthusiasm and friendship.

We are delighted to welcome Professor Betty Miller Unterberger of Texas A & M University as Miss Brand's successor on the committee. We look forward to many years of happy association with Professor Unterberger.

We express our gratitude to Professors John Milton Cooper, Jr., William H. Harbaugh, and Richard W. Leopold for their careful reading of the manuscript of this volume and to Judith May, our editor at Princeton University Press. Our special thanks go to Anne Cipriano Venzon and Manfred F. Boemeke, our two editorial assistants, who have rendered invaluable help during the past years.

THE EDITORS

Princeton, New Jersey
February 22, 1982

CONTENTS

Collateral Materials

ABBREVIATIONS

ALI	autograph letter initialed
ALS	autograph letter signed
ASB	Albert Sidney Burleson
ASBhw	Albert Sidney Burleson handwriting, handwritten
CC	carbon copy
CCL	carbon copy of letter
CCLS	carbon copy of letter signed
CLS	Charles Lee Swem
CLSsh	Charles Lee Swem shorthand
CLST	Charles Lee Swem typed
EAW	Ellen Axson Wilson
EBG	Edith Bolling Galt
EBW	Edith Bolling Wilson
EBWhw	Edith Bolling Wilson handwriting, handwritten
EMH	Edward Mandell House
FKL	Franklin Knight Lane
FR	*Papers Relating to the Foreign Relations of the United States*
FR-WWS 1916	*Papers Relating to the Foreign Relations of the United States, 1916, Supplement, The World War*
Hw, hw	handwriting, handwritten
HwC	handwritten copy
HwCL	handwritten copy of letter
HwCLS	handwritten copy of letter signed
HwLS	handwritten letter signed
HwS	handwritten signed
JPT	Joseph Patrick Tumulty
JRT	Jack Romagna typed
MS	manuscript
MSS	manuscripts
NDB	Newton Diehl Baker
RG	record group
RL	Robert Lansing
T	typed
TC	typed copy
TCL	typed copy of letter
TCLS	typed copy of letter signed
TI	typed initialed
TL	typed letter
TLI	typed letter initialed
TLS	typed letter signed
TS	typed signed
WHP	Walter Hines Page
WW	Woodrow Wilson
WWhw	Woodrow Wilson handwriting, handwritten
WWhwLI	Woodrow Wilson handwritten letter initialed
WWsh	Woodrow Wilson shorthand

WWT   Woodrow Wilson typed
WWTL   Woodrow Wilson typed letter
WWTLI   Woodrow Wilson typed letter initialed
WWTLS   Woodrow Wilson typed letter signed

ABBREVIATIONS FOR COLLECTIONS
AND REPOSITORIES

Following the National Union Catalog of the Library of Congress

AFL-CIO-Ar   American Federation of Labor-Congress of Industrial Organizations Archives
AGO   Adjutant General's Office
AzU   University of Arizona
CtY   Yale University
CSmH   Henry E. Huntington Library
DARC   American National Red Cross
DLC   Library of Congress
DNA   National Archives
FFM-Ar   French Foreign Ministry Archives
FO   British Foreign Office
GFO-Ar   German Foreign Office Archives
MH-Ar   Harvard University Archives
NjP   Princeton University
NN   New York Public Library
OClW   Case Western Reserve University
PRO   Public Record Office
PSC-Hi   Swarthmore College, Friends Historical Library
RSB Coll., DLC   Ray Stannard Baker Collection of Wilsoniana, Library of Congress
SDR   State Department Records
ViU   University of Virginia
WC, NjP   Woodrow Wilson Collection, Princeton University
WDR   War Department Records
WHi   State Historical Society of Wisconsin
WP, DLC   Woodrow Wilson Papers, Library of Congress

SYMBOLS

[Dec. 5, 1916]   publication date of a published writing; also date of document when date is not part of text
[*Jan. 16, 1917*]   composition date when publication date differs
[[Nov. 27, 1916]]   delivery date of speech if publication date differs

* * *   * * * *   text deleted by author of document

THE PAPERS OF

WOODROW WILSON

VOLUME 40
NOVEMBER 20, 1916–JANUARY 23, 1917

THE PAPERS OF
WOODROW WILSON

To Newton Diehl Baker

My dear Mr. Secretary: The White House November 20, 1916

In reply to your two letters of November nineteenth let me,

First, thank you for sending me General Bliss' written opinion addressed to General Scott on border control,[1] and to say that he seems to me to be speaking good sense throughout;[2]

And, second, say to you that I agree with you about the advisability of letting General Scott speak his views about compulsory military training as he has spoken them in the report to which you allude.[3] I can see no impropriety in that.

Cordially and faithfully yours,   Woodrow Wilson

TLS (N. D. Baker Papers, DLC).
[1] NDB to WW, Nov. 19, 1916, Vol. 38.
[2] T. H. Bliss to H. L. Scott, Nov. 15, 1916, printed as an Enclosure with *ibid.*
[3] NDB to WW, Nov. 19, 1916, TLS (WP, DLC).

To Louis Freeland Post

My dear Mr. Post: [The White House] November 20, 1916

Thank you warmly for your letter of November sixteenth[1] enclosing the letter you wrote on the evening of November seventh.[2] I have been very much touched by your feeling about the election and want to tell you how sincerely and deeply I thank you for your estimate of what I have been trying to do.

Cordially and sincerely yours,   Woodrow Wilson

TLS (Letterpress Books, WP, DLC).
[1] L. F. Post to WW, Nov. 16, 1916, Vol. 38.
[2] Printed as an Enclosure in *ibid.*

To Ralph Pulitzer

My dear Mr. Pulitzer: [The White House] November 20, 1916

In looking back over the campaign one of the things most prominent in my mind is my deep gratification at the support given me by the World. I want to express this to you in person and to say how proud I have been to have the support of such men as yourself and the admirable men on the staff of the World.

Cordially and sincerely yours,   Woodrow Wilson

TLS (Letterpress Books, WP, DLC).

To William Frederick (Buffalo Bill) Cody

[The White House]

My dear Colonel Cody: November 20, 1916

Again and again throughout the campaign I heard of the generous support you were giving me and now that the air has cooled and I can return to my desk and to the ordinary course of my thought, I want to give myself the pleasure of sending you a line of warmest appreciation. I hope that sometime I may thank you in person with the real warmth which I feel.

Cordially and sincerely yours,   Woodrow Wilson

TLS (Letterpress Books, WP, DLC).

To Adolph Simon Ochs

My dear Mr. Ochs: [The White House] November 20, 1916

May I not tell you what I hope you know already but what it gives me pleasure to put into words, how deeply I have appreciated the support of the editorial page of the Times? It was most helpful to me, not only in respect of its influence on the public, but also because I daily got useful suggestions from it for my own thought, and I feel that I am very much your debtor.

Cordially and sincerely yours,   Woodrow Wilson

TLS (Letterpress Books, WP, DLC).

From Edward Mandell House

Dear Governor: New York. November 20, 1916.

I saw Mr. Whitehouse, Liberal Member of Parliament,[1] on Saturday and I have just had an interview with Bernstorff.

Whitehouse is a pacifist, is perfectly reliable and is anxious for a move to be made for peace. He gave me as clear an insight into the situation, I think, as it would be possible to get even if I were in England.

When I cornered him and put specific questions I got this

result. He believes if you made an open move for peace at this time it would be taken into the House of Commons for discussion; that it would probably result in a close vote with the pacifists losing. Then would come resignations from the most advanced liberal members of the Government, and their places would be suppl[i]ed by reactionaries. A military dictatorship would probably ensure [ensue], and within the year there would be an overturn of the Government unless they succeeded in making a victorious peace.[2]

Young Carver, who is just back from England, rather confirms what Whitehouse told me except that he thinks that a move for peace by the first of January, after this Somme offensive has been tried out, might be successful. He has been to the front and believes that the soldiers there are almost unanimous for peace.

Whitehouse told me that there was no deep-seated feeling in England against America, but quite the contrary. When asked why the English Government tried to create this impression, he said it was for the purpose of getting us into the war—something which he believes would be in the nature of a calamity. He sees, as all clear sighted men see, that the salvation of the situation is in our neutrality.

Carver tells me that the feeling is worse in England than it was when I was there last spring. He had a talk with Northcliffe who deprecates it, and is undertaking by a series of articles, suggested by Carver, to change it.

Carver is very antagonistic to Page and attributes what feeling there is against us to what he terms Page's spineless policy. He says that Northcliffe told him we might as well have a jellyfish represent us. The last time I talked with Northcliffe he did not feel this way, but spoke in warm terms of Page, so I am wondering how far Carver's prejudice has influenced the stories he tells.

I had a satisfactory talk with Bernstorff. I told him that we were on the ragged edge, and brought to his mind the fact that no more notes could be exchanged, that the next move was to break off diplomatic relations. He appreciates this and will urge his Government again to be more careful. He says they will make an apology and reparation for the Marina, and believes this will be forthcoming tomorrow or next day.

I gave him your message that you intended to move for peace at the first opportunity. He said that peace was on the floor waiting to be picked up. He does not believe a belligerent government could refuse to parley, particularly since Germany is willing to evacuate both France and Belgium, and any refusal to negotiate would be an admission that they were continuing the war for conquest.

Bernstorff is thoroughly alive to the danger of the situation, and what the participation of this country in the war would mean and we can count upon his doing everything possible to prevent it.

In this connection I want to say that I have indisputable evidence that Bernstorff used in a quiet way what influence he could bring to bear in favor of your re-election. I did not get this from him either directly or indirectly.

If you desire to discuss the situation with me personally I will come down any time, for we now have a better understanding of it than we had last week.

Affectionately yours,   E. M. House

TLS (WP, DLC).
1 John Howard Whitehouse, former parliamentary private secretary to David Lloyd George, also a prolific writer on educational, social, and political topics.
2 Whitehouse kept a diary of his conversations with House—"The House Report, 14 November 1916 to 14 April 1917," T MS in the Papers of J. Howard Whitehouse, Bembridge School, Isle of Wight. Whitehouse left the following record of the meeting:

"14 [17] November 1916

"Colonel House sent for me today and I had a long interview with him. He had just returned from the President. His communication was delivered with great earnestness.

"He said that England was the only obstacle to peace. The President was ready to act as mediator and, he said 'he can obtain for England everything she is fighting for.'

"He continued: We have had many difficulties with Germany in this connection. There were many hostile influences which had to be overcome. We know the situation there exactly, and there is now no difficulty as to mediation. England alone is the difficulty and she controls both France and Russia.

"He went on to say that the Government of the United States had been quite unneutral in its friendliness to England. It had done everything possible for her—things which had been kept secret from the public and press. Yet notwithstanding this the official and semi-official communications from England were of the most offensive character. There was the latest dispatch from Grey publicly charging the Government with having taken no adequate steps to stop unneutral acts in the States. Other communications which reached the President from England all attempted to persuade him that the English people held America in the utmost contempt and regarded her as a nation of shopkeepers making money out of the war.

"We do not want such money, House continued. All the forces which are hostile to the President in this country are thereby strengthened. The President's only desire is to secure peace and he can do so on terms acceptable to England.

"He went on to point out the folly of the view that the entry of America into the war would help the allies. It would automatically stop the export of any munitions to England, and probably all other things. The submarine warfare would extend to all shipping and England would be in a critical position.

"He was amazed at the attacks on America in official and semi-official circles in the face of what America had done for the allies. The President had even been told that a considerable number of people in England would welcome war with America."

From Joseph Patrick Tumulty

                                         The White House.
Memorandum for the President: November 20, 1916.

Assistant Secretary Phillips of the State Department telephoned that he had been advised by the Swiss Minister[1] that the Minister was in receipt of a cable from his government directing him to request an audience with the President on a matter of immediate importance. The Minister hoped that he might see the President at the President's early convenience.[2]

T MS (WP, DLC).
  [1] That is, Paul Ritter.
  [2] See the memorandum by Ritter printed at Nov. 22, 1916.

From Newton Diehl Baker, with Enclosure

My dear Mr. President: Washington. November 20, 1916.

I beg leave to inclose herewith copies of four resolutions adopted at the annual convention of the National Consumers' League, of which I am President. The first of these resolutions is addressed to you and I was directed by the convention officially to transmit it to you for your consideration.

                    Cordially yours,   Newton D. Baker

TLS (WP, DLC).

                    E N C L O S U R E

Whereas   Congress has conferred the benefit of the 8 hours day
            upon children employed in manufacture, and upon
            men engaged in railroad transportation between
            states, thus affirming its power to regulate the hours
            of labor of wage-earners under the Commerce Clause
            and the General Welfare Clause; therefore
Resolved   that the National Consumers' League respectfully
            suggests that the legislative program of the Adminis-
            tration include a bill to limit to 8 hours in 24 hours
            the working day of women, this bill to embody the
            principle on which the federal child labor bill is based;
            and
Resolved   that a copy of this resolution be forwarded to the
            President and Congress, and to Secretary Wilson.
Whereas   It is in the interest of the health and welfare of the

nation that the working hours of women should be limited to 8 in one day in manufacture; and

Whereas the federal government has limited to these hours the working day of its direct employes both men and women, and of large numbers of its indirect employes engaged through contractors; and

Whereas the government has farther extended the benefits of the 8 hours day to children and to men engaged in interstate transportation; therefore

Resolved that the Council of the National Consumers' League authorizes the Executive Committee to support any bill appropriate to this purpose which may be introduced into Congress during the coming session; and

Resolved that whenever the Executive Committee undertakes the support of a federal 8 hours bill for women it may make itself responsible for one half the salary of Miss Falk,[1] secretary of the Consumers' League of the District of Columbia, this appropriation not to exceed one thousand dollars ($1000.), with the understanding that Miss Falk remain as secretary of that League, and also give whatever time may be necessary to work with Congress in behalf of bills already endorsed by the National Consumers' League together with the proposed 8 hours bill; and

Resolved that whenever the Executive Committee may undertake to support such a bill, a special committee to be known as the 1917 Committee on the Federal Eight Hours Bill for Women shall be created, and the president of the League is hereby requested to appoint a chairman for such committee at that time.

Whereas Any Congressional bill for the 8 hours day and 48 hours week for women can, when enacted, apply only to manufacture and must, therefore, leave to State Legislation wide areas of industry; and

Whereas in only four States and the District of Columbia do women in industry now enjoy the benefits of the 8 hours day by law; and

Whereas forty legislatures will be in session in 1917; therefore

Resolved that we recommend to all the State Leagues that they promote if not an 8 hours bill some measure for a short working day for women in industry, practicable in relation to their existing laws, and that in doing so they correspond with the Committee on legislation of which Miss Josephine Goldmark is Chairman.

Whereas   The Supreme Court of the United States has upheld
          as constitutional the California 8 hours law for wom-
          en;
Whereas   the Congress of the United States has established the
          8 hours day for women wage earners of the District
          of Columbia; and
Whereas   four States have passed 8 hours laws for women; and
Whereas   forty legislatures will be in session and can pass
          similar laws in 1917; therefore,
Resolved that it is the sense of this meeting that we urge the
          men and women here present to promote in their own
          States the passage at the earliest possible date of laws
          based upon the California statute creating the 8 hours
          day and 48 hours working week for women; and
Resolved that we approve the introduction in Congress of a
          Federal 8 hours bill for women, founded on the prin-
          ciples embodied in the federal child labor law.

T MS (WP, DLC).
  [1] That is, Zip S. Falk.

From Charles Richard Crane

Dear Mr President   [New York] November 20 1916

While we, Secretary Houston and I, were in Boston, both Dr
Eliot and Mr Olney put in strong pleas for him to remain in public life. He said that he felt under obligation to his University[1]
and Dr Eliot—who had advised Mr Brookings[2] originally about
the Secretary—told *me* that he would write to Mr Brookings that
the Secretary was very important to the country in the years to
come and hoped that Mr Brookings would make it easy for him
to continue in your service.

I think it would be well for you to ask Mr Brookings to come
to see you and also, *pretty soon*, to have a heart to heart talk with
the Secretary himself. I have seen a good deal of him during and
since the campaign and have been glad to note a distinct growth
in his combative nature, a quality not altogether wanting before.
And I know that he has entire confidence in your program and
would feel loyally bound to give every ounce of his strength to
see that it was carried out. We feel—all of us—that we are very
fortunate in having such a man so near to you.

                    Always devotedly   Charles R. Crane

ALS (WP, DLC).
  [1] That is, Washington University, of which Houston was still the chancellor.
  [2] Robert Somers Brookings, a banker and merchant of St. Louis, chairman
of the board of trustees of Washington University.

A Memorandum by Norman Angell[1]

[c. Nov. 20, 1916]

The discussion of the foreign situation shows sufficiently that the country considers the choice to lay only in one of two courses of action:

To "muddle along" and avoid conflict by maintaining somehow existing relations with Germany, keeping to the position of neutrality, or

To enforce our demands against Germany by war, which would, of course, be war on the side of the Western Allies; diplomatic rupture being the preliminary stage.

These two courses, in popular opinion, exhaust the alternatives.

Yet by neither can America's interests be defended or her present demands secure satisfaction. In joining the Allies America's object would be to make secure American life and trade at sea in wars between other nations. But, however completely Germany may be beaten, America will not know at the end of the war whether those things have been secured or not. If she were fighting for territory she could by her own victory take it. But she is fighting to compel better behavior on the part of the nations in the future; and her entrance into the war if ill-considered or ill-controlled might make international chaos worse, not better. The retention by one or more of America's Allies of such rights as that to use floating mines might, with the cheapening and increased effectiveness of that instrument, make neutral life as insecure in the next war as in this. While the acceptance by America of the interpretation of the law as put forward by the Allies of blockade, contraband, seizure of neutral mails and persons on neutral ships—which the fact of joining the Western powers against Germany would in large measure involve—would undermine neutral right far more seriously than would the acceptance of the German contention that merchant ships, in order to be immune from attack, should not carry guns. To go to war for the right of neutrals to travel on armed ships and to sanction the Allied interpretation of neutral rights would be about equivalent to pulling down the walls of a house for the purpose of fixing a weathercock on the roof.

Merely to maintain the present situation is hardly less stultifying and not likely to be capable of indefinite prolongation. To urge on behalf of such a policy that America is not concerned is to propound an untenable theory that overlooks the obvious condi-

[1] Norman Hapgood wrote on the top of the first page: "by Norman Angell return to Norman Hapgood." Wilson put it in his own personal file.

tion. America is involved whether she will or no. Her citizens are killed, her trade affected, her resources used to influence the war's issue, and resentment incurred because of the rules which she is laying down. It is not a question of whether she is concerned but of what represents her greatest concern. It is hardly indeed a question of whether she will intervene, but what manner of intervention will best subserve her chief ends. Even if we could claim that a prolongation of the present relationship to Germany would not involve a sacrifice of the rights and securities which are in question—for those are very nebulous at the best—it involves at least the risk of recurring humiliation. A situation necessitating that is likely to break down and give place—after an interval of diplomatic non-intercourse,—to a state of war, even though after the war has been fought, America will be no nearer to securing her ends. She will have drifted into it, not because it offered any real solution, but merely as the result of the irritation and humiliation of the present position. As temper rises, as it may, the mere fact that war may be futile and stultifying, leaving the country in a worse position than it was originally, will not prevent our embarking upon it. The country will do so to satisfy its temper, its indignation, its temperamental need for action of some kind.

By only one means can inaction on the one hand, or war of unlimited liability on the other, be avoided: By a general realization of the futility of both courses, and of the possibility of a third less barren one. A third policy would have no chance of securing the necessary support to its enforcement so long as there exists, as there does at present, a widespread impression on the part of one section that the country can perfectly well keep out of it all and avoid entanglements, and on the part of the other section that by going to war America can effectively enforce her claim; a public opinion averse to intervention, not only owing to the literalness of its adherence to the Washingtonian injunction about "entangling alliances," but also because of the fear that entrance into the war on the side of the Allies, even if accompanied by general declarations about the espousal of public right (similar to those made, for instance, by England on entering the war) will in reality be championing, not so much fundamental international right as the ambitions of one European group as against a rival European group.

The disregard of diplomatic precedent and form as well as what may be termed the dramatic element of the suggestion that follows are deliberately designed for the purpose of stimulating public examination of the facts; a re-consideration of accepted ideas—a necessary element in rendering any third course possible, however intrinsically sound it might be otherwise.

It is obvious that the entrance of America into the international policies of Europe would in any case be a step as radical as any taken since she became an independent state, and should be taken, if at all, with a searching of mind on the part of the American people as to their ultimate objects, and be accompanied if only "out of decent respect to the opinion of mankind" by some declaration of such ultimate purpose, some clear formulation of objects and the rights which America claims and supports and the obligations she is prepared to assume with reference to them.

The suggestion here made is that a third course is possible in some such action—its details are capable of variation, as this:

At the moment that the negotiations of Germany over the sinking of merchantmen or any other such detail, reached a deadlock the American Government, for the purpose of raising the whole matter above the plane of the mere detailed interpretation of certain law (shortly, let us hope, to be changed in any case) should make to Germany and to the world a solemn declaration of America's purpose in the dispute and her real relationship to the two combatants.

Such a declaration should set forth that the nature of the American claims which have grown up out of the war is such that the satisfaction of them is dependent in a peculiar sense finally upon re-establishing respect for international right, that both combatants have held that right lightly; that though heretofore America has, following established practice, taken no action save where her direct interest has been affected, the whole course of her own relations with the combatants and the development of the situation which faces all alike shows that only by directing efforts first to the establishment of the rights which are common to all can the particular right of each be safeguarded.

America, therefore, links her particular claims to the defense of certain general rights and abandons her position of strict diplomatic neutrality for the purpose of so doing.

Thus, while not associating herself with all the territorial ambitions of the Allies in the Balkans, Africa and elsewhere, she is ready not only to facilitate the continuance and increase of the material aid furnished by American finance and industry to the Allies, but to add to these forces and associate herself also with any coercive measure of an economic kind which the Allies may adopt until the Teutonic powers shall have accepted as a basis of peace settlement at least the following conditions:

1. The acceptance of the international principles involved in

the American claims as to neutral rights, and that their violation is an unfriendly act towards America whether American life and property are concerned or not.

2. The evacuation of Belgium, France and Servia.

3. The indemnification of Belgium.

4. The appointment of an international commission of inquiry into the violation of the rights of non-combatants on land and sea, with authority to assess damages, and an agreement on German[y]'s part to pay the damages in which she may be cast, and to punish individuals convicted of offences against the laws of war.

5. An agreement to submit all future justiciable causes of dispute to an international court, and non-justiciable causes to a council of inquiry and to submit to at least six months' delay before proceeding to hostilities on such causes on pain of opposition by all other states party to the agreement, Germany to assume reciprocal obligations in the cohersion of any other state that may violate this rule.

On the acceptance of these terms by Germany, America would obligate herself to revert to the status quo ante, and undertake:

A. Not to furnish military or naval aid to Germany's enemies.

B. To become one of the guarantors of the integrity of Belgium.

C. In the event of the creation of a buffer state in Poland, to assist in the maintenance of its inviolability by refusing to allow American citizens to furnish its invader or his allies with supplies of any nature.

D. To support the policy of the open-door in the protectorates and non-self-governing territories of the nations.

E. To enter into reciprocal and mutual undertaking with other nations as to the submission of international disputes to a court of inquiry and as to the enforcement of such decisions by the combined powers, economic and military, by the nations party to the arrangement.

Such a declaration would, of course, put an end to America's neutrality in the dispute. Whether it involved war or even rupture of diplomatic relations would depend upon Germany. It would be quite unlikely to involve war—all Germany's interests would be against that and she of herself could take virtually no effective military action towards it: her armies could not reach ours. She might not even accept it as one involving diplomatic rupture, when we remember the very unusual situations created in this war illustrated in the position of Greece, of Italy, (with reference to Germany), etc.

If this declaration of policy on America's part left Germany's conduct unaffected and she failed to meet either the general or particular demands of America, it would still be open to the United States to organize much more systematically than the position of neutrality makes possible that progressive economic pressure by which Great Britain through her sea power hopes finally to impose the essential demands of the Allies upon Germany. To this end America could:

Offer to settle the whole contraband and blockade dispute with England on the basis of making international that virtual control of the maritime trade of the world which England now exercises. America, that is, would offer not merely to cooperate with Great Britain in preventing Germany securing supplies but would offer also to organize nationally American resources in munitions, supplies, money and credit for the purpose of helping the Allies. The control of international trade necessary for the isolation of Germany would be exercised internationally by the consent of all concerned; not merely of the Allies and the United States but of the merchants of the neutral states (as apart from their governments who would thus avoid the creation of a *casus belli*) as well. American influence in South America would ensure a very large measure of cooperation on the part of the South American republics. The importance of making this world control international instead of a function of British sea power arises not so much from the fact that Britain could not be trusted to exercise it as well and as impartially as an international body, but from the fact that if admitted as a right of Britain it would become the recognized right on future wars of any belligerent—other than Great Britain and on behalf perhaps of very different causes— obtaining command of the sea. But where such right can only be exercised internationally neutrals have some security as to its future employment. By the suggested arrangement two very important results are obtained: (a) The recurring conflict between belligerent need and neutral right which renders more difficult the blockade or siege of Germany and tends to diminish its effectiveness would be avoided since such siege would be accomplished not merely by sea power but by cooperation between the non-German nations of the world as a whole, and (b) A beginning is made with international cooperation for exercising a kind of pressure upon Germany much more far-reaching in its character than that which the mere naval power of one nation, however great, could impose.

For the international bodies organized as prize courts or Boards of Control, made up of representatives of America, Britain, and her colonies, France, Russia, Italy, Belgium, Japan, and, less officially, of the Scandinavian and Balkan States. Holland, Switzerland and Greece, would not deal merely with matters of exports and imports, with trade between the various countries, but with financial arrangements as well—with exchange and credit difficulties, loans, censorship of mails and all the thorny problems that have arisen during the war. From these matters they would naturally proceed to deal with such problems as the disposal of German property—interned ships, businesses of various kinds, royalties on patents, bank balances, etc.—which would involve deciding just how far sequestrated property should be used as a means of indemnifying those directly suffering by damage done by Germany. An international body acting under the authority of an international court might decide that such source of revenue as royalties on German patents throughout the world should be applied to the reimbursement of those who in Belgium or elsewhere had suffered from German confiscation.

Such action would, of course, in turn involve some decision as to future relationship with Germany; the conditions upon which Germany should once more be admitted to the community of nations, whether on equal terms or not, and whether common action by the non-German world in such matters as tariffs, ship and mail dues, etc., might not furnish a means of controlling German action throughout the world and a leverage wherewith to bargain. A threat of commercial exclusion from virtually the whole western world for a decade or a generation in case of a refusal to evacuate Belgium might have more effect in influencing German policy than the threat of continued military pressure.

For if we can assume an international control of the world's wealth (in some such way as that indicated above) having been established for purposes of war and having gone on for some time, there would be a situation in which the channels of trade would for prolonged periods have been turned away from Germany and a situation also in which (for instance) Germany's enemies would control virtually every pound of cotton grown in the world. And when we remember how the close cooperation of war conditions would have cordinated international action and improved its working, we might well have therein the beginnings of the world organization of our common resources—social, economical, and political—for the purpose of dealing with a recalcitrant member of international society by other than purely military means; a starting point whence international law might be made a reality, a code that is not merely expressing the general interest but embodying a means of enforcing respect for it.

The proposal outlined above constitutes not only a departure from American traditions hostile to entanglement in European affairs, as old as American independence, but a departure also from one of the universally accepted principles which heretofore has governed the relations of nations, the principle, namely, that a state has no ground of action against another until its own direct interest is involved. America would in any course of action similar to that proposed base her action upon the plea that her interest is vitally involved in the maintenance of a certain international code of conduct, a general law.

The justification of so revolutionary a change in the older conception of international intercourse should be made clear.

It has already been pointed out that that accomplishment of America's object in the war would depend upon the possibility of creating at its close an international arrangement of such nature that the plain interests of nations will dictate its observance.

This will not be the case, if, at the settlement, nations feel themselves to be menaced by the power of others [(]and so are led to challenge it) or populations, like the Belgian, actually chafe under alien rule.

If international law, or the force it represents, is something which gives a nation no protection against the abuse of the power of others, and is, moreover, something which hampers it in meeting that power, international arrangements will never be observed.

The outstanding fact at the present stage of the war is that both combatants are fighting mainly for security from future abuse of their enemy's power. It is likely, for instance, that the Allies could secure from Germany an undertaking to evacuate Belgium and France; and make some arrangement concerning the erection of Poland into an autonomous or semi-autonomous buffer state; to grant autonomy to Alsace-Lorraine; and make other territorial adjustments. But what the Allies are fighting for in addition to all this is such reduction of German military preponderance that there shall be no possibility of aggression in the future. This declared object of the Allies, "The destruction of Prussian militarism," must of course seem to Germany equivalent to depriving her of self-defence and placing her at the mercy of such potentially powerful rivals as Russia.

If the entrance of America into the war results finally in such successful reduction of German military power that Germany will not be in a position to resist a "punitive" peace, America will be involved in the resentments which the territorial acquisitions of Russia, Italy, Servia, Montenegro, and England may cause, and will be included in the future intrigues of the central power to tilt once more the balance of force in their favor. In the struggle which such an outcome foreshadows, America would in future conflicts be likely to see the lives and trade of her citizens exposed to even greater risks than they have suffered in the present war.

Merely, therefore, to join the Allies, beat Germany and then retire will leave the aims now embodied in American claims where they are, because their attainment depends upon the establishment after the war of some international rule giving promise of stricter observance than in the past; whereas the foundations of international relationships would be as unstable as ever. No nation will put international law before what it deems national preservation. The only hope for international arrangement—rule, treaty, law, what you will—is to identify it with national security; to make it subserve that purpose of securing immunity from the abuse of the rival's power, for which the nations are now fighting. If it could serve the common end of all, it would be worth their support; not otherwise.

But the fundamental principle of international intercourse which America is now by implication supporting, makes it impossible for international right effectively to subserve that common aim of the nations. America says: "Until an American citizen in his life or property is touched we are not concerned." The principle should be the contrary: "We interfere not to champion the American, but the universal rule under which he was entitled to protection, whether an American is the victim or not." The international understanding now is that no nation has ground of action against others, until its own particular interests or rights are violated. Each says in effect to the rest: "However much international right is violated to your detriment we shall not interfere." Thus each is compelled to defend itself against the rest, to base its safety upon rivalry to others. Only by the contrary principle of combination with others for the purpose of defending the common right, and so the individual wronged by the violation of that common right, is it possible to get the effective protection of the individual. Until our basis of action in international affairs is, not first the defense of our rights (or rather our view of our rights, which is sometimes a very different matter) but the defense of the general right, our own particular right will be insecure as the present difficulty of defending American claims abundantly demonstrates it to be.

America at present bases her claims upon a law which the precedent and practice of nations has established. But if she washes her hands of all international acts save those against her citizens, there may grow up as the result of a large number of acts against nations not in a position to resent them, a "practice of nations" so modified in the sense of its disregard of neutral right that in the future the "general practice" will constitute no real protection of any. If, as the result of the immunity which has followed acts like the violation of Belgium, there grows up the impression that a combatant in order to be safe has merely to violate such rights one at a time; and there also grows up the impression that a hard pressed combatant may commit acts like the sinking of the Lusitania and escape penalty because his rival is also violating the law and because no one nation is likely to possess such overpowering force as to deal with both, national rights and international law must necessarily continue to be in practice unobserved.

The principle involved is worth clarification because the whole character of American action, of America's future international policy, of American influence in international affairs, the final outcome of the step America is about to take, will depend upon the decision of America's general opinion as to which of the two contrary methods of action it will most consistently support.

The individual within the state has achieved the protection of his rights only by virtue of a course of action toward others the exact contrary of that which America has heretofore adopted and is still adopting toward other individual nations. The law within the state is worth the individual support because his own security is bound up in it. He contributes to its cost because the community will enforce it for his protection.

Security for the individual is achieved only by making an aggression upon his rights under the law equivalent to an aggression upon the rights of all. A community which remained "neutral" when one of its members was the victim of such aggression, would have surrendered its law and disintegrated into chaos; would be one in which no one could be secure for long.

But that is the prevailing American conception of the community of nations. It is indeed the universal conception of international relationship—of neutrality, the right of intervention, etc.

A violation of the general rule or law is not considered as an aggression against those who have subscribed to it. It is America's position today. She is not concerned in the violation of sea law, say until an American citizen suffers. Until America abandons this principle and stands not only for her own particular right but for the observance of the rule under which the right is claimed, that rule will never be strong enough to protect her particular right.

As we have seen, her own claims are of such nature that they can only be satisfied by the observance of an international arrangement: and yet she declines to assume the position by which alone an international arrangement will become dependable, one that is which it will be to the plain interest of the nations to observe. Merely, therefore, to maintain the present relationship to Germany, or to enter the war and after its successful prosecution to revert to the former international relationship, will be equivalent to the surrender of American claims.

If, however, the policy of the United States were based upon the course of action suggested in this memorandum, such policy would embrace aims that are in one form or another common to both combatants. Each desires, as the object of its war, at least security from the abuse of the power of the other (which may not prevent, of course, it desiring other and perhaps aggressive ends as well); but it is that mainly perhaps for which both are now fighting. The attitude of America would make it more realizable for all.

If such a declaration of purpose cannot be made by the American Government, it should be made by an American party, to the end of presenting dramatically to the mind of the American people the question of the objects for which they are entering this war, and of giving precision to their aims. Without such precision victory may in reality find the American people further from their objective than ever. It may worsen the chaos of mankind and make that humanity and justice of which the President so often speaks as the purpose of American power more remote than ever.

CC MS (WP, DLC).

A News Report

[Nov. 21, 1916]

DISCUSSED NEW ALLIES' LOAN

Was Theme of Davison's Conference at
White House, It Is Admitted.

It was admitted at the White House yesterday that the purpose of the secret conference obtained by H. P. Davison, of J. P. Morgan & Co., with President Wilson last Saturday concerned another huge loan to England and her allies.[1]

Mr. Davison, it is said, desired to learn if this government would approve such a loan without security. He is understood to have repeated the assertion he made in Chicago two weeks ago, that unless the allies were given sufficient money to continue the war successfully, the financial equilibrium of the world would not be maintained.

President Wilson has made no statement concerning the conference, but individuals who have daily access to the White House say he will not oppose the plan. State Department and Treasury officials are already studying the situation.

Mr. Davison is understood to have told President Wilson that his recent investigations in Europe convinced him it was not only necessary but safe to give the allies all the additional money they needed without even a scrap of paper as security.

Printed in the *Washington Post*, Nov. 21, 1916.

[1] Davison, on behalf of J. P. Morgan and Co., had visited Great Britain and France during September and October to investigate financial conditions and discuss their financial needs. He and J. Pierpont Morgan, Jr., had met with the Joint Anglo-French Financial Committee in London from October 3 to October 10. There they learned that the French government had already exhausted its gold and dollar resources and would need £40,000,000 to £50,000,000, in addition to money already promised by the British Treasury, in order to meet France's dollar payments to the United States during the next six months. The British delegates replied that their government was in no position to help the French. Great Britain had spent $1,038,000,000 in the United States from May to September 1916. This outlay had been met three fifths by sale of gold and securities, two fifths by loans. They estimated that British expenditures in the United States, not allowing for any new outlays, would run to a total of $1,500,000,000 during the six months from October 1916 to March 1917. British-owned American securities were now virtually exhausted. The British Treasury could provide perhaps $250,000,000 out of a secret gold reserve. Canada might be able to furnish $100,000,000. If so, $1,150,000,000 would remain to be raised by American loans. The members of the Joint Committee had asked Morgan and Davison whether American banks could supply $1,500,000,000 by March 31, 1917. Morgan replied that he did not see any way to answer that "awful question." Perhaps it would be possible to meet the crisis by temporary bank overdrafts and short-term credits. Both Morgan and Davison thought that it was too risky to try to float a large, unsecured public loan in the United States.

On his return to New York, Davison and other members of the House of Morgan searched for an answer to the impending exchange crisis. The result was a temporary expedient—purchase by American banks of short-term British and French treasury notes that might be renewed over and over. Davison went to Washington on November 18 and presented the plan to members of the Federal Reserve Board. They were not enthusiastic about the proposal, mainly because they had been growing worried about American dependence upon the war trade and had been discussing ways to keep it within reasonable bounds. Davison conferred with Wilson at the White House in the late afternoon of the same day. See Arthur S. Link, *Wilson: Campaigns for Progressivism and Peace, 1916-1917* (Princeton, N. J., 1965), pp. 182-83, 200-201.

To Edward Mandell House, with Enclosures

My dearest Friend,   The White House. 21 November, 1916.

Your letter about your interviews with Whitehouse, Carver, Bernstorff et al. has given me a great deal to think about and has brought at least a ray of light, corroberating in some degree the impression I expressed to you, that this is very nearly the time, if not the time itself, for our move for peace. The enclosed despatches will interest you, I am sure.

I have completed my message to Congress and am just about to sketch the paper I spoke of when you were here. Just so soon as I can give it enough elaboration to make it a real proposal and programme I am going to beg you to come down and we will get at the business in real earnest. I will make the best haste I can consistent with my desire to make it the strongest and most convincing thing I ever penned.

All join me in affectionate messages.

Faithfully Yours,   Woodrow Wilson

WWTLS (E. M. House Papers, CtY).

E N C L O S U R E   I

Berlin (via Copenhagen) Nov. 17, 1916.

4614. HIGHLY CONFIDENTIAL.

Importance is to be attached to peace interview with Chancellor cabled by William Bayard Hale to NEW YORK AMERICAN[1] as he informs me it has been sanctioned by highest authority. Please inform Mr. Gerard. I learn in strictest confidence that recent Austrian deputation to Berlin expressed Austria's desire to avoid peace suggestions until Roumania shall have been defeated but that German Government is not in accord with this wish. The Chancellor's interview with Hale is said to be in the nature of an informal suggestion to the President whose response is awaited with eagerness. There has recently been a marked increase of peace talk and sentiment in Berlin extending to practically all parties.   Grew.

[1] Hale himself had requested Grew to send this cable and had stated that the "highest authority" mentioned was Emperor William. Joseph C. Grew, *Turbulent Era: A Diplomatic Record of Forty Years, 1904-1945*, ed. Walter Johnson (2 vols., Boston, 1952), I, 263-64. However, Hale's interview with Bethmann Hollweg was to have a curious history. On November 20, 1916, Grew cabled to the State Department that the transmission of the interview to the *New York American* had been delayed by Bethmann Hollweg's departure for General Headquarters before he could approve it. *FR-WWS 1916*, p. 67. Grew cabled again on November 25 and reported that, "in view of recent developments such as the death of the Austrian Emperor, the changes in the [German] Foreign Office, and the establishment of the auxiliary Government service," Bethmann Hollweg had "now decided that it would be preferable to base the interview primarily on those developments, and thus avoid approaching the subject of peace directly, though bringing it into the interview indirectly." Hale had submitted a new draft for the Chancellor's approval. Grew further reported that he had the original draft in his possession but assumed that he should not cable the full text of it to the State Department since "the original interview cannot now be regarded as authentic or as the Chancellor's own utterance." However, he did quote "a few disconnected excerpts from the more significant portions" of the interview. They are as follows:

"Do you think, Mr. Hale, it is possible that your countrymen think that the German people alone remain untouched by the electric vibrations of the idea of peace which throb in the air, surcharged with the agonies of 30 months of bloody conflict?

"Surely no one who knows anything of the German character, of German history, or of German ideals, can doubt the sincerity with which, on purely unselfish grounds, we desire to see brought to an end this conflict so disastrous to all western civilization.

"The mandate which continues Mr. Wilson in the high office which he has discharged through four most difficult years seems to be interpreted by some, at least, of your public men as a proposal of the initiation of a program of peace.

"We Germans neither invite it nor should we resent it.

"The question of peace lies with the enemies of the allied Central powers of Europe, whose only desire and firm determination is to defeat the conspiracy which would crush their national existence.

"If you ask me the definite question of Belgium, I will remind you that in no utterance of mine have you ever read that the retention of Belgium was a principle of German policy.

"If you inquire our views respecting a world tribunal to enforce peace, I answer that world peace is and has ever been a German ideal and that we should hail with joy any practical plan that would reasonably promise to insure it.

"If I say these things it is not because of any doubt, indecision, or weakness.

"While the will of the German people grows even more resolute to carry the struggle on to any length necessary to the complete vindication of our national integrity and destiny, it has ever been and is now our desire to resume the amicable [exertions] of peace as soon as we are allowed to do so." *Ibid.*, pp. 69-70.

On November 28, Grew cabled to the State Department the final text of the interview which, he commented, had been revised five times before it received Bethmann Hollweg's final approval. As indicated above, this version was a commentary on recent political events in Austria and Germany and contained only very general statements indicating that Germany was interested in serious peace negotiations and proposals looking toward a league of nations. *Ibid.*, pp. 71-74. A considerably edited version was printed in the *New York American*, Nov. 30, 1916.

For further commentary on the Hale interview, see Grew, *op. cit.*, pp. 252-54.

ENCLOSURE   II

Berne, Nov. 20, 1916.

435. BASLER NATIONAL ZEITUNG publishes leading article to the effect that it is informed from trustworthy diplomatic source that the United States Government is about to take steps to bring about peace. The first step would be a call for conference of belligerent and neutral powers, to be held in the United States or in one of the neurtal [neutral] countries of Europe. The article states that Germany is willing to evacuate northern France and all of occupied Belgium on condition that group of neutral powers guarantee Belgium's future neutrality. This article is much commented on here and has caused a recrudescene of peace articles in the Swiss press.

CONFIDENTIAL.

Article is undoubtedly inspired by German propaganda here and is intended as *ballon dessai*. Swiss Political Department informs me that it has no knowledge of neutral peace move but that Sweden had proposed joint action by neutrals to enforce certain neutral rights including protection of neutral vessels from illegal submarine attacks and unwarranted interference with mails between neutral countries. Stovall.

ENCLOSURE III

Vienna, (via Berne), November 20, 1916.

1539. Vienna press commenting extensively on telegraphic press reports that the President contemplates inviting at early date representatives of belligerent powers to a preliminary peace conference where all parties shall present minimum demands to lay foundation for final peace conference but no cessation of hostilities during preliminary conference. Press giving prominence to discussions of this report but maintaining position reserve. Governmental attitude not indicated.

Following summary of NEUE FREIE PRESSE, seventeenth:

"If the United States in view of possible difficulties with Japan and Mexico needs peace in Europe, England's wishes cannot be so potent as to cause the President to forego an effort to # American aims. America desires peace in Europe, not on Europe's account but in her own interest. America can impose her wishes on London, since munitions and loans are indispensable to England."

Eighteenth:

"The peace plan of President Wilson occupies public opinion in Budapest. Member of Hungarian Parliament states that the initiative of Wilson will be greeted joyfully by every one here, for we certainly desire an honorable peace. It can surely not be supposed that Wilson's project will be shattered by the Central Powers, which have given so many proofs of their wish to avoid further purposeless shedding of blood.

"A member of Hungarian delegation states that America had the duty to offer its good offices to effect an understanding between the belligerents. It was pleased however to reap financial profit and maintain a onesided neutrality. If the present report proves true, we must rejoice, for even if it should not bring peace or an armistice, it would at least encourage the hope that the United States might at least assume a position of honest and unbiased neutrality."

"Following from ARBEITER ZEITUNG, eliminated by censor seventeenth, but published nineteenth:

"Each belligerent nation can accept Wilson's invitation without appearing to be at end of its resources. We greatly desire that Wilson may not be dismayed by the difficulty of his task, that conscious of the longing of humanity, he may attack the work courageously.["]   Penfield.

T telegrams (E. M. House Papers, CtY).

From Joseph Patrick Tumulty

[The White House, c. Nov. 21, 1916]

The Secretary begs to call to the President's attention the two attached articles from the New York Times,[1] which he mentioned yesterday. *They are worth the most earnest attention.*

TL (WP, DLC).

[1] Nicholas Murray Butler, writing under the pseudonym "Cosmos," had just begun publication of a series of articles entitled "All Want Peace: Why Not Have It Now?" They appeared under this title in the *New York Times*, Nov. 20, 21, 22, 23, 24, and 25, 1916. The series continued with a new subtitle, "What Must Be Its Basis?" on Nov. 27, 28, and 30, and Dec. 2, 4, 6, 9, 12, 15, and 18. These articles were reprinted in book form as Cosmos [Nicholas Murray Butler], *The Basis of Durable Peace* (New York, 1917). As the two subtitles suggest, Butler discussed both the current political and military situation in Europe and the prospects and requirements for a durable peace settlement, including the advisability of some form of international organization. Tumulty enclosed the first two articles, which appeared in the *New York Times* on November 20 and 21. Butler argued in the first that it was becoming clear that Germany and her allies could not win the war and that, while Great Britain and her allies could and probably would win, such a victory would be a Pyrrhic one. There were increasing signs that both sides were ready to consider some means of bringing the conflict to a close. It was, therefore, appropriate to ask the British and German governments to state the objects for which they conceived themselves to be fighting. Butler pointed out that both Viscount Grey and Bethmann Hollweg had made recent statements which seemed to indicate that their nations were fighting for the right of "free development" for all nations, great and small. In his second article, Butler began a detailed investigation of the extent to which either Great Britain or Germany was in reality committed to this policy of free development. In light of their past records in dealing with other nations and with their own colonial dependencies, Butler concluded that Britain was far more likely to support such a policy than was Germany.

From Robert Lansing

PERSONAL AND PRIVATE:

My dear Mr. President: Washington November 21, 1916.

I have been more and more disturbed by the policy of the German Government in the deportation of the civil population of Belgium as the magnitude and purpose of the removals have become more apparent.

The mere fact of the deportation of civilians from a particular region by military authorities is not, in my opinion, reprehensible.

There may be ample justification for such action because of military necessity. Prior to the present case we have had two examples of the removal of civilians from their homes, the Armenians by the Turks, and the French in the neighborhood of Lille by the Germans.

In the case of the Armenians I could see that their well-known disloyalty to the Ottoman Government and the fact that the territory which they inhabited was within the zone of military operations constituted grounds more or less justifiable for compelling them to depart from their homes. It was not to my mind the deportation which was objectionable but the horrible brutality which attended its execution. It is one of the blackest pages in the history of this war, and I think that we were fully justified in intervening as we did in behalf of the wretched people, even though they were Turkish subjects.

In the case of the French at Lille and other towns in the vicinity I can conceive that military expediency may have furnished good reason for the deportation. Located near the battle lines, as they were, the difficulty of furnishing the population with food and shelter may have warranted the removal of a portion to a greater distance from the war zone. But, as in the case of the Armenians, the German military authorities showed towards the inhabitants of the Lille section a ruthlessness and inhumanity which caused needless distress by the separation of families and by deportation without due regard to age or sex and without opportunity to prepare for departure.

Of course in the case of the Armenians the Ottoman Government is by nature and training cruel and barbarous and could not be expected to conform to so high a standard of humanity as the enlightened Government of Germany, which makes the conduct more criticizable.

In the case of the Belgians the conditions seem to be utterly different. They do not appear to be deported because they are in the field of active operations or because of the difficulty of furnishing them with food, since that is being done through the Belgian Relief Commission. It is not the helpless or weak who are being transported but only males who are physically fit to work. They are being taken to Germany, according to reports, for the purpose of being placed in factories and fields in order that the Germans now engaged in manual labor may be mustered into military service, thus increasing the military strength of Germany without impairing her industrial efficiency.

Of course these Belgians are going unwillingly and are being forcibly compelled to labor for their conquerors. They are to all intents in a state of involuntary servitude. To use a more ugly phrase, they are slaves under a system of slavery which has not been practiced in regard to civilian enemies by civilized nations within modern times. It arouses in me, as I am sure it must arouse in every liberty-loving man, an intense feeling of abhorrence and a desire to find some way to prevent the continuance of a practice which is a reversion to the barbarous methods of the military empires of antiquity.

Now, Mr. President, I have nothing definite to propose. As you know I have firmly supported the policy of avoiding all protests on account of inhuman methods of warfare by belligerents which are in violation of international law. I still believe that that policy is wise and should be continued. But in all such cases the conduct complained of was never admitted to be the definite policy of a Government, nor was the inhumanity of the individual cases conclusively proven. The present case is different. Germany has not yet denied the act or the purpose of the act. Her Government appears rather to excuse it though, in my opinion, no excuse offered can in any way relieve that Government of the enormity of the crime of making slaves, not of prisoners of war (which would be bad enough), but of peaceable non-combatants who have by the fortunes of war come within its jurisdiction. It is a direct and unjustifiable blow at the principle of individual liberty—an essential element of modern political ideas, if not of our civilization.

As I say, I have nothing to propose at the present time but I feel that we ought to consider very carefully whether some way cannot be found to bring moral pressure upon Germany to cause her to abandon a policy which invites the protest of the civilized world, and which will greatly increase her difficulties when the time comes to negotiate a treaty of peace, unless I misjudge the temper of her enemies. If we desire to see peace restored in Europe, no step would be more efficacious than to convince Germany of the imperative need to abandon this policy. I do not believe that any efforts, which we might make, to bring the belligerents together could possibly succeed while Germany persisted in enslaving the civilian subjects of her enemies who have fallen into her hands. To attempt to do so would, I am sure, arouse bitter resentment and place us in a most embarrassing position.

In this connection I may call your attention to a letter which I wrote you on the 15th[1] reporting an interview with the Belgian Minister in which he desired me to ask what would be your attitude toward receiving from the King of the Belgians a request to act more formally in behalf of the deported population of his country. I have been thinking over the matter and I can see no very strong objection to receiving such a request. Indeed it might offer an opportunity to seek to prevent the carrying out of a policy which, it seems to me, if persisted in, will so arouse the Allies that the possibility of peace in the near future will be almost unthinkable.

At your convenience I would like to discuss this subject with you for I feel that we must determine upon the course of action which should be pursued.

Faithfully yours,   Robert Lansing

TLS (WP, DLC).
  1 RL to WW, Nov. 15, 1916 (second letter of that date), Vol. 38.

From Charles William Eliot

Dear Mr. President: Cambridge, Mass., 21 November 1916.

I ventured to send you this morning a telegram expressed as follows:

> I believe American people wishes for immediate imperative protest against German deportations.

Will you allow me to state the case more fully in writing? The deportation of Belgian men and women for forced labor in Germany, or in territories held by German armies, is a limited adoption of the ancient practice of carrying off the people of a conquered country into slavery in the country of the conquerors. It is not a general sweeping-up of the entire population, but only of the most available portion of the population. The means of enforcing labor are not as brutal as they were nineteen hundred years ago; but they are doubtless brutal enough considering how the standards of brutality have changed. The deportations are extremely cruel so far as the Belgians are concerned. They are also morally inexpedient in the highest degree so far as the Germans are concerned. They arouse the indignation of the entire civilized world with the exception of the Central Monarchies. In my neighborhood, I find no exceptions to the indignant state of mind, except among persons of German birth and strong German sympathies. Republicans and Democrats, educated and uneducated, rich and poor are united in common sentiments on this subject.

I hope you will see in the adoption of this deportation policy an opportunity to send a strenuous and imperative protest in the name of the American people direct to the German Chancellor, publishing it in the American newspapers as soon as it has reached the Chancellor.

Since the invasion of Belgium and the development of the

policy of the frightfulness, there has been no such sowing of the seeds of hate as this policy of deportation. The over-running of Serbia and Albania was nothing to this. The submarine policy is much less hateful. The sinking of the Lusitania did not produce the unifying effect on the American people that this policy of deportation is producing.

When you have disposed in Congress of the questions growing out of the threatened strike of the four railroad Brotherhoods, I hope you will turn with pleasure to the introduction of the merit system into the Government service with a completeness comparable with that of the Department of Agriculture under Secretary Houston. Our Government has now been charged by the people with so many new functions of great importance that it has become indispensable that the whole work of the Government should be performed from bottom to top not only honestly but efficiently in every respect.

That is far from being the case at present. For instance, the efficiency of the Post Office Department with regard to the delivery of the mails, apart from the parcel post, has declined very much since the 4th of March, 1913. I hear often testimonies to this effect. I realize it every day in regard to the mail which comes into this house and goes out of it. Book publishers, newspaper men, large advertisers by circulars, hotels, and innumerable sellers and buyers by mail testify to this same decline in the efficiency of the Post Office; but particularly to delays in transmission. I imagine, but do not know, that the decline is due: first, to a desire to economize in the Post Office Department, so that the annual deficit may be reduced or extinguished; and secondly, to the imperfect manner in which civil service rules have been applied in that Department during your Administration.

It happens that there is an important meeting of the National Civil Service Reform League at New Haven on the 5th of December next. I asked Secretary Houston if he could not come to that meeting and describe the organization of his Department and the effects of applying civil service rules to both new appointments and promotions; but he told me that on acount of an important engagement on the 4th of December he could not attend the meeting at New Haven on the 5th. Would it not be possible for you to request the Postmaster General to go to that meeting and describe what he has done in regard to the merit system in the Post Office Department, and what he wants to do?

I am, with high regard,

Sincerely yours   Charles W. Eliot

TLS (A. S. Burleson Papers, DLC).

From John Palmer Gavit

CONFIDENTIAL

Dear Mr. President: [New York] November 21, 1916.

I have taken steps to get for you as promptly as possible the information suggested by you in our conversation yesterday; I shall forward it to you as soon as it comes to hand.

Meanwhile, it will interest you to know that on the train coming over from Washington I chanced to meet Mr. Charles T. Thompson,[1] until lately chief of the Washington Bureau of the Associated Press, who returns tomorrow, I believe, to Europe where he has spent many months since the beginning of the war. I asked him about the existence in France of any substantial body of opinion in favor of an early peace. He said that in France, even more than in England, it was impossible for anyone with personal safety to express any such views; one doing so was subjected to most vigilant espionage, and even ran in danger of personal injury. Nevertheless, at a recent meeting of French Socialists, while 1,200 voted to sustain the Government in the matter of the war, 900 voted for a resolution designed to enlist the aid of the International toward peace. The Paris newspapers were not permitted to make any public reference to this resolution or the vote in its favor.

He said, moreover, that there were many signs of vast weariness of war on the part of the men in the trenches and their families and relatives at home. Of course this must be the state of affairs in all of the armies—the determination to fight to the bitter end is so largely confined to those who aren't doing the fighting! How quickly an end of war would come if the men on the fighting-line should suddenly awaken to the absurdity of the whole business, and with a loud laugh rush into each other's arms!

Of course, Mr. Thompson was talking to me privately, and with no thought of my quoting him to you.

I am very grateful for the patient hearing you gave me yesterday.   Sincerely yours,   John P. Gavit

TLS (WP, DLC).
[1] Charles Thaddeus Thompson.

From Edward Mandell House, with Enclosure

Dear Governor: New York. November 21, 1916.

I am enclosing you a letter from Sir Horace which may be of interest because of what he says about Roosevelt.

I also have a letter from Noel Buxton outlincing [outlining] what he thinks might be possible peace terms. He says this memorandum represents "an increasing body of opinion."

I will not burden you with it unless you care to read it.

There is a great deal of feeling concerning the Belgian deportations. What would you think of saying something which would show our extreme disapproval of such methods?

I am sending the leading editorial in the Times of today[1] and a letter on the editorial page signed "Cosmus."[2] They may interest you.   Affectionately yours,   E. M. House

P.S. Will not Mrs. Wilson and you take dinner with us alone on Saturday[3] and go to the theatre?

TLS (WP, DLC).
[1] "The Talk About Peace," *New York Times*, Nov. 21, 1916. The reason why there was now so much talk of peace, the editorial declared, was that Germany and Austria had, for all practical purposes, been defeated. There was no longer any realistic hope that the Central Powers could attain the objects for which they had begun the war. What kept the conflict going was, on the one hand, the determination of the Allies to destroy militarism and imperialism and thus make another war impossible, and, on the other hand, the desperate need of the German and Austrian militarists and imperialists to save themselves. This was distinct from the interests of the German and Austrian peoples, who had been deceived by their rulers into believing that they were fighting for their very existence. The road to peace lay in convincing both the Allied governments and the German people that their objectives and interests could be embodied and made secure in the terms of a peace settlement and in the international agreements which would enforce that settlement.
[2] That is, the second of the "Cosmos" articles described in JPT to WW, Nov. 21, 1916, n. 1.
[3] Wilson planned to attend the Army-Navy football game in New York on November 25. As it turned out, illness prevented his appearance.

ENCLOSURE

Sir Horace Plunkett to Edward Mandell House

Foxrock, Ireland.
My dear Colonel House: November 2, 1916.

I wish the trusty bearer of this letter could have waited a few more days; I might then have offered my congratulations (as my reading of the American mind makes me confidently hope they will be) or my condolences on a partial interruption of those great aims, the general nature of which you have been good enough to disclose to me.

A short time ago a strong impression prevailed in London that the Republicans would win, the Wall Street betting being largely responsible for the belief. I thought it well to give it as my opinion to Arthur Balfour that among these financiers the wish was father to the odds. I further gave my reasons for my fervent hope that the President would be re-elected, not the least of them being the immense possibilities of a better understanding between the two democracies, which might be brought about by utilizing to the full the personal relations you had established in this country.

At this date, our Press is informed by its American correspondents that the issue of the elections baffles prediction. So I will say now, in order that you may get my message the sooner, what my feelings will be in the event of your friend failing, on this occasion, to secure his second term.

I need not say that this result would be a grievous disappointment to me. I am, however, convinced that it would not deprive him and you of that part in the world's affairs which I am quite sure concerns you both even more than the great task of nation building at home, the need for which has been precipitated by the war. I shall in that untoward event, expect to see the President joining Taft and leading a great non-party movement for defining and declaring the attitude of the United States towards war and its prevention.

In talking about the election to influential people over here, I always point out the advantage of having a President in his second term when questions of foreign policy are of paramount importance. You will not misunderstand me in this judgment. I know your friend would not allow his prospects at the next election to affect his policy in international affairs, but the whole of his Administration are bound to be more or less Party men, and you cannot altogether eliminate the interfering influence of Party considerations. It is for this reason that his influence as a past President (and a likely President of the future) might conceivably be greater in guiding the public opinion of the leading neutral nation, and in certain eventualities he might be a more active representative of the United States in mediation between the belligerents, than if he were re-elected President. In any case you, in virtue of your European work through this awful crisis, will be as closely associated with him as heretofore.

Coming to the other eventuality, the victory, the hope of which I am cherishing, you will, I presume, at once take up again the splendid work you were engaged upon all the time you were here in England. I think you will find the task of adjusting matters between the Republic and the Empire immensely easier than it has yet been.

You must not be surprised, and I hope you will not be annoyed, if the President's re-election is badly received by British public opinion. It is safe to say that had Roosevelt secured the nomination, British opinion would have been dangerously un-neutral in regard to the Presidential election.

In the strict confidence that I impose in you as I would in few other human beings, (and this rather because I distrust their memories and discretion than that I fear they would play false to me) I may tell you that, some time ago Roosevelt wrote rather angrily to more than one correspondent over here about me. It was quite evident that some Cabinet Minister had divulged, either to Roosevelt direct or to some person who passed it on, the contents of that Memorandum of mine to the Cabinet written in February,[1] a copy of which you have. Perhaps foolishly—for I was very ill at the time—I wrote to Roosevelt and asked him what he really had heard. In his reply, he said:

"Two persons, one an American in England, the other an Englishman who said his information came indirectly from Mr. Asquith, had written me that you had told your Government that Mr. Wilson was friendly to England, that he was bringing the opinion of the Middle West round to the side of England, which I was powerless to do, and that England should recognize this inner meaning of Mr. Wilson's attitude. The Englishman wrote in joy at Wilson's supposed attitude. The American instanced your alleged statement as proof that it was a mistake on my part to have championed the cause of the Allies, that England would only respect people who opposed her, that Wilson had gained British goodwill precisely because he had been lukewarm or hostile, and that I ought to learn the lesson and pay heed to German and Irish feeling."

You will probably think me very indiscreet, but one can accomplish nothing without trusting somebody, and I thought a Cabinet document was as safe a repository as exists. I have sent you the above quotation because it illustrates the relations between Roosevelt and some members of our Government, or at least precisely the leanings of the latter.

By the way, I am not sorry that I wrote that Memorandum, for I have proof positive that it made a profound impression upon many members of the Cabinet, both as to the actual economic and potential military power of the United States, and as to its probable attitude towards peace, which I need not tell you has been the subject of grave alarm to some English and, I am told, some French statesmen.

Lord Kitchener, on reading the Memorandum, sent for me and talked to me for nearly an hour upon it. He told me that if the United States were drawn into the war, it would, in his judgment, bring it to an early end for the reasons I had given. "Otherwise," he said, "I do not change my estimate of its duration." This, you will remember, was three years from August 1914.

I should anticipate some expression of disappointment in our Press at the President's re-election, especially if his majority were a very narrow one. There would, however, be a wholly new situation to deal with and it would be most important that the Press work over here should be vigorously and understandingly prosecuted. I have done, as far as was possible in my unhappy condition, some preparatory work that I should be disappointed if, when I get over to London, I were not able to follow it up as the occasion may demand.

Yours ever sincerely,   Horace Plunkett.

TCL (WP, DLC).
    ¹ See n. 1 to H. Plunkett to EMH, March 7, 1916, printed as an Enclosure with EMH to WW, March 20, 1916, Vol. 36.

Franklin Knight Lane to Robert Lansing

Atlantic City, Nov. 21, 1916.

112. We have inserted in the withdrawal plan laid before the Mexican Commissioners the following article:

"Each of the Governments, parties to this agreement, shall guard its side of the International boundary, thereby making each Government responsible for lawless acts committed along the border by bands of men coming armed from its own territory into the territory of the other. This however does not preclude such cooperation on the part of the military commanders of both countries as may be practicable."

We have also drafted the following letter to the Mexican Commissioners which we intend submitting:

"Having arrived at an agreement as to the withdrawal of troops and border control we desire in accordance with instructions from the President of the United States to request an assurance from the citizen first Chief of the Constitutionalist Army intrusted with the executive power of the Mexican nation that when the above mentioned agreement is approved by both governments you are authorized to meet at once and take up with the American commissioners those questions deemed by the American Government of vital importance, such as protection of life and property of foreigners in Mexico, the establishment of an international claim commission, religious tolerance and such other questions as may be submitted by the American or Mexican Commissioners affecting the continuance and strengthening of the friendly relations between the two countries with a view to arriving at definite conclusions to be submitted to the two governments for their approval."

They talk as if they wished to submit our plan of withdrawal to Carranza by wire. If they do we propose to make this oral statement:

"It is essential as a matter of governmental policy that the United States reserve the right to deal with any serious hostile incursion from Mexico into American territory as may be deemed advisable at the time including the right to pursue marauders into Mexican territory when such pursuit is necessary to our own protection. Duly mindful of the obligations imposed upon us by international law such pursuit will not be intended and should not be considered an act hostile to the constitutionalist government of Mexico."   Lane[1]

T telegram (SDR, RG 59, 812.00/19920, DNA).
[1] For a full account of the meeting of the Joint High Commission on November 21, see FKL to RL, Nov. 21, 1916, printed as an Enclosure with RL to WW, Nov. 23, 1916.

From Charles Francis Joseph

Berlin, Via Sayville, N. Y., Nov. 22, 1916.

With deepest sorrow I hasten to inform your excellency that my beloved granduncle, His Imperial and Royal Majesty, Francis Joseph Roemish I, expired last night after a short illness. I feel confident that your excellency and the American nation will sympathize with the great loss that Austria Hungary has sustained by the death of his majesty.   Charles.

T telegram (WP, DLC).

To Charles Francis Joseph

[The White House] November 22, 1916.

I beg of Your Majesty and the Imperial and Royal Family to accept the sincerest sympathy of Mrs. Wilson and myself in the great loss which you have sustained in the death of your illustrious uncle for whom I entertained sentiments of the highest esteem and regard. I also extend to Your Majesty the condolences of the Government and people of the United States, and convey to you my best wishes for your personal wellbeing and prosperity.
[Woodrow Wilson]

CC telegram (WP, DLC).

To Joseph Patrick Tumulty

Dear Tumulty: [The White House, c. Nov. 22, 1916]

I suppose this[1] is in connection with the lighting of the statue of liberty.[2] I did not know they were arranging a dinner for me.

Will you please have the following names taken from the lists:
George W. Burleigh,
General Leonard Wood,
Dr. Nicholas Murray Butler,
John Hays Hammond,
Hudson Maxim,
Frank Munsey,
Theodore P. Shonts.[3]

There are others who are almost as unpalatable to me, but these are the ones that I am most desirous of seeing relieved from a duty which will no doubt be onerous to them.

The President.

TL (WP, DLC).

[1] E. Harding to JPT, Nov. 21, 1916, TLS (WP, DLC), enclosing a list of names of prominent New Yorkers proposed to attend a dinner to be given in Wilson's honor by Mayor John Purroy Mitchel at the Waldorf-Astoria Hotel on December 2.

[2] The occasion for Wilson's visit to New York on December 2 was the first illumination of the Statue of Liberty from an electric plant, constructed with funds raised by the New York *World*. Wilson was to give the signal for the illumination and to accept the plant on behalf of the federal government.

[3] Those not previously or recently identified in this series are: George William Burleigh, Princeton 1892, lawyer and capitalist, active in numerous military organizations; Hudson Maxim, inventor of many high explosives used in modern warfare and a militant advocate of preparedness; Frank Andrew Munsey, the magazine and newspaper tycoon, publisher, among others, of *Munsey's Magazine* and the New York *Sun*; and Theodore Perry Shonts, former railroad executive, chairman of the second Isthmian Canal Commission (1905-1907), at this time president of the Interborough Rapid Transit Company.

To Theodore Wright[1]

My dear Friend: [The White House] November 22, 1916

Thank you for your letter of November twentieth[2] and for your thoughtfulness in sending me the Daily News editorial.[3] I had seen quotations from it but I had not the pleasure of seeing the whole article. Gard[i]ner is certainly a very good and generous friend and I appreciate such articles very keenly.

I was very much touched by what you told me of Mrs. Wright's vote. Please give her my warm regard and tell her how I value her confidence and trust. I hope that her health is improving.

With the warmest good wishes and all grateful appreciation to yourself,

Cordially and sincerely yours,   Woodrow Wilson

TLS (Letterpress Books, WP, DLC).

[1] President of the Record Publishing Co., editor-in-chief of the *Philadelphia Record*, 1877-1912, now living in retirement in Anaheim, California. However, he still contributed an occasional editorial to the *Record*.

[2] It is missing.

[3] A. G. G[ardiner], "America & the Future," London *Daily News & Leader*, Nov. 18, 1916. Gardiner believed that Wilson's reelection was by then certain and that, for another four years, he would thus lead "the greatest single political potentiality on earth." The United States might lack fleets and armies, but these would be rapidly forthcoming if required because America was not only "unequalled" in population and natural wealth but also was acquiring more of the accumulated riches of the old world every day that the war continued. Thus, the United States would soon speak with great authority in the affairs of the world.

Gardiner maintained that, while it was true that many people in Great Britain and in Europe resented America's neutrality, they were gradually coming to appreciate the fact that it was Wilson's policy of strict neutrality which had enabled the Allies to obtain the supplies necessary to carry on the war, in contrast to what would have been the case had Bryan been elected in 1912. Gardiner argued also that Hughes' legalistic policies, if he had been elected in 1916, would soon have put the United States into the war on the side of the Central Powers.

However, Gardiner believed that there was a far more important reason to rejoice in Wilson's reelection: "It is Mr. Wilson who has got the vision of the future—the only vision that makes the future thinkable. He struggles towards the conception of a society of nations, a pooling of force, an accomodation of interests and declared principles of international affairs. He knows that henceforth there can be no such thing as a neutral, and that every war will be a world war. The ocean has been annihilated and 'splendid isolation' is, politically, as outworn a phrase in America as it is in England. . . . It is to do . . . 'something infinitely greater'—something nobler than building a higher tariff wall for the American plutocracy—that he comes back to power. It is to establish a society of nations, and to change the whole doctrine of force in the world. He cannot eliminate force, but it is in his power and the power of the American nation to make force grind the wheels of peace instead of the wheels of war. Under his A.B.C. treaty he can bring all the American republics into this grand stream of endeavour. There is half the world with all its potentialities. If the British Empire, France and the neutral States of Europe associate themselves with the movement it will be assured of a backing which will make dreams of militarist conquest too dangerous to entertain. Into such a combination, a new Russia, freed from the influence of a German bureaucracy, would not fail to enter, and ultimately mere self-interest, if no other better motive, would bring all the nations into this world society, regulated by law and backed by the force which can alone make the reign of law valid."

To John Palmer Gavit

My dear Mr. Gavit: [The White House] November 22, 1916

Thank you for your letter of the twenty-first giving the substance of your conversation with Mr. Charles T. Thompson. It is very interesting not only, but I am sure that it is probably very near to being an assessment of the actual facts. Human nature, after all, is the same everywhere and there are some things we can take for granted.

Cordially and sincerely yours, Woodrow Wilson

TLS (Letterpress Books, WP, DLC).

Two Letters to Newton Diehl Baker

My dear Mr. Secretary: The White House November 22, 1916

Thank you for the copy of the resolutions adopted at the annual convention of the National Consumers' League. I dare say these are the first of a series of suggestions of a similar kind which will grow out of the Child Labor Bill. I wonder what you yourself think as to the limits of this sort of legislation by Congress?

Cordially and sincerely yours,   Woodrow Wilson

My dear Mr. Secretary: The White House November 22, 1916

I have your letter[1] about Vice Governor Martin's[2] desire not to return to the Philippine Islands.

My present feeling is that it is extremely desirable that we should make practically all our important appointments in the immediate future out of the great West which has just been added to the Democratic ranks. I wonder if we cannot find some really live and vigorous and at the same time well-balanced person from one of the new allies? Perhaps you are in a better position to search that region with your eye than I am.

Cordially and sincerely yours,   Woodrow Wilson

TLS (N. D. Baker Papers, DLC).
  [1] NDB to WW, Nov. 21, 1916, TLS (WP, DLC).
  [2] Henderson S. Martin.

To Charles Richard Crane

My dear Friend: [The White House] November 22, 1916

I have your two letters of November twentieth[1] and shall certainly keep an eye on the matter of which you speak concerning Houston.

Moreover, I have written to the three gentlemen whose names you were kind enough to give me in response to my request, trying to express to them my very deep and genuine appreciation of their support.

In haste, with warmest regard, always

Faithfully yours,   Woodrow Wilson

TLS (Letterpress Books, WP, DLC).
  [1] The one not printed is C. R. Crane to WW, Nov. 20, 1916, ALS (WP, DLC). In it, Crane suggested that Wilson write "notes of appreciation" to Edward Wyllis Scripps and two other officials of the Scripps newspaper chain.

To Charles William Eliot

Personal.

My dear Doctor Eliot: The White House November 22, 1916

Thank you for your telegram of November twenty-first. I feel with you that a very considerable opinion is gathering about the matter of the Belgian deportation and the Secretary of State and I are in earnest conference about the proper course to pursue.

Cordially and sincerely yours,   Woodrow Wilson

TLS (C. W. Eliot Papers, MH-Ar).

From Charles Evans Hughes

Lakewood, N. J., November 22, 1916.

Because of the closemess [closeness] of the vote I have awaited the official count in California and now that it has been virtually completed, permit me to extend to you my congratulations upon your reelection. I desire also to express my best wishes for a most successful administration.   Charles E. Hughes.

T telegram (WP, DLC).

From Robert Lansing

PERSONAL AND PRIVATE:

My dear Mr. President: Washington November 22, 1916.

I enclose the report of our Consul at Cork, Mr. Frost, dated November 1st, in the case of the MARINA, to which is attached the affidavits of the American citizens who were on board the vessel.[1] I also enclose the report of the Consul dated November 2d on the same subject.[2]

It seems to me to be a case in which, from the facts sworn to, there appears to be little possible defense. Even the excuse that the vessel was laden with contraband for Great Britain is absent, in the fact that she was on her homeward voyage and practically in ballast.

I have been considering in my own mind whether it is possible for us to avoid taking definite action in the case in accordance with our SUSSEX note. I do not feel, however, that I wish to express an opinion at present, although I consider the situation very grave.   Faithfully yours,   Robert Lansing

TLS (SDR, RG 59, 841.857 M 331/42, DNA).
  [1] This enclosure is missing.
  [2] Wesley Frost to RL, Nov. 2, 1916, TCL (SDR, RG 59, 841.857 M 331/42, DNA).

From Edward Mandell House, with Enclosure

Dear Governor: New York. November 22, 1916.

I am enclosing you a copy of a note Bernstorff sent me the other day.

I have just had a talk with Frederic Palmer, the war correspondent who has represented the American Press on the Western Front since the beginning of the war.

He says no one can tell just when the hour has struck for peace proposals. The fact that the Allies contend that they will fight until their last man is exhausted in order to bring about complete victory, is, in his opinion, the usual attitude and does not mean much.

He believes Russia to be the big gamble in the situation and that in peace negotiations it may be found that both the Central Powers and the Western Allies will give but scant consideration to her claims.

I am trying in every way possible to get a clear understanding of the situation so as to give it to you when you are ready.

Thank you so much for your letter of yesterday enclosing the interesting despatches.

If you have a minute on Saturday Cleve Dodge would like to shake your hand and tell you how glad he is you have won.

If I am not at the train when you arrive, I will try and see you a moment before you leave if you cannot remain over for dinner and the theater.   Affectionately yours,   E. M. House

TLS (WP, DLC).

ENCLOSURE

Count Johann Heinrich von Bernstorff to Edward Mandell House

My dear Colonel House: New York. November 20, 1916.

I received a telephone message from Washington just now, according to which a telegram from Berlin arrived, that W. B. Hale had wired the President about an interview with the Imperial Chancellor.

According to my telegram, I was instructed to explain to the President, that this interview was not given out, because the Chancellor did not agree with the draft of the interview.

May I ask you to be good enough to make use of the above information?

With many thanks in advance,

Always sincerely yours,   J. Bernstorff.

TCL (WP, DLC).

From John Palmer Gavit

Englewood, N. J.

My dear Woodrow Wilson: November 22, 1916.

Inasmuch as I am not in the least afraid of you in your exalted job, and yet would like mightily to help you, if only by some trifling contribution in my capacity as a friend who doesn't want anything that you can give, except friendship; I feel free to write something that I find in my thought, evidently intended for you. I know you will take it as from man to man, for just what it is worth to you, assured only that it is meant to be helpful.

It seems to me that no President ever before has been in quite the position that you occupy now and will increasingly occupy, of freedom from every obligation except that of straightforward service to the people. Even the tolerably reasonable claims of expediency and political tradition of which you had to take notice in your first term have expired under the Statute of Limitations in such case made and provided. You are free now as never before to move in straight lines. No man is in a position to raise with you any question except *What is the Right Thing to do?*"

Governor Hughes won and held the confidence of the people of the State of New York, not because he was a loyal Republican or a wonderful administrator, but because they came to believe that he moved in straight lines, met questions on their merits as an honest and disinterested man must meet them, without regard to personal or party consequences, and did, regardless of expediency, what seemed the *right thing to do*. In the net outcome this proved, of course, to be the cleverest kind of politics. When he came before them as a candidate for the Presidency, they turned him down because he chose the other way, and subordinated the straight-line policy to considerations of political expediency. I am convinced more than ever that the man who in public office has the wisdom and the courage to do *the right thing* regardless of consequences to himself or his party will win and hold the confidence of the people from coast to coast, and that the little politicians of all parties and stripes can no more control or direct that force than they can control or direct the tides of the ocean.

If I were in your place, vested with the inestimable power and responsibility that have come to you in your re-election, it seems to me I would do, or try to do, these five things—all of them related very directly to the matter of "America Efficient," about which Mr. Hughes talked so much and so inefficiently:

First, I would take the public service out of Politics. Specifically, within thirty minutes after I became convinced that it was *the right thing to do*, I would issue an Executive Order placing *all* of the postoffices, with their present incumbents, in the Classified Service. There are enough Republicans holding over to rob the act of partisan significance. In New York city, in the case of Mr. Morgan,[1] it would have a tremendous moral effect. If I had the nerve, I would go on, perhaps a bit later, and cover in all of the other offices, small and large, that I could reach under the law. I need not dwell upon the sensationally dramatic character of such an act, or upon its quality as the right thing to do.

Second, I would do everything in my power to take the Tariff out of politics, by strengthening and equipping the Tariff Commission, setting it to work at the earliest possible moment, and taking its work very seriously as a matter of Administration policy. It would rob the Republicans of their last poor leg to stand on.

Third, I would in a manner of speaking take National Elections out of politics, by insisting upon Corrupt Practices legislation of the most drastic character, setting a standard for the States to rise to. Preliminary to that, by a ruthless investigation of this last campaign I would set before the American people a picture of their political machinery and practices that would set them shrieking for the legislation.

Fourth, I would continue the beneficent work of Mr. Bryan in the matter of arbitration treaties and other measures designed to compel a season of consideration in advance of hostilities. In the same spirit I would undertake all practicable measures *to take the private profit out of war*. And in the same spirit I would insist upon the principle of arbitration in all controversies between Labor and Capital. I would take each by the neck and be afraid of neither.

Fifth, I would do what I could to smash the traffic which is the chief enemy of personal, industrial and military efficiency—the Drink Business. To begin with, I would take the first opportunity to declare myself on the subject beyond the possibility of misunderstanding. I would not allow myself to forget that I had been elected by the vote of "dry" States. If I ever had said anything inconsistent with this position I would laugh and say, with Walt Whitman: "Do I contradict myself? Very well, I contradict myself."

I believe that the President who did these things on the level, would have a hard time keeping the people from making him King—to say nothing of requiring them to remember party planks or traditions about second and third cups of coffee!

Sincerely yours,   John P. Gavit

TLS (WP, DLC).
[1] That is, Edward M. Morgan, Postmaster of New York, a Republican.

From Newton Diehl Baker

Personal

Dear Mr. President: Washington. November 22, 1916.

May I suggest the possibility of securing as a bureau chief for the enforcement of the recent child labor legislation some person so well known to be in sympathy with it that our friends everywhere will realize the intention of the government to enforce the law?

Most of the difficulty of child labor legislation in the various states has come, after the passage of the law has been secured, in getting anything like sympathetic or effective enforcement of the law. We will undoubtedly have a good deal of adroit and subtle evasion of the national law. Some such man as Owen Lovejoy, McKelway, or a person whom they would suggest, would be familiar with the types of evasion which have been encountered in the enforcement of the state laws, and the appointment of such person would undoubtedly signify to the child labor advocates throughout the country the real sympathy of the administration with the measure.

Respectfully yours,   Newton D. Baker

TLS (WP, DLC).

A Memorandum by Paul Ritter

MEMORANDUM.

Washington, D.C. 22. November 1916.

Präsident Wilson empfing mich heute um 2.15 im Weissen Haus. Ich brachte ihm den Inhalt des Kabels[1] zur Kenntnis. Er war über dasselbe erfreut & sagte, dass er zur Zeit eifrig bemüht sei, Informationen zu sammeln & sammeln zu lassen darüber, wie die Volksstimmung in den kriegsführenden Ländern für den Frieden sei. Es sei dies ungemein schwierig, da überall die Presse verhindert werde, das Friedenstema zu behandeln.

Wilson führte aus, dass er daher sehr dankbar wäre, wenn die neutralen Länder ihm ihre Eindrücke, die sie in Europa erhalten, stetsfort zur Kenntnis bringen möchten, damit er auch dadurch besser zu schätzen vermöge wann der Moment zum handeln für ihn gekommen sei. Es brauche dies nicht officiell & umständlich zu geschehen, sondern wie ein Freund zum Freund & ohne Formalität. Es bestehe überhaupt viel zu viel Ceremonial zwischen den Regierungen.

Auf meinen Einwurf, dass ich bis jetzt auf dem Staatsdepartement stets die Auskunft erhalten habe, dass wenn der Präsident in Friedenssachen einen Schritt tue, er dies allein & ohne Mithilfe anderer Neutraler zu tun gedenke & auf meine Frage ob dies immer noch der Fall sei, antwortete Herr Wilson, dass die Lage einzelner Neutraler (er citirte speciell Holland) so schwierig sei, dass von ihnen nicht erwartet werden könne, dass sie normal handeln würden. (not to act normally). Ich möchte allein handeln, sagte er, um niemand in Verlegenheit zu setzen, oder gar gegen jemand discriminieren zu müssen. (I wish to embarasse no one & not to discriminate anyone.) Der Präsident fuhr fort:

Mein Plan ist noch nicht gefasst, aber es können sich unter den nächsten Nachrichten, die ich erwarte, solche befinden welche mich zu einem Handeln veranlassen möchten.

Spanien hat mir ein ähnliches Ansinnen gestellt, wie die schweizer. Regierung, allerdings nicht ein gleichlautendes. Ich hätte also eventuell auch auf Spanien Rücksicht zu nehmen.

Ich warf ein, dass das heutige Kabel meiner Regierung nicht darauf hinziele, über die Pläne des Präsidenten informiert zu werden, damit die Schweiz bei einer gemeinsamen Handlung Neutraler auch sicher mitmachen könne, denn diesen Auftrag habe ich schon früher erhalten & mich damals dementsprechend beim Staatsdepartement erkundigt & dort negative Auskünfte erhalten. Das heutige Kabel rede von ins Vertrauen gezogen werden & von der Ehre eventueller Cooperation seitens der Schweiz mit den Vereinigten Staaten.

Haben Sie denn Kenntnis was sich Ihre Regierung darunter vorstellt, fragte Herr Wilson.

Iche antwortete verneinend & sagte auf seine Anfrage was ich mir denn dabei denke, dass ich, ganz persönlich & unverbindlich

denke, dass wenn der Präsident der V.S. z.B. einen Vertrauens-
mann nach Europa senden würde, es für diesen vielleicht leichter
wäre, unter Mithilfe meiner Regierung, seine Berichterstattung
über die Meere nach dem Weissen Hause zu senden, sei doch
der schweiz. Bundesrat, durch die vielsprachige Bevölkerung, die
ihm untersteht, besser als irgendjemand in der Lage, das Seelen-
leben der uns umgebenden Kriegsführenden zu beurteilen.

Der Präsident bat mich hierauf dem Bundesrate warm zu
danken & ihn anzufragen ob ihm bei der Abfassung des Kabels
ein Plan vorgeschwebt habe, welchen er als dienliche Sug[g]estion
nutzbringend verwerten könnte. (if they have some special
method of action in mind, that would serve me with a serviceable
suggestion.)

Er erkundigte sich über die Zustände in der Schweiz, drückte
seine Bewunderung aus & erzählte zum Schlusse wie gerne er
sich der Vorlesungen, die er bei dem schweiz. Professor Guyot
an der Universität Princeton s.Z. gehört habe, erinnere.

Wir kamen auch auf die Tauchbootfrage zu reden & ich
gewann den Eindruck, dass ein Bruch zwischen den V.S. &
Deutschland, von dem jetzt wieder so viel geredet wird, nicht
zu befürchten ist.   P. Ritter[2]

TS MS (E 2001 [B], 1/17, Swiss Federal Archives).
[1] "Regarding the ever-recurring talk about peace, the press suggests that, in
view of his re-election, President Wilson may redouble his peace efforts. Since
these expectations may not be unfounded, please seek a personal interview,
if possible, and make it clear that, if Switzerland were taken into confidence,
we would be highly honored to cooperate in carrying out such plans." Political
Department to Swiss Legation, Washington, Nov. 18, 1916, T telegram (E
2001 [B], 1/17, Swiss Federal Archives).
[2] On November 23, Ritter instructed Carl P. Hübscher, Secretary of Legation, to express to Tumulty his astonishment that this very confidential meeting
had been reported in that day's *New York American*. The legation had kept
the matter strictly secret. Tumulty explained that, by long-standing tradition,
every meeting with the President was recorded in a register that was accessible
to journalists, even such a hostile one as the *New York American*. If future
meetings of this sort with Ritter were to take place, they could be held away
from the White House. Memorandum, Legation of Switzerland, Nov. 23, 1916,
T MS (E 2001 [B], 1/17, Swiss Federal Archives).

TRANSLATION

MEMORANDUM

Washington, D. C. November 22, 1916.

President Wilson received me today at the White House about
2:15. I informed him of the contents of the cable. He was pleased
at this and said that he was now busily engaged in gathering
information or having it gathered about public opinion in the
belligerent countries with regard to peace. This was uncommonly

difficult, for everywhere the press was hindered from discussing the topic of peace.

Wilson said that he would be very grateful if the neutral countries would keep him constantly informed of their impressions, as formed in Europe, so that he could thereby better judge when it was time for him to act. This need not be official and ceremonious, but as friend to friend and without formality. There was entirely too much ceremony between governments.

I remarked that, so far, I have always been told at the State Department that, if the President were to take a step in peace matters, he planned to do it alone and without the help of other neutrals. When I also asked whether this was still the case, Mr. Wilson replied that the situation of individual neutrals (he cited especially Holland) was so difficult that they could not be expected to act normally. I should like to act alone, he said, in order not to embarrass or discriminate against anyone. (I wish to embarrass no one & not to discriminate anyone.)

The President continued: My plan is not yet set, but the latest reports, which I am now awaiting, may be such as to allow me to act. Spain has made of me a request similar to but not identical with that of the Swiss government. I might therefore also have to take Spain into account.

I interjected that today's cable from my government did not seek to be informed of the President's plans so that Switzerland could take part in a common action of neutrals, for I had previously received such a proposal and spoken accordingly to the State Department, where I received negative responses. Today's cable speaks of being taken into confidence and of the honor of possible Swiss cooperation with the United States.

Mr. Wilson asked if I knew what our government proposes.

I replied in the negative and, answering his question as to what I thought about it, said quite personally and uncommittedly that, if, for example, the President of the United States should send a confidential agent to Europe, the latter, with the cooperation of my government, would find it much easier to send his reports across the sea to the White House, and, indeed, the Swiss Federal Council, through the multilanguage populace it represents, was better situated than anyone else to judge the inner life of the belligerents.

In this connection, the President asked me to thank the Federal Council warmly and ask them whether, in drafting the cable to him, they had some special method of action in mind, that would help him with a serviceable suggestion. (if they have some special method of action in mind, that would serve me with a serviceable suggestion.)

He then asked about conditions in Switzerland, expressed his admiration, and in closing told how pleasantly he recalled hearing the lectures by the Swiss Professor Guyot at Princeton University in his days there.

We also spoke of the submarine question and I gained the impression that there is no need to fear a break between the United States and Germany, about which we hear so much.

P. Ritter

To Charles Evans Hughes

The White House, Nov. 23, 1916

I am sincerely obliged to you for your message of congratulations. Allow me to assure you of my good wishes for the years to come.   Woodrow Wilson

Hw telegram (C. E. Hughes Papers, DLC).

To Jane Addams

My dear Miss Addams: The White House November 23, 1916.

Your message gave me the deepest pleasure.[1] I wish I felt more worthy of the great trust imposed in me.

Cordially and sincerely yours,   Woodrow Wilson

TLS (J. Addams Coll., PSC-Hi).
[1] It is missing.

From Robert Lansing, with Enclosure

PERSONAL AND CONFIDENTIAL:

My dear Mr. President: Washington November 23, 1916.

The Swedish Minister called upon me today and handed me the enclosed confidential memorandum relating to the plan of a conference of neutrals which was adopted last September by Sweden, Norway and Denmark, and to which they have agreed to invite Holland, Spain and Switzerland, and to afford an opportunity to this Government to take part if it so desire.

The Minister is very anxious to know our attitude to this proposed Conference and whether we would consider taking part in it. At your convenience I should like to talk the matter over.

Faithfully yours,   Robert Lansing.

TLS (SDR, RG 59, 763.72111/4329½, DNA).

ENCLOSURE

Handed me by the Swedish
Minister, Nov. 23, 1916. RL

Strictly Confidential Memorandum.

At the beginning of September last the following communication was, by agreement between Sweden, Norway and Denmark, confidentially made to the Ministers of Foreign Affairs at the Hague, Madrid and Berne through the Legations of the three northern countries:

"At the meeting of the Ministers of Foreign Affairs of Sweden, Norway and Denmark at Copenhagen in March, 1916, the question of cooperation with other neutral powers for the safeguarding of common interests, jeopardized by the world war, was the object of preliminary deliberations. It is the intention to prosecute this scheme on [at] the forthcoming meeting at Christiania by bringing up the question of issuing invitations to a conference to be held by neutral powers in order to consider common interests especially with regard to commerce, neutrality rules and the application of these rules. In choosing the subjects for discussion it is a leading principle to avoid even appearance of taking sides with either of the belligerent parties. The question of mediation is excluded from the program."

This communication was received with sympathy and interest.

Consequently at the meeting at Christiania it was moved by the Swedish delegate that steps should be taken in order to convoke such a conference.

As special subjects to be brought up at the conference were mentioned:

Treatment of submarines and airships;

Destruction of neutral prizes and the question of granting the right of asylum to such prizes;

Questions arising out of the issuing and application of "black-lists" by the belligerents;

Preparatory steps for adjusting the economic situation after the war and of apprising each other of steps taken during the war for economical-political purposes.

Both Norway and Denmark having expressed their approval of this plan, it was agreed that, as a suitable preliminary measure representatives of the three northern countries and Holland, Spain and Switzerland should meet to discuss how such cooperation as above mentioned should best be established and to draw up proposals for the organisation of a conference and for a final program.

It was also decided that the United States Government should be afforded an opportunity to take part in these deliberations, which could take place, either at a meeting of special delegates, or, if it should be deemed more practicle [practical], at a meeting of a member of the Government of the country, in which the meeting was held, and the ministers accredited to that country. Finally it was agreed that the deliberations take place at Stockholm, where all of the States invited have diplomatic representatives.

T MS (SDR, RG 59, 763.72111/4329½, DNA).

From Robert Lansing, with Enclosures

PERSONAL AND PRIVATE:

My dear Mr. President: Washington November 23, 1916.

I send you the report of Mr. Lane as to the proceedings of the Mexican Commission on November 21st.

As these papers belong to the confidential files of the Department will you kindly return them after reading?

Faithfully yours,   Robert Lansing

TLS (SDR, RG 59, 812.00/199983½, DNA).

E N C L O S U R E   I

Franklin Knight Lane to Robert Lansing

[Atlantic City, N. J.]
My dear Mr. Secretary: November 21, 1916.

Instead of sending a telegraphic report to you tonight I felt that it would be more satisfactory to forward a more detailed statement, inasmuch as today's session marks a turning point in the history of the Commission.

Early this morning the American Commissioners held a conference and reached a final decision as to the course which they would pursue in the further conducting of negotiations. It was a little before 11 o'clock before the Commission went into session and we immediately submitted the plan of withdrawal of troops and border control amended in accordance with the understanding reached at our conference in Washington. I referred to the conference at the White House[1] and am enclosing herewith (Exhibit "A"), a summary of my remarks.

After a brief discussion, the Mexican Commissioners requested a recess, inasmuch as there were several matters in the amended proposal which they wished to consider very carefully before giving their assent thereto. At 11:30 a recess was taken, with the understanding that the Commission would reassemble as soon as the Mexican Commissioners were prepared to define their attitude toward the proposed agreement.

We reassembled at 3:20. Cabrera immediately stated that the Mexican Commissioners had no fundamental objections to present. I will not burden you with the details of the discussion, as it was evident that an agreement on withdrawal of troops and border control could be reached without difficulty. In fact, early in the afternoon a tentative agreement was reached, a copy of which I am transmitting to you, designated as ("Exhibit B").

We then informed the Mexican Commissioners that the plan tentatively agreed upon covered two points, namely the withdrawal of troops and border control, but that with reference to the pursuit of marauders the Government of the United States had formulated a policy, concerning the terms of which we were authorized to inform the Mexican Commissioners and which they might transmit to their government. This statement took the following form:

"It is essential, as a matter of governmental policy, that the United States reserve the right to deal with any serious incursion from Mexico into American territory as may be deemed advisable at the time, including the right to pursue marauders into Mexican territory when such pursuit is necessary to our own protection. Duly mindful of the obligations imposed upon us by international law, such pursuit will not be intended, and should not be considered an act hostile to the Constitutionalist Government of Mexico."

To this statement Cabrera immediately took exception, on the ground that such policy was not in harmony with the principle of border control formulated in Article VI of the agreement. He did not press this point, however, and we then proceeded to submit our letter requesting from the First Chief formal assurance that immediately upon the approval of agreement on withdrawal of troops and border control the Mexican Commissioners would be authorized to proceed at once to the consideration of those other questions which the American Commissioners deem of vital importance. The text of this letter is transmitted herewith, (Exhibit "C").

Immediately after the presentation of this letter Cabrera stated that if the American Commissioners refused to submit this agreement to their government before they had received the assurance requested in the letter, General Carranza would not look upon the document as an agreement of the Commission, and that the purpose of the Commission would thus fail. This furnished us the opportunity to state a few plain truths to Mr. Cabrera. We pointed out to him, in the first place, that it was due entirely to his attitude that the assurance requested in our letter had become necessary. We pointed out to him that the correspondence between the two governments, immediately preceding the appointment of this Commission, clearly indicated that when an agreement satisfactory to both governments, with reference to the withdrawal of troops and border control, had been reached the Commission should proceed to consider "such other matters, the friendly arrangement of which would tend to improve the relations of the two countries."

I called his attention to the fact that his interpretation of the correspondence between the two governments was, and so far as we were informed still is, that the Mexican Commissioners would not proceed to the consideration of any of those questions which the American Commissioners deem so vital, until every American soldier had been withdrawn from Mexican soil. His reply was that it was true that he did not deem it advisable, while any American soldiers were on Mexican soil, to proceed to the consideration of the questions which the American Commissioners desired to submit.

Further discussion made it clear that the reason for Cabrera's attitude is that if, in the discussion of other questions, the Mexican Commissioners refused to reach constructive conclusions, the United States will delay the withdrawal of troops, and he finally said: "I do not believe that you intend to withdraw the troops from Mexican soil until we have agreed to your proposals on the other questions which you desire to submit."

I then pointed out to him that what the American Commissioners wanted to know, and were entitled to know, was whether Mr. Carranza's interpretation of the notes exchanged between the two countries was the same as Mr. Cabrera's. If so, it would be entirely useless to continue negotiations. Mr. Cabrera then said that Carranza had advised him that he, Cabrera, was right in his position.

At this point Bonillas made it clear that in his view there was not the slightest doubt that upon the approval of the agreement with reference to withdrawal of troops and border control the Mexican Commissioners should, in accordance with the terms of the notes exchanged, proceed to the consideration of the other questions.

Pani then stated that he was more interested in the questions which the American Commissioners desired to submit than the American Commissioners themselves, as he felt that they were of great importance to Mexico. He made a plea, however, that the acceptance of the proposed agreement should not be made dependent upon a condition precedent. We tried to convince him that our letter requesting assurance from the First Chief, with reference to the constructive consideration of the other questions, was made necessary by reason of the fact that the interpretation given to the powers and scope of the Commission by the Chairman of the Mexican Commission differed widely from the interpretation of the American Commissioners and that we were entitled to know the attitude of General Carranza with reference to this important matter.

I availed myself of this opportunity to say to the Mexican Commissioners that if they did not feel any real desire to work out with us a constructive program for the rehabilitation of Mexico it would be best for them not to submit anything to their government; not even the proposed agreement, because, in our minds, questions such as the protection of life and property of foreigners were of far greater moment, not only to the United States but also to Mexico than the question of border control or withdrawal of American troops. I also said to them that I was convinced that if the three Mexican Commissioners recommended to General Carranza to give the assurance requested in our letter there would be no difficulty in securing the same, inasmuch as it was asking nothing more than the fulfillment of the understanding reached by the two governments prior to the appointment of this Commission.

At this point Bonillas asserted himself, stating that he felt that there would be no difficulty in securing the assurance which the American Commissioners desired, if upon presenting the proposed agreement to the First Chief, the Mexican Commissioners requested further authority to consider such questions as either the American or the Mexican Commissioners might deem of importance. "If," he continued, "the First Chief refuses such authority then the Commission comes to an end without having accomplished anything, and the withdrawal agreement would not go into effect, but I am convinced that such authority will be forthcoming."

Soon after we had reached a tentative agreement on withdrawal and border control, the question arose as to the best method of presenting the matter to Carranza. The Mexican Commissioners are unanimous in their belief that the only way to secure adequate consideration of the whole situation is to have one of the Mexican Commissioners present the matter in person to Carranza. They feel certain that telegraphic transmittal will not bring the results which they are anxious to obtain. It is their plan, therefore, to have Pani leave for Queretaro as soon as possible.

We are to hold another session tomorrow morning at 11 o'clock, at which some matters not completely disposed of at to-day's session will be considered.

Cordially yours,   Franklin K. Lane

TLS (SDR, RG 59, 812.00/19983½, DNA).
[1] About this conference, see NDB to WW, Nov. 19, 1916, n. 1, Vol. 38.

E N C L O S U R E   I I

EXHIBITS "A," "B" and "C."

EXHIBIT "A."

Secretary Lane referred to the fact that he had a prolonged conference with the President with reference to the Mexican situation. He presented to the President the history of the negotiations of the Commission, also a mass of information which the Commission had received from various sources, some of which was favorable to the *de facto* government, but much of which indicated not only distressing conditions in Mexico, but the inability of the *de facto* government to control the situation. Continuing, Secretary Lane said, in substance:

"The desire of the President to see the *de facto* government strengthened and placed in a position to restore order in Mexico has in no way diminished. In this respect the views of the members of the American Commission are entirely in harmony with those of the President, and it was probably for this reason that they were selected to fulfill this mission. With the President, we are anxious to see a Mexico strong, independent, sovereign, and completely fulfilling her domestic as well as her international obligations. The President's purpose and our purpose in coming into this conference was to draft with you a constructive program which would strengthen the Carranza Government, and would assist in the restoration of order and prosperity in Mexico. This was our hope, and it is still our expectation.

"I must inform you, in all solemnity, that the President's patience is at an end, and that he regards present conditions in Mexico as intolerable.

"The plan of withdrawal of troops and border control which we are proposing to you this morning is but a step toward that larger constructive program which we confidently expect you to draw up with us in the same spirit of helpfulness and cooperation in which we approach these questions. Nothing short of this will satisfy either the Government or the people of the United States, and it is well for you to know this clearly and definitely at the present moment. We do not wish to do anything that will either hurt your pride or diminish your sovereignty. We have no designs on the integrity of your territory or your freedom of action in the determination of your national policy, but we are deeply and vitally interested in the fulfillment of your obligations to protect the lives and property of foreigners who have cast their lot with you, and in the satisfactory adjustment of every question which affects the cordial relations between the United States and your country. This can only be done through a policy characterized by frankness, cordiality, mutual trust and cooperation. If, however, you have reached the conclusion that you do not desire the co-operation of the United States, if you feel that you want to cut yourselves off completely, it is well for us to know this as soon as possible, as it will vitally affect our policy with reference to Mexico."

Mr. Cabrera here made the statement that it was evident from Secretary Lane's presentation that Mexico would have to follow the road indicated by the United States. To this Secretary Lane replied:

"There is no desire on the part of the United States to dictate to Mexico the policy that she should pursue. We have assured you time and again that we desire to respect your sovereignty and independence, but it is evident that many of the problems confronting you cannot be satisfactorily solved unless you have the friendship and the cooperation of the United States. It is up to you three gentlemen to determine whether Mexico is to have the benefit of such cooperation, or whether she desires to pursue a policy of isolation. This latter policy can lead to but one result, namely the downfall of the Carranza Government, with all the consequences that this will involve."

PROTOCOL OF AGREEMENT, AD REFERENDUM
WITHDRAWAL OF AMERICAN TROOPS FROM MEXICAN TERRITORY
AND
PROTECTION OF AMERICAN-MEXICAN INTERNATIONAL BOUNDARY.

Memorandum of an Agreement signed this —— day of ——, 1916, by Franklin K. Lane, George Gray, and John R. Mott, Special Commissioners of the President of the United States of America, and Luis Cabrera, Ygnacio Bonillas, and Alberto J. Pani, Special Commissioners of the Citizen First Chief of the Constitutionalist Army Entrusted with the Executive Power of the Mexican Nation:

ARTICLE I.

The Government of the United States agrees to begin the withdrawal of American troops from Mexican soil as soon as practicable, such withdrawal, subject to the further terms of this agreement, to be completed not later than —— (that is to say forty (40) days after the approval of this agreement by both Governments).

ARTICLE II.

The American commander shall determine the manner in which the withdrawal shall be effected, so as to comport with the dignity of the United States as a friendly power, and so as to ensure the safety of the territory affected by the withdrawal.

ARTICLE III.

The territory evacuated by the American troops shall be occupied and adequately protected by the Constitutionalist forces, and such evacuation shall take place when the Constitutionalist forces have taken position to the south of the American forces so as to make effective such occupation and protection. The Mexican commander shall determine the plan for the occupation and protection of the territory evacuated by the American forces.

ARTICLE IV.

The American and Mexican commanders shall deal separately, or wherever practicable in cooperation, with any obstacles which may arise tending to delay the withdrawal. In case there are any further activities of the forces inimical to the Constitutionalist Government which threaten the safety of the international border along the northern section of Chihuahua, the withdrawal of American forces shall not be delayed beyond the period strictly necessary to overcome such activities.

ARTICLE V.

The withdrawal of American troops shall be effected by marching to Columbus, or by using the Mexican Northwestern Railroad to El Paso, or by both routes, as may be deemed most convenient or expedient by the American commander.

ARTICLE VI.

Each of the Governments parties to this Agreement shall guard its side of the international boundary. This, however, does not preclude such cooperation on the part of the military commanders of both countries, as may be practicable.

ARTICLE VII.

This Agreement shall take effect immediately upon approval by both Governments. Notification of approval shall be communicated by each Government to the other.

In testimony whereof, we have signed, sealed and interchanged reciprocally this Protocol of Agreement, at Atlantic City, New Jersey, this ——— day of ———, in the Year of our Lord, one thousand nine hundred and sixteen.

EXHIBIT "C"

To The Honorable Luis Cabrera,
   The Honorable Ygnacio Bonillas,
   The Honorable Alberto J. Pani.

Gentlemen: November 21, 1916.

Having arrived at an agreement as to the withdrawal of troops and border control, we desire, in accordance with instructions from the President of the United States, to request an assurance from the Citizen First Chief of the Constitutionalist Army Entrusted with the Executive Power of the Mexican Nation that when the above mentioned agreement is approved by both Governments, you are authorized to meet at once and take up with the American Commissioners those questions deemed by the American Government of vital importance; such as protection of life and property of foreigners in Mexico, the establishment of an international claims commission, and such other questions as may be submitted by the American or Mexican Commissioners affecting the continuance and strengthening of the friendly relations between the two countries, with a view to arriving at definite conclusions to be submitted to the two Governments for their approval.

We beg to remain,

          Most respectfully yours,   Franklin K. Lane
                                  George Gray
                                  John R. Mott

To The Honorable Luis Cabrera,
 The Honorable Alberto J. Pani.
 The Honorable Ygnacio Bonillas,

Gentlemen: November 22, 1916.[1]

Having arrived at an agreement as to the withdrawal of troops and border control, we desire, in accordance with instructions from the President of the United States, to request an assurance from the Citizen First Chief of the Constitutionalist Army Entrusted with the Executive Power of the Mexican Nation that when the above mentioned agreement is approved by both Governments, you are authorized to meet at once and take up with the American Commissioners those questions deemed by the American Government of vital importance; such as protection of life and property of foreigners in Mexico, the establishment of an international claims commission, and such other questions as may be submitted by the American or Mexican Commissioners affecting the continuance and strengthening of the friendly relations between the two countries, with a view to arriving at definite conclusions to be submitted to the two Governments for their approval.

We understood from the examination of the notes exchanged between the Departments of State of the two countries that as soon as an agreement satisfactory to both countries with reference to the withdrawal of troops and border control was reached, we should immediately pass to the consideration of the other questions deemed vital to the strengthening of cordial relations between the two countries. This view has not been accepted by all of the Mexican Commissioners. It is essential therefore for us to know whether the First Chief's interpretation of the authority of this Commission is such as to empower you to proceed, as soon as the agreement relating to the withdrawal of troops and border control is approved, to the consideration of the other questions which the American Commissioners deem of vital importance. It is of course understood, as we have repeatedly stated, that the fulfillment of the terms of the agreement as to the withdrawal of troops and border control shall not be made dependent in any way upon our agreement concerning the questions referred to in the body of this letter.

We beg to remain,

 Most respectfully yours,   Franklin K. Lane
                            George Gray
                            John R. Mott.

T and CC MSS (SDR, RG 59, 812.00/19983½, DNA).
 [1] Lane wrote at the top of this document: "This is a corrected copy of letter sent you last night marked 'Exhibit C'"

From Arthur Yager

My dear Mr. President: Washington. November 23, 1916.

Upon arriving in Washington from Kentucky some days ago I had a consultation with the Secretary of War and General McIntyre of the Bureau of Insular Affairs and we all concluded that it would be better for me to hasten on to Porto Rico rather than wait in Washington for the reassembling of Congress. We were led to this conclusion partly by the recent political developments in Porto Rico, but chiefly by the fact that we could get no assurance in advance that the Senate would take up the Porto Rican bill immediately upon their reassembling or even before the Christmas holidays, and as I was needed now in Porto Rico it seemed unwise to linger in Washington for so long a time upon an uncertain contingency. I had hoped for a brief conference with you in the last few days but in default of that I am writing this letter upon the eve of my departure to beg of you that you make mention in your forthcoming message to Congress of the Porto Rican bill as one of the most urgent items of unfinished legislation. In support of this request I submit the following considerations:

First. The Philippine bill has already been passed and is in operation and as this bill and that of Porto Rico have usually been classed together it seemed to the Porto Ricans an unfair discrimination for Congress to pass the one and omit the other.

Second. As you doubtless remember, Congress suspended the elections in Porto Rico which were to take place November 7th until some future date to be fixed by the President. This action was received with gratification in Porto Rico because it seemed to imply a serious intention on the part of Congress to complete and pass the Porto Rican bill at the short session this winter. It would be a grievous disappointment to have to fix a date for and to hold these suspended elections without having first passed the new organic act.

Third. As explained in my previous letter, recent political developments in the Island, due to the sudden death of the Resident Commissioner, Mr. Muñoz Rivera, have made still more urgent the prompt passage of the Porto Rican bill. The remnants of the anti-American party in the Island have seized upon the occasion to renew their agitation for independence and to try to prevent the passage of the new bill, to which they are naturally opposed. It is, therefore, not only of urgent importance that it be passed at this session but that it be passed promptly, so that the elections can be held under its provisions and the new government organized promptly in the spring. I am perfectly confident that this will allay all political discontent and place the Island in a condition of peace and progress.

As I am leaving today for my post of duty, I submit this suggestion to you in the hope that it will stimulate the Senate to prompt action upon this urgent matter.

The bill has passed the House. It has been unanimously reported to the Senate with some amendments and, therefore, is in the most favorable position possible for prompt and early action upon it by the Senate, before the ways have been filled with other matters that may distract the attention of the Senate from the little island and its interests.

Assuring you of the highest personal regard and friendship and congratulating you afresh upon your most remarkable reelection to the great office of President, I am, and always, sincerely

Your friend,   Arthur Yager

TLS (WP, DLC).

From Edward Nash Hurley

Dear Mr. President: Washington November 23, 1916.

If the cost accounting system introduced by the Federal Trade Commission could be extended to the whole economic life of the nation, I believe it would facilitate the solution of most of the problems which we, as a country, are facing.

In 1912, if you will remember, you said that our greatest national weakness was dependent [dependence] upon artificial stimulants for our industrial life.

Your recent addresses have convinced me that there can be a wider application of the cost accounting system which we are urging business men everywhere to adopt.

Since 1912, under your leadership, we have made wonderful humane progress. We have made great strides in improving the conditions of labor; in eliminating child labor and in reducing the hours of adult labor.

Admittedly we have made greater progress in that direction than have other countries, but we have made less progress in applying efficiency to our business, manufacture and trade.

The cost accounting system which we inaugurated and which has your approval, if generally extended and made a basic principle for the teaching of all government agencies, would give the nation accurate information as to just where it stands in efficiency with respect to the rest of the world; would accelerate all the nation's processes; would make possible stupendous economies by the elimination of waste, and would open the doors to social justice.

If the cost accounting system could be extended by the Federal Trade Commission so that it might be placed at the disposal of all business men and manufacturers, there could be no demand for nursing any of them on the bottle of special privilege. Each business man would know precisely what it costs to produce a given article. Each could figure into his costs an eight hour day, a pension-retirement system, a stock ownership or profit participation plan or such other remedies as may be deemed desirable to bring about complete community of interest between capital and labor.

While his profit would be more certain, the consumer would be the chief beneficiary in that his prices would be based on a more economical production.

If the new Tariff Commission were then to build upon the work done by the Federal Trade Commission, exacting from each manufacturer a definite statement of his cost of production, tariff schedules soon would be based upon the sound foundation of American efficiency and not, as so often has been the case in the past, upon inefficiency and misinformation.

Under the old system, tariffs were frequently fixed with a view to protecting high cost of production which an accurate cost accounting system would have reduced almost automatically. I believe the system which I have outlined is the groundwork for a solution of the problem of industrial unrest. I believe it might be applied ultimately, if not immediately, to the railroad problem.

It is because it is a problem requiring leadership and general governmental cooperation, and the working of one agency with another, that I transgress upon your time to lay the matter before you. If I did not believe that it goes to the very roots of the grave problems that now confront you, I would not presume to ask your indulgence for this letter.

To put into effect the program I have outlined requires no additional legislation. It merely requires the formulation of a policy by the President and extending through existing government agencies. I have refrained from going into details because I am aware of your tremendous burdens; but the whole purpose of the program would be to establish a firm foundation for national economy and increased energy; tending surely to a decrease in the cost of living, and opening the door to such concessions to labor as will make the interests of labor and capital identical.

I believe your leadership alone is necessary to vitalize the program and make it part of our national life in the next four years.　　　　　　　Sincerely yours,　　Edward N. Hurley

TLS (WP, DLC).

From Edward Mandell House, with Enclosure

Dear Governor:　　　　　　　　New York. November 23, 1916.

I am enclosing you a copy of a letter which has just come from Vi[s]count Grey. It gives me an opportunity to write him whatever I wish.

Captain Gaunt is going to England Saturday, but this [is] not to be known to anyone excepting the British Ambassador. There is some reason for secrecy.

Gaunt has caught a conversation between Bernstorff and a certain lady here. Bernstorff told her that they were trying to negotiate a loan in America and when that was arranged they did not intend to pay further attention to America. This conversation is not mere hearsay.

Baruch tells me that Kuhn, Loeb & Co. are preparing to make a loan to the German cities just as they did sometime ago to the French cities. Before doing it they want to be sure that our relations with Germany are satisfactory, otherwise they will refuse to go on. I am wondering what, if anything, you want done in regard to this.　　　Affectionately yours,　E. M. House

TLS (WP, DLC).

E N C L O S U R E

Viscount Grey of Fallodon to Edward Mandell House

Private.

Dear Colonel House:　　　　　　London. November 2, 1916.

I send you a report of a speech I made the other day[1]: in the turmoil of the Election it may not have reached the United States.

I am writing without any knowledge of what the result of the Presidential Election will be, but whether it leaves you in touch with public affairs or whether it removes you from them by displacing your friend, please remember that I hope always to maintain the friendship and to see you again whenever there is opportunity.

It seems of little use to write about public matters such as mediation or submarines till the Election is over and we know what the President's position is, but I should like to hear from you after the Election, especially as to the prospect of a League of Nations to keep future peace being effectively supported and pressed by the United States.

Yours sincerely, Grey of Fallodon.

TCL (WP, DLC).

[1] It was Grey's speech to the Foreign Press Association at the Hotel Cecil in London on October 23. Grey began with a brief review of the origins of the war; he threw all of the blame upon Germany. Grey then declared that the Allies were determined that the war should not end until they could be certain that future generations would not be subjected to such a terrible trial. Later in the speech, Grey made it clear that this meant that the war had to continue until German militarism was destroyed. Grey then turned to the question of what neutrals could and should do to insure the future peace of the world. He urged that they promote discussion of a postwar league to prevent another world war. He also hailed the movement in the United States for a league of nations and the statements of both Wilson and Hughes as steps in the right direction. Great Britain favored such a league and also international agreement for more humane methods of warfare. London *Times*, Oct. 24, 1916; extensive extracts also appeared in the *New York Times*, Oct. 24, 1916.

From Richard Heath Dabney

Dear Woodrow: [Charlottesville, Va.] 23 Nov., 1916.

While attending a meeting of the Association of American Universities at Worcester, Mass., I sent you a telegram to Williamstown congratulating you upon your election.[1] As it was not then absolutely certain that you *were* elected, I ran a small risk of being premature with my message. But, as the papers today contain the congratulatory telegram of Mr. Hughes, I cannot refrain from writing a line to tell you how heartily I rejoice in your splendid victory. No one can now say that you are a minority President. Your vote is the largest that any candidate ever received for any office on earth, and your plurality over the candidate of the reunited wings of the Republican party is considerably more than four hundred thousand. Moreover, the fact that your vote was nearly always larger than that received by Democratic candidates for Congress, Governorships, etc., shows that the people have even more confidence in *you* than in the measures passed, upon your recommendation, by Congress. Many a man voted for you who, for instance, did not approve of the Adamson Eight-Hour Law; and many a man who desired much sterner action against Prussianism than you have taken voted for you none the less. It was a wonderful personal truimph, and I glory in the fact that popular instinct has overcome the shrewd ratiocination of the privileged class. It is needless to say that I both hope and believe that the consciousness of having the people back of you will hearten you to go on and make your second term even more successful & satisfactory than the first.

Faithfully & affectionately   R. H. Dabney.

ALS (WP, DLC).
¹ It is missing.

From Felexiana Shepherd Baker Woodrow

My dear Tommy: Marietta, Ga., Nov. 23, 1916.

The glorious news of your wonderful victory seems almost too good to be true.

With warmest congratulations to you and your dear Wife and love to you both,   Affectionately,   "Aunt Felie"

ALS (WP, DLC).

From Joseph R. Wilson, Jr.

Baltimore, Md., November 23, 1916.

I congratulate you upon having received congratulations from Mr. Hughes.   Joseph R. Wilson.

T telegram (WP, DLC).

To Edward Mandell House

My dearest Friend,   The White House. 24 November, 1916.

I have had a really overwhelming cold during nearly the whole of the week, and it has sadly thrown my plans out. The paper I had intended to write needed the clearest thinking I could do, and not until to-night have I ventured to begin it. Even now I have gone no further than a skeleton outline.

I wanted to make these suggestions:

First, that you convey to Kuhn, Loeb & Co. through Mr. Schiff, who would be sure of my personal friendship, the intimation that our relations with Germany are now in a very unsatisfactory and doubtful state, and that it would be most unwise at this time to risk a loan.

Second, that you write to Lord Grey in the strongest terms to the effect that he could be sure that the United States would go any length in promoting and lending her full might to a League for Peace, and that her people were growing more and more impatient with the intolerable conditions of neutrality, their feeling as hot against Great Britain as it was at first against Germany and likely to grow hotter still against an indefinite continuation of the war if no gre[a]ter progress could be shown than now appears, either for the Allies or the Central Powers.

It might be well to intimate to him that Page no longer represents the feeling or the point of view of the United States any more than do the Americans resident in London.

I hope that these suggestions commend themselves to you. I do not think that he ought to be left in any degree in ignorance of the real state of our opinion. It might even be well to intimate that we, in common with the other neutral nations, look upon the continuation of the war through another winter with the utmost distaste and misgiving.

I am so sorry I am not to see you to-morrow, but it would be folly for me to risk the exposure at the present stage of my cold. All join in affectionate messages.

Faithfully Yours,   Woodrow Wilson

WWTLS (E. M. House Papers, CtY).

From Walter Hines Page

Dear Mr. President: London, Nov. 24, 1916

We have all known for many years that the rich and populous and organized states in which the big cities are do not constitute the political United States. But, I confess, I hardly expected so soon to see this fact proclaimed at the ballot-box. To me that's the surprise of the election. And your popular majority as well as your clear majority in the Electoral College is a great personal triumph for you. And you have remade the ancient and demoralized Democratic party. Four years ago it consisted of a protest and of the wreck wrought by Mr. Bryan's long captaincy. This rebirth, with a popular majority, is an historical achievement— of your own.

You have relaid the foundation and reset the pillars of a party that may enjoy a long supremacy for domestic reasons. Now, if you will permit me to say so, from my somewhat distant view (four years make a long period of absence) the big party task is to build up a clearer and more positive foreign policy. We are in the world and we've got to choose what active part we shall play in it—I fear rather quickly. I have the conviction, as you know, that this whole round globe now hangs as a ripe apple for our plucking, if we use the right ladder while the chance lasts. I do not mean that we want or could get the apple for ourselves, but that we can see to it that it is put to proper uses. What we have to do, in my judgment, is to go back to our political fathers for our clue. If my long-time memory be good, they were sure that their establishment of a great free Republic would soon be imitated by European peoples—that democracies wd. take the place of autocracies in all so-called civilized countries; for that was the form that the fight took in their day against organized Privilege. But for one reason or other—in our lifetime partly because we chose so completely to isolate ourselves—the democratic idea took root in Europe with disappointing slowness. It is, for instance, now perhaps for the first time in a thorough-going way, within sight in this Kingdom. The dream of the American Fathers, therefore, is not yet come true. They fought against organized Privilege exerted from over the sea. In principle it is the same fight that we have made, in our domestic field, during recent decades. Now the same fight has come on a far larger scale than men ever dreamed of before.

It isn't, therefore, for merely doctrinal reasons that we are concerned for the spread of democracy nor merely because a democracy is the only scheme of organization yet wrought out that keeps the door of opportunity open and invites all men to their fullest development. But we are interested in it because under no other system can the world be made an even reasonably safe place to live in. For only autocracies wage aggressive wars. Aggressive autocracies, especially military autocracies, must be softened down by peace (and they have never been so softened) or destroyed by war. The All-Highest doctrine of Germany today is the same as the Taxation-without-Representation of George III—only more virulent, stronger, and further-reaching. Only by its end can the German people recover and build-up their character and take the permanent place in the world that they—thus changed—will be entitled to. They will either reduce Europe to the vassalage of a military autocracy, which may then overrun the whole world or drench it in blood, or they must through stages of Liberalism work their way towards some approach to a democracy; and there is no doubt which event is impending. The Liberal idea will win this struggle, and Europe will be out of danger of a general assault on free institutions till some other autocracy which has a military caste try the same Napoleonic game. The defeat of Germany, therefore, will make for the spread of the doctrine of our Fathers and our doctrine yet.

An interesting book might be made of concrete evidences of the natural antipathy that the present German autocracy has for successful democracy and hence for us. A new instance has just come to me. My son, Arthur, who succeeded to most of my activities at home has been over here for a month and he has just come from a visit to France. In Paris he had a long conversation with Delcassé, who told him that soon after he became Foreign Secretary the last time (I think about 1909), the Kaiser himself made a proposal to him to join in producing "the complete isolation" of the United States. What the Kaiser meant was that if the Great Powers of Europe wd. hold off, he wd. put the Monroe Doctrine to the test and smash it.

The great tide of the world will, by reason of the war now flow towards democracy—at present alas! a tide of blood. For a century democracies and Liberal governments have kept themselves too much isolated, trusting prematurely and too simply to international law and treaties and Hague conventions. These things have never been respected, except as springes[1] to catch woodcock, where the Divine Right held sway. The outgrowing or the overthrow of the Divine Right is a condition precedent to the effectiveness of international law and treaties.

It has seemed to me, looking at the subject only with reference to our country's duty and safety, that somehow and at some early time our championship of democracy must lead us to redeclare our faith and to show that we believe in our historic creed. Then we may escape falling away from the Liberal forces of the Old World and escape the suspicion of indifference to the great scheme of government which was set up by our fathers' giving their blood for it. I see no other way for us to take the best and biggest opportunity that has ever come to prove true to our faith as well as to secure our own safety and the safety of the world. Only some sort of active and open identification with the Allies can put us in effective protest against the assassins of the Armenians and the assassins of Belgium, Poland, and Serbia and in a friendly attitude to the German people themselves, as distinguished from their military rulers. This is the attitude surely that our fathers would have wished us to take—and would have expected us to take—and that our children will be proud of us for taking; for it is our proper historic attitude whether looked at from the past or looked back at from the future. There can be no historic approval of neutrality for years, while the world is bleeding to death.

The complete severance of relations, diplomatic at first and later possibly economic as well, with the Turks and the Germans would probably not cost us a man in battle nor any considerable

[1] That is, snares.

treasure; for the moral effect of withdrawing even our formal approval of their conduct—at least our passive acquiescence—would be—that the Germans would see that practically all the Liberal world stands against their system, and the war wd. end before we should need to or could put an army in the field. The Liberal Germans are themselves beginning to see that it is not they but the German system that is the object of attack because it is *the* dangerous thing in the world. Maximilian Harden presents this view in his Berlin paper. He says in effect that Germany must get rid of its predatory feudalism. That was all that was the matter with George III.

Among the practical results of such action by us would, I believe, be the following

(1) the early ending of the war and the saving of, perhaps, millions of lives and of incalculable treasure,

(2) the establishment in Germany of some form of more liberal government

(3) a league to enforce peace, ready-made, under our guidance—*i.e.* the Allies & ourselves,

(4) the sympathetic coöperation and the moral force of every Allied government in dealing with Mexico,

(5) the acceptance—and even documentary approval, of every Allied government of the Monroe Doctrine,

(6) the warding off and no doubt the final prevention of danger from Japan, and,

most of all, the impressive and memorable spectacle of our Great Democracy thus putting an end to this colossal crime, merely from the impulse and necessity to keep our own ideals and to lead the world right. We should do for Europe on a large scale essentially what we did for Cuba on a small scale and thereby usher in a new era in human history.

I write thus freely, Mr. President, because at no time can I write in any other way and because I am sure that all these things can quickly be brought to pass under your strong leadership. The United States would stand, as no other nation has ever stood in the world—predominant and unselfish—on the highest ideals ever reached in human government. It is a vision as splendid as the Holy Grail. Nor have I a shadow of doubt of the eager and faithful following of our people, who wd. thereby reëstablish once for all our weakened nationality. We are made of the stuff our Fathers were made of.

And I write this now for the additional reason that I am within sight of the early end of my service here. When you calld. me I answered, not only because you did me great honor and laid a

definite patriotic duty on me but because also of my personal
loyalty to you and my pride in helping forward the great principles in which we both believe. But I understood then (and I
am sure the subject lay in your mind in the same way) that my
service would be for four years at the most. I made all my arrangements, professional and domestic, on this supposition. I
shall, therefore, be ready to lay down my work here on March
4 or as soon thereafter as meets your pleasure.

I am more than proud of the confidence that you have shown
in me. To it I am indebted for the opportunity I have had to give
such public service to my country as I could as well as for the
most profitable experience of my life. A proper and sympathetic
understanding between the two English-speaking worlds seems
to me the most important duty of far-seeing men in either country. It has taken such a profound hold on me that I shall, in
whatever way I can, work for its complete realization as long as
I can work for anything.

I am, Mr. President, most faithfully and gratefully,

yours,   Walter H. Page

ALS (WP, DLC).

An Unpublished Prolegomenon to a Peace Note

[c. Nov. 25, 1916]

When the air is burdened with peace rumors and the diplomatic wires which girdle the world are hot with overtures and
suggestions of peace, it is a pertinent question to ask, What are
the terms of a lasting peace? For, with the horrible nightmare
still upon it, the world will listen to no suggestion which does not
seek to safeguard it against such a recurrence in the future.
When this unprecedented eruption subsides, if we are still to
live over the volcano, we must know that the last spark of life
in it is extinguished. War, before this one, used to be a sort of
national excursion, a necessary holiday to vary the monotony of
a lazy, tranquil existence on which the population turned out to
celebrate their freedom from conventional restraint, with brilliant
battles lost and won, national heroes decorated, and all sharing
in the glory accruing to the state. But can this vast, gruesome
contest of systematized destruction which we have witnessed for
the last two years be pictured in that light, in which all the great
nations of Europe were involved, wherein no brilliant battles such
as we thrill to read about were either lost or won, but few national figures decorated above the rest, and no particular glory

accrued to any state; wherein the big, striking thing for the imagination to respond to was the untold human suffering?

In assessing the terms of a lasting peace, we are too apt to allow our sympathies with one side or the other to override our judgment. If we are pro-Ally, German militarism must first be crushed ere a lasting peace is tenable. If our sympathies are the other way, then the first essential to a lasting peace is the defeat of British navalism. Both contentions, it must be admitted, are sound, convincing arguments, not only to their respective authors, but to the unprejudiced neutral who has no interest in the war except to bring it to an end. In the extreme point to which Germany has carried its military organization, he sees a serious menace to the permanent peace of Europe and of the world. But in no less a degree does he recognize the source of international friction existent in the absolute control of the seas by Great Britain, or any other one power. There are other objects to be attained, however, which the partisan does not usually consider in his assessment of the case.

Assuming that German militarism were crushed by the decisive defeat of German arms, would that be the prelude to a lasting peace? Is it necessary to answer the question? Would the breaking of British navalism bring it on? It is only necessary to go back to the war of 1870 to disprove either assumption. With France then hopelessly beaten, a huge indemnity levied upon her, and two of her fairest provinces torn from her bosom, it was thought that, thus crippled, she would reconcile herself to the superiority of German arms and in time forget the ravishment of her territory. On the contrary, then was born one of the germs of the present war: she paid the indemnity and reconstructed her whole life, with the single object of excelling German military organization and regaining Alsace and Lorraine.

On the other hand, Germany, flushed with victory and puffed up at the ease with which it had broken the vaunted military power of France, began to dream greater dreams of conquest and power. Another germ was hatched which was to develop into the dreadful malady of the present conflict. We see it abundantly demonstrated in the pages of history that the decisive victories and defeats of wars are seldom the conclusive ones. One Sedan brings on another, and victory is an intoxicant that fires the national brain and leaves a craving for more.

Were Germany, by a decisive victory, to bring her enemies to their knees, the partitioning of territory would at once be begun and a huge indemnity levied to stand her cost of the war; and from that minute on she would have to prepare herself for another conflict which would inevitably come. Even she, with her unmatched genius for military organization, could never hope to keep the whole of Europe in military subjection. With the defeat of Germany, the inevitable procedure would be the annexing of her colonies, the allot[t]ing out of the territory of her allies, and an indemnity collected for the rehabilitation of Belgium, Serbia, and Rumania; perhaps, too, for the reimbursement in part of the military expenses of the Entente. Needless to say, such an outrage to her pride would never be forgotten; it would rankle in her breast as did the rape of Alsace-Lorraine to the French. Based on either of these hypotheses, an enduring peace is the empty talk of partisan dreamers.

The crowned victor in a mighty conflict too easily forgets the suffering and the agony endured in achieving the end. The memory of the death struggle which all but overpowered it is dimmed by the growing sun of glory and is finally eclipsed altogether. In the language of the street, the victorious nation, as the man, gets "cocky" again, places another chip on its shoulder and becomes unendurable as a neighbor. As a consequence, it has another fight on its hands ere its sword grows rusty.

What, then, are the terms which make for an enduring peace? The present war, with its unprecedented human waste and suffering and its drain of material resource, presents an unparalleled opportunity for the statesmen of the world to make such a peace possible. Never before in the world's history have two great armies been in effect so equally matched; never before have the losses and the slaughter been so great with as little gain in military advantage. Both sides have grown weary of the apparently hopeless task of bringing the conflict to an end by the force of arms; inevitably they are being forced to the realization that it can only be brought about by the attrition of human suffering, in which the victor suffers hardly less than the vanquished. This may require one year, maybe two.

To bring about a peace with these circumstances prevailing, when the big, outstanding thing to be remembered by all nations was the uselessness of the utter sacrifices made, would be to give it the essential basis of endurance—the psychological basis. Deprived of glory, war loses all its charm; when the only attribute of it is suffering, then it is something to be detested. In the revelation of the modern processes of battle, it has already lost some of its halo. The mechanical game of slaughter of today has not the same fascination as the zest of intimate combat of former days; and trench warfare and poisonous gases are elements which detract alike from the excitement and the tolerance of modern conflict. With maneuver almost a thing of the past, any given point can admittedly be carried by the sacrifice of enough men and ammunition. Where is any longer the glory commensurate with the sacrifice of the millions of men required in modern warfare to carry and defend Verdun? With this experience conducing, the aim of far-sighted statesmen should be to make of this mightiest of conflicts an object lesson for the future by bringing it to a close with the objects of each group of belligerents still unaccomplished and all the magnificent sacrifices on both sides gone for naught. Only then would war be eliminated as a means of attaining national ambition. The world would be free to build its new peace structure on the solidest foundation it has ever possessed.

In the event of such a peace, the objects for which all the belligerents are fighting will be entrusted for accomplishment to the convention which is to assemble after the war, as should be.

T MS (C. L. Swem Coll., NjP).

A Draft of a Peace Note

[c. Nov. 25, 1916]

1 I take the liberty of addressing to you very frankly certain questions which seem to speak out almost of themselves from the circumstances and present progress of the war and of which I feel justified in making myself the spokesman not only because I am privileged to speak as the head of a great nation whose vital interests are being more and more seriously and profoundly affected with each week of the war's continuance but also because both my heart and my reason tell me that the time has come to take counsel lest a violence be done civilization itself which cannot be atoned for or repaired.

2 In every quarter of the world the life of mankind has been altered and disturbed. Everywhere it is hindered and perplexed, rendered harder, more hazardous, more difficult to plan or to live upon any terms. The task of every government, the task of caring for and promoting the interests of its own people, has been hampered and impeded; and the burden falls, as always, upon those least prepared, least able to bear it.

3 The position of neutral nations, in particular, has been rendered all but intolerable. Their commerce is interrupted, their industries are checked and diverted, the lives of their people are put in constant jeopardy, they are virtually forbidden the accus-

tomed highways of the sea, their energies are drawn off into temporary and novel channels, they suffer at every turn though disengaged and disposed to none but friendly and impartial offices.

4 And[1] yet the objects which would, if attained, satisfy the one group of belligerants or the other have never been definitely avowed. The world can still only conjecture what definitive results, what actual exchange of guarantees, what political readjustments or changes, what stage or degree of military success even, would bring it to an end.[2] If any other nation now neutral should be drawn in, it would know only that it was drawn in by some force it could not resist, because it had been hurt and saw no remedy but to risk still greater, it might be even irreparable, injury, in order to make the weight in the one scale or the other decisive; and even as a participant it would not know how far the scales must tip before the end would come or what was being weighed in the balance!

5 Authoritative spokesmen of the nations engaged have, indeed, spoken in general terms[3] of the issues involved; but they have nowhere, so far as I know, made any definite statement of the measures which would in their judgment bring those issues to a practical settlement. Whatever may have brought the war on, they believe the very life and political integrity of the nations they represent to be involved. They are fighting, they have declared, to be quit of aggression and of peril to the free and independent development of their peoples' lives and fortunes. They feel that they must push the conflict to a conclusion in order to make themselves secure in the future against its renewal and against the rivalries and ambitions which brought it about. But to what conclusion? These are very general terms. What sort of ending, what sort of settlement, what kind of guartantees [guarantees] will in their conception constitute a satisfactory outcome, promising some prospect of perman[en]cy and safety?

6 Leaders on both sides have declared very earnestly and in terms whose sincerity no one can justly doubt that it was no part of their wish or purpose to crush their antagonists, make conquest of their territories or possessions, deprive them of their equal place and opportunity among the great peoples of the world. They have declared also that they are fighting no less for the rights of small and weak nations and peoples than for those

[1] In his shorthand draft, Wilson began this sentence as follows: "And yet the reasons for the war remain obscure and the objects. . . ."
[2] This sentence, in Wilson's shorthand draft, reads: "As it is not known what motives led to its sudden outbreak, it is not known what results. . . ."
[3] The shorthand draft: "spoken very definitely."

of the great and powerful states immediately involved. They have declared their desire for peace, but for a peace that will last, a peace based, not upon the uncertain balance of powerful alliances offset against one another, but upon guarantees in which the whole civilized world would join, that the rights and privileges of every nation and people should be the common and definite obligation of all governments.

[7] With these objects the people and government of the United States whole-heartedly sympathize. And they are struck by the circumstance that, stated in the general terms in which they have been stated, they are the same,—are the same even in specific detail, as, for example, the security of all nations alike, whether they be weak or strong, against a[g]gression and competitive force.[4] We are ready to join a league of nations that will pledge itself to their accomplishment and definitely unite in an organization not only of purpose but of force as well that will be adequate to assure their realization. They are ready to lend their every resource, whether of men or money or substanc[e] to such a combination, so purposed and organized. If that be the object of the present war, they are ready when the right moment comes to cooperate to bring it about. But how are they to know when that moment comes unless they be apprised by what test the nations now at war will judge the time of settlement and definition to have come? What must constitute victory by the one side or the other, and what must that victory mean?

[8] The conflict moves very sluggishly. Only upon one or two separated fields here and there do armies move with definite success. Along the main lines of battle, so far as we can judge, there can be no rapid change, until———? Must the contest be decided by slow attrition and ultimate exhaustion, the slow expenditure to [of] millions of human lives until there are no more to offer up on the one side or the other? Triumph so gained might defeat the very ends for which it had been desired.[5] Upon a triumph which overwhelms and humiliates cannot be laid the foundations of peace and equality and good will. A little while and it may be too late to realize the hopes which all men who love peace and justice entertain and which all statesmen must see to be the only hopes worthy to serve as the motive of great and permanent plans for mankind. Exhaustion, reaction, political upheaval, a resentment that can never cool would make such

[4] This sentence is not in the shorthand draft.
[5] Thus in the shorthand draft: "Triumph might bring disaster because upon a triumph which overwhelms. . . ."

hopes vain and idle. An irreparable damage to civilization cannot promote peace and the secure happiness of the world.

9. In such circumstances and moved by such considerations, I deem myself to be clearly within my right as the representative of a great neutral nation whose interests are being daily affected and as the friend of all the nations engaged in the present struggle, and speaking with the utmost respect for the rights of all concerned, in urging as I do most earnestly urge, that some means be immediately taken, whether by conference or by a separate formulation of demands and conditions, to define the terms upon which a settlement of the issues of the war may be expected. It has become necessary that the nations that are now neutral should have some certain and definite guide for their future policy. It is necessary that they should have some certain means of determining what part they shall henceforth play should the terms defined be impossible of realization and the end of the war be indefinitely postponed.

The simplest means of arriving at this end would be a conference of representatives of the belligerent governments and of the governments not now engaged in the war whose interests may be thought to be most directly involved, and it is such a conference that I take the liberty of urging, whatever its outcome may be. If that be not feasible, it is possible that other means may be found which will in effect accomplish the same result.

10. My object, my sole object, in pressing this essential issue now is to assist, if I may, in bringing the war to an end before it is too late to remedy what it has done; to bring about an early reconsideration of peace on the basis of the rights alike of the weak and of the strong, the rights of peoples as well as of governments; and to afford an opportunity to form such a league of nations as all now desire, a league united and powerful enough in force and purpose to guarantee the peace of the world against further breach by injustice or aggression,—guarantee it by the sheer might of an intelligent and irresistable organization of the major force of mankind in the common interest of civilization.[6]

Let me say, in order that there may be no danger of any misunderstanding, that I am not renewing or seeking to press my offer of mediation made at the outset of the war. I then expressed my desire to be of service to the belligerents by any offices of accommodation looking towards an end of the contest that they might any of them suggest or encourage; and that offer of course stands. But I am not now returning to that. Neither am I pro-

[6] All new text from this point on.

posing peace. I am doing a very simple, a very practical, and a very different thing. I am asking, and assuming that I have the right to ask, for a concrete definition of the guarantees which the belligerents on the one side and the other deem it their duty to demand as a practical satisfaction of the objects they are aiming at in this contest of force, in addition to the very great and substantial guarantee which will, I feel perfectly confident, be supplied by a league of nations formed to unite their force in active cooperation for the preservation of the world's peace when this war is over. To answer these questions need not commit any belligerent to peace at this time; but until they are answered no influential nation of the world not yet involved in the struggle can intelligently determine its future course of action. The United States feels that it can no longer delay to determine its own.

WWT MS (WP, DLC).

To Edward Mandell House

My dearest Friend,   The White House. 25 November, 1916.

I have completed a first draft of the paper. Would it be convenient for you to come down and spend Monday evening and night with us to talk it over (and of course as much longer as you can)? I think things are thickening and we should choose our course at once, if we have data enough to form a judgment on.

I am better. I hope that I had a clear head enough for the draft.

All join in affectionate messages.

In haste,   Affectionately Yours,   Woodrow Wilson

WWTLS (E. M. House Papers, CtY).

From Edward Mandell House, with Enclosure

Dear Governor: New York. November 25, 1916.

I hope you will soon be rid of your cold. It would have been a mistake to have come today as it is so cold and windy.

I am enclosing a copy of a letter from Bernstorff.

What would you think of Bill Edwards[1] for Postmaster of New York? He would please the Independents and the regulars, I think. Just how well he could do it, I do not know, but it would be a popular appointment.

Affectionately yours,   E. M. House

TLS (WP, DLC).
[1] That is, William Hanford Edwards, Princeton 1900, former Commissioner of Street Cleaning in New York, at this time an insurance broker.

ENCLOSURE

Count Johann Heinrich von Bernstorff to Edward Mandell House

Washington, D. C.
November 23, 1916.

My dear Colonel House:

On Tuesday I sent a long cable to Berlin as I promised you.

There is no intention on the part of my Government to make any change in the principle of submarine warfare. I am, therefore, sure, that Berlin will be prepared to make all necessary reparation for the mistakes in the "Arabia" and "Marina" cases. If these two ships were really not—as the submarine commanders believed them to be—armed transport ships, they certainly came very near it.

I hope the whole question of *"armed merchantmen"* will not be brought up, but that we can limit the discussion to *"armed transports"* so that a long controversy is avoided, and I *do* hope that the President will be satisfied, if my Government goes as far as it can.

I shall call on Mr. Lansing as soon as I receive definite information. If *you* wish to see me on this subject, please wire or phone and I will come over to New York immediately for a few hours.

What do you think of Lord Derby's speech?[1] It seems to confirm my opinion, that the Allies *could* not and would not refuse to *talk*, and that is all they are to be asked to do. Whether the negotiations would lead to peace, is, of course, quite a different matter, but I am confident that they would.

Yours very sincerely,   J. Bernstorff.

TCL (WP, DLC).

[1] He meant the interview with Lord Derby printed in the *New York Times*, Nov. 23, 1916. Asked about the prospects for early peace negotiations, Derby replied: "All I can say is that any peace proposal that would come from Germany would be met by the Allies with all the consideration it deserved." He expressed doubt that Germany would offer any peace plan "worth seriously considering." When asked about possible American proposals to end the war, he answered: "The Allies would, of course, listen to any word from America, but that is not saying they would come at this time to any peace agreement."

From Henry Pomeroy Davison

My dear Mr. President: New York. November 25th, 1916.

In keeping with my promise to give you information regarding the external debts of both Great Britain and France, I am in receipt of a cable from the Chancellor, through our London house, stating that the external debt of Great Britain on November 18th, 1916, was approximately £225,000,000, being about 7% of the total debt; that the budget revenue of the British Government for the current year is about £500,000,000. He adds that there has been no recent official estimate of the national income, but upon the basis of calculations made by expert statisticians, he puts the normal income at about £2,500,000,000 sterling, adding that the income at the present time owing to high prices and profits is considerably higher.

Through our Paris house we are informed that the total exterior debt of France is Fcs. 5,925,000,000, of which Fcs. 1,813,-000,000 is held in the United States and Fcs. 3,960,000,000 is held in England. The aggregate of these totals 7.8% of the entire obligations of the French Republic including the Bank of France, and the bonds and notes of the Defense Nationale.

Both of these percentages are higher than I had supposed, but in each case I had not taken into consideration the obligations between the Allies, which owing to the extraordinary conditions would, I should suppose, find a practical offset in case of need.

In furnishing you with this information I beg to avail of the opportunity to assure you that we will take the greatest satisfaction in furnishing you with any information which we may have upon this or upon any other subject at any time.

Believe me, my dear Mr. President,

Most respectfully yours,   H. P. Davison

TLS (WP, DLC).

From the Diary of Charles Sumner Hamlin

Nov 25 Sat. [1916].

Met early in morning and went over letter or rather a statement for insertion in the Bulletin along lines of Agents letter.[1] Warburg furnished a draft wh. to my mind was offensive to Allies —it even complained of the prospectuses of their loans (presumably the Russian loans) as false and misleading and laid down rules as to what facts the offering Bankers should state in the prospectus. It also admitted that conservatism in purchasing the British Exchequer Notes would cause our exports to fall off, but said that as to certain exports (munitions, I suppose) it would be a good thing for the country. I insisted on striking out all about prospectuses as unnecessary and also as to the Notes as investments from point of view of endowed investors, and pointed out that at the interview w. Davidson[2] many of the Board

—especially Dr Miller—said they were a first class investment say up to 500 millions.

Delano pointed out that the reference to falling exports being beneficial would give the embargo advocates a great weapon.

The President sent word he would see Harding at 2.30 and finally we put the proposed draft in rough shape for the President to see.

3. P.M. Gov. H. said had seen President who said he agreed w. the Board that great caution shld be exercised by the Banks in investing in these Notes; that he had hoped the Board would make a public statement but he had not felt like suggesting it; that he would read this proposed announcement and return it with suggestions Monday.

Warburg is in 7th heaven of delight; while he talks fairly I can not but feel he is so prejudiced against the Allies that he will go to almost any extreme to injure them & this feeling has made me very cautious as to what we should say & insistent on confining our remarks to the Banks & not to the investing public. If we were to issue the statement as any drawn by Warburg I am confident it would have precipitated great confusion & trouble financially.

Bound diary (C. S. Hamlin Papers, DLC).
[1] About this problem, see Link, *Campaigns for Progressivism and Peace*, pp. 200-201, and the Enclosure printed with WW to W. P. G. Harding, Nov. 26, 1916.
[2] He of course meant Henry P. Davison.

To William Procter Gould Harding, with Enclosure

CONFIDENTIAL

The White House.
My dear Mr. Harding,   26 November, 1916.

I am taking the liberty of using my own pen (for so I regard this typewriter) to make reply to the question you put to me yesterday about the enclosed statement.

I like it. I am glad that the Board has determined that it is its duty to make it. Such advice to the banks seems to me very timely and indeed very necessary. My only suggestion is that the statement be made a little stronger and more pointed and be made to carry rather explicit advice against these investments, as against the whole policy and purpose of the Federal Reserve Act, rather than convey a mere caution. The securities spoken of, though nominally liquid, will in the event, I should say, certainly not be so, and our domestic transactions might be seriously embarrassed and impeded should the national banks tie up their resources in them.

Thank you very much for consulting me on this extremely important matter, which might at any time be radically affected by a change in the foreign policy of our government.

Cordially and sincerely Yours,   Woodrow Wilson.

TCL (E. M. House Papers, CtY).

E N C L O S U R E

November 27, 1916.

The Federal Reserve Board today made public the following statement relating to foreign credits, which is to appear in the next issue of the Federal Reserve Bulletin:

In view of contradictory reports which have appeared in the press regarding its attitude toward the purchasing by banks in this country of Treasury bills of foreign governments, the Board deems it a duty to define its position clearly. In making this statement the Board desires to disclaim any intention of discussing the finances or of reflecting upon the financial stability of any nation, but wishes it understood that it seeks to deal only with general principles which affect all alike.

The Board does not share the view frequently expressed of late, that further importations of large amounts of gold must of necessity prove a source of danger or disturbance to this country. That danger, the Board believes, will arise only in case the inflowing gold should remain uncontrolled and be permitted to become the basis of undesirable loan expansion and of inflation. There are means, however, of controlling accessions of gold by proper and voluntary cooperation of the banks or if need be by legislative enactment. An important step in this direction would be the anticipation of the final transfer of reserves contemplated by the Federal Reserve Act to become effective on November 16, 1917. This date could be advanced to February or March 1917. Member banks would then be placed on the permanent basis of their reserve requirements and fictitious reserves would then disappear and the banks have a clearer conception of actual reserve and financial conditions. It will then appear that while a large increase in the country's gold holdings has taken place the expansion of loans and deposits has been such that there will not remain any excess of reserves, apart from the important reserve loaning power of the Federal Reserve Banks.

In these circumstances the Board feels that member banks should pursue a policy of keeping themselves liquid; of not loaning down to the legal limit, but of maintaining an excess of reserves—not with reserve agents, where their balances are loaned out and constitute no actual reserve, but in their own vaults or preferably with their Federal Reserve Banks. The Board believes that at this time banks should proceed with much caution in locking up their funds in long-term obligations or in investments, which are short term in form or name but which, either by contract or through force of circumstances, may in the aggregate have to be renewed until normal conditions return. The Board does not undertake to forecast probabilities or to specify circumstances which may become important factors in determining future conditions. Its concern and responsibility lie primarily with the banking situation. If, however, our banking institutions have to intervene because foreign securities are offered faster than they can be absorbed by investors—that is their depositors—an element would be introduced into the situation which, if not kept under control, would tend toward instability, and ultimate injury to the economic development of this country. The natural absorbing power of the investment market supplies an important regulator of the volume of our sales to foreign countries in excess of the goods that they send us. The form which the most recent borrowing is taking, apart from reference to its intrinsic merits, makes it appear particularly attractive as a banking investment. The Board, as a matter of fact, understands that it is expected to place it primarily with banks. In fact it would appear so attractive that unless a broader and national point of view be adopted, individual banks might easily be tempted to invest in it to such an extent that the banking resources of this country employed in this manner might run into many hundreds of millions of dollars. While the loans may be short in form, and severally, may be collected at maturity, the object of the borrower must be to attempt to renew them collectively, with the result that the aggregate amount placed here will remain until such time as it may be advantageously converted into a long-term obligation. It would, therefore, seem as a consequence that liquid funds of our banks, which should be available for short-credit facilities to our merchants, manufacturers and farmers, would be exposed to the danger of being absorbed for other purposes to a disproportionate degree, especially in view of the fact that many of our banks and trust companies are already carrying substantial amounts of foreign obligations, and of acceptances which they are under agreement to renew. The Board deems it therefore its duty to caution the member banks that it does not regard it in the interest of the country at this time that they invest in foreign Treasury bills of this character.

The Board does not consider that it is called upon to advise private investors but as the United States is fast becoming the banker of foreign countries in all parts of the world, it takes occasion to suggest that the investor should receive full and authoritative data—particularly in the case of unsecured loans—in order that he may judge the future intelligently in the light of present conditions and in conjunction with the economic developments of the past.

The United States has now attained a position of wealth and of international financial power, which, in the natural course of events, it could not have reached for a generation. We must be careful not to impair this position of strength and independence. While it is true that a slowing down in the process of credit extension may mean some curtailment of our abnormally stimulated export trade to certain countries we need not fear that our business will fall off precipitately should we become more conservative in the matter of investing in loans, because there are still hundreds of millions of our own and foreign securities held abroad which our investors would be glad to take over, and moreover trade can be stimulated in other directions.

In the opinion of the Board, it is the duty of our banks to remain liquid in order that they may be able to continue to respond to our home requirements, the nature and scope of which none can foresee, and in order that our present economic and financial strength may be maintained when, at the end of the war we shall wish to do our full share in the work of international reconstruction and development which will then lie ahead of us, and when a clearer understanding of economic conditions as they will then exist, will enable this country more safely and intelligently to do its proper part in the financial rehabilitation of the world.

TC MS (E. M. House Papers, CtY).

To Robert Lansing

The White House.

My dear Mr. Secretary, 26 November, 1916.

I would be very much obliged to you if you would discuss this with me orally at the earliest opportunity,—say after the meeting of the Cabinet on Tuesday next, the 28th. I do not feel certain yet of my insti[n]ctive judgment in the matter, which is adverse to any participation by our government in the conference proposed.[1]   Faithfully Yours,   W.W.

WWTLI (SDR RG 59, 763.72111/4330½, DNA).
[1] See RL to WW, Nov. 23, 1916 (first letter of that date). Lansing left the following record of his meeting with the Swedish Minister: "MEMORANDUM of Conversation with SWEDISH MINISTER, on Friday, December 1, 1916
"I told the Minister that I had requested him to come to the Department in regard to the Memorandum which he left with me on November 23d in which was outlined a plan for a conference of neutrals regarding certain subjects mentioned in the memorandum, and which proposed to invite Holland, Spain and Switzerland to join with Sweden, Norway and Denmark in such conferences, stating that it was decided to afford an opportunity to the United States Government to take part in these deliberations.
"I informed the Minister that after very careful consideration of the subject, and after a conference with the President in regard to the proposed meeting, we had reached the conclusion that it would be inadvisable for this Government to participate in a neutral conference at this time; that the reasons for this decision were that on account of our geographical location our problems in regard to the subjects proposed for discussion were so different from those of countries contiguous to the belligerents that there would be no common ground for discussion; that, furthermore, we were peculiarly related to the American Republics and they were not included as possible conferees; and that it had been our policy heretofore, and seemed to be a wise one, to act independently of other countries although, as far as possible, obtaining identic action with them.
"The Minister said that he appreciated our attitude in regard to the proposed conference and would communicate our decision to his Government. Robert Lansing." TS MS (SDR, RG 59, 763.72111/4331½, DNA). The substance of this memorandum was sent as RL to All Diplomatic Missions, Dec. 4, 1916, T telegram (SDR, RG 59, 763.72/3039A, DNA).

To Robert Lansing, with Enclosure

The White House.
My dear Mr. Secretary,   26 November, 1916.

It is with the deepest reluctance that I approve and authorize the course here proposed, but I am convinced that it is the least of the evils in sight in this very perplexing situation. I therefore authorize you to issue the necessary instructions in the premises.

I have stricken out the sentence in the proposed proclamation which authorizes the commanding officer to remove judges and others in certain circumstances. It may be necessary to resort to such extreme measures, but I do not deem it wise to put so arbitrary an announcement in the proclamation itself.

Faithfully Yours,   W.W.

WWTLI (SDR, RG 59, 839.00/1952, DNA).

E N C L O S U R E

From Robert Lansing

PERSONAL AND PRIVATE:

My dear Mr. President: Washington November 22, 1916.

The situation in the Dominican Republic is approaching a crisis and we ought to determine immediately a course of action, as otherwise revolution and economic disaster are imminent.

After reviewing conditions with Mr. Stabler, Chief of the Latin American Division, I requested him to embody the conclusions we reached in a letter to me, which he has done and which I enclose to you together with other papers bearing on the subject.[1] You will also perceive that Mr. Polk has taken up the matter with Mr. Stabler, Minister Russell, Admiral Benson and Captain Knapp. Captain Knapp is a most competent officer and has been since the beginning of the war a member of the Neutrality Board. He has just been given command of the squadron in Dominican waters. I know him well and place great reliance upon his judgment and discretion.

I will be glad to receive at your earliest convenience your instructions as to the course which should be taken.

Faithfully yours,   Robert Lansing.

TLS (SDR, RG 59, 839.00/1952, DNA).

[1] J. H. Stabler, "*Re Santo Domingo*," Nov. 21, 1916, TS MS; John Brewer to Secretary of State, Nov. 20, 1916, TC telegram; W. W. Russell, "Memorandum," Nov. 9, 1916, TS MS; J. H. Stabler, "Re Dominican Situation," Oct. 31, 1916, TS MS; "Tentative Draft" of proclamation, T MS, all SDR, RG 59, 839.00/1952, DNA. These documents all reviewed recent developments in the Dominican Republic. Stabler, in his memorandum of November 21, said that both the State and Navy departments "thought that the only solution of the difficulty would be the declaration of martial law and placing of Santo Domingo under military occupation." Most of the documents listed above are printed in *FR 1916*, pp. 239-47. For discussions of events leading to the military occupation of the Dominican Republic by the United States, see Sumner Welles, *Naboth's Vineyard: The Dominican Republic, 1844-1924* (2 vols., New York, 1928), II, 700-96; Dana G. Munro, *Intervention and Dollar Diplomacy in the Caribbean, 1900-1921* (Princeton, N. J. 1964), pp. 269-325; and Arthur S. Link, *Wilson: The Struggle for Neutrality, 1914-1915* (Princeton, N. J., 1960), pp. 538-48.

To Robert Lansing, with Enclosure

The White House.

My dear Mr. Secretary,   26 November, 1916.

I think there is undoubtedly sufficient ground here for a very solemn protest, and I suggest that it be made orally, to the following effect:

That this Government has heard of this action with the greatest regret and wishes to enter its most friendly but most solemn protest as in contravention of all precedent and the long accepted principles of international practice;

That its effect upon Belgian relief, so humanely planned and so successfully car[r]ied out, will probably be fatal, to the great embarrassment, we should assume, of the German government; and

That I feel that it has placed a new and vehy [very] serious obstacle in the way of efforts looking towards peace which I had hoped made [might] soon be made and which I was anxiously seeking an opportunity to make.

I hope that the suggestion of the last paragraph can be successfully withheld from any, even the least, publicity, by the most painstaking precautions. I believe, from Mr. Grew's recent despatches, that it will be the most persuasive part of the protest.

Faithfully Yours,   W.W.

WWTLI (SDR, RG 59, 763.72115/3782, DNA).

E N C L O S U R E

Frank Lyon Polk to Robert Lansing

My dear Mr. Secretary   [Washington, c. Nov. 25, 1916]

The Belgian Minister has just handed the enclosed note to me. I thought you might wish to show it to the President

Yours in haste   Frank L Polk

ALS (SDR, RG 59, 763.72115/3782, DNA).

The situation in Belgium becomes more and more terrible every day. The rounding up of able-bodied Belgians is now being carried out throughout the country. When not compelled to work in Germany in munition factories they are sent to occupied France and made to build trenches and strategic railways. The Germans announce that they will deport 350,000 Belgians. Requisitions continue with the avowed object of ruining the country's industries. All materials which could be of use to the Germans are carried off by them, all other materials are sold at ridiculously low prices. The Governor General has declared to the "New York Times" that the deportations are made without any complaint from those deported: this is false. As a matter of fact the victims endure moral torture, acute physical suffering and all the disgrace of slavery. The German Government seek to justify their action by pleading the necessity of checking unemployment; they have in fact promoted unemployment by obstructing the municipalities in their attempts to engage the unemployed on public works, and forbidding the opening up of coal mines in Limbourg. Belgium is abandoned to the violence of the military authorities, and this is approved of and acquiesced in by the civil authorities. You should beg the Secretary of State to urge the German Government to consider the consequences of the crimes against the laws of humanity committed in their name. Germany before being forced to evacuate Belgium desires to leave her in the condition of a lifeless body, but while intent on torturing her she makes herself an outcast among nations, and instead of imposing peace by intimidation raises the whole civilised world against her.

T MS (SDR, RG 59, 763.7115/3782, DNA).

From the Diary of Colonel House

The White House, Washington. November 26, 1916.

Polk met me at the station and gave me the despatches he referred to over the telephone. I dropped him just before we reached the White House.

The President received me in the hall and asked me to take tea with Mrs. Wilson and Mrs. Gerard. After tea I dressed for dinner and joined the President in his study where we talked of things of minor importance.

After dinner we went to the study and began the discussion of the object of my visit. He read several letters and despatches from abroad which Polk had already shown me. He then read a draft of the proposed note to the belligerents urging them to state what terms they demanded as a basis for peace.

It was a wonderfully well written document, yet, strangely enough, he had fallen again into the same error of saying something which would have made the Allies frantic with rage. I have called his attention to this time after time and yet, in almost every instance where he speaks of the war, he offends in the same way.

The sentence to which I objected was: "the causes and objects of the war are obscure." I told him the Allies thought if there was one thing clearer than another it was this; that their quarrel with him was he did not seem to understand their viewpoint. They hold that Germany started the war for conquest; that she broke all international obligations and laws of humanity in pursuit of it. They claim to be fighting to make such another war impossible, and to so break Prussian militarism that a permanent peace may be established.

I urged him to insert a clause in lieu of the one to which I objected which would make the Allies believe he sympathized with their viewpoint. I thought he could do it in a way to which Germany would not object and might even take as vindication of her own position.

I also suggested another clause, which he inserted, stating specifically he was not trying to mediate or demand peace.

He again insisted that I go over and be in England when this note was delivered. I should dislike to do this for many reasons. His note may be received with great indignation and con[s]trued as a move in favor of Germany and, besides that, my going may bring about a crisis with Page. I called the President's attention to this phase and he expressed indifference to Page's attitude. He thought it would not affect anyone excepting Page, and he felt quite content to have him resign in any way he would.

I do not share this view. Page could resign stating that he did not approve the President's overtures and it would make him popular in England and the President correspondingly unpopular. It would also be a blow at the proposal. We argued this earnestly from various angles, but I did not convince the President that it was a serious obstacle. He asked me to think out the best way of sending the note without cabling it. He thought if it were cabled, it would become public property immediately and before it reached the distant belligerents. It would reach England and France within a few hours, but would take days to reach Russia, Germany and Austria.

I thought he should prepare a better background than he now has for the reception of the note, particularly in the Allied countries. This, I thought, might be done by making a firm protest in regard to Belgian deportations. I told of my having a cable sent over, with the consent of Lansing, giving the true story of the part our Navy took in the activities of U53. This I felt would create a favorable impression. My whole idea is to delay until the time seems propitious. It is too important a matter to bungle, and if he is not careful, that is what he will do.

I repeated my conversation with Mr. Bryan.[1] Bryan has gotten upon the nerves of the President because of the insistence of the Bryan clique that Bryan has again won the election for the President by his campaign in the Far West. The dinner to be given Mr. Bryan in Washington also seemed to disturb him. This is a foolish move on the part of Bryan enthusiasts, and if they wished to give him a dinner it should have been held elsewhere.

The President wished to know how much of his former influence I thought Bryan had recovered. My opinion was that he stood about where he stood before the election and that he need not be considered as a menace to the President's leadership unless the President himself aided him by treating him unkindly.

I outlined my views as to what the situation would be four years from now. I do not share the general view that the Western States that voted for the President this time can be counted upon in the future, and if we assumed that the solid South and the Trans-Mississippi country will work together, we should labor under a delusion. I thought the pendulum in the East would swing back to the Democratic Party, and if the democrats four years from now nominate an Eastern man, the republicans would probably nominate Hiram Johnson of California and the old alignment of the East and South would again be successful. The President expressed some astonishment at this view because, since the election, everyone seems to hold a contrary one.

The President had a letter from Gavit, of the New York Evening Post, which he read to me. Gavit desires him to do several things and, strangely enough, the President was rather inclined to do them all. I shall arrange to see Gavit when I return and have a talk with him.

One of the things the President wished to talk about was the advisability of taking up prohibition and advocating it. I did not give a definite opinion but was inclined toward acquiescence. Politically it would be bad for the Democratic Party, but I have come to believe that prohibition carries with it so much more of good than evil, that it must eventually prevail. It cannot become effective until it is nation-wide, and if the President threw the weight of his great influence in its behalf, I am not sure that he could do anything better. The result in Russia during the war must have convinced fair-minded people of the beneficent effects of prohibition. It was about the last thing I thought the President would suggest or consider doing, and I am sure from what he said, that Mr. Bryan's advocating it as an issue in 1920 had much to do with his leaning in that direction. His idea is, I feel certain, to take the question out of Mr. Bryan's hands into his own, which would eliminate Bryan as a political force in the party.

Mr. Bryan originates many great ideas, and someone more practical than he uses them. Among others Roosevelt robbed him in this way.

T MS (E. M. House Papers, CtY).

¹ "I called on Mr. Bryan at the Holland House on my way to the station. It is the first time we have met since he left the Cabinet. He was most cordial. He asked me to say to the President that he expected to be at the Peace Conference in any event, that is, if the President did not commission him to represent the United States, he would go in the capacity of a private citizen. He also said that, in his opinion, he could stop the war if the President would give him proper authority and credentials and allow him to go to Europe. He said, 'They are all Christians and not pagans, and I could talk to them in a christianlike way and I am sure they would heed.'" House Diary, Nov. 26, 1916.

From the Diary of Charles Sumner Hamlin

Nov 27 Monday [1916]

Board met 11 am. Gov H. read confid. letter from Presdt stating that he had read our proposed statement as to the Brit. Exch. Notes and fully approved it. The only suggestion he would make was that it was not strong enough and could be made more positive; that he believed it most dangerous for banks to invest in this kind of security as it was not liquid & would prove very embar[r]assing *if there should be any change in our foreign policy.*

Board then amended the statement to make it stronger.

From William Procter Gould Harding, with Enclosure

Dear Mr. President: Washington November 27, 1916.

Will you permit me to thank you for your memorandum and to say that the Board has strengthened its statement somewhat and that it will be given to the press for publication tomorrow morning.

I enclose a copy of the revised statement with the new matter underlined.   Respectfully yours,   W P G Harding.

TLS (WP, DLC).

E N C L O S U R E

*STATEMENT FOR THE PRESS*¹

November 27, 1916. . . .

The Board deems it, therefore, its duty to caution the member banks that it does not regard it in the interest of the country at this time that they invest in foreign Treasury bills of this character.

The Board does not consider that it is called upon to advise private investors but as the United States is fast becoming the banker of foreign countries in all parts of the world, it takes occasion to suggest that the investor should receive full and authoritative data—particularly in the case of unsecured loans— in order that he may judge the future intelligently in the light of present conditions and in conjunction with the economic developments of the past.

T MS (WP, DLC).
    1 What follows is the new text; otherwise, this statement is identical with the copy printed as an Enclosure with WW to W. P. G. Harding, Nov. 26, 1916.

To William Procter Gould Harding

[The White House]
My dear Mr. Harding: November 27, 1916
    Thank you sincerely for the revised copy of the statement. The addition seems to meet very adequately what I had in mind.
        Cordially and sincerely yours,   Woodrow Wilson

TLS (Letterpress Books, WP, DLC).

To Robert Lansing, with Enclosure

My dear Mr. Secretary: The White House November 27, 1916
    This paper enclosed emanates from a group of men who are anything but our friends and many of whom would be very glad indeed to embarrass us, and I would value a suggestion from you as to what reply should be made to the inquiry.
        Cordially and faithfully yours,   Woodrow Wilson

TLS (SDR, RG 59, 763.72115/2632½, DNA).

E N C L O S U R E

From Frederick Wallingford Whitridge and Others

New York, November 25, 1916.
    There are many of our citizens who wish to do their part toward an expression of public opinion regarding the deportation of Belgians into Germany and France, which as now reported appears to be in violation of law and humanity. We should be glad to have all the information possible so as to be sure of the facts before taking public action. May we have such information as may be proper as to what facts the State Department has, what our Government has done and what so far as known other neutral

governments have done about the violation of international law in this respect. If the facts are not now known by our Government cannot they be obtained from our Minister to Belgium?

Fredrick W. Whitridge,	S. R. Bertron,
Rev. Dr. W. T. Manning,	Pierre Mali,
Senator Root	Rev. Dr. Slattery.
A. J. Hemphill,	R. Fulton Cutting
Thos. Ryan	Joseph H. Choate
Rob't Bacon	Benj. T. Calle,
Francis L. Stetson,	Robert T. Brides
James M. Beck,	John M. Parker, New Orleans;
H. L. Stimson,	W. H. King.[1]

T telegram (SDR, RG 59, 763.72115/2632½, DNA).

[1] Individuals not already identified in this series are: the Rev. Dr. William Thomas Manning, rector of Trinity Episcopal Church; Alexander Julian Hemphill, chairman of the board of the Guaranty Trust Co.; Pierre Mali, Belgian Consul General; the Rev. Dr. Charles Lewis Slattery, rector of Grace Episcopal Church; and Robert Fulton Cutting, financier, civic leader, and philanthropist, all of New York. W. H. King may have been William H. King, proprietor of a paint business in New York. Calle and Brides cannot be identified; perhaps the telegrapher garbled their names.

To Charles William Eliot

Personal and Confidential.

My dear Doctor Eliot: The White House November 27, 1916

It really was not necessary for you to add argument to your brief telegram of the twenty-first of November about the sad Belgian business. The case argues itself and I am taking steps which I hope will be influential, if not effective.

As to the second matter touched on in your letter, you may be sure the purpose you have in mind has my entire sympathy and I shall at once consult the Postmaster General about the possibility of his attending the meeting of the Civil Service Reform Association on December fifth.

In haste, with much respect,

Sincerely yours,   Woodrow Wilson

TLS (C. W. Eliot Papers, MH-Ar).

To Albert Sidney Burleson

My dear Burleson: The White House November 27, 1916

Will you be kind enough to look particularly at the last part of this letter and tell me what you think? It might be a ten-strike for you to go to the meeting and let the whole crowd know exactly what is going on.

   Always

           Cordially and faithfully yours,   Woodrow Wilson

Went against my will. Made speech & was introduced by Presdt Hadley.[1]

TLS (A. S. Burleson Papers, DLC).
   [1] ASBhw.

To Richard Heath Dabney

My dear Heath: The White House November 27, 1916
   You may be sure that your letter of November twenty-third warmed the cockles of my heart and was one of the most welcome letters I ever received. Your telegraphic message sent to Williamstown reached me, but I am only now beginning to come to the surface after being submerged in messages from many quarters and looking around to pick out the people I especially want to write to.
   With warmest thanks for every word you say,
                   Affectionately yours,   Woodrow Wilson

TLS (Wilson-Dabney Corr., ViU).

To Joseph R. Wilson, Jr.

Dear Joe: [The White House] November 27, 1916
   Your telegram about Mr. Hughes' message amused me very much. It was a little moth-eaten when it got here but quite legible.
                   Affectionately yours,   Woodrow Wilson

TLS (Letterpress Books, WP, DLC).

To Arthur Yager

                                          [The White House]
My dear Governor Yager: November 27, 1916
   I was sincerely sorry not to see you before you left for Porto Rico. I did not know that your early departure had been planned.
   I fully appreciate the importance of the Porto Rican Bill and have embodied a strong recommendation of its passage in the address which I shall make to Congress now in a few days.

I shall try to interest myself continuously in the matter until something is accomplished.

In haste, with warmest regard,

Cordially and faithfully yours, Woodrow Wilson

TLS (Letterpress Books, WP, DLC).

To John Palmer Gavit

My dear Mr. Gavit: [The White House] November 27, 1916

Thank you for your letter of November twenty-second. It is just the sort of letter I like to receive and you may be sure it has made a deep impression on me, because whether we agree as to the items or not, we certainly agree as to the method.

Cordially and faithfully yours, Woodrow Wilson

TLS (Letterpress Books, WP, DLC).

To Felexiana Shepherd Baker Woodrow

My dear Aunt Felie: The White House November 27, 1916

Thank you with all my heart for your message of the twenty-third. It was delightful to get it.

My own feeling is one of rather overwhelming responsibility, because I must live up if I can to the confidence the people have reposed in me, but in the midst of the responsibility I feel, of course, the delightful warmth at my heart which comes from such apparently personal trust as the people have shown.

With affectionate messages from us all,

Faithfully yours, Woodrow Wilson

TLS (received from James Woodrow).

From Newton Diehl Baker

My dear Mr. President: Washington. November 27, 1916.

I have your letter of the 22d, acknowledging the receipt of the resolution adopted at the Annual Convention of the National Consumers League, and note that you ask how far I think legislation like that in the recent Child Labor Bill can properly go.

This problem is in part at least the old puzzle of the limitations of State authority and State adequacy as against National intervention. Things which 20 years ago seemed to me exclusively matters of State concern have come with the passing years to be obviously appropriate subjects for National legislation because of the changed character of the things themselves, and so I do not know that I have reached any clear conclusion as to where the Federal Government ought to stop in this kind of police regulation, but for practical purposes I am entirely clear that at present we ought not do anything more than we have done. The Child Labor law still has to run the gauntlet of the Supreme Court, and still has to be put into practical operation. In the meantime, the 8-Hour Railroad Employees Bill is still in the courts and with those two problems still only partially solved, I personally think it would be unwise to complicate the situation by other legislation of like sort. Perhaps in the next Congress we will be able to have a clearer view of the possibilities of Federal action as the result of what the Supreme Court says about these two laws and our efforts to enforce them.

Respectfully yours, Newton D. Baker

TLS (WP, DLC).

From Samuel Reading Bertron

My dear Mr. President: New York November 27, 1916.

Our Belgian Relief Commission has been importuned to take every possible action in this Country to aid in protesting against the removal of the Belgians from their homes by the Germans, in contravention of the law. In order to be of some service, the Commission, joined by citizens here, are proposing to have a large meeting here for the purpose of protesting against such unwarranted action. Being a member of the Commission, I was asked that my name be used, with a view of first ascertaining from Washington the exact position and then in joining in the protest of citizens here. I agreed to do so on condition that no action should be requested of the Administration that could be in the slightest degree embarrassing. On my return to town I find that a telegram had been sent you asking for information, in which my name and that of several other Democratic friends was used, without my having seen the telegram. I want to say to you, Sir, that if there is anything in the slightest degree embarrassing in this respect my name and that of my Democratic associates will be withdrawn.

Please permit me to thank you heartily for your kind communication to John M. Parker.[1] He deserved it and his co-operation, as the result of the election proved, was invaluable.

There is every disposition in the large cities, by those who were formerly opposed to your election, to get in now and help the Administration in every possible way. This is certainly true of the business community. Mr. Reynolds, President of the largest bank in Chicago, assured me of this when I met him last Friday and stated that he was going to give out interviews to this effect in Chicago. Mr. Hepburn, the Dean of our banking fraternity here is equally emphatic in making such assurances of support.

Never before has a President had such a compliment or such an opportunity and I pray that your strength will be such as to permit you to solve the great problems before you. Please rest assured that I and all other friends are ready to be of aid when we can.

Please command me when I can be of any assistance possible, and believe me,   Faithfully yours,   S R Bertron

TLS (WP, DLC).
1 WW to J. M. Parker, Nov. 15, 1916, Vol. 38.

From Annie Wilson Howe Cothran

New York City
My dear Uncle Woodrow,   November 27th [1916]

I was sadly disappointed when I learned a cold had prevented your coming to the game, for I looked forward to, at least, a glimpse of you all. I hope your cold is entirely gone by now. It would have been very risky to sit through the game   They said it was dreadfully cold. I did not go myself for I was going just to be with you all. Thank you just the same for sending the tickets to me   Some friends here were overjoyed to receive them. They had the box to themselves.

I am mighty sorry to trouble you when you are not well, and when you have a million and one things to worry over, but I have wanted you to know my plans and how they were working out.

I am delightfully situated among very dear friends who help to make my lonliness a little more bearable. Coming back here was very hard. I never realized how dreadful it could be, or I fear I should never have found the courage to come alone.

I am paying $75.00 a month for Room rent light, heat, linin & service. The place is furnished. Baby and I together pay $72.00 a month for table board. I have had to get a nurse girl too   My strength gave out and I could not sing more than five songs without becoming exhausted.

I pay her five a week $20.00 a month then $12.00 a month for her table board. She saves me my laundry bills which have always been a big item and I feel that in her I have a bargain. About $9.00 or $10.00 a month covers incedentals such as phone, fees, car fare back and forth to Mr Davids. The milk and eggs I have been ordered to take by Dr Davis in Phila. and anything in addition.

Dr Davis made me promise I would get my strength by making it a business of my life. I have gained already and am doing hard work in my music. Mr. David says I am ready to sing at my concert tomorrow if I needed to. I want to show you dear, dear people what I have done and can do when I see you next. Margaret says you want me and baby down in Wash on Xmas, if so I am going to sing for you and see what you think. May I? I know that you have not had a moment to try and have what mother had transfered to me and therefore I shall have to ask you to please let me have a little cash to go on. I am all paid up to the 30th of Nov. but my bank is growing slim—very slim. Do you think I can be trusted, dear Uncle Woodrow to run my own affairs and open an account in the bank? I want to prove to you and my precious brothers how well I can do. I have had some experience with Mother and she and I went over things together, always. I am keeping an itemized account of even a penny paper and am learning to keep my books very neatly and accurately.

I am well—thin as always, but I believe gaining a pound at a time. Baby is fine so well & so full of joy! I shall leave here for Pittsburg on December 10th for my concert on the 12th and return the 13th. I hope, with some money of my own in my pocket.

Give Edith and Helen my dearest love and keep a world full of very real, very warm love for yourself.

Devotedly yours Annie.

ALS (WP, DLC).

To Robert Lansing

The White House.

My dear Mr. Secretary,   28 November, 1916.

Let me suggest the following as the confidential part of the instructions to Grew, and let me express the hope that unusual pains will be taken to make it indeed confidential.

Please represent to the Chancellor confidentially and very earnestly the very serious unfavourable reaction in the public opinion of this country caused by the Belgian deportations at a time when that opinion was more nearly approaching a balance of judgments as to the issues of the war than ever before; and also, and more particularly, the serious embarrassment that reaction has caused the President in regard to taking steps looking towards peace. Say that the President is watching the whole situation with the utmost solicitude with a desire and a definite purpose to be of service in that great matter at the earliest possible moment and has again and again been distressed to find his hopes frustrated and his occassion destroyed by such unhappy incidents as the sinking of the MARINA and the ARABIA and the Belgian deportations. Say that the President has noted with the deepest interest what you reported in one of your recent despatches about the evident distress and disappointment of the Chancellor that nothing had come of his intimations about peace and that what the President is now earnestly pleading for is practical cooperation on the part of the German authorities in creating a favourable opportunity for some affirmative action on his part in the interest of early peace.[1]

Cordially and faithfully Yours,   W.W.

WWTLI (R. Lansing Papers, NjP).
[1] For the telegram as sent, see RL to J. C. Grew, Nov. 29, 1916.

From William Cox Redfield

My Dear Mr. President: Washington November 28, 1916.

The inclosed correspondence with Judge Adamson refers to the matter of which I spoke in the Cabinet.[1] The bill is pending before Adamson's committee, and as you will see he seems to block the way.

The glory of your Administration has been and is its human outlook, but in leading thought along such noble lines must we not ourselves be careful lest we be found wanting? I feel that the failure to treat the field officers of the Lighthouse Service, whose duties are peculiarly dangerous, just as we are treating the officers of the Coast Guard, not only does injustice by prefer[r]ing one class of Government servants over another equally worthy, and bearing the same risks or worse, but continues a condition whose inhumanity is obvious to all who understand it.

Yours very truly,   William C. Redfield

TLS (WP, DLC).
[1] W. C. Redfield to W. C. Adamson, Nov. 25, 1916, CCL; W. C. Adamson to W. C. Redfield, Nov. 26, 1916, TLS; W. C. Redfield to W. C. Adamson, Nov. 28, 1916, CCL; all in WP, DLC. Redfield urged the passage of S. 4225, or at least that portion of the bill which provided pensions for members of the field force of the Lighthouse Service. Adamson, in his reply, professed high regard for Red-

field but flatly refused to "change the great principles of a lifetime" by "opening the doors to fraud by permitting civil service employees to raid the Treasury with civil service pensions." In his rejoinder to Adamson of November 28, Redfield denied that he was "insisting on civil service pensions." He pointed out that, under recent legislation, the Lighthouse Service would become a part of the navy in time of war and argued that its members were therefore entitled to the same benefits as were those of the Coast Guard, who received pensions.

From Joseph Patrick Tumulty

| | The White House. |
| Memorandum for the President: | November 28, 1916. |

Senator Ashurst telephones that he has been delegated as a committee of one to invite the President to attend a dinner which is to be given Mr. Bryan in this city on December 6th. It is not important, he says, that he present this invitation in person, but it is important that he know within twenty-four hours, if possible, if the President is or is not coming to the dinner. He asks if he may not have the President's acceptance or declination without delay in order that he may proceed with the plans for the dinner.[1]

TL (WP, DLC).
[1] See the extract from the diary of Henry F. Ashurst printed at Dec. 2, 1916, n. 2.

From the Diary of Colonel House

November 28, 1916.

I had breakfast alone, the President and Mrs. Wilson deciding to play an early game of golf. He offered to forego this if I had anything of importance to discuss, but I told him I had finished last night so far as I was concerned. They wished me to go to the links with them but I thought I had better see Lansing, Polk and Phillips at the State Department.

Polk came to the White House from his home and we went to the State Department together where I had nearly an hour's conference with Lansing. I spoke of the President's desire for me to go abroad and asked him to use his influence toward postponing it, since I did not dare express my own views too strongly for fear the President might think I was unwilling to go.

Lansing does not think much of the League to Enforce Peace. He believes if it is inaugurated, only democracies should be elegible for membership. Forming a league with such limitations would be difficult and would give offence.

After leaving Lansing, I went to Phillips' office, and had him walk with me to the White House in order that we might talk en-route. When I reached the White House I found the President had returned, and I left Phillips and went into the study where the President was signing answers to innumerable congratulatory election telegrams and letters. It was mechanical work and we talked for nearly an hour.

The President indicated a purpose not to be bound by party ties, but to appoint the best men to office he could find. We took up the Postoffice Department and outlined a way by which he could bring practically the entire service under the Civil Service law. He asked whether I thought the country would approve and whether it was desired and would be popular. I believed it would.

He was sorry to have me leave and expressed the hope I would soon come again. Polk and I took the 12.30 train and were soon joined by Carter Glass who was also going to New York.

To Martin Travieso, Jr.

[The White House]
My dear Governor Travieso: November 29, 1916.

Your kind message of congratulation has been transmitted to me by General McIntyre.[1] Allow me to thank you most warmly for the good will which prompted you to send it.

Cordially and sincerely yours,   Woodrow Wilson

TLS (Letterpress Books, WP, DLC).
[1] F. McIntyre to JPT, Nov. 11, 1916 (second letter of that date), Vol. 38.

From William Bauchop Wilson

My dear Mr. President: Washington November 29, 1916.

The recently threatened railway strike has clearly demonstrated the danger to the country in the possibility of the entire transportation systems being tied up at the same time. Through the introduction of railway transportation our populous centers have been educated to rely on supplies coming from long distances in the interior for their food and other necessities. Our industrial and commercial system has been built up on a reliance on railway facilities. If a strike occurs, involving all of the railways at the same time, within one week every industrial and commercial establishment in the country would be idle and their workers out of employment. Every farmer having perishable crops ready for the market would lose them. Starvation would stalk abroad in our great cities, and the first to feel the effect would be the little children, dependent on their daily milk supply.

Food riots would follow in every part of the country at the same time, with the police powers having neither the force nor the inclination to suppress them. No one can foretell what the ultimate issue would be. It is evident that some method must be found that will prevent the recurrence of such a menace in the future.

As you know, I have been opposed to compulsory arbitration, primarily because I did not believe any man or set of men should be compelled to work against their will for the profit or convenience of any other man or set of men, and, secondarily, I believe that in any system of general arbitration the final protection of the wage-workers against unfair decisions would be the standard of living, which is flexible and may be raised or lowered and the workmen still live, while the employer would have as his final protection the clean cut inflexible line between profit and loss, which he would be able to show specifically from his cost accounts, thereby giving a greater measure of protection to the employer than to the employee against the possibility of unfair decisions. I realize that the second objection is more or less academic, but the first one involves a fundamental principle of human liberty. For that reason I have been opposed to the Australian system of compulsory arbitration, because it penalizes the workers who collectively refuse to work under an award, and for the same reason I have been opposed to the introduction of the Canadian system compelling the employees to continue at work thirty days pending an investigation. I have given a great deal of thought to the subject matter, but it is only recently that there has begun to develop in my mind an idea that seems to me would prevent the possibility of a general strike and yet leave the workers free to quit work, individually or collectively, if they so desired, and the employers free to shut down their operations so far as their charter rights would permit them to do so. Men may here or there in small numbers quit work for malicious purposes. The number of such instances is few. When strikes occur it is almost invariably the case, and is invariably the case when large numbers are involved, that they engage in them because they hope to gain something as a result of the strike. If you can create a system by which nothing can be gained by striking and provide other machinery by which gains can be made, you will thereby remove the incentive to strike and you could then leave the workers free to work or not to work, individually or collectively, with absolute confidence that they would continue to work.

It seems to me that the object sought can be accomplished by the establishment of a Railway Labor Commission, to be composed of nine members, three to be representative of the employees, three to be representative of the employers, and three to be representative of the public generally. Three of them to be appointed for nine years, three for six years, and three for three years, and thereafter the term of office to be nine years, if that is possible within the terms of the Constitution. The Commission to have jurisdiction in labor disputes between employees engaged in the moving and dispatching of trains used in interstate commerce, such as engineers, firemen, conductors, trainmen, switchmen, telegraphers, etc., and their employers. The jurisdiction of the Commission to extend to cases:

(A) Where a dispute is presented to the Commission by any citizen representing twenty per cent. or more of any of the classes of labor enumerated or any group of them, or presented to the Commission by the representatives of any railway, steam or electric, engaged in interstate commerce.

(B) When any strike order is about to be taken or has been taken.

(C) When any strike order has been issued or a strike has occurred.

The Commission to have power to compel the attendance of persons and papers and to administer oaths, to hear and determine the issues and to have power to grant the full demands of either side or any modification of them; the awards to apply to the places to be filled rather than to the men who at the time the award was made occupied the places; the award to be for three years, and thereafter, unless either side shall, after the expiration of three years, seek to re-open the case, and, except that upon either side showing that an emergency or abnormal condition has arisen since the dispute was decided, the Commission may re-open the case. That all awards made shall be upon the basis of an eight-hour schedule or less for the operation of trains, and may include extra time for overtime, if deemed necessary for the enforcement of the schedule. That the Department of Justice be directed to prosecute in the courts of competent jurisdiction claims for wages arising out of an award when the wage rate is not being complied with. That the workmen shall be free to individually or collectively refuse to work under the award and the employers shall be at liberty to cease to operate their roads in so far as their charter rights may permit them to do so, but if they do work or do operate it must be in accordance with the terms of the award.

The important difference between this suggestion and that of other compulsory arbitration laws which have been suggested is that it makes it useless for railway employees to strike and therefore abolishes the likelihood of their doing so instead of endeavoring to secure the enforcement of an award by penalizing the strikers.

I am submitting to you the foregoing for your consideration, and may add that I do not know what the attitude of the leaders of labor would be in connection with it, as I have not discussed the suggestions with any of them.

Faithfully yours,   W B Wilson

TLS (WP, DLC).

From Newton Diehl Baker, with Enclosures

My dear Mr. President: Washington. November 29, 1916.

I inclose you a copy of General Funston's reply to my inquiry, and I attach a copy of my telegram to him upon its receipt. The whole purpose of this inquiry is of course merely to have a soundly thought-out plan in the event of its being determined here that it is wise to act, and I am keeping General Funston under orders not to act without definite and positive instructions from the Department.   Cordially yours,   Newton D. Baker

TLS (WP, DLC).

E N C L O S U R E   I

Fort Sam Houston, Texas [Nov. 28, 1916].

Number 3807. Confidential. Replying your number 4999, in case conditions developed as suggested by you, I recommend that as soon as Villa and his main body are known to be approaching Juarez,[1] that is, shall have passed north of Ahumada, General Bell inform General Pershing, who will then start column number one, consisting of two infantry, one regiment of cavalry, one battery of heavy artillery, and one battery of mountain artillery, one pioneer company, Corps of Engineers, one ambulance company Hospital Corps, one field hospital company Hospital Corps now at El Valle, with view to cutting railroad at Gallego. Infantry and engineers to move by trucks. The distance of 70 miles could be covered by infantry in approximately seven hours. Cavalry, artillery and other units to follow, arriving within approximately 24 hours. At same time column number two consisting of three regiments of cavalry from Dublan should move towards railroad at Ahumada. It would require from 36 to 48 hours for these troops to cover this 90 miles. As soon as column number one started, General Bell to start column number three from El Paso, Texas, consisting of two or three infantry, depending upon size of Villa's force, two batteries, pioneer company Corps of Engineers, motor cycle company, one motorized ambulance company Hospital Corps and one field hospital company Hospital Corps, all to be moved in auto trucks, to cross river at Fabens, Texas, following automobile roads and striking railroad at Samalayuca or Ahumada, depending on the location of Villa's force. Column number three to be followed by two regiments of cavalry. Each one of these columns would in all probability be strong enough to attack Villa's force and certainly could protect itself against attack. Closing in as they would, Villa would be left but little opportunity to escape except in southeasterly direction, where there are but few roads which lead into mountainous country. If circumstances made it necessary and advisable, cavalry columns could pursue. Supply for columns numbers one and two to be maintained by autotrucks from Columbus, N. M., there being sufficient number companies at that point for this purpose. Supply for column number three to be maintained by autotrucks from El Paso, Texas. After all columns had united on railroad, all supplies to be sent from El Paso, Texas, by way of Fabens, Texas.

Funston.

[1] Villa, on the rampage again, had captured Chihuahua City on November 26, and there was much talk to the effect that he would attempt to capture Juárez and perhaps attack El Paso also.

E N C L O S U R E   I I

[Washington, Nov. 28, 1916]

Your number 3807 received. Plan will be considered here. Take no action upon it without explicit directions from War Department. We will use information transmitted by you and that from State Department and other sources to keep informed, and will give you all information promptly.

Baker,   Secretary of War.

T telegrams (WP, DLC).

From George Carroll Todd[1]

Dear Mr. President: Washington. November 29, 1916.

The Attorney General, who is away for a brief period, left directions that I submit to you an outline of the course of action of the Department of Justice in the matter of the increasing cost of the necessaries of life.

Two broad limitations upon the power of this Department in the field in question should be stated at the outset:

First. Increases in prices, brought about not by agreement or conspiracy but by a common selfish impulse of traders to take advantage of the extraordinary conditions of the times, are not punishable under any Federal law, no matter how completely lacking in economic justification, no matter how extortionate.

Second. Sales of commodities by retailers to consumers in the various cities and communities generally fall outside the field of interstate commerce and therefore outside the jurisdiction of the Federal Government.

Within these limitations the Department of Justice has brought to bear its full energy. Immediately after the outbreak of the European War in August, 1914, when the first marked increases took place, the Attorney General instructed the various United States District Attorneys and the various agents of the Bureau of Investigation throughout the country to make inquiry in their respective communities for the purpose of ascertaining whether any such increases were due to agreements or conspiracies in restraint of interstate trade. These instructions have been repeated from time to time since.

In the course of the inquiries operations on several of the leading produce exchanges of the country, including the Chicago Board of Trade and the Minneapolis Chamber of Commerce, have been carefully looked into for possible violations of existing Federal statutes, but none thus far has been disclosed.

As regards anthracite coal, the recent abnormal increases in the price of which have caused so much public concern, the Department of Justice during the present Administration has been especially active.

The control of this commodity has become centered in a few railroads. The backbone of the combination is the Reading Holding Company, which controls two of the great railroads from the anthracite field, namely, the Philadelphia & Reading and the Central of New Jersey, and two great coal mining companies, namely, the Philadelphia & Reading and the Lehigh & Wilkes-Barre, which together possess about 63 per cent of all the unmined anthracite coal. A suit to dissolve the Reading Holding Company was instituted under the Anti-Trust Laws and the Commodities Clause shortly after the present Administration came into power. The decision of the lower court was in part favorable and in part adverse to the Government. Appeals were taken to the Supreme Court, where the case was argued early in October.

Suits have also been instituted under the Anti-Trust Laws and the Commodities Clause against the Delaware, Lackawanna & Western Railroad Company and its affiliated coal companies and the Lehigh Valley Railroad Company and its affiliated coal companies—branches of the combination.

In the case against the Lackawanna Companies the decision of the lower court was adverse to the Government, but on appeal to the Supreme Court the decision of the lower court was reversed and the relief asked by the Government granted. In the suit against the Lehigh Valley Companies the decision of the lower court was also adverse to the Government. An appeal was taken to the Supreme Court, where the case was argued early in October. As this case is similar to the Lackawanna Case it is expected that the decision of the lower court will be reversed and the relief asked by the Government granted.

In addition to these proceedings under the Anti-Trust Laws and the Commodities Clause the Attorney General in a letter to the Trade Commission, after the recent advance in wages but *before* the increase in prices, called the attention of the Commission to the fact that on three prior occasions when wages were increased, namely, in 1900, 1902 and 1912, the price of anthracite coal was increased out of all proportion to any increased cost of production due to the higher wages; and in view of past history he recommended to the Commission that in the event the recent advance in wages should be followed by an advance in price (as subsequently it was), a thoroughgoing investigation be made for the purpose of ascertaining whether there was any justification for the increase in the price.

Subsequently, Senator Hitchcock brought the matter before the Senate, calling attention especially to the letter of the Attorney General, and the Trade Commission was directed by resolution of the Senate to conduct such an inquiry as the Attorney General had recommended. A copy of the Attorney General's letter is attached hereto.[2]

The investigations of the Department will, of course, be continued. A special legal and investigating force has been organized for this single purpose, under the immediate charge of District

Attorney Anderson of Boston, who has so arranged the regular work of his district as to permit him to give such time as may be necessary to this pressing matter.

The Attorney General also stated that you desired this Department to submit any suggestions it might have for providing new governmental means of dealing with the general problem of preventing extortionate prices.

There can be little doubt that the great produce exchanges and stockyards of the country, which constitute the primary market places for our food stuffs, should be under much closer governmental scrutiny and regulation than now prevails, to the end, amongst others, of assuring against the employment of their facilities in transactions which create false impressions of the conditions of supply and demand and artificially affect prices. Without stopping now to inquire how far the Federal Government could directly regulate such exchanges, it could doubtless accomplish the same objects by prescribing the conditions upon which they should be permitted to use the mails, the telegraph and other instrumentalities of interstate communication in carrying on their business.

Very respectfully,   G. Carroll Todd

TLS (WP, DLC).

[1] Assistant to the Attorney General in charge of enforcement of the Sherman Antitrust Act.

[2] This enclosure is missing. However, it is printed in *Cong. Record*, 64th Cong., 1st sess., pp. 9747-48.

From Don Niko Grškovićᶜ[1]

Pittsburgh, Pa., Nov. 29, 1916.

The delegates of the Societies and the colonies of the South Slavs, viz the Croats, Serbs and Sloven[e]s, assembled at the Second Slavic National Congress, at the City of Pittsburgh, Penna., this twenty ninth day of November, nineteen sixteen, for the purpose of deliberating upon the endeavors of their brethren in Europe who want to liberate themselves of all and every foreign rule and united in a national state of their own desire to bring into existence and to preserve the great principles of equality fraternity and humanity, extend their most respectful greetings to you, Mr. President, and express herewith their unconditional loyalty to you and to the institutions of this land of liberty. In so doing we are moved by the profound conviction that it is necessary that the great principles of the American democracy be preserved and developed by all free peoples whether American citizens or not; whether living on American soil or elsewhere. For the defense of those liberties and principles and assuming that America should be attacked on this account or provided that she should be compelled to defend them from whomsoever in the world, we are ready at any time to place at her disposal our strength and our lives. Whereas heretofore we desire to support the progress of the preparedness for America which is necessary for this country in order to enable the same to defend those principles at any time, and against every enemy whether foreign or domestic and we shall continue to repel all elements disloyal to those principles. We who are American citizens as well as those among us who as yet did not have the opportunity to become Americans are convinced that we are going to best display our loyalty to the American spirit if we thoroughly acquaint America with the conditions and wishes of our people, knowing that generous America will understand our struggle and employ her powerful influence in behalf of our people, in accordance with her so many times proven mission among humanity. Encouraged by your historical words uttered May 27th, of this year, according to which America takes interest in the cause of other peoples, as well as in her own, and that it is the desire of America disinterestedly and justly to defend the principles that every nation has the right to choose the sovereignty under which she intends to live, that smaller nations of the world, too, are entitled to liberty and integrity as well as the larger ones and that the world has the right to enjoy protection from every oppressor of her rights. We therefore hail you, Mr. President, as the champion of those principles and as the first citizen of this great free country.   Don Niko Grskovich

T telegram (WP, DLC).
  [1] Croatian Catholic priest, pastor of the parish of St. Paul in Cleveland; owner and editor of *Hrvatski Svijet*, an influential Croatian weekly newspaper; and a leader of the South Slav movement in the United States.

From the Right Reverend Arsène E. Vehouni[1]

The President: Worcester [Mass.], Nov. 29, 1916.

In behalf of Kevork V., Catholicos of all the Armenians,[2] and as his representative in the United States, I beg leave to extend our most sincere compliments and best wishes to yourself.

His Holiness Kevork V. has caused to be prepared and framed a parchment setting forth his appreciation and that of all Armenians to the President and people of the United States for their humane and generous interest in the Armenian people.[3] As a representative of His Holiness I have the very distinguished honor of requesting the President to appoint a time when representative Armenians, in the presence of others who may be invited with the approval of the President, may present to the United States the parchment herein referred to.

I most respectfully ask the President to make an appointment in December of this year for the purpose of such presentation,[4] and in the words of His Holiness Kevork V. I have the honor to express the hope that "you may be given long life and strength in the grace and help of the Lord."

Very respectfully,   Arsène E. Vehouni

TLS (WP, DLC).

[1] Prelate of the Armenian Apostolic Church in America.

[2] At the Metropolitan See of Ararat, at Etchmiadzin, Vagharshabad. His name is also often transliterated as Gevorg V.

[3] A translation of the text (printed copy, WP, DLC) follows:

"KEVORK, THE SERVANT OF JESUS CHRIST, AND BY THE WILL OF GOD PRIMATE AND CATHOLICOS OF ALL THE ARMENIANS AND SUPREME PATRIARCH OF THE NATIONAL SEE OF ARARAT, THE APOSTOLIC MOTHER CHURCH OF THE CATHEDRAL OF ETCHMIADZIN, TO WOODROW WILSON, PRESIDENT OF THE UNITED STATES OF AMERICA, GREETINGS. WE SEND YOU BENEDICTION FROM OUR PATRIARCHAL SEE, AND PRAY FOR YOU LONG LIFE AND STRENGTH IN THE LORD.

"MR. PRESIDENT

"We are deeply grateful for the many works of kindness which the people of your great Nation have extended to our little flock scattered throughout the world. Exiled as they are in barren deserts, you extended to them a helping hand that they might be preserved in life, and might steadfastly maintain that faith in Christ for the sake of which many of them have been martyred, as the saints were slain of old by the sword of the wicked.

"Orphans and widows, old men and children, young brides and tender virgins, deprived of their possessions and bereaved of those dear to them, fed on grass, starving and desolate, raise their hands in prayer that the Lord may assist you to protect those who are living in distress that they may be spared in their places of banishment, and by your care and that of other sympathetic nations may be returned in safety to their homes.

"Joining our children in these their prayers, we beseech the Lord of all that the humane compassion of yourself and your Nation may not diminish, and that we may not be left forsaken under the hand of the oppressor, but by your assistance may be delivered and rescued from this heavy yoke. May you be given long life, and strength in the grace and help of the Lord.

"KEVORK V. Catholicos of all the Armenians.

"April 10-23, 1916.

"In the year 1365 of our Calendar, in the fifth year of our Primacy. At the Metropolitan See of Ararat, at Etchmiadzin, Vagharshabad."

[4] Wilson received the Prelate and others at the White House on December 14.

Robert Lansing to Joseph Clark Grew

Washington, November 29, 1916.

3621 You are instructed to obtain as soon as possible an interview with the Chancellor and repeat verbatim to him the following:

"The Government of the United States has learned with the greatest concern and regret of the policy of the German Government to deport from Belgium a portion of the civilian population for the purpose of forcing them to labor in Germany and is constrained to protest in a friendly spirit but most solemnly against this action which is in contravention of all precedent and of those humane principles of international practice which have long been accepted and followed by civilized nations in their treatment of non-combatants in conquered territory. Furthermore the Government of the United States is convinced that the effect of this policy, if pursued, will in all probability be fatal to the Belgian relief work, so humanely planned and so successfully carried out, a result which would be generally deplored and which, it is assumed, would seriously embarrass the German Government." Paragraph.

You will also leave a copy in writing of the foregoing with the Chancellor. Paragraph.

STRICTLY CONFIDENTIAL TO BE DECIPHERED BY MR. GREW.

You will please to represent to the Chancellor confidentially and very earnestly the very serious unfavorable reaction in the public opinion of this country caused by the Belgian deportations at a time when that opinion was more nearly approaching a balance of judgments as to the issues of the war than ever before; and also, and more particularly, the great embarrassment which that reaction has caused the President in regard to taking steps looking towards peace. You are authorized to say that the President is watching the whole situation with the utmost solicitude having the desire and definite purpose to be of service in that great matter at the earliest possible moment and has been repeatedly distressed to have his hopes frustrated and his occasion destroyed by such unhappy incidents as the sinking of the MARINA and the ARABIA and the Belgian deportations. You are also authorized to say that the President has noted with the deepest interest your report in a recent despatch of the evident distress and disappointment of the Chancellor that nothing had come of his intimations about peace, and that what the President is now earnestly desiring is practical cooperation on the part of the German authorities in creating a favorable opportunity for some affirmative action by him in the interest of an early restoration of peace.   Lansing

T telegram (SDR, RG 59, 763.72115/3101A, DNA).

To William Jennings Bryan

My dear Mr. Bryan,   The White House. 30 November, 1916

Now that the result of the election is nowhere questioned I want to express to you the feeling, not of triumph, but of profound encouragement and real elation that the cause which we believe to have been the cause of the people should have been so emphatically and unmistakably sustained and my gratitude to all who, like yourself, have assisted to make the verdict clear. I am sure that all Democrats admire your course during the campaign as I did

Cordially and sincerely Yours,   Woodrow Wilson

ALS (W. J. Bryan Papers, DLC).

To Annie Wilson Howe Cothran

Dearest Annie,   The White House. 30 November, 1916.

Of course I will depend on you to manage your affairs carefully and practically. I am enclosing my cheque for one thousand dollars, as I would have done about this time to dear Sister. You know that I promised her that so long as I could and you needed it I would try always to see that she had a couple of thousand each year; and I made her promise, besides, to send Mr. David's bills for the music lessons to me, as I shall expect you to do.

I am sorry to say that I have had so many things to do since I got back here that I have not yet got a lawyer to wind up dear Sister's affairs for me and effect the transfers to you. Do you like the lawyer[1] with whom you have been dealing in Philadelphia? Your mother was legally a resident of Pennsylvania, and it is there that her affairs must be wound up. If you have found the lawyer I speak of satisfactory, I will consult him and get his assistance.

I am so glad you are so satisfactorily fixed and that you are surrounded by friends whom you like and can depend on. And it pleases us all very much to learn that you and the baby are prospering physically. That is the root of the matter. If you keep well, and build up your strength, all the rest will come easily in time, as you get first an entrance and then a recognized standing in your profession.

We are all well. It will be jolly to see you and Josephine at Christmas time. We shall look forward to it. We are hoping to have Jessie and Frank too and their little ones.

We shall want to know all about your experience at your

concert. I hope with all my heart that it will be a great success. We shall be most interested to hear you sing when you come down to see us.

All send messages of love to you both.

In haste (this is written on my own typewriter),

Affectionately,   Woodrow Wilson

WWTLS (WP, DLC).
[1] Abram Heebner Wintersteen, Princeton 1878.

From Newton Diehl Baker, with Enclosure

My dear Mr. President: Washington. November 30, 1916.

I inclose a copy of a telegram, which has just come from General Funston, and, as you see, is from General George Bell at El Paso.

It has not seemed to me that General Bell showed any particular discretion or judgment in valuing rumors and reports which come to him, but as the facts here stated are interesting, if true, I think you ought to see them.

Cordially yours,   Newton D. Baker

TLS (WP, DLC).

E N C L O S U R E

Ft. Sam Houston, Texas, November 30, 1916.

Number 3819. Following received from General Bell. Quote: Replying to your eight fifty five shall keep you fully posted. Have been sending General Pershing whatever information came into our possession. The fall of Chihuahua took place Monday afternoon and was reported to you a few hours later that same evening. The capture of Juarez is believed to be only a question of a very short time perhaps even of hours. Villa has Trevino's secret code and the other day sent a message to Trevino signed Murgia[1] that he would arrive shortly at Chihuahua thus gaining access and deceiving the Chihuahua people into believing that Murgia was actually close to Chihuahua. He also sent a message to General Gonzales[2] in Juarez signing Trevino's name to telegram directing him to send some ammunition which Gonzales sent and which of course Villa captured. These two cases are undoubtedly substantially as stated and it is believed Villa also sent a telegram Monday evening from Sauz to General Gonzales to which he attached General Ozuna's[3] name asking for ammunition and a consultation regarding further plans. General Gonzales left early yesterday morning with about one hundred eight men and a car of ammunition and has not yet returned although due back in Juarez over fifteen hours ago. He has not been heard from since reaching Sauz. The telegraph operator at Guzman at seven o'clock this morning says that a man coming from Santa Sophia on horseback reported that four men well armed and well mounted rode into Santa Sophia about four yesterday afternoon looked around and rode off and that about midnight fifty men rode into Santa Sophia and went north along the railroad. Last night there was a meeting of Legalistas[4] and Villistas in El Paso at which one of my men was present. They discussed a plan for the capture of Juarez the details of which were in my possession within an hour or two after they were made. Every eventuality has been prepared for and I believe that if an attack is made on Juarez it will be so conducted that no shots will fall on American territory. Whether Villa has a force at Sauz or not there is a large body of bandits estimated at about one thousand between Sauz and Juarez. It is not believed that Villa himself will attempt to come to Juarez. It has just been reported a number of people are shouting viva Villa in the streets of Juarez and are not being disturbed.

Unquote. Bell. Funston.

T telegram (WP, DLC).
    [1] General Francisco Murguia, new *Carrancista* military commander in the State of Chihuahua.
    [2] That is, Francisco González.
    [3] Gregorio Osuna.
    [4] The Legal Peace Party, a recently formed union of *Zapatistas, Villistas*, and a new group called *Legalistas*. The party was committed to the overthrow of Carranza and the establishment of a legally constituted government in Mexico.

From Edward Mandell House

Dear Governor: New York. November 30, 1916.

I have been thinking a lot of your proposed note to the belligerents and I cannot bring myself to believe that it should be done immediately or without further preparation.

You have before you the biggest opportunity for service that was ever given to man and I hope you will not risk failure. Since you first suggested your plan I have talked with everybody within my reach, whose opinion I value, many of them having an intimate knowledge of the situation in the Allied countries, and there is not one that believes it could be successful at this time.

I have just talked to Gavit of the Evening Post, without telling him or anyone, of course, what you had in mind, but merely drawing him out and getting an opinion. Gavit thinks you should make a public statement expressing the feeling of neutral nations in regard to the war so there could be a general discussion. He does not think that a direct note to the belligerents would be advisable or effective.

Whitehouse, the pacifist member of Parliament about whom I wrote you sometime ago, does not think that such a demand as you have in mind would bring a favorable response, although he would like to see you make it.[1]

I believe you have the situation in your own hands and if you do not act hastily you can bring about the desired result. If you do it now, there does not seem to me one chance in ten of success and you will probably lose your potential position for doing it later.

The Germans are the only ones that believe it can be done now, and the wish with them is father to the thought. They do not care how you come out of it so it is done and they reap a certain measure of profit in any event.

Before the step is finally taken a good many things I think should be done. A background should be laid in both France and England so that public opinion would listen with favor to any proposal from you. This can be done, and quickly, if we get at it.

Bernstorff telephoned me this morning and asked for an appointment for Saturday at half past ten. If there is anything in particular you want me to say to him please let me know.

Affectionately yours,   E. M. House

TLS (WP, DLC).

[1] "I received an urgent message from House to visit him. He said he should much value any suggestions I could offer for the guidance of the President at this time. The time was coming when he would have to decide upon his future action. At present all was in the melting pot. I said that I had never wavered in my belief that he should offer mediation. Christmas was now coming and people's thoughts would be turned towards peace. This was the right time to strike. I described very fully to House what would be the probable result of an offer of mediation and especially that though it might not be immediately successful, its ultimate success was certain. I found House most responsive all the time and unusually excited and animated for him." J. H. Whitehouse, "The House Report . . . ," Dec. [1], 1916.

William Jennings Bryan to Joseph Patrick Tumulty

New York, Nov. 30, 1916.

Shall be in Washington December first fifth and sixth. Shall be pleased to call on President if convenient.[1]

W. J. Bryan.

T telegram (WP, DLC).

[1] See the extract from the diary of Henry F. Ashurst printed at Dec. 2, 1916, n. 2.

From the Diary of Charles Sumner Hamlin

Nov 30 Thursday [1916].

Telephoned Harding & met him at Metrop. Club—told him whole story. He spoke of several papers, espec. Phila Ledger, wh. said Warburg was respsn. for our circular. This irritated him very much. He said the Presdt told him at his interview that our relations w. Gt Britain were more strained than w. Germany.

To Francis Burton Harrison

[The White House]
My dear Governor Harrison: December 1, 1916.

I have received through General McIntyre your cablegram conveying the congratulations of the members of the Philippine Legislature.[1] Will you not be good enough to express to them my warmest thanks and appreciation?

Cordially and sincerely yours,   Woodrow Wilson

TLS (Letterpress Books, WP, DLC).
[1] F. McIntyre to JPT, Nov. 15, 1916, Vol. 38.

To Manuel Luis Quezon

[The White House]
My dear Mr. Quezon: December 1, 1916.

The generous words of your kind message of congratulation, which has been transmitted by Governor Harrison through General McIntyre,[1] gave me the keenest gratification, and my warmest thanks go out to you for having sent it.

Cordially and sincerely yours,   Woodrow Wilson

TLS (Letterpress Books, WP, DLC).
[1] F. McIntyre to JPT, Nov. 18, 1916, Vol. 38.

Two Letters from Robert Lansing

[Washington]
My dear Mr. President: December 1, 1916.

It is evident to my mind that the gentlemen making the request for information regarding the deportation of Belgians desire to obtain some official statement from the Government which they can reproduce in quoted form in printed circulars to be distributed broadcast over the country for the purpose of arousing pub-

lic opinion and forcing the Government to take some action unfavorable to Germany, which could be construed as favoring the
Allies. If I am correct in this surmise, I think that no good purpose would be served by giving out officially the information
desired. As a matter of fact, it has always been a rule of this
Department not to make official statements to inquirers regarding confidential matters under diplomatic discussion unless the
inquirers are parties in interest. This rule is based on the fact that
the correspondence is with foreign governments, who may not
desire to have the subject matter given out without their consent. This is peculiarly true in the present case, which is passing
into a very delicate stage. I think, therefore, that it is not only
appropriate, but necessary, for the moment at least, to answer
the committee substantially along these lines. Somewhat later,
I suppose, it may be possible, with the consent of the German
Government, to give out some of the correspondence in the
Belgian matter. Of course, if Germany should prefer to give the
matter out without asking us, we could then give out so much as
may be desirable to make our position clear.

Faithfully yours,   Robert Lansing

CCL (SDR, RG 59, 763.72115/2632½, DNA).

Dear Mr. President: Washington December 1, 1916.

Mr. John W. Garrett has accepted the Mission to The Hague
and I have therefore telegraphed Dr. van Dyke to obtain the
agrément of the Dutch Government to his appointment. Following your direction Dr. van Dyke has been asked to remain at
The Hague until early next year, or until the confirmation by
the Senate of his successor, and he has been assured of your
regret at his retirement and of your appreciation of his considerate method of action in the matter.

With assurances of high respect, etc., I am, my dear Mr.
President,   Very sincerely yours,   Robert Lansing

TLS (WP, DLC).

From Baron Erich Zwiedinek

Your Excellency,   Washington, Dec. 1st 1916

I am deeply grateful for the honor of Your Excellency's and
Mrs Wilson's gracious presence at the religious services held at
St Patrick's Church on November 29th in memory of the late
Emperor and King Francis Joseph I.

Permit me also to thank Your Excellency most heartily for the beautiful wreath which you had the great kindness to send.

I have the honor to remain most respectfully and obediently yours,   E Zwiedinek

ALS (WP, DLC).

From Franklin Knight Lane, with Enclosures

My dear Mr. President: Washington December 1, 1916.

I am sending to you herewith a copy of the agreement made with the Mexican Commissioners,[1] a copy of the notice which I read to them regarding the right of pursuit, a copy of the letter asking assurance as to the discussion of other questions,[2] and a note from our minutes.

We shall make to you an extended and formal report later. There are one or two matters which might be drawn to your attention now as illustrating the attitude of the Mexicans, which is one of undisguised hostility. The Commissioners said frankly that the people of Mexico hated Americans, and that Villa's strength was his anti-American attitude. My personal belief is that this hostility does not reach down to the peons, but that they are the victims of agitators and demagogues, who fight among each other for official position.

After your visit to the Mexican Commissioners at New London, we gave a dinner to them at which Mr. Cabrera sat opposite me. Early in the dinner I rose and toasted the First Chief, Mr. Carranza, and the Republic of Mexico. There were perhaps thirty at the dinner, including a number of newspapermen. All rose and joined in the toast. There was no response from Mr. Cabrera. I waited a course, and still no response came. I waited another course, and seeing that no reply toast was forthcoming and that the newspapermen had their eyes on Cabrera, I wrote on the back of my menu card these words: "You will please rise and offer a toast to the President of the United States," and passed it to him. In a few minutes he rose and made a speech upon Mexico's history, and, without a word of appreciation of your generous and noble attitude, ended by saying: "Let us drink to the President of the United States." The newspapermen who saw the incident, including Mr. O'Laughlin, suppressed it at my request.

Samuel Gompers came to Atlantic City saying that he thought he could make the Mexican Commissioners realize the importance of coming to an agreement with us, and after two interviews with them he returned to me saying that they were impossible,—bad-natured children who should be soundly spanked into a proper frame of mind. Henry Bruere, of New York, also volunteered his services, but his high optimism was destroyed when they repudiated a proposition which they themselves had dictated to him and which we had accepted.

During the discussion of the translation from English into Spanish of the proposed agreement, Cabrera had the impudence to suggest that possibly we have it translated into Japanese.

When our sessions closed in Atlantic City the three American Commissioners expressed the hope that we would reunite to take up the constructive policies which had been considered and again, as a hundred times before, expressed our desire to be given an opportunity to prove to Mexico our willingness to help her. The only response that Cabrera made was that he had heard much of America's desire to help Mexico, but no evidence of our desire to have Mexico help the United States. Whereupon Judge Gray moved an adjournment.

Faithfully yours,   Franklin K. Lane

TLS (WP, DLC).
 [1] It is printed in Enclosure II with RL to WW, Nov. 23, 1916.
 [2] *Ibid.*

E N C L O S U R E   I

STATEMENT TO MEXICAN COMMISSIONERS
READ BY
SECRETARY LANE
NOVEMBER 21, 1916

It is essential, as a matter of governmental policy, that the United States reserve the right to deal with any serious hostile incursion from Mexico into American territory as may be deemed advisable at the time, including the right to pursue marauders into Mexican territory when such pursuit is necessary to our own protection. Duly mindful of the obligations imposed upon us by international law, such pursuit will not be intended, and should not be considered an act hostile to the Constitutionalist Government of Mexico.

Read to the Joint Commission by the Chairman of the American Commission, November 21, 1916, and not inserted in the Minutes, at the request of the Mexican Commissioners.

E N C L O S U R E　I I

EXCERPT FROM MINUTES OF THE AMERICAN AND
MEXICAN JOINT COMMISSION OF WEDNESDAY,
NOVEMBER 22ND, 1916.

The American Commissioners informed the Mexican Commissioners that they would submit the agreement regarding withdrawal of troops and border control, to their Government for approval when the assurance asked for in the letter of November 22nd, 1916, was given.

T MSS (WP, DLC).

From John Gardner Coolidge[1]

The President:　　　　　　　　　　Paris. December 1, 1916

I take the liberty of writing to you to express my deep sense of gratitude for the high honor conferred upon me in your offer of the Mission to Colombia.

I was unable to accept for reasons which appeared to me imperative, but I feel that the only return that I can make for the confidence reposed in me, is to pledge to you my absolute loyalty and the best work that in me lies, so long as it shall please you to retain me in the service of the Government.

I have the honor to be, Sir,

Your obedient servant　　John Gardner Coolidge

ALS (WP, DLC).
[1] Boston gentleman of independent means; Republican; Secretary of Legation in Peking, 1902-1906; Secretary of Embassy in Mexico City, 1907-1908; appointed Minister to Nicaragua, July 1, 1908, but resigned on November 26, 1908, because of a dispute over policy; since November 1914 a special agent of the Department of State to aid the American Ambassador in Paris.

From Ambrose White Vernon

My Dear Mr. Wilson:　　　　　　Brookline, Mass Dec. 1, 1916

May I tell you how I rejoiced in your re-election to the great office of President?

I wouldn't have dared to encroach upon your time to say so, were it not for the fact that Mr. Gifford Pinchot seems greatly distressed over the passage of the Shields Bill.[1] So does my dear friend, Charles Gill, the former Yale Captain and now in the Rural Church Commission of the Federal Council of Churches, who, I think piloted you partially through the City of Columbus,

Ohio. They are very anxious for you to give most serious consideration to what they deem a most iniquitous bill. I remember
that you valued Mr Pinchot's opinion very greatly when I was last
privileged to speak to you and so I thought you might like to know
his present position on these bills.

You may be interested to know that *here* in Boston, the home
of political Conservatism, the Minister's Club made up mostly
of older men were in *your* favor on a straw-vote and that in a
younger group of Congregational Clergymen, not a single one of
them voted for Hughes! New England is open to high-minded
democratization!

Most Sincerely & rejoicingly yours

Ambrose W. Vernon

ALS (WP, DLC).
1 For the recent history of the Shields bill, see M. D. Foster to WW, July 4,
1916, n. 1, Vol. 37.

From Albert Shaw

Dear Mr. President: New York December 1, 1916

I am sending you a copy of a volume that has been privately
printed here, by the League for Political Education, in memory
of our old friend, the late Elgin R. L. Gould.[1] I was asked to write
the chapter on Gould's student days at Baltimore, and it occurs
to me you may like to glance it over as referring to a period that
does not seem so long past, although more than thirty years have
gone by since that time.

I had meant to ask you for a few words of recollection about
Gould, but the compilers of the volume put me under some
pressure to prepare the copy, and it was at a moment when you
were greatly absorbed by acute foreign situations and could not
be bothered with outside details.

I beg to congratulate you upon your reëlection and to express
confident wishes for an administration that will witness world
peace on terms of justice and honor, with our own country helping to bring about the desired readjustment.

I have found myself heartily in accord with most of the undertakings and achievements of your administration, though
I have had a view of America in relation to the European War
that has been different from yours on the one hand and quite
different from Mr. Roosevelt's on the other. I have from the
start believed in a somewhat aggressive assertion and enforcement of our own rights as a neutral, regardless of sentiment or

sympathy for one side or the other. But we are all standing loyally behind your conduct of affairs, and I have in the main had a great regard and esteem for the personnel of the Administration.

Again with heartiest wishes for the success of your second term in its public policies, and with the wish that your health—which seems to have improved all the time—may continue to be vigorous, I am,   Faithfully yours,   Albert Shaw.

TLS (WP, DLC).
   1 [League for Political Education], *Elgin Ralston Lovell Gould: A Memorial* (n.p., 1916). This pamphlet is in the Wilson Library, DLC.

Robert Lansing to Edward Mandell House

STRICTLY CONFIDENTIAL:

My dear Colonel: [Washington] December 1, 1916.

I have just returned from an hour's interview with the President on the subject in which we are both so deeply interested. The form it has taken is far less objectionable than the one originally proposed. I have not yet given a final opinion to the President on the subject but feel disposed to the opinion that it will possibly accomplish much good. However, there will be time to go over the matter after it is put in final form.

I also took up the subject of the proposed visit by you to London and believe that the matter is satisfactorily disposed of. I argued that in view of the fact that you had visited the belligerent countries on previous occasions, to sound them in regard to peace, I thought your presence in connection with this new communication would cause an unfavorable impression as to the purpose of the communication and would injure, rather than help its favorable reception. The President seemed to be impressed with that point of view and asked me to consider some other person who could explain matters both to Page and to the British officials in case questions arose as to the object of the communication.

I will communicate with you further in case there is a change of attitude in regard to this latter matter. I presume the President will submit to you a draft of the proposed communication when it is finally drawn. I have no copy yet.

With warm regards believe me—
                    Very sincerely yours,   Robert Lansing

CCL (R. Lansing Papers, NjP).

Remarks Upon Giving the Signal to Light the Statue of Liberty[1]

Dec. 2, 1916

I light this Statue with the thought that it may always stand as a symbol of our purpose to throw upon liberty, out of our own life as a Nation, a light which shall reveal its dignity, its serene power, its benignant hope and spirit of guidance.

W.W.

EBWhw MS (WP, DLC).
[1] For the occasion of these remarks, see WW to JPT, Nov. 22, 1916, n. 2. Wilson gave the signal on board the presidential yacht *Mayflower* in New York harbor. For accounts of the event, see the *New York Times* and the New York *World*, Dec. 3, 1916.

After-Dinner Remarks[1]

December 2, 1916

Mr. Toastmaster, ladies and gentlemen: Those who conceived and arranged this interesting program of today were generous enough to relieve me of the responsibility of making a speech. But they gave me the privilege of coming here to accept, in the name of the Government of the United States, the lighting plant from which has proceeded the illumination thrown upon the statue. I would certainly be lacking in feeling if I did not express some of the things that have come into my thought as I have taken part in these ceremonies.

There are many moving circumstances connected with this day, connected with the things it recalls, connected with the things that it suggests. I was reflecting, as we saw the light streaming upon that beautiful statue, that its source was outside the statue, that it did not proceed from liberty but proceeded from the light we were throwing upon liberty. And it occurred to me that, after all, it was a proper symbol of our life. Because we can take to ourselves the dignity of liberty only as we illustrate the fact in the true spirit of liberty. The only light that we can contribute to the illumination of the world is the light that will shine out of our life as a nation on that conception and upon that image.

There is a great responsibility in having adopted liberty as our ideal, because we must illustrate it in what we do. I was struck by the closing phrase of Mr. Pulitzer's admirable little speech. He said that there would come a day when it was perceived that the goddess of liberty was also the goddess of peace; and, throughout the last two years, there has come more and more into my heart the conviction that peace is going to come to the world only with liberty.

With all due and sincere respect to those who represent other forms of government than our own, perhaps I may be permitted to say that peace cannot come so long as the destinies of men are determined by small groups who make selfish choices of their own.

It is very true, as more than one of the speakers this evening have either said or intimated, that our long-standing and delightful friendship with the people of France has come from a community of ideals and identity of purpose. One republic must love another republic, just as one body of human beings must understand and sympathize with another body of human beings. There is a common pulse in us all. There is a common contact with life. There is a common body of hope. There is a common stock of resolution. All the world over, the life of the individual means the same thing to him. It means opportunity, not only, but it also means his relationship to others. And he comes to his full dignity only when he stands upon the same level with others, and, looking in his neighbor's eye, knows that he belongs with him to a common, free community of purpose and thought and action.

The peace of the world is not going to be assured by the compact of nations, but by the sympathies of men. I was present once at a very interesting little conference on foreign missions.[2] The conference was the most interesting of the kind I have ever attended, because the purpose of it was to wipe out the lines between Christian churches in the work in foreign fields and, forgetting denominational differences, unite in a common enterprise of enlightening the world with the spirit of Christ. I couldn't help saying that, while I entirely sympathized with the position of the conference and hoped that it might be realized, I hoped that those who were converted by this kind of uniting influence in foreign fields did not come and look at us. Because, while we were uniting for their benefit, we were divided for our disadvantage.

And so, sometimes, when I see this Statue of Liberty and think of the thrill that must come into some hopeful heart as, for the first time, an immigrant sees that statue and thinks that he knows what it means, I wonder if, after he lands, he finds the spirit of liberty truly represented by us. I wonder if we are worthy of that symbol. I wonder if we are sufficiently stirred by the history of it, by the history of what it means. I wonder if we remember the sacrifices, the mutual concessions, the righteous yielding of selfish right that is signified by the word and the conception of liberty. I wonder if we all wish to accord equal rights to all men.

And so it is profitable that occasions like this should be frequently repeated, and that we should remind ourselves of what sort of image we have promised to be. For the world is enlightened, my fellow citizens, by ideals, by ideas. The spirit of the world rises with the sacrifice of men. The spirit of the world rises as men forget to be selfish and unite to be great.

This, then, to repeat that beautiful phrase of Lincoln's in his Gettysburg Address, "is not a time of congratulation but a time of rededication."

Let us determine that the light that shines out of our lives upon the uplifted image of liberty shall be a light pure and without reproach.

JRT transcript (WC, NjP) of CLSsh (C. L. Swem Coll., NjP).

[1] About the dinner in Wilson's honor, see WW to JPT, Nov. 22, 1916, n. 1. The other honored guest was Jean Jules Jusserand. Mayor John Purroy Mitchel was toastmaster; the other speakers were Jusserand, Chauncey M. Depew, Ralph Pulitzer, and Henry Latham Doherty, president of the Society for Electrical Development. See the *New York Times*, Dec. 3, 1916.

[2] About this meeting, a "China dinner" in New York on January 14, 1909, and Wilson's remarks, see W. H. Grant to WW, Dec. 19, 1908, Vol. 18, and the news report printed at Jan. 28, 1911, Vol. 22.

To Henry Pomeroy Davison

My dear Mr. Davison: The White House December 2, 1916

May I not thank you very sincerely for your letter of November twenty-fifth and for the interesting information it conveys? It was very kind of you to think of my desire to have this information and I value your promise to keep me informed from time to time upon these matters.

Cordially and sincerely yours,   Woodrow Wilson

TLS (DARC).

From Lillian D. Wald

Dear Mr. President: New York City. December 2, 1916.

My colleagues on the Committee of the American Union Against Militarism and I are deeply interested in your reply concerning the best method for removing the offending "Joker"[1] and while you are taking up that detail, may I draw your attention to Section 59 of the Defense Law approved June 3rd, 1916 which grants exemption to persons from military service whose religious belief forbids it. It makes provision for the establishment of the sincerity of such persons, but only in a combatant capacity and states in a clause "that no person so exempted shall be exempt from military service in any capacity that the President shall declare to be non-combatant." This according to Quakers and others who are anti-militaristic would mean the possibility of drafting into what is known in England as alternative service; in the making of munitions, taking care of camps, doing garrison duty and so forth, and this under penalty of the laws of war. You know so well that many people base their opposition to carrying arms because of moral scruples rather than the so called religious grounds. Of these there are many, not only here but in England, and the numerous conscientious objectors in England who are in the jails belong to this class.

You will be glad to know, I am sure, that Miss Addams is improving and that we will be in Washington in conference concerning measures that relate to anti-militarism.

With apologies for this lengthy letter, I beg to remain, dear Mr. President   Yours very sincerely,   Lillian D. Wald

TLS (WP, DLC).

[1] About the so-called "Joker" clause in the Army Reorganization Act of 1916, see WW to A. R. E. Pinchot, Aug. 19, 1916, n. 1, Vol. 38. Lillian D. Wald to WW, Nov. 23, 1916, T telegram (WP, DLC), had suggested that Wilson urge repeal of the clause in his forthcoming Annual Message. In his reply (WW to Lillian D. Wald, Nov. 27, 1916, TLS [Letterpress Books, WP, DLC]), Wilson said that he thought the "Joker" should not be dealt with in a public message. Instead, he went on, he would "consult with the proper committee to see if it is not possible to get the law amended in the way we desire."

From Robert Lansing

PERSONAL AND CONFIDENTIAL:

My dear Mr. President: Washington December 2, 1916.

I enclose a report appearing in the NEW YORK WORLD of this morning[1] which is, I understand, an Associated Press dispatch as it appears also in other papers, relative to a protest to Germany on the part of this Government in behalf of the deported Belgians. When I read it I was astonished at the accuracy of the statement because it conforms practically to the telegram which went forward and which was guarded with so much care.

I immediately instituted an inquiry to find out the source of this report and learned from Mr. Polk that he obtained the information last evening from one of his newspaper friends that the Associated Press correspondent at the White House had the story.

I am sure that you will feel the same annoyance that I do in regard to the publicity given to certain of our delicate diplomatic negotiations. Two or three days ago a statement very similar in its accuracy, as to the Tarnowski affair,[2] was also obtained by the Associated Press—whether from the same source or not I do not know. In any event it is very discouraging to take every precaution for secrecy and have these matters appear in the public press.

I am writing you in this matter because I thought you ought to know what I had learned as to the source of this publication and also to relieve the members of this Department from responsibility for so unfortunate a statement.

Of course it is possible that Mr. Gerard said something to some of his intimate newspaper friends who, in turn, reported it at the Executive Offices to some other man. I do not like to think that Mr. Gerard would do this even unintentionally, in view of the fact that I warned him very plainly against speaking of our protest to anyone. I have heard, however, that he is not very discreet in private conversation—but this I do not know of my own knowledge.   Faithfully yours,   Robert Lansing.

TLS (F. L. Polk Papers, CtY).
    [1] The enclosure is missing. Lansing describes it well.
    [2] That is, the difficulty that the State Department was encountering in obtaining from the Allies assurances of safe conduct for Count Tarnowski.

From Newton Diehl Baker

My dear Mr. President: Washington. December 2, 1916.

I inclose you a copy of a despatch which I have prepared and have in my office in code, but have not yet sent, for the reason that General Scott is clear, from a study of the despatches, that there is not yet, and will not be for several days, any occasion to undertake the movement here suggested.[1] He thinks it entirely safe to wait until Tuesday or Wednesday, and even believes that we could send this despatch by registered mail and still have it reach General Funston before the people in Chihuahua will have been able to organize any movement north and get it started. Meantime I am keeping close watch on all reports; and, if any occasion arises to act before you can see this despatch, I shall do so.

I am submitting this because I want it to express exactly your views; and if, after you have read it, you desire any change, I will be glad to come on a telephone call at any time, to get your corrections or further ideas.

          Respectfully yours,   Newton D. Baker

TLS (N. D. Baker Papers, DLC).
    [1] Not found, but see WW to NDB, Dec. 3, 1916.

From John Palmer Gavit, with Enclosure

Dear Mr. President: Englewood, N. J. December 2, 1916.

The enclosed letter from the Rev. D. Anderson,[1] addressed to me, was written in accordance with my request for a candid, unexaggerated statement regarding the state of public opinion in England regarding an early cessation of the war. In connection with our recent conversation on this subject[2] I transmit it to you without comment save to say that I have much confidence in the sanity and candor of this man. The letter will speak for itself.

I am much chagrined and deeply indignant to find that in a letter sent out to certain persons in connection with the publication of the text of Mr. Trevelyan's article, some mention was made of the fact that the document had "been presented to the President for his consideration."[3] It is of no great consequence of course, but it is in direct violation of the pledge which was given to me before I consented to have anything to do with the matter. It is to me only another brilliant illustration of the fact that the mischief in this world is done, not by wicked people, but by well-meaning fools.   Sincerely yours,   John P. Gavit

TLS (WP, DLC).

[1] The Rev. D. Anderson cannot be further identified except to say that he was well acquainted with the peace movement in Great Britain and wrote to Gavit on the stationery of the Church of the Pilgrims (Congregational) of Brooklyn, N. Y.

[2] At their meeting on November 20. See J. P. Gavit to WW, Nov. 21, 1916.

[3] The "article" was Charles Philips Trevelyan, "Hands Across the Sea: An Open Letter to Americans," *The Survey*, XXXVII (Dec. 9, 1916), 261-62. Trevelyan, the son of Sir George Otto Trevelyan, was a Liberal M.P. and a radical pacifist, whose opposition to the war alienated him both from his own family and the British ruling class. Charles Trevelyan asserted that the peoples of the belligerent nations in general, and those of Great Britain in particular, were growing "heartily sick" of the war. Only governments and the press insisted upon continuing the conflict to final victory. No one wished for peace at any price, but there was a rapidly growing popular movement for a negotiated peace on "reasonable" terms. The problem was that the peoples of the warring nations were deliberately kept in ignorance of their opponents' war weariness and desire for peace. "If, however," he continued, "some voice so loud that it reverberated across the seas, so important that the censorship could not exclude it, *spoke not to the governments but to the peoples*, a change would begin to come. Suppose that to the British people, for instance, an American president were to be able to say in quite simple and direct language that Germany was ready to give up Belgium and France if the British government would negotiate. . . . There might be no open response at once. But from the day of the utterance public opinion would begin to form on the irrefutable knowledge that a peace could be obtained satisfactorily on the question which was most vital to the British people." It was true that Wilson's pledge of American support for a league to enforce peace in his speech of May 27, 1916, had elicited little public response in Europe. However, Trevelyan said, the British people were aware of Wilson's declaration but did not yet perceive its bearing on an early end to the war. What the people of all nations were seeking was security. A league of nations, Trevelyan went on, offered the only real hope of security. At this point, Trevelyan appealed directly to Wilson: "My countrymen do not yet see—but they will if you are persistent—that your approval of the League of Peace amounts to American cooperation in the objects for which they profess to be fighting—a secure civiliza-

tion. Sooner or later your espousal of that plan will affect the course of the war. It will shorten it. They do not yet see that your plan ought to be the first of the terms of peace."

On an unpaginated introductory page just preceding Trevelyan's article, the editors of *The Survey* noted that he had sent it "by hand messenger to the American Neutral Conference Committee." Rebecca Shelly, the secretary of that organization, had forwarded it to *The Survey*. The *New York Times*, Dec. 5, 1916, reported that the American Neutral Conference Committee had discussed and endorsed Trevelyan's article during a luncheon meeting in New York on December 4. The *New York Times* also quoted a few of its key passages.

The Editors have found no copy of, or reference to, the "letter sent out to certain persons." However, the statement that Trevelyan's article had been "presented to the President" was correct. There is an undated T MS in WP, DLC, which is a verbatim copy of the article; it is prefaced by a Hw pencil notation: "What the President Can Do by Charles Trevelyan, M.P." As Gavit makes clear, he was the person who delivered the manuscript to Wilson, on November 20.

E N C L O S U R E

D. Anderson to John Palmer Gavit

Dear Mr. Gavit: Brooklyn, New York, Dec. 1. 1916.

It is difficult in the nature of things to express a decided opinion on the state of public opinion in Great Britain on the war and its continuance. It may be freely admitted at the outset that the great majority of people are behind the Government in its determination to continue the war because very few people believe that at the present time real and lasting peace on reasonably satisfactory terms can be made.

But there are certain facts that go to show that the people in general would gladly respond to any authoritative suggestion that an equitable peace could be attained without further fighting.

Fifty members of the House of Commons voted against the Conscription Act and the whole of this number can be relied upon to further any efforts toward peace by negotiation at the present time. Behind them again stand a number of liberal and labor Members of Parliament of moderate view who would welcome any tolerable suggestion which might lead to a shortening of the war.

I know too that, behind the comparatively small minority in the churches which has taken the Quaker position, objecting to war on religious grounds, there is a fairly large body of people who would welcome the prospect of negotiations leading to a real peace which might rebuild international relations on a basis of mutual good will rather than of sullen acceptance of the inevitable by a conquered foe.

Again it is quite certain that a large section of the Labor Party has never been whole-hearted in support of the war and could be rallied to a reasonable peace movement.

There is further the fact that a recent petition to the Government, asking that negotiations for peace should be set on foot, secured 150000 signatures. I, a professed pacifist, did not sign this petition myself because I felt that the time was not yet ripe, that no peace worth having was yet in sight, and I know others who shared that view. It is certain, therefore, that behind the more active peace parties stand many others who would welcome a serious effort towards peace. And this feeling has been growing rapidly within the last two or three months.

It is a fact coming within my own observation that the general temper of the people is changing; there is a more subdued and chastened feeling; no longer anywhere does one hear the light-hearted talk of crushing Germany and occupying Berlin, which was common enough even in responsible quarters, at the beginning of the war.

There is also the undoubted fact that on the whole Peace Meetings are more largely attended and better received than a few months back. That rests not alone on the testimony of pacifists; in the House of Commons on Oct. 13th. last, Sir Henry Dalziel (who has been a strong supporter of the war throughout) said: "It would be a mistake for the House to shut its eyes to the fact that in large industrial centres throughout the country huge Mass Meetings had been held week after week at which the doctrine of peace had been received with the most hearty applause." It is on the authority of Mr. H. W. Massingham in the Nation of Nov. 11th. that "Every week the Independent Labor Party hold about 150 large or crowded meetings which end in commending unanimously, or almost unanimously, a more moderate view of the war." And I observe that in recent messages from the other side, published in the American papers, it is stated that the Cabinet are planning a Campaign, the avowed object of which is to combat this growing sentiment.

Another fact beyond dispute or question is that all the romance of war has been knocked out for those taking part in it. As a minister I have had opportunities of talking to a number of men at home from the front and I have not come across one who really wants to go back, although all are willing to "stick it out" as a horrible but necessary duty. Moreover, in discussing this point with ministers of all shades of opinion I have only heard of one man who was glad or anxious to go back.

Another interesting sign of the times is the starting, by a group of influential business men of a new Weekly Paper "Common Sense" under the editorship of Mr. F. W. Hirst, until recently editor of the "Economist." In his first leading article he repudiates as "no policy at all" the suggestion that England should "fight on after the right terms can be secured for the sake of what is called in bruising circles a knockout."

Another fact of some significance is that in the North Ayrshire by-election the Rev. Humphrey Chalmers, standing as an independent *Peace* Candidate, secured 1300 votes against the 7100 of his coalition opponent who had behind him the whole strength of both the great political party organizations.

All these things taken separately do not seem to amount to much, but taken together (and I have tried to set them down without exaggeration), they do indicate I think that there is a real and growing body in England which would gladly respond to any suggestion that the war could be ended on reasonably satisfactory terms. I think the great difficulty in the way is the feeling that Germany at present is taking the attitude of a conqueror. Our people will not consent to any negotiation on such a basis. They feel naturally that Germany started with every advantage, that now after enormous sacrifices and exertions, we have just made good the initial disadvantage, and that as Germany has had free course in the first act of the drama so to speak, so we must be left to play our part in what remains. If any authoritative indication could reach our people that the German Government recognized the situation, not only in esse but in posse, and was willing to treat on some such basis, then I think all these moderate forces of which I have spoken would gain the necessary focus and would at once begin to make their influence felt upon the Government.   Sincerely yours,   D. Anderson

TLS (WP, DLC).

From Annie Wilson Howe Cothran

My dearest Uncle Woodrow,   New York City Dec. 2nd, 1916.

Thank you so much for your lovely letter. It has put new hope and life into me. Your trust and faith and love are helping me more than I can tell you. It makes me very, very happy to be told that you love me though! and very proud that you trust me.

My work is growing more and more fascinating and I am making progress. I shall leave New York on the 10th for Pittsburg. Think about me and pray for me I shall be very lonly and heartsick, dear Uncle Woodrow.

Thank you so much for your check. You dont know how grateful I am to you for helping me as you are to make me self supporting. I love both you and Edith very deeply and warmly.

Mr. Wintersteen in Phila. is very very fine and I think would settle mother's estate for us. Dr. Davis introduced him to me and to mother. His name is A. H. Wintersteen, Room 1601 c/o Morris Building 1421 Chestnut Street, Philadelphia.

Baby and I are both very well and I am well pleased with the nurse I have secured. With unbounded love from us both to you and Edith and Margaret and Cousin Helen.

Devotedly   Annie.

ALS (WP, DLC).

Paul Samuel Reinsch to Robert Lansing

Peking, China, December 2, 1916.

CONFIDENTIAL. The Chinese Government apprehend that if insisted on the claim of the British, French, Russian and Japanese group banks to the effect that they represent the five power syndicate together with their broad interpretation of article seventeen of the loan agreement so as to include administrative loans of whatever kind threatens to destroy equal opportunity and reduce China to fiscal dependence on certain powers under the leadership of Japan. It considers very important the right of independent banks to do business not specifically preempted and will appreciate the assistance of the American Government in safeguarding this.

A rumor has been circulated emanating from Japanese sources to the effect that alleged strongly German Character of the Continental Commercial Bank accounts for making of the loan which is represented as directed against the interests of allied powers. While this clumsy invention will not make much impression it indicates a possible line of attack on independent American enterprise in China.   Reinsch.

T telegram (SDR, RG 59, 893.51/1715, DNA).

From the Diary of Henry Fountain Ashurst

December 2, 1916.

Senator Vardaman, Mr. Pickford[1] and myself of the Committee of the Bryan Banquet called on W.W. at the White House.

I told the President of the proposed banquet to Colonel Bryan in recognition of the services rendered by Bryan in stumping the western states in the recent Presidential campaign and I added that a special feature of the banquet would be a suitable reference to California which was the pivotal state.

By W.W:

"I shall be glad to send a letter[2] which may be read at the banquet but you surely must perceive that were I to attend, my presence would draw attention from the character whom you seek to honor and the fact that I am the President would have a tendency to throw him into the shade. At whatsoever function the President is present, under our system he is the first figure and must precede all others and this might prove embarrassing at some juncture of the banquet."

I saw the force of this statement and told him he was correct. Senator Vardaman's face grew dark and he indicated that my reply to W.W. did not suit him.

We were preparing to leave, when W.W. said:

"Another reason for my not attending the banquet is that I have no sympathy with all this talk that California should be specially honored because the returns from that State were in favor of the Democratic Party. I owe no especial thanks to California for casting its vote for me and certainly no gratitude is due to any person or to any State for performing a duty. California but did her duty and I am not inclined to engage in fulsome expressions of gratitude."

This from W.W. infuriated Senator Vardaman and I was taken aback but said:

"Good Morning, Mr. President. Send us the letter."

T MS (AzU).
[1] Thomas H. Pickford, real estate broker of Washington.
[2] Wilson did not attend the dinner in honor of Bryan at the Lafayette Hotel on December 6. He conveyed his felicitations in WW to O. P. Newman, Dec. 5, 1916, which was read aloud at the dinner. He and Mrs. Wilson also had Bryan and Mrs. Bryan to lunch at the White House on December 6.

Three Letters to Robert Lansing

The White House.

My dear Mr. Secretary,   3 December, 1916.

I thank you very much for this.[1] Would you be kind enough to answer these gentlemen to the effect you suggest, as by reference from me? I would be very much obliged to you indeed if you would. I think that the wisest way to handle the case.

Faithfully Yours,   W.W.

WWTLI (SDR, RG 59, 763.72115/2633½, DNA).
[1] RL to WW, Dec. 1, 1916 (first letter of that date).

The White House.

My dear Mr. Secretary,   3 December, 1916.

This[1] disturbs me very much indeed. I mentioned the matter to not a soul except Gerard. It did not go through my Office in any form, and I can therefore feel sure that no one there had access to any information about it.

These things make me feel quite desperate sometimes; and I feel like advising that we make a clean sweep in the telegraph office of your Department. Is it now arranged so that *no* one has access to that room except the telegraphers?

We *must* get to the bottom of these incidents if we have to put detectives on the job. Some very serious consequence to the country might easily sometime be brought about.

What do you think of this suggestion?

Faithfully yours,   W.W.

WWTLI (F. L. Polk Papers, CtY).
[1] RL to WW, Dec. 2, 1916.

The White House.

My dear Mr. Secretary,   3 December, 1916.

This interference on the part of the entente bankers annoys me intensely, and I think we ought to put our protest into pretty plain terms. You have followed the detail of this whole business of a Chinese loan much more attentively than I have: what would you advise?   Faithfully yours,   W.W.

WWTLI (SDR, RG 59, 893.51/1718½, DNA).

To Newton Diehl Baker

The White House.

My dear Mr. Secretary,   3 December, 1916.

Thank you for letting me see the enclosed. It exactly expresses what I had in mind, wit[h] items added which I had not thought out.

Query: Would it not be safer to instruct Pershing, with an inevitable hint of what was in mind, not to disturb the movement of Villista forces northward towards Juarez until it was pretty clear that all had got north of him that there was any immediate purpose of sending?[1] He might by his own scoutings and other movements frighten them back or arouse their suspicions.

The news in this morning's papers[2] makes it look as if our plan would not have to [be] acted upon in the near future at least, but perhaps it is wise to let Pershing have as much of our mind as is safe at once.   Faithfully Yours,   Woodrow Wilson

WWTLS (N. D. Baker Papers, DLC).
  1 *Sic!*
  2 The newspapers of December 3 reported that General Murguia and his forces had routed a band of *Villistas* in a battle about thirty miles south of Chihuahua City on December 1. See, for example, the *New York Times* and the *Washington Post*, Dec. 3, 1916.

To Edward Mandell House

The White House.

My dearest Friend,   3 November [December], 1916.

I was deeply disappointed that we did not get a chance to have a talk yesterday, though of course I had foreseen that it would be difficult in the midst of such a programme.

The situation is developing very fast and if we are going to do the proposed thing effectively we must do it very soon. In your last letter (the one of the thirtieth) you say, "Before the step is finally taken a good many things, I think, should be done. A background should be laid in both France and England so that public opinion would listen with favor to any proposal from you. This can be done, and quickly, if we get at it[.]" I wish you would expand that suggestion into concrete items and let me know just what sort of a programme, with what steps in it, you have in mind.

One of the reasons why early action is necessary is W.J.B. Gerard told me yesterday: 1) that W.J.B. was intent (as you already knew) on going abroad to fix the whole matter up himself and wanted him (Gerard) to prepare the way for him by getting the consent of the Kaiser and the men at the Foreign Office to see him. I instructed Gerard to do nothing of the kind; but simply to show him every courtesy if he came but let it be distinctly understood that he represented nobody but himself.

2) That W.J.B. had told him in a previous interview that he was going actively to oppose me in this country if I showed any signs of breaking off diplomatic relations with Germany.

3) That he had (I think most indiscreetly) told W.J.B. (in a later interview) that he could not consistently oppose me if I merely insisted on knowing what they were fighting for, showing W.J.B. a declaration of that very policy in the COMMONER;[1] and that it was evident that W.J.B. took to a renewal of that line of action very quickly and would probably make it the basis of his own mediation. I did not gather that he actually told W.J.B. what

I had in mind; but that he must have made it easy to guess that I had talked to him along those lines.

I think it would be well if you would have a talk with Gerard and put him on his guard and get from him more of the detail of his last interview with W.J.B. than it was possible for me to get amidst the events of yesterday.

Evidently a great deal of deliberate mischief is brewing COM-MONERwards.

Mr. B. told him that he would "expect" to be the peace commissioner if any were at any time appointed by me; but that, whether a commissioner or not, he would go and act as he thought best,—substantially what he said to you.

Gerard hopes that I will do what we discussed, and do it at once, and thinks, with us, that it is not what Germany wishes and not what either side could object to or decently decline if done in the terms I suggested,—as a neutral demand.

We enjoyed very much indeed having Mrs. House with us, and the sight done [down] the Bay was most inspiring.

With affectionate messages from us all,

Faithfully Yours,　Woodrow Wilson

WWTLS (E. M. House Papers, CtY).
  [1] W. J. Bryan, "The Road to Peace," *The Commoner*, XVI (May 1916), 5. *The Commoner* was Bryan's monthly magazine.

From Edward Mandell House

Dear Governor:　　　　　　　　　New York. December 3, 1916.

Gerard had just telephoned to ask me to say that if he is not to sail on the Frederick 8th it will be necessary to know by tomorrow afternoon. If he misses this boat he will not be able to sail again for a month unless he goes through England or France.

How would it do to send Gerard over in a battleship anyway even if Tarnowski has safe conduct. They would be more likely to give him safe conduct if they knew you were sending a battleship over that could bring him back if necessary.

Jusserand told Gerard yesterday that the reason they objected to Tarnowski was because he was a Pole and they were afraid he would stir up agitation with that element here.

Affectionately yours,　E. M. House

7:30 I have just finished a long conference with Jusserand. I will write you of it tomorrow. It is important.

I would let Gerard go tomorrow if I were you and not hold him for a battleship.

TLS (WP, DLC).

From Edward Mandell House, with Enclosures

Dear Governor: New York. December 3, 1916.

I am enclosing you a copy of a letter I received yesterday from Howard, President of the United Press, which may be of interest.

I am watching with a good deal of concern the crisis in the English Cabinet. If the Lloyd-George-Northcliffe-Carson combination succeed in overthrowing the Government and getting control, there will be no chance for peace until they run their course. England will then be under the military dictatorship that Whitehouse spoke about.

I am also sending you a copy of a cable from Lady Paget. This American Matinee is for the American Red Cross on the Allied Fronts. If it would be possible to cable her it would have a good effect in England and France.

I spoke to Bernstorff about it yesterday and he thought it would not be misunderstood in Germany and there could be no objection to such a cable. I let Bernstorff know that the best thing for peace was to strengthen you in the Allied countries, particularly in England. He understands this.

He told me yesterday that his government were in hopes that you might think fit to keep Gerard home. He said they put this suggestion to him mildly but constantly. The main objection, as far as I could gather, was Gerard's brusqueness which makes him unpopular. I think I talked Bernstorff into the belief that it was best to let Gerard go back and for his government to treat him cordially. He is to send a cable to this effect.

I told him Gerard was loyal and would carry out your views as nearly as it was possible, and that they would find him working steadily for peace.

You made your friends very happy last night and we are all talking about it today. Mrs. Cornelius Vanderbilt[1] who sat in a box next to ours and who has republican sympathies, told me that she did not know there was an American who could make such a speech. She said she understood now why we were such partisans of yours.

I do not think I was ever prouder of you than last night, and as old Bill[2] would say "that is going some."

Affectionately yours,   E. M. House

I hope you will not give Von Wiegand (the World's Berlin correspondent) the interview he wants and for good reasons which I will give you if you wish them.

TLS (WP, DLC).
[1] Either Alice Claypoole Gwynne (Mrs. Cornelius II) Vanderbilt or Grace Graham Wilson (Mrs. Cornelius III) Vanderbilt.

2 That is, William Jesse McDonald, the former Texas Ranger and Wilson's bodyguard during the campaign of 1912. See the index references in Vol. 26 of this series.

E N C L O S U R E   I

Roy Wilson Howard to Edward Mandell House

Personal & Confidential:

My dear Colonel: New York City. December 1, 1916.

While reading the following, please be good enough to forget, just for a moment, that I happen to be a newspaperman and take this from the viewpoint of a common or garden American.

The rumor is kicking about again that you are contemplating another European trip soon. Quite naturally the papers have jumped to the conclusion that you are going gunning for peace prospects. I hope that the rumor is without foundation. I believe that for you to make another swing around at *this time* would be a costly mistake.

You know that my point of view is neither that of an editor nor of a partisan. I was once regarded as a reasonably good reporter. The outstanding discovery which I made, as a reporter, during the last few months spent in South America and Europe was that at the time of my visit, the President stood higher in the respects of every foreign nation I visited, than he had ever stood before, and he had compelled a respect for America that did not exist in Europe a year and a half ago.

There is no doubt in my mind but that Germany intends to coax, if possible, or bull-doze if necessary, America into starting a peace move. When I was in Berlin, the threatening tactics appeared more popular. Should you start on this trip now, Germany and the Allies, despite anything you or anyone else can say, will believe your trip is in some way connected with peace-making efforts. Germany will be confirmed in the belief that bull-dozing pays in dealing with America and the improved standing of the country in the eyes of the Allies and neutral countries abroad will be set back three years.

I don't believe the game is worth the candle. If the President could advance the cause of permanent peace three months by sending you now—why, to hell with three years' improvement in our foreign standing. But I am convinced that he not only will not advance it, but that he will surely set it back. Today, Woodrow Wilson is the biggest peace asset in the world—if he is cashed in at the right time. This is not the right time. If you move now, Europe will say Wilson is moving. If the President moves now, he, in my judgment will injure and perhaps destroy his great potential power for good, a power that will be measured by the timeliness of its application.

You have established a credit for yourself among the leaders over there and have achieved a position and a recognition that is absolutely unique. This position is an asset both to this country and to the cause of permanent peace. I went just ahead of you twenty-one months ago and I know, possibly better than you even, with what distress and misgiving your coming was awaited, especially among some of the leaders in the Allied countries. I followed you more than a year later and I know that as a result of the confidences you inspired, you hold in your hands today, wonderful possibilities for good if these possibilities are not subjected to an early frost. But from what I saw and heard, I am convinced that if the President sends you now, the chance of good resulting would be far outweighed by the probability of harm being done.

All of which is passed along in the friendliest spirit for whatever value you may care to attach to it. I am anxious to have a real chat with you one of these days when each of us have a few moments to spare.   Faithfully yours,   Roy Howard.

TCL (WP, DLC).

E N C L O S U R E   I I

Please discover if the President can send me a cable wishing success to the American Matinee on December 8th.

Lady Paget,
35 Belgrave Square, London.

A reply something like this could not offend anyone.

It is deeply gratifying to me to find Americans in the belligerent countries working so hard to alleviate suffering and I sincerely hope that your efforts may be crowned with success.

Lady Paget is one of your warmest admirers in England and is a true American.

T and Hw MS (WP, DLC).

Sir Cecil Arthur Spring Rice to the Foreign Office

Personal & very Secret.
Confidential:

Washington 3 Dec. 1916

My tel No. 3619

Crawford reports:[1] "Yesterday evening Mr. Polk asked me by telephone whether I had seen the explanation issued by the Federal Reserve Board of their action in respect of British Treasury Bills[2] & whether I thought it satisfactory.

I replied that I had seen the statement to which he referred but that personally I did not find in it any explanation, nor had it in my view improved the situation. He then asked me whether I would see the Governor of the Federal Reserve Board and tell him what I felt should be done. I answered that I had already expressed my views to Mr. Harding. The mischief had been done and no useful purpose would be served by pursuing the matter further.

This morning (Sunday) Mr. Harding called at my house after ten. He said that he had called at the suggestion of the Counsellor of the State Department to discuss the Treasury Bill incident. I told him that further discussion seemed useless. We had already covered the ground in our conversation of last Thursday night and I could add, or withdraw, nothing from what I had said on that occasion. He confessed that the explanatory statement issued by the Board had not mended matters from my point of view. I observed that the mischief was irreparable. He then produced a telegram from Secretary McAdoo, who he said would endeavour to make amends in the speech he was to deliver in N. Y. about the 11th. Dec. He continued in strictest confidence that he knew he could speak to me as a friend without my forgetting that he was a servant of the U.S.G. Later on he would tell me the whole inner history of the incident, and even now he desired that I should know that the paragraph "warning individual investors" to which I had the strongest objection was not in the draft of the Boards statement as prepared by him, but that he had been instructed to insert it by the "highest authority." He further advised me carefully to watch the future foreign policy of the President Wilson in relation to H.M.G.

I should add that I have confidence in Governor Harding's friendliness & sympathy. I was almost daily in conference with him last year throughout the negotiations leading to the declaration of cotton as contraband, when he was deputed by the President to negotiate with me the arrangements and assurance to the

U.S.G. which accompanied that declaration. It was also with him and with Governor Strong that I made the arrangements for the approval and recognition of Lord Reading's mission[3] by the U. S. Treasury. Throughout I have found him helpful & sincere. His remarks to me today should be regarded as strictly confidential"

This information is very serious and must be regarded as strictly confidential. I have received a similar warning from another quarter. The object of course is to force us to accept Presidents mediation by cutting off supplies. We shall take quiet measures here to counteract this policy.

Hw telegram (FO 115/2084, pp. 309-310, PRO).
  [1] R. A. Crawford, "MEMORANDUM," Dec. 5, 1916, TS MS (FO 371/2800, No. 255636, PRO).
  [2] Upon receipt of the news that the British and French governments had instructed J. P. Morgan & Co. to withdraw their treasury notes from sale in the United States, Harding spoke briefly to the press. He declared that the portion of the Federal Reserve Board's statement of November 27 dealing with the foreign treasury bills had been "intended in no way to slight the financial status of any foreign country or to reflect on any American banking firm." He added: "The statement was issued merely to prevent the confusion of the discount and the investment markets. The effect, I believe, will mean that foreign government paper will be entirely of the investment charact[e]r, which it should be. Of course, the Reserve Board has no authority to give advice as to investments, but it is only fair to recommend to purchasers of foreign securities that all facts about them should be considered." *New York Herald*, Dec. 2, 1916.
  [3] That is, to arrange to float a $500,000,000 public Anglo-French bond issue in the United States. The negotiations took place in September and October 1915. See Link, *The Struggle for Neutrality, 1914-1915*, pp. 625-26.

From Edward Mandell House

Dear Governor: New York. December 4, 1916.

Gerard is sick this afternoon and may not be able to sail tomorrow. It depends upon the verdict of his doctor. I took down verbatim his version of that part of his conversation with Mr. Bryan in which you are interested.

Bryan asked Gerard to please write or cable him whether or not the Kaiser would receive him. Bryan said that everybody must concede that he should be a peace delegate. Gerard told him that it would be a mistake for you and him to conflict in these matters and that it would be a mistake for him (Bryan) to insist that you call a peace conference.

Bryan wanted to know what Ge[r]ard thought was best to do at this time to bring about peace. Ge[r]ard said he did not know of any particular thing excepting perhaps to call on the belligerents to state what they were fighting for. Bryan replied that was his idea also. That the neutral nations had a right to demand what the belligerents were fighting for. He produced a copy of the COM-

MONER and showed Gerard a paragraph where he had advocated that idea.

Gerard replied that possibly he, Bryan, and you might not be very far apart, but that he could find out when he lunched with you. Gerard told him that in his opinion it would be a mistake for him (Bryan) to antagonize you for there was nothing so likely to create war as the belief that we were divided in this country. Bryan then wanted to know why it would not be well to get Germany and Austria to sign one of his peace treaties. Gerard replied that this would make you the laughing stock of the world because the Germans would immediately begin an unrestricted submarine warfare and you would not be able to prevent it until after a year had passed.

This, I think, is all of any importance that passed. I cautioned Gerard about mentioning what you had in your mind and I rather led him to think that you had only an indefinite idea of doing anything. I thought it best to do this in order to insure silence.

In my opinion, Bryan cannot muddy the waters to any appreciable extent. He may try, and probably will try, but he has but little influence here and none abroad. If he went to England or France he would be politely frozen. Germany would use him, but everyone would know what they were doing and it would not have the slightest effect anywhere. As I said before, the only way Bryan can resuscitate himself would be by your creating a sentiment for him by unfriendly treatment. This is not only my opinion, but that of Carter Glass and others like him with whom I have talked.

What I meant by preparing a proper background in England and France was to do certain things which you are doing, and certain things which you might do. For instance, the protest against the Belgian deportation. Your speech of Saturday night will have a favorable effect. A telegram to Lady Paget will also help.

I saw Robert Fleming on Friday. He is one of the foremost financiers of England and I enlisted his cooperation towards forming such a sentiment. I upbraided him, and those like him, for sitting still and permitting the war party to create the impression that no one in England was in favor of peace upon any reasonable terms and permitting the press to rebuff any suggestion of help in a solution of their troubles by you. Fleming is a very rich man and can organize a propaganda that would be formidable.

I shall see Whitehouse again tomorrow and try to persuade him to return to England immediately upon a similar mission. I shall write Lord Loreburn, Buxton and others like them, discreetly urging their cooperation.

I had a long and spirited conversation with Jusserand yesterday. He promised to send a cable to his Government embodying the things we have done for France since the war began. Jusserand was inclined to be critical because we had not sent Bernstorff home and had not held Germany to strict accountability in the submarine controversy. He mentioned the Sussex, marina and several of the latest incidents.

I turned on him when he had finished and made him confess that if Germany started an unrestricted submarine warfare, there was a possibility of practically isolating England. He admitted that the course you had followed was the one most favorable to the Allies. The substance of my reply was that the Allies did not seem to know what was best for them and that they had better take our guidance.

He admitted that it was probable that no material change in the western line could be made at least for a year or more, and I suggested the wisdom of accepting your offer of last spring to mediate. He seemed to concur in this, but at the last moment upon leaving, he veered away into the high-flown, foolish declaration that France would fight to the last man.

Bernstorff is the only Ambassador of the belligerent countries that seems to have any sense of proportion, and who never criticizes this Government in the slightest for anything that occurs. He takes what comes philosophically, and tries to make a favorable impression if possible. The others seem at times to say what they can to irritate.

Jusserand told me that his Government had sent him a long cable just before he left Washington, all of which had not been decyphered up to the time of his leaving, but that he got enough of it to know that they would probably reject our request for a safe conduct for Tarnowski.

I went into this with him in some detail, and he wanted to know whether I thought it important enough for him to see you. I thought that it was.[1] He was not pleasant about it. For some reason they seem to be bitterly opposed to his coming over.

He asked if it were true that you had any thought of sending a battleship to bring Tarnowski over. I veered away from a direct answer to this telling him that you had not discussed that feature with me.

He was excited over the action of the Federal Reserve Board. I tried to smooth it over.

In the event you want someone to take a verbal message to

Page and Sharp, the best man to do it I think would be W. H. Buckler of the London Embassy. He is the one man there who has not lost his bearings, and he seems in sympathy with your purposes. He is friendly with Trevelyan, Massingham of the Nation and men of that kind. If you will look him up in Who's Who you will find he has had ample experience. He should be cabled for immediately I think if you approve the suggestion.

When you get your note finished will you not let me come over? There are many things that I can explain better in person, and I think the matter you have in mind deserves constant attention.

Affectionately yours,   E. M. House

TLS (WP, DLC).
1 Jusserand did not talk to Wilson about this matter. The Allies did grant safe conduct, and Tarnowski arrived in Washington on February 1, 1917.

From Robert Lansing, with Enclosure

PERSONAL AND PRIVATE:

My dear Mr. President: Washington December 4, 1916.

I assumed from your note to me of yesterday, in reference to the Chinese Loan, that it was advisable to make an immediate statement to Minister Reinsch. I therefore had prepared and sent a telegram—of which a copy is enclosed. Do you feel that we should go further and make representations to London, Paris, Petrograd and Tokio?

My own view is that it would be well to wait and see if they propose to take any further steps in the matter. Possibly they will let it rest as it is.   Faithfully yours,   Robert Lansing.

TLS (SDR, RG 59, 893.51/3010, DNA).

E N C L O S U R E

December 4, 1916.

Amlegation, Peking.   NOT TO BE DISTRIBUTED.

Your confidential telegram of December 2, one p.m.

You may say to the Chinese Government that in the opinion of this Government there is nothing in the terms of the Chicago loan which conflicts with any agreements between China and foreign bankers. Opposition would seem to imply a claim on the part of some to greater privileges in China than enjoyed by Americans.

This Department last summer gave every encouragement to

participation by group banks in loan to China and met with nothing but rebuffs.

CC telegram (SDR, RG 59, 893.51/1715, DNA).

From Robert Lansing, with Enclosure

PERSONAL AND CONFIDENTIAL:

My dear Mr. President: Washington December 4, 1916.

I enclose you a very interesting despatch from Mr. Grew as to the general situation in Germany—(No. 4503, November 7, 1916). I am sure you will find it very interesting reading.

Faithfully yours,   Robert Lansing

TLS (SDR, RG 59, 763.72/3036, DNA).

E N C L O S U R E

Joseph Clark Grew to Robert Lansing

No. 4530 *Strictly confidential.*

Sir: Berlin, November 7, 1916.

With reference to my confidential despatch No. 4322 of October 16, 1916, reporting on the political situation in Germany, particularly in its bearing on the question of a possible resumption of the relentless and indiscriminate form of submarine warfare, I have the honor to bring to the Department's attention certain further information on this subject, which comes to me from a trustworthy, well informed and confidential source in direct touch with sentiment in naval circles at the naval ports.

Much irritation has been caused in certain high naval quarters owing to the delay in an official announcement of a general submarine campaign against England, which is generally interpreted as a temporary victory for those opposed to the von Tirpitz policy. An outspoken declaration for the indiscriminate destruction of enemy ships without warning would, it is said, have been made before this, could those in authority agree that the present was an opportune time to launch the campaign. While the entire Navy is in favor of it, they are divided into three separate groups on the question as to the time when it should begin. The first group, the great majority, hold that action should not be taken until after the presidential election in the United States. A second group believe that the early spring would be the opportune time, both on account of the weather conditions and because the sub-marine fleet would by that time be greatly augmented in tonnage. A third group, who are in the minority, have for the past two months been in favor of opening hostilities immediately.

The naval authorities are apparently much worried at the strength of the opposition to their plan. They realize that it would probably involve the United States in the war and they know that the Emperor is emphatically opposed to it, but they appear to believe that they can act independently of his wishes. They declare that he has always been opposed to the Zeppelin raids over London, but that the Admiralty has pursued that method of warfare regardless of his wishes or opinions and they pretend to believe that his opposition, as well as that of his close advisers, to the indiscriminate submarine warfare, can be overcome through a campaign of pressure from high military as well as high naval authorities. In any case, the idea that the submarines will even-tually operate against all enemy ships without giving warning still dominates the wishes of the naval commanders, not only of the submarines but of all other grades in the Navy, and it is said that there is not one dissenting voice in the entire Navy against what they deem to be a necessary undertaking to avoid a long continuance of the war and an ultimate defeat.

The food situation must to a great extent be regarded as bound up with the submarine issue, for the greater the growth of dis-satisfaction and unrest among the people owing to difficult con-ditions of living, the greater will be the pressure to meet these conditions with some strong, and what the Navy considers decisive, action.

It is an open secret that this food question is becoming alarm-ing to those in a position to know the exact conditions. The authorities are becoming nervous over the growing dissatisfac-tion of the people in the decrease of the supply of food stuffs and the difficulty of finding even the amounts which their food cards call for. Riotous demonstrations of the working people have oc-curred in Kiel and other places, which necessitated the calling out of the marines and soldiers to enforce order, and though nothing of this appears in the press, it is probable that the unrest is wide-spread.

In this connection the Consul General at Dresden[1] writes me as follows under date of November 4th: "On Thursday afternoon some two thousand women made a pacific descent upon the city hall at Dresden and demanded not bread, but potatoes. They re-

[1] Leo Allen Bergholz.

ceived the promise of a larger quantity and an exhortation not to disturb the peace. The women were of the lower classes and were very orderly in their behavior. Papers of Dresden have, of course, made no mention of the demonstration.

"The normal quantity of potatoes allowed each person a day in Dresden is a pound, but for weeks many even of the well-to-do families have been unable to secure any. Through bad packing, I learn from an excellent source, two thousand tons stored in Dresden rotted. Eight thousand pounds of butter, also through faulty packing, had to be sold to soap factories. All this is known to the people and, naturally creates certain hostility towards the local authorities who are held responsible.

"There is virtually no meat, butter, eggs, or sugar to be had and very few vegetables and very little milk, and the little there is, is sold at least between a hundred and two hundred per cent above the prices before the war. Cards for every kind of food are in use with the exception of fish and vegetables, but unhappily the amounts they call for, although insignificant, are not to be had. For instance each adult person is supposed to receive an eighth of a pound of butter a week, but in fact he is very fortunate if he secures this quantity every ten days or even two weeks. Butter costs seventy cents a pound, just twice what it was sold for before the war. One receives a pound and a half of sugar, half a pound of coffee, and a quarter pound of tea a month. Each inhabitant is allowed an egg a week which costs twelve cents and which in normal times could be had for a cent and a quarter. We are supposed to receive nine ounces of meat a week, but in fact we get about the half. If one is rich one can buy geese, costing from $7.50 to $10.00 each, ducks from $3.73 to $6.25 each, and hens at $2.50 each. In ante bellum times geese sold for $2.00 to $2.50 each, ducks for $0.75 to $1.25 and chickens for $0.50 to $0.75 each. The best meats, when obtainable, cost on the average $1.00 a pound, but before the war never more than forty cents a pound.

"The result of all this is that there is, if not actual starvation, at least woeful distress among the poor, want among the middle class, and a great deal of grumbling among the rich who can still live on geese, ducks, and game and who, it must be frankly stated, seem to be favored by the Government as no meat cards are required for these luxuries.

"I think that it is now generally admitted that the trouble lies with the Government which seems not to be able to adapt itself to changed conditions. It makes regulations which do not work and apparently has not the capacity to enact new ones. The trouble is that, although an Imperial Food Director has been appointed, there is no single governmental control of its distribution due largely to the independent Kingdoms of Prussia, Saxony, Bavaria, and Wurttemberg declining to surrender their surplus supplies to their less fortunate neighbors. Saxony is a manufacturing country and not an agricultural one, and it is, therefore, almost wholly dependent upon the other German states for its food. Even the local Saxon municipalities retain for possible lean months the products they do not actually need instead of turning them into a single distributing centre. Dresden, for instance, grants nominally an eighth of a pound of butter a week, but Blasewitz, a suburb of the city, but with its own Municipal Government, permits the purchase of a quarter pound a week. Hundreds of pounds of fish, meats, butter, and potatoes have been allowed to spoil, due either to indecision or lack of adaptability on the part of the officials.

"Wholesale dealers and hotels could purchase tons of meats, sausages and supplies of all kinds from the Scandinavian countries, but are not permitted to do so as the Government is unable to devise a plan for the supervision of their distribution."

These conditions, which obtain in a greater or less degree throughout the entire country, must be met, and met in a way that will prevent the growth of ill-feeling and riotous manifestations, just as the successful operations of the enemy on the Somme and elsewhere and the consequent discouragement of the people were met with the campaign against Roumania. To offset the dissatisfaction over the lack of food, the people's minds must be turned to something that appeals to their imagination and which holds out a prospect of an early peace with victory. The submarine campaign is the solution chosen by the Navy and probably by a great number of the high military officers in the field. They fully realize, however, that their present stumbling block is the Emperor and his immediate advisers, including von Hindenburg, upon whom the decision of the question of plunging into a general submarine warfare, will probably ultimately rest.

The return of the submarines "U-53" and "U-69" from the Atlantic coast of the United States is the cause of much elation in the Navy. They pretend to see in this a demonstration that they can carry on a successful submarine warfare along the full ocean highway, even to the gateways to American waters, and they regard it as a successful test and an experience to be availed of in case the much desired submarine campaign should ultimately be launched.

For the past three weeks it is said that from four to five new submarines a week have been put into commission. This rapid increase is believed to be but temporary and due to the completion of submarines of all types which were under construction when the new type, now in use, was agreed upon. Almost the whole strength of the naval constructive force, however, is diverted to the rapid building of submarines and little attention is now being given to the building of the larger or dreadnought type of ships. Those under construction are of the Ersatz or replacing order and are of the small cruiser class only.

There are at present believed to be nearly 100 qualified submarine commanders awaiting assignments, which are being made as rapidly as the boats are put into commission. The men for 100 more boats are awaiting places on these boats. Even with this qualified force on hand, as many more are undergoing training for the service and the school ships are busy with this work.

It is said that the Zeppelin raids over London will probably be discontinued and that airship activity will be directed to places in the British Isles outside of that city. The recent death of Kapitänleutnant Mathey and the destruction of his Zeppelin[2] have had a depressing effect on the air division, for he was the oldest and most capable Zeppelin commander in the fleet and his ship was the latest and best equipped model. Mathey always operated at an altitude of 4000 meters and considered himself safe at that height. His only danger was in case an aeroplane could get above him, and he reasoned that it required so much time for a machine to do that after getting notice that he was within the zone of operations that he would have dropped his bombs and returned out of danger. It now develops that before they started, the British agents in Germany communicated with their people and the British aeroplanes had arisen to a height of 5000 meters before the Zeppelins arrived and therefore had no trouble in dropping inflammable bombs on the high airship. Kapitänleutnant Koch,[3] who was under Mathey at an altitude of 2500 meters saw his machine fall and he himself with his machine had a narrow escape, two inflammable bombs hurled at him passing his Zeppelin at a distance of less than ten meters.

Heretofore it has been considered by the Zeppelin authorities that in case a ship was struck it would ignite and those in it would be incinerated before having time to even hurl themselves from the boats. In view of the fact that Mathey and his companions were not burned nor was their clothing even scorched, they now

[2] Heinrich Mathy and his crew were killed when their airship *L31* was destroyed by incendiary machine gun fire from an intercepting British airplane over London on October 2, 1916. See Douglas H. Robinson, *The Zeppelin in Combat: A History of the German Naval Airship Division, 1912-1918* (London, 1962), pp. 194-96, 387.

realize that had the Zeppelin been supplied with parachutes they could probably have been saved. The Zeppelins are now to be given this contrivance for future use.

I have indications from various sources that since von Hindenburg became Chief of Staff there has been a great increase in the number of men called to the ranks who were previously passed as unfit or excused from service for one reason or another. A great number of Jews are being reexamined and forced into service. My reports are that since von Hindenburg's appointment approximately 100,000 new men in Berlin, 60,000 in Hamburg and similar quotas in other cities have been taken.

In connection with the general political situation and the submarine campaign, I would respectfully refer to my confidential telegrams Nos. 4503, 4553, 4558 and 4569, of October 20, November 3, 4, and 7, respectively, sent since my despatch of October 16, as well as to the press summaries cabled daily.

I have the honor to be, Sir, Your obedient servant, J. C. Grew Chargé d'Affaires *ad interim*

TLS (SDR, RG 59, 763.72/3036, DNA).
[3] Robert Koch, commander of airship *L24*. See *ibid.*, pp. 193-94, 217, 387, 389.

From Samuel Gompers, with Enclosure

Sir: Washington, D. C., Dec. 4, 1916.

I beg to hand you herewith a copy of a letter which I have received from Mr. Santiago Iglesias,[1] President of the Free Federation of Workmen of Porto Rico, the organization affiliated to the American Federation of Labor and representing the best interests of the workers of the Island. I bespeak for the letter and its contents your sympathetic consideration and action which I am sure it deserves.   Very respectfully yours,   Saml. Gompers

TLS (WP, DLC).
[1] Santiago Iglesias Pantín (1870-1939), a friend and associate of Gompers in the labor movement since 1901, president of the Federación Libre de Trabajadores de Puerto Rico and president of the Socialist party of Porto Rico.

E N C L O S U R E

Santiago Iglesias Pantín to Samuel Gompers

Dear Sir and Brother: [Washington] December 4, 1916.

As you know, for years the Free Federation of Workingmen of Puerto Rico has repeatedly asked that a Congressional investigation be made of the economic and social conditions of the workers of Puerto Rico prior to any change in the Organic Act or to any new law which might be enacted by Congress. You, being fully informed of the deplorable conditions of the workers of Puerto Rico in general, I have therefore nothing more to add to the reports already made to you in regard to the subject matter.

I now want to make particular reference,to the constant failure of Congress during the last few years, in regard to framing a law as to the statutes of the people of Puerto Rico. There is now pending before the Senate a bill which, if it become law, certainly will define, for ever, the status of the people of Puerto Rico. The bill itself contains several clauses of a reactionary character to which the Free Federation of Workingmen of Puerto Rico emphatically protest, and instructed me to come again to the mainland to inform you of such a decision taken in the name of the labor movement of the whole Island.

Before entering into the presentation of the features of the bill to which the labor people, as well as may be said the people in general of Puerto Rico, protest, let me quote the Honorable John J. Shafroth, Chairman of the Committee of the Senate on the Pacific Islands and Puerto Rico, in an address to the Senate:

"Mr. President, in the formation of our Republic we put forth to the world new principles of government, which seemed so plain to us that we declared them to be self-evident truths. We declared that all men are created equal, not in intellect, not in height, not in strength, not in color, and not in many other respects, but equal in rights. We declared that man is entitled, as an unalienable right, to life, liberty, and the pursuit of happiness. We said in that declaration that so sacred are these rights against tyranny that they not only shall not be invaded by others, but they cannot be bartered away even by ourselves."

The working people of Puerto Rico wonder why the policy outlined by Senator Shafroth in the splendid remarks above has not been followed by himself in the framing up of the Puerto Rican bill.

Section 26 of the Jones Bill, with amendments by the Senate Committee of which Senator Shafroth is Chairman, says:

"No person shall be a member of the Senate of Puerto Rico * * * who does not own * * * taxable property in Puerto Rico to the value of no less than $1000.00 * * * *"

Section 27 of the same bill says: "No person shall be a member of the House of Representatives * * * who does not own

* * * and pay taxes upon property of the assessed value of no less than $500.00 * * * *"

The only argument which Governor Yager advanced in advocating the property and the literacy qualifications is that he has proof that the corporations practically control the votes of large groups of the working people.

In regard to this statement I want to inform you that the labor movement of Puerto Rico, as expressed through the Free Federation of Workingmen, affiliated with the American Federation of Labor, has been and is now the most potential and influential factor in the Island that is trying to Americanize the people of Puerto Rico to the American standard of political action and freedom, and they have succeeded in a great measure to free them from the influence of the employers, politically as well as economically. I advise you that it is a dangerous proposition at this time to impose a property qualification on members to be elected for the Senate, as well as for the House of Legislature of Puerto Rico. To give the property qualification only the right to rule the affairs of the people of the Island will have a tendency to strengthen and encourage the agitation and propaganda of those who are already preaching anti-American sentiments and striving for the independence of the Island.

Section 35 of same bill states: "That no person shall be allowed to register as a voter or to vote in Puerto Rico unless * * * he is able to read and write or * * * he is a bona fide tax payer." This has been amended by adding these words: "That all legally qualified electors of Puerto Rico at the last election shall be entitled to register and vote at elections for ten years from and after the passage of this Act."

I do not believe, sir, that more can be said in regard to this subject matter than has been already said by you before the Senate Committee on the Pacific Islands and Puerto Rico at the last session of Congress; nevertheless, in the name of justice and to the credit of the American nation, it will be wise to eliminate from the Jones Bill this most objectionable feature. If Congress enacts the Bill with that clause, it will disfranchise three out of every four voters of Puerto Rico; it will practically disfranchise one hundred and seventy-five thousand workingmen out of a total of two hundred and five thousand voters of the whole island. Besides it would be a great political mistake and a national wrong imposed upon the people of the Island.

The people of Puerto Rico have been exercising such a franchise for the last sixteen years, and even in the Spanish monarchy. Such rights were recognized to our people by Congress of Spain and our local legislature, and now the Congress of the United States is being advised to take away those rights that our people enjoy and possess. *It is indeed a very serious question, that the same bill which purports to grant American citizenship to the people of Puerto Rico shall take away the civil rights that our people enjoy and possess, so it will clearly appear to the minds of the people that in being honorably bestowed with citizenship of the United States they are going to lose their civil rights, and a property clause is going to be created to make the laws and to rule the working people who constitute ninety odd per cent of the people of the Island.* On the other hand, no means are provided to enable some 300,000 children to attend school, which amounts to 60 per cent of the total electoral population, who because of the inability to obtain an education will be deprived the right of franchise. Moreover, only such citizens who pay a tax are privileged to be representatives in the Legislature of the Island. Workingmen, however bright and intelligent they may be, if they pay no taxes will be disqualified and robbed of the right to be representatives.

On that point I want to declare emphatically, and advise you, that in the probable enactment of the Jones Bill, unfortunately containing those clauses mentioned above, it will be more than likely that the political agitators and anti-American propagandists will obtain a strong argument to encourage and stimulate the discontent among the masses of the people.

Recently, in a conversation with General Frank McIntyre, Chief of the Bureau of Insular Affairs in the War Department, I tried to convey to him the above influences, ideas and political conditions that now exist in Puerto Rico, and I am glad to inform you that he made the following remark, referring specially to that section of the bill relative to the civil rights of Puerto Rico: *"Those clauses are not essential to the principles of the bill and could very well be eliminated."* While the Jones Bill grants to the people of Puerto Rico American citizenship, that same bill forces upon our people theories of government which have long ago been repudiated by the progressive force of American democracy, as well as the progressive force of Puerto Rico.

If the condition of the people of Puerto Rico is ever to be raised to a standard at all compatible with that prevailing in the United States, our civil and political rights that we now enjoy and possess must be guaranteed and extended in the new Organic Law now pending before the Senate. In conclusion, speaking in regard to the civil rights of the people of Puerto Rico, let me quote from your statement made before the Senate Committee that has charge of the Jones Bill:

"But, gentlemen, let me say this, that the idea of making the Government of Porto Rico a government based upon property qualifications is not conducive to the development of democratic ideals among the people of our country or elsewhere. You can not deprive the Porto Rican people of their inherent right of self-government and continue very long to maintain self-government and democratic ideals in the United States. Tyranny disrupts the character of even the tyrant. Those who inflict injustice themselves inevitably feel its reflections."

Referring now to another subject matter, you know that we have time and again petitioned Congress that there should now be in the Island, a department of agriculture and labor, with the same power, dignity, and authority of other departments, and the Jones Bill contains that provision in section 18: at the same time, in section 37 we find the following amendment:

"No executive department not provided for in this Act shall be created by the legislature, but the legislature may, in the interests of economy, consolidate departments or abolish any department with the consent of the President of the United States."

Certainly this amendment puts in an absolute dangerous position, the department of labor now created by the Jones Bill. The working people of Puerto Rico look upon that amendment as a means of finally abolishing the only department which the bill creates to protect the working people of the Island.

The Free Federation of Workingmen of Puerto Rico maintains fully the same declarations and petitions duly made to the President of the United States and Congress year after year.

The people of the Island want to solve a great economical problem and ought to have the right guaranteed by the new constitution to use the government, whose upholders they are, to obtain loans at a low rate of interest, and the government in making such loans should also do away with the dreadful usury prevailing throughout the country. In so doing the government would also hamper and lessen the social and industrial oppression of the masses and help thereby in diffusing the wealth.

The banking system and the credit have both been left in the hands of private manipulation, and both speculation and monopoly, as well as the control of the local government, has fallen into the hands of the most powerful corporations.

The private monopoly of vital interests of the community of the Island is detrimental to the well-being of the people, and such monopoly and control of the wealth produced by the people is creating among the popular minds a moral state of indignation against the hateful industrial oppression which has been the cause for so much wretchedness, privation, and hunger among the working masses.

We hope the United States Congress will enact a constitution furthering the common good of all the people of Puerto Rico and in the general interest of the Island, ridding the masses from the social and industrial oppression they suffer, oppression which is casting discredit upon the American flag. Congress should suppress the monopoly affected by the corporations; the exportation of the wealth produced by Puerto Rican workers should be regulated so as to retain the greater part for the benefit of the inhabitants of the Island; now more than 60 per cent is exported, a circumstance which turns the Island into a trading post operated by underfed and barefoot laborers, and in this way the constitution would benefit the whole people, and not a specially privileged class or party. Such a measure would promote the diffusion of wealth and comfort, intelligence, virtue, and equal opportunity, which are the chief aims and aspirations of the wise, democratic American institutions.

In the event that a resolution for a general investigation should not prove successful in the affairs of the Island, then we request Congress to stand by and adopt the amendments and additions that are absolutely necessary, democratic, and such as will concede the right for the safeguard of the interest of the laboring people of Puerto Rico, and of being included in the Jones Bill pending before the Senate; the petitions are as follows:

1. If Puerto Rico is to be American forever, we should be declared citizens of the United States collectively.

2. Popular suffrage must not be restricted, and all citizens, adults, men of 21 years of age or over, should have the right of suffrage for elective offices in all the branches of the government, such as they now enjoy and possess.

3. A department of labor should be established and vested with the same authority and prestige as the other departments of the Government, and its executive head should receive his appointment from the President of the United States. And the purposes of the department of labor shall be to foster, promote, and develop the welfare of the wage earners of the Island of Puerto Rico, to improve their working conditions, and to advance their opportunities for profitable employment.

4. Eight hours shall constitute a day's work in all cases of employment by and on behalf of Puerto Rico or any county or municipality, or by and on behalf of any contract for labor and supplies for the Island or any county or municipality thereof.

5. No children under the age of 14 years shall be employed, allowed or permitted to work in any factory, sugar, tobacco, or coffee field, workshop, mill establishment, or at any other place where goods of any kind are manufactured, and penalties shall be provided by laws for any violation therein.

6. The Legislature of Puerto Rico ought to pass a law fixing a minimum wage salary per day's work for the women, and under no circumstances shall a woman be allowed to work over eight hours per day nor after 7 p.m. until 7 a.m. of the following day in any factory, shop, or manufacturing, or agricultural establishment of any kind, and provisions will be made in the law to punish all violations that may be committed against these provisions.

7. The legislature shall, by appropriate legislation, create and enforce a liability on the part of all employers to compensate their employes for any injury incurred by the employes in the course of their employment, irrespective of the fault of either party. The legislature shall provide for the settlement of any dispute arising under the legislation contemplated by this section of the constitution either by arbitration or by an industrial-accident board or by the courts, or by either, any, or all of these agencies; anything in this constitution to the contrary notwithstanding.

8. Every person may freely speak, write, or publish his sentiments on all subjects, being responsible for the abuse of that right, and no law shall be passed by the legislature to restrain or abridge the liberty of speech or of the press. Nor shall any officer or court of any political division of Puerto Rico abridge the liberty of speech or of the press. In all criminal prosecutions for libel, the truth of the matter alleged to be libelous may be given in evidence to the jury, and if it shall appear to the jury that the matter charged as libelous be true and was written and published with good motives and for justifiable ends, the party shall be acquitted.

9. The using and contracting of convict labor by any officer of the Island is hereby prohibited.

10. No corporation shall be permitted or authorized to carry on or own land in excess of 500 acres.

11. Lawyers employed as officers of the government of Puerto Rico in any department or office are hereby prohibited and under no circumstances will be permitted to appear as lawyers in any

court of the Island unless they appear as counsel representing the Government.

With best wishes and regards, I remain

Fraternally yours,   Santiago Iglesias

TCLS (WP, DLC).

From Robert Russa Moton

Personal

Tuskegee Institute,
Dear Mr. President: Alabama December 4th, 1916

I was in Washington a week ago today and had hoped through Secretary Redfield to have a five minutes talk with you, but I thought it unwise for me to see you, that it might be embarrassing to you and perhaps interfere with the very thing that I wished to call to your attention.

I have appreciated the delicacy of your situation throughout your administration, and I need not tell you that I appreciate also the splendid service you have rendered this nation. I realize that it was embarrassing and perhaps unwise for you to make any reference to the race question as it might perhaps hazard in some way the other important policies of your administration, but now that your election is assured and your policies are pretty definitely established and accepted by the nation as a whole, I am wondering if you could refer in some way to the ten or eleven millions of Negroes in our country.

The South is very much stirred by the migration of Negroes Northward, and I think thoughtful colored people in the South are equally stirred. The South is also stirred on the lynching question, as indicated by the enclosed editorial from the Atlanta Constitution of November 24.[1]

Of course it may not be possible for you to say anything in your forthcoming message to Congress, but it might be possible for you, in your inaugural address or in some other way to refer to this group of people who constitute at least one-tenth of the population of our country.

It would hearten my race more I think than even you realize if you should now make a statement calling for justice for these millions of people, especially condemning burning and lynching. While the South has been much the greater sinner, the North is not free for there have been lynchings in Delaware, Pennsylvania and Ohio as well as other Northern states, I think.

I am writing this, of course, in the strictest confidence, and want to assure you I would not only do nothing that would in any way embarrass your administration, but knowing the conditions as I do and knowing how discouraged not to say despondent many of our people are, I felt that I owed to them and to you also to write thus frankly.

May I add my prayerful good wishes for your good health.

Yours very truly,   R. R. Moton

TLS (WP, DLC).
[1] "Keeping the Negro at Home." It admitted that lynching was a prime factor motivating increased black migration from the South to the North and East: "Loss of much of the state's best labor is one of the prices Georgia is paying for unchecked mob activity against negroes often charged only with ordinary crimes. . . . Lynching for causes less serious has been the outgrowth of mob execution for the one more heinous crime, in connection with which many have felt there was justification for it. Mob activity has fed upon itself and grown from bad to worse, until it has become not only a social and moral, but a serious business problem. It is imperative that we get back to a basis of law and order." Moton also enclosed a clipping from the *Atlanta Constitution*, Dec. 2, 1916, of an editorial entitled "Would Help Both Races." It argued that the education of blacks was as important to whites as to blacks.

John B. Densmore[1] to Joseph Patrick Tumulty

My dear Mr. Tumulty: Washington December 4, 1916.

I have been requested to write you, asking to obtain an appointment to see the President on Monday, the 11th, or Tuesday, the 12th, for Mr. Frank P. Walsh, of Kansas City, Mr. John P. White, President of the United Mine Workers, and "Mother" Jones. They desire to discuss briefly with the President some matters in connection with the parole of some of the labor people now in prison.

Will you please direct your reply to Secretary Wilson, as I may be absent from the city.

Sincerely yours,   J B Densmore

TLS (WP, DLC).
[1] Solicitor of the Department of Labor.

To Joseph Patrick Tumulty

Dear Tumulty: [The White House, Dec. 5, 1916]

I am willing to see these gentlemen at 2:15 on Monday, the eleventh, here at the house.[1]   The President.

TL (WP, DLC).
[1] Wilson received Walsh, White, and "Mother" Jones in the Oval Office on December 11 at 2:15 P.M.

An Annual Message

[Dec. 5, 1916]

Gentlemen of the Congress: In fulfilling at this time the duty laid upon me by the Constitution of communicating to you from time to time information of the state of the Union and recommending to your consideration such legislative measures as may be judged necessary and expedient I shall continue the practice, which I hope has been acceptable to you, of leaving to the reports of the several heads of the executive departments the elaboration of the detailed needs of the public service and confine myself to those matters of more general public policy with which it seems necessary and feasible to deal at the present session of the Congress.

I realize the limitations of time under which you will necessarily act at this session and shall make my suggestions as few as possible; but there were some things left undone at the last session which there will now be time to complete and which it seems necessary in the interest of the public to do at once.

In the first place, it seems to me imperatively necessary that the earliest possible consideration and action should be accorded the remaining measures of the programme of settlement and regulation which I had occasion to recommend to you at the close of your last session in view of the public dangers disclosed by the unaccommodated difficulties which then existed, and which still unhappily continue to exist, between the railroads of the country and their locomotive engineers, conductors, and trainmen.

I then recommended:

First, immediate provision for the enlargement and administrative reorganization of the Interstate Commerce Commission along the lines embodied in the bill recently passed by the House of Representatives and now awaiting action by the Senate; in order that the Commission may be enabled to deal with the many great and various duties now devolving upon it with a promptness and thoroughness which are, with its present constitution and means of action, practically impossible.

Second, the establishment of an eight-hour day as the legal basis alike of work and of wages in the employment of all railway employees who are actually engaged in the work of operating trains in interstate transportation.

Third, the authorization of the appointment by the President of a small body of men to observe the actual results in experience of the adoption of the eight-hour day in railway transportation alike for the men and for the railroads.

Fourth, explicit approval by the Congress of the consideration by the Interstate Commerce Commission of an increase of freight rates to meet such additional expenditures by the railroads as may have been rendered necessary by the adoption of the eight-hour day and which have not been offset by administrative readjustments and economies, should the facts disclosed justify the increase.

Fifth, an amendment of the existing federal statute which provides for the mediation, conciliation, and arbitration of such controversies as the present by adding to it a provision that, in case the methods of accommodation now provided for should fail, a full public investigation of the merits of every such dispute shall be instituted and completed before a strike or lockout may lawfully be attempted.

And, sixth, the lodgement in the hands of the Executive of the power, in case of military necessity, to take control of such portions and such rolling stock of the railways of the country as may be required for military use and to operate them for military purposes, with authority to draft into the military service of the United States such train crews and administrative officials as the circumstances require for their safe and efficient use.

The second and third of these recommendations the Congress immediately acted on: it established the eight-hour day as the legal basis of work and wages in train service and it authorized the appointment of a commission to observe and report upon the practical results, deeming these the measures most immediately needed; but it postponed action upon the other suggestions until an opportunity should be offered for a more deliberate consideration of them. The fourth recommendation I do not deem it necessary to renew. The power of the Interstate Commerce Commission to grant an increase of rates on the ground referred to is indisputably clear and a recommendation by the Congress with regard to such a matter might seem to draw in question the scope of the Commission's authority or its inclination to do justice when there is no reason to doubt either.

The other suggestions,—the increase in the Interstate Commerce Commission's membership and in its facilities for performing its manifold duties, the provision for full public investigation and assessment of industrial disputes, and the grant to the Executive of the power to control and operate the railways when necessary in time of war or other like public necessity,—I now very earnestly renew.

The necessity for such legislation is manifest and pressing. Those who have entrusted us with the responsibility and duty of serving and safeguarding them in such matters would find it hard, I believe, to excuse a failure to act upon these grave matters or any unnecessary postponement of action upon them.

Not only does the Interstate Commerce Commission now find it practically impossible, with its present membership and organization, to perform its great functions promptly and thoroughly but it is not unlikely that it may presently be found advisable to add to its duties still others equally heavy and exacting. It must first be perfected as an administrative instrument.

The country cannot and should not consent to remain any longer exposed to profound industrial disturbances for lack of additional means of arbitration and conciliation which the Congress can easily and promptly supply. And all will agree that there must be no doubt as to the power of the Executive to make immediate and uninterrupted use of the railroads for the concentration of the military forces of the nation wherever they are needed and whenever they are needed.

This is a programme of regulation, prevention, and administrative efficiency which argues its own case in the mere statement of it. With regard to one of its items, the increase in the efficiency of the Interstate Commerce Commission, the House of Representatives has already acted; its action needs only the concurrence of the Senate.

I would hesitate to recommend, and I dare say the Congress would hesitate to act upon the suggestion should I make it, that any man in any occupation should be obliged by law to continue in an employment which he desired to leave. To pass a law which forbade or prevented the individual workman to leave his work before receiving the approval of society in doing so would be to adopt a new principle into our jurisprudence which I take it for granted we are not prepared to introduce. But the proposal that the operation of the railways of the country shall not be stopped or interrupted by the concerted action of organized bodies of men until a public investigation shall have been instituted which shall make the whole question at issue plain for the judgment of the opinion of the nation is not to propose any such principle. It is based upon the very different principle that the concerted action of powerful bodies of men shall not be permitted to stop the industrial processes of the nation, at any rate before the nation shall have had an opportunity to acquaint itself with the merits of the case as between employee and employer, time to form its opinion upon an impartial statement of the merits, and opportunity to consider all practicable means of conciliation or arbitration. I can see nothing in that proposition but the justifiable safeguarding by society of the necessary processes of its very life. There is nothing arbitrary or unjust in it unless it be arbitrarily and unjustly done. It can and should be done with a full and scrupulous regard for the interests and liberties of all concerned as well as for the permanent interests of society itself.

Three matters of capital importance await the action of the Senate which have already been acted upon by the House of Representatives: the bill which seeks to extend greater freedom of combination to those engaged in promoting the foreign commerce of the country than is now thought by some to be legal under the terms of the laws against monopoly; the bill amending the present organic law of Porto Rico; and the bill proposing a more thorough and systematic regulation of the expenditure of money in elections, commonly called the Corrupt Practices Act. I need not labor my advice that these measures be enacted into law. Their urgency lies in the manifest circumstances which render their adoption at this time not only opportune but necessary. Even delay would seriously jeopard the interests of the country and of the government.

Immediate passage of the bill to regulate the expenditure of money in elections may seem to be less necessary than the immediate enactment of the other measures to which I refer; because at least two years will elapse before another election in which federal offices are to be filled; but it would greatly relieve the public mind if this important matter were dealt with while the circumstances and the dangers to the public morals of the present method of obtaining and spending campaign funds stand clear under recent observation and the methods of expenditure can be frankly studied in the light of present experience; and a delay would have the further very serious disadvantage of postponing action until another election was at hand and some special object connected with it might be thought to be in the mind of those who urged it. Action can be taken now with facts for guidance and without suspicion of partisan purpose.

I shall not argue at length the desirability of giving a freer hand in the matter of combined and concerted effort to those who shall undertake the essential enterprise of building up our export trade. That enterprise will presently, will immediately assume, has indeed already assumed, a magnitude unprecedented in our experience. We have not the necessary instrumentalities for its prosecution; it is deemed to be doubtful whether they could be created upon an adequate scale under our present laws. We should clear away all legal obstacles and create a basis of undoubted law for it which will give freedom without permitting unregulated license. The thing must be done now, because the opportunity is here and may escape us if we hesitate or delay.

The argument for the proposed amendments of the organic law of Porto Rico is brief and conclusive. The present laws governing the Island and regulating the rights and privileges of its people are not just. We have created expectations of extended privilege which we have not satisfied. There is uneasiness among the people of the Island and even a suspicious doubt with regard to our intentions concerning them which the adoption of the pending measure would happily remove. We do not doubt what we wish to do in any essential particular. We ought to do it at once.

At the last session of the Congress a bill was passed by the Senate which provides for the promotion of vocational and industrial education[1] which is of vital importance to the whole country because it concerns a matter, too long neglected, upon which the thorough industrial preparation of the country for the critical years of economic development immediately ahead of us in very large measure depends. May I not urge its early and favourable consideration by the House of Representatives and its early enactment into law? It contains plans which affect all interests and all parts of the country and I am sure that there is no legislation now pending before the Congress whose passage the country awaits with more thoughtful approval or greater impatience to see a great and admirable thing set in the way of being done.

There are other matters already advanced to the stage of conference between the two Houses of which it is not necessary that I should speak. Some practicable basis of agreement concerning them will no doubt be found and action taken upon them.

Inasmuch as this is, Gentlemen, probably the last occasion I shall have to address the Sixty-fourth Congress, I hope that you will permit me to say with what genuine pleasure and satisfaction I have cooperated with you in the many measures of constructive policy with which you have enriched the legislative annals of the country. It has been a privilege to labour in such company. I take the liberty of congratulating you upon the completion of a record of rare serviceableness and distinction.[2]

Printed reading copy (WP, DLC).

[1] That is, the Smith-Hughes bill, about which see W. C. Redfield to WW, March 23, 1916, n. 1, and WW to W. C. Redfield, March 27, 1916, n. 1, both in Vol. 36.

[2] There is a WWsh draft of the paragraph relating to the Smith-Hughes bill in WP, DLC. There is a WWT draft of this message from the first sentence through the paragraph beginning "This is a programme of regulation, prevention, and administrative efficiency. . . ." in the C. L. Swem Coll., WC, NjP. Wilson then dictated the balance of the message to Swem on November 20, and there is a CLST transcript of this latter portion in *ibid.*

To Robert Lansing

The White House.

My dear Mr. Secretary,   5 December, 1916.

I do not know that this matter has gone far enough to justify protests direct to the several capitals, but I think that it would be well to authorize Reinsch to let the representatives of those governments in Peking know that any strained construction of existing agreements between the Chinese government and their bankers or any attempt to exclude our bankers from a fair participation in Chinese affairs would meet with very decided resistance from this government; and that it might be well for you to convey the same intimation, orally, to the representatives of those governments near us here.

Faithfully Yours,   W.W.

WWTLI (SDR, RG 59, 893.51/3010, DNA).

To Edward Mandell House, with Enclosure

[The White House, Dec. 5, 1916]

I know you would like to see this.   W.W.

WWhwLI (E. M. House Papers, CtY).

E N C L O S U R E

Berlin via Copenhagen December 1, 1916.

4671. Strictly confidential.

Actuated by the allusions to peace contained in the Chancellor's interviews with Hale and myself and in the Reichstag Wednesday, already reported to the Department, I have drawn the following impressions of the general situation here:

Germany as a whole, with the exception of a certain element in the army and navy and certain politicians of the Reventlow type, would appear ready to welcome steps toward peace as the food situation, while by no means critical, is becoming more and more difficult and as there is a general weariness of war. As it is not generally believed here that peace can yet be effected, owing principally to the (resources of?) England and the growing doubt that Russia can be induced to make a separate peace, the *Empire* is gathering all of its potential resources with a veiw [view] to augmenting the supply of trained soldiers, ammunition and guns in order to meet and if possible to exceed the enemy's increasing output. The three principal steps taken in this (significant?) and large scale movement are the organization of the government auxiliary service and the impressment of laborers in Belgium and Poland which will release a large number of men to the front and provide a great increase in the number of available munition workers. By this method it is hoped that Germany will be able to conduct a successful offensive against Russia next spring or earlier and to check a similar offensive on the part of the Allies. For this reason the army leaders are probably averse to present steps toward peace as they appear to believe that they can secure more favorable terms after their spring offensive than now. The navy, as I have already reported, will never feel that its trump card has been played until the indiscriminate submarine warfare against British commerce shall have been reopened.

The Chancellor however is to all appearances sincerely in favor of any steps which might lead to peace and I am of the opinion that Zimmerman,[1] although a more determined man than von Jagow, shares the Chancellor's sentiments in this respect. They feel, as far as I am able to judge, that the war can now only result in a draw, that the continued loss of life is and will be futile and that although Germany is able to maintain the present situation indefinitely if not *to end*, humanity calls for an end.

To what extent the Chancellor would encounter opposition here should his repeated peace suggestions be acted upon I am not yet able to say. Whatever criticism might be evoked however would, as far as I am able to gauge the situation, be based upon the fear of a confession of weakness rather than upon any lack of desire for peace among the people, officials and politicians of Germany as a whole.

I may add that I have shown the above statement to the military attache of the Embassy[2] who informs me that his views and impressions coincide with my own.   Grew

T telegram (E. M. House Papers, CtY).
[1] Arthur Zimmermann had succeeded Gottlieb von Jagow as Foreign Secretary on November 23, 1916.
[2] That is, Col. Joseph Ernst Kuhn, U.S.A.

Two Letters to Franklin Knight Lane

My dear Lane: The White House December 5, 1916

Thank you for yours of December first, enclosing the copy of the agreement made with the Mexican Commissioners and a copy of the notice which was read to them with regard to the right of pursuit and a copy of the letter asking assurance as to the discussion of other questions, together with a note of the minutes of the Commission. I am very glad to have an exact and official record.

You certainly have had the greatest discouragements and rebuffs to overcome and I value the service which you and your colleagues have performed all the more.

Cordially and faithfully yours,   Woodrow Wilson

TLS (CSmH).

[The White House]

My dear Mr. Secretary: December 5, 1916

It is with the deepest distress that Mrs. Wilson and I learn of the death of your brother,[1] and she joins with me in sending you our heartfelt sympathy. I know how anxious you have been about him for a long time and how distressing it must be to you that his health failed to take a favorable turn. We shall think of you as I am sure you would wish us to think in your distress.

Cordially and sincerely yours,   Woodrow Wilson

TLS (Letterpress Books, WP, DLC).
[1] Frederick T. Lane of Berkeley, California, died on December 5, 1916.

To Bainbridge Colby

My dear Mr. Colby: The White House December 5, 1916

I am happy to know that I am going to have an opportunity to see you Thursday evening,[1] but that must not deprive me of the pleasure of saying to you in a somewhat more permanent form than I could give it by word of mouth how deeply I have appreciated your generous course throughout the recent campaign, how it has reinforced my own resolution and given me a sense of comradeship with men of high ideals working in the public interest and with no thought of themselves. The work that you did was everywhere spoken of with the greatest admiration and was by no one valued so highly, I think, as by myself.

Cordially and sincerely yours,   Woodrow Wilson

TLS (B. Colby Papers, DLC).
[1] December 7, when Wilson was to give a dinner at the White House to honor Vance C. McCormick and other Democratic and Progressive party leaders who had worked for Wilson's reelection.

To William Charles Adamson

My dear Judge: [The White House] December 5, 1916

May I submit the enclosed[1] to you in the same frank way in which we always treat each other about everything and ask you what you think about the subject matter?

Cordially and sincerely yours,   Woodrow Wilson

TLS (Letterpress Books, WP, DLC).
[1] Part of the Redfield-Adamson exchange, cited in W. C. Redfield to WW, Nov. 28, 1916, n. 1.

To Lillian D. Wald

My dear Miss Wald: The White House December 5, 1916

I have not yet had a chance to confer with the new chairman of the Committee on Military Affairs about the so-called joker and I am obliged to you for calling my attention to Section 59 and the possible inferences from it. I shall try to have it in mind when the subject is discussed. Just at present I am caught in a drift which carries me very rapidly in other directions.

Cordially and sincerely yours,   Woodrow Wilson

TLS (L. D. Wald Papers, NN).

To Robert Lansing

My dear Mr. Secretary,   The White House. 5 December, 1916.

Thank you. This is indeed most interesting.[1]

Faithfully Yours, W.W.

WWTLI (SDR, RG 59, 763.72/3064½, DNA).
[1] That is, J. C. Grew to RL, Nov. 7, 1916, printed as Enclosure with RL to WW, Dec. 4, 1916 (second letter of that date).

To Vance Criswell McCormick

My dear McCormick: [The White House] December 5, 1916

Thank you for your letter of the first.[1]

I am quite content that Col. Robert N. Harper[2] should be appointed Chairman of the Inaugural Committee.

I want to confirm your impression that it is my wish that there should be no inaugural ball, and I hope that that will be the understanding of Colonel Harper when he assumes his duties.

We are looking forward with a great deal of pleasure to seeing you on the seventh. Mrs. Wilson and I are both deeply disappointed that your mother and sister[3] cannot come. We hope that the pleasure of meeting them is only postponed.

　　With the warmest regard from us all,

　　　　Cordially and sincerely yours,　Woodrow Wilson

TLS (Letterpress Books, WP, DLC).
　[1] V. C. McCormick to WW, Dec. 1, 1916, TLS (WP, DLC).
　[2] Robert Newton Harper, president of the District National Bank of Washington.
　[3] Annie Criswell (Mrs. Henry) McCormick and Anne McCormick, both of Harrisburg, Pa.

To Benton McMillin

My dear Mr. Minister:　　　[The White House] December 5, 1916

　　I highly value your kind letter of November fifteenth.[1] It is very gratifying to me that my attitude towards Latin America should be so well understood and so generously interpreted in Peru, and I hope that if you have an opportunity to do so you will convey to the President and the Minister for Foreign Affairs my greetings upon some early occasion, and express the gratification I feel that the work in which I am so deeply interested, the drawing together of the two continents in cordial mutual understanding and co-operation, is to be extended for another presidential period.

　　With the best wishes and renewed thanks for your generous letter,　Cordially and sincerely yours,　Woodrow Wilson

TLS (Letterpress Books, WP, DLC).
　[1] B. McMillin to WW, Nov. 15, 1916, Vol. 38.

To John Palmer Gavit

My dear Gavit:　　　　　[The White House] December 5, 1916

　　Thank you sincerely for the letter written by the Reverend D. Anderson. I shall read, ponder, and inwardly digest it, and I am warmly obliged to you for sending it to me. I know that you will keep it in mind that I want every tip of this kind that I can get.

　　I am obliged to you for explaining how the statement that it had been presented to me for consideration got published in connection with the publication of the text of Mr. Trevelyan's article. It is astonishing how indiscreet and stubborn good people can be.

　　　　Cordially and faithfully yours,　Woodrow Wilson

TLS (Letterpress Books, WP, DLC).

To Don Niko Grškovič

My dear Sir: [The White House] December 5, 1916

May I not express to you and through you to the members of the Second Slavic National Congress, recently assembled in the City of Pittsburgh, my very profound appreciation of your telegram in their behalf of November twenty-ninth? Such sentiments of loyalty and national patriotism as your message expresses constitute to my mind one of the best assurances of the future unity and influence of the great nation to which we should devote the very best that is in us.

Cordially and sincerely yours, Woodrow Wilson

TLS (Letterpress Books, WP, DLC).

To Francis Griswold Landon[1]

[The White House]
My dear Captain Landon: December 5, 1916

If you are so glad[2] why did you support the other man?
Woodrow Wilson

TLS (Letterpress Books, WP, DLC).
[1] Princeton 1881, gentleman of independent means of Dutchess County and New York City; long active in the New York National Guard; Republican assemblyman from Dutchess County, 1901-1903 and 1915.
[2] The communication to which Wilson is replying is missing.

To Albert Shaw

My dear Shaw: The White House December 5, 1916

I am glad you sent me the memorial volume to Gould and I shall take a great deal of interest in examining particularly the part about our old association at the Hopkins.

I appreciate very warmly what you say about your feeling concerning my reelection and about the administration in general. Some day we will get together and thresh out such differences of opinion as we may happen to have. I often think of our old association and have a strong appetite for some of the old talks.

Cordially and sincerely yours, Woodrow Wilson

TLS (A. Shaw Coll., NjP).

To John Appleton Haven Hopkins

[The White House]

My dear Mr. Hopkins: December 5, 1916

If I have not earlier expressed to you the deep appreciation I have felt throughout the campaign in the consciousness of your approval and support, it has not been because my thought has not been often upon it but only because public duties demanded my attention which I knew you would wish and expect me first to address myself to.

I want now to express my thanks in the most cordial and heart-felt way.

We are looking forward with the greatest pleasure to seeing you on Thursday evening.

Cordially and sincerely yours,   Woodrow Wilson

TLS (Letterpress Books, WP, DLC).

To Francis Joseph Heney

My dear Mr. Heney: [The White House] December 5, 1916

I am sincerely sorry to know that you have found it impossible to come on to the dinner on Thursday evening. I knew it was a great deal to ask of you and I do not wonder that you have found it impracticable. But I wanted to tell you in person what I must for the present content myself with writing you, how proud I have been of your support and of the sense of strength it has given me to feel my association with men who like yourself have devoted their full energies to disinterested service to the great people whom we are trying to stand by and whose interests we are trying to advance in the policies of the country. My heart goes out to you in genuine gratitude.

Cordially and sincerely yours,   Woodrow Wilson

TLS (Letterpress Books, WP, DLC).

To Matthew Hale

My dear Mr. Hale: [The White House] December 5, 1916

The waters of piled-up duty that rose in a flood about me when I got back here to Washington are subsiding a little bit and I now have breathing space enough in which to turn, as I do with the greatest pleasure, to say to you how much throughout the campaign I have valued your support and the sense of association with you which your course has afforded me. My heart goes out to you in genuine and heartfelt thanks.

Cordially and sincerely yours,   Woodrow Wilson[1]

TLS (Letterpress Books, WP, DLC).
[1] Similar letters are WW to Solomon Bulkley Griffin, editor of the *Springfield* (Mass.) *Republican;* WW to Ole Hanson, real estate dealer and Progressive party leader of Seattle; and WW to John P. Dwyer, managing editor of the *Philadelphia Record*, all dated Dec. 5, 1916, and all TLS (Letterpress Books, WP, DLC).

To Samuel Reading Bertron

My dear Mr. Bertron: [The White House] December 5, 1916

Of course, I knew without your saying it that you could have had no part in anything which might in any way embarrass us down here, and so I knew that the use of your name on the telegram to which you refer had occurred in some routine way and without your personal knowledge, for, to tell the truth, the telegram was not very wisely conceived.

But you need not fear that your taking part in any such meetings as the one you referred to would be embarrassing to us in any way.

I thank you with all my heart for your consideration in making the explanation, though it was unnecessary.

I am very much pleased by what you say of the resolution of even our opponents to stand back of the administration, now that the contest is settled. I am sure that nothing is in our minds which need trouble any business man who is willing to work in a spirit which is unselfish and unexclusive.

Cordially and faithfully yours,   Woodrow Wilson

TLS (Letterpress Books, WP, DLC).

To Oliver Peck Newman

[The White House]
My dear Mr. Commissioner: December 5, 1916

Will you not be kind enough to convey my very cordial greetings to Mr. Bryan and to those who are assembled to do him honor at the dinner on Wednesday evening? In the recent campaign no one rendered more unselfish service than Mr. Bryan, and I am happy to know that this dinner expresses the genuine admiration of all Democrats for him. May I not by this means convey to him my warmest congratulations and best wishes for his continued health and happiness?

Cordially and sincerely yours,   Woodrow Wilson

TLS (Letterpress Books, WP, DLC).

From John Sharp Williams

My dear Mr. President: [Washington] Dec 5 1916

I am very much pleased to see that our Government is making protest against Germany's reducing the population of Belgium to slavery. It is worse than that, because they are deporting them from their homes as well as forcing involuntary servitude upon them. I hope our protest will be strongly and manfully worded. Of course, we have no treaty basis upon which to stand, but surely any member of the family of civilized nations has a right to protest against this abom[inable] violation of the recommendations of the Hague, and all the precedents of international law. Since Chri[s]-tianity became a vogue it has ceased to be the custom of civilized countries to reduce the population of conquered territories to slavery. It is still worse to make them work in munition factories to make things wherewith to kill their own brethren.

God knows, Belgium has suffered enough solely for having been accidentally placed geographically between two great antagonists who wanted to cut each others throats. There is not a pretense that either her Government or people committed an offense against anybody in the world, or wanted war or invited or gave occasion for it.

I am, with every expression of regard,
                    Very truly yours,   John Sharp Williams

TLS (WP, DLC).

To John Sharp Williams

Confidential.

My dear Senator: The White House December 5, 1916

I entirely agree with you about the Belgian deportations, and the protest we have sent to the German Government is very earnestly worded. It is one of the most distressing and, I think, one of the most unjustifiable incidents of the present war, and I wish I were not obliged to express judgments of this sort in private only.

                    Cordially and sincerely yours,   Woodrow Wilson

TLS (J. S. Williams Papers, DLC).

To Percival Chandler Norris[1]

My dear Mr. Norris: [The White House] December 5, 1916

Your letter of Thanksgiving Day[2] gave me the deepest pleasure. A public man can hear nothing better than the sort of confidence which you so generously express.

And I want to send a special message to your mother[3] whose confidence in me and interest in my reelection have touched me very deeply. I hope with all my heart that her health is restored. I wish that it might be possible for me some day to say to her in person how much such messages as hers gratify and sustain me.

It was certainly a very generous impulse which led you to write and I thank you for it warmly.

Cordially and sincerely yours,   Woodrow Wilson

TLS (Letterpress Books, WP, DLC).
[1] Princeton 1902, teacher of Latin at the Lawrenceville School, Lawrenceville, N. J.
[2] It is missing.
[3] Lydia Hutton Shortlidge (Mrs. Augustus C.) Norris.

To Laura Isabelle Moore Wylie[1]

My dear Miss Wylie: [The White House] December 5, 1916

I am very much interested to hear of the plan of the Writers Club to observe the birthday of Joel Chandler Harris this year in a suitable way,[2] and avail myself of the opportunity to beg that you will express my own very great personal debt of unalloyed pleasure to Joel Chandler Harris. My old nurse brought me up on some of the stories that he so admirably revives and elaborates in his Uncle Remus, and I have always kept the book in my heart as well as in my head.

Cordially and sincerely yours,   Woodrow Wilson

TLS (Letterpress Books, WP, DLC).
[1] Mrs. Hart Wylie, a free-lance journalist of Atlanta. A widow for many years, she customarily called herself Lollie Belle Wylie.
[2] Her letter is missing.

To Lucius Hopkins Miller

Personal.

My dear Miller: The White House December 5, 1916

I am sincerely distressed to know that you are going to give up at Princeton, but I do not wonder.[1] I know the extreme embarrassments and impediments under which you have been working and have wondered at your courage and steadfastness.

My experience down here, I am sorry to say, leads me to say that I think it would be a mistake for you to try to undertake any work in connection with the Government if that is what you have in mind, unless, indeed, your resources are such as to render you entirely independent. Unhappily, no part of the public work, except that which is routine and uninspiring, affords anything like the assurance of a career. Again and again I have had to discourage the idea of official public service in men whose services would, I knew, be of genuine value and inspiration, but until the conditions grow more permanent I am obliged in candor (and confidence) to say what I have.

I wonder if there is any other way in which I could serve you?[2]

With warm regards to Mrs. Miller,[3]

Cordially and faithfully yours,   Woodrow Wilson

TLS (L. H. Miller Coll., NjP).
[1] L. H. Miller to WW, Nov. 30, 1916, CCL (WC, NjP).
[2] Miller became an investment banker in New York.
[3] Mae Coffeen Miller.

To Bella Wilson Shope[1]

My dear Cousin: [The White House] December 5, 1916

Your note[2] was very welcome and I thank you for it very warmly.

You may be sure that no personal desire of mine prompted me to run again. I was willing only because it seemed to me that it was necessary for me to do so in order to hold together what had already been accomplished. I must admit that I look forward to the next four years with something of a sinking heart, because I am afraid the problems of those years may be even more difficult than the problems of the years that have gone by, but no one who is serving this great nation can afford to have a faint heart.

With warmest appreciation,

Sincerely yours,   Woodrow Wilson

TLS (Letterpress Books, WP, DLC).
[1] Mrs. William Krebs Shope, Wilson's first cousin. She was the daughter of John Wilson and lived in Brooklyn.
[2] It is missing.

From Robert Lansing, with Enclosure

My dear Mr. President: Washington December 5, 1916.

I enclose to you a letter from the King of the Belgians which has just been handed to me by the Belgian Minister.

At the same time he left with me a more extended note of protest than the one which he had received by cable, and which you have already seen. As soon as the protest is translated I will send you a copy.   Faithfully yours,   Robert Lansing.

TLS (WP, DLC).

ENCLOSURE

From Albert, King of the Belgians

Monsieur le Président,   La Panne, le 11 novembre 1916.

Des renseignements surs, venant de la Belgique occupée, nous apprennent les mesures récentes prises par l'occupant relativement au travail forcé et à la déportation en Allemagne.

Cette nouvelle violation des lois que les peuples s'étaient engagés à observer en temps de guerre me détermine à solliciter la haute intervention du Président des Etats Unis d'Amérique.

Vous tiendrez, j'en suis sur, à vérifier ces renseignements concernant les Belges civils deportés en Allemagne pour y être employés à des travaux pénibles contre leur gré. C'est là une méconnaissance des engagements solennellement contractés lors de la signature des conventions de La Haye. Le Président de la grande et libre République américaine ne pourrait il pas protester contre cette atteinte aux droits de la personnalité humaine?

Tous ceux qui aspirent à voir mettre un terme aux horreurs d'une guerre, qui comptera parmi les plus longues et les plus dévastatrices, comprendront combien de tels procédés rendent plus difficile toute tentative de pacification et compromettent le rétablissement des relations normales entre les nations.

C'est en faisant appel à vos sentiments si connus d'équité et d'impartialité que je vous prie, Monsieur le Président, de me croire   Votre tres dévoué   Albert

HwLS (WP, DLC).

TRANSLATION

Mr. President,   La Panne, November 11, 1916.

From authoritative sources in occupied Belgium, we learn of the measures recently taken by the occupying state relative to forced labor and deportation to Germany.

This fresh violation of the laws which nations are pledged to observe in time of war causes me to solicit the high intervention of the President of the United States of America.

You will have, I am sure, verified these reports concerning the deportation of civilian Belgians into Germany to be employed there in hard labor against their will. Such an act is a violation of the solemn engagement agreed to by the signing of The Hague conventions. Cannot the President of the great and free American republic protest against such violations of human rights?

All those who long to see a termination of the horrors of a war, which will be counted among the longest and most devastating, will understand how such measures make more difficult even tentative suggestions of peace and jeopardize the reestablishment of normal relations among nations.

In making this appeal to your well-known sentiments of justice and impartiality, I beg you, Mr. President, to believe me to be

Your friend,   Albert

From Edward Mandell House

Dear Governor: New York. December 5, 1916.

Whitehouse came this morning. I wanted to confirm my judgment as to the cause of and the probable effect of the present British Cabinet crisis.

It is the old fight between Asquith and Lloyd George, with Asquith too timid, as usual, to accept the challenge and go before the country. Most of the Liberals are urging him to do this, and he may do it, but the chances are that he will make further compromises which will lead to the resignations of the more advanced liberals in the Government and replacing them with reactionaries.

Whitehouse believes that in a contest between the Liberals on the one hand and the Tories and Lloyd George on the other, that the Liberals would win.

Whitehouse is a man that one can talk to freely and I asked him the point-blank question what he thought you could do at this time to help bring about peace, and when it should be done. He suggested the very thing you have in mind, and thought the psychological time would be just before Christmas.

He thinks the present British Cabinet would receive the communication with reserve and dignity. That it would open up such a discussion in Parliament and in England that within a short time they would have to accept mediation. He feels very confident of this.[1]

Gerard was better this morning and is sailing. I had a final talk with him and urged him to be discreet and more diplomatic with the Germans, and as sympathetic with them as he could bring himself to be.

Bernstorff's cable has evidently brought good results for, as Gerard was leaving, he had a cable from Germany saying that Zimmermann had consented to preside over a banquet which was to be given upon his arrival in Berlin.

I asked Gerard to urge upon the Government the necessity for doing their share, by discontinuing all acts tending to irritate the English and French as well as ourselves.

Burleson was in this morning. I suggested that Bryan was a candidate for 1920. Burleson declares that he is not, but that he is grooming Josephus Daniels for the place, with prohibition and womans suffrage to be the issues.

With Lansing, McAdoo, Baker, and Burleson with their lightning rods erect and with Crane grooming Houston, and Bryan grooming Josephus, you have a Cabinet with a single hearted purpose. Lane and Wilson were unfortunately born in British possessions. It is too bad that it could not be made unanimous.

Affectionately yours,   E. M. House

TLS (WP, DLC).
[1] He summarized very accurately J. H. Whitehouse, Hw memorandum, Dec. 5, 1916, E. M. House Papers, CtY.

From Norman Hapgood, with Enclosure

Dear Mr. President: [New York] Dec. 5/16.

I have thought for two days about the best way to handle the inclosed. Knowing your feeling about Mr. Kent I have decided that the best way is the most direct. I therefore give you his letter, instead of describing the situation. You doubtless know his tariff speeches and his bold tariff votes, as well as his general ability: and of course you know his enthusiastic following among Independents.   Very sincerely yours   Norman Hapgood

ALS (WP, DLC).

E N C L O S U R E

William Kent to Norman Hapgood

My dear Norman: Kentfield, Cal., Nov. 29, 1916

I understand that there was a statement in the paper this morning that I was being considered as a member of the Tariff Commission. I have heard nothing about it and have no reason to believe that there is any basis for the rumor. The report, however, brought the matter to my consideration. I believe this is a position in which I could do good work without being tied down to an extent detrimental to my health. It would open up the possibility of economic study and investigation in which I believe I could be of good service.

Please think it over and if you agree with me you might suggest it at headquarters. If you have any doubt about it, please say so frankly.

It is extremely hard for me to contemplate entire release from federal service. I probably could secure the governorship here if I wanted it, but I do not like the idea of getting down to state matters when my view has been directed to national affairs regardless of state lines.

I shall leave for the East on Friday and shall be in Washington either Tuesday or Wednesday dependent on whether I stay over a day in Chicago.   Yours truly,   William Kent

TLS (WP, DLC).

From Melvin A. Rice

My Dear Friend: New York City December 5, 1916.

Permit me to report further progress in the matter of Fraulein Clara Bohm. I am advised by an American newspaper man, via Holland, under date of October 14th., that Miss Bohm is in receipt of your last remittance, that she is in ordinary health and filling her days with prayers for the cessation of the war. Miss Bohm sends her love and best greetings to you.

May I again remind you that, so far as my newspaper friend knows, I alone am interested in this relief.

With my love to you and yours, I am, Sir,

                    Very respectfully,   Melvin A. Rice

TLS (WP, DLC).

From Samuel Gompers, with Enclosures

Sir: Washington, D. C., December 5, 1916

Yesterday at the conference you so kindly accorded some friends and the undersigned, you asked that the subject matter of the petition presented to you for executive clemency in the case of some of the men now in Leavenworth, Kansas Penitentiary be presented to you in writing. Messrs. Ed. Nockels, Secretary of the Chicago Federation of Labor, and Messrs W. J. McCain and Benj. Osborne,[1] vice-presidents of the Bridge and Structural Iron Workers of America have written the enclosed letter addressed to you and which I have the honor to respectfully submit for your consideration.

The formal petition for executive clemency has already been submitted to you through Hon. William B. Wilson, Secretary of the Department of Labor.

May I join in the petitions presented to you and respectfully urge that they be given your sympathetic consideration and action. It is true that the charge made against these men was very serious but they have already served long terms of imprisonment in expiation of the charge. The health and constitution of several of them have been undermined. No further good purpose can be served by their longer incarceration. Government, society have meted out punishment to them. Would it not be a most gracious and kindly act if in the good will of the coming Yuletide these men were restored to their families who are hoping and yearning for their return?

Sincerely hoping that this entire matter may commend itself to your favorable consideration and action I have the honor to remain,   Yours very respectfully,   Saml. Gompers.

N.B. Enclosed is the memorandum upon the subject matter which was brought to your attention yesterday.   S.G.

TLS (WP, DLC).
[1] Edward M. Nockels, William J. McCain, and Benjamin Osborne.

ENCLOSURE I

Memorandum

F. B. and W. G. Simpson,[1] (Bankers) were defended by Governor Holly[2] at Boise, Idaho.

Tried at the district term in Boise, February, 1915, convicted and sentenced to five years at McNeill Island, off the coast of Washington.

Affirmed by the Federal Court of Appeals, February, 1916

Petition for rehearing was denied in March, 1916.

Petition for writ of certiorari was denied by the United States Supreme Court in April, 1916.

The President on June 30, 1916, granted them a pardon.

T MS (WP, DLC).

¹ Actually, S. D. Simpson and W. G. Simpson, who had been convicted on a charge of issuing a false certificate of deposit while serving as officers of a national bank in Caldwell, Idaho. There is extensive correspondence about their case in Case File No. 2975, Series 4, WP, DLC, but nowhere are their full names given.

² James Henry Hawley, Governor of Idaho, 1911-1913, and a lawyer of Boise.

ENCLOSURE II

From Edward M. Nockels and Others

Sir:　　　　　　　　　　Washington, D. C., December 4, 1916.

In furtherance of our conference today in reference to securing Executive clemency for members of the International Association of Bridge and Structural Iron Workers who are now serving their sentences in the federal prison at Leavenworth, Kansas, to wit:

Frank M. Ryan, sentenced to seven years, has served thirty months up to December 1, 1916.

Eugene A. Clancey, sentenced to six years, has served thirty-one months up to December 1, 1916.

John T. Butler, sentenced to six years, has served forty-seven months up to December 1, 1916.

Frank C. Webb, sentenced to six years, has served forty-seven months up to December 1, 1916.

Michael J. Young, sentenced to six years, has served thirty-four months up to December 1, 1916.

Philip A. Cooley, sentenced to six years, has served forty-seven months up to December 1, 1916.

J. E. Munsey, sentenced to six years, has served forty-seven months up to December 1, 1916.

John H. Berry, sentenced to four years, has served thirty months up to December 1, 1916.[1]

All of these men have been eligible to parole and five of them have served two-thirds of their sentence. Their full time will expire June, 1917.

Referring to John T. Butler, we desire to direct your attention to the fact that he has been in the hospital practically all of the time that he has been in prison and is now propelled in a roller chair. He has lost the use of his hands and is in a very poor physical condition at the present time and may not live to serve his full sentence.

In regard to Eugene A. Clancey, he was transferred from the prison at Leavenworth to the prison at San Quentin, California, on account of being affected with a weak heart, and his condition, as the reports will show, has been critical for a long time and is so at the present time.

We also desire to say that Frank M. Ryan's health is failing of late very noticeably and he has also been confined in the hospital. Mr. Ryan is close on to sixty years of age.

Respectfully, yours,   Ed Nockels
164 Washington St Chicago, Ill.
W. J. McCain
Labor Temple Kansas City Mo.
Ben. Osborne
347 Hall St Portland Ore

TLS (WP, DLC).

[1] These men had been convicted in the so-called Dynamite Conspiracy Trial, held in the federal district court in Indianapolis from October 1 to December 28, 1912. This trial was a direct outgrowth of the dynamiting of the *Los Angeles Times* building on October 1, 1910, and the subsequent trial and conviction of two brothers, James B. and John J. McNamara for that crime. John J. McNamara had been secretary-treasurer of the International Association of Bridge and Structural Iron Workers. Frank M. Ryan and John T. Butler were, respectively, president and vice-president of the union. Ryan, Butler, and the other men named in the above letter—all associated with the union in one capacity or another—were convicted of transporting dynamite on passenger trains for unlawful purposes or of conspiring to cause such violations of federal law. For all of these events, see Louis Adamic, *Dynamite: The Story of Class Violence in America*, rev. edn. (New York, 1934), pp. 187-248. For a detailed account of the Dynamite Conspiracy Trial, see the *New York Times*, Oct. 2-Dec. 31, 1912, *passim*.

To Samuel Gompers

My dear Mr. Gompers: The White House December 6, 1916

I have yours of the fifth transmitting the memorandum I asked for in the matter of executive clemency for some of the men now in Leavenworth Penitentiary. Of course, I need not assure you that the matter will receive my most careful consideration.[1]

Cordially and sincerely yours,   Woodrow Wilson

TLS (S. Gompers Corr., AFL-CIO-Ar).

[1] Wilson did not pardon any of the men mentioned in this correspondence at this time. However, see S. Gompers to WW, Aug. 18, 1917.

To Melvin A. Rice

My dear Rice: The White House December 6, 1916

Thank you for the report about Fraulein Bohm. I am sincerely obliged to you for letting me know. If you are sending anything more to her at any time, do let me have a share in it.

In haste

Cordially and sincerely yours,   Woodrow Wilson

TLS (Letterpress Books, WP, DLC).

To Lady Mary Fiske Stevens Paget

[The White House] December 6, 1916.

It is deeply gratifying to me to know that Americans in the belligerant countries are working so hard to alleviate suffering and I sincerely hope that your efforts may be crowned with success. Woodrow Wilson.

T telegram (Letterpress Books, WP, DLC).

From Edward Mandell House, with Enclosures

Dear Governor: New York. December 6, 1916.

I am enclosing a letter to you from Trevelyan and a copy of one from Buckler to me. They came this morning. I still think Buckler is the man you need to interpret your note not only to Page but to such others as you might think wise.

I also have a letter from Noel Buxton in which he says: "Mr. Carver will I think confirm my statement that there is a current of independent and reasoning opinion in this country."

Thank you for sending me Grew's despatch. It is of more than usual interest.

Grew has proved the estimate I had of him when I told you our interests would not suffer in his hands while Gerard was away. Affectionately yours, E. M. House

I have a long letter from Page, the substance of which is, that the only way to end the war is for us to participate.

TLS (WP, DLC).

ENCLOSURE I

From Charles Philips Trevelyan

Dear Mr. President, Westminster. Nov. 23. 1916.

I am venturing to write to you on your reelection, though I am only an Englishman and a stranger to you. I am speaking for many more Englishmen than you imagine when I say that we watched for the results of the Presidential election with more anxiety than we ever felt about an election at home, and that on the morning when your defeat was reported we felt as if the only near hope of better things had gone out. I am not using the language of hyperbole. I and a few others in this country have openly in the face of unpopularity and misrepresentation spoken against hate and war passion, pleaded for reason in the House of Commons, declared that the discussion of our national aims was as vital to a true peace as military effort and success, and recently have urged that negotiations ought to be attempted. Above all we have preached the cooperation of nations as the only security. This we have done at a thousand meetings, though unreported owing to the influence of the official censorship. And we know by experience that a vast opinion really agrees with us, but that fear of authority, of military coercion, and of the apparent uselessness of discussion keeps men silent. In the middle of the darkest night of these efforts of ours we suddenly found that you had held up to the world the ideals for which we were struggling. We know that our own people and indeed all the belligerent peoples have to find their own salvation from their terrors and unreason before peace can come. But your declarations are heard even through the censorship and are stirring to thought masses of men who will not listen to us or to others who are trying to say the same in the other war-sodden countries.

The difference between you and the other rulers of the world today is that you have imagination and faith in what men can do if they can once get out of this welter of hate. As you have trusted the instinct of your own people and won a most remarkable victory because you believed in their capacity to respond to high standards, my earnest prayer to you is to have the same faith in the multitudes of common men and women in our poor countries. Do not be discouraged by the cold refusal of Governments to welcome your offers of help. Do not judge of opinion by the base press of our capitals. Here, in the least ruined country, there is universal war-weariness except among the politicians and the press, and a yearning for a great solution, which will make your opportunity before much time has passed. But, as you have faith in democracy, have faith also in its necessary processes. However much you try to influence Prime Ministers and Chancellors, it is far more important that your great, sane policy should be heard and understood by the peoples. They wait for some voice of authority repeating loudly and constantly enough to create conviction that a reasonable settlement is possible which will give them all security, and that their enemies are disposed to agree to it. They will never believe it of their enemies if left to the teachings of their own press, and their governments are committed to impossible policies. I do not know if you can become a mediator; but I am certain that you can evoke the spirit which will make mediation possible.

This letter is perhaps too presumptuous. But it does not do to be nice about etiquette in such times. You alone may be able with any rapidity to turn the mind of great masses of men from war thoughts to peace thoughts. The popular belief of the moment in England that an honourable peace is unattainable from Germany prevents our people from demanding peace. But if you can persist in placing before them a policy which promises security from future war—even if your earlier efforts seem to fail—they will be listening and before long there will be a great response.

I remain,   yours respectfully,   Charles Trevelyan.

ALS (WP, DLC).

E N C L O S U R E   I I

William Hepburn Buckler to Edward Mandell House

Dear Colonel House: London. November 24, 1916.

I was somewhat taken aback when requested to send you this letter, but I agreed to do so provided that (1) it should be left open and (2) that the writer would entrust its fate entirely to you. He said he was perfectly satisfied that you should do with it whatever you thought fit.

Whether one thinks his policy wise or foolish one cannot but respect his sincerity. The effectiveness of his public speaking has greatly increased since the war began because of the consuming conviction which now inspires him.

Massingham of "The Nation" has now come round in favor of "peace by negotiation," and the prospects of this hitherto negligible group of Radicals are distinctly improving.

It is amusing to remember that Sir George Trevelyan—Charles' father—has for years corresponded with Roosevelt.

Yours sincerely,   W. H. Buckler.

TCL (WP, DLC).

From Robert Lansing

PERSONAL AND PRIVATE:

My dear Mr. President: Washington December 6, 1916.

I send you a translation of the note of the Belgian Government on "the Forced Labor and Deportation to which the German authorities subject the Belgian people," to which I referred in my letter to you of yesterday as having been handed me by the Belgian Minister.[1]   Faithfully yours,   Robert Lansing.

TLS (WP, DLC).

[1] "Translation: Note of the Belgian Government on the Forced Labor and Deportation to which the German authorities subject the Belgian people," c. Dec. 5, 1916, T MS (WP, DLC). This document set forth the alleged facts of the German deportations of Belgian citizens and denounced the German rationale for these actions.

From John Skelton Williams

Dear Mr. President: Washington December 6, 1916.

This office for some time past has been requiring all National Banks in their reports of condition from time to time to show the amount of Foreign Government and other Foreign Securities held by them.

Immediately before the outbreak of the European War the total amount of Foreign Securities reported on hand by National Banks was $15,627,000. On May 1, 1916, this amount had increased to $158,500,000.

These figures were not regarded as excessive. The amount, I think, was very much less than it was generally supposed the banks were holding. In fact, several New York bankers stated to me that they estimated the amount of Foreign Securities thus held by the National Banks about the time of the May call from 300 to 500 million dollars.

After conference with Secretary McAdoo, it was decided not to make the figures public, the idea being that if it should be charged during the campaign that the National Banks were overloaded with foreign bonds, we could then with perfect propriety print the exact figures, which we both thought would be reassuring.

Between May 1, 1916, however, and September 12, 1916, the National Banks largely increased their holdings of Foreign Securities, so that the total amount of Foreign Government and other Foreign Securities held by National Banks on September 12, 1916, was shown to be $239,566,000.

This was an increase since June 30, 1914, of $223,939,000, and an increase since May 1, 1916, of $81,066,000.

Last week I telegraphed Secretary McAdoo as follows:

"Do you or do you not think it would be best to give out at this time gross figures regarding foreign Government bonds held by our National Banks? There has been material increase in holdings past six months but the amount held is probably less than is generally surmised,"

and upon receipt of his telegram saying that he saw no objection to publishing the figures at this time, I prepared a statement for the press, of which I beg leave to enclose you a copy.[1]

After this statement had been prepared, however, and before it had been given out, it was thought that it might be best to withhold its publication until the return of Secretary McAdoo, in order that he might be fully informed as to the whole situation, before making the publication.

As I think you may be interested in these facts, I am taking the liberty of handing you with this a copy of the statement as prepared for publication, but which is now being withheld from publication, pending the return of Secretary McAdoo.

Respectfully and faithfully yours,

Jno. Skelton Williams

TLS (WP, DLC).
¹ Press release, Dec. 4, 1916, T MS (WP, DLC). This document gave figures for the total holdings of foreign securities by United States national banks on various dates between June 30, 1914, and September 12, 1916. It also provided figures on the holdings of domestic securities for some of the dates for comparative purposes.

From William Charles Adamson

Dear Mr. President: Washington, D. C. December 6, 1916.

I have this day received your note of the 2nd instant enclosing part of the correspondence between Secretary Redfield and myself about pensioning the Lighthouse people. The Secretary didn't submit to you our entire correspondence. In my first letter to him I detailed fully the different phases of the subject and my reasons for opposing the entering wedge of a civil service pension list.

Pensions are not proper subjects for my Committee's consideration anyway. The late Senator Frye¹ sent over annually from the Senate a bill for pension and retirement fees for the Life Savers. At first we answered his appeal by increasing the salaries of the Life Savers, but every time we informed him that all the Life Savers had to do to entitle them to the benefits they desired was to go back into the fighting organization from which they had voluntarily separated. After fourteen or fifteen years they finally consented, and by the creation of the Coast Guard we restored them to a fighting organization which ipso facto entitled them to the benefits they wished. They would have done that long before had they not been discouraged and persuaded against the step by the other several hundred thousands of civil service employees who were desirous of using the Life Savers as the entering wedge because they thought them more worthy in popular estimation and more likely to enlist sympathy and thereby help them secure what they all wanted.

At the time that was done there was a proposition to provide also for the Lighthouse Keepers, but we couldn't arrange that or consent to it, though we are perfectly willing, if the Lighthouse people are not paid enough, to increase their compensation. It cannot be denied that they have an arduous calling and subjected to some dangers and privations, but it is not as bad as the Secretary portrays. I have inspected a number of their establishments. They seem to be comfortable and well fixed. The only difficulty is that they are like other people, they get old and reach the point where they can't earn a salary, and like millions of people in every vocation of life, they find it hard to eke out an existence in the ebb tide of life without any reserved fund and without ability to earn a salary. That is the common lot of humanity. There are millions of people in this country who regard the people in the civil service as exceedingly fortunate to be enabled to draw stated salaries through life as long as able to work. I have many thousands in my District who would be glad to take the places of those civil service appointees and would be perfectly willing to perform the services, and more than at present performed, for the salaries, but if the salaries are not large enough they ought to be increased, and as we have jurisdiction of the Lighthouse Keepers we are perfectly willing to consider a bill to increase their salaries, but one of the greatest perils that threaten us now economically is the proposition to saddle on the Government a list of pensions and retirement fees for all civil service people. That is contrary to my principles and my ideas of Governmental economy and I cannot vote for it, but if Secretary Redfield wants a pension and retirement bill let him have it drafted and sent to the Pension Committee or the Committee on Reform in the Civil Service. But I don't know that my opposition to it need conclude it, if he thinks he can get it reported out of my Committee in spite of my objection it is all right with me. I am not dictating to anybody at all. I am responsible for my own conscience, and my own conscience and judgment oppose that proposition. If there were none but the Lighthouse Keepers the evil would not be so great, but I realize that that is only the entering wedge and pitched upon as the most likely to arouse sympathy and perhaps succeed.

With high regards and best wishes, I remain,

Yours truly,   W. C. Adamson

TLS (WP, DLC).

[1] William Pierce Frye (1831-1911), Republican senator from Maine, 1881-1911.

From Samuel Reading Bertron

My dear Mr. President: New York December 6, 1916.

Please pardon me for troubling you with the enclosed copy of letter received from a very good friend of mine in Belgium, Chevalier de Wiart.[1] I think our Country resents this recent move on the part of Germany as much as it did the invasion of Belgium and we should be strong in this instance and I know the Country will back vigorous action on the part of the Administration.

Permit me to thank you for the most delightful speech I have ever heard any one make on last Saturday night.

Very respectfully,   S R Bertron

TLS (WP, DLC).
[1] E. Carton de Wiart to S. R. Bertron, Nov. 21, 1916, TCL (WP, DLC).

From Robert Lansing, with Enclosure

PERSONAL AND CONFIDENTIAL:

By dear Mr. President: Washington December 7, 1916.

I enclose herewith a confidential telegram received from Mr. Grew in answer to our telegram of November 29th—which is the one we took such care to prevent from becoming public.

I cannot say that I find Mr. Grew's telegram very encouraging but I suppose no judgment should be formed until the Chancellor has had an opportunity to consult with Mr. Zimmerman and make a formal answer.

Faithfully yours,   Robert Lansing.

TLS (SDR, RG 59, 763.72115/2612, DNA).

E N C L O S U R E

Berlin via Copenhagen, Dec. 5, 1916.

CONFIDENTIAL.

4689. Department's 3621, November 29, 3 p.m.

I saw the Chancellor today at the first possible opportunity and made representations as instructed. After I had repeated to him verbatim and given him a copy in writing of the Department's representations regarding the Belgian deportations, he said that he would reply formally within a few days, but for the present he wished to say informally that he could not acknowledge that these deportations were contrary to international law. He understood America's interest in Belgium, but called attention to the forcing by the Entente of Roumania and Greece and asked how this had impressed America. He spoke of the unbelievable conditions in Greece and asked if they could be compared to those obtaining in Belgium. He then said that this policy in Belgium was not his wish, but that the German Government had been forced to it by the Entente.

After some further informal conversation regarding the deportation measures in Belgium, I turned to the subject contained in the latter part of the Department's telegram and made representations as directed. The Chancellor listened respectfully, but made no comment and said that he would send for me in a few days as he wished to talk the matter over with Zimmerman before replying.   Grew.

T telegram (SDR, RG 59, 763.72115/2612, DNA).

From Edward Mandell House, with Enclosures

Dear Governor: New York. December 7, 1916.

I am enclosing you a memorandum which Whitehouse has just left with me.

I am also enclosing a letter which I have thought to send Lloyd George if you approve. It might bring a favorable answer, and yet it might bring such a reply as would prevent you from carrying out your plan. This will have to be determined.

If you decide to let it go, please have the State Department send it in the pouch.

I have a letter from Governor Glynn today in which he says:

"At a meeting the other day I fell in with George W. Perkins. In the course of the conversation he offered to make me a bet that the next presidential race would be run by two third term candidates—Wilson on our side, Roosevelt on the republican side. I write you this because I thought it well for you to know what Perkins is thinking of."

Affectionately yours,   E. M. House

TLS (WP, DLC).

ENCLOSURE I

Edward Mandell House to David Lloyd George

Dear Mr. George: New York. December 7, 1916.

The cables tell us that you have accepted the Premiership and I wish to congratulate you. I have looked for a long while for some such denouement.

Do you recall the dinner at the Savoy, and are you still of the opinion you expressed then as to what action the President should take?[1]

You have the courage and the force to do great things, and could you do a greater thing than to lend your influence to this?

Sincerely yours,   E. M. House

TLS (WP, DLC).

[1] House had dinner with Lord Reading and Lloyd George at the Savoy Hotel on January 14, 1916. Lloyd George did most of the talking. He agreed with House that neither side could achieve a decisive victory and said that peace could come only through Wilson's intervention, probably in September. Lloyd George also said (according to House) that Wilson could dictate the terms of peace. Among them were the evacuation of France and Belgium, the return of Alsace-Lorraine to France, the restoration of Poland, the end of militarism, and compensation for Germany in Asia Minor. EMH to WW, Jan. 15, 1916, Vol. 35.

E N C L O S U R E   I I

A Memorandum by John Howard Whitehouse

7th. Decr., 1916.

The news from England this morning of the succession of Mr. Lloyd George to the Prime-ministership enables me to submit to the President more definite information as to the political position in England and to supplement my memorandum of Tuesday last.

The new ministry will not be a coalition ministry in the sense in which Mr. Asquith's was. It will not include many—if any—of the liberal members of the late cabinet. A new position will be immediately created in the House of Commons. The greater part of the liberal party will resent Mr. Asquith's fall and at heart will be hostile to the new government; so, too, will be the Labour party and the Irish party. The party system will probably come into operation once more, and, indeed, this is certain to happen if Mr. Asquith remains the leader of the liberal party in the House (as distinct from the leader of a coalition government) or if the liberal party in the House chooses as their leader some person other than Lloyd George.

This will mean a great and immediate consolidation of all the moderate forces, both in Parliament and the country, especially in view of the extreme legislation which the new Government will certainly propose to Parliament, and I feel even more strongly than I ventured to say in my memora[n]dum of Tuesday that the new situation is most favourable for action by the President.

That action would tend to give all these moderate forces a common constructive policy.   J. Howard Whitehouse

TS MS (WP, DLC).

William Hepburn Buckler to Edward Mandell House[1]

Dear Colonel House: London, England. December 7, 1916.

I enclose, as of possible interest to you, a copy of a private memorandum drawn up here on September 30, when the Rumanians were in Transylvania and when the press here expected great things of their army.

The situation is of course darker now after two months of German triumphs, and is likely to become still blacker before the new Ministry—whether Lloyd George's or anyone else's—has long been in power.

Asquith has been astute to retire now, and let the impending discontent be confronted by his successor.

It has been for some time evident enough that things were going badly for the Entente on land, but the sea blockade is now the outstanding feature which causes far greater uneasiness than appears in print. From three ships sunk per day in July-September, the average has risen last month to seven per day. Irving Thomas, the Standard Oil man in control of shipping here—with close relations to the Admiralty and F. O. said today that there is dismay among his official friends ("their tails are between their legs" was his phrase). He has hitherto been to my mind ludicrously optimistic as to the prospects of the Entente, but today he admitted that unless this submarine thrust can be parried a defeat, not a draw, must be the outcome. He says the Admiralty have lately been haunted by the receipt from Germany of plans of new and far more powerful super-submarines which are to be ready in the spring. Perhaps this country will at last have the sense to see that the price of peace is going higher, and that she would do well to join the bidding before it is prohibitive. This notion must, I should think, ere long penetrate even the ignorance and complacency of the ruling class here, and if so we may have the pleasure of seeing you soon again in 1917.

I am hoping for peace simply because I dislike to see the drubbing of the Entente become more severe, as it is bound to be if peace is long postponed.

Sincerely yours,   W. H. Buckler.

P.S. Lloyd George now appears to be in. He was bound to be tried as a strong well advertised quack medicine, but is I think unlikely to cure the patient.

Grasty[2] of the New York Times says that Northcliffe is in the highest glee and now expects the war to be won in short order.

TCL (WP, DLC).
    [1] House sent this letter to Wilson on December 19. See EMH to WW, Dec. 20, 1916.
    [2] Charles Henry Grasty was now treasurer of the New York Times.

Remarks to a Social Insurance Conference[1]

December 8, 1916.

Mr. Chairman, ladies and gentlemen: I believe it is unnecessary to explain to you why I am not here to make an address. I think time would fail a man, occupied as I am, to make all of the addresses expected of him; but I could not deny myself the pleasure of coming here tonight to bid you a very genuine welcome. You are associated in this conference with members of the government, and the government is, in a certain sense, your host. And, as a representative of the government, I want to bid you a very hearty welcome and to say how much it pleases all of us who live here, whether permanently or temporarily, that this should be a gathering place for men and women who come together to discuss some of the most serious aspects of the life of the nation.

We are living in an extremely interesting time. We have drifted away from purely political questions. We have, fortunately enough, ceased to make constitutional questions the center of discussion and are turning our attention, more and more, to those things which affect the daily life and fortunes of the rank and file of great nations. We are studying the people whom long ago we ought to have served better than we have served them. And, as we get in closer and closer touch with the daily lives of men and women, we know how to counsel better, we know how to govern better, we know how to conduct our own individual lives better, with a deeper insight and a truer sympathy.

A conference such as this—to discuss social insurance—gives evidence of the dominant interest of our own time, and one of the best elements of social insurance is social understanding—an interchange of views and a comprehension of interests which for a long time was only too rare. It used to be confined to those who were supposed to be restricted to what the general public regarded as the useless precincts of the university. Now it has spread to the ranks of practical men and has come to be regarded as a practical study.

I had a very startling insight not long ago into the popular view of a university. A man who had not often appeared outside of university circles made an address, which struck some men who had never been university students as very interesting. And one of them said to another, "That man has got brains." The other said, "Yes, he has got brains to burn." Then the first said, "What gravels me is how a man with as much brains as that should waste twenty years hanging around a university." That is a not uncommon view of the university man, but it is more uncommon than it used to be, just because the fundamental studies characteristic of universities have come out into the field of practical life.

I wish that it could be my privilege to take part in your conferences. I would learn a great deal and profit very much, but the exigencies of public duty confine me to the very pleasant and agreeable task of bidding you heartily welcome.

T MS (WP, DLC).
1 At the Continental Hall of the Daughters of the American Revolution. William C. Redfield served as chairman of the meeting. The other speakers included William B. Wilson and Samuel Gompers. The conference was held under the auspices of the International Association of Industrial Accident Boards and Commissions. *New York Times* and *Washington Post*, Dec. 9, 1916.

To Edward Mandell House

My dearest Friend,   The White House. 8 December, 1916.

That was a most impressive letter from Mr. Trevelyan,—and a most interesting memorandum from Mr. Whitehouse. The time is near at hand for *something*!

But that something is not mediation such as we were proposing when you were last on the other side of the water, and therefore I do not think that it would be wise to send the letter you were kind enough to submit to me to Lloyd George. We cannot go back to those old plans. We must shape new ones.

Members of Congress have been sucking the life out of me, about appointments and other matters affecting the destiny of the world, and I have been prevented from perfecting the document. I shall go out of town (on the MAYFLOWER no doubt) for the purpose, if it can be done in no other way.

In enforced haste,   Faithfully,   W.W.

WWTLI (E. M. House Papers, CtY).

To Robert Lansing

The White House.

My dear Mr. Secretary,   8 December, 1916.

This is certainly most disappointing,[1] but it is just about what I expected. Protests that there is no likelihood the government making them will follow up with action make very little practical difference, as this war is going.

Faithfully Yours,   W.W.

WWTLI (SDR, RG 59, 763.72115/2634½, DNA).
1 That is, Grew's telegram of December 5.

To John Sharp Williams

My dear Senator,   The White House. 8 December, 1916.

Will you not let me be very frank indeed and say that it is extremely embarrassing to me to see candidates for appointment personally, particularly candidates for offices of such dignity and importance as federal judgeships?

I would like very much, on general principles, to meet any friend of yours, but if I were to see the friend who is desirous of being appointed to the place created by Judge McCormick's[1] death I would be very ill at ease, very unlike myself, and quite unable to assess the man.

Faithfully Yours,   Woodrow Wilson

WWTLS (J. S. Williams Papers, DLC).
[1] Andrew Phelps McCormick, United States circuit court judge, who had died on November 2, 1916.

From Robert Lansing, with Enclosure

PERSONAL AND PRIVATE:

My dear Mr. President: Washington December 8, 1916.

The information which we now have regarding the MARINA, ARABIA, and other vessels sunk during the past two months seems to me to create a very serious situation in the submarine matter. We took a very definite stand in the SUSSEX case declaring that we could not continue diplomatic relations with a government which attacked merchant vessels without warning. Germany has done this and attempts to defend her submarine commanders on the ground of mistake, a defense which I do not see how we can accept without receding from our position that there can be no such things as mistakes when American lives are lost or put in jeopardy as a result of the acts of submarine commanders. If we do take that position, and I do not see how we can avoid it, and if we live up to our SUSSEX declaration, as I feel we are honorably bound to do, what course remains other than to reject the explanations offered and announce that we have no alternative but to break off diplomatic relations?

I feel that a crisis has come in the submarine matter which ought to be met promptly and squarely. We ought not to let the matter drift along with Germany continuing at intervals to sink vessels on which Americans have taken passage. The longer we delay the more frequent I believe will be these outrages and the less regard will Germany give to our declaration in the SUSSEX case. Delay, in my opinion, will accomplish no ultimate good, as there seems to be a very definite determination on the part of the German Government to make submarine warfare more effective by pursuing more reckless methods, which I am convinced will increase as more submarines are launched.

It is with increasing anxiety that I have seen the progress of events, hoping that in some way the issue might be avoided, for I realize fully how serious a step it will be to sever our relations with Germany. I do not think that we can longer avoid facing the situation with firmness and definitely deciding whether our declaration in the SUSSEX case will be carried out or abandoned.

The facts, on which the foregoing statements are made, are given in the enclosed memoranda.[1] The MARINA and ARABIA cases are dealt with more fully than those included in the list entitled "Vessels carrying American Citizens sunk by Submarines," which is a continuation of the list dated November 13, 1916, previously sent you. I would in the list call special attention to the CHEMUNG, the PALERMO, and the JOHN LAMBERT.

I am also sending to you a copy of a letter dated today which I have just received from the German Ambassador.

Faithfully yours,   Robert Lansing.

TLS (WP, DLC).
  [1] It is missing in the files of the State Department. For an updated version, see RL to WW, Jan. 15, 1917, n. 1.

E N C L O S U R E

Count Johann Heinrich von Bernstorff
to Robert Lansing

Washington, D. C.,
December 8, 1916.

My dear Mr. Secretary:

Late yesterday evening I received from Berlin the information about the "ARABIA," which had already reached you through Mr. Grew and had been published yesterday. I, therefore, need not trouble you to-day for the purpose of transmitting the information I received.

With reference, however, to our last conversation, I beg to repeat, that my Government has instructed me to put myself at your disposal in view of a speedy and satisfactory settlement of the MARINA and ARABIA cases. I should, therefore, be very much obliged, if you would kindly let me know *confidentially* as soon as you have reliable evidence concerning the two cases. My Government has received very little information on these matters, as the state of war makes communication very difficult, and is, therefore, prepared to draw its conclusions from any confidential information you may transmit to me.

I remain, my dear Mr. Lansing,

Yours very sincerely,   J. Bernstorff

TLS (SDR, RG 59, 841.857/256½, DNA).

From Edward Mandell House

Dear Governor: New York. December 8, 1916.

I have a letter today from A. G. Gardiner the last paragraph of which reads:

"I cannot tell you how much I rejoice at the result of the Election. Had it gone otherwise, I should have felt that the one visible hope in this sad world had been extinguished."

Affectionately yours,   E. M. House

TLS (WP, DLC).

From William Kent

Washington, D. C.

My dear Mr. President: December 8, 1916.

I am extremely anxious to see you concerning the grazing homestead bill[1] at an early date. The bill is in conference with practically no disagreement between the House and Senate and will therefore perfunctorily be made law.

It is a matter of such vast importance to the meat industry of the country, both in its private and public aspects, and has such a bearing on costs, as to deserve the most careful attention. It is one of these seemingly unimportant bits of legislation that to my opinion would prove tremendously destructive.

I realize fully that this measure is a popular bill and that it will take not only courage to stop it but there is due a clear explanation of the reasons upon which a veto is based.

I have talked with Mr. Ferris, Chairman of the Public Lands Committee, who is violently in favor of its adoption upon the assumption that it will tend to create profitable homes in the West. He furthermore compares the opposition to it to similar opposition on the part of cattle men in Oklahoma, where fertile, arable lands were used for pasturage. He furthermore states his belief that no bureau in Washington should pretend to state that a piece of land is too poor to be taken up for this purpose, but that that should rest with the individual opinion of the entryman.

I sincerely hope that you have consulted with Secretary Houston or will do so at an early date.

Yours truly,   William Kent

TLS (WP, DLC).

¹ H.R. 407. It provided for homesteads of 640 acres on unappropriated, unreserved public lands. The land was to be chiefly valuable for grazing and raising forage crops and was not to contain merchantable timber or be susceptible of irrigation. All coal and mineral rights were to be reserved to the United States. The areas subject to entry were to be designated by the Secretary of the Interior, and no entries were to be permitted until such designation was made. Wilson signed the bill on December 29, 1916. 39 *Statutes at Large* 862. For the significance of the measure, see E. Louise Peffer, *The Closing of the Public Domain: Disposal and Reservation Policies, 1900-50* (Stanford, Cal., 1951), pp. 160-63.

From Franklin Knight Lane

City Dec 8 [1916]

It was very good of you, My dear Mr President, to write me at this busiest of times. Fred was a redheaded boy, always in scrapes and I especially loved his daring. He died as he lived a gallant figure. He rose from his bed and was wheeled to the polls to vote for you. When he returned home he wrote me his last line saying how proud he was of the chance.

His death came as a great surprise. I had thought he was growing stronger and beginning to doubt the doctors.

You have a fine faith which supports you in the dark days and I envy you, but I have not yet given up the struggle for it.

Always yours faithfully   Franklin K. Lane

ALS (WP, DLC).

An After-Dinner Talk¹

December 9, 1916

Mr. Chairman, gentlemen of the Gridiron Club: The night is so far spent that it would not be in good taste to detain you for a speech, but it is always very delightful on an occasion like this to come last and attempt to interpret the spirit of the occasion. I think the spirit of the occasion can never be mistaken at the Gridiron Club. There is a great deal of fun made of individuals, and sometimes of policies, but it never cuts very deep. Particularly does it not cut deep when you know the men who are making the fun. I know these men; I know their temper, and they could not ruffle mine.

I am of that temperament not to be hurt except when something gets under my skin, and I want to say to the amiable gentlemen who conducted the recent campaign on the other side that nothing got under my skin. I have been accustomed to reading fiction all my life. I remember the story—which will be familiar to Mr. Rhett[2]—for example, told of old Mr. Louis Petigru of Charleston, South Carolina, a very dignified and forcible man. On one occasion he lost a civil suit, and his client was very much exasperated. He followed him out of court abusing him, calling him a thief and a liar and everything else that was vile. And Mr. Petigru paid not the least attention to him, until he called him a Federalist. Then he knocked him down. And someone said, "Why, Mr. Petigru, why did you knock him down for that? That was the least offensive thing he said." "Yes, damn him," said he, "it was the only true thing he said. I never knock an opponent down until he says something that is true."

After all, the campaign was a very great interruption to business. It was not interesting, because it was not a discussion of what we ought to do. It was only a discussion of who ought to do it, and the discussion of who ought to do it is very much less interesting than the discussion of what should be done. The Republican editors—I say it with all deference to them—were singularly lacking in inspiration as to any ideas as to what ought to be done, and only such suggestions are interesting. For, gentlemen, we are in a world which means business now if it never meant business before. Now, if never before, the motto is "Put up or shut up." If you have got nothing to suggest, the world will be impatient of the noise made by your vocal organs.

And a great deal has to be suggested, a great deal that is of vital importance. In the charming and playful speech just made by the distinguished Ambassador from Japan, he intimated that diplomatists would not be needed to accommodate differences, but they will be needed to interpret the spirit of nations to each other, for that is the foundation of peace. Nations are led into war with one another because they do not understand each other, or because the interests of their rulers is not consistent with their own interests in matters of national life and relations. And the thing that the world does need is interpretation, is the kind of vision which sees beneath the surface into the real needs and motives and sympathies of mankind.

It is a fearful thing that is going on now, this contest of bloody force, but it is going to do one fine thing. It is going to strip human nature naked, and, when it is over, men are going to stand face to face without any sort of disguise, without any sort of attempt to hoodwink one another, and say to one another, "Men and brethren, what shall we do for the common cause of mankind?" And when that question is asked, what answer are we going to make and what contribution is America going to make to that answer? It will have to be made in candor. It will have to be made in sympathy. It will have to be made with the conviction that sacrifice is the basis of common helpfulness and the basis of common happiness. The nation hereafter that tries to get advantage of another nation will be the nation that is discountenanced and rejected of the rest.

So it was to that counsel that the recent campaign was an interruption. We were engaged in trying to find out—for we have not yet learned—what the object of this war is, not in general terms, but in specific terms. And, having found out what the object of the war is, to bring the counsel of the world to bear upon the means of attaining that object as soon as possible and the coming into conference to determine how we shall for the future see that the balance of power in the world is not disturbed; that aggression is held back; that selfishness is condemned; and that men regard each other upon the same footing as human beings.

Gentlemen, there is only one meaning to democracy. Democracy means that the man who considers himself as belonging to a class, with a separate set of interests from his fellow men, is an enemy of mankind. He does not belong to the family; he does not deserve to be taken into counsel; he is by temperament and point of view an antagonist of the great mass of mankind. That is the meaning of democracy. It is a deep spiritual meaning. Democracy is not a form of government. It is a vision of sympathy. It is an insight into the essential relationship of men to each other. It is what in the past, when there was not the same general information and contact that there is now, only the poet could perceive.

Why is it that, on an occasion like this, though we laugh at the jokes, we cheer all those things that touch our sentiment and our sense of comradeship? Why do we never cheer a biting jest? Why do we always cheer a generous sentiment? Why do we love the old songs that call us back to the simplicity of childhood and the comradeship of quiet neighborhoods, where all knew each other, where all cooperated with each other, where the simpler days were spent, when there did not seem to be any problem, except the problem of cooperation? Why is it that they stir us? Why, because that is the life of mankind. And, in proportion as we lose that simple touch, we lose the capacity to think out the problems which are, in the last analysis, the problems of statesmanship as well as the problems of humanity.

I am happy, for one, to live in a time when the great problems of statesmanship are no longer political problems at all, but problems of how to work out common rights, how to relieve common suffering, how to see that those who lack the ordinary equipment of mankind are assisted by the rest who have that equipment, and how all the levels are raised and all the needs served as at a common table. Those are the problems of the modern time. That is the reason, among other things, that the movement for woman suffrage is becoming irresistible. Women feel further than we do, and feeling, if it be comprehending, feeling goes further in the solution of problems than cold thinking does. The day of cold thinking, of fine-spun constitutional argument, is gone, thank God. We do not now discuss so much what the Constitution of the United States is as what the constitution of human nature is, what the essential constitution of human society is. And we know in our hearts that, if we ever find a place or a time where the Constitution of the United States is contrary to the constitution of human nature and human society, we have got to change the Constitution of the United States. The Constitution, like the Sabbath, was made for man and not man for the Constitution. I have known of some judges who did not perceive that. I have known of some judges who seemed to think that the Constitution was a straitjacket into which the life of the nation must be forced, whether it could be with a true regard to the laws of life or not.

But judges of that sort have now gently to be led to a back seat and, with all respect for their years and their lack of information, taken care of until they pass unnoticed from the stage. And men must be put forward whose whole comprehension is that law is subservient to life and not life to law. The world must learn that lesson—the international world, the whole world of mankind.

Now, that is not a party question. I have had to deal in my short career in politics with a great many questions that were not party questions, and I have had the good fortune to be associated with a great many men who realized that they were not party questions. I remember when Senator Frelinghuysen[3] had to vote with me in New Jersey because we were dealing with questions of education which had nothing to do with whether he was a Republican and I was a Democrat or not. I was just as much for his scheme of education as he was for some of my schemes that had nothing to do with the fortunes of party. And I want to serve notice on Senator Frelinghuysen now that I expect his cooperation in the future. He can explain it to his neighbor, Senator Calder.[4] I expect it just because we are all doing the same thing. There has been a very noticeable tendency of Republicans in the last four years to vote with the Democrats, not because one side were Republicans and the other Democrats, but because they were all alike Americans and interested in things that served America. I want to say here and now that I do not respect a Republican or a Democrat who does not put America before his party. Now the happy circumstance of the time is that we can forget about the campaign and remember the United States.

T MS (WP, DLC).
¹ At the annual dinner of the Gridiron Club at the New Willard Hotel. Louis William Strayer, president of the club and Washington correspondent of the *Pittsburgh Dispatch*, presided.
² Robert Goodwyn Rhett, financier of Charleston, S. C.
³ Joseph Sherman Frelinghuysen, newly elected Republican senator from New Jersey.
⁴ William Musgrave Calder, newly elected Republican senator from New York.

To Robert Lansing, with Enclosure

The White House.

My dear Mr. Secretary,   9 December, 1916.

Here is the demand for definitions. I would be very much obliged if you would give me your detailed criticism of it, being kind enough to note them on other sheets since these are so small. I have numbered the paragraphs for your convenience in reference.

I think that the time is at hand for something of this kind to be done with effect. And it does not seem to me that that time is very distant. Affairs may disclose it at any moment.

Faithfully Yours,   W.W.

WWTLI (WP, DLC).

E N C L O S U R E

1. I take the liberty of addressing to you very frankly certain questions which seem to speak out almost of themselves from the circumstances of the present war and of which I feel justified in constituting myself the spokesman not only because I am privileged to speak as the head of a great nation whose vital interests are being more and more seriously affected with each week of the war's continuance but also because both my heart and my reason tell me that the time has come to take counsel lest a violence be done civilization itself which cannot be atoned for or repaired.

2. In every quarter of the world the life of mankind has been altered and disturbed. Everywhere it is hindered and perplexed, rendered harder, more hazardous, more difficult to plan or to carry through upon any terms. The task of every government,

the task of caring for and promoting the interests of its own people, has been hampered and impeded, and the burden falls, as always, upon those least prepared, least able to bear it.

3. The position of neutral nations, in particular, has been rendered all but intolerable. Their commerce is interrupted, their industries are checked and diverted, the lives of their people are put in constant jeopardy, they are virtually forbidden the accustomed highways of the sea, their energies are drawn off into temporary and novel channels, they suffer at every turn, though disengaged and disposed to none but friendly and impartial offices.

4. And yet the objects which would, if attained, satisfy the one group of belligerents or the other have never been definitely avowed. The world can still only conjecture what definitive results, what actual exchange of guarantees, what political changes or readjustments, what stage of military success even, would bring the war to an end. If any other nation, now neutral, should be drawn in, it would know only that it had been drawn in by some force it could not resist, because it had been hurt and saw no remedy but to risk still greater, it might be even irreparable, injury in order to make the weight in the one scale or the other decisive; and even as a participant it would not know how far the scales must tip before the end would come or what was being weighed in the balance!

5. Authoritative spokesmen of the nations engaged have, indeed, spoken in general terms of the issues involved, but they have nowhere made any definite statement of the measures which would in their judgment bring those issues to a practical settlement. Whatever may have brought the war on, they deem the very life and political integrity of the nations they represent to be involved. They are fighting, they have declared, to be quit of aggression and of peril to the free and independent development of their peoples' lives and fortunes. They feel that they must push the contest to a conclusion in order to make themselves secure in the future against its renewal and against the rivalries and ambitions which brought it about. But to what conclusion? These are very general terms. What sort of ending, what sort of settlement, what kind of guarantees will in their conception constitute a satisfactory outcome, promising some assurance of permanency and safety?

6. Leaders on both sides have declared very earnestly and in terms whose sincereity no one can justly doubt that it was no part of their wish or purpose to crush their antagonists, make conquest of their territories or possessions, deprive them of their equal

place and opportunity among the great peoples of the world. They have declared, also, that they are fighting no less for the rights of small and weak nations and peoples than for the rights of the great and powerful states immediately involved. They have declared their desire for peace, but for a peace that will last, a peace based, not upon the uncertain balance of powerful alliances offset against one another, but upon guarantees in which the whole civilized world would join, that the rights and privileges of every nation and people should be the common and definite obligation of all governments.

7. With these objects the people and Government of the United States whole-heartedly sympathize. They are struck by the circumstance that, stated in the general terms in which they have been expressed, the objects of all the belligerents are the same,— are the same even in specific detail, as, for example, the equal security of all nations alike, whether they be weak or strong, against aggression and competitive force. We are ready to join a league of nations that will pledge itself to the accomplishment of these objects and definitely unite in an organization, not only of purpose, but of force as well, that will be adequate to assure their realization. We are ready to lend our every resource, whether of men or money or substance, to such a combination, so purposed and organized. If that be the object of the present war, we are ready, when the right moment comes, to cooperate to bring it about. But how are we to know when that moment comes unless we be apprised by what test the nations now at war will judge the time of settlement and definition to have come? What must constitute victory by the one side or the other, and what must that victory mean?

8. The conflict moves very sluggishly. Only upon one or two separated fields here and there do armies move with definite success. Along the main lines of battle, so far as we can judge, there can be no rapid change, until ——— ? Must the contest be decided by slow attrition and ultimate exhaustion, the slow expenditure of millions of human lives until there are no more to offer up on the one side or the other? Triumphs so gained might defeat the very ends for which they had been desired. Upon a triumph which overwhelms and humiliates cannot be laid the foundations of peace and equality and good will. A little while and it may be too late to realize the hopes which all men who love peace and justice entertain and which all statesmen must see to be the only hopes worthy to serve as the motive of great and permanent plans for mankind. Exhaustion, reaction, political upheaval, a resentment that can never cool make such hopes vain and idle. An

irreparable damage to civilization cannot promote peace and the secure happiness of the world.

9. In view of such circumstances and moved by such considerations, I deem myself to be clearly within my right as the representative of a great neutral nation whose interests are being daily more and more affected, and as the friend of all the nations engaged in the present struggle, in asking the belligerent nations to define the terms upon which a settlement of the issues of the war may be expected. I do so with the utmost respect for the rights of all concerned and without any desire to intervene in any sense, and only because it has become necessary that the nations that are now neutral should have some certain and definite guide for their own future policy. It is necessary that they should have some assured and definitive criterion by which to determine what part they shall henceforth play should the terms defined seem impossible of realization and the end of the war likely to be indefinitely postponed.

10. Let me say, in order that there may be no danger of a misunderstanding, that I am not now renewing or seeking to press the offer of mediation which I made at the outset of the war. I then expressed my desire to be of service to the belligerents by any offices of accommodation that they might any of them suggest or encourage; and that is, of course, still my earnest wish. But I am not now returning to that. Neither am I proposing peace. I am doing a very simple, a very practical, and a very different thing. I am asking, and believe that I have a right to ask, for a concrete definition of the guarantees which the belligerents on the one side and the other deem it their duty to demand as a practical satisfaction of the objects they are aiming at in this contest of force; for an explicit statement of what they want in addition to the very great and substantial guarantee which will, I am confident, be supplied by a league of nations formed to unite their force in active cooperation for the preservation of the world's peace, of the rights of peoples and of governments, when this war is over. To answer these questions need not commit any belligerent to peace at this time; but until they are answered no influential nation of the world not yet involved in the struggle can intelligently determine its future course of action. The United States feels that it can no longer delay a final decision of its own.

WWT MS (WP, DLC).

From Edward Mandell House

Dear Governor: New York. December 9, 1916.

The Lloyd George suggestion was not the one we made to them but one of his own.

The dinner I referred to was one at which no one was present excepting Lloyd George, Reading and myself. It was evidently planned for the purpose of giving George an opportunity to tell me his idea as to ending the war.

The proposal was that in the Autumn (this last Autumn) you should arbitrarily demand that the war cease. He said the Allied Governments would demur but that later they would yield. He also had the theory that you could dictate the terms of peace and he outlined what he thought you could do.

When I spoke to Grey, Asquith and Balfour about it, they thought his plan was grotesque, but since he is now Premier he has the power to carry it through if he is still of the same mind, which, of course, I very much doubt.

It would not surprise me if the George Ministry was very short lived. The fact that Asquith refused an earldom is significant. I believe he thinks he will be returned before a great while.

I am counting upon seeing you Tuesday afternoon since Mrs. Wilson and you have been good enough to invite us to the Cabinet Dinner.   Your affectionate,   E. M. House

TLS (WP, DLC).

From John Sharp Williams

                                                    [Washington]
My dear Mr. President: December 9th, 1916.

I have your very frank note of the 8th anent the proposed interview that I wanted to get for an applicant for the judgeship. I don't blame you a bit,—not even a little bit. One thing though, I would like to mention to you: We are forced now and then to ask these interviews. The answer one way or the other makes very little difference, but having people wait around until you get a reply for two whole days is rather embarrassing.

I am, with every expression of regard,
                    Very truly yours,   John Sharp Williams

TLS (WP, DLC).

From John Skelton Williams

Dear Mr. President: Washington December 9, 1916.

I thank you for your personal note of yesterday.[1] I shall do nothing further in the matter of the press statement referred to until hearing from you.

I am taking the liberty of handing you with this a copy of my address which I shall deliver at Norfolk on Monday, before the Southern Commercial Congress,[2] in which I advocate the making of foreign "investments" of a kind and in a way which I am sure you will approve.

Respectfully and faithfully yours,

Jno. Skelton Williams

TLS (WP, DLC).
  [1] It is missing.
  [2] John Skelton Williams, *Samson and Good Samaritan: Address . . . To be Delivered December 11, 1916 . . .* , printed press release (WP, DLC). Williams said that both prudence and morality dictated that the American people devote a sizable portion of the wealth that they had gained as a result of the European war to alleviate the suffering and devastation which it caused.

From Newton Diehl Baker, with Enclosure

My dear Mr. President: Washington. December 9, 1916.

The inclosed is a fair copy of a telegram just received from General Funston. With your permission I will try to speak to you about it tomorrow on the telephone, unless you desire me to come to the house for a word of conference before I leave in the evening for Kansas City. I will be in my office all of to-morrow morning if you wish to call me on the telephone there.

Respectfuly yours,   Newton D. Baker

TLS (WP, DLC).

ENCLOSURE

Fort Sam Houston, Texas, December 9, 1916.
Following received from General Pershing:

Quote: Villistas gathering cattle, horses, Santa Clara Valley. Entire district said now to be for Villa. Small parties Villistas reported operating between Lake Guzman and Ahumada. Number Villistas detrained San Antonio and marched north to San Diego Delmonte on fourth instant. Local guards various towns previously reported said to be concentrating at Providencia. Generally rumored that Villa intends to go south. In view of Villa's daring, and the comparative inefficient Carrancista forces, Villa's power almost certain to increase. Reports regarded as authentic place his forces at 6,000. Four trainloads of supplies captured at Chihuahua arrived San Ysidro fifth instant. A swift blow delivered by this command should be made at once against this pretender. Our own prestige *in Mexico* in Mexico [*sic*] should receive consideration at this time. In the light of Villa's operations during the past two weeks, further inactivity of this command does not seem desirable, and there is no longer doubt as to the facts. As stated in previous communications, aggressive action would probably meet no resistance by Carrancist[a]s and should meet their approval. Civilian element would welcome us, as they now wonder at our inactivity. Unquote.

I approve of the foregoing recommendation. Villa's successes are rapidly placing him in control of a large part of State of Chihuahua. Carranza force(s) opposed to him have not been successful; on the contrary they have been seriously and decisively defeated several times during the last month. I can see no reason for believing that they will be more successful in months to come, as Villa is constantly gaining in strength, influence and power and is extending area over which he has complete control. Secret service report(s) show that there is strong Villa sympathy in *Coahu[i]la* and Nuevolon [Nuevo León], and I believe if he is allowed to continue his career unchecked that in the course of a few months he will control all of northern Mexico. A quick decisive blow directed against him now by John J. Pershing's (Major General) command would check this rising power, and if allowed to continue until Villa is captured would put an end to the whole movement, thereby greatly benefiting de facto Government. John J. Pershing (Major General) states that he believes such action would meet with no resistance by Carrancistas. It would certainly seem that it should meet not only with their approval but with their cooperation. This would involve the use of the Mexico Central or Mexico North Western railroads from Juarez, as John J. Pershing must have one of these railroads for his line of communications. There could be *not* assurance of success in pursuing Villa without provision being made for following him into Durango, Distrito Federal.   Funston.

T telegram (WP, DLC).

Two Letters from Franklin Knight Lane

My dear Mr. President: Washington December 9, 1916.

I quoted to you from memory a despatch sent by the German Chancellor to Austria July 29, 1914. This was published in the London "Nation" of November 11, 1916. The whole paragraph in the "Nation" is as follows:

"A very important speech has been made by the German Chancellor in reply to Lord Grey's powerful indictment of Germany's culpability for the war. He dealt, not at all conclusively, with the 'Lokal-Anzeiger's' report of a German mobilization in [on] July 30th, 1914. We all know that this statement was verbally at least untrue, and that the issue was stopped. The point is—Why was the statement made at all? The inference at once arises that it was made in order to produce the effect of alarm, which it did actually bring about in Petrograd. Of more consequence, however, was the Chancellor's strong affirmation that he did in fact telegraph to Vienna the famous despatch published in the 'Westminster Gazette,' suggesting that Austria should come to an understanding with Russia, and that if Germany's advice were disregarded, she could not be drawn into a 'world conflagration.' To this the Chancellor adds the statement that he also transmitted to Vienna, as 'a suitable basis for the maintenance of peace,' Lord Grey's mediation proposal of July 29th, coupled with 'a most peremptory recommendation.' The Chancellor adds that in his telegram these words occurred:

'Should the Austro-Hungarian Government refuse all mediation, we are confronted with a conflagration in which England would go against us, and Italy and Rumania, according to all indications, would not be with us, so that with Austria-Hungary we should confront these three great Powers. Germany, as a result of England's hostility, would have to bear the chief brunt of the fight. The political prestige of Austria-Hungary, the honor of her arms, and her justified claims against Serbia can be sufficiently safeguarded by the occupation of Belgrade or other places. We therefore urgently and emphatically ask the Vienna Cabinet to consider the acceptance of mediation on the proposed conditions. Responsibility for the consequences which may otherwise arise must be extraordinarily severe for Austria-Hungary and ourselves.'

"We can only describe this declaration as momentous. But it leaves the later evolution of German policy absolutely obscure. Why did not Austria yield if she was thus solicited in good faith? And why did the Kaiser send his peremptory telegrams to the

Tsar? And why was the German mobilization hurried on? Was this unspeakable calamity really the result of a muddle or a misunderstanding?"   Cordially yours,   Franklin K Lane

My dear Mr. President: Washington December 9, 1916.

I have been asked by Senator Phelan to suggest some amendment that would be satisfactory to the administration regarding relief to the California oil men. I have drafted the inclosed,[1] which is in effect this:

1. That all men entitled to patents to their lands shall have them. This no statute could take away.
2. That wherever a producing oil well has been sunk the claimant to that land or his assignee shall have a lease to the extent of his claim, (this, however, not to exceed 160 acres,) on surrendering all his claims to a patent and paying to the Government a back royalty of one-eighth (which is the commercial royalty figure) on all the oil that he has heretofore produced, as well as one-eighth for the future.

This gets rid of all the troublesome questions so difficult of adjudication, it protects the large investment made by the oil men (which it is estimated approximates $15,000,000) and reserves to the Government fifty percent. of the land now claimed. That is to say, under this scheme leases would be given for approximately 16,000 of 36,000 acres of land.

I have submitted this proposition to no one, and would like to have your judgment on it before I even tentatively present it to anyone else.

As to the naval oil reserves, I would recall to you these facts: That reserve No. 1[2] contains a large amount of railroad land which the lower court has held was obtained by fraud. The case is to be appealed to the Circuit Court of Appeals. I believe we will win it, there and in the Supreme Court. Other than this, patents have been granted by the state to two bodies of land, one to the Standard Oil and one to the Associated Oil Company, a reversion of which to the Government can, I believe, be obtained if this matter can be straightened out. I say this upon a statement made to me by one of the oil men that they had secured such a promise from these oil companies in the event that relief was given as to other lands. In this event reserve No. 1, which contains 32,000 acres and upon which there is one producing well, would be freed as a naval reserve and could be held indefinitely without being pumped.

As to reserve No. 2,[3] one-half of this land is owned by the Southern Pacific Railroad Company and other private holders, and suit has been brought to cancel these patents which are some twenty years old. There is unquestionably additional land which under the law that obtained when the claims were made and under subsequent law will have to be patented to the claimants. Nevertheless, a considerable body of this land should be available for the Navy.

Naval reserve No. 3, which is in Wyoming,[4] is entirely free from claims, excepting one, which our reports indicate may prove invalid. You will recall that recently I recommended two shale oil reserves, which you approved, in which it is estimated by the Geological Survey there is 1,000,000,000 barrels of oil. There is in California also a large body of withdrawn land which so far as we know has not been proved but which may be as valuable as any yet discovered, and any portion of this can be withdrawn for a naval reserve.

If in your opinion some such measure as that inclosed would deal equitably with the claims of the oil producers, most of whom are outside of the large companies such as the Standard Oil and the Associated Oil, and represent small individual investments, I suggest the advisability of your talking with members of the Public Lands Committee of the Senate and House regarding the matter.

Cordially and faithfully yours,   Franklin K. Lane

TLS (WP, DLC).
  [1] T MS (WP, DLC). Lane explains the proposed amendment well.
  [2] Elk Hills, located near Bakersfield, Cal.
  [3] Buena Vista Hills, also near Bakersfield.
  [4] Teapot Dome, located near Casper, Wyo.

From Franklin Knight Lane, with Enclosure

My dear Mr. President: Washington December 9, 1916.

I inclose a proposed water power bill, along the line of our talk yesterday. It has these advantages:

1. The administration would be held responsible for whatever terms and conditions were made as to such leases.

2. These terms and conditions would be known and fixed before the lease was made.

3. The terms and conditions could be made so as to draw a distinction between the use of navigable waters and others.

4. Such a measure would eliminate all controversy in Congress over details.

5. By regulation everything could be accomplished that is sought to be accomplished by the Ferris, Myers, Adamson or Shields bill.

6. There would be no danger of the caprice of any single Cabinet officer, or his prejudice or favor, controlling the conditions of the leasing.

I am sending this to Secretary Baker and Secretary Houston. Secretary Baker tells me that he cannot take the matter up specifically until next Friday. Does it not look to you that if we are to get any legislation through it will have to be some such general measure as this, especially as to navigable waters?

Cordially and faithfully yours, Franklin K Lane

TLS (WP, DLC).

E N C L O S U R E

Proposed Water Power Act
Suggested by Secretary Lane.

Section 1. This Act shall be known as the Water Power Act.

Section 2. The Secretary of War, the Secretary of the Interior, and the Secretary of Agriculture shall compose a Water Power Commission.

Section 3. This Commission shall have power to grant leases for the use of all public lands (including reservations) and navigable streams for the development of water power, under such terms and conditions as shall be by them prescribed by general regulations; no such lease to extend for longer than fifty years.[1]

T MS (WP, DLC).

[1] This proposed act was the germ of the Federal Water Power Act finally adopted in 1920.

Mary Harris ("Mother") Jones
to Edward Mandell House

My dear Col. House: Washington, D. C. Dec. 9, 1916.

I hope you will pardon me if I take the liberty to write you in behalf of the structural ironworkers who are incarcerated in Levenworth prison and who have been separated from their homes and families and from society for several years. I write you because I know your abiding faith in the goodness of human nature and because of your close relation with the President who I know, is a man of kind heart and tender sympathies. The men for whom I appeal were convicted under stress of public excitement and it is not unfair to say that the mind of the court and the public was inflamed against them.

If in desperation over real or fancied wrongs men commit acts of violence, who is there to say that there is no extenuating circumstance? We do not all entertain the same viewpoint towards society. Imagine men engaged in the hazardous work of erecting iron and steel for tall buildings. Suppose one of them fell to the ground and was crushed, who would take care of his family? You can realize that these men do not earn enough to insure the future let alone provide sufficient for the daily needs of themselves and their families? These men cannot entertain the same beneficent attitude of men in easier and more comfortable circumstances. And who shall say that these men are not more sinned against by society than sinning?

We all go through this life but once my dear Colonel and it behooves us all to render as much aid to our fellowbeings as we can while here. If we could raise up all humanity and obviate all strife, what a glorious world this would be. But constituted as it is, society inflicts many hardships on those least able to bear them.

When I visited the penitentiary a few weeks ago, one of those whom I am trying to help asked me "Mother, will it be possible for us to see our families at home this Christmas?" I responded that I thought it might be and I said this in the hope that my appeal in their behalf would bear fruit. The world is growing better in spite of the terrible slaughter on the other side, or maybe because it is awaking people to "man's inhumanity to man" so aptly described by Pope. We should try to raise this country above the Greed for Gold that has produced such horrible disaster abroad. In my long years I have seen many men sacrificed on the Altar of the Dollar and I hope that the last of such sacrifice in this country has been made. Let us all work for a better day when this nation will stand forth as an exemplar for the world; when Greed will be banished and when the strife for gain will no longer afflict us.

With faith in the humane interest of the President and confident that he will aid me in the effort to restore these men to their families, and to society, I remain

Yours faithfully,   Mother Jones

TLS (WP, DLC).

From Robert Lansing, with Enclosure

My dear Mr. President,   Washington December 10, 1916.

I have little comment to make on this communication as a whole because it is so admirably presented, and is certainly justified by our own situation which grows constantly more intolerable. We cannot continue much longer to attempt by peaceable means to secure our rights. We are certainly drifting nearer and nearer, and it seems to me that unless something is done we will soon be forced to act as I indicated to you the other day in my letter on the submarine matter.

I am not at all sure what effect this communication would have on the respective belligerents; and yet it is probably the only step which can be taken offering a possible way to prevent an open rupture in the near future with one side or the other. On the other hand the answers may compel more speedy action on our part. Of course that is the problem which causes anxiety, but I do not see that it causes much greater anxiety than to watch the steady drift toward an impossible situation, in which self-respect as well as interest will compel this country to take sides in the conflict.

While this course of action has its uncertainties which I think should be very carefully considered before being finally adopted, there can be no question whither the logic of events is leading us if some step is not taken to bring this war to an end.

I think, among other questions, we should consider these: Unless the answers of *both* parties are made in the right spirit, will there be any other course than to declare in favor of the one most acceptable and abandon a neutrality which is becoming more and more difficult? But suppose that the unacceptable answer comes from the belligerents whom we could least afford to see defeated on account of our own national interests and on account of the future domination of the principles of liberty and democracy in the world—then what? Would we not be forced into an even worse state than that in which we are now? I think that we must consider the possibility of such a situation resulting; and if it does result, which seems to me not only possible but very probable, can we avoid the logic of our declarations? And if we act in accordance with that logic, would it not be a calamity for this nation and for all mankind? I have told you how strongly I feel that democracy is the only sure guarantee of peace, so you will understand how these questions are worrying me, and why I think that they should be considered with the greatest deliberation and care before we take a step which cannot be withdrawn once it is taken.

I enclose the communication with comments on the text.

Faithfully yours   Robert Lansing.

ALS (WP, DLC).

E N C L O S U R E

Washington Dec. 10, 1916.

COMMENTS AND SUGGESTIONS

General Note. In making certain suggestions as to changes in the text I had in mind the probability that the communication would have to be put into a foreign language, undoubtedly French and possibly Italian, and whether certain expressions used would render themselves to proper translation.

Paragraph 1.

In place of "certain questions which seem to me to speak out almost of themselves" &c. I would suggest "certain question which present themselves" &c.

In place of "of which I feel justified in constituting myself the spokesman" read "which I feel justified in asking not only because" &c.

Paragraph 2.

"Interrupted" in place of "hindered" in the 3rd line.

I think that, as "hampered" and "impeded" have almost the same meaning, the words "hampered and" might be left [out], or else some other word used in place of "hampered" (lines 7 and 8).

Paragraph 3.

Merely as a query. Is it the *position* of neutrals or the *situation* of neutrals? The word "situation" conveys to me the idea of an involuntary state more than "position."

I think that "and diverted" (line 4) might be omitted and that "diverted" might be substituted for "drawn off" (line 7).

Paragraph 4.

In place of "drawn in" (line 9) substitute "involved in the conflict," and in place of "drawn in" (line 10) "involved."

Paragraph 5.

In place of "indeed" (line 2) the phrase "it is true."

In place of "as I know" (line 4) substitute "as I am aware."

In place of "Whatever may have brought the war on," the phrase, "Whatever may have caused the war."

In place of "involved" (top of p. 3) put "at stake," which I think is the claim.

In place of "push" (p. 3, line 5) put "press."

In place of "will in their conception constitute" (p. 3, line 11) substitute "do they conceive to constitute."

Paragraph 7.

In place of "struck" (line 3) put "impressed."

I would omit in line 13 the words, "not only of purpose, but of force as well." I do not think that this commitment to the use of force essential to the strength of the declaration. I would leave the character of the pressure to be exerted open to inference. I may be prejudiced as to this because the more I consider the idea of the use of force jointly to preserve peace the more doubtful I am as to a practical method of applying it. Until the ambition of rulers for power and their greed for territory and glory are eliminated by the domination of the will of the people through the establishment of democratic institutions I do not think that universal peace will come.

For the same reason I would omit the sentence beginning "We are ready to lend"—

Paragraph 10.

In place of "that they might any of them suggest" &c. (line 6 and 7) substitute "which any of them might suggest" &c. The other could hardly be rendered in a foreign language.

In place of "aiming at" (line 3 from bottom of p. 6) put "seeking to attain."

In place of the words "to unite their force in active cooperation["] (p. 7, line 3) put "to cooperate." This is following my suggestion as to omission of reference to the use of force stated under Paragraph 7.

In place of "decision" (last line on p. 7) put "determination" to correspond with "to determine" (line 3 from bottom of p. 7), or else leave "decision" and change "to determine" to "to decide."

Hw MS (WP, DLC).

From Edward Mandell House, with Enclosure

Dear Governor: New York. December 10, 1916.

I cabled Lord Grey the other day asking if he could give us any information that would be useful for our guidance here. Today I have the following answer:

"I am in compliance with my request now out of office. Drummond has same position with Balfour at the Foreign Office as he had with me. My personal views remain unchanged. Do yours?"

Drummond is his private secretary and will also be Balfour's. This is fortunate for it gives us direct communication in the event you desire it. I know Drummond well and have a good opinion of him.

If Grey had to leave, the next best man in the Kingdom for us is Balfour. This will give Sir Horace great influence upon American affairs since Balfour and Plunkett are the closest friends and Balfour will look largely to him for guidance. This, again, is fortunate.

I do not know what Grey means when he says his personal views remain unchanged. Is there anything you think I could cable to either Grey or Balfour that would be of value at this time?

I am enclosing a letter which I have just received from Bernstorff. I also enclose the letter to which he refers.[1]

Your affectionate,   [E. M. House]

TL (WP, DLC).
[1] Minnie Heuermann to J. H. von Bernstorff, Nov. 22, 1916, TCL (WP, DLC). She wrote concerning the neglect of German prisoners of war in Russia.

E N C L O S U R E

Count Johann Heinrich von Bernstorff
to Edward Mandell House

My dear Colonel House: Washington, Dec. 9, 16.

I am sending you these lines only for the purpose of keeping you posted about current topics as they look from my point of view.

The Arabia and Marina cases have been dealt with as I told you beforehand they would be. There was no other way available, as every other one would have caused still more trouble.

I very much regret the *publication* of the note about the Belgian deportations,[1] because I am afraid that the publication will im-

pair the success of the steps taken. It will arouse German public opinion which was dormant, and the usual answer will be
hurled back that American humanity is *one sided.* People at
home will say, that the Belgian deportations are nothing compared with those from East Prussia to Russia, and with the
treatment of German prisoners in Russia—cases in which the
American Government has not achieved anything and not even
seriously protested.

Several ladies from St Louis are working in this matter in
Washington and now are trying to see the President, after having conferred with Senator Stone and the State Department. Confidentially I enclose copy of a letter from one of these ladies,
which was written when she was on her way back from Russia.

Apart from the above special point of view a humanity campaign seems a very good thing to me, as the most *humane way*
out of all trouble would be to end the war. If this could be accomplished, all deportations, etc. would end automatically. With
this goal in view, I think the change in England from Grey to
Balfour is very hopeful. The war may have influenced the latter, but in the days when I knew him very well, he was a reasonable man, brought up in the ideas of his uncle, Lord Salisbury,
who always regarded it as necessary for the welfare of Europe
that England and Germany should be on good terms. He then had
nothing of Grey's anti-German bias, which led the latter from the
first day he was in the Foreign Office to work at consolidating a
coalition against Germany—a policy which could only end as it
did.

I have always considered the two Edwards (King Edward and
Sir Edward Grey) as really and practically *solely* responsible
for the present war, and I think I know what I am talking about
because I have seen them both at work in London.

As always I am entirely at your disposal, if you have anything
you wish to talk over.

Yours very sincerely,   J. Bernstorff.

TCL (WP, DLC).
¹ Lansing made public on December 8 the first paragraph of RL to J. C.
Grew, Nov. 29, 1916. *New York Times*, Dec. 9, 1916.

To Samuel Gompers

The White House
My dear Mr. Gompers: December 11, 1916

Thank you for sending me a copy of the letter from Mr.
Santiago Iglesias, President of the Free Federation of Workmen

of Porto Rico. I am very much puzzled what to think of the conditions in Porto Rico and am glad to have every possible source of light.

    Cordially and sincerely yours,   Woodrow Wilson

TLS (S. Gompers Corr., AFL-CIO-Ar).

To John Skelton Williams

[The White House]
My dear Mr. Comptroller: December 11, 1916

Thank you warmly for the very important copy of your address which is to be delibered [delivered] before the Southern Commercial Congress. I am going to give myself the pleasure of reading it very carefully.

I appreciate your withholding the statement of the national bank investments for the present. I am not sure what indirect effect the publication might have on some of our foreign relations.

    In haste

        Cordially and sincerely yours,   Woodrow Wilson

TLS (Letterpress Books, WP, DLC).

To Franklin Knight Lane

[The White House]
My dear Mr. Secretary: December 11, 1916

Thank you very much indeed for your suggestions about the water power bill and about the vexatious oil question. You may be sure I will study them very carefully.

        Cordially and sincerely yours,   Woodrow Wilson

TLS (Letterpress Books, WP, DLC).

To William Kent

My dear Mr. Kent: [The White House] December 11, 1916

I wonder if you have seen the Secretary of Agriculture recently about the grazing homestead bill? We discussed it in Cabinet the other day and the Secretary seemed to be of the opinion that if certain provisions he had suggested were inserted, the best practicable solution within our reach just now would be achieved. If you have not seen him, I wish you would have a talk with him.

    In haste

        Cordially and sincerely yours,   Woodrow Wilson

TLS (Letterpress Books, WP, DLC).

To Joseph Morris Price[1]

My dear Mr. Price: [The White House] December 11, 1916

You are such a generous friend and supporter that I am sure you will understand why I have not been able to make an appointment to see you. The weeks of a short session of Congress are always so extraordinarily crowded with pressing duties that cannot wait, and I am just now under such unusual pressure in the business which office appointments so certainly interrupt and which must yet be done at some hour of the day or night, that I have thought it literally impossible to add to my office appointments until I in some shape and degree cleared my docket.

Drop me a memorandum, won't you, about what it was you wanted to discuss? I cannot bear to put you off indefinitely.

Cordially and sincerely yours,   Woodrow Wilson

TLS (Letterpress Books, WP, DLC).
[1] President of the Improved Mailing Case Co. of New York and active in political reform in that city; also chairman of the Fusion executive committee which ran John Purroy Mitchel's campaign for mayor in 1913.

To Ambrose White Vernon

Personal.

My dear Vernon: [The White House] December 11, 1916

I, too, was disturbed over the passage of the Shields Bill and we are working very hard to bring something genuine and reliable out of the conservation controversy. I think that there is no danger of the extreme views presented by Senator Shields prevailing.

It was a pleasure to hear from you and I thank you with all my heart for the friendly cheer your letter brings.

Cordially and sincerely yours,   Woodrow Wilson

TLS (Letterpress Books, WP, DLC).

To Robert Somers Brookings

[The White House]
My dear Mr. Brookings: December 11, 1916

I have just heard of your reply to the letter of Doctor Eliot about Secretary Houston.[1] It is another evidence of your genuine public spirit and of your willingness to make sacrifices to serve the public interest. It is, indeed, in a very real sense necessary that Secretary Houston should remain for the present in public life. His services are of a very unusual quality and there is no one among my advisers whose advice and judgment I more confidently rely upon. May I not express my deep gratification at the generous conclusion reached?

Cordially and sincerely yours,   Woodrow Wilson

TLS (Letterpress Books, WP, DLC).
¹ C. W. Eliot to R. S. Brookings, Nov. 21, 1916, and R. S. Brookings to D. F. Houston, Nov. 24, 1916, both TLS (WP, DLC). Eliot told Brookings that Houston felt under obligation to return to the chancellorship of Washington University, if Brookings so desired. Eliot urged Brookings to tell Houston to feel free to resign the chancellorship in order to remain in the cabinet. Brookings did so very graciously in his letter to Houston. Houston forwarded the two letters to Wilson on December 11.

To George Wilkins Guthrie

[The White House]
My dear Mr. Guthrie: December 11, 1916

Your gracious letter of the tenth of November¹ about the result of the election has gratified me very deeply. To feel your personal friendship and your sincere and ardent devotion to the objects we are all seeking to promote is a constant pleasure and encouragement to me.

You may be sure that though I do not often send messages your way, I do very often indeed send thoughts and that they are always thoughts of real gratification that we have such a representative at one of the most important posts in the disturbed world of our day.

Cordially and sincerely yours,   Woodrow Wilson

TLS (Letterpress Books, WP, DLC).
¹ G. W. Guthrie to WW, Nov. 10, 1916, ALS (WP, DLC).

From Robert Lansing, with Enclosure

PERSONAL AND CONFIDENTIAL:

My dear Mr. President: [Washington] December 11, 1916.

This copy of a CONFIDENTIAL TELEGRAM from Grew may explain how some matters become public.

In view of the reference in the telegram to the contents of the one to Grew I would suggest its immediate destruction. The original I shall retain as strictly confidential.

Faithfully yours,   Robert Lansing

CCL (SDR, RG 59, 763.72119/192, DNA).

E N C L O S U R E

Berlin, Dec. 8, 1916.

CONFIDENTIAL.

4707. To my great astonishment the correspondent of the Associated Press informed me today that a certain official in the Foreign Office had just given out to him the nature of my interview with the Chancellor on December fifth regarding the attitude of the President towards taking steps looking towards peace. He said that he was going to send a telegram on the subject to the Associated Press in the United States this afternoon. I immediately went to Foreign Office and told them with emphasis that my communication to the Chancellor had been confidential, that I had so stated when delivering it, and that it was my duty to call their attention to this fact before the telegram was released. Foreign Office acknowledged that a mistake had been made and stated that they would suppress the telegram at the censor's office.

In this connection I desire to record that no word regarding my interview with the Chancellor has been divulged by this Embassy.   Grew.

T telegram (SDR, RG 59, 763.72119/192, DNA).

From John Philip White and William Green

Indianapolis, Ind.,
Dear Mr. President: December 11, 1916.

In behalf of the international organization of the United Mine Workers of America we heartily thank you for your action in commuting the sentences of Frank Ledvinka, Fanny Sullens, James Oates, et al, who had been sentenced to serve a certain length of time in prison by Judge Dayton for an alleged violation of an injunction issued by him.[1] Your prompt action in this matter is very much appreciated.

Very sincerely yours,   John P. White President.
Wm Green. Secretary-Treas.

TLS (WP, DLC).
[1] The three persons named and Hiram Stephens, all officials of, or organizers for, the United Mine Workers of America, had been sentenced to six months in prison for contempt of court for failure to obey an injunction issued by Federal District Judge Alston Gordon Dayton in connection with coal strikes in West Virginia in 1913 and 1914. The Supreme Court, in October 1916, had refused to review the convictions, and the cases had been brought to Wilson's attention on November 21.

To William Charles Adamson

My dear Judge: [The White House] December 12, 1916

Thank you for your letter of December sixth about your correspondence with Secretary Redfield concerning the pensioning of the lighthouse people.

I need not tell you I appreciate to the full the strength of the argument you use. I must admit, however, that I have been troubled about the question of a pension for civil service employees and am not as certain of my negative conclusions as I used to be. Some day we must get together and see how far we really are apart.

Cordially and faithfully yours,   Woodrow Wilson

TLS (Letterpress Books, WP, DLC).

To Franklin Knight Lane

[The White House]

My dear Mr. Secretary: December 12, 1916

Thank you for your kindness in sending me the quotation from the London Nation of November 11, 1916, about the German Chancellor's efforts to prevent the war. It is certainly a very remarkable statement and raises fresh wonders and conjectures.

Always

Cordially and faithfully yours,   Woodrow Wilson

TLS (Letterpress Books, WP, DLC).

To Robert Russa Moton

Personal.

[The White House]

My dear Principal Moton: December 12, 1916

Your letter of December fourth appeals to me very strongly. I have again and again wondered, as you may be sure, what it would be possible for me to do or say, and the truth is that I have not been able to form a confident judgment as to what would be effective and influential.

I am not in saying this dismissing the subject, of course; I am only telling you that I have long been trying to choose a wise course, and shall not cease to try.

With warm appreciation of your generous letter,

Cordially and sincerely yours,   Woodrow Wilson

TLS (Letterpress Books, WP, DLC).

To Garrett Droppers

Personal.   [The White House]
My dear Mr. Droppers: December 12, 1916

Your very generous letter written on October twenty-fifth[1] has reached me at last and I want you to know how deeply and sincerely I appreciate it. It is worth while to go through anything to feel the warmth of such friendship and trust as you give me.

The campaign was indeed one of the most virulent and bitter and, I must believe, one of the most unfair on the part of the Republican opposition that the country has ever seen, but I think that very circumstance worked to my advantage. I think the country resented the methods used, and that a very strong resentment was felt which was characterized by strong and generous feeling.

The results show themselves more truly in the popular vote than in the electoral vote, and I am heartened by the feeling that it can no longer be said that I represent a minority of the nation.

My thoughts often turn to you, particularly in these days of deep trouble for Greece and, therefore no doubt, of increased anxiety for you. My heart goes out to the little nation and I hope that she will come out of the fire better and not worse for these days of travail.

Cordially and sincerely your friend,   Woodrow Wilson

TLS (Letterpress Books, WP, DLC).
[1] G. Droppers to WW, Oct. 25, 1916, Vol. 38.

To Charles Williston McAlpin

My dear Friend: [The White House] December 12, 1916

For some inexplicable reason, your kind letter of November eleventh[1] never came under my eye until this morning. I feel that I owe you an apology for not having acknowledged it before with my heartfelt appreciation of the affectionate congratulations which it conveys.

Of course, I am quite willing that you should have my next inaugural privately printed. I have not even yet thought of what it should contain, but I dare say I must turn my thoughts in that direction very soon after the holidays.

It was delightful to us all to have you and Harry Fine down at Shadow Lawn.[2] So far from being an intrusion it was a great pleasure to us.

In haste, with many apologies,
Cordially and faithfully yours,   Woodrow Wilson

TLS (Letterpress Books, WP, DLC).
¹ C. W. McAlpin to WW, Nov. 11, 1916, ALS (WP, DLC).
² McAlpin and Fine had luncheon with the Wilsons at Shadow Lawn on November 8.

From Robert Lansing, with Enclosure

My dear Mr. President: Washington December 12, 1916.

I have the honor to enclose herewith copy of a translation of a Note of December 12th received from the Belgian Minister expressing the gratitude of his Government for the action of the Government of the United States in the matter of the deportations of Belgians to Germany.

I am, my dear Mr. President,
Very sincerely yours,   Robert Lansing

TLS (WP, DLC).

ENCLOSURE

Emmanuel Havenith to Robert Lansing

Washington, D. C.,
Mr. Secretary of State: December 12, 1916.

I have the honor to inform Your Excellency that I am instructed to express to you the heartfelt gratitude of the King's Government for the noble action the Government of the United States was pleased to take with the German Government in regard to the deportations of Belgian civilians to Germany and for the great interest it takes in the defence of the unfortunate Belgian people who have already been so sorely tried. In the exile and slavery whither they have been dragged by an oppressor who no longer respects any divine or human law, those unfortunates will find great moral support in hearing the voice of this noble country again proclaim the immutability of those fundamental principles of justice and liberty that are so dear to all the civilized peoples and above all to the United States for it was in the defence of those principles that one of its greatest presidents, Abraham Lincoln, offered up his all, even his blood and his life.

Be pleased to accept, Mr. Secretary of State, the assurances of my highest consideration.   E. Havenith.

TCL (WP, DLC).

From Bainbridge Colby

My dear Mr. President:　　　　New York December 12th, 1916.

How can I express the pleasure your letter gave me? I am carrying it in my pocket, unable to part with it, even to the framer (for whom it is destined), and I fear I am violating all the proprieties in exhibiting it to those of my intimates whom I can trust to forgive my pride in it.

I thank you from my heart, Mr. President, for your generous praise. It is far more than I deserve. Nothing I have ever been permitted to do has given me the deep satisfaction I have had in my work in this campaign. My complete confidence in you made it a joyous thing to uphold you, and to defend your policies and measures, and to demand your continuance in power. The victory, which is yours and no one else's, and which you accept so simply and self-forgetfully, was sweet indeed, I can tell you, to your fighting men.

The dinner Thursday night was, from every point of view, most delightful. You could not possibly have been in happier vein and, will you allow me to add, the honor you did Mrs. Colby[1] gave me a very genuine thrill.

Please remember us both to Mrs. Wilson, of whose charming qualities I had new proofs in our conversation at dinner.

With fervent good wishes always, believe me,
　　　　　　Sincerely yours,　Bainbridge Colby

TLS (WP, DLC).
[1] Nathalie Sedgwick Colby.

From Hollis Burke Frissell

Dear Mr. President:　　　　Hampton. Virginia
　　　　　　　　　　　　　December 12, 1916.

I had a talk the other day with Mr. George Foster Peabody, in regard to the race situation in the South. The movement of large numbers of blacks to the Northern States, seems to some of us a very serious matter. I feel that if it were possible for you to publicly express the kindly interest in the negro race which I am sure that you feel, your words would carry comfort and help to an extent you perhaps hardly realize.

Dr. John R. Mott, in one of his public utterances, expressed a belief that we in this country must work out the race problem of the world. As you know, here at Hampton we are struggling to bring about kindly feeling between the two races, and we have succeeded to some extent in our endeavor. I realize how weighted your days have been, and what serious problems you have to meet, but I should like to press upon your consideration, this problem which seems to many of such great importance.

I wish that we might have the privilege of seeing you at Hampton sometime this year, and I should be very glad if on some special occasion we could invite the Governor[1] and other leading men of Virginia to meet you here, when I feel sure some words from you might accomplish great good.

Yours very truly,   H. B. Frissell

TLS (WP, DLC).
[1] Henry Carter Stuart.

A Draft of a Note

[Dec. 13, 1916]

TO ENTENTE POWERS.

In presenting this communication on behalf of the Imperial German Government[1] you are instructed to say to the Secretary of State for Foreign Affairs that the Government of the United States takes advantage of this unexpected opportunity to make representations to His Majesty's Government which it begs that His Majesty's Government will bear in mind in discussing the German overture. You will then read to him the following, a copy of which you will be kind enough to leave with him:

The request to present this note has come as a surprise to the Government of the United States; but it is a very welcome surprise because it seems to the Government of the United States to promise at least a beginning of interchanges of view between the governments now at war which may presently afford relief to the neutral nations of the world from a situation which has become all but intolerable. The effects of the present war upon the fortunes, the policies, and the rights of neutral nations seem to the President of the United States to give him a clear right to speak now with great candour with regard to this overture for peace. As a sincere friend of the nations at war and as a friend of humanity he, like all other men who look with deep sorrow and anxiety upon the present tragical circumstances of the world, earnestly and eagerly desires peace; but he ⟨of course has no right to constitute himself the spokesman of humanity. He⟩[2] can speak only as the representative of the people and Government of the United States. He, therefore, speaks now ⟨only⟩ particularly of the rights of the great neutral nation of which he is the head, and speaks, not of sentiments, but of concrete interests which it is his duty to safeguard.

In every quarter of the world the life of mankind has been altered and disturbed. Everywhere it is hindered and perplexed, rendered harder, more hazardous, more difficult to plan or to carry through upon any terms. The task of every government, the task of caring for and promoting the interests of its own people, has been hampered and impeded, and the burden falls, as always, upon those least prepared, least able to bear it. The commerce of neutral nations is interrupted, their industries are checked and diverted, the lives of their people are put in constant jeopardy, they are virtually forbidden the accustomed highways of the sea, their energies are drawn off into temporary and novel channels, they suffer at every turn, though disengaged and disposed to none but friendly and impartial offices. The time has come to take counsel lest a violence be done civilization itself which cannot be atoned for or repaired.

Until now, no opportunity for counsel has been suggested. Neither group of belligerents has avowed the objects which would, if attained, satisfy them that the war had been fought out. The world has been obliged to conjecture what definitive results, what actual exchange of guarantees, what political changes or readjustments, what stage of military success even, would bring the war to an end. Neutral nations have felt themselves constantly in danger of being drawn in because their rights were being constantly set aside or directly violated, and yet have been aware that, should they become involved, it would be only because they had been hurt and saw no remedy but to risk still greater, it might be even irreparable, injury in order to make the weight in the one scale or the other decisive; and that even as participants they would not know how far the scales must tip before the end would come or what was being weighed in the balance.

Authoritative spokesmen of the nations engaged have, it is true, spoken more than once in general terms of the issues involved, but none has yet definitively stated the measures or agreements which might be expected to bring those issues to a conclusive settlement. They have said that they deemed the very life and political integrity of the nations they represented to be involved, and that they felt that they had no choice but to push the fearful contest to a conclusion in order that they might be secure in the future against its renewal and against the rivalries and ambitions which brought it about; but they have not said what sort of ending, what manner of settlement, what kind of guarantees would afford the assurance of safety and of permanency they desired.

Here at last, in the overture now made by the Imperial German Government, is an opportunity for definition. The Government of the United States has, of course, no opinion to express, no counsel to offer as to the advisability of acting upon the offer of discussion now so explicitly made, but it does feel that it has the right to say that the governments of Great Britain and her Allies owe it to the nations not yet involved, whose vital interests, like those of the United States, are being, through no fault or act of their own, more and more seriously affected with every week of the war's continuance, to state, even if that offer is declined, what concrete objects they are seeking to attain and would be willing to discuss.

The Government of the United States understands it to have been agreed from the first that it was not the wish or purpose of either side to crush their antagonists, make conquest of their territories or possessions, deprive them of their equal place and opportunity among the great free peoples of the world. This has been the explicit assurance of the leading statesmen of both sides. They have declared, also, that they are fighting no less for the rights of small and weak nations than for the rights of the great and powerful states immediately involved. And throughout they have earnestly affirmed their desire for peace, but only for a peace that would last, a peace based, not upon the uncertain balance of powerful alliances offset against one another, but upon guarantees in which the whole civilized world would join, that the rights and privileges of every nation and people should be the common and explicit obligation of all governments alike.

With these objects the people and government of the United States whole-heartedly sympathize. When once the particular issues at stake between the belligerents, the issues as yet undefined, are settled, the people of the United States are ready to express that sympathy in action. They are ready to support their Government in joining a league of nations that will pledge itself to an accomplishment of these objects and definitely uniting in an organization that will be adequate to assure their realization. They are ready to contribute every influence and resource at their command to such a combination, so purposed and organized. If that be the ultimate object of the war, they are ready when the right moment comes to cooperate to bring it about. They are impatient to learn how they may know when that moment comes. They wait to be told for what sort of concrete results they must look before these final guarantees will be asked for and matured.

The Government of the United States hopes, therefore, that the governments of Great Britain and her Allies will in no case now withhold a very definite avowal of the immediate objects they seek to attain and whose attainment they are resolved shall precede the concert of nations upon which in any event the permanent peace of the world must depend. A little while and it may be too late to realize the hopes which all men who love peace and justice entertain and which all statesmen must see to be the only hopes that are worthy to serve as the motive of great and permanent plans for mankind. If the contest must continue to proceed towards undefined ends by slow attrition to the ultimate exhaustion of the one group of nations or the other, if million after million of human lives must be offered up until there are no more to offer on the one side or the other, if resentments must be kindled that can never cool, and despairs engendered from which there can be no recovery, hopes of peace and of the willing concert of free peoples will be rendered vain and idle. An irreparable damage to civilization would make peace itself meaningless and futile.

These very solemn and earnest representations are made with the utmost respect for the rights of all concerned and in sincere friendship; and they are made very frankly because with no motive except the motive avowed. The reply which the governments of Great Britain and her Allies shall make to the present overtures of the Imperial German Government the Government of the United States is not at liberty to suggest. But it is directly and of right concerned that it and the other nations of the world which are in like case with itself should be told what immediate objects the governments of Great Britain and of her Allies have in mind; and it requests that this be made the occasion for their explicit avowal. It has no desire to intervene. It is not itself proposing peace between the nations now at war or suggesting any terms upon which peace might be concluded. It is asking simply that, in view of the daily effects the war is having on the essential rights and privileges of its own people, it be informed what the entente powers have it in mind to demand of their opponents when they shall come to the point at which they shall deem it to be consistent with their duty to their people to conclude a peace.[3]

T MS (WP, DLC).

[1] It is printed as Enclosure I with RL to WW, Dec. 14, 1916. However, it had been published in full in the morning newspapers in the United States on December 13.

[2] Words in angle brackets in this document and the following one deleted by Wilson.

[3] There is a WWT draft of this note in WP, DLC.

A Draft of a Note

TO CENTRAL POWERS.

Seek a personal interview with the Imperial Chancellor and say to him that the Government of the United States very cheerfully undertakes to transmit to the governments of Great Britain, France, and Serbia the note which he handed you on December 12th; and take advantage of that opportunity to read to him the following, a copy of which you will be kind enough to leave with him:

The Government of the United States welcomes this expression of the willingness of the Imperial German Government to discuss terms of peace as affording at least a promise of an interchange of views between the Governments now at war with all the more gratification because the war has created a state of affairs throughout the world which has become almost as burdensome to the nations which have remained neutral as to the nations directly engaged. The effects of the war upon the fortunes, the policies, and the rights of neutral nations seem to the President of the United States to give him a clear right to request the Imperial German Government to add to its present overtures a definite official intimation of the practical agreements and actual terms upon which it would deem it possible to conclude peace. In the opinion of the Government of the United States a preliminary indication from each group of belligerents of the terms which may be made acceptable to them will be found to be an indispensable introduction to discussion.

The President is confident that a frank expression of this opinion on his part will be accepted as entirely justified by the direct and very serious effects which the war is having upon the international rights of the United States. As a sincere friend of the nations at war and as a friend of humanity, he, like all other men who look with deep sorrow and anxiety upon the present tragical circumstances of the world, earnestly and eagerly desires peace; but he ⟨, of course, he has no right to constitute himself the spokesman of humanity. He⟩ can speak only as the representative of the people and government of the United States. He speaks now, therefore, ⟨only⟩ particularly of the rights of the great neutral nation of which he is the head, and speaks, not of sentiments, but of concrete interests which it is his duty to safeguard.

In every quarter of the world the life of mankind has been altered and disturbed. Everywhere it is hindered and perplexed, rendered harder, more hazardous, more difficult to plan or to carry though upon any terms. The task of every government, the task of caring for and promoting the interests of its own people, has been hampered and impeded, and the burden falls, as always, upon those least prepared, least able to bear it. The commerce of neutral nations is interrupted, their industries are checked and diverted, the lives of their people are put in constant jeopardy, they are virtually forbidden the accustomed highways of the sea, their energies are drawn off into temporary and novel channels, they suffer at every turn, though disengaged and disposed to none but friendly and impartial offices. The time has come to take counsel lest a violence be done civilization itself which cannot be atoned for or repaired.

Until now, no opportunity for counsel has been suggested. Neither group of belligerents has avowed the objects which would, if attained, satisfy them that the war had been fought out. The world has been obliged to conjecture what definitive results, what actual exchange of guarantees, what political changes or readjustments, what stage of military success even, would bring the war to an end. Neutral nations have felt themselves constantly in danger of being drawn in because their rights were being constantly set aside or directly violated, and yet have been aware that, should they become involved, it would be only because they had been hurt and saw no remedy but to risk still greater, it might be even irreparable, injury in order to make the weight in the one scale or the other decisive; and that even as participants they would not know how far the scales must tip before the end would come or what was being weighed in the balance!

Authoritative spokesmen of the nations engaged have, it is true, spoken more than once in general terms of the issues involved, but none has yet definitely stated the measures or agreements which might be expected to bring those issues to a conclusive settlement. They have said that they deemed the very life and political integrity of the nations they represented to be involved, and that they felt that they had no choice but to push the fearful contest to a conclusion in order that they might be secure in the future against its renewal and against the rivalries and ambitions which brought it about; but they have not said what sort of ending, what manner of settlement, what kind of guarantees would afford the assurance of safety and of permanency they desired.

Here at last, in view of the overture now made by the Imperial German Government, is an opportunity for definition. The Government of the United States sincerely hopes that neither party to the war will fail to take advantage of it.

The Government of the United States understands it to have been agreed from the first that it was not the wish or purpose of either side to crush their antagonists, make conquest of their territories or possessions, deprive them of their equal place and opportunity among the great free peoples of the world. This has been the explicit assurance of the leading statesmen of both sides. They have declared, also, that they are fighting no less for the rights of small and weak nations than for the rights of the great and powerful states immediately involved. And throughout they have earnestly affirmed their desire for peace, but only for a peace that would last, a peace based, not upon the uncertain balance of powerful alliances offset against one another, but upon guarantees in which the whole civilized world would join, that the rights and privileges of every nation and people should be the common and explicit obligation of all governments alike.

With these objects the people and government of the United States whole-heartedly sympathize. When once the particular issues at stake between the belligerents, the issues as yet undefined, are settled, the people of the United States are ready to express that sympathy in action. They are ready to support their Government in joining a league of nations that will pledge itself to an accomplishment of these objects and definitely uniting in an organization that will be adequate to assure their realization. They are ready to contribute every influence and resource at their command to such a combination, so purposed and organized. If that be the ultimate object of the war, they are ready when the right moment comes to cooperate to bring it about. They are impatient to learn how they may know when that moment comes. They wait to be told for what sort of concrete results they must look before these final guarantees will be asked for and matured.

The Government of the United States hopes, therefore, that the Imperial German Government and the governments of the entente powers will in no case now withhold a definite avowal of the immediate objects they seek to attain and whose attainment they are resolved shall precede that concert of nations upon which in any event the permanent peace of the world must depend. A little while and it may be too late to realize the hopes which all men who love peace and justice entertain and which all statesmen must see to be the only hopes that are worthy to serve as the motive of great and permanent plans for mankind. If the contest must continue to proceed towards undefined ends by slow attrition to the ultimate exhaustion of the one group of antagonists or the other, if million after million of human lives must be offered up until there are no more to offer on the one side or the other, if resentments must be kindled that can never cool and despairs engendered from which there can be no recovery, hopes of peace and of the willing concert of free peoples will be rendered vain and idle. An irreparable damage to civilization would make peace itself meaningless and futile.

These very solemn and earnest representations are made with the utmost respect for the rights of all concerned and in sincere friendship; and they are made very frankly because made with no motive except the motive avowed. The Government of the United States deems itself to be directly and of right concerned that it, and the other nations of the world which are in like case with itself, should be told what immediate objects the governments of the belligerent nations have in mind. It therefore requests that this be made the occasion for their ⟨explicit⟩ avowal. It has no desire to intervene. It is not itself proposing peace between the nations now at war or suggesting any opinion of its own as to the terms upon which peace might be concluded. It is asking simply that, in view of the daily effects the war is having upon the essential rights and privileges of its own people, it be informed what the several powers have it in mind to demand of their opponents when they shall come to the point at which they shall deem it to be consistent with their duty to their people to conclude a peace.

You are instructed to inform the Imperial Chancellor that an identic note in the same sense as the foregoing is being sent to each of the entente powers and to each of the powers now allied with Germany.[1]

T MS (WP, DLC).
[1] There is a WWT draft of this note in WP, DLC.

From Robert Lansing

PERSONAL AND PRIVATE:

My dear Mr. President: Washington December 13, 1916.

I wish you would read the enclosed quotation of the LONDON DAILY NEWS editorial on the German peace proposals.[1] It is, to my mind, a very sensible statement of the British position—or, rather, what should be the British position.

                    Faithfully yours,   Robert Lansing

TLS (WP, DLC).

1 London *Daily News*, Dec. 13, 1916, quoted in "Northcliffe Glad 'Old Gang' is Out; Scorns Hollweg," New York *World*, Dec. 13, 1916, clipping (WP, DLC). The editorial in the *Daily News* read in part:

"We have reached one of the great landmarks of the war and upon the action of the allies in the next few days enormous issues depend. Bethmann-Hollweg has seized a moment when the facts of the war are most obviously favorable to issue a proposal which will put the allies on defense and if possible in the wrong.

"The move may be supposed to have three main objects in view. The first is to compel the allies to face a problem which must be faced eventually, a problem, that is, of the terms on which they are prepared to make peace. . . .

"In the second place, his aim is to put us wrong with the neutral world. *Especially his eye is on the United States, where several significant incidents have happened of late which are disquieting to the allies.*

"In the third place, his aim is obviously to justify his Government in the eyes of his own people. There is undoubtedly a strong and widespread desire for peace in Germany and a powerful and growing suspicion of the Government. That suspicion he hopes to allay by putting the allies in the position of refusing all overtures and consolidating the country on the conviction that Germany is being reduced to wage a sheer defensive war of existence. . . .

"The allies cannot enter into peace negotiations on the basis Bethmann-Hollweg offers them, but they must put their case before the enemy and before the world. They must state the terms on which they are prepared to negotiate and throw on Germany the responsibility of rejecting or accepting that basis of negotiation. A mere non possumus will be a fatal mistake. It will be the greatest diplomatic victory German [has] achieved in the war. We must not permit her to have that victory."

From Thomas Riley Marshall

Dear Mr. President,   Washington. [Dec. 13, 1916]

I trust you did not glean from the table talk with Mrs. Marshall last evening that I was dissatisfied with the conduct of the National Committee touching money matters or vouching for the truth of statements made to me. I simply repeated various reasons given to me as to why we lost Indiana. So far I can not tell to my own satisfaction. I am suspending judgment.

Let me thank for your kind note about my Christmas vacation,[1] and say that whatever I did was gladly done—so the work while hard was agreeable.

Regardfully Yours,   Thos. R. Marshall

ALS (WP, DLC).

1 It is missing.

From Robert Lansing, with Enclosures

STRICTLY CONFIDENTIAL:

My dear Mr. President: Washington December 14, 1916.

I hasten to send you the text of a despatch received late last night from Berlin, which has just been deciphered. I have not waited to compare the text which we are requested to transmit to certain of the Allied Governments with the note as it appears in the newspapers. That is being done.

I also enclose a copy of another telegram marked "Strictly Confidential" from Mr. Grew, giving a statement made by the Spanish Ambassador at Berlin, relative to the identic note.

As a matter of interest, and as showing the uncertainties of communication, I would call your attention to the fact that while the latter telegram was filed six hours after the principal one it was received here three hours earlier.

Faithfully yours,   Robert Lansing.

TLS (WP, DLC).

E N C L O S U R E   I

Berlin via Copenhagen, December 12, 1916.

4722 The Chancellor has just sent for the Spanish Ambassador,[1] the Swiss Minister[2] and myself as representatives of the powers protecting German interests in the enemy countries and delivered to us separately a communication offering to enter into peace negotiations which he requested us to transmit through our respective governments to the governments of the various enemy powers. The Government of the United States is asked to transmit the communication to the governments of France, Great Britain, Japan, Roumania, Russia and Servia. Spain is asked to do the same to Belgium and Portugal, and Switzerland to Italy. I understand that a special note has also been sent to the Pope. It is said that the Chancellor will inform the Reichstag of this step at the special session this afternoon. An English translation of the communication which the Chancellor handed to me both in German and French and which he said would be given out similarly by Austria-Hungary, Turkey and Bulgaria to-day follows:

"The Imperial Chancellor, Berlin, December 12, 1916

"Mr. Chargé d'affaires: For nearly two and a half years the most terrible war which history has ever seen has been raging in a large part of the world. This catastrophe, which the bonds of a common civilization of a thousand years did not avail to stay, strikes humanity in its most costly attainments. It threatens to reduce to ruins the moral and material advance which formed Europe's pride at the commencement of the Twentieth Century.

"German and its allies, Austria-Hungary, Bulgaria and Turkey, have proven their invincible power in this struggle. They have gained tremendous successes over their adversaries who have the superiority of numbers and war material. Their lines withstand unshaken the continually repeated attacks of the armies of their enemies. The latest storm attack in the Balkans has been repulsed quickly and victoriously. The latest events demonstrate that even further continuation of the war cannot break their power of resistance but that on the contrary the whole situation justifies the expectation of further successes.

"The four allied powers were forced to take up arms for the defense of their existence and their national freedom of development. Even the glorious deeds of their armies have not altered this at all. They have ever been tenacious of the creed that their own rights and well-founded claims do not conflict with the rights of the other nations. They do not seek to crush or destroy their adversaries.

"Filled with the consciousness of their military and economic power and prepared if necessary to continue the struggle forced upon them to the very last, but at the same time imbued with a wish to avoid further bloodshed and to put an end to the horrors of war, the four allied powers propose to enter into peace negotiations immediately. The proposals which they will bring with them for these negotiations, and which are directed towards insuring the existence, honor and freedom of development of their nations, form, according to their convictions, a suitable basis for the establishment of a permanent peace.

"(*) (If?) in spite of this offer of peace and reconciliation the struggle should continue the four allied powers are determined to carry it through to a victorious conclusion. However, they solemnly decline all responsibility therefor before humanity and history.

"The Imperial Government has the honor to request the Government of the United States of America through your kind mediation, to be good enough to bring this communication to the cognizance of the Government of the French Republic and the Royal Britannic, the Imperial Japanese, the Royal Roumanian, the Imperial Russian and the Royal Servian Governments.

"I avail myself of this occasion to renew to you, Mr. Chargé d'affaires, the assurances of my most distinguished consideration. (signed) von Bethmann Hollweg. To Mr. Joseph Clark Grew, Chargé d'affaires of the United States of America."

Grew.

1 Luis Polo de Bernabé.
2 Alfred de Claparède.

ENCLOSURE II

Berlin (via Copenhagen) December 12, 1916.

STRICTLY CONFIDENTIAL.

4724. The Spanish Ambassador called on me shortly after we had seen the Chancellor separately this morning and said in the course of informal conversation that the Chancellor's offer to enter into peace negotiations had come as a surprise to him and that when he was summoned to the Chancellor he thought it likely that the latter was going to announce a resumption of the indiscriminate submarine warfare. He said that he thought it improbable that the enemy governments would accept the Chancellor's offer to enter into peace negotiations and in that case he believed that there would be a radical change in German policy involving a reopening of the ruthless submarine activity in the near future.   Grew.

T telegrams (WP, DLC).

From Edward Mandell House

Dear Governor: New York. December 14, 1916.

Both Brooks and Whitehouse have been here this afternoon. I therefore obtained a view of both sides of the question.

Strangely enough, Brooks thinks that the British reply should be that they would be willing to go into a discussion with Germany provided Germany will consent to disarmament and a league to enforce peace as a basis of settlement. Brooks has cabled this view to Northcliffe and Lloyd George.

Whitehouse thinks that when you send the German note to England that you should ask whether or not they would permit you to be the medium for a wider discussion of terms which would embrace disarmament and a league to enforce peace afterwards.

Whitehouse thinks we are on the eve of peace discussions. Brooks does not think it will lead to anything—but the wish to him is father to the thought.

One of the difficulties Whitehouse says in the situation, and this he told me in the deepest confidence, was that the British Government was not properly represented at Washington, and that we were not properly represented in London. He expressed the hope that in the event the pending matters admitted of discussion, you would send someone to England to present your views in a way which he was sure Page did not have the disposition to do. This, however, is something that we can discuss later.

What is important, I think, is that in the transmission of the note you say something that will call forth an answer and do it before either Switzerland or Spain has a chance to forestall you.

Affectionately yours, E. M. House

TLS (WP, DLC).

A Memorandum by Robert Lansing

December 14, 1916.

THE GERMAN PROPOSAL TO ENTER ON PEACE NEGIOTIATIONS.
WHAT IS THE PURPOSE OF THE GERMAN GOVERNMENT IN
PROPOSING NEGIOTIATIONS FOR PEACE AT THIS TIME?

A. If it is induced by a sincere desire to end the war, the reasons would seem to be—

1st. That its military operations against Roumania have been successful to an extraordinary degree.

2d. That Belgium, northern France, Poland, Serbia and Montenegro are in the hands of the Central Powers, and only a small portion of Hungary is in Russian occupation.

3d. That the offense [offensives] by Great Britain and France in the West, of Russia in the East, and of the Allies in Macedonia have been checked.

4th. That the Greek situation presents to the Allied Governments a problem of increasing difficulty and discouragement to those governments.

5th. That the political situations in Great Britain, in France and, to a less degree, in Russia indicate popular discontent with their governments resulting apparently from dissatisfaction at the failure to accomplish marked military successes in spite of the sacrifices made by the nations.

6th. That the submarine warfare has been recently conducted with such vigor that much tonnage of the Allies has been destroyed.

7th. That the sinking of the vessels of certain neutrals has reached an alarming extent and would induce those neutrals to be strong advocates of any effort made to end hostilities.

8th. That the apparent impossibility of either group of belligerents winning a decisive victory over their opponents without a long continuance of the conflict, even if it can

ever be won which some doubt, has aroused a strong
sentiment among the people of neutral nations that the
war should end.

Less evident but undoubtedly as influential in determining this
action would seem to be—

9th That the German people are growing discontented because of the failure of their Government to bring the
war to a successful conclusion, because of the vast numbers of lives sacrificed, and because of the want and
hardship caused by the economic pressure of Great
Britain's control of sea.

10th. That there is growing a strong peace sentiment among
the German people, which may result in political up-
risings.

11th. That the blame for the suffering and sacrifices which
the German nation has been called upon to bear has
been placed more and more on the Government, and it
is a matter of expediency for the dominant class to end
the war before this feeling crystalizes and becomes a
menace to their power after peace is restored.

It would appear from the foregoing reasons that the German
Government may be entirely sincere in this movement to
negotiate peace. The military situation, the Greek crisis, the
political state of the Allies, the success of submarine warfare, the
peace sentiment among neutrals, and the domestic situation
politically and economically in Germany make the present a most
opportune time to suggest a conference of the belligerents looking toward peace.

B. It [If] the purpose of the proposal is not sincere but is advanced with the conviction that it will be rejected by the enemy,
the reasons would seem to be—

1st. That the blame for the continuance of the war would
be placed upon the Allies.

2d. That by thus making her opponents responsible for continuance Germany would gain sympathy among neutral
nations.

3d. That she would arouse resentment among the advocates
of peace in the Entente nations and cause increased
political dissensions thus materially weakening their
Governments in the prosecution of the war.

4th. That the German people, whatever they might be called
upon to endure in the future, could not blame their Government for the war's continuance.

    5th. That with a change of sentiment toward the Government there would result united political action in its support, and less, if not little, probability of political antagonism on the restoration of peace.

    6th. That the rejection of the proposal would offer an excuse for the renewal of ruthless submarine warfare as a means of bringing the war to end.

It would appear from these reasons that even if the German Government was certain, when the proposal for a conference was made, that it would be rejected or accomplish nothing, it was an expedient move to make from the international as well as the national standpoint.

Whether the purpose of the German Government in proposing negotiations for peace are sincere or insincere, the course it has pursued is wise and shows great astuteness in seizing upon this particular time to make overtures for a parley.

That Government could never find a more favorable time to conduct negotiations. It could never find a better time to have its enemies refuse to negotiate. Whatever answer the Allies make, if it is confined to a simple acceptance or rejection, Germany gains. Only a counter proposal, which will shift the blame, can prevent the advantage being to the German Government.

T MS (WP, DLC).

Oswald Garrison Villard to Joseph Patrick Tumulty

                               [New York]

Dear Sir Joseph of the Warm Heart: Dec 14, 1916.

As J. P. Gavit remarked: "In this peace matter W.W. is now fishing behind the net. He let another fellow get the jump on him." Which is but what a certain "grouch" said to the honorable Mr. Secretary to the President at the New Willard on Sunday morning last.

Of course, the grouch, being human, and very fallible, cannot resist saying: "I told you so. I knew the single-track mind would get side-tracked while the express went by."

But: This *gloating* is not the real purpose of this note; which is to point out that while now, because of hesitation, the pride and glory of having initiated peace negotiations has passed forever from Woodrow Wilson's grasp, there is still one opportunity left to achieve immortality. It is to lead the way toward disarmament and a peace league of nations. Is that, too, to go to Germany? Are we who have been so severely criticized as caring only for our own skins and pockets to lose this chance to serve the world? And establish our desire to serve all mankind by a glorious deed?

Well, the danger is that the same vacillation, the same old heartbreaking wondering if just the right moment, or the right time, has come is likely to let that opportunity slip by. The trouble with Col. House & the White House is that that vilest of creatures, Madame Expediency, rules. One does not ask: "Is this right and just and deserved of humanity?" "Yes?" "Then here and now is it done!" One gets blocked by a submarine, or held up by a letter from Bryce, or the opinion of Mr. War Correspondent —and so Madame Expediency wins. Why in God's name not try once, *just once*, going ahead and doing the right thing & letting the rest go hang?

They used to tell Wendell Phillips that the South would be a hell if he freed the slaves. To which he said: "I entrench myself on the principle of human liberty and leave the working out of details to Almightly God." Isn't there one principle on which the White House can entrench at any cost? If so the W.W. stock (S.T.R.R. Co. Limited, First Preferred) would go beyond par at once.

Here's hoping. I know you would if you could, fidus Achates!

There'll be a monument to your loyalty & devotion one of these days, Sir Joseph! And among those present will be

Oswald Garrison Villard.

ALS (WP, DLC).

From the Diary of Colonel House

December 14, 1916.

I have been too busy again to keep a daily diary. The number of people I have seen, the telephone calls and other matters have kept me on the run from morning until night.

Sunday evening we dined with the Mezes. Robert Underwood Johnson was there and read us some of his unpublished poems. He invited us to dine with them Saturday to meet James M. Beck.

On Tuesday, at eleven o'clock, we took the train for Washington to attend the first Cabinet Dinner of the year given by the President. There were a number of acquaintances on board the train to prevent my getting any quiet or rest. Governor Glynn, Walter Lippmann, Albert Roberts[1] and others.

[1] Albert S. Roberts, Texas-born businessman of New York.

Besides ourselves the house guests at the White House were President and Mrs. Garfield of Williams College, Thomas Jones of Chicago, Joseph Wilson and several others.

The President handed me the memorandum he had prepared to send the belligerents and asked me to read it carefully and give him my opinion. Lansing had already gone over the note and his letter and notes were attached.

The President seemed depressed because the Germans had launched their bolt today asking for a peace conference. I tried to show him it would be of advantage rather than otherwise. As a matter of fact, my desire for peace is so much keener than my wish to bring it about personally that I feel a certain elation not felt for a long while. In my opinion, it will be impossible for the belligerents to get together completely without the aid of the United States.

I did not altogether agree with Lansing's criticism of the note, which was largely as to verbiage rather than ideas. Lansing's excuse for criticising some of the President's expressions was that they could not be translated into foreign languages. This I suppose is true, but the substitutions made the document less forceful and less characteristic of the President.

I did agree with Lansing's suggestion that there should be no threat in the note in the event one side or the other failed to respond. I told the President I felt strongly about this, since it would not do to place ourselves in an attitude which might make us an ally of Germany.

I had an opportunity of talking to Secretary Daniels at the Cabinet Dinner. I obtained enough from him to know that my worst fears as to our unpreparedness were confirmed. I asked Daniels how well our coast was defended by mines. He replied we were getting mines now from England, but he was insisting that they permit us to manufacture them over here under their patents. I asked how well we were prepared for war if it should come tomorrow. He said "war with whom?" I replied with Great Britain. There was no need to await a reply since his face told the story. He thought in a year we should have enough mines to protect the coast fairly well.

I am convinced that the President's place in history is dependent to a large degree upon luck. If we should get into a serious war and it should turn out disastrously, he would be one of the most discredited Presidents we have had. He has had nearly three years in which to get the United States into a reasonable state of preparedness and we have done nothing. Neither the Army nor the Navy are in condition to meet an enemy of the class of Roumania or Bulgaria, provided they could reach us. The few machine guns we have in the Army are borrowed or requisitioned from the British. If we had the 75,000 or 100,000 we need we have not the men to use them. We have no large guns. If we had them we have no trained men who would understand how to handle them. We have no air service, nor men to exploit it, and so it is down the list.

A combination of Great Britain and Japan could put us out of business just as rapidly as they could march through the country. It would be utterly impossible in these days of secrecy and censorship to know what troops Great Britain and Japan were transporting to Canada. They could assemble a large army there without our knowledge and we should be as helpless to resist them as Belgium or Serbia were to resist the Germans. If Great Britain and Japan wished to combine against us they could pretend to be conveying Japanese troops through Canada to France, and in this way we could not know just what they were doing or how many men were in Canada.

I believe the President will pull through without anything happening, but I could not sleep at night if I had this responsibility upon my shoulders and had not properly met it. The European countries are just as well aware of our condition as we are ourselves. The greatest security for peace at this time would be complete preparedness for war. If Great Britain and Russia had kept pace with Germany in military affairs, this war could not have happened because Germany would never have attempted to bring it about.

I told the President what Daniels said, and I urged him not to place our country in the position where we should either have to back down or fight the Allies. The trouble is the President does not know what is going on in any of the departments. He does not follow their work and has an idea that every department of the Government is running smoothly and well. As a matter of fact, most of them are, but a few are inefficient. I have complained of this from the beginning of his administration. He could remedy it easily if he would go at it in the right way.

Domestic legislation is the President's forte. No one has ever done that better or perhaps so well. But as an administrator he is a failure, and it is only because of a generally efficient Cabinet that things go as well as they do.

I dislike to record this criticism of the President because he is one of the great men of the world today, but he sadly lacks administrative ability.

After the dinner Tuesday the different Cabinet officials took me aside for talks. Lansing is disturbed over the foreign situation. He also wished to discuss the selection of a proper man for First Assistant Secretary of State in Osborne's place. We decided sometime ago to give Billy Phillips first place and get a new man for Third Secretary. There is great difficulty in finding a democrat, a man of means and one with ability to do the work creditably.

Gregory still wishes to resign. I told him to leave it in abeyance for the moment because I thought it unfair to upset the President at this time.

I asked Phillips to come over to the White House Wednesday to discuss foreign appointments. We both think it would be well to send Morris[2] to Argentine and give Norman Hapgood Stockholm. In suggesting this to the President he said he did not want to do anything Senator Lewis of Illinois would even indirectly feel was done for him. The President exhibited his usual prejudice in this. Nearly every time I see him there is some new man in his blacklist and he seldom removes one when once there. I cannot understand how he permits such small matters to disturb his equinimity. I mentioned The Independent to him the last time I was here, and found it had come under the ban of his displeasure simply because it did not support him, although it was certainly fair and nearly all the staff voted for him.

On Wednesday, the President undertook to revamp his note to the belligerents so as to have it conform with changed conditions brought about by Germany's offer to parley. He read me most of what he had written, not having finished it all before I left. He has done it exceedingly well as, indeed he does everything of this kind.

I suggested that it might happen that a peace agreement might stall upon the question of indemnity for the restoration of Belgium, Poland and Serbia, in which event, I was in favor of the United States stepping into the breach and offering to restore the devastated part of the countries at our own expense. This interested him, but he did not express an opinion; something he seldom does.

The President has a letter from Walter Page which he says he has not read but which he has given Mrs. Wilson to look over and get the sense of it. He now seldom reads Page's letters. He often holds them for my coming. This is the usual penalty for verbosity. I find myself doing the same thing when my correspondents cannot hold themselves within reasonable limits.

2 That is, Ira Nelson Morris, Minister to Sweden.

The President said Page had offered his resignation and he asked whether I thought he should accept it. I did not answer directly, but asked how sincerely Page had offered it. Mrs. Wilson thought he had offered it with a view of having it refused. I proposed Thomas Jones of Chicago as a suitable man[.] The President was afraid Jones could not be confirmed by the Senate since he was once rejected for the Federal Reserve Board. I then proposed Hugh Wallace. He did not think Wallace sufficiently serious minded, and while he did not say so, I could see he did not think he was of the intellectual caliber needed now. I may suggest Frank Polk as a suitable man for the place.

We left for New York on the 12.30 with Secretary McAdoo and a number of other acquaintances. McAdoo talked to me a large part of the way over. He feels discouraged at the President's attitude. He feels he should revamp his Cabinet and get rid of the weak members. He also feels that the President is not following the work of the departments as he should. In other words, he feels just as I do. McAdoo said the President had no business head, and what the office needs now is someone with that kind of ability. It is to be remembered, however, one seldom finds a man who has what the President has and administrative ability as well, so I suppose we should be content.

To Robert Lansing, with Enclosure

[The White House]

My dear Mr. Secretary,   15 December, 1916.

Subsequent thought has developed the enclosed. I think it best to be perfectly frank and explicit. This frees what we intend to do of all possible irritation to the Allies, and prepares the way for what we ought to do in any case unless their immediate action renders it unnecessary.   Faithfully Yours,   W.W.

Here is a remarkable editorial from the SPRINGFIELD REPUBLICAN.[1]

WWTLI (WP, DLC).

[1] It is missing, but it was "Mr. Wilson's Opportunity," *Springfield* (Mass.) *Republican*, Dec. 14, 1916. It declared that the German peace note gave Wilson the best opportunity he had yet had to impress upon the belligerents "the desire of the neutral world for the early restoration of peace." "In particular," it continued, "the president may without giving offense urge the entente powers to present to the central powers what they believe would furnish 'an appropriate basis for the establishment of a lasting peace,' in case the proposals now to be made by the central powers seem impossible of serious consideration. The president could thus get before mankind, and especially before the peoples of the warring nations, statements by the two sides sufficiently specific, perhaps, to indicate what they are now fighting for. These statements would hereafter at

least furnish the material for popular discussion and the revision of opinion in the respective countries and help to clear away the fogs of chauvinist fanaticism and ignorance which now darken the popular understanding of the real issues of the conflict. There has been too much self-anointing rhetoric hitherto in the explanations of the war aims of the belligerent governments composed for home consumption. . . . In every country engaged in this ghastly struggle the inhabitants believe what they have been told by their leaders and rulers, but in every country also the truth has been varnished so as to make it appear like the last indisputable and sacred word of the Almighty to his chosen people. The supreme value at this time of proposals designed to form 'an appropriate basis for the establishment of a lasting peace' may consist simply in this, that they force the hostile governments to face concrete realities before the world, and above all before their own people. . . . In view of the blighting effect of the censorships in every belligerent nation and the black atmosphere of misconception and fear in which the millions who compose the masses have lived since the first gun was fired, no more important service at this juncture could be performed by the president than to bring both sides authoritatively to make known to everybody precisely what conditions would seem consistent with an honorable peace."

There were other reasons for Wilson to promote peace discussions. Further prolongation of the conflict threatened a collapse of western civilization which might engulf even the neutral nations. Moreover, the United States wished to disprove the slander that she was fattening on the woes of Europe. There was also a racial problem: "Nor does the white race in the new world relish the continued decimation of its members in the old world—a decimation that, in the light of the arrested birth rate of Europe, must be figured ultimately in scores of millions of souls. Every year that this gigantic conflict between nations of the white race continues must see that race lose somewhat in strength as compared with the human hordes of Asia."

"This is not an appeal for an ignoble peace, nor for an inconclusive peace," the editorial concluded. "The final test of a peace is the living of it; and no peace can be adjudged inconclusive without being tried. But the alternative to peace is what? For 2½ years Europe has experienced the agony of it. The result of the greatest military efforts history has known is a war that is certainly not conclusive, whether or not one may call it noble. The question is whether another year, or two years, or even three years more of this conflict, could possibly solve Europe's problems more advantageously or decisively than they could be solved by the processes of peace."

ENCLOSURE[1]

INSTRUCTIONS to each of our representatives who are to present the German overtures.

In bringing this note to the attention of the foreign office, as requested ⟨, by the Imperial German Government,⟩ intimate quite explicitly that⟨,⟩ while you are submitting it on behalf of the ⟨German⟩ *respective* governments only and in no sense as the representative of the Government of the United States, this Government is deeply interested in the result of these unexpected overtures, would deeply appreciate a confidential intimation of the character and purpose of the response that will be made, and will itself presently have certain very earnest representations to make on behalf of the manifest interests of neutral nations and of humanity itself to which it will ask that very serious consideration be given. It does not make these representations now because it does not wish to connect them with the ⟨German⟩ *proposed* overtures, *or have them construed in any way as an attempt at mediation* notwithstanding the fact that these overtures afford an admirable occasion for their consideration. The Government of the United States had it in mind to make them entirely on its own initiative and before it had any knowledge of the present attitude or suggestions of the ⟨German⟩ *Central* governments. It will make the same representations to the governments of the Central Powers and wishes to make them almost immediately, if necessary, but not as associated with the overtures of either group of belligerents. The present overtures ⟨of Germany⟩ have created an unexpected opportunity for looking at the world's case as a whole, but the United States would have itself created the occasion had it fallen out otherwise.

WWT MS (WP, DLC).
1 Words in angle brackets deleted by Lansing; words in italics inserted by him.

To Herbert Bruce Brougham[1]

[The White House]

My dear Mr. Brougham: December 15, 1916

I am deeply interested in what you tell me of the extensive and important newspaper project which Mr. Curtis has in mind.[2] I wonder if you could come down to see me next Wednesday, the twentieth, to tell me something more about it? I am quite sure that I could see you at 3:30 at the house, not at the office.

Cordially and sincerely yours,   Woodrow Wilson

TLS (Letterpress Books, WP, DLC).
1 At this time associate editor of the Philadelphia *Public Ledger*.
2 Brougham's letter is missing. However, he (with the approval of Cyrus Hermann Kotzchmar Curtis, president of the Curtis Publishing Co. of Philadelphia) planned to organize a newspaper syndicate or news bureau, with special correspondents in the United States and abroad. As Brougham explained to House, he planned "to organize a bureau by which better and more accurate news could be disseminated throughout the country." Brougham, House added, had "a list of papers that would cooperate in the plan." Moreover, "It is intended that the men doing the actual news service shall be selected by the President and myself as a guaranty of good faith." House Diary, Dec. 29, 1916.

To Thomas Riley Marshall

[The White House]

My dear Mr. Vice President: December 15, 1916

Thank you for your note, though I beg to assure you that it was unnecessary. I perfectly understood the spirit of what Mrs. Marshall told me and of your own explanation of the result in Indiana and did not draw any wrong inferences.

It was very delightful to have you with us the other night, and I hope that your vacation is going to be a genuine one.

Cordially and faithfully yours,   Woodrow Wilson

TLS (Letterpress Books, WP, DLC).

From Samuel Jordan Graham

Dear Mr. President: Washington. December 15, 1916.

May I congratulate you on not having committed yourself to the general proposition that the Government can relieve the situation connected with the high cost of living,[1] and may I offer briefly one or two suggestions?

1st. I do not think that it is possible for the Government to check the rise in prices and I expect to see it continue.

2nd. The Government can only, in possibly several ways, somewhat alleviate it.

As to the first of these propositions, and I have not seen this noticed, we are in a condition of world-wide inflation. The nations at war have piled up an indebtedness of fifty billion dollars which is represented by *promises to pay*, now afloat in the world, causing a tremendous, unexampled expansion of its currency and credits. It is known that we in this country have absorbed two millions of our securities, which are nothing but promises to pay and are being used as a basis of expanding credits. We have also purchased, in the form of loans, about two billions of their promises to pay, and no one knows how much we have taken through the medium of payment to private sellers for their goods—some billions more, undoubtedly.

While the production of the world for the last year is very little, if anything, more than it was two years ago, the volume of currency, or the promises to pay and credits based thereon, has increased five or six fold. It is this enormous inflation that is causing the high prices, and it is a situation which this Government cannot possibly control as it is world-wide. I feel that in some form this thought should be frankly brought to the attention of the people so that they may understand it and your administration be cleared of the current false impression that the Federal Government can give relief.

What has been happening during the last two years is that we have been transferring our production and wealth to the warring nations and receiving their promises to pay in return. It is true that we have received a large amount of gold, but this gold of itself is so abnormal in amount that it is adding to the inflated condition by being used as a basis for extending credits. We have now more than $30. per capita. The more we get of it the worse this situation will become.

This is too big a subject to discuss in a letter. I am simply trying, briefly, to throw out some suggestions.

As to the second proposition, the alleviation of the situation.

It seems to me, that the high cost of living is due, among other things, to two causes in particular:

1st. The great increase in the number of local combinations in cities and in the states which have greatly increased in the last two years and which can only be dealt with by the local authorities under the state law, and that at present practically nothing is being done along this line by the state authorities. All that can be done as to this is to direct attention to the necessity for the states to enforce their local laws in the matter of restraint of trade and monopoly.

2nd. The big problem of distribution, which is now being studied in the different localities along the line of what is called "better marketing." Approximately, it costs twelve per cent. to distribute from the producer to the wholesaler, while it costs forty per cent. to distribute from the wholesaler through the retailer to the consumer. This increase is due, to some extent, to combinations, but is largely due to the fact that the expense of the business of the small grocer is paid by the consumer. Take a grocer doing a business of $500 a month; the hire of clerks, wagon driver, rents, his own services, etc., in addition to a profit, has to be added to his purchase price from the wholesaler. This is where the chief cost in distribution occurs. It, of course, cannot be reached by the Federal Government in the courts or under any existing law. Just how this is to be worked out I am not prepared to say. My real purpose in writing this note is to suggest the importance of letting the people know exactly what the situation is so that they will not rest under the false impression that it is possible for the Federal Government either to prevent these high prices or to very materially affect them.

I also do not see how the Federal Reserve Board can remedy this inflation to any material extent. The raising of the interest rate would not affect the situation appreciably.

If our people would stop taking these promises of people of foreign nations to pay in exchange for their goods, it would, to a certain degree, prevent the situation from becoming immeasurably worse, but the inflation is already so tremendous that the highest prices to meet it, I don't think, have anything like been reached. I look for them to continue to advance until the readjustments incident to the ending of the European war occur.

Faithfully,   Saml J Graham

TLS (WP, DLC).

¹ Wilson had conferred on December 11 with George Weston Anderson, who was heading an investigation by the Department of Justice into the high cost of living. The *New York Times*, Dec. 12, 1916, reported: "The President will continue the examination of facts collected by various departments before deciding whether any remedial legislation shall be recommended to Congress."

From Francis Griffith Newlands

My dear Mr. President: Washington, D. C. Dec. 15, 1916.

I endeavored yesterday through the telephone to inform you of the action of the Committee.¹ Senator Robinson and myself made a strenuous effort to secure the immediate reporting of the bills relating to the Governmental investigation of wage disputes and the taking over of the railroads in case of military necessity, but the overwhelming sentiment of the Committee was that a hearing should be had and only our two votes were registered in favor of immediate action.

Among other things, it was stated that the railway executives and employes were about to get together at Evansville, Indiana, in an agreement that would make further legislation unnecessary and would practically annul the eight hour legislation already adopted.² The conclusion of the Committee was that the hearing should be fixed for January 2, next.

I enclose you herewith the two tentative measures upon which the hearing will be had, and the statement issued by me to the press, regarding them.³ As I observed that the legislation is referred to in the press as involving the consideration of a compulsory arbitration bill, I have today, at the suggestion of the Associated Press, upon my complaint as to the use of this phrase, made the enclosed statement, marked "2," for publication.⁴

Believe me, my dear Mr. President,

Most sincerely yours,   Francis G. Newlands

TLS (WP, DLC).

¹ The Senate Committee on Interstate Commerce.

² Whoever "stated" that railway executives and employees were about to get together at Evansville to solve their problems was somewhat confused. What did convene in Evansville on December 14-15 was the Central States Conference on Rail and Water Transportation. Among the speakers who discussed transportation problems was William Granville Lee, president of the Brotherhood of Railway Trainmen. After a lengthy review of events leading to the passage of the Adamson Act, Lee turned to the subject of continuing negotiations between the railroad managers and the four railroad brotherhoods: "Perhaps no better opportunity than this moment could come to say to you that we, both sides to this

controversy, are carefully considering plans to settle this entire controversy out of court, to settle it before January 1st by applying something satisfactory to both interests. . . . It is only in a crude state yet, but I know I am not betraying confidences when I say, some of the very best friends, high up in the chambers of the operating departments of the railroads, favor something of that kind. They have discussed it with us. I only left them night before last in New York and will go back there again very soon." *Official Proceedings of the Central States Conference on Rail and Water Transportation Held Under the Auspices of the Evansville Chamber of Commerce, Evansville, Indiana, December 14 and 15, 1916* (n.p., n.d.), pp. 72-73.

After several informal discussions between the National Conference Committee of Railways and the heads of the four brotherhoods in late December, the talks broke down on December 28 over the issue of whether the Adamson Act should take effect on January 1, 1917, as the brotherhoods demanded, or be suspended pending a Supreme Court decision on its constitutionality, as the railroad managers desired. *New York Times*, Dec. 29, 1916.

3 "A Bill to amend an Act entitled 'An Act providing for mediation, conciliation, and arbitration in controversies between certain employers and their employees' approved July fifteenth, nineteen hundred and thirteen" and "A Bill to authorize the President of the United States in certain emergencies to take possession of railroad, telephone, and telegraph lines, and for other purposes," printed bills (WP, DLC). Since these were only tentative versions for the use of the committee, they had no official bill numbers. Their content is summarized in n. 4 below. The third enclosure here mentioned was F. G. Newlands, CC press release, Dec. 14, 1916 (WP, DLC), which gave the same description of the committee meeting of December 14 as in the above letter.

4 F. G. Newlands, CC press release, Dec. 15, 1916 (WP, DLC). Newlands said in part: "I observe that the press refer to the measure recommended by the President as a compulsory arbitration bill. This is a misnomer and should be corrected. No measure for compulsory arbitration is proposed. The legislation desired is an amendment to the Mediation and Conciliation Act providing that where mediation and conciliation have failed there shall be an investigation of the facts by a Government Commission appointed by the President, instructed to report within ninety days, accompanied by a stay of the power of strike or lock-out during the period of investigation and for thirty days thereafter. Another measure provides for taking possession of railroad, telephone and telegraph lines in case of military necessity."

Walter Hines Page to Robert Lansing

London December 15, 1916.

5320. The following is confidential for the Secretary and the President only.

Concerning the German proposal to hold a peace conference responsible men here of course are waiting to see what terms will be proposed. But the undoubted overwhelming feeling in and out of official life is opposed to the acceptance or even to serious consideration of any proposal unless definite and favorable terms are put forward by the German Government. Nobody believes that such terms will be authorititively put forth. The language and the tone of the proposal are considered insulting because of its boastfulness and its threat. The proposal itself is regarded as an indication of severe economic strain and of greater weakness than the English had suspected. The purposes of it are considered to be to hearten the German people and to affect neutral opinion favorably toward Germany especially pacifist opinion and if possible to break the solidarity of the Allies. There is also a suggestion of feeling that the German declaration is made to prepare an excuse for further deliberate frightfulness. It is believed here that the Germans are proposing separate secret considerations to such of the Allies as they hope to detach from the others. One instance such as follows:

I have it from a wholly reliable source that Villalobar,[1] Spanish Minister (at?) Brussels, whose strong pro-German sympathies and leanings are well known and who is regarded in well-informed quarters as an active agent of Germany recently wrote to the Belgian Minister of War at Havre stating that he had been authorized, either by the German Emperor or the German Government in Belgium, to approach the Minister of War with regard to the possibility of peace. He had been empowered to say that if the Belgians would make peace now Germany would evacuate his country, pay them a full indemnity, and assist in their financial rehabilitation, but that if they refused the Germans would see to it that when the Belgians recovered control of their country, if they ever did, not one stick would stand upon another in any city or town in Belgium—that every (village?) would be razed to the ground. Under the circumstances Villalobar added that he thought the Belgian Government's course was clear and that they should consent to peace at once.

The only immediate result expected here of this latest German maneuver is a grimmer renewal of hostilities in France as soon as the weather permits; and the (warring?) military commanders confidently expect success since they will then for the first time have sufficient munitions for indefinite continuous use.

The British Government have bought all the exportable food in the Scandanavian states, Iceland and Holland and this purchase will still further lessen the supply that leaks to Germany. The British Government having an enormous oversupply of fish is now selling so many Dutch herring in New York that the Canadian maritime provinces have complained to the British Government of this invasion of their market.

For all these complaints the British Government do not seem likely to give favorable attention to any proposal which would seem to leave the German military power unbroken expecially since the newly formed Government here, which was chosen for a more vigorous prosecution of the war, has not had time to try itself at the task.   Page.

T telegram (WP, DLC).
[1] Rodrigo de Saavedra, Marquis de Villalobar.

Sir Cecil Arthur Spring Rice to the Foreign Office

Personal.   Washington   R. December 15th. 1916.

United States Government have now received German Note and will transmit it to the Powers concerned. Question under consideration is, as I understand, whether United States Government will simply act as postman or make some suggestion of their own, officially or otherwise, in making formal communication of German Note.

There is a strong movement here amongst Pacifists and pro-Germans in favour of the latter course. Senator Stone will make a speech to-day urging United States Government to intervene in name of neutral interests to stop war and to use means at its command to force Allies to consent to peace. A journalist who saw President yesterday conveyed an intimation to me that President was considering what measures should be taken (cutting off supplies, refusing clearances to armed merchant vessels etc.) in case Great Britain returned categorical refusal to treat.

I venture to observe that from point of view of situation here (quite irrespective of all other considerations of which I am of course no judge) our wisest course would be to make a statement expressing our strong desire for peace but that our action must be guided solely by nature of terms offered and agreement of our allies and that therefore our attitude remains expectant. Meanwhile we propose to continue fighting with all our strength until a real and permanent peace is secured.

Germans are counting on influence of peace party among allies and agents of this party here and expect that a direct and unqualified refusal of any peace proposition will increase strength of this party. If Germany can be forced to propose detailed terms situation would be reversed. German Embassy is giving out that conquered territory will only be surrendered on payment of heavy ransom.

German proposal is simply a declaration of willingness to treat. But since no terms have been stated natural answer would be that we entirely share their desire for peace and will be prepared to discuss terms when disclosed. If President should make any comments of his own, any observations which we make might be accompanied by some friendly and non-committal expression of appreciation of motives prompting him.

T telegram (FO 371/2805, No. 254012, pp. 278-88, PRO).

To Walter Hines Page[1]

[Washington] December 16, 1916.

The American Missions at Berlin, Vienna, Constantinople and Sofia have received from the Governments of Germany, Austria Hungary, Turkey and Bulgaria, respectively, identic notes for transmission to the Entente Powers. The note from the German Government, which has been received in the English Language, reads as follows: . . .

In bringing this note to the attention of the foreign office, as requested, intimate quite explicitly that, while you are submitting it on behalf of the respective governments only and in no sense as the representative of the Government of the United States, this Government is deeply interested in the result of these unexpected overtures, would deeply appreciate a confidential intimation of the character and purpose of the response that will be made, and will itself presently have certain very earnest representations to make on behalf of the manifest interests of neutral nations and of humanity itself to which it will ask that very serious consideration be given. It does not make these representations now because it does not wish to connect them with the proposed overtures, or have them construed in any way as an attempt at mediation, notwithstanding the fact that these overtures afford an admirable occasion for their consideration. The Government of the United States had it in mind to make them entirely on its own initiative and before it had any knowledge of the present attitude or suggestions of the Central Governments. It will make the same representations to the governments of the Central Powers and wishes to make them almost immediately, if necessary, but not as associated with the overtures of either group of belligerents. The present overtures have created an unexpected opportunity for looking at the world's case as a whole, but the United States would have itself created the occasion had it fallen out otherwise.

Same telegram to Paris, Petrograd, Rome, Tokio, Havre, Bucharest and Belgrade.

T telegram (R. Lansing Papers, NjP).
[1] The following telegram is printed in *FR-WWS 1916*, pp. 94-95.

From Edward Nash Hurley

Dear Mr. President: Washington December 16, 1916.

In response to the suggestion that more details would be desirable in connection with *the plan to apply cost accounting to the large problems now facing the Government,* I desire to submit to you the following:

There is now before the Appropriations Committee of the House an estimate of $100,000 for the extension of the cost accounting system under the supervision of the Federal Trade Commission.

This relatively insignificant item, if made secure by a personal recommendation from you and accompanied by educational processes, would be virtually all that would be necessary to carry out the effective program for the solution of the major portion of our industrial problems, which you have outlined in several of your public addresses.

The program to which I refer is the accommodation of the large differences between capital and labor; the steady growth of the cost of living; and the economic struggle which probably will be the aftermath of the European war.

The practical remedies which I believe can be specifically applied, and which will be set forth definitely and concisely later on, were suggested, if I may be permitted to say so, by several of your addresses prior to the election. Before setting forth these practical remedies, however, it is necessary to call attention to the fact that just as most differences of opinion are due to vague definitions, so most economic differences are due to conflicting data or insufficient facts.

Ninety per cent of the manufacturers of the United States do not know what it costs them to produce their goods.

Seventy per cent of the commercial paper of the United States is accepted by banks without any request for a statement as to what that paper represents. The commercial paper is accepted, in other words, from a business man who does not himself know whether his business is profitable or unprofitable. And the United States Government is issuing currency based on that sort of commercial paper.

Ninety per cent of the manufacturers in Germany know precisely what it costs them to produce their goods.

There is not a bank in Germany that does not insist on assuring itself of the efficiency and economical operation of a business firm before lending money.

Where an American manufacturer, no matter how efficient otherwise, is without an accurate cost accounting system which reveals automatically what products are profitable and what products are not profitable, and where waste and duplication exist, the inevitable result is that he arbitrarily bases his prices on the prices fixed by his competitors. Yet the competitors may be incompentent, wasteful, and tending swiftly and surely towards bankruptcy, selling actually below cost. The result is that there are two failures where there should have been one.

This is one of the individual effects of such lack of information. The larger effect is that upon the consumer. The consumer pays for all the waste due to the failure to keep an accurate record of costs. He pays for the inefficient system. He does not get the benefit of moderate prices, based upon economical manufacture plus a reasonable profit.

If we had cost accounting, as a sound foundation for all American business, fixed as a prerequisite by the Federal Trade Commission in adjusting unfair trade practices; by the Federal Reserve Board with reference to the kind of paper that should be accepted by the banks; by the new Tariff Commission when appeals for modification of tariff rates are made; and by whatever cooperative associations may be created under the pending Webb bill, we would be taking an important step toward an effective, systematic handling of the problem of the high cost of living. With such a system in general operation, it would be possible to ascertain at any given moment whether the producer, middleman or retailer was charging the exorbitant profits. We know the wide difference between the producer's price and the price paid by the ultimate consumer. We do not know where the bulk of the money goes because we have no national records of costs for any industry or business.

At tariff hearings, one manufacturer has said that it costs him $10 to produce a given article; another says it costs him $12 to produce the same article; another fixes his cost at $14. In the past we have given protection to safeguard the interest of the man whom it costs $14. Yet it has not been possible for any committee of Congress—and it will not be possible for the Tariff Commission—to call for the accounting sheets. There are no such sheets kept in a uniform manner.

When the suggestion is made that employers should get closer to their employees, and make their interests identical by pension-retirement or stock-ownership plans, whereby the employees would become stockholders, the objection is usually raised that the employer can not afford to put such a plan into operation. As a matter of fact, he does not know whether without a loss to himself he can afford to install a system of mutual cooperation between himself and his employees. What he needs is an accurate cost accounting system.

Such a cost accounting system encourages and takes care of the stock-ownership, pension, and other plans for bringing the employee into the partnership. It is all figured as part of the cost of production which the cost accounting system automatically will make economical. Every humane move made by a firm will be covered by the books. If humane legislation costs an American manufacturer anything, it will appear on his cost sheets. Whatever tariff schedules are then revised, will be revised upon the actual cost of production, and there will be a definite method of determining whether the cost of production is higher here, rightfully because of better working and living conditions, or whether solely because of inefficiency and waste.

The man with the accurate cost sheets will be able to obtain larger credits from the banks than his inefficient competitors.

It is a large problem—too large to be dealt with in such short space—but I trust I have made clear how national cost accounting, worked into the whole business and financial fabric, by the Trade Commission, the Tariff Commission, the Federal Reserve Board, and by whatever associations may be created under the Webb bill, will make the whole nation more economical and efficient. For the inauguration of this program, I believe very little need be done. What has already been done, and what should now be done, can be stated briefly as follows:

Arrangements have already been made by the Federal Trade Commission with the Institute of Public Accountants to approve of a uniform set of rules along the lines of which chartered accountants henceforth should make their reports.

I have personally taken up with the members of the Federal Reserve Board, in an informal manner, the question of having the Federal Reserve Board, as well as the Federal Trade Commission, give approval to these rules.

If the plan receives the educational impetus that would be given to it by any public comment from the President, I feel sure the Federal Reserve Board will go further and make some requirements for cost accounting before commercial paper is accepted. That, however, can wait until the more necessary immediate steps are taken.

The Tariff Commission, if the matter is brought to its attention, may establish cost accounting as a prerequisite in all tariff hearings. This could be brought about by informal suggestion from the President when the commission is being organized.

Aside from these informal suggestions from the President, and any reference that might be made to Congress, thus attracting the attention of business, I believe that the only definite step necessary to put the program into execution is to induce Congress to make the appropriation of $100,000 with which the Federal Trade Commission at once can divide the country into zones, placing in each zone cost accounting experts to educate the business men as to the need of better business methods.

Upon this first step, the others will follow normally and without legislative expedients.

The Federal Trade Commission received for the present fiscal year an appropriation of $390,000. Of that amount the bulk was spent on economic investigations and legal proceedings necessary for the adjustment of trade discrimination and unfair practices. Only $10,000 of it was available for what I consider the most necessary and constructive work—the establishment of a cost accounting system as a permanent foundation for prosperity, national economy, efficient industry and the mutuality of interest between capital and labor.

If you give your approval to the plan I have outlined, I believe it will be wholly practicable to invite the cooperation of the business men of the country, and persuade them to install cost accounting systems, by working with their own associations and the Government.

It will be possible through Government agencies, and with the cooperation of business men, to gather complete information about business. There is at present no information available regarding the costs in any industry; nothing that can be given out by the Federal Trade Commission in response to the many demands for such information from manufacturers who desire information as to the conditions under which their industry, as a whole, is operating. Government should assist in making business intelligent.

With the appropriation available, all this necessary work for the improvement of business and manufacturing methods can be undertaken; American business will know where it stands and what it must do; and there will be a sound foundation for economy, efficiency, and national unity and cooperation, in which labor will work in greater harmony with capital because, among other things, labor will know what share it is getting, and should have.

If an announcement could be made by you that this program is to be undertaken, in connection with a recommendation for the appropriation of the $100,000 needed for the extension of the cost accounting system, I believe that would be all that would be needed to launch the plan. I believe the program is constructive, and I know, from the countless requests we are receiving from small business men for the accounting system, that the business world will welcome it. Big business is already highly organized; a bare score out of 250,000 commercial corporations are handling the bulk of the foreign trade. Cost accounting will bring the benefits of efficiency to the smaller manufacturers and business men and make the nation, commercially and financially, indomitable.

As showing the vital relation which national cost accounting holds to the solution of the problems of labor and capital, I am taking the liberty to send you herewith a copy of a short address which I made recently before representatives of both labor and capital in the garment business in New York. It points the way to an intelligent distribution of the product, and that, after all, is the end sought by all who seek to mediate between labor and capital.   Sincerely yours,   Edward N. Hurley

TLS (WP, DLC).

From Winthrop More Daniels

My dear Mr. President: Washington 16 Dec. 1916.
    Your renomination of me to succeed myself in the Interstate Commerce Commission pleases me not least in that I interpret it as an approval of my work for the last three years. I said the other night to Mr. Tumulty that I felt more confident of your approval than I did of some of our Senatorial friends. But I am not disposed to borrow trouble, and trust they will not be disposed to interpose any unreasonable obstacle to confirmation. In case they should, and any embarrassment to you is caused thereby, you will not hesitate, I trust, to withdraw the nomination. The work is engrossing in interest, but I have always felt that release from the constant drive of it would be a solid consolation, if for any reason, I had to discontinue it. From my experience in public service, I wonder often that so many covet high administrative positions. The more one gets into it however, the more disposed he becomes, as Brackett[1] used to say, "to live with a vengeance and die with a *jerk!*" I am sure you will believe how very deeply I appreciate your implied approval and how earnestly I hope to continue to deserve it. I am, with truest regard,
                    Very Sincerely,   W. M. Daniels.

ALS (WP, DLC).
    [1] Cyrus Fogg Brackett, late Joseph Henry Professor of Physics at Princeton University.

To Robert Lansing, with Enclosure

The White House
My dear Mr. Secretary,   17 December, 1916.

Here is the note we promised to send and which I think it highly necessary to send at once before it be too late to inject new elements into the debate now going on among the nations at war.

I append to the paper itself certain memoranda on a separate sheet which will speak for themselves.

I would be very much obliged if you would as early as possible make any comments upon the matter or manner of the paper which may occur to you, in order that we may get the message off at the earliest possible moment.

Have you any special instructions to suggest to Page in London to make him realize what is expected of him?

Faithfully Yours,   W.W.

WWTLI (WP, DLC).

E N C L O S U R E

INSTRUCTIONS.

The President directs me to send you the following communication to be presented immediately to the Secretary of State for Foreign Affairs—the Minister of Foreign Affairs and he requests that you present it with the utmost earnestness of support. He wishes the impression clearly conveyed that it would be very hard for the Government of the United States to understand a negative reply. After yourself reading it to the Secretary of State for Foreign Affairs—the Minister of Foreign Affairs and making the oral representations suggested please leave a copy of this paper with him.[1]

The President of the United States has instructed me to suggest to His Majesty's Government or, etc., substituting the name of the particular government addressed a course of action with regard to the present war which he hopes that His Majesty's Government or the government addressed will take under consideration as coming from a friend not only, and suggested in the most friendly spirit, but also as coming from the representative of a neutral nation whose interests have been most seriously affected by the war and whose concern for its early conclusion arises out of a manifest necessity to determine how best to safeguard those interests if the war is to continue.

The suggestion I am instructed to make has long been in the mind of the President to offer. He is somewhat embarrassed to offer it at this particular time because it may now seem to have been prompted by the recent German overtures. It is in fact in no way associated with them in its origin and the President would have delayed offering it until the German overture had been answered but for the fact that it also concerns the question of peace and may best be considered in connection with other proposals which have the same end in view. The President can only beg that his suggestion be considered as entirely on its own merits as if it had been made in other circumstances.

The President suggests that an early occasion be sought to call out from all the nations now at war a frank comparison of views as to the terms upon which the war might be concluded and the arrangements which would be deemed satisfactory as constituting a guarantee against its renewal or the kindling of any similar conflict in the future. He is indifferent as to the means taken to accomplish this. He would be happy himself to serve in its accomplishment in any way that might prove acceptable, but he has no desire to determine the method or the instrumentality. One way will be as acceptable to him as another, if only the great object he has in mind be attained.

He takes the liberty of calling attention to the fact that the objects which the statesmen of the belligerents on both sides have in mind in this war are virtually the same, as stated in general terms to their own people and to the world. Each side desires to make the rights and privileges of weak peoples and small states as secure against aggression or denial in the future as the rights and privileges of the great and powerful states now at war. Each wishes itself to be made secure in the future, along with all other nations and peoples, against the recurrence of wars like this, and against aggression or selfish interference of any kind. Each would be jealous of the formation of any more rival leagues to preserve an uncertain balance of power amidst multiplying suspicions; but each is ready to consider the formation of a league of nations to enforce peace and justice throughout the world. Before that final step can be taken, however, each deems it necessary first to settle the issues of the present war upon terms which will certainly safeguard the independence, the territorial integrity, and the political and commercial freedom of the nations involved.

In the measures to be taken to secure the future peace of the world the people and government of the United States are as vitally and as directly interested as the governments now at war. Their interest, moreover, in the means to be adopted to relieve the smaller and weaker peoples of the world of the peril of wrong and violence is as quick and ardent as that of any other people or government in the world. They stand ready, and even eager, to cooperate in the accomplishment of these ends when the war is over with every influence and resource at their command. But the war must first be concluded. The terms upon which it is to be concluded they are not at liberty to suggest; but the President does feel that it is his right and his duty to point out their intimate interest in its conclusion, lest it should presently be too late to accomplish the greater things which lie beyond its conclusion, lest the situation of neutral nations, now exceedingly hard to endure, be rendered altogether intolerable, and lest, more than all, an injury be done civilization itself which can never be atoned for or repaired.

The President, therefore, feels altogether justified in suggesting an immediate comparison of views as to the terms which must precede those ultimate arrangements for the peace of the world which all desire and in which the neutral nations as well as those at war are ready to play their full responsible part. If the contest must continue to proceed towards undefined ends by slow attrition until the one group of belligerents or the other is exhausted, if million after million of human lives must continue to be offered up until on the one side or the other there are no more to offer, if resentments must be kindled that can never cool and despairs engendered from which there can be no recovery, hopes of peace and of the willing concert of free peoples will be rendered vain and idle.

The life of the entire world has been profoundly affected. Every part of the great family of mankind has felt the burden and terror of this unprecedented contest of arms. No nation in the civilized world can be said in truth to stand outside its influence or to be safe against its disturbing effects. And yet the concrete objects for which it is being waged have never been definitively stated.

The leaders of the several belligerents have, it is true, stated those objects in general terms. But, stated in general terms, they seem the same on both sides. Never yet have the authoritative spokesmen of either side avowed the precise objects which would, if attained, satisfy them and their people that the war had been fought out. The world has been left to conjecture what definitive results, what actual exchange of guarantees, what political or territorial changes or readjustments, what stage of military success even, would bring the war to an end.

It may be that peace is nearer than we know; that the terms

which the belligerents on the one side and on the other would deem it necessary to insist upon are not so irreconcilable as we have feared: that an interchange of views would clear the way at least for conference and make the permanent concord of the nations a hope of the immediate future, a concert of nations immediately practicable.

The President is not proposing peace; he is not even offering intervention. He is merely proposing that soundings be taken in order that we may learn, the neutral nations with the belligerent, how near the haven of peace may be for which all mankind longs with an infinite and increasing longing. He believes that the spirit in which he speaks and the objects which he seeks will be understood by all concerned, and he confidently hopes for a response which will bring a new light into the affairs of the world.

MEM. ONE

This to be sent to each of the belligerent governments on both sides, and also to the neutral nations for their information.

MEM. TWO

In the copy sent to the Central powers the first two sentences on page *two* to be altered as follows: He is somewhat embarrassed to offer it at this particular time because it may now seem to have been prompted by a desire to play a part in connection with the recent overtures of the Central Powers. It has in fact been in no way suggested by them in its origin and the President would have delayed offering it until those overtures had been independently answered but for the fact,—etc., etc.

WWT MS (WP, DLC).
    ¹ Wilson retyped this paragraph after reading Lansing's following letter and memorandum. Wilson then pasted the new paragraph on the first page.

From Robert Lansing, with Enclosure

My dear Mr. President,   Washington December 17, 1916.

In returning to you this draft of instructions I wish to say that I consider the document a most excellent one and far superior to the one which you previously drafted. It is much more logical and direct and in presentation is much more forceful and convincing. I think too that you have eliminated the expressions which I feared would cause offense among some of the belligerents, particularly among the Entente Powers which are especially sensitive—unreasonably so—but which on account of this must be handled gently if the purpose of the communication is to be attained.

If I were to make a general criticism I would say that possibly the dire effects of the war on the interests of this country as a neutral are not emphasized quite enough to impress the belligerents with the fact that we can no longer submit to having our people deprived of their rights on the plea that belligerent necessity compels such deprivation. I have read and reread the draft but do not find a suitable place to insert this thought without destroying the harmony of treatment. Probably it cannot be incorporated but I thought you were entitled to have every possible suggestion.

As to the comments and suggestions enclosed I hope that you will understand that I have written them with great frankness because I was sure you would wish it. You possibly may think I am a purist in certain suggested changes of language, and probably I am, but I felt that this will be read some day as one of the greatest state papers ever produced and that therefore every word and every sentence ought to be critically considered. I have attempted to do this. I do not think in view of the superior importance of this paper that too much care can be expended in weighing the exact meaning of each expression and the possible interpretations to which it is open not only in English but also when translated into a foreign tongue.

I do not think that anything can be added to the instruction to Page in London. It is explicit and shows very clearly what is expected of him. I do not think that he will say anything to moderate the effect because I do not see what he can say. He will see, I am sure, that you are in downright earnest.

Faithfully yours   Robert Lansing.

ALS (WP, DLC).

E N C L O S U R E

December 17, 1916
Robert Lansing.
The lines on each page of the
draft are separately numbered.

Page 1   COMMENTS AND SUGGESTIONS

Lines 1-3.   Substitute— "The President directs me to send you the following communication to be presented immediately to the Secretary of State for Foreign Affairs (the Minister of Foreign Affairs) and he requests that you present it with the utmost earnestness of support"

Line 4.   After the word "impression" insert "clearly."

Line 10.   In place of "the Foreign Office" read "him."

Lines 17-19.   Read "will take under consideration as suggested in the most friendly spirit and as coming not only from a friend but also coming from—"

Line 26.   Read "The suggestion which I am instructed to make—," and strike out "it" at the end of the line.

Page 2.

Line 4.   In place of "German overtures" read "overtures of the Central Powers."

Line 7.   In place of "the German overture" read "these overtures."

Line 12.   Strike out the first "as" in the line and insert the word "and" after the word "merits."

Lines 15-16.   The expression "to call out—a frank comparison" I do not quite comprehend. Does it mean frank statements by all the nations at war as to the terms &c which could be compared? Or does it mean a frank exchange of views between the belligerents as to terms? I think the latter meaning would be unfortunate but assume that it carries the former meaning and would suggest that the lines read "to call forth from all the nations now at war in order that they may be frankly compared their respective views as to the terms—."

Page 3.

Line 11.   In place of "this" read "the present one."

Line 17.   In place of the word "enforce" I would suggest "insure" in order that we may not be charged with assuming a too definite commitment by the belligerents on this subject.

Page 4.

Lines 5-7.   Read "to cooperate when the war is over with every influence and resource at their command in the accomplishment of these ends."

Line 20.   Read "justified in suggesting an immediate opportunity for the comparison—" I am a little doubtful as to the exact meaning as stated in my comment on Lines 15-16 on Page 2, and therefore make this suggested reading with hesitation.

Page 5.

Line 18.   In place of "it is true" read "as has been said." See Lines 3-4 on Page 3.

Page 6.

Lines 3-4.   In place of "as we have feared" read "as might be
                concluded from the course of events" or some other
                sentance (this is not a good one) which removes the
                idea that we fear or have feared that the terms of the
                belligerents cannot be reconciled.

Line 10.   Would it not be well to use "mediation" in place
                of "intervention," since the latter word might be con-
                strued as a threat of interference with force?

Lines 12-13.   Ought not "belligerent" to be plural?

Line 14.   "Infinite and increasing." I only raise the ques-
                tion as to whether an *infinite* longing can also be an
                increasing longing. Infinity conveys to me the idea of
                being beyond increase.

HwS MS (WP, DLC).

From Edward Mandell House

Dear Governor: New York. December 17, 1916.

The British Ambassador has sent Sir William Wiseman of
the Embassy[1] to see me.

He suggested that I find out unofficially Germany's terms.
This, I told him, could not be done before Friday or Saturday
since I was sure that Bernstorff did not know them. That what
Bernstorff had was what his Government had given him for
public consumption, and they were not intrusting him with what
they really had in mind.

The British Embassy is cabling their Government today asking
whether or not it would be possible for the Prime Minister to
delay his answer until Friday or Saturday, telling them of their
conversation with me and what is planned. They expect an
answer by tomorrow afternoon at five o'clock.

If it is favorable, I am to get in touch with Bernstorff and see
what can be done there.

It looks as if you might soon be having the belligerents talking
—at least there is hope.

I am writing in great haste because of the lateness of the hour.
Will you not advise me promptly by telegraphic code, or letter,
if you have anything further to suggest?

                        Your affectionate,   E. M. House

TLS (WP, DLC).

[1] Captain Sir William George Eden Wiseman, formerly an artillery officer
in the British army, at this time nominally a member of the purchasing commission of the Ministry of Munitions, in fact the head of British counterin-

telligence operations in the United States. He was soon to become a very important informal liaison between House and Wilson and the Foreign Office and other agencies of the British government. See Wilton B. Fowler, *British-American Relations, 1917-1918: The Role of Sir William Wiseman* (Princeton, N. J., 1969), pp. 8-19, and Arthur Willert, *The Road to Safety: A Study in Anglo-American Relations* (London, 1952), pp. 15-27, 61-62.

From Franklin Knight Lane

My dear Mr. President: Washington December 17, 1916.

Governor Kendrick,[1] the newly-elected Senator from Wyoming, came to see me yesterday, and as I am going away I wish to report to you what he said. He opened by saying:

"I am the largest stock raiser in my part of the country, and have made my fortune out of raising stock upon the public domain. I wanted to see the President upon this matter and sought an interview which I could not obtain excepting on Saturday afternoon, when I was going down the river with Mr. Daniels at his request, primarily for the purpose of talking over some matters which he was interested in.

"I am a member of the National Live Stock Growers Association and I find the hotels here filled with members of that association who are assiduously carrying on a lobby against the 640-acre homestead bill. That bill will put me out of business, probably, and if it does the country will be better off, for it is better to have many people with small ranches than one man or a few men with large ranches. The country gets more beef as the result. They have tried to get me to oppose the bill. On the contrary, I have gone to Mr. Ferris and advocated the measure, not only because I think that it will build up our state in population but because it will increase the nation's food supply. The Live Stock men have suggested to me that it would give opportunity for blackmailing them. I take no stock in this idea. Whatever interferes with the Live Stock man's free use of public lands he is opposed to, and he conjures bugaboos to scare Congress. In Western Nebraska, with which I am familiar, the 640-acre homestead has worked well. There are many more cattle on the land than there were before it was divided.

"I wanted the President to know this, and so I am telling it to you."   Faithfully yours,   Franklin K Lane

TLS (WP, DLC).
[1] John Benjamin Kendrick, Democrat.

Remarks at a Press Conference

December 18, 1916

It is understood that nothing that I say shall be quoted outside. And I want to say another thing. There are some things that I ought not to discuss just now, and if I decline to discuss them, I beg that you won't draw the inference that I am trying to hold something back. It won't be for that reason. It will be merely for this, that anything that is said now will lead to speculation, and there ought not to be speculation. That will be my only motive. I won't hold anything back because sometimes, when a man declines to discuss a thing, the inference is drawn that he would rather not discuss it for some reason that he doesn't want to explain. For example, these peace negotiations. And I judge that it is a source of irritation on the part of the belligerents to have foreign nations discussing whether they will come in and tell them how to settle their own affairs or not, and, therefore, the discussion back and forth, whether they will or won't, is disadvantageous to the thing that we all ought to serve with every devotion that is in us, and that is the peace of the world. It is inconceivable that we should put any slightest grain of difficulty in the way of arriving at some basis of peace. And, therefore, since the Government of the United States is doing nothing, I think perhaps it is best not to discuss whether it is going to do anything or not.

Mr. President, to start with a harmless topic, what is the status of this cost of living investigation?

I haven't followed it the last half week, and I dare say you know about as well as I do. We are pushing it along every channel that is open to us under federal law. You, of course, understand that, so far as the Department of Justice is concerned, the difficulty is that the only thing we can attack men for is combinations affecting interstate commerce, and it is precious hard to prove that, in many instances. But the investigation itself, I think, is helping and is helping clear up a great many of the details.

Mr. President, as a result of the difficulties that exist, is it likely that any additional legislation will be asked for?

It is possible, but, you see, Congress, in any case, would have to keep within the limits of its power, and it has no power over any trade that is not interstate.

There is a bill that has been introduced by Mr. Fitzgerald that limits the holdings of cold storage companies by seeking to prohibit the interstate transportation facilities to companies that violate these provisions.

> That hasn't been brought to my attention. We tried the regulation of cold storage in New Jersey by state legislation, and, while we accomplished something, I must say we didn't accomplish enough to be very encouraging.

Mr. President, are there any other bills which have been introduced which have your approval, which you are looking over?

> None that I have any knowledge of.

Mr. President, there is a good deal of interest now in this public buildings bill in view of Secretary McAdoo's warning regarding the condition of the Treasury, and attracted particularly to the public buildings legislation. Has that matter been brought to your attention, this specific bill, providing for thirty-eight million or thirty-nine mililon dollars?

> Yes, it has, by the Treasury Department.

Is there anything you could say on it with regard to expressing your opinion?

> No, I will have to reserve what I have to say until it gets here.

Mr. President, it is reported that the brotherhood men and the railroad managers are about to come to an understanding with regard to the Adamson Act. Will that in any way affect the need of action on the railroad program at this session which you submitted?

> I don't think so.

You think that that program will be carried out at this session of Congress?

> Yes, I think it will.

Does the request of the Newlands Commission for an extension of time in any way affect that possibility?

> Oh, no. That request was made merely because Senator Newlands wanted to release himself and other members of the committees of both houses to give their entire time to this legislation. You see, the Congress had set a limit of time on them, had set a date by which they would report.

Yes. The eighth of January.

> And they can't get through their investigation and, at the same time, to release members [blank]

There is no need of Congress waiting for a report of this committee before acting on the program submitted?

> Oh, no, because the program submitted has nothing to do with the subject matter of that investigation.

Of course this is a hypothetical-type question, but, if this program would fail, do you think an extra session would be essential?

I don't know. It would depend upon how much it failed. I can't imagine its failing. If it failed, it would be for lack of time.

Mr. President, have you any idea when they are going to pay attention to this—your recommendations in Congress?

They will pay attention to those now in the committees. The bad part is starting at the Senate end, because the pending part was at the Senate end—the bill to increase the Interstate Commerce Commission—and, therefore, that seemed the natural end for it to begin at. That is the only reason why the House committees have not taken it up, I understand.

Have these labor leaders said anything to you in regard to their attitude?

I haven't seen them since I got back except just to shake hands.

I thought you had seen Mr. Gompers?

Oh, I did see Mr. Gompers, but he didn't say anything about that. I thought you meant the brotherhood men.

The American Federation of Labor seems to be just as much interested as the brotherhoods in the matter of compulsory investigations?

Yes, they do seem to be, very naturally, because the principle of it might be adopted in other legislation, though Congress has very little to do with most of the elements that the Federation of Labor deals with, because their activities are local and not interstate. You see, this legislation of Congress is specifically limited to those employees of the railroads that are actually engaged in the running of trains in interstate transportation.

It has been stated, Mr. President, from time to time, that you are in favor of this proposal to federalize more effectively the control of the railroads. Have you expressed any opinion on that subject?

No, I haven't, because I was waiting for the conclusions of that investigation. I don't know enough about it.

The proposition seems to be, as presented by the commission now, that they can't conclude their investigation in a proper way unless they are allowed an extension of time.

Well, I dare say that is true also, but that is not because the subject matter is shifting in any way. I mean because that isn't because the field of inquiry is being enlarged or altered. It is merely because of want of time.

Mr. President, has either side brought to your attention this settlement of the Adamson Act out of court—by an agreement among themselves?

No. We can't settle our part of it out of court.

Mr. President, about two or three weeks ago *Sea Power*, which is the organ of the Navy League, said it had reason to believe that you were in favor of universal military training, and we have never been able to find out whether you were or not.

Well, some of the gentlemen who represent the navy, particularly the retired officers of it, know a great deal that is not so. They are very accomplished in that. I haven't expressed any opinion on that at all.

Would you care to say anything at all? I am making a distinction between universal training and universal service.

No, because in that case, as in every similar case, my attitude would be entirely dependent on the plans. The idea is easy enough, and it is attractive enough, but how it is to be done is the essential matter. It is the way I feel about every big public question—I want to see the bill before I form an opinion.

That is implied in a measure in the Chamberlain bill.[1]

Yes, in a measure, but it is not thoroughly worked out.

Mr. President, has the immigration bill reached you?[2]

No. Has it passed?

It passed both houses this morning by a two-thirds vote.[3] Would that influence your action on it?

[1] Senator George Earle Chamberlain had introduced on December 13, 1915, a bill (S. 1695) "to provide for the military and naval training of the citizen forces of the United States." Based upon Swiss and Australian models, the bill provided that all able-bodied males should receive occasional military training between the ages of twelve and twenty-three, beginning with a Citizen Cadet Corps and ending in a Citizen Army or Citizen Navy. Since the spring of 1916, the bill had been in metamorphosis in accordance with the advice of various military experts and civilian preparedness groups. The final result, reported to the Senate by Chamberlain, the chairman of the Committee on Military Affairs, on February 10, 1917, was a very different bill. It called for six months of intensive training for all able-bodied males age nineteen, followed by membership in a Reserve Citizen Army or a Reserve Citizen Navy until the age of twenty-eight. A Senate subcommittee, headed by Chamberlain, was holding public hearings on the measure at this time; General Leonard Wood testified in favor of the bill on December 18. For a careful analysis of the original Chamberlain bill, see "To Raise Every Boy to Be a Soldier," *New York Times*, Dec. 26, 1915, Sect. IV. For the final form of the measure, see 64th Cong., 2d sess., Senate Report No. 1024. See also John Garry Clifford, *The Citizen Soldiers: The Plattsburg Training Camp Movement, 1913-1920* (Lexington, Ky., 1972), pp. 203-14, and John Patrick Finnegan, *Against the Specter of a Dragon: The Campaign for American Military Preparedness, 1914-1917* (Westport, Conn., 1974), pp. 112-13, 179-83.

[2] A revised version of the Burnett bill which Wilson had vetoed in 1915 (see WW to the House of Representatives, Jan. 28, 1915, Vol. 32).

[3] The new version of the Burnett bill had passed the House of Representatives on March 30, 1916, by a vote of 307 to eighty-seven. A slightly different version passed the Senate on December 14 by a vote of sixty-four to seven. Both bills were now in a conference committee, and the two houses took no further action upon them until January 8, 1917.

Better wait and see. I didn't know that it had passed, to tell you the truth.

Mr. President, with regard to this matter of universal military training, have you been urged recently to take some measures with reference to the federalized militia? Have you been told that it was a failure, or asked to take up the question with that in mind?

> I have heard a great many men say very loudly that it was a failure, but they are the same men who said it was a failure before it was tried. It hasn't been thoroughly tried out yet by any means.

Mr. President, do the amendments of the Senate, put in the immigration bill with regard to the literacy test and legal offenders, meet with your approval?

> I don't know what they are. What were they?

Yes, sir, the literacy test is amended so as to permit those that are religiously persecuted and political offenders to be exempted from the literacy test.

> Let in whether they could read or write?

Yes, sir.

> That is interesting! Well, I have several times pointed out the difficulty about exempting from the literacy test those who have been subject to religious persecution. It throws on the United States Government the very unpleasant and invidious task of determining which governments have been guilty of religious persecution. It is a very delicate thing to undertake.

Mr. President, is it your intention to make any further recommendations to Congress with reference to legislation that may be required to meet conditions that will arise after the war?

> No, sir. We have got the instrumentalities created now that are intended to assess those changes as they take place, which is as it should be, and, until they are assessed, I don't see that we know our ground well enough. Had you something special in mind?

Oh, no. Naturally, the tariff and the progress in the Congress on action with regard to the Webb bill.

> But I thought that the country, for the time being, had got the tariff off its mind. I am going to urge the passage of the Webb bill. I have already done that. I though you meant something in addition.

Oh, no.

One thing that is interesting, Mr. President, is Mr. Hurley's suggestion about the cost accounting system. I wondered whether that had come before you or not?

> Suggestion about legislation about it?

He wanted that generally discussed from a larger approach—greater extended Trade Commission service in the matter.

> That is a matter of appropriation, not legislation. There is not any legislation that could oblige the adoption of a cost accounting system.

Mr. President, in this connection, when may we expect an announcement on the Tariff Commission?

> Why, I am pretty nearly ready, but one man has eluded me and I am looking for a man.

Does the same apply to the shipping board?

> Yes. There, I am one man shy, too.

Mr. President, when you speak of instrumentalities, do you mean the Tariff Commission as one of them?

> I mean that, so far as legislation is concerned, we are supplied with instrumentalities.

Mr. President, have the conferees on the water power bill communicated with you as to any plan as to working out the bill?

> I have had one conference with a group of them, and incidental talks with individuals about it. I think they are going to work something out. That is my present impression.

You haven't gotten any impression [blank]

> No, I haven't, because the conferees didn't indicate.

Mr. President, have you taken any position on Senator Owen's bill or any other bill with regard to the expenditures of campaign funds?

> No, I haven't.

Mr. President, nobody has mentioned Mexico.

> No. We wouldn't be at home if they didn't.

Will you tell us something about that situation?

> I dare say that you know as much as I do. I merely know that the commissioners will meet again to receive the suggestions, I would call them, with which Mr. Pani has returned, and I haven't yet learned what those suggestions are.

Mr. President, Mr. Fitzgerald on Saturday said there would be a deficit of $300,000,000. Have you any views as to revenue measures?

> Mr. Fitzgerald didn't just discover that, did he? That had been discovered sometime before. That of course, is for the fiscal year 1918, not for the present fiscal year.

Mr. President, just about the time that the general revenue law was being passed by the Senate, Mr. Simmons read a statement from the Treasury Department to the effect that it would cost, I think, $130,000,000 to pay the expenses of the Mexican trouble that—

You mean of the border patrol?

Yes.

And if that trouble, with the necessity of keeping those troops there, continues after January first, it would cost us another $86,000,000. Now, I said that this new revenue measure wouldn't provide for raising revenue to meet those expenses, as I would call it. The Treasury Department suggested that we would have to issue bonds.

Now that we are getting very near to the first of January, I wonder if anything had been done in connection with meeting those expenses?

We are all right until the end of the present fiscal year.

Until next July?

Oh, yes. There is plenty of margin until then.

Yes, sir. I understood that we were getting sufficient revenues, but it was my impression that we would have to make up those revenues in some way.

I can't answer that as clearly as I would like to. I don't think so. I think the whole difficulty is for the succeeding year, when there will be very much of an increase in the expenditures on the preparedness program, as well as a possibility of continuing this large expense on the border. Of course, in that case, that would have to be met and added as unusual expense.

Won't it be necessary to meet that at this session, Mr. President.

It will be necessary to provide by legislation as to how it will be met, certainly—how it is to be met by revenue arrangements after the first of July.

You don't mean raising any additional revenues?

They will have to provide for raising additional revenue, yes.

Well, just now we are getting enough revenue to meet current expenses.

Yes, and expenses that are enacted—that are provided by statute during the present fiscal year.

Hasn't the Secretary of the Treasury reported that June 1917 will show a surplus of $105,000,000 in the present fund?

At the present rate, yes. In the year later, there will be a deficit, according to his figures, of $135,000,000, but that

has been increased by various means that have been arranged, until some people estimate it at $300,000,000.

Will this Congress have to make provision to guard against that
deficit?

It will have to make provision to increase the revenues in
an arithmetical proportion as they go along.

Mr. President, as I recall, the Secretary of the Treasury, he has
reported—he said that that $115,000,000 did not take into con-
sideration a continuation of the troops on the border after December 31, 1916.

No, it doesn't, but it takes in this calendar year.

Do you not hold that additional taxes will have to be levied at
this session of Congress?

I am talking about—I am going on scraps of paper. I have not
heard from the Secretary of the Treasury, and I ought not
to consider it because I don't know enough about it. I don't
know when the legislation to meet the deficit will have to be
enacted. My impression is that part of it, at any rate, will
be proposed at this session.

Then there is no comprehensive program as yet, regarding the
raising of this revenue?

No. There have been a great many suggestions. That was
one of the things we were discussing in cabinet, not because
it is our business to suggest it, but we wanted, if called on,
to know just what we thought it was wise to suggest.

Do you think, Mr. President, the Tariff Commission will be able
to make any report so as you could take action in that regard?
Will they be ready to do that?

I shouldn't think so.

Mr. President, last session you went before Congress and outlined
what you thought ought to be done to raise revenue. If you do
arrive at the point where you think it is necessary, will you go
before Congress to make a similar suggestion?

Whenever I have anything to say, I will go.

Mr. President, it has been suggested that bonds be sold. Could
you tell us your attitude on that question?

That depends entirely on the particular circumstances. My
general attitude is that it is bad finance to issue bonds
for permanent expenses, that the only excuse for bonds are
extraordinary and temporary expenses. You see, that was
the idea that Congress had in mind when it authorized
the Panama bonds—that we were not going to build canals
all our life. That was a temporary and extraordinary thing
and, therefore, we were providing for the expense of that
canal over and above what we could not appropriate, by

bonds. That illustrates the principle I have in mind. If it is clearly temporary and something one generation ought not to be made to pay for, I think it is legitimate to issue bonds. But I don't think it is wise to issue bonds for permanent expenses when a nation can pay the bill, as we undoubtedly can.

Will the expenses of the border patrol be considered in that light? Extraordinary or temporary?

I don't know yet whether it is going to be permanent or temporary.

Mr. President, this question of a nitrate plant, this is being held up now until we hear from these experts?

It isn't exactly being held up. We are waiting for the necessary information.

Senator Smith of South Carolina was over to see you, I think, about a place on the Savannah River.

Yes. It would be hard to miss a senator who hasn't been.

Mr. President, some of us are interested in the appointment of a postmaster in New York. Can you tell us anything about that?

I can't.

Anything on the half holiday, Mr. President?

No, sir. I am looking for one myself. You see, it doesn't seem all the departments [blank] . . .

Mr. President, there is a lot of talk about the result of the sinking of the *Marina* and *Arabia*. Could you give us anything you know on that?

No, sir, because we haven't yet settled the question of fact.

JRT transcript (WC, NjP) of CLSsh (C. L. Swem Coll., NjP).

To Robert Lansing

The White House.

My dear Mr. Secretary,   18 December, 1916.

Thank you for your note and for your comments. You will see that I have adopted almost all of your suggested changes.[1]

I felt the omission of which you speak (the omission to dwell on the things the United States has suffered in consequence of this war) but, like you, saw no logical place to bring them in without breaking the course of the argument.

Will you not be kind enough to see that this is coded and despatched at once, with the utmost possible privacy, and that as fast as possible (as nearly synchronously as possible) it be sent to all the governments at war?

Faithfully Yours,   W.W.

WWTLI (R. Lansing Papers, NjP).

¹ After reading Lansing's "Comments and Suggestions," Wilson made numerous changes in his draft and returned it to Lansing. Lansing then had the following document typed as a matter of record.

An Appeal for a Statement of War Aims[1]

INSTRUCTIONS.

The President directs me to send you the following communication to be presented immediately to the Minister of Foreign Affairs *of the Government to which you are accredited* and he requests that you present it with the utmost earnestness of support. He wishes the impression clearly conveyed that it would be very hard for the Government of the United States to understand a negative reply. After yourself reading it to the Minister of Foreign Affairs and making the oral representations suggested please leave a copy of this paper with him.

The President of the United States has instructed me to suggest to (His Majesty's Government) *the Government to which you are accredited* a course of action with regard to the present war which he hopes that—*substitute name of Government to which you are accredited*—will take under consideration [*as suggested in the most friendly spirit and*]² as coming (from a) [*not only from a*] friend (not only, and suggested in the most friendly spirit,) but also as coming from the representative of a neutral nation whose interests have been most seriously affected by the war and whose concern for its early conclusion arises out of a manifest necessity to determine how best to safeguard those interests if the war is to continue.

The suggestion [*which*] I am instructed to make (it) [*the President*] has long (been) [*had it*] in (the) mind (of the President) to offer. He is somewhat embarrassed to offer it at this particular time because it may now seem to have been prompted by the recent (German) overtures [*of the Central Powers.*] It is in fact in no way associated with them in its origin and the President would have delayed offering it until (the Germans) [*those*] overtures had been answered but for the fact that it also concerns the question of peace and may best be considered in connection with other proposals which have the same end in view. The President can only beg that his suggestion be considered (as) entirely on its own merits [*and*] as if it had been made in other circumstances.

The President suggests that an early occasion be sought to call out from all the nations now at war (a frank comparison of) [*such an avowal of their respective*] views as to the terms upon which the war might be concluded and the arrangements which would be deemed satisfactory as (constituting) a guarantee against its renewal or the kindling of any similar conflict in the future [*as would make it possible frankly to compare them.*] He is indifferent as to the means taken to accomplish this. He would be happy himself to serve [*or even to take the initiative*] in its accomplishment in any way that might prove acceptable, but he has no desire to determine the method or the instrumentality. One way will be as acceptable to him as another, if only the great object he has in mind be attained.

He takes the liberty of calling attention to the fact that the objects which the statesmen of the belligerents on both sides have in mind in this war are virtually the same, as stated in general terms to their own people and to the world. Each side desires to make the rights and privileges of weak peoples and small states as secure against aggression or denial in the future as the rights and privileges of the great and powerful states now at war. Each wishes itself to be made secure in the future, along with all other nations and peoples, against the recurrence of wars like this, and against aggression or selfish interference of any kind. Each would be jealous of the formation of any more rival leagues to preserve an uncertain balance of power amidst multiplying suspicions; but each is ready to consider the formation of a league of nations to (enforce) [*ensure*] peace and justice throughout the world. Before that final step can be taken, however, each deems it necessary first to settle the issues of the present war upon terms which will certainly safeguard the independence, the territorial integrity, and the political and commercial freedom of the nations involved.

In the measures to be taken to secure the future peace of the world the people and Government of the United States are as vitally and as directly interested as the governments now at war. Their interest, moreover, in the means to be adopted to relieve the smaller and weaker peoples of the world of the peril of wrong and violence is as quick and ardent as that of any other people or government (in the world). They stand ready, and even eager, to cooperate in the accomplishment of these ends when the war is over with every influence and resource at their command. But the war must first be concluded. The terms upon which it is to be concluded they are not at liberty to suggest; but the President does feel that it is his right and his duty to point out their intimate interest in its conclusion, lest it should presently be too late to accomplish the greater things which lie beyond its conclusion, lest the situation of neutral nations, now exceedingly hard to endure, be rendered altogether intolerable, and lest, more than all, an injury be done civilization itself which can never be atoned for or repaired.

The President, therefore, feels altogether justified in suggesting an immediate [*opportunity for a*] comparison of views as to the terms which must precede those ultimate arrangements for the peace of the world which all desire and in which the neutral nations as well as those at war are ready to play their full responsible part. If the contest must continue to proceed towards undefined ends by slow attrition until the one group of belligerents or the other is exhausted, if million after million of human lives must continue to be offered up until on the one side or the other there are no more to offer, if resentments must be kindled that can never cool and despairs engendered from which there can be no recovery, hopes of peace and of the willing concert of free peoples will be rendered vain and idle.

The life of the entire world has been profoundly affected. Every part of the great family of mankind has felt the burden and terror of this unprecedented contest of arms. No nation in the civilized world can be said in truth to stand outside its influence or to be safe against its disturbing effects. And yet the concrete objects for which it is being waged have never been definitively stated.

The leaders of the several belligerents have, (it is true,) [*as has been said,*] stated those objects in general terms. But, stated in general terms, they seem the same on both sides. Never yet have the authoritative spokesmen of either side avowed the precise objects which would, if attained, satisfy them and their people that the war had been fought out. The world has been left to conjecture what definitive results, what actual exchange of guarantees, what political or territorial changes or readjustments, what stage of military success even, would bring the war to an end.

It may be that peace is nearer than we know; that the terms which the belligerents on the one side and on the other would deem it necessary to insist upon are not so irreconcilable as (we) [*some*] have feared; that an interchange of views would clear the way at least for conference and make the permanent concord of the nations a hope of the immediate future, a concert of nations immediately practicable.

The President is not proposing peace; he is not even offering (intervention) [*mediation.*] He is merely proposing that soundings be taken in order that we may learn, the neutral nations with the belligerent, how near the haven of peace may be for which all mankind longs with an (infinite) [*intense*] and increasing longing. He believes that the spirit in which he speaks and the objects which he seeks will be understood by all concerned, and he confidently hopes for a response which will bring a new light into the affairs of the world.

T MS (WP, DLC).

[1] In the following document, words in parentheses were deleted by Lansing. Words in italics, with the exceptions noted below, were added by Lansing. The note as sent conformed to this document. It was dispatched at 9:30 P.M. on December 18 and is printed in *FR-WWS 1916*, pp. 97-99.

[2] Words in square brackets, although italicized, are WWhw changes in and additions to the WWT copy which is printed as an Enclosure with WW to RL, Dec. 17, 1917. In most cases, Wilson, in making these changes, was responding to the suggestions in RL to WW, Dec. 17, 1917. Italicized words in square brackets should be read as part of the text of the note as sent.

To Edward Mandell House

My dearest Friend,   The White House. 19 December, 1916.

I sent yesterday to *all* the belligerent governments the message of which I enclose a copy. Things have moved so fast that I did not have time to get you down here to go over it with you. It was virtually in response to the suggestion you quoted from Whitehouse (Brooks seems to me to be quite of the most common breed of British extremists and fools) and was written and sent off within a very few hours, for fear the governments of the Entente might in the meantime so have committed themselves against peace as to make the situation even more hopeless than it had been. I hope you will like and approve the note. It proceeds along a different and, I hope, more effective line than the other which you saw.

Thank you warmly for your letters. They are just what I want.
          Affectionately Yours,   Woodrow Wilson

This is the original. Could you without trouble have it returned?   W.W.

WWTLS (E. M. House Papers, CtY).

To Robert Lansing

                              The White House.
My dear Mr. Secretary,   19 December, 1916.

This is so interesting a paper,[1] and is so *true* that it distresses me to suggest that its utterance at this particular time would be unwise. But I must frankly say that I think the considerations it urges, and the policy, are what we ought to have *in mind* in the weighty international transactions which we are (I hope) approaching, but ought not to make explicit before the event and before the necessity to do so.

Perhaps it would be possible for you to maintain the general theory of the first part of the paper without making the very specific application of what follows; though that, too, would be difficult, I see.

Thank you warmly for having consulted me.

Faithfully Yours,   Woodrow Wilson

WWTLS (R. Lansing Papers, NjP).
 1 Entitled "Americanism," it is dated December 5, 1916, and is a T MS in the R. Lansing Papers, NjP. Lansing defined true Americanism as devotion to that principle of individual liberty in organized society which finds its expression in democratic institutions. Governments so constituted, whether they be republican or monarchical, he said, are invariably peace-loving, not aggressive, and never violate their word. By implication, Lansing condemned the Central Powers as aggressors, because their governments were not subject to the will of their peoples. Any international league to preserve the peace, Lansing continued, would have to be made up of nations which trusted each other. It followed, therefore, that such a league could not be open to all nations since such inclusiveness would make it "inherently defective" because it would be "constantly menaced by factions resulting from inharmonious conceptions of duty and right and from radically different motives by the governments bound to carry out its objects." It would be well, therefore, Lansing concluded, to limit membership in any future league to democratic nations whose governments were responsible to their peoples.

To Pleasant Alexander Stovall

Personal.

My dear Stovall: [The White House] December 19, 1916

Thank you very warmly for your letter of November twenty-fourth.[1] It warmed the cockles of my heart. To have you thinking of me away off there in Switzerland girt about by the war is very delightful to me. You may be sure our thought constantly goes out also to you.

Things go normally here. We are just now, of course, holding our breath for fear the overtures of the Central Powers with regard to peace will meet with a rebuff instead of an acceptance.

With warmest regards,

Cordially and sincerely yours,   Woodrow Wilson

TLS (Letterpress Books, WP, DLC).
 1 P. A. Stovall to WW, Nov. 24, 1916, TLS (WP, DLC).

To Francis Griffith Newlands

My dear Senator: [The White House] December 19, 1916
Thank you warmly for your letter of December fifteenth.

Senator Robinson had already told me how vain the opposition to a hearing on the bills had been. I am very sorry.

I hope that the Committee will not share the feeling that any agreement between the railroad managements and their employees relieves us of the obligation to safeguard the country in the future against the recurrence of such threats to its life as the recent one. My very earnest conviction is that it will not affect that duty in the least, and that we ought in conscience and in obedience to the express promises made during the campaign to press on towards the completion of our legislation.

I am sure that you will share these feelings.
Cordially and sincerely yours,   Woodrow Wilson

TLS (Letterpress Books, WP, DLC).

To Franklin Knight Lane

My dear Lane: [The White House] December 19, 1916
Thank you for your letter about your interview with Governor Kendrick. It will serve me as a valuable memorandum of my own conversation with him, for I did manage to see him at last and was very much impressed by what he said.
Always   Faithfully yours,   Woodrow Wilson

TLS (Letterpress Books, WP, DLC).

To Edward Nash Hurley

My dear Hurley: [The White House] December 19, 1916
Thank you warmly for your kindness in sending me under date of December sixteenth further details in connection with the plan to apply cost accounting to the large problems now facing the Government. I am going to give myself the pleasure of studying the paper at as early a date as possible.
Cordially and sincerely yours,   Woodrow Wilson

TLS (Letterpress Books, WP, DLC).

To Winthrop More Daniels

My dear Daniels: The White House December 19, 1916

Thank you for your letter. I am sure you must know what genuine pleasure it gave me to renominate you. I have been very proud that you should have been my selection, for I believe that the whole country feels that your service on the Commission has had unusual distinction in every way.

I don't wonder that you would relish a release. I can subscribe to that feeling with the greatest heartiness, but then, after all, I feel with you that we must all subscribe to Brackett's programme.

With warmest regards from us all, in haste
Cordially and faithfully yours, Woodrow Wilson

TLS (Wilson-Daniels Corr., CtY).

From Robert Lansing, with Enclosures

My dear Mr. President: Washington December 19, 1916.

I have just received the enclosed report from Secretary Lane. After reading it will you please return it to me for my files?
Faithfully yours, Robert Lansing.

TLS (WP, DLC).

E N C L O S U R E I

Franklin Knight Lane to Robert Lansing

Bellevue-Stratford Hotel,
Philadelphia, Pennsylvania,
My dear Mr. Secretary: December 18, 1916.

I am inclosing herewith a report of the session of the American and Mexican Joint Commission held today.
Cordially yours, Franklin K Lane

TLS (SDR, RG 59, 812.00/20143½, DNA).

ENCLOSURE II

SESSION OF THE
AMERICAN AND MEXICAN JOINT COMMISSION
MONDAY, DECEMBER 18, 1916.

The Commission met at 10.45 a.m., Mr. Cabrera presiding. Mr. Cabrera informed the Commission that Mr. Pani had brought from Mexico the views of Mr. Carranza with reference to the protocol. He then requested Mr. Pani to present the situation to the Commission. Mr. Pani's statement was made in somewhat broken English, and it was difficult at times to get at his precise meaning. The substance of his statement was that while the First Chief approved of the fundamental principles upon which the protocol was based, he deemed it important to have certain changes made in order that the sovereignty of both countries might be fully safeguarded under the agreement. The First Chief deemed it most important that any agreement be so clearly worded that there would be no possibility of misunderstanding or misinterpretation.

Secretary Lane then requested Mr. Pani to take up the protocol article by article and present to the Commission the specific objections of the First Chief. All the Mexican Commissioners stated that they had made a mistake in urging the fixing of a definite date for the withdrawal of the troops.

Article 1 provides that the troops shall be withdrawn within forty days from the date of the approval of the agreement. To this the First Chief objected because of the fact that if anything should occur to delay withdrawal beyond the date fixed, it would be interpreted as sanctioning the occupation of Mexican soil by American forces. The First Chief therefore proposed a redrafting of Article 1 as indicated on accompanying comparison between the protocol of November 24th and the new Mexican proposal (Exhibit A). In commenting on this article both Messrs. Pani and Bonillas made much of the fact that under the terms of Article 1 as proposed no definite time was set for the period necessary for withdrawal and that the American Government might therefore use its discretion in fixing the time. Mr. Bonillas even went so far as to say that this withdrawal could take 60, 90, or even 100 days.

Proposed changes in the other articles are fully indicated in the accompanying comparison (Exhibit A) and did not give rise to much comment by the Mexican Commissioners. Mr. Pani stated that the First Chief was impressed by the fact that the proposed protocol did not deal adequately with the safeguarding of the border and that for this reason a new article was proposed (see Article 4 of new Mexican proposal).

Having presented the amendments to the protocol, Secretary Lane inquired whether Mr. Pani had brought with him a reply of the First Chief to the letter of November 24th, in which the American Commissioners had requested assurance that when the proposed protocol was approved by both governments the Mexican Commissioners would be authorized to meet at once and take up with the American Commissioners those questions deemed by the American Government of vital importance; such as protection of life and property of foreigners in Mexico and the establishment of an international claims commission. To this Mr. Pani replied that the view of the First Chief was that it would be best for both countries to have Mexican soil entirely free from American troops before discussing any other questions. He feels that the two countries will be dealing on a plane of equality and they will then be able to deal more effectively with the other international questions pending between the two Governments.

Mr. Cabrera then stated that all the matters discussed at the morning session would be presented to the American Commissioners in the form of a letter.

At 11.45 a.m. a recess was taken.

After reassembling the Mexican Commissioners submitted the attached communication. (Exhibit B)

A discussion of this communication brought out the fact that the First Chief had instructed his Commissioners to remain in the United States and to proceed to the discussion of the other questions which the American Commissioners deemed important as soon as the withdrawal was completed. Secretary Lane inquired of the Mexican Commissioners whether this position was in harmony with the understanding reached between the two governments leading up to the appointment of the Commission. To this Mr. Pani replied that the view of the First Chief was that the agreement reached at Atlantic City did not cover fully both subjects contemplated by the two governments, namely, the withdrawal of troops and border control. This fact, combined with the notice served on the Mexican Government with reference to the policy of the United States to pursue marauders across the border, represented a situation unsatisfactory to the First Chief, and that he felt, therefore, that the two countries could not be placed upon a plane of equality when dealing with the other questions, nor could they be solved satisfactorily until after the troops had been withdrawn. Mr. Mott inquired of Mr. Cabrera whether the immediate withdrawal of troops from Mexican soil would not complicate the situation for the *de facto* government, owing to the fact that Villa might immediately occupy such territory. To this Mr. Cabrera replied that the immediate local situation in that part of Chihuahua now occupied by American troops might take a change for the worse, but that the situation throughout the country would be greatly improved because the withdrawal would strengthen the Carranza government.

Adjournment was taken at 5.15 p.m. until tomorrow, Tuesday morning, at 10 o'clock. The American Commissioners will hold a conference this evening to formulate a reply to the proposal to the Mexican Commissioners.

EXHIBIT A

THE AMERICAN AND MEXICAN JOINT COMMISSION.

PROTOCOL OF AGREEMENT,
AD REFERENDUM, SIGNED
AT ATLANTIC CITY,
NOVEMBER 24TH, 1916.

PROPOSED PROTOCOL

ARTICLE I.

The Government of the United States agrees to begin the withdrawal of American troops from Mexican soil as soon as practicable, such withdrawal, subject to the further terms of this Agreement, to be completed not later than _____; that is to say, forty (40) days after the approval of this Agreement by both Governments.

ARTICLE I.

The Government of the United States agrees to begin the withdrawal of American troops immediately after the ratification of this Agreement, and to effect the same in a continuous manner until the complete evacuation of said troops, either by land towards Columbus, or making use of the Mexican Northwestern Railway to El Paso, or through both routes as the American commander may deem more convenient and practicable.

ARTICLE II.

The American commander shall determine the manner in which the withdrawal shall be effected, so as to ensure the safety of the territory affected by the withdrawal.

ARTICLE II.

Omitted in Proposed Protocol.

ARTICLE III.

The territory evacuated by the American troops shall be occupied and adequately protected by the Constitutionalist forces and such evacuation shall take place when the Constitutionalist forces have taken position to the south of the American forces so as to make effective such occupation and protection. The Mexican commander shall determine the plan for the occupation and protection of the territory evacuated by the American forces.

ARTICLE IV.

The American and Mexican commanders shall deal separately, or wherever practicable in friendly cooperation, with any obstacles which may arise tending to delay the withdrawal. In case there are any further activities of the forces inimical to the Constitutionalist Government which threaten the safety of the international border along the northern section of Chihuahua, the withdrawal of American forces shall not be delayed beyond the period strictly necessary to overcome such activities.

No corresponding Article in Protocol of November 24th, 1916.

ARTICLE II.

(Of proposed Protocol)
The territory evacuated by the American troops shall be occupied and protected by the Constitutionalist forces. The Mexican commander shall determine the plan for the occupation and protection of the territory evacuated by the American forces.

ARTICLE III.

The American and Mexican commanders shall deal separately, or wherever practicable in friendly cooperation, with any obstacles which may arise tending to bar or interfere with the withdrawal.

ARTICLE IV.

Both Governments bind themselves to cooperate in the protection and vigilance of the boundary line, by means of:
(a) Full and mutual interchange of information between the military commanders on both sides to the end that such

lawless incursions may be anticipated and defended against

(b) Mutual use of railroads on both sides of the border for the carriage of troops, or supplies, or war material, and

(c) Mutual scouting within a distance of ten miles of the border, providing that the corresponding permits, between the respective military commanders, be requested and granted in writing, and that said scouting expeditions shall never proceed further than ten miles from any military camp or village of more than one hundred inhabitants.

ARTICLE V.

The withdrawal of American troops shall be effected by marching to Columbus, or by using the Mexican Northwestern Railroad to El Paso, or by both routes, as may be deemed most convenient or expedient by the American commander.

ARTICLE V.

Omitted because included in Article I of Proposed Agreement.

ARTICLE VI.

Each of the Governments parties to this Agreement shall guard its side of the international boundary. This, however, does not preclude such cooperation on the part of the military commanders of both countries as may be practicable.

ARTICLE V.

(of proposed Protocol)
Until a satisfactory Agreement is reached for the reciprocal crossing of both countries over the boundary, in pursuit of outlaws, each of the contracting governments shall protect its own side of the boundary line

ARTICLE VII

This Agreement shall take effect immediately upon approval by both Governments.

ARTICLE VI.

This Agreement shall remain in full force for a period of four months from the date of its

Notification of approval shall be communicated by each Government to the other.

ratification. If neither of the Governments parties to this Agreement shall give notice to the other, ten days previous to its expiration, of its intention to terminate the same, it shall further remain in force until thirty days after either of the Governments shall have given notice to the other of its intention to end it.

EXHIBIT B.
COMMUNICATION OF MEXICAN COMMISSIONERS
TO THE AMERICAN COMMISSIONERS.

Gentlemen: Philadelphia, Dec. 18, 1916.

In order to place concretely in writing the points treated verbally during the session of today, we have the honor to inform you that the Citizen First Chief of the Constitutionalist Army has not ratified the Protocol submitted to his consideration for reasons which we desire briefly to present:

The First Chief of the Constitutionalist Army is of the opinion that, the presence of American troops on Mexican soil constituting as it does a violation of Mexican sovereignty, the acceptance of any agreement for the withdrawal of troops, subject to conditions which might subsequently justify a delay in such withdrawal, would be interpreted as constituting a tacit consent of the Government of Mexico to the actual occupation of Mexican territory.

The Government of Mexico does not desire to place itself in a position in which, because of unforeseen circumstances which might subsequently arise, it might appear to be sanctioning a posteriori the presence of American troops on Mexican territory. Viewed from this standpoint, the Mexican government desires that the wording of the agreement should be so explicit as to leave no room for future difficulties in interpretation or execution.

The Government of Mexico could not approve the Agreement after having received notice of the declared purpose of the American Government, to reserve to itself the right to send future expeditions into Mexico, in pursuit of marauders. Under such conditions, the Mexican Government was confronted with the following choices:

First   Either to refrain from signing the Protocol, because such approval would have been equivalent to tacit agreement to the policy announced by the American Government, or

Second In the event of signing the Protocol, the Mexican Government would have been compelled to make clear its protest against any new attempt to violate Mexican territory. Such protest would tend to create an unstable situation, dangerous to the maintenance of peace between both countries, which is precisely what the Mexican Government desires to avoid in proposing the holding of these conferences.

The Citizen First Chief believes that, in view of the fact that the mutual respect of sovereignty is the only solid basis for the preservation of peace and amicable relations between Mexico and the United States, the solution of our difficulties should be sought in a plan of cooperation for the protection and safeguarding of the border, thus preventing and avoiding the causes of friction instead of following the policy outlined by the American Government of sending future military expeditions into Mexico, which will only serve to disturb the relations between the two countries. As regards the discussion of the other questions which the American Commissioners desire to submit to the Mexican Commissioners, the First Chief approves the attitude assumed by the latter, namely that they proceed to discuss such questions after the withdrawal of troops has been completed, and if, fortunately, it is possible to reach a conclusion with reference to the sovereignty and protection of the border.

In short, the Constitutionalist Government believes that whatever may be the form of agreement arrived at with reference to the withdrawal of troops from Mexican territory, such agreement should avoid:

First   Any implication of express or tacit consent of the Mexican Government to the present occupation of its soil

Second Any assent to future occupation of such soil, and

Third   Any authorization or tolerance of a new expedition of American troops into Mexican territory

The Mexican delegates are confident that it will be possible to arrive at a formulation which meets the conditions suggested by the First Chief, especially in view of the earnest desire which they have no doubt exists on the part of the American Commissioners to arrive at an agreement compatible with the respect for the sovereignty of our country.

We beg to assure you of our distinguished consideration.

Luis Cabrera
Ygnacio Bonillas
Alberto J. Pani

T MSS (SDR, RG 59, 812.00/20143½, DNA).

From the White House Staff

The White House.
Memorandum for the President: December 19, 1916
Senator Walsh asks for an appointment with the President for himself, Mr. Lane and Mr. Ferris on the water-power bill. He stated that he thinks Senators Bankhead and Shields will yield to the suggestion as to a modification of the bill. He asks if they may have an early appointment.

Thursday 4:30

T MS (WP, DLC).

From William Kent

Dear Mr. President: Washington, D. C. December 19, 1916.
Concerning H.R. 407, known as the stock-raising homestead bill, in accordance with your suggestion, I have taken the matter up with Secretary Houston and Secretary Lane, and have furthermore consulted with Mr. H. S. Graves, Forester.[1]
The bill, after passage in the House and Senate, went to conference, and in conference was amended in some particulars, to my mind beneficially, but the main contention has not been met, and could not be met in such conference, as that contention brought in new matters of legislation and was not subject to conference.
The most important feature of the bill, as far as the public welfare is concerned, is found in the classification of the lands "chiefly valuable for grazing" and the right to refuse homestead entries on lands "chiefly valuable for grazing" if they be of a sort that could not be reasonably expected to support a family on 640 acres.
If lands below the standard of creating substantial, self-supporting homes on 640 acres should be permitted to be taken up under this legislation, there would exist an obvious source of disappointed hopes, of encouragement to illegal and fraudulent

entries, and the possibility of taking up lands for strategic or blackmailing purposes, which dangers are conceded by Secretary Houston and recognized by Secretary Lane in his proposed policy of refusing to designate such unfit lands as eligible to homesteading under this Act.

Pardon me if I quote that portion of the Act that to my mind permits entry of lands below the margin contemplated by the purposes of the bill. The only interpolation made by me is in capitals.

"That from and after the passage of this Act it shall be lawful for any person qualified to make entry under the homestead laws of the United States to make a stock-raising homestead entry for not exceeding six hundred and forty acres of unappropriated unreserved public land in reasonably compact form: *Provided, however*, that the land so entered shall theretofore have been designated by the Secretary of the Interior as 'stock-raising lands.'

"Sec. 2. That the Secretary of the Interior is hereby authorized, on application or otherwise, to designate as stock-raising lands subject to entry under this Act lands the surface of which is, in his opinion, chiefly valuable for grazing and raising forage crops, do not contain merchantable timber, are not susceptible of irrigation from any known source of water supply, and are of such a character that (AT LEAST) six hundred and forty acres are reasonably required for the support of a family."

It is perfectly obvious that under this definition there is an exclusion of lands of such a nature that 640 acres exceeds the amount necessary to support a family. By such exclusion, there are excepted from entry, lands eligible for homestead under tillage requirements of the 160 and 320 acre acts, and also lands that may be declared irrigable and therefore not needed in such a large quantity for the support of a family. The final clause "of such a character that six hundred and forty acres are reasonably required for the support of a family" is but a reiteration of the exemption of such high quality of land from entry under this 640 acre act.

The opinion has been expressed by Secretary Lane and others to whom the matter has been referred that this final clause may be interpreted as excluding from entry lands "of such a character that 640 acres *may not be reasonably expected* to support a family." This, to my mind, is clearly torturing the language of the section out of shape. The limitation was intended to prevent entry of lands of higher character, and specifically to permit entry of all lands below the higher classification.

My interpretation is based, first, on the clear language of the bill, and second, on the history of the bill, which first passed the House after a long contest in the Public Lands Committee with a clause inserted which limited the right to take up lower class lands by specifically stating that such lands must, in the opinion of the Secretary of the Interior, be of such a quality as might support a family. This definition was deliberately and carefully eliminated from the present bill.

Secretary Lane has stated that it would not be his intention to designate lands as eligible for stock-raising homestead entry, unless of such a character that 640 acres might be reasonably expected to be adequate for the support of a family. However beneficial such an interpretation might be, I respectfully submit that it is not justified by the language of the bill, and if not adversely construed by the courts, it would not entail upon any successor a similar interpretation. It will furnish a continuing source of agitation in every specific location where requests are made. Such a shift from law to the opinion of the Secretary will breed bitterness and unnecessary trouble. For these reasons, I believe that, in the public interest, this measure should be vetoed, and sent back to Congress with the statement that such an important feature should not be left in discussion as between the powers and the discretion of the Secretary of the Interior and the language of the law.   Yours truly,   William Kent

TLS (WP, DLC).
[1] Henry Solon Graves, Forester and Chief of the United States Forest Service since 1910.

From Robert Bridges

Dear Mr. President: [New York] Dec 19, 1916

I want to thank you personally, and all your family for a very good time. It was, as always with you, a meeting of old friends which no official position can swamp. It was a delight to me to see you so well and fit for the hard job ahead of you.

Talcott[1] and I had some mighty pleasant chats. He evidently enjoyed his fight, though he felt he could not win—but it was up to him to make it.[2] Of course the "interests" were all opposed to him. He says it does not make any difference in his friendships but "they don't throw any business his way." I fear that his law practice has been badly scattered.

With my regards to Mrs. Wilson and your family, and best wishes for the holidays and the coming year I am, as always,
                    Faithfully Yours   Robert Bridges

ALS (WP, DLC).

[1] That is, Charles Andrew Talcott. Talcott and Bridges attended the cabinet dinner at the White House on December 12 and remained overnight as house guests.

[2] Talcott had been defeated for reelection to Congress in 1914 by his Republican opponent, Homer Peter Snyder. In 1916, Talcott ran again against Snyder, who defeated him by a majority of 6,339 votes.

Two Letters to William Kent

My dear Mr. Kent: [The White House] December 20, 1916

I warmly appreciate your frank letter of December sixteenth[1] and am heartily glad to know how you feel about the matter Secretary Lane mentioned to you. I hope to follow it up just as soon as possible.

In haste

Cordially and sincerely yours,   Woodrow Wilson

TLS (Letterpress Books, WP, DLC).

[1] It is missing.

My dear Mr. Kent: The White House December 20, 1916

Thank you for your letter about the stock-raising homestead bill. After getting your former letter, I interested myself in making myself familiar with the questions as far as I could amidst a multitude of distractions, and I have had more than one conference about it. Secretary Lane and Secretary Houston have been cooperating with me in trying to advise the committee particularly with regard to a provision for classifying the lands, and I hope from what Mr. Ferris told me in the moment I saw him last night that it has been possible to alter the terms of the bill in a way that will in part, at any rate, guard against the worst of the results you fear.[1]

Cordially and sincerely yours,   Woodrow Wilson

TLS (W. Kent Papers, CtY).

[1] Kent's objections were not met in the bill reported out of conference committee and approved by the House on December 22. Wilson signed it on December 29, 1916. *Cong. Record*, 64th Cong., 2d sess., pp. 688-89, 754.

From William Cox Redfield

My Dear Mr. President: Washington December 20, 1916.

The Alaska General Fisheries Bill[1] is at the point where a word from you may at a stroke destroy a miserable monopoly and do inestimable service to the people of Alaska and to all who consume the vast products of her fisheries. The bill represents the nearly or quite unanimous views of the House Committee on Merchant Marine and Fisheries. It represents the results of ten years of administrative experience, plus special studies for the purpose on the spot, and is a measure that was drawn by the committee itself after exhaustive hearings in which every interest, pro and con, was given a chance. Today one fishing company has taken up for itself nearly or quite thirty fishing sites for its own exclusive use, not for the purpose of legitimate fishing but to exclude competitors. Two other similar cases, one grasping seventeen sites, another about twenty, are just reported to us.[2] This deliberate attempt to monopolize an important food supply will be destroyed by the bill which makes such action impossible. The bill requires that sites must be actually used, and become forfeited after disuse.

The bill for the first time affords adequate means for conserving the fisheries, now seriously threatened by reason of deficiencies in existing law. It brings to an end many disputes regarding fishery locations. The only present right in this matter is the possessory claim arising under common law. From this condition endless quarrels arise, always at the expense of the fish supply. It abolishes the existing unfair system of dual taxation and furnishes revenue alike to the Government for the specific needs of the fisheries and for the Territory of Alaska. It discontinues the rebating of license taxes to operators of private hatcheries, and brings all hatcheries under the supervision of the Government. It brings to a close in three years the objectionable practice of utilizing food fishes in the manufacture of fertilizer and oil.

In brief, the bill has been drawn solely with the view to perpetuating the fisheries of Alaska in the interests of her people and in those of the entire nation. If this legislation is deferred, two to four fishing seasons may elapse before the present obsolete laws can be replaced. At this time of high prices for food it is almost an offense for anyone to get in the way of a measure of this kind.

The bill is so placed in the House that a special rule is necessary to get it consideration. For this rule the committee is ready to ask if there is hope the measure will pass the Senate. I have written Judge Alexander today a letter of which copy is inclosed.[3]

In the Senate a strange thing has happened. The bill has not been introduced there and is not pending. Nevertheless, Senator Lane, Chairman of the Senate Committee on Fisheries, called together his committee 18th instant, Senators Martin and Fletcher being absent, and gave a hearing on the bill to Mr.

Wickersham, Delegate from Alaska, and others, all in opposition to the measure. No notice was sent the Bureau of Fisheries or the Department. The committee adopted a resolution adverse to the bill. Promptly on learning this I wrote the Chairman a letter of which copy is attached.[4] I have no reply. On 19th I spoke of this to Mr. Burleson, and today at his request sent him letter of which copy is inclosed.[5]

The subject is one not only of grave money value (products worth over twenty million dollars annually), but directly affects the cost of food of the consumer all over the country. I therefore respectfully ask your earnest assistance in this matter that the bill may be considered on its merits. If assured that the Senate will so do I am confident a rule can be obtained in the House to that effect.   Yours very truly,   William C. Redfield

TLS (WP, DLC).

[1] H.R. 17499, the main provisions of which Redfield summarizes very well.

[2] James Wickersham, delegate from Alaska, in the discussion of the bill in the House on December 13, asserted that three companies monopolized the best salmon-fishing sites: the Alaskan Packers' Association, Booth Fisheries, and Libby, McNeill and Libby. The latter two, according to Wickersham, each controlled about one hundred fish trap sites. *Cong. Record*, 64th Cong., 2d sess., pp. 288-89.

[3] W. C. Redfield to J. W. Alexander, Dec. 19, 1916, CCLS (WP, DLC).

[4] W. C. Redfield to Harry Lane, Dec. 18, 1916, CCL (WP, DLC).

[5] W. C. Redfield to A. S. Burleson, Dec. 20, 1916, CCL (WP, DLC).

To William Cannon Houston[1]

[The White House]
My dear Mr. Houston: December 20, 1916

There is a bill now pending in which my interest is so great that I take the liberty of dropping you a line in the hope that I may enlist your valuable assistance in its support and passage. It is the bill providing for the protection, regulation and conservation of the fisheries of Alaska. I have had more than one conference with the gentlemen in the Department of Commerce about this bill. I know, therefore, with what thoughtfulness and with what full knowledge of the facts and conditions it has been drafted, and I want very earnestly to bespeak for it your most favorable consideration. It seems to me that it would be a distinct detriment to the interests alike of Alaska and of the United States if it were not passed.

Cordially and sincerely yours,   Woodrow Wilson

TLS (Letterpress Books, WP, DLC).

[1] Democratic congressman from Tennessee, chairman of the House Committee on Territories.

To Claude Kitchin

[The White House]
My dear Mr. Kitchin: December 20, 1916

May I not express to you and through you to those who have charge of the bill my very great interest in the bill for the protection, regulation and conservation of the fisheries of Alaska? I know how studiously and with how complete a knowledge of the facts the bill has been worked out, and I should consider it very detrimental to the public interest if it were to fail. I take it for granted that you have not had time to give your personal attention as yet to this matter. I am hoping that it may be possible for you to do so.

Cordially and sincerely yours, Woodrow Wilson

TLS (Letterpress Books, WP, DLC).

To Hollis Burke Frissell

[The White House]
My dear Professor Frissell: December 20, 1916

I have your letter of December twelfth.

Of course, I need not say to you that I have the most sincere and kindly interest in the negro race. I wonder if there is some specific thing in connection with which I could in your judgment properly express that interest. There does not seem just at this moment to be anything which is, so to say, a specific matter of discussion.

In great haste

Cordially and sincerely yours, Woodrow Wilson

TLS (Letterpress Books, WP, DLC).

From Edward Mandell House

Dear Governor: New York. December 20, 1916.

Thank you for the original manuscript of the note which you have sent to the belligerent nations and which I herewith return.

There are some sentences in it that will live as long as human history.

I have felt for a long time that it was foolhardy for the English to refuse peace upon reasonable terms, and Buckler's letter, a copy of which I sent you yesterday, confirms this.[1] I believe the submarine is a serious menace to them and that the main protection they have had has been the attitude of this country—an attitude which they in no way appreciate.

Sir William Wiseman admitted to me yesterday that he considered the unpopularity of the United States among the masses in England as something to be reckoned with.

I am not at all afraid of Germany after the war unless, indeed, England is put out of commission, but it is conceivable that we might have trouble with England in the event she is victorious. Conditions have changed in as much as she now has a navy equal perhaps to all the other navies of the world, and an army equal to that of any single nation. In my opinion it will not be safe for this country to be as belligerent towards her in the future as we have been in the past.

Most of Great Britain is as war mad as Germany was when I visited there in 1914, and we can no longer count upon their looking at things from the same viewpoint as heretofore.

Wiseman says that all the belligerents resent the tone of our press, even those papers that are pro-Ally. He quoted the World as an example. He says his Government understand and appreciate our attitude, but they find it difficult to make their people understand it.

No matter who brought on the war or what the governments know the cause to be for which they were fighting, the people, he said, of every belligerent nation had worked themselves up to an exalted enthusiasm of patriotic fervor, and they resent any suggestion that they have selfish motives and [are] not fighting solely for a principle.

I think we ought to keep this constantly in our thoughts and not try to argue with them as if they were in an ordinary frame of mind.   Affectionately yours,   E. M. House

I have just seen Sir Horace Plunkett and he confirmed Sir Wm. Wiseman's statement.[2]

TLS (WP, DLC).
    [1] W. H. Buckler to EMH, Dec. 7, 1916.
    [2] In his diary (Hw bound diary, Horace Plunkett Foundation, London), Plunkett, on December 20, recorded his conversation with House as follows:
"Lunched with Col. House. I was not well enough to talk to him as I should have wished but I gathered a good deal about his mind and the President's. He told me that Wilson was not going to blunder into premature peace proposals but was going to ask both belligerents, the Central Powers and the Allies, to state specifically their peace terms. Regarding the attitude of America to the war generally House had changed his view somewhat. He agrees that the best hope of peace in the world lies in a friendly understanding of the American and British peoples and that to bring about such mutual understanding is the best work a man can do. But he no longer seems to regard American intervention in the war as practical politics. He did not say this but he gave his reasons for doubting Lord Kitchener's statement of opinion (made to both of us) that it would quickly end the war. The Germans have a strong belief in their long distance submarines and if they become desperate (from privations at home)

they would argue that unrestricted sinking of ships would help Germany (by bringing Britain to her knees) far more than anything America could do would hurt her. He said too that many people felt the British would never give America due credit for her part in the war.

"We had some talk about the future of America. House thinks she has nothing to fear from Germany. Apart from Japan (in control largely of China) England was the only power which could imperil the U. S. He said few people realize that England is going to be not only a naval but a first rate military power. Apart from officers the new army he considers the best in the field."

From William Bauchop Wilson

My dear Mr. President: Washington December 20, 1916.

Supplementing the rather crude statement I made to you yesterday with reference to the bill to provide a Civil Government for Porto Rico and for other purposes,[1] now pending in the Senate, I desire to call your attention to Sections 26, 27 and 35, to be found on pages 23, 24, 36 and 37 of the Senate print, a copy of which I am inclosing herewith.

In doing so I am not unmindful of the great necessity of securing legislation on this subject at this Session of Congress. Being strongly impressed with the need of extending a greater amount of self-government to the people of the Island, I appeared several years ago (May 2, 1912) before the Committee on Insular Affairs and urged the enactment of legislation of this general character. I realize, of course, that all legislation must of necessity be more or less compromise; that there must be a meeting of a sufficient number of minds to constitute a majority in order to secure the enactment of any measure. But I feel that this phase of the problem is extremely important, and that is my excuse for again bringing it to your attention.

If my information is correct, the Sections referred to will disfranchise tens of thousands of people who were entitled to vote even under the Spanish regime. There has been considerable unrest amongst the people of Porto Rico, growing partly out of the sentimental consideration that under the existing Organic Act they are not citizens of any country and partly out of the economic conditions on the Island. Consequently there has been an underlying disposition in some quarters to resent the authority of the United States. There has been and is a larger percentage of loyalty to America and its institutions amongst the masses of the people than is to be found in the ranks of the "higher ups." This because they have hoped that affiliation with our country would bring them the political liberty and economic advancement enjoyed by the people of the United States. To disfranchise these people would be a serious blow to their aspirations and I fear would lead to a greater spirit of unrest than has as yet manifested itself on the Island. As the disfranchising provisions are to be contained in the Organic Act, relief could not be obtained except through Act of Congress, which could not be expected to respond as promptly to the pressure of public opinion in a small insular possession as it would to similar pressure at home.

Section 26 provides a property qualification of one thousand dollars for membership in the Porto Rican Senate, and Section 27 provides a property qualification of five hundred dollars for membership in the Porto Rican House of Representatives. Section 35 provides that citizens of Porto Rico must be tax payers in amount not less than three dollars per annum and must be able to read and write in order to be qualified electors, except that the legally registered electors at the last general election shall be entitled to register and vote at elections for ten years after the passage of the Act.

The theory that only those who are possessed of property are entitled to participate in the affairs of Government is based upon the assumption that the taxing power is the primary, if not the greatest, duty developing upon a legislative body, while as a matter of fact it is only secondary and incidental to the accomplishment of the other great functions of Government. The man without property is just as much interested and in some instances more interested in the proper exercise of those functions than the man with property. That applies particularly to that class of measures that has come to be spoken of as "Social Justice Legislation," but it also applies to every police power exercised by the State, and I speak of police power in its broadest sense. To impose a property qualification upon the electorate and upon the representatives of the electorate intrusted with the powers of Government would mean that no progress could be made except in so far as a spirit of justice or generosity might find expression amongst property owners in spite of the pressure of their property interests.

So far as Section 35 is concerned, I have no serious objection to a literary qualification for electors, provided that the opportunity is given during childhood to acquire an elementary education. That is not and has not been the case in Porto Rico. Much progress has been made under American direction, but there are still tens of thousands of children of school age on the Island for whom educational opportunities have not as yet been provided, and it is not to be expected that any considerable percentage of the illiterate adult population will at any time hereafter acquire the ability to read and write. Yet Section 35 extends the voting privilege for ten years to the legally qualified electors of Porto Rico at the last general election and thereafter disfranchises them. Until the opportunity for primary education has been made universal in the Island, it does not seem to me to be just to the mass of the people who have been denied educational opportunities in the past to provide a literary qualification for voting. There is no race problem in Porto Rico of sufficient import to justify taking steps of this character. The problems are political and economic. The fear that the illiterate person not possessed of property may be dominated by his employer is not sufficient reason for withholding the franchise. The same condition would apply whether he is literate or illiterate so long as he is unable to protect himself against dismissal, directly or indirectly, for political reasons. The same condition exists in the industrial establishments on the Mainland. To disfranchise these people for this reason would simply place employers in the position where they would have absolute power without the necessity of using intimidation, coercion or suggestion with their employees, and would place the employees at the additional disadvantage of having no political power to correct existing evils when they had temporarily or permanently thrown off the industrial yoke.

I would not want to jeopardize the pending bill nor do anything that would prevent its passage at this Session of Congress, but I suggest that an effort to secure the changes referred to could scarcely result in the defeat of the measure itself.[2]

Faithfully yours,   W B Wilson

TLS (WP, DLC).
[1] That is, the Jones-Shafroth bill, H.R. 9533.
[2] All the sections to which Wilson objected were removed in the conference committee.

From Franklin Knight Lane

My dear Mr. President: Washington December 20, 1916.

At the conference of the American and Mexican Joint Commission on Monday, the Mexican Commissioners presented a letter criticizing our attitude and expressing their own, signed by themselves but said by Mr. Pani to be an epitome of his conversation with Mr. Carranza. They also suggested very extensive modifications in the proposed protocol. The two most serious matters raised in their letter touched our announcement as to the proposed policy of pursuit in case of invasion by bandits, and an explicit refusal to discuss matters vital to us while any American troops are on Mexican soil.

Yesterday we sent them a reply, standing by the protocol in full, and suggesting to them that if they desired they could add to their consent to the protocol, or in any other way they saw fit, a statement of their position as to our pursuit with their territory. They said that they were afraid that we would use the presence of our troops to coerce them into yielding upon other matters if they entered upon a discussion, and we told them that we had no such desire and that they could not be coerced because they need not reach an agreement if they did not desire to do so until the troops were out.

The main change proposed in the protocol was one which provided that we should begin withdrawal immediately. They said, in private conversation, that this meant little more than that we would have to withdraw a half dozen men at a time. The purpose of this undoubtedly was to make a paper record by which we agreed to withdraw, and then when we did not withdraw because of conditions, they would be able to shout as loudly as Villa against the "Gringos'" bad faith.

We are to hear from them in one week. If their response is favorable we meet again the following week. If unfavorable the conference is at an end.

Cordially yours,   Franklin K Lane

TLS (WP, DLC).

From Robert Lansing, with Enclosures

PERSONAL AND CONFIDENTIAL:

My dear Mr. President: Washington December 20, 1916.

I enclose yesterday's report from Secretary Lane as to the meeting of the Commissioners. It appears to me that the Secretary has followed the only course which was open to him. Kindly return the report for my files after reading.

Faithfully yours,   Robert Lansing

TLS (WP, DLC).

E N C L O S U R E   I

Franklin Knight Lane to Robert Lansing

Philadelphia, Pa.,
My dear Mr. Secretary: December 19th, 1916.

The American Commissioners spent last evening discussing the terms of the reply to be made to the communication submitted at the session of yesterday afternoon, transmitted to the Department, attached to the report sent to you of yesterday's session.

At this morning's session the Mexican Commissioners submitted a new series of modifications to the Protocol, attached hereto as Exhibit A. After careful consideration of the situation, we reached the conclusion that it would be inadvisable to reopen the questions, the discussion of which had been the subject of prolonged conferences both at New London and at Atlantic City, and that it would only lead to a useless prolongation of the conference without tangible results.

After receiving the modified Mexican proposal at the session of this morning we adjourned at a little after eleven o'clock, for the purpose of placing our reply in final form. The Commission reassembled at 2.30 P.M., and we immediately submitted to the Mexican Commissioners the following communication:

Philadelphia, Pennsylvania,

Gentlemen:
December 19th, 1916.

After careful consideration of the proposals of the Mexican Commissioners as to changes in the Protocol, the American Commissioners are unanimously of the opinion that the proposed changes are impracticable and unwise. Each of the suggested changes was the subject of extended discussion by the entire Commission, and the members of the Commission could not come to an agreement upon them.

There is no reason, in the opinion of the American Commissioners, why this Protocol should not be approved by both governments. After months of study and discussion, the Protocol was agreed to by all the members of the Commission. It was the result of their best united effort to compose the differences between the two countries. It was submitted to the First Chief, with the request for an assurance from him that, if it were satisfactory to him, the Mexican Commissioners would be authorized to proceed to the discussion of other vital questions.

We have not insisted nor urged that the Mexican Government recognize our right to occupy Mexican territory, even under such novel and necessitous conditions as have existed; and it will not be contrary to the spirit of our discussion for the approval of your Government to be given to this instrument with such expression of Mexican authority and rights as to you may be desirable. Such expression could be spread upon the Minutes, or could be added to the Protocol.

For Mexico to reject the Protocol as unsatisfactory ends the function of this Commission. For Mexico to refuse to give the assurance asked for must have the same effect. If an agreement is reached the United States will withdraw her troops in strict compliance therewith, but the agreement to do this must be taken as equivalent to the fulfillment of the promise. To refuse to recognize this makes an issue of the good faith of the United States.

We would view with keenest regret such an inevitable termination of the work of the Commission, upon which we all entered with high hopes. We earnestly trust that the situation will be so met as to permit us to advance to the constructive consideration of those questions, the proper settlement of which will tend to strengthen the ties of friendship between Mexico and the United States.

We beg to remain,   Most respectfully yours,
                                     Franklin K. Lane
                                     George Gray
                                     John R. Mott

In order to smooth the way for the acceptance of the Protocol in its present form by the First Chief, we decided to inform the Mexican Commissioners that if the Protocol was approved, and the assurance with reference to the consideration of the other vital questions given, we would be willing to assure the Mexican Commissioners that we would not ask for a final agreement on the other questions while the American troops were on Mexican soil. This would remove the objection which they have constantly urged, that the presence of American troops was a means of exerting pressure upon them, and that they could not deal with the United States on terms of equality while subjected to such pressure.

At the close of today's session the Commission adopted the following motion:

It was moved, seconded and carried that the Commission adjourn to meet at 11 o'clock on the morning of Tuesday, January 2, 1917, provided that by one week from today, namely Tuesday, December 26th, 1916, the Chairmen of the American and Mexican sections of the Commission find it necessary to reconvene the Commission.

Our understanding with the Mexican Commissioners is that the Commission will only reconvene in case the First Chief accepts the Protocol, and in addition gives assurance that the Mexican Commissioners are authorized to proceed to the other questions which the American Commissioners deem vital to the development of amicable relations between the two countries.

I beg to remain, my dear Mr. Secretary,

Most sincerely yours,   Franklin K. Lane

TLS (SDR, RG 59, 812.00/20144½, DNA).

ENCLOSURE II

THE AMERICAN AND MEXICAN JOINT COMMISSION.

PROTOCOL OF AGREEMENT AD REFERENDUM, SIGNED AT ATLANTIC CITY NOVEMBER 24TH, 1916.

ARTICLE I. The Government of the United States agrees to begin the withdrawal of American troops from Mexican soil as soon as practicable, such withdrawal, subject to the further terms of this agreement, to be completed not later than _____; that is to say, forty (40) days after the approval of this Agreement by both Governments.

ARTICLE II. The American Commander shall determine the manner in which the withdrawal shall be effected, so as to ensure the safety of the territory affected by the withdrawal.

ARTICLE III. The territory evacuated by the American troops shall be occupied and adequately protected by the Constitutionalist forces, and such evacuation shall take place when the Constitutionalist forces have taken position to the south of the American forces

CHANGES PROPOSED BY MEXICAN COMMISSIONERS, TUESDAY DECEMBER 19, 1916.

ARTICLE I. The Government of the United States agrees to begin the withdrawal of American troops from Mexican soil, immediately after the ratification of this agreement, and to continue the same until the complete evacuation of said troops.

Omitted in proposed protocol.

ARTICLE II. The territory evacuated by the American troops shall be occupied and protected by the Constitutionalist forces, in accordance with the plan determined by the Mexican commander.

so as to make effective such occupation and protection. The Mexican commander shall determine the plan for the occupation and protection of the territory evacuated by the American forces.

ARTICLE IV. The American and Mexican commanders shall deal separately, or wherever practicable in friendly cooperation, with any obstacles which may arise tending to delay the withdrawal. In case there are any further activities of the forces inimical to the Constitutionalist Government which threaten the safety of the international border along the northern section of Chihauhua, the withdrawal of American forces shall not be delayed beyond the period strictly necessary to overcome such activities.

ARTICLE V. The withdrawal of American troops shall be effected by marching to Columbus or by using the Mexican Northwestern Railroad to El Paso, or by both routes, as may be deemed most convenient or expedient by the American commander.

ARTICLE VI. Each of the Governments parties to this agreement shall guard its side of the international boundary. This, however, does not preclude such cooperation on the part of the military commanders of both countries, as may be practicable.

ARTICLE III. The American and Mexican commanders shall deal separately, or wherever practicable in friendly cooperation, with any obstacles which may arise tending to bar or interfere with the withdrawal.

ARTICLE IV. The withdrawal of American troops shall be effected by marching to Columbus or by using the Mexican Northwestern Railroad to El Paso, or by both routes, as may be deemed most convenient or expedient by the American commander.

ARTICLE V. Until a satisfactory agreement is reached for the mutual protection of the border and pursuit of outlaws, each of the contracting Governments shall protect its own side of the boundary line. This, however, does not preclude such cooperation on the part of the military commanders of both countries as may be practicable.

| ARTICLE VII. This agreement shall take effect immediately upon approval by both Governments Notification of approval shall be communicated by each Government to the other. | ARTICLE VI. This agreement shall take effect immediately upon approval by both Governments. Notification of approval shall be communicated by each Government to the other. |

CC MS (SDR, RG 59, 812.00/20144½, DNA).

From William Lea Chambers

My dear Mr. President: Washington December 20, 1916.

The Board[1] has information from interested sources, which I think we can rely on, that leads me to believe there is little if any sincerity in the reported movements of the parties to reach an agreement on the controversies which the Adamson bill was intended to settle; and if you will pardon me, I will also say that I believe the whole purpose is to postpone legislation at this session of Congress.

If you desire it, I will be pleased to answer your call and give you orally the information I have and its sources.

Very respectfully,   W. L. Chambers

TLS (WP, DLC).
[1] That is, the United States Board of Mediation and Conciliation.

From Robert Somers Brookings

My dear Mr. President: St. Louis, December 20, 1916.

I have just returned from the East and find your very gracious letter of the 11th awaiting me.

I am deeply conscious of the fact that few men are more gifted for public service than Secretary Houston, and if even in a limited way he can assist you in bearing the great responsibilities of your high office, I should feel more than compensated for any sacrifice that we have been called upon to make.

With much appreciation of the kind thought which inspired your letter, believe me, Mr. President, with great respect and earnest best wishes for the continued success of your Administration,   Sincerely yours,   Robt. S. Brookings

TLS (WP, DLC).

Joseph Edward Willard to Robert Lansing, with Enclosure

Personal.   Washington, D. C.,
My dear Mr. Secretary: December 20, 1916.

Referring to our conversation of last evening, I enclose herewith, for your approval, copy of cable to our Charge d'Affaires in Madrid, which I am sending today, and, as instructed by the President, in cipher. I am retaining personally one copy.

Thanking you for your uniformly courteous consideration, please believe me, my dear Mr. Secretary,

Very sincerely yours,   Joseph E. Willard.

TLS (R. Lansing Papers, DLC).

ENCLOSURE

December 20, 1916.

In relation to the communication which the President has sent to the belligerent nations, and of which a copy has been sent you for delivery to the Spanish Government; I am directly authorized by the President to cable that you may say to his Majesty's Government, that having the same end in view, the time seems opportune for that Government to act, and, if willing, to support the position taken by this Government.   Willard

TC telegram (R. Lansing Papers, DLC).

From the Diary of Colonel House

December 20, 1916.

The President sent me today the original draft of the note which he has sent to the belligerents and neutrals. He asked me to return it so I took a copy with the eliminations and changes just as he had made them. I thought it might sometime be interesting since the President may destroy the original.

I have seldom seen anything he has written with so many changes. My letter to him tells of my thought on this subject. They do not tell, however, that I deprecate one sentence which will give further impetus to the belief that he does not yet understand what the Allies are fighting for. That one sentence will enrage them. I talked to him for ten minutes when I was there and got him to eliminate from the original draft a much more pronounced offense of the same character, but he has put it back in a modified form. He seems obsessed with that thought, and he cannot write or talk on the subject of the war without voicing it. It has done more to make him unpopular in the Allied countries than any one thing he has done, and it will probably keep him from taking the part which he ought to take in peace negotiations.

I find the President has nearly destroyed all the work I have done in Europe. He knows how I feel about this and how the Allies feel about it, and yet the refrain always appears in some form or other. Lansing, too, is afflicted with the same disease, but in his case it is not so serious as with the President.

Sir Horace Plunkett took lunch with me. He shows the result of his recent illness. He, too, confirms everything I have heard about the dislike of the United States among the people of England, and he did not deny there was a possibility of future trouble between Great Britain and this country. I am writing the President about this tonight. I wish I could make him realize the seriousness of the international situation and could open his eyes to the state of mind and their feeling toward us. I do not see how he can figure largely in an international adjustment as long as they feel toward him as they do. It is all so unnecessary. He could have done and said the same things if he had said & done them in a different way.

Whitehouse came to make some further suggestions.

Miss Ida Tarbell called to discuss the President's offer of a place on the Tariff Commission which I made her on Sunday. We talked for nearly an hour. She has an interesting mind. I did not try to persuade her as I could see she is not strong and should not undertake such arduous work. Then, too, her personal affairs are not in shape to allow it. She has a fine sense of public service and does not desire to decline a call of duty.

Vance McCormick brought Breckenridge Long of Saint Louis in order that I might look him over as a possible Assistant Secretary of State.

To William Cox Redfield

[The White House]
My dear Mr. Secretary: December 21, 1916

I yesterday wrote two letters about the fisheries matter, one to Mr. Claude Kitchin and the other to Mr. Houston, whose opposition was said to be one of the difficulties. I will be very glad to have your suggestion as to whom it would be most serviceable to write to in the Senate.

In haste   Faithfully yours,   Woodrow Wilson

TLS (Letterpress Books, WP, DLC).

To Robert Lansing

                                          The White House
My dear Mr. Secretary: December 21, 1916
     May I not return the enclosed papers[1] for your files and thank you for having sent them to me?

          Cordially and faithfully yours,   Woodrow Wilson

TLS (SDR, RG 59, 812.00/20145½, DNA).
  [1] RL to WW, Dec. 19, 1916.

From Joseph Patrick Tumulty, with Enclosure

Dear Governor   [Washington, Dec. 21, 1916]
     This statement was given out by the Secretary of State this morning. I thought you should know about it & send it.

                                               Tumulty

ALS (WP, DLC).

E N C L O S U R E

The reasons for the sending of the note were as follows:
"It is not our material interest we had in mind, when the note was signed, but more and more our own rights are becoming involved by the belligerents on both sides, so that the situation is becoming increasingly critical. *I mean by that, that we are drawing nearer the verge of war ourselves*, and therefore we are entitled to know exactly what each belligerent seeks in order that we may regulate our conduct in the future.

No nation has been sounded. No consideration of the German overtures or of the speech of Lloyd-George was taken into account in the formulation of the document. The only thing the overtures did was to delay it a few days. It was not decided to send it until Monday. Of course, the difficulties that face the President were that it might be construed as a movement toward peace and in aid of the German overtures. He specifically denies that that was the fact in the document itself."[1]

T MS (WP, DLC).

[1] The full text of Lansing's statement follows:

"The reasons for the sending of the note were as follows:

"It isn't our material interest we had in mind when the note was sent, but more and more our own rights are becoming involved by the belligerents on both sides, so that the situation is becoming increasingly critical.

"I mean by that that we are drawing nearer the verge of war ourselves, and therefore we are entitled to know exactly what each belligerent seeks, in order that we may regulate our conduct in the future.

"No nation has been sounded. No consideration of the German overtures or of the speech of Lloyd George was taken into account in the formulation of the document. The only thing the overtures did was to delay it a few days. It was not decided to send it until Monday. Of course, the difficulties that faced the President were that it might be construed as a movement toward peace and in aid of the German overtures. He specifically denies that that was the fact in the document itself.

"The sending of this note will indicate the possibility of our being forced into the war. That possibility ought to serve as a restraining and sobering force, safeguarding American rights. It may also serve to force an earlier conclusion of the war. Neither the President nor myself regard this note as a peace note; it is merely an effort to get the belligerents to define the end for which they are fighting." *New York Times*, Dec. 22, 1916. About Lloyd George's speech on the German peace offer, see H. Plunkett to EMH, Dec. 27, 1916, n. 4.

To Robert Lansing

The White House.

My dear Mr. Secretary,   21 December, 1916.

I quite understand that you did not realize the impression of your reference to war in your statement of this morning would make,[1] but I feel so strongly that the whole atmosphere of our present representations may be altered by that reference that I wrote to suggest this:

Would it not be possible for you to issue another statement, for the papers of to-morrow morning, saying that you found that your utterance of this morning had been radically misinterpreted, and explaining that your intention was merely to suggest the very direct interest the neutral nations have in the question of possible terms of peace and that it was not at all in your mind to intimate any change in the policy of neutrality which the country has so far so consistently pursued in the face of accumulating difficulties. You will know how to phrase it and how to give your unqualified endorsement to the whole tone and purpose of our note.

I write this because caught in a net of engagements from with [which] it seems impossible to extricate myself on short notice.

Faithfully Yours,   W.W.

WWTLI (RSB Coll., DLC).

[1] In fact, Wilson was so upset or infuriated by Lansing's statement that he nearly decided to demand Lansing's resignation. See the extract from the House Diary printed at Jan. 11, 1917.

Lansing conferred with Wilson at the White House in the afternoon of December 21; Wilson then wrote the foregoing letter; and Lansing issued the following statement:

"I have learned from several quarters that a wrong impression was made by the statement which I made this morning, and I wish to correct that impression.

"My intention was to suggest the very direct and necessary interest which this country, as one of the neutral nations, has in the possible terms which the belligerents may have in mind, and I did not intend to intimate that the Government was considering any change in its policy of neutrality, which it has consistently pursued in the face of constantly increasing difficulties.

"I regret that my words were open to any other construction, as I now realize that they were. I think that the whole tone and language of the note to the belligerents show the purpose without further comment on my part. It is needless to say that I am unreservedly in support of that purpose and hope to see it accepted." *New York Times*, Dec. 22, 1916.

Both Lansing and House set to work at once to reassure the British and French governments whose leaders were in a state of shock following the receipt of Wilson's note.

Spring Rice and the other Allied representatives in Washington agreed that Jusserand should speak for them all in protesting against Wilson's initiative. However, Spring Rice did report: "I received visit from a friend of the President who assured me that sentiments of entire Government towards us were most friendly, . . . and I was urged to impress on you the danger of treating the President's proposal as anything but a friendly step. A high official speaking most confidentially and in his own person thought statement should be made to the effect that only adequate security for permanent peace would be a popular and responsible Government in Germany." C. A. Spring Rice to the Foreign Office, No. 3808, Dec. 21, 1916, received 9:50 P.M., Dec. 22, 1916, T telegram (FO 371/2805, No. 259910, pp. 496-97, PRO).

As it turned out, Lansing called Jusserand to his office on the afternoon of December 20. Lansing explained that Wilson was not trying to mediate but did wish to help bring the war to an early end. Jusserand replied that he was surprised at such an appeal from a head of state who had repeatedly said that he was ignorant of the causes of the war and had no concern about them. It was as if a doctor said, "I am ignorant of the causes of your disease and have no cure. Permit me to cure you." Wilson and Congress were threatening the Allies at the very time that the dead of the *Lusitania* remained unavenged.

Lansing replied that it was not a parallel question, and that everyone knew where the President's preferences lay as between the democracies and the autocracies. Wilson wanted nothing that would cause harm to the Allies, particularly France, and only wanted to know what the Allies aspired to: Alsace-Lorraine; a correct and considerable indemnity for France, Belgium, and Serbia; the restoration of conquered territory; the settlement of the Balkan problem by a commission, and so on. Lansing said that he thought that these were very legitimate terms. Moreover, the Allies should make it clear that they would deal only with a liberalized Germany after a reform of the German electoral system and constitution. Finally, Lansing said that he was speaking only in his personal capacity; however, the material and spiritual conditions in Germany were such that he would not be surprised if Germany accepted all these terms. J. J. Jusserand to the Foreign Ministry, Nos. 928-30, Dec. 20, 1916, TC telegram (Télégrammes Washington, Vol. 46, pp. 97-98, FFM-Ar). Lansing called Spring Rice to his office on December 21 and repeated everything that he had said to Jusserand. However, Lansing was even more specific in his suggested peace terms. He added that he thought that the Allies might also demand the Trentino for Italy, an autonomous Poland under Russian sovereignty, and expulsion of Turkey from Europe. J. J. Jusserand to the Foreign Ministry, Nos. 933-34, Dec. 21, 1916, TC telegram (Télégrammes Washington, Vol. 46, pp. 99-100, FFM-Ar).

Someone in the Foreign Office in London burned three telegrams from the British Embassy in Paris. One was dated December 20; two were dated December 21. Among them undoubtedly were copies of Jusserand's telegrams to the French Foreign Ministry just cited. Stephen A. Oxman, "British Responses to President Wilson's Peace Efforts, 1914-1917" (D. Phil. dissertation, Oxford University, 1973), p. 385.

In New York, Colonel House was hard at work to repair what he thought was the disastrous damage done to Anglo-American relations by Wilson's peace initiative. House saw Sir Horace Plunkett on December 22 and assured him that the

Wilson administration's attitude toward Great Britain had not changed; that the administration thought that the German submarine menace was "appallingly serious for England, so much so that the President would hesitate to bring about a breach with Germany for fear he should do far more harm to England than American intervention on the side of the Allies would do good"; and that Wilson was convinced that he was restraining Germany. H. Plunkett to A. J. Balfour, Dec. 22, 1916, TLS (A. J. Balfour Papers, Add. MSS 49792, British Library). Plunkett also sent the following cablegram to Lord Robert Cecil at the Foreign Office through Wiseman: "Colonel House, to whom I deprecated the peace note, has positively assured me that the attitude of the Administration towards Britain has not changed from that which he explained to Balfour in February. I cable you as Balfour is reported absent." Quoted in H. Plunkett to A. J. Balfour, just cited.

Such reassuring messages continued to flow from Washington and New York to Paris and London during the next few days. Perhaps the most important were reports from Jusserand and Roy Howard. Jusserand cabled the Foreign Ministry on December 23: "Mr. Lansing's second statement has less credibility than the first, and they very generally believe here that to the well known desire of the President to play a role in the peace settlement has come to be added (in effect, to determine his decision) the fear that, if the war lasts, his country will be drawn into it at a time when it is so badly prepared to make war." J. J. Jusserand to the Foreign Ministry, Dec. 23, 1916, No. 938, TC telegram (Télégrammes Washington, Vol. 46, p. 101, FFM-Ar). But even more explicit was the following message from Roy Howard: "Tell Northcliffe privately Colonel House says that Lansing's *first* statement on the morning of the twenty-first in which he said that America was on the verge of war, is the secret of the Note's real purpose. Incidentally, its frankness almost caused war." Quoted in Northcliffe to D. Lloyd George, Dec. 27, 1916, TLS (D. Lloyd George Papers, F/41/7/2, House of Lords Record Office).

Subsequent documents in this volume will reconfirm the fact that Wilson regarded his note of December 18 as a prelude to the peace conference over which he hoped to preside. It is clear from the foregoing discussion that Lansing and House were, at the minimum, seeking to assure the French and British governments that Wilson believed that the United States would soon be forced into the war, and that he had sent the note to prepare American public opinion for such an eventuality. Lansing, of course, went further and suggested terms (indeed, he intimated that Wilson approved them) that the Allies could have imposed only through a decisive military victory. The only possible inference from this fact is that Lansing wanted the Allies to reply to Wilson in such a manner as to tip the scales in Germany in favor of an all-out submarine campaign which, Lansing believed, would force the United States into the war. As we will see, this did in fact happen.

Soon after issuing the "verge of war" statement, Lansing wrote a memorandum explaining the motives behind his action. Lansing wrote that he had issued his first statement because he was convinced that Wilson's note, standing alone, would be generally perceived as supportive of and in fact supplemental to the German peace overture. The Allies would be deeply hurt, would believe that the United States would support Germany, and would return a curt refusal to Wilson's appeal for a statement of war aims. "The essential point in the situation," Lansing explained, "was *that the only explanation which would satisfy public opinion that the note was not sent to support the German overture, was the announced belief that the danger of a break of diplomatic relations was so imminent that steps to prevent it could not be delayed until the overture was answered.* No other course seemed possible to avoid the logic of the circumstances as to the real purpose of the note."

Lansing continued:

"The results which I sought to accomplish by the statement were two: *First*, to destroy any belief which the German Government had that the identic note was induced by its overture or was intended to support it, since that would apparently deprive the note of its impartial character and incline the German Government not to comply with the request for a statement of terms on the assumption that the request was directed in reality to the Allies. *Second*, to show to the Entente Governments that there was an excellent reason for the United States on its own account to ask both sides at this particular time to declare frankly the specific conditions which they would demand before making peace.

"The line of thought was this: If the United States is forced unwittingly to act, it is necessary for it to determine which side it will join in the conflict. To reach an intelligent determination it is entitled to know specifically the demands of the respective parties so that it can decide which demands are just and to what the United States is obligated by becoming a belligerent. Furthermore there was the possibility that on comparing the respective demands of the two parties some basis can be found for the negotiation of a peace, which would remove the imminent danger of the United States being dragged into the war. This possibility was the result most earnestly hoped for by this Government, though it seemed doubtful of being realized.

"I realized that it was possible that the Allies might conclude from a statement that the peace of the United States was threatened that, if this country entered the war, it must enter it on their side because of the acute situation caused by the continued outrages by German submarines; and that there was danger, if the Allied Governments were convinced of this, that they would deem it for their interest to leave everything *in statu quo* on the theory that the course of events would compel the United States to break with Germany. On the other hand they had to face the possibility that the German Government would respond frankly to the request in the note, and that, if it did and if the Allies refused, the United States would be compelled to view the German reply as friendly and that of the Allies as in a measure unfriendly.

"I assumed that the Allied Governments would, therefore, not be influenced to refuse to reply to our request by a statement as to the imminent menace to the peace of this country. But, even if they were so influenced and failed to perceive the logical consequence of a refusal, the situation would be no worse than rejection by the Allies and noncompliance by their enemies, which seemed to be certain if no statement was made. With the issuance of a statement that the critical situation of American interests required immediate action there was the possibility that the note would receive favorable replies; without such statement there seemed to be no possibility. Convinced of this and earnestly desiring that the note should accomplish its purpose I made the first statement at the first opportunity feeling that no time should be lost in counteracting the opinion which was bound to be formed from the circumstances surrounding the sending of the note.

"However, after discussing the statement with the President, I found that he feared that it might give the impression that this Government had actually decided to enter the war in case the terms proposed by one group of belligerents appeared to be more just and lenient than those of the other group, so that instead of being an attempt to avoid becoming a party by finding some basis for peace negotiations the note of this Government was in fact a threat that the United States would exert its physical might in favor of one side or the other. The President also gave more emphasis to the possibility that the statement might cause the Allies to seek to continue the present critical situation than I had done. As to the underirable [undesirable] impression which the statement might create, I agreed with him for I saw that my words were open to such an erroneous interpretation. I, therefore, issued at once a second statement declaring that the United States had no intention of abandoning its policy of neutrality."
R. Lansing, "CONFIDENTIAL MEMORANDUM IN RE: THE TWO STATEMENTS WHICH I ISSUED TO THE PRESS ON DECEMBER 21, 1916 . . . " TS MS (R. Lansing Papers, NjP).

The evidence is overwhelming that Lansing thought that Wilson's efforts for peace were foolhardy and unwise, and that the Secretary of State was doing everything that he could to promote American entry in the war against Germany. As the documents have revealed, he had already urged Wilson to break relations with Germany over the *Marina* and *Arabia* cases. He wrote in his so-called diary (T MSS, R. Lansing Papers, DLC) on December 3, 1916, that he was sure that Wilson's hope of making peace could not succeed, and that he was not sure that it would be a good thing for the world if Wilson did succeed. "Our present position is becoming impossible. We are very near the edge of the precipice. When we do go into the war, and we might as well make up our minds that we are going in, we *must* go in on the side of the Allies, for we are a democracy."

In another memorandum which he wrote on December 3, Lansing wrote that Wilson cherished the idea of a negotiated peace. But there could be no hope for peace on just terms until Germany's power had been broken. A peace move would alienate the Allies; it was imperative that the United States be drawn closer to them. "What will the President do?," Dec. 3, 1916, T MS (R. Lansing Papers, DLC).

Lansing came near to telling the truth when he wrote to a friend as follows:

"In regard to my statements concerning the notes to the belligerents I will one of these days tell you the whole story. The inside facts are most interesting and I believe that you will find my course was justified. Of course I have been generally criticized by the press but I do not blame the editors as on the face of it they are right. Unfortunately I can not make public the real reason now—I do not know as I ever can although I hope it may be possible to do so some day. For the present, however, I must bear the blame of having made an unpardonable blunder, and I do so with perfect equinimity knowing that my action accomplished what it was intended to accomplish.

"Of course I am talking in enigmas to you but one of these days I will explain the whole thing to you for your personal enlightenment as I do not want you to think me quite so lacking in judgment as the papers charge and the known facts seem to prove." R. Lansing to Edward N. Smith, Jan. 21, 1917, HwCLS (R. Lansing Papers, DLC).

This carries the story to December 26, when an Anglo-French conference met in London for the purpose, among other things, of framing a reply to Wilson's note.

To the Right Reverend Arsène E. Vehouni

Your Eminence: [The White House] December 21, 1916

I was very much touched to receive at your hands the other day[1] the address[2] which His Holiness, Kevork V, Primate and Catholicos of all the Armenians and Supreme Patriarch of the National See of Ararat, was gracious enough to send me in recognition of such services as the representatives of the United States have been able to render to the distressed Armenians upon whom the burden of the present war has fallen with circumstances of especial tragedy. I am sure that I am expressing the feeling of the people of the United States when I say that the little we have been able to do has been done with hearts full of sympathy, and that the suffering people of Armenia may rest assured that they will continue to receive at our hands an unqualified sympathy and, whenever it is possible, generous assistance.   Cordially and sincerely yours,   Woodrow Wilson

TLS (Letterpress Books, WP, DLC).
[1] December 14, 1916.
[2] It is printed in A. E. Vehouni to WW, Nov. 29, 1916, n. 3.

From John Hessin Clarke

My dear Mr President: Washington, D. C. [c. Dec. 21, 1916]

Doubtless I am a partial judge in your case, but I can not refrain from writing you how wise, and timely and noble your note to the Powers seems to me to be. It is worthy the best that is in us as a nation. Let the critics rave!

Cordially and Sincerely   John H. Clarke

ALS (WP, DLC).

To John Hessin Clarke

My dear Mr. Justice: The White House December 21, 1916

Your note about the representations I have just made to the belligerent governments gives me the deepest and truest gratification, and I want you to know how sincerely I appreciate your generous judgment. The thing was certainly done with a full heart.

Cordially and sincerely yours,   Woodrow Wilson

TLS (J. H. Clarke Papers, OCIW).

To William Lea Chambers

My dear Judge: [The White House] December 21, 1916

Thank you for the information contained in your letter of December twentieth. I would not in any case have consented to a postponement of the legislation and I am taking steps now to press it as far as possible.

In haste, with much appreciation,

Sincerely yours,   Woodrow Wilson

TLS (Letterpress Books, WP, DLC).

To Rudolph Spreckels

Personal.

[The White House]

My dear Mr. Spreckels: December 21, 1916

Thank you for writing me again about the abuse of proxy votes in stockholders' meetings. The suggestion you make interests me very much indeed and I am going to take it up with those who can best advise me here.

This is only a line to tell you that I am going to see what can be done.

In haste

Cordially and sincerely yours,   Woodrow Wilson

TLS (Letterpress Books, WP, DLC).

To William Gibbs McAdoo

My dear Mac: [The White House] December 21, 1916

I wish you would read this letter from Mr. Rudolph Spreckels.[1] It seems to me to contain a most interesting suggestion which may lead to something useful.

I happen to have heard very recently that there is a deliberate intention on the part of many of the controlling interests in the country to throw men out of employment just so soon as it may be possible to do so by reason of a slackening of the war orders.

In haste Affectionately yours, Woodrow Wilson

TLS (Letterpress Books, WP, DLC).
[1] Spreckels' letter is missing in WP, DLC, and in the W. G. McAdoo Papers, DLC. Wilson's reply to Spreckels, however, suggests that Spreckels had again raised the subject of his letter to Wilson of Aug. 21, 1916, printed in Vol. 38. In that letter, Spreckles had complained that the proxy system of voting at stockholders' meetings of large corporations and banks was responsible for keeping a "selfish and arbitrary minority in control." He had suggested that Congress pass legislation prohibiting the use of proxies at stockholders' meetings of corporations doing interstate business. He further urged that Congress designate a federal official in each of the states in which such stockholders' meetings were held to vote the stock of absentee shareholders. Thus, Spreckels had claimed, the power of the few who dominated almost everything in the country would be ended.

From Robert Lansing

PERSONAL AND PRIVATE:

My dear Mr. President: Washington December 21, 1916.

I laid before you some days ago the present status of the submarine controversy and gave it as my opinion that we were approaching, if we had not reached, a time when we must either make good by some action or else withdraw from the position which we took in the SUSSEX case. I do not think that we can continue this uncertain state much longer, and ought, therefore, determine on a definite course of action.

In some of the cases all the evidence possibly obtainable has been received and we can offer no further excuse, which seems valid, for delaying action. Meanwhile new cases are becoming of almost daily occurrence, from which it may be concluded that the German Government has assumed that we intend to submit to the sinking of American vessels with Americans on board without carrying out our threat. I cannot but feel that to have this impression prevail in Germany, and it is having its effect here as well, puts us in a more or less humiliating position and may seriously affect our prestige as a government which means what it says. I know that you will agree with me that we cannot afford

that impression to become a conviction, and I, therefore, urge
that we determine at once upon a definite course of action and do
so without delay. I am firmly convinced that we ought not to
longer avoid a decision.

I hope, therefore, you can consider my former letter and the
general subject and advise me as to your wishes.

Faithfully yours,   Robert Lansing

TLS (WP, DLC).

From William Jennings Bryan

Miami, Florida, December 21, 1916.

You have rendered an invaluable service to a war-stricken
world in asking the belligerent nations to set forth in specific
terms the concessions and assurances which they deem necessary to the establishment of a lasting peace. It would be a reflection upon the nations at war to doubt that they know the ends
for which they are fighting or to assume that they have any purposes which they are unwilling to reveal. A definite statement by
both sides, no matter how far these statements may be apart,
will clear the air and afford a basis for negotiations, and when
negotiations begin they are not likely to terminate until an agreement is reached, because neither side will consent to assume
responsibility for continuing the unspeakable horrors of this conflict, if any reasonable terms can be secured. Accept cordial
congratulations and my earnest wish for the success of the movement which you have had the honor to inaugurate.

William Jennings Bryan.

CC telegram (WP, DLC).

From Harry Augustus Garfield

Dear Mr. President: [Williamstown, Mass.] Dec. 21, 1916

With profoundest gratitude for your message to the Powers,
which was sent, as I knew it would be, when the moment for its
fullest influence came, & with Christmas greetings from all of us
to you & to each of your household, I remain, as always, with high
and affectionate regard,

Faithfully yours,   H. A. Garfield.

HwCLS (H. A. Garfield Papers, DLC).

From William Cannon Houston

Washington, D. C.
Dear Mr. President: December 21, 1916.

I beg leave to acknowledge the receipt of your letter this after-noon, just as I am preparing to leave for home, in reference to the bill to regulate the fisheries in Alaska and I note with deep interest the fact that you approve and favor the enactment of this measure.

I have been fearful that this measure, in its present form, would give exclusive and perpetual rights to parties now operat-ing these fisheries to such an extent that they would have absolute control of this great interest in Alaska, and in view of the fact that the measure does not, to the extent I think it should, prevent the methods in use there, which as I understand are destroying the fish that come to these waters, I have enter-tained grave doubts as to the wisdom of this measure.

I am much impressed by the fact that the measure meets your approval and you desire its passage and this causes me to feel that I should give it my most serious thought, and I assure you that I shall do so.   Respectfully,   W. C. Houston.

TLS (WP, DLC).

From Herbert Bruce Brougham

Dear Mr. President: Philadelphia 21st December 1916.

While we are actively canvassing the question which I dis-cussed with you yesterday, some notion of the character of the men who shape the editorial policy of the Public Ledger may be gained from the inclosed clippings of its editorial articles on your appointment of Justice Brandeis, and the series of articles by William Hard on this appointment, together with clippings of the special articles by George Creel and Charles Ferguson, and of our editorial approval of the movement which Ferguson has started in New York.[1]

I greatly appreciate your reception of me and extended talk on a day which must have had its special cares and anxieties.
          Very sincerely yours,   H. B. Brougham

TLS (WP, DLC).
[1] The clippings which he enclosed were as follows: (1) An undated editorial, "Will It Be 'Mr. Justice Brandeis'?" supporting Wilson's nomination of Brandeis; (2) Three articles by William Hard, a freelance writer: "Brandeis The Conserva-tive Or A 'Dangerous Radical'?", May 12, 1916; "Brandeis The Adjuster And Private-Life Judge," May 14, 1916; and " 'Regularization' Of Shops By A Business Individual," May 16, 1916. Hard praised the selection of Brandeis and said he

was a free spirit and a man of deep culture with a uniquely judicial temperament. (3) A letter to the editor from Charles Ferguson, Nov. 22, 1916, in which Ferguson deplored the continual antagonism between manufacturers and organized labor and called for the formation of a group of intelligent men "who can do things—who are determined to do them and do them well." Such a group, if sufficiently impatient with theories and endowed with practical sense, he claimed, could put an end to the wars of capital and labor and lower the price of bread as well. (4) A news report, " 'New Machine' Fights High Cost," Dec. 10, 1916, which described the organization by fifty members of the American Society of Mechanical Engineers, then meeting in New York, of a schismatic group dedicated to increasing the purchasing power of the dollar by eliminating managerial inefficiency in the planning, building, and operation of industrial plants and in the distribution of foodstuffs. (5) An editorial, "The New Machine" Dec. 10, 1916, which commented favorably on the objectives of the new group. And (6) an article by George Creel, "What Men Four Years Hence Will Lead Nation's Parties?", which said that Wilson's reelection had smashed the conservative wings of both the Republican and Democratic parties, and that the membership of each party would henceforth find it necessary to regroup behind a progressive candidate if they wished to appeal to the new electorate which had emerged during the Wilson years.

Sir Cecil Arthur Spring Rice to Arthur James Balfour

Washington December 21st, 1916.

No. 3807. There is little doubt in minds of all allied representatives here that although President's strong wish is to play great part as peace maker main reason for his action is fear of German submarines and of his being involved in war. Belgian Minister saw House in New York and was convinced of this.[1]

President believes Allies incapable of coping with this warfare and does not wish to be forced into alternative of war or ignominious surrender. Germans say United States Government must prohibit Americans from travelling on any but certain marked ships and that all other ships with allied destination will be destroyed. To avoid this alternative President is determined to arrange a peace or at any rate peace negotiations.

T telegram (FO 371/2805, p. 478, PRO).
[1] House did not record this meeting in his diary nor report on it in a letter to Wilson.

From James Viscount Bryce

Private

My dear Mr. President   [London] Dec. 22nd 1916

Will you pardon me for venturing to trouble you with a few lines prompted by a wish to lay before you the state of public sentiment here. I have not yet seen to-day's newspapers; but if the current sentiment should find warm expression in them, the reason may not be fully understood in America. I write for and from myself only, knowing nothing of the views of the present British Government beyond what they have said in Parliament.

Our people, and the French also, do not understand how it can appear to be thought in any neutral country that the moral position and aims of the Allies can be put on the same plane as those of Germany and Austria and the Turks. We have conducted the war, first and last, upon the recognized principles of humanity and have respected the lives of innocent civilians. We entered the war with no selfish aims, and mainly to save Belgium. We have been feeding her people for the last twenty months. We honestly wish to save her, to secure reparation for her, and to deliver the Eastern Christians from Turkish massacres. What Germany has done in Belgium and what she has permitted in Armenia you know. I need say nothing about the Lusitania and the constant slaughter of innocent non combatants over the whole East of England by aircraft. Now it hurts us that our motives and our conduct should be spoken of as if they bore any resemblance to those of Germany Austria and Turkey. Moreover our experience of German faithlessness, and unblushing disregard of honour and the principles of right, have made it impossible for us to attach the slightest value to any protestations she utters or any promises she makes

I wish the German Government would state its terms, but am sure they would be such as the Allies could not accept. Neither will she accept any terms we could offer. The German Government is too much afraid of its own Junkers and Jingoes to do that, and its recent successes in Rumania make it all the harder for it to abate its demands. I believe that [the] offer it has just made to negotiate is designed partly as bluff, partly to appease the hungry crowds, partly to entrap us into negotiations which would give the Germans time to improve their position, and could have, under present conditions, no practical result.

We are as heartily anxious for peace as any people could be. Every household is mourning sons brothers husbands. But a peace concluded on any terms the German Government would now accept would be a hollow truce They, being what they have shewn themselves to be (by their whole conduct and principles), would not honestly enter into any League of Peace. A regenerated Germany, delivered from the rule of soldiers, might do so.

That is why we must fight on at whatever cost. It is the best chance for safety & for peace itself.

I need not say how heartily I sympathize with your desire for the establishment, after the war, of a system to prevent future wars, nor how grateful I am to you for what you have said about that in your speech last June,[1] which some of us here, who have been working for a League of Peace, have often quoted for the hopes it held out of America's participation. But I am sure such a system could not be established on the basis of any terms the German military caste would embrace or observe With a democratic Germany it would be different. Believe me, with many apologies for so long a letter, written in haste—for mail.

Very sincerely yours   James Bryce

ALS (WP, DLC).

[1] He referred to Wilson's speech to the League to Enforce Peace, printed at May 27, 1916, Vol. 37.

From John Sharp Williams

My dear Mr President   Washington, D. C. Dec 22/16

I tried several times yesterday to get Tumulty ovver the phone to transmit a personal message to you, which is in itself of no importance, except in so far as importance may be reflected upon it by the subject-matter.

I wanted only to say that while you have as governor of New Jersey and as president of the United States done several very fine things—in the good old English significance of the word— fine in phraseology, in taste, in sentiment & in thought, in purpose & in effect—the finest thing you ever did was your identic note to the governments of the belligerent countries.

It was actuated at once by Americanism & by a cultured & true "International Mind." It went to the centre. Germany must now say whether a *sine qua non* with her is the subjection of Belgium to herself, the subjection of Servia to Austria, a resur- [r]ected Poland with out regard to German & Austrian Poles, the retention in Europe of "the unspeakable Turk" & the subjection to him of Armenian, Syrian & other Christians in Asia; or whether she is willing to let the world live on a basis of independence & self-evolution of languages & nationalities. With more regard than ever before even—

Yours truly   John Sharp Williams

ALS (WP, DLC).

From Claude Kitchin

Dear Mr. President: Washington, D. C. December 22, 1916.

Please permit me to acknowledge receipt of your letter of the 20th, expressing your great interest in the bill for the protection, regulation and conservation of the fisheries of Alaska.

I wish to assure you that I will take pleasure in cooperating with Judge Alexander, Chairman of the Committee from which the bill is reported, with a view to pass it at this session.

Sincerely yours,   Claude Kitchin

TLS (WP, DLC).

Walter Hines Page to Robert Lansing

London, December 22, 1916.

5363, Confidential. Your circular 18th. The dominant tone in public and private comment on the President's suggestion is surprise and sorrowful consternation and all public comment so far is visibly restrained. The Foreign Office gave the British press a hint last night to maintain its comments cautiously and not to question the President's sincerity. Beneath open comment is a deep feeling of dissappointment and in many quarters even of anger. The only section of opinion that is pleased is the small group of pacifists.

The President's suggestion itself would have provoked little or no criticism if it had been made at another time. But his remarks accompanying his suggestion are interpreted as placing the allies and the central powers on the same moral level. The WESTMINSTER GAZETTE this afternoon, alone among all the London dailies, explains that such an interpretation is not warranted by a careful reading of the note.

The opinion even in the least excitable and most friendly circles is that the note was a mistake because they judge it ill-timed and because they interpret it to show a misunderstanding of the aims of the allies. The British feel that this is a holy and defensive war which must be fought to a decisive conclusion to save free government in the world from a military tyranny and that even to suggest ending it indecisively is a blow at free government.

Bryce came to see me profoundly depressed. He has written the President a personal letter which I send in tonight's pouch.

Northcliff tells me that his papers the TIMES and the DAILY MAIL are saying and will continue to say as little as possible but that "the people are as mad as hell." I am told that Mr. Asquith when asked about the note replied sadly, "Dont talk to me about it. It is most disheartening." A luncheon guest at the palace yesterday informs me that the King wept while he expressed his surprise and depression.

It is perhaps too soon to venture an opinion about the permanent effect of the note on British feeling towards our government; but there is reason to fear that it will for a long time cause a deep, even if silent, resentment because as the British interpret it, it seems to them to mean that the President fails to understand the motives and high necessities, the aims and the sacrifices of the allies who regard themselves as fighting, now with good hope, to save the world from a despotic inundation.

I presume the comments of the chief London newspapers have been telegraphed to the American press. The following sentences are from today's morning CHRONICLE which has always been sympathetic and friendly. The editorial from which they are taken is thought in newspaper circles to reflect the opinion of the Prime Minister. They are typical of the restrained comment thus far made:

"As a liberal newspaper which has always made a special feature of endeavoring to bring Britain and America more closely together and has through evil report as well as good consistency [consistently] championed United States in this country, we may ask our friends across the Atlantic to believe us when we say that no American state paper within our generation has been calculated to cause so much pain not merely to Englishmen but to liberal opinion throughout Western and Southern Europe as the note from President Wilson communicated to our Foreign Office on December twentieth.

The President beyond all doubt whatever did not intend his words as an insult but they are deeply insulting none the less and none of the allied peoples can be expected to relish them."

Page

T telegram (SDR, RG 59, 763.72119/253, DNA).

Paul Ritter to Arthur Hoffmann

FRIEDE.

Herr Bundesrat,   [Washington], den 22. Dez. 1916.

Ihr Kabel vom 18. Dezember[1] betr. engerer Fühlungsnahme mit Wilson in Friedenssachen war gerade eingelaufen, als am Morgen des 19 ten. mich Herr Lansing telephonisch ersuchte um 11 Uhr 45 im Staatsdepartemente vorzusprechen. Ich traf im Wartezimmer den spanischen Botschafter RIANO, welcher vor mir eintrat & mir beim Zurückkommen zuflüsterte: "er wird Ihnen etwas Angenehmes mitteilen."

Herr Lansing sagte, dass da die Lage der Neutralen ganz unerträglich geworden sei, (has become intolerable) der Präsident sich zur Absendung einer Note, (deren Inhalt er mir darlegte) an die Regierung der Kriegsführenden, sowie der neutralen Staaten entschlossen habe. Diese sei gestern Abend auch für Bern an Minister STOVALL abgegangen.

Ich nahm als selbstverständlich an, dass Herr Stovall Ihnen mitteilen werde, dass die Note an alle Neutralen gegangen sei & beschränkte mich daher in meinem Kabel vom 19. Dez. Sie wissen zu lassen, dass ich informiert sei.

Am 20. Dez. Nachmittags 6 Uhr wurde der Wortlaut der Npte [Note] den hiesigen Botschaftern & Gesandten mitgeteilt & erregte, da sie überall als vollkommene Ueberraschung kam, ungeheueres Aufsehen. Bei den andern Neutralen insbesondere erzeugte das bald durchsickernde Faktum, dass Riano & ich allein schon vorher von Lansing ins Vertrauen gezogen worden waren, Misstimmung.

Gleichen Abends war ich zu einem grossen Diner bei Lansings eingeladen, an welchem auch der italienische Bot & der japanische Botschafter teilnahmen. Im Rauchzimmer setzte sich der Staatssekretär ausschliesslich mit mir in eine Ecke & wir kamen überein, dass es besser sein werde ein paar Tage zuzuwarten, ehe ich dem Präsidenten Ihren Kabelauftrag vom 18. Dez. zur Kenntnis bringe, da Herr Wilson später besser als gerade jetzt mir eine Antwort zu geben im Stande sein werde.

Am nächsten Morgen, den 21ten, veröffentlichte die Presse den Wortlaut der Note. Noch in höherem Masse als dies nach dem Friedensschritte Deutschlands der Fall gewesen, brachte diese Publikation nicht nur einen neuen Kursfall der Papiere aller Industrien, welche mit Kriegslieferungen zu tun haben hervor, sondern auch Weizen, Baumwolle etc. fielen lebhaft im Preise.

Die N. Y. Staatszeitung vom 21. Dez. enthält ein gutes Stimmungsbild & erspart es mir heute ausführlicher zu werden.

Der 22te brachte neue Aufregungen in die officielle Welt. Von den Zeitungsreportern gepresst sich über die Wilsonsche Note weiter zu äussern, hat LANSING, nervös & überarbeitet, den Leuten im Interview ein Diktat gegeben, welches in nackten Worten darstellt, was verschleiert & zwischen den Zeilen schon aus der Note vom 18. Dez. herauszulesen gewesen war. Lansing sagte nämlich: "das Absenden unserer Note deutet an, dass Möglichkeit vorhanden ist uns in den Krieg hineinzuzwingen. Weder der Präsident noch ich betrachten sie als eine Friedensnote, sondern lediglich als einen Anlauf um endlich die Kriegführenden zu veranlassen das Ziel anzugeben für welches sie kämpfen."

Der Präsident,—vielleicht in übertriebenr Weise—von seinem Privatsekretär TUMULTY, welcher mit LANSING auf gespanntem

Fusse steht, auf die Tragweite dieses Interviews sofort aufmerk-
sam gemacht, hatte eine heftige Auseinandersetzung mit dem
Staatssekretär, dahin resultierend, dass in den heutigen Morgen-
blättern die nicht sehr würdige Erklärung Herrn Lansings zu
lesen ist: "ich bedauere & sehe es ein, dass meinen gestrigen
Worten ein anderer Sinn unterlegt werden kann, als ich ihnen zu
geben wünschte * * * *"

Da nun gerade heute Morgen Ihre Kabelanfrage einlief, ob
alle Neutralen die Note vom 18. erhalten haben, so fügte ich der
bejahenden Antwort eine kurze Skizze über das unglückliche
Lansing-Interview an.

Bei den Kollegen im diplomatischen Corps hat diese Ent-
schleierung der tieferen Absichten Wilsons naturgemäss wilde
Mutmassungen hervorgerufen & jeder glaubt sich berechtigt
sie in dem für ihn günstigsten Sinne zu interpretieren.

Im Staatsdepartemente sind die aufgeregten Vertreter der
verschiedenen Mächte gleichzeitig eingetroffen & es bedurfte
geschickten Manoeverierens seitens des Personals um Zusam-
menstösse zu verhindern.

Auch für diese jüngsten Vorkomnisse gestatte ich mir, Sie auf
die soeben einlaufende heutige Ausgabe der N. Y. Staatszeitung,
welche ich hier beilege zu verweisen.

Die Kurse an der Börse fallen immer noch & es herrscht dato
hier ein wildes, noch selten gesehenes diplomatisches, politisches
& geschäftliches Chaos, für welches die Presse wie Sie den Aus-
schnitten entnehmen wollen, kurzerhand den Staatssekretär
Lansing verantwortlich macht.

Genehmigen Sie, Herr Bundesrat, die erneute Versicherung
meiner ausgezeichneten Hochachtung

Beilangen.   (Ges.) Ritter

TCL (E2300 Washington, No. 33, Swiss Federal Archives).
    [1] Dated December 17, 1916, it follows (our translation): "With reference to
the conversation held on November 22, 1916, with President Wilson and to our
cable of November 18, we simply had in mind getting in closer contact with
President Wilson so that he could tell us in great confidence any plans that he
might have so that we could work together. We are ready to inform the President
of what we have learned of opinion in the warring countries. Political Department." TC telegram (E2001 [B] 1, Vol. 81, Swiss Federal Archives). The Editors
have not found a copy of this telegram in any repository in the United States.
    Ritter left a copy of this telegram with Tumulty on about December 26.
P. Ritter to Swiss Foreign Ministry, n.d., received December 29, 1916, Hw
telegram (E2001 [B] 1, Vol. 17, Swiss Federal Archives). Wilson received
Ritter at the White House on January 9, 1917. See P. Ritter to A. Hoffmann,
Jan. 12, 1917.

PEACE.

Mr. Federal Councilor: Washington, December 22, 1916.

Your cable of December 18 about closer contact with Wilson on peace matters had just come in when, on the morning of the 19th, Mr. Lansing asked me by telephone to meet him at the State Department at 11:45. In the reception room I met the Spanish Ambassador, Riaño, who went in first and, on coming out, whispered to me: "He has good news for you."

Mr. Lansing said that, the position of the neutrals having become quite intolerable, the President had decided to send a note (whose contents he described to me) to the belligerent governments as well as to the neutral states. This went also to Minister Stovall at Bern last [the same?] evening.

I took it for granted that Mr. Stovall would inform you, since the note went to all neutrals, and accordingly limited myself in my cable of December 19 to letting you know I had been informed.

At 6 p.m. on December 20 the text of the note was given to the ambassadors and ministers here and, coming as a complete surprise to all, it caused an enormous sensation. Among the other neutrals, especially, there was much displeasure at the fact, which quickly leaked out, that Lansing had let only Riaño and me in on the secret ahead of time.

That same evening I was invited to a large dinner at Lansing's, with the Italian and Japanese Ambassadors also present. In the smoking room, the Secretary of State sat alone with me in a corner, and we agreed that it would be better to wait a few days before I brought the proposal in your cable of December 18 to the President, as Mr. Wilson would be in better position to reply later rather than just now.

On the next morning, the 21st, the press published the text of the note. Even more than in the case of the German peace move, this news brought not only a further drop in stock prices of all industries concerned with war deliveries, but also a sharp drop in the prices of grain, cotton, etc.

The *N. Y. Staats-Zeitung* of December 21 contains a good review of public opinion and spares me from going into detail on this today.

The 22d brought new excitement in the official world. Being pressed by newspaper reporters to say more about Wilson's note, Lansing, nervous and overworked, gave those at the interview a statement that said in naked words what in the note of December

18 was hazy and to be read between the lines. Lansing said, in fact: "The sending of our note indicates the possibility of our being forced into the war. Neither the President nor myself regard it as a peace note, it is merely an effort at last to get the belligerents to define the end for which they are fighting."

The President's Private Secretary, Tumulty, whose relations with Lansing are strained, immediately informed the President of the burden of the interview, perhaps in exaggerated terms, and he (Wilson) then had a great disagreement with the Secretary of State, with the result that today's morning newspapers publish the not very dignified clarification by Mr. Lansing: "I realize and regret that my words yesterday could be taken in another way than I had intended. . . ."

Since there came just this morning your cable inquiry as to whether the neutrals have received the note of the 18th, I added to an affirmative reply [by telegram] a short sketch on the unfortunate interview by Lansing.

This unveiling of Wilson's deeper plans has naturally aroused wild conjectures among colleagues in the diplomatic corps, and everyone feels justified in interpreting the situation in the terms most acceptable to himself.

The excited representatives of the various powers converged simultaneously at the State Department, and it took skilled maneuvering by its personnel to prevent collisions.

For these latest events too I allow myself to enclose the newly-arrived issue of today's *N. Y. Staats-Zeitung*.

Prices on the stock market are still falling, and as of now there prevails a wild and seldom-seen diplomatic, political, and commercial chaos, for which, as the enclosed clippings show, the press in sum holds Secretary of State Lansing responsible.

Accept, Mr. Federal Councilor, the renewed assurance of my highest respect. (Signed) Ritter

To Robert Lansing, with Enclosure

The White House.
My dear Mr. Secretary, 23 December, 1916.

It has occurred to me that it might serve our present objects better if we were to send instructions such as the enclosed to our representatives at the capitals of the several belligerents, to whom our recent note went. What do you think? I wish to remove every possible ground of hesitation that we are in a position to remove.

If you see no serious objection, will you not be kind enough to have this message coded and despatched at the earlies[t] practicable time, and with the most careful precautions against a leak?   Faithfully Yours,   W. W.

WWTLI (R. Lansing Papers, NjP).

E N C L O S U R E

In regard to the Department's No. (the note addressed to all the belligerent governments) please say to the Minister for Foreign Affairs of the government to which you are accredited that the Government of the United States sincerely hopes that the note will be considered as carrying none of the implications which have been attributed to it in the press and elsewhere and as meaning nothing but what it plainly and in entire frankness expresses. Intimate also that what this Government ventures to suggest is that whatever reply is made, if the request of the note is complied with, be made, not publicly, but in strict confidence; it being understood that the Government of the United States may in its turn convey it in like confidence to the governments of the other group of belligerents, in order that it may in that way be ascertained without publicity whether there is any present ground or basis to hope for negotiations or conferences of any kind.[1]

WWT MS (R. Lansing Papers, NjP).
[1] This was sent, e.g., as RL to Amembassy, Paris, Dec. 24, 1916, CC telegram (SDR, RG 84, Foreign Service Posts: Paris, Vol. 43, DNA).

From the Swiss Federal Council[1]

[Bern, Dec. 23, 1916]

The President of the United States of America, with whom the Swiss Federal Council, guided by its warm desire that the hostilities may soon come to an end, has, for a considerable time, been in touch, had the kindness to apprise the Federal Council of the peace note sent to the governments of the Central and Entente Powers. In this note President Wilson discusses the great desirability of international agreements for the purpose of avoiding more effectively and permanently the occurrence of catastrophes such as the one under which the peoples are suffering today. In this connection he lays particular stress on the necessity for bringing about the end of the present war. Without making peace proposals himself or offering mediation, he confines himself to sounding as to whether mankind may hope to have approached the haven of peace.

The most meritorious personal initiative of President Wilson will find a mighty echo in Switzerland. True to the obligations arising from observing the strictest neutrality, united by the same friendship with the States of both warring groups of Powers, situated like an island amidst the seething waves of the terrible world war, with its ideal and material interests most sensibly jeopardized and violated, our country is filled with a deep longing for peace, and ready to assist by its small means to stop the endless sufferings caused by the war and brought before its eyes by daily contact with the interned, the severely wounded and the evacuated *those expelled*,[2] and to establish the foundations for a beneficial cooperation of the peoples.

The Swiss Federal Council is therefore glad to seize the opportunity to support the efforts of the President of the United States. It would consider itself happy if it could act in any, no matter how modest a way, for the rapprochement of the peoples now engaged in the struggle, and for reaching a lasting peace.[3]

TC telegram (E2300 Washington, No. 33, Swiss Federal Archives).
  [1] Delivered to the White House on December 23, 1916. For details of delivery, the suggested change by Lansing, and publication of the text, see P. Ritter to A. Hoffmann, Dec. 28, 1916.
  [2] Lansing's suggested change.
  [3] This telegram is printed in *FR-WWS 1916*, p. 117.

From the Diary of Colonel House

December 23, 1916.

I have been in constant communication with Washington regarding foreign affairs. The State Department is worried sick over the President's *laissez-faire* policy. Every day Lansing and Polk urge me to come to Washington to talk to him. I have promised to go next week, but I have no stomach for it. It is practically impossible to get the President to have a general consultation. I see him and then I see Lansing, and the result is, we get nowhere. What is needed is consultation with the three of us, and a definite program worked out and followed as consistently as circumstances will permit.

From Robert Lansing

Personal and Confidential

My dear Mr. President,   Washington December 24, 1916.

I have, as you requested, given careful consideration to the draft of instructions to be sent to our representatives in the various belligerent capitals, which you sent me last night. I believe that such instructions would materially help the situation especially the intimation that the replies would not be made public. Publicity in a situation such as this prevents frankness and makes all parties color their statements to meet the demands of public opinion at home. I have, therefore, had the instruction sent forward under the strictest injunction of secrecy and I most sincerely hope that it will help in accomplishing the objects sought.

Would it not be well, while this delicate state of affairs continues and in order that I may be kept fully acquainted with your views and wishes, as to any steps which it would be advisable to take, for me to see you for me to see you [*sic*] for a few minutes every day so that we could talk over the general situation and any new developments?

Faithfully yours   Robert Lansing.

ALS (WP, DLC).

To George Dewey

The White House.

My dear Admiral Dewey,   26 December, 1916.

May I not wish you many happy returns of the day?

You have earned the best sort of happiness, that which comes from a sense of the admiration and confidence of those whom you have so conscientiously and so gallantly served. I congratulate you with all my heart.

Cordially and sincerely Yours,   Woodrow Wilson

WWTLS (G. Dewey Papers, DLC).

From Newton Diehl Baker, with Enclosure

Dear Mr. President: Washington. December 26, 1916

I hand you herewith a memorandum made by the Judge Advocate General on the two sections of the National Defense Act containing draft provisions. Section 111 deals only with the power of the President to draft the National Guard into the Federal service when, and therefore after, Congress shall have authorized the use of these forces.

Section 79 is an attempt on the part of Congress to provide in time of peace a method of recruiting and maintaining troops in reserve when the National Guard shall have been called out of the States and is actually engaged in military operations. Such search as I have been able to make indicates that both of these provisions were made by the Committee of the Senate, neither of them having been suggested by the War Department, at least I have not been able to find as yet any such suggestion emanating from the Department.

I assume it is the provision contained in Section 79 that has been called to your attention as containing a power in the President not hitherto granted in our history except after actual war has begun. I can find no precedent for such a power granted in time of peace, although this power is to be exercised only in time of war. Frankly, I do not find myself offended by it, nor do I regard it as a departure from the general spirit of this National Defense Act. It seems to me that the experience of the European countries was in large part responsible for the theory upon which our National Defense Act was based, namely, that anticipatory preparation had to be made and that it was not safe for a country to wait until it was in a great emergency to make its preparations. With that thought in mind, Congress, in the National Defense Act, gave the President many new powers, as for instance those in Section 120, whereby the President "in time of war, *or when war is imminent*," is authorized practically to conscript manufacturing plants and supplies for the use of the Army. Here the President is not even obliged to wait until actual war has been declared, but is intrusted at his discretion to determine when war is imminent and to exercise powers of the most drastic kind with regard to property. As I understand it, those who have criticised the provisions of Section 79 feel that it is giving the President power in time of peace which he is to use in time of war, but which has hitherto been conferred only after actual war has begun. It would seem that if the power is appropriate to the national defense, vesting it in the President in a time free from the excitement of war would be a very wise thing to do rather than to wait until the confusion of war has busied everybody's mind with the complicated problems which such an issue presents, and then have to pass rapidly legislation which might not be well digested and would therefore be less appropriate to its object than such legislation as could be worked out in a time free from excitement.

The theory of our National Defense Act plainly is that our international policies are defensive and not offensive. Such is the condition of our Government and such is the obvious trend of our policies. The legislative control over the power to declare war is the constitutional safeguard, and I am inclined to feel that the critics of this provision would criticise any other plan which might be made looking to things to be done in a state of war, and for the same reason, namely, that to them it seems to imply that we are getting ready to make war rather than providing for our safety in the event of war being made upon us.

Respectfully yours,   Newton D. Baker

TLS (WDR, RG 94, AGO Numerical File, No. 256159, DNA).

E N C L O S U R E

A Memorandum by Enoch Herbert Crowder

Washington. December 26, 1916.

INFORMAL MEMORANDUM FOR THE SECRETARY OF WAR.

Subject: Draft provisions of National Defense Act of June 3, 1916.

Upon a hasty examination of the National Defense Act I find but two sections dealing with the draft.

The general provision is in Sec. 111, which authorizes the President to draft into the military service any and all members of the National Guard and of the National Guard Reserve during a period of war, but only "when Congress shall have authorized the use of the armed land forces of the United States for any purpose requiring the use of troops in excess of those of the Regular Army." There is here no advance delegation of authority to the President to impose a draft. Congress must act before the power may be authorized.

In Sec. 79 of the Act there is an advance delegation to the President of a limited power of draft in time of war. That section provides that when members of the National Guard and the enlisted reserve thereof of any State, Territory, or the District of Columbia shall have been brought into the service of the United States in time of war, there shall be immediately organized for each regiment of infantry or cavalry, each nine batteries of field artillery and each twelve companies of Coast Artillery brought into the service, one reserve battalion; and further provides:

"If for any reason there shall not be enough voluntary enlistments to keep the reserve battalions at the prescribed strength, a sufficient number of the unorganized militia shall be drafted into the service of the United States to maintain each of said battalions at the proper strength."

No further action by Congress is necessary and the President proceeds under the authority of this section when war exists to exercise the drafting power, but it plainly appears that it is not an unlimited power, and may be exercised only in so far as necessary to keep recruit battalions of the National Guard in a position to supply vacancies occurring by death or other cause in any organization of the National Guard brought into the service of the United States.

As it is the effect of the draft provided for in said Section 79 to place the drafted individual in the service of the United States from date of notice of the draft, any failure on his part to meet his obligations may be enforced, under the Articles of War, by trial by court-martial and punishment at the discretion of the court.   E. H. Crowder Judge Advocate General.

TS MS (WDR, RG 94, AGO Numerical File, No. 256159, DNA).

Two Letters to Newton Diehl Baker

                                                      The White House.
My dear Mr. Secretary,   26 December, 1916.

Thank you for letting me have this memorandum, which I return for your files.

I am inclined to agree with the Judge Advocate General's opinion, and your own, that the scope and purpose of these sections of the defense act have been misunderstood and that those sections are really not an accidental but perhaps an essential part of the general plan.   Cordially and faithfully Yours,

WWTLI (WDR, RG 94, AGO Numerical File, No. 256159, DNA).

                                                      The White House.
My dear Mr. Secretary,   26 December, 1916.

I have read this letter of Professor Johnson's with a great deal of interest.[1]

I wish every day that there were more *mere* Americans in this country. Almost all of our fellow citizens this side the Rock Mississippi seem to think in terms set by the thinking or the prepossessions of one side or the other across the water. If Professor Johnson had lived with the English statesmen for the past two years and seen the real inside of their minds I think he would feel differently. The point of view is all the more interesting because so evidently honest and genuine.

                                                      Faithfully Yours,

WWTL (N. D. Baker Papers, DLC).
  [1] W. H. Johnson to NDB, Dec. 24, 1916, TLS (N. D. Baker Papers, DLC). William Hannibal Johnson, Professor of Latin at Denison University, urged

Baker not to "be led into the advocacy of universal compulsory military training." "The country," Johnson wrote, "will make short work of any party which
attempts that under any circumstances short of an actual condition of war."
He then went on to express great disappointment at Wilson's note to the
belligerents of December 18: "I have consistently supported the President's
attitude in maintaining a strict official neutrality as regards the actual war on
the other side, but when it comes to an official declaration that the two sides
are apparently alike in their aims, I can only register an indignant dissent.
There was no occasion for any note of the kind, and it wholly and offensively
misrepresents the attitude and moral feeling of a very large portion of the President's most ardent adherents. . . . Why should the President's hand be put out
now to stay the fall of the most reactionary manarchical [monarchical] regime
left to curse the modern world? Shall he interfere to strangle a German democracy in the very hour of its birth?"

James Watson Gerard to Robert Lansing

Berlin (via Copenhagen) December 26, 1916.

4782. Referring to the Department's circular of December
eighteenth, the following note was given to me by Zimmerman
after lunching with me today:

"Foreign Office, Berlin, December twenty-six, 1916. With reference to the esteemed communication of December twenty-first,
Foreign Office number 15118, the undersigned has the honor
to reply as follows: To His Excellency the Ambassador of the
United States of America Mr. James W. Gerard.

The Imperial Government has accepted and considered in the
friendly spirit which is apparent in the communication of the
President, noble initiative of the President looking to the creation
of bases for the foundation of a lasting peace. The President dis-
closes the aim which lies next to his heart and leaves the choice
of the way open. A direct exchange of views appears to The Imperial Government as the most suitable way of arriving at the
desired result. The Imperial Government has the honor therefore, in the sense of its declaration of the twelfth instant, which
offered the hand for peace negotiations, to propose the speedy
assembly, on neutral ground, of delegates of the warring States.

It is also the view of The Imperial Government that the great
work for the prevention of future wars can first be taken up
only after the ending of the present conflict of exhaustion. The
Imperial Government is ready, when this point has been reached,
to cooperate with the United States at this sublime task.

The undersigned, while permitting himself to have recourse
to good offices of His Excellency the Ambassador in connection
with the transmission of the above reply to the President of the
United States, avails himself of this opportunity to renew the
assurances of his highest consideration. Zimmerman."

Gerard.

T telegram (SDR, RG 59, 763.72119/265, DNA).

Walter Hines Page to Robert Lansing

London, Dec. 26, 1916.

5374. CONFIDENTIAL. Your circular twenty-fourth, received December twenty-fifth, presented this morning to Cecil[1] in charge of Foreign Office. I again explained first sentence to him at length.

To your suggestion that the Allies' reply to President's note, if it be favorable, be not made public, he said that he could give no definite or official answer. This subject would have to be referred to his Government and to the Governments of her Allies.

This is all that he said to me officially.

But he talked at length personally, remarking several times that he was expressing only his individual views and that I must not understand them as the views of his Government. He informed me that he was deeply hurt by the President's note because it seemed to pass judgment on the Allied cause by putting it on the same moral level as the German cause and because one sentence (the sentence about the position of neutrals becoming intolerable) might be a veiled threat. I assured him that in my judgment no threat was intended. He was sure too that the British people were surprised and hurt. Since the President's note was promptly made public and British public feeling was deeply stirred, he for his own part saw difficulties in keeping the British reply secret. The public would demand publicity. Again he reminded me that this was only his personal opinion.

Then he remarked that there is nothing that the American Government or any other human power can do which would bring the war to a close before the Allies had spent their utmost force to secure victory. A failure to secure a victory would leave the world at the mercy of the most arrogant and the bloodiest tyranny that had ever been organized and that it is better to die in an effort to defeat that tyranny than to perish under its success. He had always been almost a pacifist. No man hated war more than he. No man had believed more earnestly than he that great wars were impossible. But since European civilization had been thus murderously assaulted, there was nothing to do but to defeat its desperate enemy or to perish in the effort. He had hoped that the United States understood what is at stake. He went so far as to say that if the United States should come into the war it would decide which would win—freedom or organized tyranny. If the United States should help the Germans, civilization would perish and have again to be slowly rebuilt if it should ever appear again. If the United States should help the Allies civilization would triumph.

My inference from this long conversation, from the comments of the Allied press, and from my reading of British public opinion, is that the answer to the President's note will be courteous but very frank; that it will initiate [intimate] or directly declare that no efforts by any neutral government, however well meant, can help towards peace; that unless and until the Allies have spent their whole force no compromise terms will be considered; that peace will be made by those who have fought and by nobody else; and that Allied public opinion will not permit a secret reply to the President's note. Comment here shows that the British would regard secret discussion now as a German wish and a German suggestion. Cecil, however, did not say this.

Cecil informed me that a reply to the German note would soon be ready and that a reply to the President's note would be got ready as soon as possible. The Allies are now in consultation about it.

I regret to report that I fear no explanation can remove from the British mind the conviction that the President's note put the two sides on the same moral level. It is this that public opinion resents. I have seen only one newspaper (the WESTMINSTER GAZETTE) which gave a more friendly construction; and I hear privately but I think authoritatively that its article was directly suggested by Asquith.   Page.

T telegram (SDR, RG 59, 763.72119/263, DNA).
    [1] That is, Lord Robert Cecil.

To William Jennings Bryan

My dear Mr. Bryan: The White House December 27, 1916

Yours was a very generous telegram and I thank you for it with all my heart.

We all join in sending to Mrs. Bryan and you the warmest good wishes of the season.

Cordially and sincerely yours,   Woodrow Wilson

TLS (W. J. Bryan Papers, DLC).

To Manuel Castro Quesada[1]

                                    [The White House]
My dear Mr. Minister: December 27, 1916

It is with a deep sense of gratification that I have read your letter congratulating me on my reelection to the Presidency of the United States of America,[2] and I respond to the high honor you bestow upon me by saying to you and the Government and people of Costa Rica that I shall strive to carry out those high ideals which in no small part will be to foster and nourish the traditional bonds of friendship existing between our two countries.

I am, my dear Señor Quesada,

Very truly yours,   Woodrow Wilson

TLS (Letterpress Books, WP, DLC).
[1] Costa Rican Minister to the United States.
[2] It is missing.

To Julio Betancourt

[The White House]
My dear Mr. Minister: December 27, 1916

I have received your cordial note of congratulations on my re-election to the Presidency[1] and I beg to express my thanks and deep appreciation of the high value you place on my judgment, which I assure you will at all times prompt me to advocate and promote a close and friendly attitude towards the country you so worthily represent.

I am, my dear Señor Betancourt,

Very truly yours,   Woodrow Wilson

TLS (Letterpress Books, WP, DLC).
[1] It is missing.

To Harry Augustus Garfield

My dear Garfield: The White House December 27, 1916

Your letter of December twenty-first touched me very deeply and I send you my thanks out of a very full heart.

There have been many discordant voices about my recent circular message to the Powers, but I believe that all those who know how to judge generously will see what its true meaning and purpose were.

With the warmest best wishes from all of us for the Christmas and New Year season,

Faithfully yours,   Woodrow Wilson

TLS (H. A. Garfield Papers, DLC).

To Jane Addams

My dear Miss Addams:

The White House
December 27, 1916

Thank you sincerely for your telegram of December twenty-fifth.[1] I appreciate the messages which you so graciously convey and hope with all my heart that some effect will be wrought which would at least make peace a little nearer.

With warm regard,
Cordially and sincerely yours,   Woodrow Wilson

TLS (PSC-Hi).
[1] It is missing.

To Paul Samuel Reinsch

My dear Mr. Minister:

The White House
December 27, 1916

Your very generous letter of congratulations[1] has given me the greatest pleasure and in return I want to say how glad I have been to have a representative like yourself at so difficult a post as that of Pekin, where many things are happening which it seems so difficult, so next to impossible to handle wisely amidst the present disturbed conditions of the world.

I believe that I am expressing also the feeling of the Secretary of State when I say that we have the greatest confidence in your discretion and judgment and should be very sorry indeed to lose you in times when clear heads and steady hands are so absolutely necessary.

With the warmest good wishes for the New Year,
Cordially and sincerely yours,   Woodrow Wilson

TLS (P. S. Reinsch Papers, WHi).
[1] P. S. Reinsch to WW, Nov. 11, 1916, Vol. 38.

To William Winter[1]

My dear Mr. Winter,

The White House.
27 December, 1916.

I know that you will pardon a typewritten note from a man whose pen hand was long ago tired out. This little machine has so long been my pen that it seems to me to produce my own handwriting.

I want you to know how I value the books you have been so generous and so gracious as to send me. I have long been an admirer of your work, not only for its unusual quality, but also for the spirit in which it was done, and this volume which has just reached me, the third series of "Shakespeare on the Stage" is most acceptable. The inscription has touched me very deeply and I thank you for it with all my heart.[2]

Your sincere friend,   Woodrow Wilson

WWTLS (Berg Coll., NN).
 [1] Drama critic of the *New York Tribune*, 1865-1909; noted historian of the stage.
 [2] *Shakespeare on the Stage*, 3d series (New York, 1916). This book is in the Wilson Library, DLC. The inscription reads as follows: "To Woodrow Wilson. With profound respect and admiration. William Winter December 5, 1916"

To Lucy Marshall Smith and Mary Randolph Smith

The White House.

My very dear Cousins,   27 December, 1916.

It was sweet of you to think of us and send us such charming Christmas presents. The handkerchiefs are just the sort I dote on and yet I do not like to use them for fear of wearing them out. I hope that you will enjoy the Littell.[1] I have not seen it recently but it ought just now to have rather poignant interest as reflecting the thoughts of the nations at war.

We had a very happy Christmas. Jessie and Frank came down (leaving the precious little ones in good hands, you may be sure) and at our Christmas dinner we had all three of the girls, all Edith's family who are here,—in all twenty-two very jolly people. After dinner we had a fine time playing charades, and, as usual, the three Wilsons showing alarmingly finished histrionic gifts! Stock. was here, too, and did some "tough" parts in the scenes with great ability! It was fine to see him so well.

Little Josephine is the only little one in the house, so that the Christmas tree was not so exciting a function as usual. Some of the toys she received have been played with more by Stock. and Frank than by her. "Boys like that kind of thing," was her comment as *she* played happily putting her new doll to bed in a charming four-poster toy bed.

All join me in the most affectionate messages. May the best conceivable things of the new year come to you both, along with what you are already sure of, the continued love of your friends!

Dear Cousin Mary's letter about the election brought happy tears to my eyes.[2]

Affectionately Yours,   Woodrow Wilson

WWTLS (photostat in RSB Coll., DLC).
 [1] The Boston *Living Age*, a weekly compilation chiefly of material from British periodicals. Its name had been changed from *Littell's Living Age* in 1896,

following the death of Robert Smith Littell, the son of the founder, Eliakim Littell.

² It is missing.

From Edward Mandell House

Dear Governor: New York. December 27, 1916.

Bernstorff came to see me this morning by appointment.

He was disappointed in his Government's reply to your note. While he does not believe that any one of the belligerents could state their terms excepting in conference, he thinks that it might be done confidentially. He says that his Government would not want the State Department to be cognizant of what was going on until later for the reason that so many leaks have occurred there.

I told him I would write to you and get your views concerning this method and would then tell him whether or not to go ahead upon the lines discussed this morning. In the event you give the word I advised that he cable his Government suggesting that Germany should answer somewhat as follows:

No matter what caused the war, the dominant feeling in Germany today is that the essential object to be accomplished at a peace conference is to agree upon some plan by which such another war can never again be possible. That all territorial questions should be subservient to the main one.

I thought if they would send this reply it would give us a working basis with the Entente, and would put Germany in an unassailable position.

Bernstorff thought well of the suggestion, and will send it just as soon as I have heard from you.

If you prefer for me to come over for a personal conference please wire me tomorrow, and I will come on Friday.

I feel sure if we are persistent and ingenious enough a start can be made, and having once started, final negotiations will follow.   Affectionately yours,   E. M. House

TLS (WP, DLC).

From Herbert Bruce Brougham

                                Daylesford, Pa. Berwyn P.O.
Dear Mr. President: 27th December 1916

Would you feel easier in your mind if Ralph Pulitzer and Frank Cobb were to form the proposed organization of newspapers, rather than Mr. Curtis?

Although it would be at some personal sacrifice, I should be quite free to put the matter in their hands. I say this in full recognition of the advantages of control that should accrue in making the World leader of the undertaking.

Very sincerely,   H. B. Brougham

ALS (WP, DLC).

From Cleveland Hoadley Dodge

My dear old Friend   New York. December 27th, 1916

If Who's Who is right tomorrow is your sixth ten year milestone and I must send you my hearty congratulations and best wishes for many happy returns of the day. I remember ten years ago when we celebrated your fiftieth birthday. How big the lively scraps of those days seemed at the time, and how small they seem now

When I think of the last fifteen years, aside from family blessings, I am most thankful for all that my association with you has brought me, and for all the inspiration to better things which I have got from you.

You have tackled a good many large jobs in your life, but you now have on your hands the hardest proposition, even you ever undertook. Your friends are with you, heart & soul, and pray God that you may be successful, if not at once, at least in the not distant future

We thank God for all you mean to the World, and trust that your life and strength may be spared for many years, to solve the great problems which you, better than anyone else, can solve.

Mrs. Dodge joins me in much love to you and Mrs. Wilson, wishing you all possible blessings in the New Year

Your's devotedly   Cleveland H. Dodge

ALS (WP, DLC).

From George Dewey

My dear Mr. President: Washington December 27, 1916.

Thank you a thousand times for your very kind note of congratulations on my seventy-ninth birthday.

What you say of my duty performed thouches [touches] me very much. The last few years of my life have been full of happiness, and expressions such as yours have made them so.

Faithfully yours,   George Dewey.

TLS (WP, DLC).

William Phillips to Joseph Patrick Tumulty

Dear Mr. Tumulty: Washington December 27, 1916.

The Spanish Ambassador has been instructed to convey personally to the President the congratulations of the Pope on the President's recent notes to the belligerents. In order to carry out his instructions the Ambassador asks that an audience may be arranged for him at the President's convenience.

Will you kindly take up the matter with the President and let me know his wishes so that I may inform the Ambassador?[1]

Sincerely yours,   William Phillips

TLS (WP, DLC).
[1] Wilson saw the Spanish Ambassador, Juan Riaño y Gayangos, at the White House at 2 P.M. on January 16, 1917.

Sir Horace Plunkett to Edward Mandell House

My dear Colonel House

Battle Creek Michigan
Dec 27, 1916

In thinking over our two long conferences during my brief stay in New York last week it has occurred to me that criticisms of mine upon certain utterances of the President may have left an impression on your mind that I myself feel the resentment to which those utterances have unhappily given rise in England. I should have made my position perfectly clear but for the multiciplicity [multiplicity] of subjects we had to discuss. I am sure you will pardon me for sending the explanation which follows.

I hold, even more strongly than when we were together in London last February, that the best hope of a lasting peace lies in a right mutual understanding between the peoples of the American Republic and of the British Empire. For this reason, I have as you know, done my best to explain to our Government the difficulties of the President's position which my long acquaintance with the middle Western States enables me to understand. I wish to continue this slight service and I should not have come across the Atlantic this year had I not wished to make it more efficient by further study of public opinion in those parts of your country which count most politically and of which least is known in England. But the point I was trying to make clear was that a series of unfortunate expressions used by the President and widely published seem to show that he has not appreciated the change which has come over the sentiment of the British and possibly also of the French people as the result of over two years of war. One would expect large changes of view from such a ghastly experience, but the most important change to understand has I think been missed. The President's last note ignores it in one or two passages.

It is as certain as anything can be that the British Democracy would not have permitted their government to become involved in the European war (as it was at the outset) but for the invasion of Belgium. It took many months for our people to realise how this action violated the main principles for which the Allies (the British and French at any rate) are now consciously fighting. In the British Democracy's view—and I had better confine myself to this—the war in Europe is fundamentally a struggle between brute force in the form of militarism and the very imperfect idea of world law and public right which is already in existance and which the teaching of this war will, it is hoped, define more clearly and establish more firmly. For the fourth time in nine years, Germany rejecting international conference, attempted to impose her will on Europe by war or threat of war, and that in defiance of the two fundamentals upon which the comity of nations hitherto rested—the sanctity of treaty law and the freedom of weaker independent civilized states from coercion by the stronger, except in accordance with the principle of justice, and after all attempts to secure justice by negotiation and conference have failed. In this case there was no attempt to prove Serbia guilty and no attempt to confer with her. She was to be coerced, and as everbody believed, annexed, partly because she stood across the road to the East and partly because her incorporation was necessary to the racial ascendency of Germans and Magyars over the Slavs. And this coercion was to be done under the threat that if the rest of Europe did not acquiesce in this settlement, by force of arms and without conference, of a question which had always been regarded as a European question, there would be a general war in which Germany would seek to establish a tyranny over Europe by violating the neutrality of Belgium—the security erected by statesmen of an earlier day for the very purpose of protecting Europe against that very event.

It is needless to say that such a survey of the situation was not wholly in the mind of the British Democracy at the outbreak of the war but it is so now. The British workingmen, speaking through their union leaders, are extraordinarily clear as to the object for which they are fighting. They feel that there can be no liberty in Europe unless this attempt to overthrow liberty and public right by military force has clearly and demonstrably failed.

Hence they will not entertain negotiations for peace until Germany is willing to concede as the basis from which the negotiations are to start, that Belgium, France and Serbia are to be restored and indemnified. To a people so feeling and believing the President's expressed doubts as to how the war began and what the British people are fighting for are extremely difficult to explain satisfactorily by any theory of neutrality.

I gathered in our conversation that the President's only concern in the matter is to decide in what manner America can best serve the common cause of Democracy. It has been stated in the press that he regards the submarine menace as so grave that he fears too openly friendly an attitude towards Great Britain might remove all restrictions upon submarine activity, and so, by inflicting a fatal blow upon British sea-borne commerce, do more harm to the Allies than even active American intervention on their side would do good. My considered opinion is that the straight-forward comradeship of America would be a thousand times more valuable in the eyes of the British people, no matter what its price in the extra dangers involved, than peace proposals which seem to be based upon a total failure to appreciate the fact that the British Democracy is upholding at an appalling sacrifice of blood and treasure, principles which it hitherto believed were identical with those upon which your great Republic is founded.

It is a happy circumstance that an intimate friend of mine who has also taken you into his confidence, is now Secretary of State for foreign affairs.[1] Before I left New York I assured him by cipher cable that after full discussion with you I was convinced that, notwithstanding recent utterances of the President, his general attitude towards the war was that which you explained to both of us in London last February. I thought it well to do this because when I left England the misunderstandings of which I told you had gone so far that people felt America was in danger of becoming an enemy to freedom in Europe only second to Germany itself. I do not think we over there shall ever get it out of our heads that, had the United States taken her stand for liberty and public right, declaring she would never recognize obliteration of the liberties of France, Belgium and Serbia by force and arms and without conference, the war would have been over now, and that without America taking any military part in it. Of course, I understand the President's difficulties and yet I believe as strongly as I did when I wrote that memorandum to our

[1] Arthur Balfour.

Cabinet,[2] that if the President combined with the human[i]tarian plea of saving human life a definite stand against the militarist contention the whole American people would follow him as they would follow no other leader and that the war would still be brought to an early conclusion.

Just one more point I should like you to consider. It is quite possible that the number and the influence of the British peace groups may be greatly over-estimated. The fact is that the best known pacifist agitators admit they have no considerable following. It is very significant that Sir John Simon,[3] acknowledged leader of the dissenting radical members of Parliament spoke in favor of Lloyd George's speech the other day.[4] By the way, that speech as well as the German so-called peace proposals were an ill preparation for a favorable reception to the President's last note in Great Britain.

You must not infer from anything I have said above that I shall be less anxious in the future than I have been in the past to render you any small service of which I am capable in bringing about a better understanding between your country and mine. I only wish to look the difficulties in the face which is always the best way of overcoming them.

Believe me yours ever sincerely,   Horace Plunkett[5]

TLS (WP, DLC).

[2] See n. 1 to H. Plunkett to EMH, March 7, 1916, printed as an Enclosure with EMH to WW, March 20, 1916, Vol. 36.

[3] Sir John Allsebrook Simon, Liberal M.P., who had been Home Secretary from May 1915 until January 1916, when he resigned on the issue of conscription.

[4] David Lloyd George, in his first speech as Prime Minister in the House of Commons on December 19, had asserted that the German Chancellor had not in fact put forth any concrete proposals of peace terms either in his note to the Allies of December 12 or in his speech to the Reichstag of the same day. In contrast, he declared, the position of the Allies had long been well known: they demanded "complete restitution, full reparation," and "effectual guarantees" against a future repetition of the war. Lloyd George declared that the Allies would not end the conflict until these terms had been secured, and he quoted from Abraham Lincoln's speech of June 16, 1864: "We accepted this war for an object and a worthy object, and the war will end when that object is attained. Under God I hope it will never end until that time." However, Lloyd George did not rule out serious peace discussions. "We will, therefore," he concluded, "wait until we hear what terms and guarantees the German Government offer other than those, better than those, surer than those which she so lightly broke, and meanwhile we shall put our trust in an unbroken Army rather than in a broken faith." *Parliamentary Debates: Commons*, 5th Ser., LXXXVIII, cols. 1333-38.

In brief remarks to the Commons on December 21, Simon supported the position set forth by Lloyd George. Simon concluded as follows: "On these two points every patriotic citizen is agreed: first, that it would be an unpardonable crime for any Government to allow the War to go on for an unnecessary hour, and, secondly, that it would be the deepest treachery to falter in securing, by force of arms if need be, by more reasonable methods if and when the opportunity comes, those objects, essentially defensive and essentially unaggressive, for the sake of which, I am convinced, we were compelled to go to War." *Ibid.*, cols. 1714-17.

[5] H. Plunkett to A. J. Balfour, Jan. 4, 1917, TLS (A. J. Balfour Papers, FO 800/211, PRO), enclosed a copy of this letter to House.

To Edward Mandell House

The White House. Dec 28 1916

Yours of yesterday received. I had already instructed our representatives in the several belligerent countries to suggest that quote whatever reply is made, if our request is complied with be made not publicly but in strict confidence; it being understood that the Government of the United States may in its turn convey it in like confidence to the governments of the other group in order that it may in that way be ascertained whether there is any ground or basis for conference or negotiation of any kind end quote. This is consistent with your suggestion to Bernstorff. It might be well for him to get his reply personally from his government and himself convey it to me through any channel he thinks secure but not in person.

WWT telegram (WP, DLC).

To Ida Minerva Tarbell

[The White House]
My dear Miss Tarbell: December 28, 1916

I am really distressed to learn through Colonel House that you do not feel that your health will permit you to accept a place on the Tariff Commission. I had quite set my heart on seeing you on that Commission. Its work will indeed be arduous, no doubt, but I do not think that it would be overwhelming at all, and I hope that your decision does not mean that you are really unwell. It would distress me to think that.

With the highest esteem and with genuine regret,
    Cordially and faithfully yours,   Woodrow Wilson

TLS (Letterpress Books, WP, DLC).

To Jane Addams

My dear Miss Addams: The White House December 28, 1916

Alas, I am sorry to say that Miss Tarbell feels that her health will not permit her undertaking the arduous duties of the Tariff Commission. I cannot help hoping that she will yet alter her resolution in the matter, but at present there seems no prospect and I must hurry the appointment as much as I can.

Thank you very warmly for your word about the note to the

belligerent Powers. I knew that you would sympathize and am happy to think of your sympathy.

Cordially and sincerely yours,   Woodrow Wilson

TLS (PSC-Hi).

To John Sharp Williams

My dear Senator: The White House December 28, 1916

I want to tell you how much I appreciated your generous letter of December twenty-second. It is delightful to have you hold such an estimate of the things I have been doing, and particularly of my recent effort in the matter of peace. I thank you with all my heart for your letter.

Cordially and sincerely yours,   Woodrow Wilson

TLS (J. S. Williams Papers, DLC).

To Hiram Woods

My dear Hiram: [The White House] December 28, 1916

It amuses me a little bit that men such as those who asked you to write me about the Belgium deportation[1] should think that it was necessary to call my attention to the matter or to its tragic significance, and I think that what the Government has done is all that could possibly be done unless we are to go to the length of declaring war on Germany. But I, of course, appreciate the circumstances which led to your letter and do not mean any of this criticism even by implication for yourself.

We all join in wishing you and yours the best possible things of the New Year.

Affectionately yours,   Woodrow Wilson

TLS (Letterpress Books, WP, DLC).
[1] H. Woods to WW, Dec. 18, 1916, TLS (WP, DLC). The text reads as follows: "I have been asked by a number of prominent professional men of different political opinions to write you about the Belgian Deportation. Knowing you as I do, a 'conventional' letter is out of place. And yet I would be lacking in courtesy to these men if I failed to carry out their request. The action you have already taken has met with general and hearty approval. The mass meeting called here [Baltimore] for Friday night [December 22] will add such public support as private citizens can give. There is full confidence in you to do all possible to stop this horrible cruelty."

From Edward Mandell House, With Enclosure

Dear Governor: New York. December 28, 1916.

I am enclosing you a letter from Howard of the United Press.

It is a fact that there is a general misunderstanding of your position, and it is also a fact that if you wanted the widest dissemination for a statement you could get it better through a sympathetic organization like the United Press than any other source. I think it is a mistake to use one of the great daily papers, or any single paper where wide publicity is desired.

Your code message has come. I will tell Bernstorff to proceed as you indicate. The more we talk to Germany regarding peace just now, the less danger there will be of a break because of submarine activity.   Affectionately yours,   E. M. House

TLS (WP, DLC).

E N C L O S U R E

Roy Wilson Howard to Edward Mandell House

Personal

Dear Colonel: New York City December 26, 1916.

Before I sailed for South America July 1st, we discussed the possibility of Germany attempting, along about mid-October, to *force* the President to make a peace move.

When I reached England on Sept. 21st, there was evidence that this propaganda was under way.

After becoming convinced that any peace move by Washington was certain to be misunderstood and certain to be prejudicial to America's standing in the Allied countries, I went to Lloyd George. I suggested that if the British were disposed to resent any overtures by America, it seemed only fair that, as a counterbalance to the German propaganda, Lloyd George should set forth in simple, direct language which everyone could understand, the actual British attitude toward peace proposals through the medium of an interview.[1]

You are familiar with the interview and its results. It went round the world, was printed in every civilized language and is still referred to almost daily in the news and editorial—not because it was a great state document, but because it was a human statement by an intensely human individual talking to the ordinary folks of America.

Three weeks later, in talking of the interview to Briand in Paris, he said, "Oh yes, I concur absolutely in all that Mr. Lloyd George has said, but you know, really, it was a reiteration of my speech of a month ago on the convening of our chamber."[2]

I did *not* know it—had no recollection of the speech to which he referred. I'll venture to say you cannot now recall the "speech." I have an idea you do recall the Lloyd-George "interview." One was purely official, and as news, withered and died over night. The other was human and is still alive.

Now, we have tried hard as newspapermen—reporters, not editors—to make and keep clear, the situation presented by the President's note to the belligerents. We, and everyone else, have failed. The matter has been so scrambled that even the public here at home does not understand exactly where the President or the nation stands. Naturally, the belligerents know even less and each has shown a tendency to put the worst possible construction on the note. Further official explanation or modification will not help much.

The President has spoken officially. Now, I would like to have him drive home the idea of America's position in an interview in which he can talk *to*, *at* and *for* the ordinary folks of all nations. I can't tell you what I would like him to say because I'm damned if I know myself where America stands. I want him to pick out *me* as one of the millions of ordinary folks—skull of good, average thickness—and get it across to me. If he gets it over to me, I'll guarantee to spread it from Tierra del Fuego to Gjaesvaer and from Nome to Hobart.

Can you help?

If the A.P. should happen to have asked for this same interview, and if the President believes it is advisable to give it, let him decide which of us shall have it. To us, it is highly desirable that the United Press should be the medium. To the country, it is important only that one of us should be. If we cannot have it, the Associated Press should. To give it to both would be to lose the effect of the punch.

Faithfully yours,   Roy W. Howard

TLS (WP, DLC).

[1] About this interview, see RL to WW, Sept. 30, 1916, n. 1, Vol. 38.

[2] For a summary of Briand's speech to the Chamber of Deputies on September 14, see the *New York Times*, Sept. 15, 1916.

From John Howell Westcott

Dear Woodrow: Princeton Dec 28, 1916

Mary's[1] twelfth birthday reminds us that today is your sixtieth and we want to wish you many happy returns.

It is doubtful whether there is any house in the country where they think and talk about you as much. Certainly there is none where they believe in you more thoroughly

We spent some anxious days after the election—before settling down to thankful joy. Yesterday & today we have been reading over the final figures. They certainly give ground for a manifold satisfaction. I can well believe that personally you might have preferred to be freed from the tremendous responsibility of another term. But we realize that the situation is the most difficult since Lincoln's time & we do not wish to change our pilot now.

One little thing may amuse you. Pyne's butler[2] voted for you. He told some of the faculty while playing golf.

God bless you and grant you many years!

                    Yours faithfully   J.H.W.

ALS (WP, DLC).
 [1] Mary Dunton Westcott, born December 28, 1904.
 [2] Henry Egglesfield, charter member of the Springdale Golf Club and later a trustee of the club.

From Mary Randolph Smith and Lucy Marshall Smith

My dear Mr. Wilson   [New Orleans] December 28 [1916].

We are perfectly happy. To have you for our President again filled our cup, and now to own those wonderful books, has caused it to overflow in every direction. To possess that history has always been in our plan. So to have the books and the inscription on the front page makes life all poetry and weariness a name.

We wish you all a Happy New Year with Peace on Earth to round out the Good Will to Men you have ever felt.

Thank you again and for the ever welcome Littell

                    Yours as always   Mary and Lucy Smith.

ALS (WP, DLC).

From William Gibbs McAdoo

Dear Mr. President: Washington December 28, 1916.

I am very happy to tell you that Secretary Houston has succeeded in inducing Professor Taussig to accept appointment on the Tariff Commission. I enclose copy of Secretary Houston's letter to Professor Taussig and copy of Professor Taussig's telegram in reply.[1] I want you to see this in order that you may know just what I authorized Secretary Houston to say in your behalf and mine in connection with this appointment. It occurs to me that it would be wise to ask Professor Taussig to run down to Washington and confer with us about the other appointments, but I do not want to do this unless you think well of it.

Cordially yours,   W G McAdoo

TLS (WP, DLC).
[1] D. F. Houston to F. W. Taussig, Dec. 26, 1916, CCL (WP, DLC); F. W. Taussig to D. F. Houston, Dec. 28, 1916, TC telegram (WP, DLC).

Paul Ritter to Arthur Hoffmann

III. 4 Friede   Washington, den 28. Dezember 1916.
Herr Bundesrat,

Seit meinem letzten Berichte vom 22. Dez. (Beilage 1)[1] lief am 23. Nachmittags die Note des Bundesrates ein. Während sie entziffert (Beilage 2)[2] und übersetzt (Beilage 3)[3] wurde, zeigte ich die Ankunft dem Sekretär des Praesidenten an und bestätigte Ihnen telegraphisch den Empfang. Gleichen Abends 6 ½ Uhr gab ich die Note, im Originaltext und in der englischen Uebersetzung, im Weissen Hause ab.

Am Sonntag den 25 [24]. kam Staatssekretär Lansing persönlich auf die Gesandtschaft, änderte mit meinem Einverständnis in der Uebersetzung (Absatz 2 am Ende) die Worte "the evacuated" in "those expelled" um und teilte mir mit, dass, sofern ich keinen Einspruch erhebe, der Praesident die gute Nachricht am Weihnachtsmorgen veröffentlichen werde.

Dies meldete ich Ihnen mit Kabel No 31 und lege Ihnen heute zahlreiche Ausschnitte grösserer Zeitungen vom 25. Dez. bei, damit Sie daraus die Freude ersehen, welche durch die schweiz. Note hier erweckt worden ist.[4]

Die von Ihnen gebrauchte Wendung "has been for a considerable time in touch with the President" hat vereinzelt die Meinung aufkommen lassen, dass es sich um eine bestehende Vereinbarung oder beabsichtigtes künftiges Zusammengehen handle (Beilage 4).[5] Dieser Ansicht trat Herr Lansing in sehr oberflächlicher Weise in der Presse entgegen, hervorhebend dass Herr Wilson für die Abfassung seiner Note mit Niemand, auch nicht mit der Schweiz "in touch" gewesen sei (Beilage 5, Seite 2[6] und Beilage 10 Seite 1 unten, blau).[7]

Mehrere Zeitungen hoben hervor, und sprechen ihre Verwunderung darüber aus, dass der Text der Schweizernote nach Washington und nach London nicht identisch sei. Während man hier lese, dass der Bundesrat "seit geraumer Zeit" mit Praesident Wilson Fühlung gehabt habe, stehe in der Note nach London, dass man "seit 5 Wochen" mit ihm in Fühlung gestanden habe (Beilage 5, pag. 2 und Beilage 10).

Einige wenige, der Administration feindliche Blätter, wie z.B. die N. Y. Sun vom 25. Dez. versuchten die Handlungsweise der Schweiz als eine Begünstigung Deutschlands darzustellen (Beilage 6 pag.2).[8] Als ich am 26. Dez. dem Sekretär des Praesidenten mein Befremden darüber aussprach, erliess er sofort für mich ein Statement (Beilage 7 pag. 1),[9] dass diese falsche Auffassung bedauerlich sei, indem das Vorgehen meiner neutralen Regierung einzig und allein als im Interesse des Friedens geschehend gedeutet werden dürfe. Ein hübsches Bild hat die "World" vom gleichen Tage (Beilage 8 pag. 2).[10]

Ich kabelte Ihnen am 26. Dez. die "high appreciation" des Praesidenten für Ihre Note und dass er mich in einigen Tagen zu empfangen gedenke. Auch fügte ich bei, dass die Presse unsere Note preise und dass die Hoffnung allgemein sei, dass andere Neutrale bald folgen werden.

Man vernimmt, dass auch süd- und centralamerikanische Diplomaten ihren Regierungen vorgeschlagen haben Aeusserungen im Sinne wie von der Schweiz geschehen, zu erlassen. Gestern Abend meldeten einzelne Zeitungen (Beilage 10), dass Schweden ebenfalls mit einer Note gefolgt sei; doch scheint sich die Nachricht bis jetzt nicht zu bewahrheiten, den[n] auf dem Staatsdepartement, wo ich heute vorsprach, wusste man nichts davon.

Wie immer in diesem Lande, ist auch dieses Mal wieder, die Politik zu unlauteren Geschäften benützt worden. Mitglieder der republikanischen Partei im Kongresse verlangen nun eine Untersuchung darüber, wer für das verfrühte Durchsickern der Wilson'schen Friedensnote an die New-Yorker Börse verantwortlich gemacht werden könne. Es geht das Gerücht um, dass der Schwiegersohn des Praesidenten, Schatzamts-Sekretär McAdoo sich bei diesem Anlass spekulativ immens bereichert habe.[11] Lansing und Polk erklärten vor einigen Tagen öffentlich (Beilage 9)[12] sie seien es nicht gewesen. Heute brachte die Washington Post einen Artikel besagend, dass auch amerikanische Diplomaten das Amtsgeheimnis zu eigenem Vorteile gebrochen haben sollen. (Beilage 9) Dieser Artikel ist aber derart ungenau abgefasst, dass darunter leicht auch Botschafter Riaño und ich (die einzigen, welche hier 2 Tage im Voraus eingeweiht waren) verstanden werden konnten. Ich teilte daher heute Herrn Lansing mit, das ich nicht die leiseste derartige Anspielung der Presse dulden würde und bat ihn meine Aussage entgegenzunehmen, dass ich nicht spekuliere und dass Einsichtsnahme in meinen Bankverkehr frei stehe. (In den Vereinigten Staaten muss beim Aktienhandel der Name des Käufers und Verkäufers in die Bücher eingetragen werden. Es ist somit eine gewisse Kontrolle möglich).

Der Staatssekretär sagte mir ferner, dass ihm erst heute den 28. Dez. der Wortlaut der deutschen Antwort, deren Text seit 2 Tagen in den Blättern zu lesen ist, (Beilage 7) zugegangen sei. "Haben Sie jemals etwas Aehnliches von diplomatischer Handlungsweise erlebt?" fragte er mich.

Dass der Praesident vom Inhalt der deutschen Note, als zu wenig in Detail der thatsächlichen Friedensbedingungen eingehend, enttäuscht ist, weiss man bereits und ich beehre mich Sie auch dieses Mal wieder auf die beiliegenden Ausführungen des wohlinformierten Korrespondenten der N. Y. Staatszeitung in der heutigen Nummer vom 28. Dez. zu verweisen (Beilage 10).

Die soeben erscheinenden Abendzeitungen bringen offiziell den Wortlaut der deutschen Antwort an die V. S. Zufällig steht im "Evening Star" (Beilage 11)[13] auf der gleichen Seite auch der Text der deutschen Antwort an den Bundesrat und es ist derart der wärmere Ton der letzteren besonders in die Augen springend.

Ich hoffe sehr den Praesidenten in allernächster Zeit sehen zu dürfen, um Ihnen alsdann seine Meinungsäusserungen speziell über die deutsche Antwort kabeln zu können. Es verlautet heute Abend, dass, was der Praesident bezw. die Administration in Friedenssachen künftig vorzukehren gedenke, geheim geschehen werde. Es seien für die zu erwartenden langwierigen Verhandlungen bessere Antworten aller Parteien unter Ausschluss der Oeffentlichkeit zu erwarten.

Dieser Entschluss ist—soweit er die Vereinigten Staaten anbetrifft—sehr zu begrüssen.

Ich erwähne noch gerne, dass die Schweizerkolonie in den V.S. grosses freudiges Interesse an der Handlungsweise des Bundesrates nimmt und ich beehre mich Ihnen auch die soeben einlaufende jüngste Nummer der Amerik. Schweiz. Zeitung (Beilage 12)[14] hier beizulegen.

Genehmigen Sie, Herr Bundesrat, die Versicherung meiner ausgezeichneten Hochachtung.   P. Ritter

TLS (E2300 Washington, No. 33, Swiss Federal Archives).
  ¹ Printed at December 22, 1916.

2 German-language text not printed.

3 English translation of note from Swiss Federal Council, printed at Dec. 23, 1916.

4 Many of the newspaper clippings mentioned throughout this report are filed with it in the Swiss Federal Archives. Others could not be identified.

5 Annex 4 is a clipping from the front page of the *New York Herald*, Dec. 26, 1916, with a marked report which referred to the concern which some members of Congress felt because Wilson planned a league of nations to enforce peace and because membership in such an organization would mean the abandonment of the Monroe Doctrine and increase the need for American military preparedness.

6 Annex 5 is missing.

7 Annex 10 consists of clippings from pages 1 and 2 of the *New-Yorker Staats-Zeitung*, Dec. 28, 1916.

8 Annex 6 consists of clippings from pages 1 and 2 of the New York *Sun*, Dec. 25, 1916. It included the text of the Swiss note of December 23 to all the warring powers as well as an account of reactions to it. The *Sun* reported that the prevalent opinion in diplomatic circles in Washington was that Swiss diplomacy there was "distinctly pro-German," and also that there had long been cordial relations between Ritter and Von Bernstorff.

9 Annex 7 consists of clippings from pages 1 and 4 of the Washington *Evening Star*, Dec. 26, 1916.

10 Annex 8 is a clipping from the editorial page of the New York *World*, Dec. 26, 1916.

11 William Robert Wood, Republican congressman from Indiana, introduced on December 22, 1916, a resolution calling for an investigation of an alleged leak of advance information about Wilson's peace note of December 18 to favored persons in Wall Street, which had led to an orgy of speculation on the stock market on December 20 and 21. It soon developed that the leak charges had been made by Thomas William Lawson, Boston speculator and author of the famous muckraking exposé, *Frenzied Finance* (New York, 1905). Tumulty, McAdoo, and other members of the administration were implicated, and Bernard M. Baruch was alleged to have been the principal Wall Street beneficiary. The House of Representatives, on January 3, instructed its Rules Committee to investigate. The highly publicized hearings took place in January and February but led only to a report which completely exonerated all governmental officials implicated. Baruch had indeed made a great deal of money by successful speculation, but not through inside knowledge. The only "leak" had been that of two indiscreet newspapermen who, being informed at Lansing's news briefing on the morning of December 20 that there was to be an important announcement that afternoon, had guessed its nature and so informed several brokerage houses. See Link, *Campaigns for Progressivism and Peace*, pp. 251-52, and John M. Blum, "The 'Leak' Investigation of 1917," *American Historical Review*, LIV (April 1949), 548-52. The complete hearings are printed in *Alleged Divulgence of President's Note to Belligerent Powers: Hearings Before the Committee on Rules, House of Representatives, Sixty-Fourth Congress, Second Session on H. Res. 420 . . . H. Res. 429 . . .* (2 vols., Washington, 1917).

12 Annex 9 consists of clippings from the *Washington Post*, Dec. 23 and 28, 1916.

13 Annex 11 is a clipping from page 1 of the Washington *Evening Star*, Dec. 28, 1916.

14 Annex 12 is missing.

T R A N S L A T I O N

Mr. Federal Councilor: Washington, December 28, 1916.

After my last report, December 22 (Annex 1), the Federal Council's note arrived on the afternoon of December 23. While it was being deciphered (Annex 2) and translated (Annex 3) I reported its arrival to the President's secretary and acknowledged receipt by telegram to you. At 6:30 the same evening, I gave the note, in original text and English translation, to the White House.

On Sunday the 25th [24th] Secretary of State Lansing came in person to the legation. With my agreement he amended the translation (next to last paragraph) to read "those expelled" instead of "the evacuated," and told me that, if I had no objection, the President would publish the good news on Christmas morning.

I reported this to you in cable No. 31, and I now send you several clippings from the more important newspapers of December 25, in which you can see the joy aroused here by the Swiss note.

The phrase you used, "has been for a considerable time in touch with the President," has in scattered cases given rise to the notion that a standing arrangement or an intended future cooperation is involved (Annex 4). Mr. Lansing, in a very superficial manner, has contradicted this in the press, emphasizing that, in composing his note, Mr. Wilson had not been "in touch" with anyone, including the Swiss (Annex 5, page 2, Annex 10, foot of page 1, marked in blue).

Several newspapers stress and express surprise that the texts of the Swiss notes to Washington and to London are not identical. Whereas here one reads that the Federal Council has been in touch with President Wilson "for a considerable time," the note to London says it was "for five weeks" (Annex 5, page 2, and Annex 10).

A very few newspapers hostile to the Administration, e.g., the N. Y. *Sun* of December 25, try to depict the Swiss mode of procedure as favoring Germany (Annex 6, page 2). When I expressed my displeasure over this to the President's Secretary, he immediately issued a statement on my behalf that this false conception was deplorable because the activity of my neutral government could only be seen as solely and completely in the interest of peace (Annex 7, page 1). The *World* of the same day gave a fair picture (Annex 8, page 2).

I cabled you on December 26 of the President's "high appreciation" for your note and said that he intended to receive me in a few days. I added that the press commended our note and there was general hope that other neutrals would soon follow.

We hear that South and Central American diplomats have proposed that their governments issue statements similar to the Swiss one. Some newspapers (Annex 10) reported last evening that Sweden, too, had followed with a note; this seems not to be verified so far, since the State Department, where I dropped in today, knew nothing about it.

As always in this country, and now again this time, policy is taken advantage of for sordid dealings. Members of the Republican party in Congress are now demanding an investigation as to who was responsible for a premature leak of Wilson's peace note to the New York stock market. It is rumored that the President's son-in-law, Secretary of the Treasury McAdoo, had thereby enriched himself immensely through speculation. A few days ago, Lansing and Polk declared publicly (Annex 9) that they had not done so. Today the *Washington Post* said in an article that American diplomats had broken official secrets for their own advantage (Annex 9). This article is, however, so loosely written that it casually mentions Ambassador Riaño and me (the only two who were in on the secret beforehand) as among those involved. I told Mr. Lansing today that I would not tolerate even the most casual insinuations of this nature and asked him to accept my assurance that I do not speculate and that my banking transactions are open to inspection. (In the United States the names of buyers and sellers of securities must be entered in the books. A certain control is thereby possible.)

The Secretary of State also told me that only today, December 28, did he receive the text of the German reply, which could be read in the newspapers two days ago. He asked me: "Have you ever heard of anything like this in diplomatic practice?"

We already know that the President is disappointed at the contents of the German note, which goes into too little detail about actual peace conditions, and I have the honor once again to refer you to the enclosed statements of the well-informed correspondent of the N. Y. *Staats-Zeitung* in today's issue, December 28 (Annex 10).

The evening newspapers, just out, give the official text of the German reply to the United States. As it happens, the *Evening Star* (Annex 11) also carries on the same page the text of the German reply to the Federal Council, so that the warmer tone of the latter is especially striking.

I hope very much to be able to see the President in the very near future, so that I can cable you his views, especially about the German reply. It was announced this evening that, whatever the President or the administration will do in the future in matters of peace, will be done in secret. In the negotiations, which will probably be protracted, one can expect better replies all around if publicity is ruled out.

So far as it relates to the United States, this decision is most welcome.

I am glad to mention that the Swiss colony in the United States is taking a great and happy interest in the activities of the Federal Council and I have the honor also to send you the latest number, just out, of the Amerik. Schweiz. Zeitung (Annex 12).

Accept, Mr. Federal Councilor, the assurance of my highest respect.   P. Ritter

To Roland Cotton Smith[1]

                                                    [The White House]
My dear Doctor Smith: December 29, 1916

I had, as you know, looked forward with pleasure to the possibility of attending the anniversary service[2] to be held at St. John's on Saturday afternoon, January thirteenth, though I think I had intimated to you and the gentlemen who accompanied you that I feared it would be impossible for me to make an address on that occasion.

I find upon examining the programme which accompanied the formal invitation that Senator Henry Cabot Lodge of Massachusetts is announced as one of the speakers. Senator Lodge's conduct during the recent campaign makes it impossible for me with self-respect to join in any exercise in which he takes part or to associate myself with him in any way.

I would not refer to this matter if I did not feel that I owed you the most candid statement of my quandary, and I want to beg that you will make no change in your arrangements. It would not be possible for me in any case to speak and I should be very much distressed if I felt that I had in any way interfered with arrangements already consummated.

I say all this, my dear Doctor Smith, in the greatest simplicity and sincerity and beg that you will take me exactly at my word and excuse me without anything said one way or the other outside our own confidence.

With the best wishes for the success of the celebration,
         Cordially and sincerely yours,   [Woodrow Wilson]

CCL (WP, DLC).
[1] The Rev. Dr. Roland Cotton Smith, rector of St. John's Protestant Episcopal Church in Lafayette Square, Washington.
[2] Celebrating the centennial of the church.

To William Jennings Bryan

My dear Mr. Bryan: The White House December 29, 1916

I have your letter of December twenty-third[1] about the possibility of appointing Senator Kern to some federal position.

There is no man in the Senate for whom I have a warmer personal feeling than Senator Kern, and you may be sure I will not overlook his claims if it is possible at any time to consider them.

Again wishing Mrs. Bryan and you all the best things of the season and the New Year,

Cordially and sincerely yours,   Woodrow Wilson

TLS (W. J. Bryan Papers, DLC).
¹ It is missing.

To John Howell Westcott

My dear John: [The White House] December 29, 1916

Your letter written on Mary's birthday and my own has given me, you may be sure, a great deal of genuine pleasure. Will you not wish Mary many, many happy returns for me and tell her I wish I had as much time ahead of me to do interesting things as she has?

In haste, with the warmest messages of good will and good wishes to you all for the New Year,

Faithfully yours,   Woodrow Wilson

TLS (Letterpress Books, WP, DLC).

From Walter Hines Page

[London] December 29th 1916.

5390 VERY CONFIDENTIAL AND URGENT FOR THE PRESIDENT

Since Lloyd George became Prime Minister he has till now been ill or constantly engaged with the War Council or with conferences with members of Allied Governments and hence inaccessible. But this morning I succeeded in breaking through red tape and secured an early informal and confidential conference with him.

I asked him flatly what the Allies' answer to your note would be and requested a frank personal and confidential statement of his feeling about your action and towards our Government and I expressed the conviction that the friendly relations between our Governments and my own constant and absolute frankness gave me warrant in making such an enquiry. I remarked also that the fierce criticism of the English press and public and even as I have heard of some members of his own Government seemed to give an additional warrant for such frank and direct enquiry.

His response was equally frank and most emphatic. In the first place, he said that he would talk to me personally and confidentially quite apart from my official and formal relations with his government. Would I quite understand this and welcome it? I expressed my gratification.

Then he went on to say that he had deprecated all the peace talk in the press of both countries and by persons official or private who had spoken directly or indirectly because all that had so far been said was premature and confusing. He feared it had done harm. He made it clear that he regarded your peace enquiry as premature.

He went on to speak most earnestly and eloquently of the relations of our two Governments and peoples saying, quote,

"We are friends. We are kinsmen. We have common ideals and a common destiny. A capital danger to one is a capital danger to the other. I, therefore, talk to you as one great democracy must talk to another and not as a stranger nor as a foreigner. Our relations must and shall be friendly; must and shall be the relations of kinship and of common aims and common character. And in a time like this of danger to all democracies for the sake of the larger things involved we must be forebearing. We must forget incidental irritations and forgive mistakes. The future of the whole world depends on our understanding one another." Unquote. He added, quote, "Do I make myself quite clear? We do make mistakes. We do have irritations. They will be forgotten if we are both conciliatory. But the harm done to all mankind if we drift apart will never be forgotten nor forgiven." Unquote.

He then expressed the opinion that your note was premature and he wished that some understanding could have been reached about it before it was sent. Neither his Government nor their Allies could now consent to talk peace to say nothing of meeting the enemy in conference. As it appears on the map the Germans now have the advantage. But their defeat had already been begun and was now certain and inevitable. While this condition lasted the Allies could not stop. They could not waver. They could not even talk of peace. The British were determined. If he were now to consent to a peace conference his Government would be swept out of power over night, and the people would become ferocious. The British are determined but they yet have no spirit of hatred nor of revenge. As things now stand they would fight on even if the United States should put an embargo on munitions and food and everything else. Peace talk now therefore is harmful to the Allies' cause.

He spoke philosophically of the German Chancellor who, he knew, did not want this war and who now withstands as best he can the fierce war spirit of his people. He did not believe that the Emperor wished this war. The crime lay with the vast and strong military caste which therefore must be defeated and permanently driven from power. That was a military and political necessity and a preliminary necessity to a permanent peace which was the only kind of peace worth having.

Such was the British and Allied position and this position was not the mere dictum of any government nor of any groups of men, but it was the logic of events which no government could change. Only a military defeat could change it and the Allies would spend every man and every shilling and an indefinite time if need be to win victory.

Although he regarded your note as premature, his Government and the French Government recognized and appreciated your high motive and had received it and would reply in good will. The British and the French had agreed on an answer which they had sent to the Russian and Italian Governments. They had set down their terms of peace as specifically as possible which were concrete enough to be clearly understood. One of their conditions was that the Turks must be cleaned out of Europe and the Christian inhabitants of the Turkish Empire be set free. Another was a quite definite proposal about Poland which he did not explain. The reply of the Allies must be published, and not used for secret conferences or negotiations.

Then the Prime Minister came to what he regarded as the most important part of his conversation. He said that you are the only man in the world to bring this carnage to an end when the time for it to end should come. This was true because not only of your detachment and your high character and disinterested aims but also because you were the head of the great democracy which is as vitally interested as Great Britain itself. You only could bring sufficient pressure on both Germany and the Allies to force an end of war when the time should come.

I asked how you should know when the Allies thought that the opportune time had come. His reply was: quote.

"That's what I am coming to. I am now talking to you quite privately. I wish to establish a relation of confidential privacy with you as the representative of the President so that we may talk so to speak, in an extra-ambassadorial way. I wish if the President will permit me to know his mind through you and I will open my mind to him through you. Of course you will do your official business with the Foreign Office. What I shall tell you lies outside and beyond that. If this is agreeable I shall ask you to call when I have anything to say. I shall promptly inform you when conditions seem to me to call for the President's good offices. It is not yet come. More peace agitation now would be unfortunate and almost or quite unfriendly." Unquote.

The foregoing is a brief summary of a very long and earnest conversation.

Later in the day I had a brief conversation with Mr. Balfour to whom of course I said nothing about what the Prime Minister had said. Balfour spoke in the same conciliatory and friendly fashion, supplementing the Prime Minister's declarations with similar assurances of his own. He spoke of Lord Grey's invitation to Mr. Polk to come to London for a friendly conference about the Blacklist which if Polk would come Grey promised very substantially to (quote) "whittle down" (unquote). Please see my two telegrams to the Department on this subject, numbers 5169 Nov. 16th. and 5219 Nov. 27th.

I venture again most earnestly to suggest that Polk come and bring his evidence in every case. This invitation I interpret as an invitation by the British Government to our Government for a friendly man-to-man conference not only about the Blacklist, but about other such subjects. It would take the friendly advances of this new Government at full tide and make for the clearing up of differences.

I hope, too, that the tone of many of the Department's routine dispatches may be modified. Written, I am sure, by subordinates, many of them make peremtory demands which defeat their purpose and leave irritation. Some of them show ill concealed hostility. I will thank you to refer to the concluding paragraph of my notes on British feeling which I left with you.[1] That programme, it seems to me, is now in order.

May I have a telegraphic acknowledgment of this telegram with such comment as you may care to make.   Page.

T telegram (SDR, RG 84, Foreign Service Posts: London, DNA).
[1] They are printed at Sept. 23, 1916, Vol. 38.

From Robert Lansing, with Enclosure

PERSONAL AND PRIVATE:

My dear Mr. President: Washington December 29, 1916.

I enclose herewith a translation copy of a communication which has just been received in French from the Norwegian Legation, being a note which that Government has today addressed to the Governments of the Belligerent Nations. A similar communication has also been received from the Danish Legation.
          Faithfully yours,   Robert Lansing.

TLS (WP, DLC).

E N C L O S U R E

T R A N S L A T I O N

Note addressed on December 29, 1916, by the Norwegian Government to the Governments of the Belligerent countries.

It is with the keenest interest that the Norwegian Government learned the propositions just made by the President of the United States with a view to facilitating measures tending to the establishment of a lasting peace while desiring to avoid any interference that might hurt legitimate feelings. The Norwegian Government would consider itself remiss in its duty to its own people and the whole of mankind if it should fail to express its most profound sympathy with every effort that might contribute to bringing to an end the progressive accumulation of suffering and moral and physical losses. It indulges the hope that the initiative of President Wilson will end in a result worthy of the lofty spirit by which he was inspired.

T MS (WP, DLC).

From Edward Mandell House

Dear Governor,   [New York] Friday night [Dec. 29, 1916].

Wilcox[1] asked me today to ascertain whether you would attend a dinner which the New York Bar Ass. is to give in January. Hughes is president of it. I said I was sure you would not, but I would ask. If I do not hear from you by Sunday, I shall tell him you cannot accept.   Affectionately yours,   E. M. House

ALS (WP, DLC).
[1] That is, William R. Willcox, chairman of the Republican National Committee.

From Edward Mandell House, with Enclosure

Dear Governor: New York. December 29, 1916.

Josiah Wedgwood,[1] a Member of Parliament and cousin to Lord Robert Cecil, has given me the enclosed memorandum to send you. It is an even more fantastic proposal than that of Lloyd George made to me when I was in London.

Hubert Croly of the New Republic writes:

"The way in which the President's note has been received in England makes me wonder whether something could not be done to explain to some of the more responsible leaders in that country just what the President is driving at in interfering in favor of a discussion of peace. It seems to me to be extremely necessary to have some one in London who understands the real purposes that underly the President's policy and its real value, and who would make a business to see as many Englishmen as he could, and try to put before them a vigorous and persuasive account of America's position and the reasons that lie behind it.

It would need a man of a great deal of tact, a certain amount of position, and a good deal of ability to do this job properly, and it is entirely possible that this need has been anticipated and that there is already someone on the spot to whom the task is being confided. But in case such an arrangement has not been made I am wondering whether it would not be worthwhile to send someone at a comparatively early date. It is fairly certain that our present Ambassador in London is quite incapable of doing work of this kind; at any rate, it is work that ought to be confided in part to an unofficial emissary rather than to our diplomatic representative at the Court of St. James.

In case you think there is anything in this idea Mr. Lippmann and I will be glad to have an opportunity of talking it over with you some time soon. In any event, I hope we can see you at fairly frequent intervals in the near future. Both Mr. Lippmann and I are more interested in doing what little we can to back the President up in his work than in anything else we have ever tried to do through the New Republic, and we are only too glad to give whatever ability we have and whatever influence the paper may have to presenting to our public the underlying purposes of the President's policy. In case you read anything we write upon the matter I should be very much obliged if you would occasionally let us know whether or not we are misinterpreting what the President is trying to do, or whether we are understating or overstating the real motives of his policy. We merely want to back him up in his work and be the faithful and helpful interpreter of what seems to us to be one of the greatest enterprises ever undertaken by an American president."

Affectionately yours,   E. M. House

TLS (WP, DLC).

[1] Josiah Clement Wedgwood, Liberal M.P., single-tax advocate, a veteran of the Gallipoli campaign, at this time on a private goodwill mission to the United States.

ENCLOSURE

A Memorandum by Josiah Wedgwood[1]

The press of England understand their duty, even without instigation from the Foreign Office. That duty is to attack President Wilson, and his note, and the terms of peace which he may lay down.

It would be fatal to his proposals if met, particularly at this stage, with English approval. German acceptance of the proposals would be seriously compromised if any British approval was shown.

President Wilson has asked both sides to say what they want. Both sides will refuse to tell him. The President will then be in the position to say that he could get no information and must come to his own conclusions as to what peace terms would be just.

(He may be informed secretly by Germany as to their maximum (and even possibly minimum) demands. He will get no such secret information from the Allies, since England (1) will not betray her allies, and (2) knows that it is not necessary to betray them since she can trust America to look after her interests without coaching.)

(It is well known that arrangements have been made, as to Asia Minor between France and England, as to the Adriatic countries between Italy and Russia, as to Constantinople between France, Russia and England, as to Transylvania with Roumania—which arrangements depend on success, and which the Allies cannot of themselves go back on)

If the President is not personally annoyed by the diplomatic abuse, and America is not offended, (as to which move caution will be necessary in England,) then he is in a good impartial position to take the next step.

That step would seem to be the drawing up of Peace Terms that would suit American ideals,—drawing them up not on general lines, but in the most exact possible detail. American information will be bad, but in the face of the refusal of the combatants to help the President he must do the best he can,—and he will of course say so at the end. (I can personally give all information wanted on British Colonial questions).

The Peace Terms will be drawn up privately, and in any case there should be no modesty about the American terms. The President and the Americans will be charged with waiting till the fighters were exhausted and then pocketing the spoils. They can face this charge (from both Germans and English) with a clear conscience, as they really want nothing.

The stronger American control is made both over Turkey and over the internationalized tropical colonies, the better,—in spite of all that Europe may say. Behind all the noise we shall be judging fairly.

Make the terms to suit American ideals. Freedom of the seas; Irish, Zionist, Szeck, Autonomy; Polish freedom—a Republic; No war after the war.

Then publish to the American people that if the combatants will make peace on these terms and no other, without any bargaining, America will enter into an alliance to maintain those terms.

The immediate result will be unlimited abuse; which will continue so long as either side believe there is a chance of (a) getting the American terms modified, or of (b) beating their enemy in the field.

Gradually public opinion will accept the boon of a guaranteed peace, and will force the hands of their governments.

You must not expect applause from this generation, but no race will ever have started its rule of the world with a cleaner conscience.

T MS (WP, DLC).
1 Drawn up in collaboration with Noel Edward Noel-Buxton. See Cicely Veronica Wedgwood, *The Last of the Radicals: Josiah Wedgwood, M.P.* (London, 1951), p. 120.

Count Johann Heinrich von Bernstorff to the German Foreign Office

Washington, den 29. Dezember 1916.
Ankunft: den 3. Januar 1917.

Nr. 192. House sagte mir als Wilsons Meinung, dass eine Friedenskonferenz ohne vorherige vertrauliche Verhandlungen nicht zustandekommen werde, da unsere Feinde, wie die Dinge jetzt lägen, die Einladung ablehnen bezw. ihre Annahme von Bedingungen abhängig machen würden. Diese Mitteilung von House war begleitet von einer Aufforderung zu unbedingt vertraulichen Verhandlungen, von denen nur er, Wilson und ich etwas wissen sollten. Unter diesen Umständen wäre völlige Diskretion sicher, da Wilson und House beide ziemlich geschickt im Gegensatz zu anderen Amerikanern Geheimnisse zu wahren wissen.

Ich bitte um baldigste Weisung, ob ich solche Verhandlungen

ablehnen soll oder ob Euere Exzellenz mich dazu ermächtigen und mit entsprechenden Instruktionen versehen wollen. Wie ich früher immer berichtet, legt Wilson verhältnismässig wenig Wert auf die territoriale Seite der Friedensbedingungen. Ich (Gruppe fehlt) nach wie vor der Ansicht, dass das Hauptgewicht auf das zu legen sei, was hier abermals als die "Garantien für die Zukunft" bezeichnet wird. Wenn wir Wilson solche so weitgehend wie möglich geben könnten, glaubt er die Friedenskonferenz zustande bringen zu können, denn damit würde das Hauptargument unserer Feinde entwaffnet. Letztere behaupten nämlich immer, dass wir jetzt nur Frieden machen wollten, um bei günstigerer Gelegenheit den Krieg wieder auzufangen, während unsere Feinde genötigt seien, die gegen uns gebildete Koalition solange wie möglich zusammenzuhalten, um einen dauernden Frieden zu erreichen. Die Wilson'schen Gedanken über solche Garantien sind Euerer Exzellenz bekannt. Sie bestehen in erster Linie in einer beschränkten Abrüstung zu Lande und zu Wasser (Freiheit der See), schiedsrichterliche Einrichtungen und Friedensliga. Glaube auf Grund Euerer Exzellenz Reichstagsrede, dass die Kaiserliche Regierung solche Garantien unter der Bedingung geben würde, dass ein Friede zustande käme.

Ich habe mich House gegenüber vorwiegend zuhörend verhalten, um Euerer Exzellenz in keiner Weise vorzugreifen. Indessen schliesse ich mich der Auffassung des Herrn House an, dass eine Friedenskonfer[e]nz ohne Hilfe der Vereinigten Staaten nicht zustande kommen wird. Unsere Feinde werden versuchen, uns ins Unrecht zu setzen, indem sie sagen, dass wir zwar eine Konferenz vorgeschlagen, aber nichts über unsere Bedingungen und Garantien hätten verlauten lassen. Ich kann natürlich nur vom hiesigen Standpunkt aus ein Urteil abgeben. Wir haben durch unser Friedensangebot eine grosse Umstimmung der hiesigen öffentlichen Meinung hervorgebracht. Diesen Vorteil werden wir gänzlich verlieren, wenn sich der von unseren Feinden kolportierte Gedanke festsetzt, dass wir nur eine für unsere eigene öffentliche Meinung berechnete theatralische Friedensgeste gemacht hätten. Welche Schritte Wilson tun wird, wenn mich Euere Exzellenz zu solchen Verhandlungen ermächtigen, ist noch nicht bestimmt und hängt wesentlich von Euerer Exzellenz Instruktionen ab. House dachte daran eventuell selbst nach England zu reisen, da der britische Botschafter hier kein Vertrauen geniesst. Je mehr Euere Exzellenz mir über unsere Bedingungen und Bereitwilligkeit zu Garantien mitteilen wollen, desto besser von hier aus gesehen. Indessen weiss ich nicht, ob Euere Exzellenz nicht vielleicht lieber die Verhandlungen scheitern lassen wollen, als amerikanische Hilfe anzunehmen. Es braucht m.E. nicht zugestanden zu werden, dass die Vereinigten Staaten an allen Verhandlungen teilnehmen. Notwendig wäre nur die Verpflichtung unsererseits zu den Garantien, welche in einer allgemeinen Konferenz im einzelnen festzusetzen wären, nachdem eine Konferenz der Kriegführenden einen Präliminarfrieden zustande gebracht hätte.

Ich unterbreite Euerer Exzellenz obigen Vorschlag, weil ich überzeugt bin, dass unsere Feinde nicht auf Verhandlungen eingehen werden, wenn nicht von hier, aus ein starker Druck ausgeübt wird. Letzteres wird aber m.E. geschehen, wenn Euere Exzellenz im übrigen glauben, amerikanische Vermittelung annehmen zu können. Mit Ausnahme der belgischen Frage dürfte die hiesige Regierung uns bei allen Verhandlungen mehr Vorteil als Nachteil bringen, da die Amerikaner jetzt erst zur Erkenntnis gekommen sind, was die Seeherrschaft Englands bedeutet.

Bernstorff.

T telegram (Der Weltkrieg, No. 23, geheim, Die Friedensaktion der Zentralmächte, 4058/909920-23, GFO-Ar).

T R A N S L A T I O N

Washington, 29 December 1916.
Received: 3 January 1917.

No. 192. House told me that, in Wilson's view, there will be no peace conference without prior confidential negotiations, because, as things now stand, our enemies would refuse the invitation or accept only conditionally. House accompanied this statement with a request for absolutely confidential negotiations, which only he, Wilson, and I were to know about. In these circumstances complete discretion would be assured, since (in contrast to other Americans) both Wilson and House are rather skilled in keeping secrets.

I request the earliest possible guidance as to whether I should refuse such negotiations or whether Your Excellency would authorize me to undertake them and would provide appropriate instructions. As I have reported often before, Wilson attaches relatively little importance to the territorial side of peace conditions. I [am] as before of the view that main emphasis is on what will once again be called "guarantees for the future." If we could give Wilson these to the fullest extent possible, he believes he could bring the peace conference into being, for our enemies' main argument would thereby be disarmed. They continue to maintain that we would make peace now only in order to resume the war later at a more favorable opportunity, whereas our enemies are obliged to hold together the coalition formed against us as long as possible in order to achieve a lasting peace. Your Excellency knows the Wilsonian ideas about such guarantees. They consist, first of all, of a limited disarmament on land and water (freedom of the seas), adjustments by arbitration, and a league for peace. On the basis of Your Excellency's Reichstag speech, I believe that the Imperial Government would give such guarantees if they would bring a peace.

For the most part I merely listened to House, in order not in any way to anticipate Your Excellency. I did, however, associate myself with Mr. House's statement that, without the help of the United States, no peace conference would be held. Our enemies will try to put us in the wrong, for they will say yes, we propose a peace conference, but we divulge nothing about our conditions and guarantees. I can of course offer a judgment only from the point of view here. Through our peace offer we have produced a great change of mind in public opinion in this country. This advantage we shall lose completely if the idea being hawked by our enemies catches on, i.e., that we have merely made a theatrical peace gesture aimed at public opinion in our own country. What steps Wilson will take, should Your Excellency authorize me to enter into such negotiations, is not yet clear and really depends on Your Excellency's instructions. House is thinking of going perhaps to England himself, since there is no confidence here in the British Ambassador. As seen from here, the more Your Excellency will confide in me as to our conditions and readiness to offer guarantees, the better. On the other hand, I do not know if Your Excellency may not perhaps prefer to let the negotiations collapse rather than to accept American help. In my view, we need not concede that the United States take part in all the negotiations. The only thing necessary would be commitment on our part to the guarantees, which would be worked out in detail at a general conference, after a conference of the belligerents had brought about a preliminary peace.

I present to Your Excellency the above proposal, because I am convinced that our enemies will not enter into negotiations unless strong pressure is exerted from here. In my opinion, however, this will come to pass, if, in other respects, Your Excellency believes American mediation to be acceptable. In all negotiations, except on the Belgian question, the government here would be more to our advantage than not, since the Americans now for the first time have found out the meaning of England's domination of the seas.   Bernstorff.

From William Cox Redfield

My dear Mr. President: Washington December 30, 1916.

I appreciate your helpful courtesy in the matter of the Alaska general fisheries bill as shown in your kind favor of the 21st.

May I say, pursuant to your suggestion as to whom it would be serviceable to write in the Senate, that we feared serious opposition from Senator Lane, who had announced his opposition to the measure. The Postmaster General kindly called on him, however, at my request, and officers of this Department familiar with the facts put them before him. This resulted in an interview between Senator Lane, the Commissioner of Fisheries, and myself on the 28th, in which we came to a common understanding agreeable to all. On yesterday I transmitted to Senator Lane a copy of the bill revised as he wished, and he has promised to introduce it in the Senate and to confer with Judge Alexander respecting it.

I am in hopes that the Rubicon has thus been crossed, but I am venturing to send the drafts of two letters, one to Senator Lane and one to Judge Alexander, for your signature if on reading you approve them.[1]   Yours very truly,   William C. Redfield

TLS (WP, DLC).
[1] See WW to H. Lane, Jan. 3, 1917, and WW to J. W. Alexander, Jan. 3, 1917.

From Walter Hines Page, with Enclosure

Dear Mr. President: London, 30 Decr. 1916

I made my telegram about Lloyd George so full last night that I have little left to write on that score. The Prime Minister has been ill, the Foreign Secretary has been ill (there's an epidemic of influenza), the Christmas holidays came—so far as any outsider's experience with the new Government goes, they have till now been inaccessible. But so far as any outsider can say, they have made an exceedingly good start. Of course Lloyd George's enemies predict that he will not last six months. But they are his enemies. His friends and the public in general expect him to finish the war successfully, and (many think) pretty quickly. To me the new Government seems to promise well—very well. There's a snap about it that the old Government lacked. Lloyd George is not a spent force, but one of the most energetic projectiles that I've ever watched or come in contact with. He said more in half an hour yesterday than Asquith ever told me in his life.

They are not going to yield their contention about the block-ade, nor about the mails. They are so hard-pressed for ships that they will keep all they can and dare within their reach. But on most other subjects I think they will be conciliatory; and we can help (I come back to my old text) if we will be more courteous. The Department is too blustering, as, I think, it has always been. Its "will-not-stand-its," its "intolerables," its "demands" and such-like belong to a war-vocabulary or to the time of George III. This tone provokes many a denial when a courteous tone wd. get what we want. The Department, my dear Mr. President, is under-manned. Of course I am not criticising any man in it: I am saying only that it has about routine things a tone and a manner that de-feat its own purposes, because, I think, there are far too few responsible men in it and because none of them knows the men they write to. Hence the vast importance of Polk's coming here if for ever so brief a visit. He will not find enemies, as, I fear, he thinks, but most courteous gentlemen who wish to retain our real friendship. *Morituous sum* and I can speak even more frankly than ever.

To come to a subject of smaller importance to the nation, I shall be glad when you can tell me your wishes about the end of my service.[1] My arrangements were made in the beginning for my official demise on March 4. My lease expires then. My servants were engaged till then. If I am to retain either or both, I must soon speak to land-lord and butler. And if it shd. be your wish that I shd. remain 3 months or 6 longer (in wh. time the war may end—a circumstance that might make my successor's induction somewhat easier), I shall be happy to serve you, as I am in that and in all other ways. But it wd. be a convenience to know, at your earliest pleasure. My affairs at home could wait even for a year, but not longer.

My own guess is—and it is a guess—that the Germans will give in within a year—perhaps within half-a-year. Then several months will be consumed by the peace-making quarrel. Their "in-vincibility" legend is fading out, between guns and hunger. The man who really makes the blockade lives around the corner. (You never heard of him, a man named Harris, a mere plain, Rt. Honble. Harris.[2]) He and Lloyd George are the two most energetic men that I know in this Kingdom. Now Mrs. Harris,[3] an estimable and loquacious lady, is one of Mrs. Page's good friends and neighbors. That's the way I've come to know Harris very well; and he tells me things that no Cabinet Minister wd. ever whisper—perhaps doesn't know—such as the price of fish in any city in Germany, the calories that a man in Leipsig gets, the number of eggs that reach Berlin from Poland and the value in dollars of a goose in Dresden. He knows, for he gets daily reports. "At 10 o'clock every night, I take up the food-reports from Germany and Austria: they are getting hungry and they will get hungrier yet before Spring."

What a glimpse of war! It's the blockade that will conquer. This gentle, resolute, quiet man sits guardian at all the gates into Germany; and, tho' he wouldn't kill a hare, he watches Hunger beginning to stalk its victims, and he methodically tabulates its approach and maps the shadow that it casts before. I think he wd. gladly lie down and die tonight to have the horrors of this infernal business ended.

But what I sat down to write you was my belief that Lloyd George will keep the programme that he sketched to me as far as you are willing he should. He will be frank. He is most friendly. He has often expressed his admiration for you—long before he could have known that he wd. now become Prime Minister and during the year he has shown and expressed to his intimates his confidence in me. He wishes confidentially to use me as a medium to reach you and for you to reach him whenever either of you have need or even an impulse. He is very direct. He does not use circumlocution. He doesn't "intimate": he says things straight out. "Call me on the telephone any time you like," was his parting word. This from the present ruler of the British Empire; for the Prime Minister is, of course, not only the Chief Executive but the chief and leader also of the House of Commons. I am sure he is quite sincere. Much may come of it, or little may come of it, as you or he will.

This change of Government is quite as complete as a change of Administration at Washington—when one party goes out and the other comes in. All that I can yet say about it is that it promises well for us.   Yours Sincerely,   Walter H. Page.

ALS (WP, DLC).
    [1] About this time, Page sent a telegram, WHP to RL, No. 5391, also asking whether Wilson wanted him to remain in London. The Editors have been unable to find No. 5391 in any collection or repository.
    [2] Frederick Leverton Harris, M.P., parliamentary secretary to the Ministry of Blockade.
    [3] Gertrude Richardson Harris.

ENCLOSURE

Memoranda

London, 30. Decr. 1916.

Written, not for the sake of the gentlemen mentioned but for possible help to the President and the Service

I

Hoover.

Mr. Herbert C. Hoover, chm. of the Commission for Relief in Belgium, would, if opportunity shd. offer, make a useful officer in the State Dp't. He is probably the only man living who has privately (i.e. without holding office) negotiated understandings with the British, French, German, Dutch, and Belgian Gov'ts. He personally knows & has had direct dealings with these Gov't's, and his transactions with them have involved several hundred million dollars. He is a man of very considerable fortune—less than when the war began, for this Relief work has cost him much. But even now his private income is perhaps $50,000 to $75,000 a year. He was approachd. on behalf of the British Gov't with the suggestion that if he wd. become a British subject the Gov't wd. be pleased to give him an important executive post and with the hint that if he succeeded a title might await him. His answer was, "I'll do what I can for you with pleasure, but I'll be damned if I'll give up my American citizenship—not on your life!" Within the last 6 months two large financial organizations, each independently, have offered him $100,000 a year to enter their service; and an industrial company offered him $100,000 "to start with." He declined them all. When the Belgium-Relief work recently struck a financial snag, Hoover by telegraph got the promise of a loan in the U. S. to the British & French Gov't's for Belgian relief, of $150,000,000! I do not *know*, but I think he wd. be glad to turn his European experience to the patriotic use of our Gov't. He is 42 years old, a graduate of Leland Stanford Jr. University

II

Laughlin

There's nothing in our diplomatic service open to Laughlin in the way of promotion after he leaves this Embassy—except an important post in the Dp't or the head of a foreign mission. If I were President, I'd make him an Ambassador. He has served in most capitals; he knows the game thro' and thro'; he's conscientious to a fault; he's patriotic to the marrow. He, too, has a fortune. After he quits the service he will retire from active life. The Service oughtn't to lose one of the best men that has ever grown up in it, especially at so young an age.

Men like these, who have had experience abroad, wd. add much to the Dp't. I needn't say that neither of them knows of my writing this memorandum.   W.H.P.

Hw MS (WP, DLC).

From Francis Joseph Heney

Los Angeles California
December 30, 1916

My dear Mr President:

It was good of you to take the time to write to me. Your letter has given me genuine and lasting pleasure, and I cordially and earnestly reciprocate the sentiments so well expressed therein. If I have been of any service to you, and thereby to our fellow-countrymen, I am more than repaid by that fact alone.

No thoughtful, intelligent observer can fail to realize that you are performing in a big way the biggest job that any President has faced since Lincoln's time. The terrible world's drama now being enacted is fraught with consequences to civilization and to the weal or woe of humanity which are not only immeasurable but well nigh inconceivable. As each new act in this tremendous drama has developed, your own actions and utterances have strengthened my confidence in your ability to handle the unprecedented situation with marvelous understanding and profound wisdom. It may be gratifying to you to know that this feeling is shared by many who voted against you at the recent election. Since the result thereof has been declared, scores of prominent men in both the Progressive and Republican parties have told me that they voted for Hughes with many misgivings, and that they felt greatly relieved when they learned that you had been re-elected. They feel that our country and our national honor are safe in your hands, and that we will not be needlessly plunged into war with any nation either great or small. Curiously enough, only one woman who voted for Hughes has so expressed herself to me. The mental attitude of such men is an interesting and important psychological study, because in a democracy we are compelled to get results from human averages.

Your note to the European powers is a masterpiece of wise and humane statesmanship. It has met with almost universal approval in this part of our country. It is certain to help mightily in bringing about a better understanding by all parties of the reciprocal rights and duties of nations. It will inevitably help to shorten the period of the present gigantic struggle for supremacy, and aid materially in bringing about the organization of a league of the strongest nations of the world to maintain lasting peace and protect the rights of smaller and weaker nations. The vindication of your foreign policies by posterity is as certain as anything ever can be.

It is a pity that the Mexican situation still remains so troublesome. One week ago I heard Lincoln Steffens deliver a lecture on Mexico, at a public meeting here. It was a more forceful and convincing endorsement of your Mexican policy than any political speech that I either heard or read during the campaign.

I take a deep interest in our domestic problems, and, with your permission, shall take the liberty of dropping you a few lines from time to time, in the hope that I may be of some service in directing your attention to certain matters which, in the press of other apparently more momentous business, might escape your close attention.

With assurances of the highest esteem, and with best wishes for the success of your administration and for your personal happiness, I am   Very sincerely yours   Francis J. Heney

TLS (WP, DLC).

From Herbert Bruce Brougham

Dear Mr. President: Philadelphia 30th December 1916

While the question of a select organization of newspapers for their special service is being discussed, and in deference to your doubt about the wisdom of forming such an organization at this time, I have gained Mr. Curtis's consent to engage Mr. Lincoln Colcord,[1] who has been designated by Colonel House,[2] the Public Ledger to bear the expense of sending him to Europe as its correspondent, and, further, to undertake the dissemination of his dispatches and articles in the best morning newspapers covering all sections of the country.

Where cases shall arise of newspapers that do not feel warranted in undergoing expense for this particular service, Mr. Curtis has agreed to furnish it gratis in order to assure the wide publication of Mr. Colcord's reports among the people of the nation.

Mr. Colcord will go quite unfettered by instructions that shall restrict in any way his statements of fact or of opinion based upon the facts as he shall find them. Colonel House has undertaken, on his part, to give Mr. Colcord unusual facilities for reaching the chief sources in Europe of information that may lead to a clear exposition of the community of interest among the nations from which peace may reasonably be expected.

We understand, also, that Colonel House will afford opportunity for Mr. Colcord to meet you and to enable you to judge of his character and capabilities; if your judgment is favorable, he has no doubt that you will be able to give your certification of Mr. Colcord as a correspondent in the integrity of whose character and in the trustworthiness of whose reports the reading public should have especial confidence, and that we may publish this certification.

Meanwhile the plan which, personally, I have much at heart[3] is in abeyance. I cannot see that it could work very well if selfish interests got control of it, for that would instantly discredit it; on the other hand, so long as men of liberal spirit controlled it the American public would recognize in it an instrument of effectual enlightenment. But I am not downhearted, for I feel that you sympathize both with the end sought and with the means proposed, the only question in your mind being that of present expediency.   Very sincerely yours,   H. B. Brougham

TLS (WP, DLC).
    [1] Lincoln Ross Colcord, journalist, poet, and short-story writer. As it turned out, Colcord became the Washington correspondent of the Philadelphia *Public Ledger*.
    [2] House had recently taken on Colcord as a kind of journalistic protégé and was soon to see him frequently to give him ideas for his political journalism. See Christopher Lasch, *The New Radicalism in America, 1889-1963: The Intellectual as a Social Type* (New York, 1965), pp. 225-50.
    [3] See WW to H. B. Brougham, Dec. 15, 1916, n. 2.

From Ida Minerva Tarbell

My dear President Wilson: New York, December 30, 1916.

I am deeply touched by your letter. You must know how honored I feel that you should have thought of me for a place on the Tariff Commission. I hope you realize how much I regret that I cannot accept. I came very reluctantly to the conclusion, for I of course realized that there was a public obligation involved; and that is the last thing that I should want to shirk. I believe, my dear Mr. President, that I appreciate, perhaps better than most people, what this Commission ought to do. I am not physically fit to give it what it deserves.

It is really humiliating to me to confess this. I have worked steadily all my life, and, until the last year, almost entirely at a desk. I realized at least three years ago that I must make a change, if I was to keep to the end the physical and mental vigor which I feel is both the privilege and the duty of a sane worker. Some months ago I gave up all editorial work; and have substituted three or four months a year of Lyceum and Chautauqua talking. It has always seemed to me that this was a legitimate way of reaching the public with the things in which one was interested. My experience has given me a real respect for the work, and an ambition to help develop it into a more serious medium than it seems to most people.

I would give a great deal, however, if I might help the Tariff Commission in some way. It might be possible that I could aid in interpreting its task to the public through my writing. I have even thought of preparing a lecture to be called "Our Tariff." Possibly this is only a way of salving my conscience for the twinge it feels in refusing to do anything that you, who carry such heavy burdens, ask; nevertheless it would give me real satisfaction if I could help educate the public to an understanding of what it ought to expect from the Commission, and to a realization that it should be given time.

I want to take this opportunity to say how glad I was of your peace note, and how rejoiced I am to see the way that much of the best opinion in all of the belligerent countries receives it. You did a great and courageous thing, my dear Mr. President, when you sent that note, and I am thoroughly convinced that the whole world is going to come one day to that belief.

I am giving myself the pleasure of sending you a copy of my last book, "New Ideals in Business."[1] It is a report of things I have been following for three or four years in certain factories and shops of the country. I went out to see what I could find that was hopeful. Here are the results. I have been made bold to send you the book, because of certain things you said to me when I had the pleasure of talking to you last fall at Shadow Lawn. I am convinced that wherever any or all of these ideas are worked out intelligently and honestly, they make for the thing which you so deplored the lack of in your talk with the men concerned in the railroad controversy, that is, the ability to consider without suspicion and ill-will questions which concern them both.

Forgive me, dear Mr. President, for this long letter. It simply says two or three things which I have wanted much to say to you, but which I have refrained from saying because I hesitated to swell in the slightest degree the flood of correspondence which I know pours upon you. I have always felt that keeping silence was the most useful thing that a citizen could do in such periods as you have had to face in the last four years.

May I not say now how much I regretted to be obliged to refuse the invitation to dinner on December 12th with which you and Mrs. Wilson honored me. I feel that this is the kind of thing which is not done, but I was under bond to speak in New Orleans, and though I tried to get a release, both my lecture bureau and the people having the course in hand refused to let me go. They were good, progressive Democrats, so though I paid the price of missing the dinner, I had the consolation that I was indirectly at least serving the cause. I go out again in a few days, and it will be with renewed energy and enthusiasm because of the confidence you have shown in me, in believing me fit for a position so important as that of a member of the Tariff Commission.

With the very best of New Year wishes to you and Mrs. Wilson, believe me, my dear Mr. President,

Faithfully yours,   Ida M. Tarbell

TLS (WP, DLC).
 [1] Ida Minerva Tarbell, *New Ideas in Business: An Account of their Practice and their Effects upon Men and Profits* (New York, 1916). It is in the Wilson Library, DLC.

From Edward Mandell House

Dear Governor: New York. December 31, 1916.

Brougham of the Curtis Publications wanted me to send you the enclosed articles of Lincoln Colcord's in order to give you an idea of how he writes.[1] Colcord is a man of fine integrity, is a progressive and an ardent admirer of yours. He is, I think, the best man we could have to make a start in the direction planned.

I have suggested Ray Stannard Baker, George Creel and Lincoln Steffins for further additions to their staff, subject to your approval. Colcord they think of sending to Europe, Steffens would be a good man for Mexico and the Spanish republics, while Creel and Baker could write upon domestic matters.

I am sorry you could not see Roy Howard when he was in Washington the other day. He understood from Tumulty that you would see him, and he returned deeply hurt.

The United Press together with the Scripps-McRay[2]—(which are really one concern) did more in the election than any single factor. In Ohio, in Minnesota, in North Dakota and in California it was the most potential influence you had.

I am told that 75% of the news that gets into the British Press and into Australia and New Zealand is through their service.

Cleve Dodge and some other representatives of charity organizations have a plan to coordinate all the foreign relief societies. They believe they can raise something like a hundred million of dollars for European relief now and after the war. They have suggested a commission and a plan which they would like you to approve.

If it is agreeable to you I will come over to Washington on Wednesday arriving there at 4.20 P.M. in order to talk this and other matters over with you. They have requested me to do so.

Your affectionate,   E. M. House

TLS (WP, DLC).

[1] Lincoln Colcord, "The Truer Germany," *New Republic*, III (July 24, 1915), 300-11, and "The United States as a Sea Power," *ibid.*, IX (Dec. 30, 1916), 240-42.

[2] The Scripps-McRea chain of newspapers.

From Karl H. von Wiegand

Mr. President: New York December 31 1916

Just before departing from Berlin on December tenth, to sail from Bergen for New York for a conference with my paper (New York WORLD) and to spend Christmas with my family, Maximillian Harden, your great admirer in Germany and who as perhaps no other man in Germany has endeavored to make your ideals clear to the German peoples and to interpret to them your high and noble aims as he conceives and understands them, requested me to extend to you his most grateful appreciation for a verbal message he said you had sent him.[1] He assumed that I might see the President but I told him that was only possible when the request came from the White House.

On the eve of my departure Harden wrote me a letter, the contents of which he requested me to communicate to you as a favor to him. Perhaps I should explain that Harden has been my friend since first I went to Germany in the summer of 1911 and that no American knows him as intimately as do I. His admiration for me, he often tells me, is only exceeded by mine for him. He was so generous and kind as to say that his wonderful article "If I were Wilson,"[2] could largely be attributed to the hours of conversation we have had on political topics in which I had given him, he said, the American, more especially what he calls the "Wilson viewpoint." I doubt whether there is a single American who believes more in you Mr. President, who admires you more, than does Maximillian Harden. And what he did to help to avert war between Germany and America more than once in submarine situation, I can only write some day when the war is ended. That is equally true of many confidential talks I have had with the highest statesmen of the Central Powers.

Herr Harden's style is most difficult of translation but I shall do the best I can. Mr. President, you will see how Harden in this letter written December 8, intuitively anticipated your Peace action, of which, of course, he could not have had any knowledge. He writes:

"My Dear von Wiegand:

As you are about to return to your peaceful country and because you have treated our cause in so high and just a journalistic manner, it would be especially friendly of you and I would be grateful to you if you could take the opportunity to tell your most honored President, how I appreciated his communication to me and how I have rejoiced in the fact that the people of the United States have elected the first man of the nation for the second time as head of their government.

I would willingly have written the President directly, but you know every word would be read and questioned, and then too I have a doubt as to the advisability of such a step at this time—a doubt which connects itself with the idea that unwittingly I might bring harm, not to me a private citizen—but to the President.

In the article I prepared at the request of your paper (This article is entitled "Wilson in Germany," and has not yet appeared[3]) I have outlined a few of my thoughts. Perhaps the President may find time to devote a moment to it.

To suggest a course of action to the all comprehending brain of a Wilson, would be a presumption on my part, I believe that the very high ethical spirit (Edle vergeistigte Sittlichkeit), which, emanating from him becomes a potent force, will set him the task of an attempt to make peace. And, I hope most intensively that he will not wait with this attempt until the undertaking becomes so simple that any King of Spain can master it.

A Crown of humanity is here to be acquired—a Crown such as has not shown its light in thousands of years, and the path in this radiance need not lead over a Golgotha. The world desires to become democratic. Therefor I hope that in a spirit of harmony with the genius of the times, this Crown might be won by the head of the greatest and most mighty Democracy. It would be the most extraordinary example for monarchies and monarchs—a lesson which would strike deeper than the bloody one given them by the Condotterie genius of Bonaparte spurred on by all to[o] eager an ambition. The message, for which Christmas would be a most fitting time, should be directed, without asking if it is agreeable to any group of powers, to the PEOPLES of the Earth and not to the chancellories. This message should in the name of mankind and humanity—the white race and its common civilization, only put forth the noble demand;

'Speak with one another! TRY! Make the attempt before in the Spring means of warfare grewsome beyond conception, shall have been put forth and again at least half a million human beings shall have been slaughtered. Make the attempt to see if not an understanding is possible with restraint exercised and yielding on all sides. I Woodrow Wilson, as the mouthpiece of the United States of America, charge before mankind and history, him who closes his ear to this appeal, with the responsibility. I could not take the responsibility to refrain from making this appeal simply because it is not convenient or agreeable to one party or to both. I do *not* desire to be arbiter mundi, only if it is demanded, will I serve as "ehrlicher Makler" (Bismarcks phrase) who will bring the parties together BUT in any case I will be the Voice of Mankind that may not and will not longer be stilled. This Voice, without being prompted either by advantage or selfishness, asks all who wish for peace organized internationally, for an ending of the horror of the times—an unproductive destructive competitive armament; for dignified freedom of all nations, to assist this last attempt towards a humane and noble understanding worthy of mankind—to assist it with all forces of national ethical consciousness, before the world experiences the realization of the tragic fate prophesied in the German mythology and in the Apocalypse.'

From *all* peoples, from the trenches of *all* nations, chants would rise to the bearer of this Evangel. The government or group which remained deaf, would have placed itself before the world in the wrong. Should only preliminary negotiations *begin*, relapse into war would be out of the question. Only then would it be revealed how resigned *everywhere* behind the boasting that today is still considered necessary on both sides, the peoples have become to to [sic] demands or expectations in a Treaty of Peace.

And whose fame in all history, could could [sic] compare to that of the man who has boldly ventured forth into the horror (or out of the horror), and just 1900 years after the Saviour, calls out across a devastated world 'Peace on Earth, good will to man.' "

This, Mr. President, is what Herr Harden requested me to say for him. As I am not known to you, I have not ventured to ask you to receive me that I might deliver this verbally, therefor have taken the liberty of writing it. In the wonderful though very involved phraseology of Harden, his letter to me sounds far loftier and I know I have not been able to do it or him justice in this.

Herr Harden further asked if I would not extend to you the "heartfelt good wishes of a humble citizen of of [sic] Germany" for the New Year.

Did I not know the situation in Germany as well as I do, did I did [sic] not know personally practically all the leading figures who are making history there, and had I not been on the inside of the submarine controversy since the day that I first startled the world with the announcement in 1914, that it was coming, I would be somewhat alarmed about what I read in the press here since I have come, that there is danger of a break between the two countries. Knowing the personal views held by Bethmann, Ludendorff, and Hindenburg, as I believe I do—together with the fact that leaders of the big parties in parliament have adopted a resolution opposing any change of Chancellor during the war, I cannot see the danger that so many of the newspapers here profess to see.

May I, as an American, also extend to you Mr. President, a humble citizen's good wishes for the successful culmination of the herculean task you have set yourself. For two and half years I have, as few outsiders have, seen the horrors and misery of war—the suffering of noncombatants with the combatants—that I know what war means. And every time that I write a dispatch I feel as never before, the responsibilities that rests upon those who write and print insidiously distilled mental poisons which can dethrone the reason of a world.

Very Sincerely Yours,   Karl H. v Wiegand

TLS (WP, DLC).
[1] Wilson sent it by Herbert Bayard Swope. See H. B. Swope to M. Harden, Sept. 1, 1916, Vol. 38.
[2] See n. 1 to the letter cited in the preceding note.
[3] Harden's article apparently was never published.

A Memorandum by Robert Lansing

MEMORANDUM OF INTERVIEW
WITH THE SPANISH AMBASSADOR,
SUNDAY, December 31, 1916.

The Spanish Ambassador called at my residence at 12:30 p.m. by appointment.

He asked me if we had received the reply from his Government which he understood had been delivered to our Chargé at Madrid. I told him that we had not.

He then said that he had been instructed by his Government to say that they had taken into consideration the present situation and, acting independently as the United States had, they thought that in view of the apparent way in which the identic note had been received in the Allied nations the time was not opportune for them to participate, but that they were prepared to take steps when a more favorable time should come. He went on to say that he was particularly instructed to express the great appreciation of the Spanish Government of the high motives of the President in the action taken and to assure this Government of the very sincere friendship of the Spanish Government and people with the hope that its present course would not be misconstrued.

He asked me if there had been a statement given out that the note had been sent without a previous understanding with other neutrals. I replied that I may have answered some question to that effect in the negative, because we had not done so, but I recalled no formal statement.   RL.

TI MS (WP, DLC).

To Edward Mandell House

The White House Jan 1 1917

Delighted you are coming over on Wednesday   We shall expect you with great pleasure   Happy New Year to you all
Woodrow Wilson

T telegram (E. M. House Papers, CtY).

From Alice Paul

Mr President: Washington, D. C. January 1, 1917.

I am writing to ask for an appointment to bring to you resolutions drawn up at memorial meetings in honor of Mrs Inez Milholland Boissevain,[1] and held in San Francisco, California, New York City, and in Washington, D. C. at the Capitol.

The bearers of these resolutions are Mrs Sara Bard Field, sent from San Francisco; Mrs John Winters Brannan[2] and Mrs Clarence Smith,[3] sent from New York, and Miss Maud Younger[4] of San Francisco.

I am requested to ask that this appointment be next Sunday afternoon at half past four o'clock. If this day is impossible, the following Monday at half past four is requested.
Very sincerely yours,   Alice Paul.

TLS (WP, DLC).
[1] Inez Milholland (Mrs. Eugen Jan) Boissevain, lawyer, feminist, socialist, pacifist, and suffragist, had died in Los Angeles on November 25, 1916, at the

age of thirty. Although she suffered from pernicious anemia, she had undertaken a western tour on behalf of the National Woman's party to rally enfranchised women against the Democratic party because of its failure to support a federal suffrage amendment. She had collapsed while speaking in Los Angeles on October 23.

2 Eunice Dana Brannan.

3 Jane Norman (Mrs. Clarence Meserole) Smith.

4 Labor leader and suffrage advocate who had delivered a memorial oration for Mrs. Boissevain in Statuary Hall in the Capitol in Washington on December 25.

Herbert Bruce Brougham to Irwin Hood Hoover

My dear Mr. Hoover: Philadelphia 1st January 1917

I wired you to-day as follows: "At suggestion of Colonel House, may I have appointment to see the President for myself and Lincoln Colcord who sails next Saturday, January sixth, on Nieuw Amsterdam as correspondent for Public Ledger? Please wire reply collect."

When I spoke with the President the other day he kindly expressed his belief that any person whom Colonel House might recommend for the mission contemplated by us would be approved by him. It is necessary, of course, that Mr. Colcord should meet the President, and that the President should have some acquaintance with his character as shown in his writings.

I believe The New Republic has already sent to the President advance proofs of an article by Mr. Colcord appearing in the current issue of that publication. I inclose a clipping of the same article, which is one of a number contributed by Mr. Colcord to The New Republic.[1]

The quality which marks Mr. Colcord's essays, poetry and fiction, and which prompted Colonel House to recommend him above better known writers, is that of a vigorous moral idealism as applied to practical affairs. His book of short stories entitled "The Game of Life and Death"[2] is really a criticism of Western standards, and his "Vision of War, 1915"[3] drives at the heart of the war in its indictment of modern materialism.

Mr. Colcord is a young man of 33, he is not yet well known to the American public, and he is not known at all to the newspaper press of this country. In order that our plan of circulating his reports and dispatches in every part of the country may be put into execution, and that the public may have an intimation of our purpose to put the American press on a higher plane of credibility, we bespeak the President's aid.

It is not necessary, or, in fact, advisable that Mr. Colcord should go officially to Europe as representing the administration. He should go for the Public Ledger. But a certification from the

President of his singular fitness and ability for this mission and of his personal character, as well as the President's commendation of the enterprise itself, would convey to the public the necessary note of distinction and of credibility. It should be of benefit both to the press and to the public.

Very sincerely yours,   H. B. Brougham

I find that The New Republic of 30th December is not yet on sale, owing to some delay, but will send it on as soon as obtainable.   H.B.B.

TLS (WP, DLC).
  1 "The United States as a Sea Power," cited in EMH to WW, Dec. 31, 1916, n. 1.
  2 *The Game of Life and Death: Stories of the Sea* (New York, 1914).
  3 *Vision of War* (New York, 1915).

To Roy Wilson Howard

My dear Howard: [The White House] 2 January, 1917

You were down here the other day and were unable to see me, and I have been very much distressed to learn through common friends that you were hurt.

You must really try to understand, my dear Howard, my real attitude towards you. I know your genuine friendship and if there were any personal aspect to the matter, you may be sure I would go the limit, but this is just the whole case:

I had learned from Mr. House that your errand was to assist me in clearing up a misunderstanding on the other side of the water as to the meaning of my note in some respects and if I had been going to make a statement through any medium, I certainly would have made it through you. But what I resolved was not that I would not see you, but that I would not make a statement or an explanation.

I think that an explanation would have weakened the whole effect of the thing. Nothing could have stated my position more plainly than the note stated it (of course, I do not mean any implied criticism of anybody in saying that), and I believe that as the days go on the note is better and better understood. Neither side in the war is pleased with anything I write unless it can be construed as favorable in feeling to them (I say this, of course, in the closest confidence) and the misunderstanding arises out of that sensitive bias:

Please make up your mind once for all that I am incapable of giving you any personal offense, and decide every matter such as this on public and not on private grounds.

With the best wishes of the New Year,
Cordially and sincerely your friend,   Woodrow Wilson

TLS (Letterpress Books, WP, DLC).

From Josephus Daniels

My dear Mr. President: Washington. January 2, 1917.

The question of securing the western half of the Osage Indian
Reservation in Oklahoma as a possible Naval Oil Reserve, brought
to your attention by Secretary Lane's letter of December 17,
1916,[1] has heretofore been discussed by representatives of the
Departments of the Interior and the Navy, and has been the subject of correspondence between the two Secretaries.

Both Departments are in accord as to the desirability of securing this area for the purpose indicated, and the recently submitted
report of the Naval Fuel Oil Board contains the following statement:

"In the western half of the Osage Nation there are several
geological structures which will undoubtedly yield a large amount
of oil, the possible production being estimated by the Geological
Survey at three hundred and fifty million barrels.

This is the only large, compact area of probably productive oil
land in the United States remaining in single ownership. Furthermore, it is the only field over which the Government has any control whose yield can be piped to the eastern coast of the United
States. This area is held in common by the Osage Nation, and it
has not been opened to development, but can be opened at any
time by the action of the Osage Council, approved by the Secretary of the Interior. There is such an urgent demand from the
Indians, the oil interests, and the State of Oklahoma for the opening of this area that, unless early action is taken to secure this
promising reserve of oil for the Nation, the opportunity will have
passed.

The Osage area presents the following advantages:

(a) The structures are independent and are therefore incapable of being drained by drilling on adjacent territory.

(b) Their location makes these lands of greatest strategic
value, since they can be connected to near by pipe lines to the
Gulf and Atlantic Coasts.

(c) If this area is opened to commercial development at an
early date it will result in converting into money the reserve
resources of the Osage Nation at a time when the Indians' financial needs are already adequately provided for. It will probably

result in the depression of the petroleum industry of the Mid-Continent field, and the sale of the oil at less than its intrinsic worth, and the export of a large part of it."

Since the securing of this area as a Naval Oil Reserve will require the approval of the two interested Departments, and the Osage Council and the action of Congress, it has been difficult to devise a plan for accomplishing the desired result, but I will be glad to make an investigation of the worth of the land and negotiate for a price as suggested by the Secretary of the Interior.

I am sending a copy of this letter to the Secretary of the Interior, and I will talk it over with him to-day.

Cordially and faithfully yours,   Josephus Daniels

TLS (WP, DLC).
¹ It is missing.

From Roland Cotton Smith

My dear Mr. President: [Washington] Jany. 2d, 1917

I returned from New York today to find your letter awaiting me.

The friendliness and courtesy of your note relieves me of a part of my embarrassment, making it necessary for me to assure you that I was very far from intending any discourtesy to you.

I was ingenuously stupid and for that I apologize.

The White House and St. Johns have had close and cordial relations for a hundred years, and it is a bitter disappointment to me that you find it impossible to be present at the Hundreth Anniversary. But I must do as you say, and take you exactly at your word. I do it with great regret.

Secretary Lane attends St. Johns, and I have great admiration for him. Is there any objection to his speaking at the Anniversary? I will not approach him until I have heard from you.

Sincerely Yrs,   Roland Cotton Smith

ALS (WP, DLC).

James Watson Gerard to Robert Lansing

Berlin via Copenhagen, January 2, 1916 [1917].

4814. Had a talk with Chancellor yesterday. He had seen the reply of Allies to German peace proposal as published by Wolff Bureau.¹ He expressed regret about failure of Germany's peace move. I said if you sincerely want peace are you willing to confide your peace terms to the President in confidence if the Allies will do the same, so that the President can see if you are near enough together to warrant a hope for peace. He said not now but I shall consider it. He is not willing to do anything about deportation of Belgians. I learn good authority deportation was a military measure demanded by General Ludendorff on the ground that he feared a British landing in Belgium and deportation was opposed by von Bissing. I learn best authority that a positive reign of terror exists in Belgium and that quantities of food contrary to guarantees are being exported to Germany.   Gerard.

CC telegram (R. Lansing Paper, NjP).
   1 The note of the Allies was transmitted to the State Department on December 29, published in Paris on December 31, and sent by the State Department to the Central Powers on January 2. It asserted that the German peace note of December 12 was in fact a propaganda document which contained no concrete peace proposals. It accused the German government of attempting to throw the onus for prolonging the war upon the Allies while seeking to impose a German peace on Europe at the moment when the Germans held a transitory military advantage. The Allies, it said, would not consider any German peace offer as genuine unless it was accompanied by definite conditions, especially conditions for the restoration of Belgium. The full text of the Allied note is printed in translation in W. G. Sharp to RL, Dec. 29, 1916, *FR-WWS 1916*, pp. 123-25. See also Link, *Campaigns for Progressivism and Peace*, p. 237.

To Ida Minerva Tarbell

My dear Miss Tarbell: [The White House] 3 January, 1917

   Thank you with all my heart for your letter of December thirtieth. I knew that you had good reasons or that you would not have declined service on the Commission, and I honor you for facing the difficult task of assessing your own physical strength and doing the thing that seemed wisest in all the circumstances.

   I think your suggestion is an excellent one that you can do no small service to the Tariff Commission by interpreting it and its task after it gets to work, or even before it begins.

   I am very much obliged to you for having thought of me in connection with your book. I shall look forward with genuine pleasure to reading it. What you write always has solid facts and real human circumstances back of it and I always feel as if I were really getting something.

   I am happy to believe that your fear about your health does not mean that you do not now feel well and fit, but only that you have had to come to a definite conclusion as to the kind of work you ought to do.

   With the most sincere and cordial good wishes for the New Year,

        Cordially and faithfully yours,   Woodrow Wilson

TLS (Letterpress Books, WP, DLC).

To Robert Lansing, with Enclosure

My dear Mr. Secretary: The White House 3 January, 1917

Apparently this letter from Senator Stone was written the very day you and I consulted about the matter it deals with. I am sure you will be interested to know that his thought is substantially our own.

I hope that you will find it possible to confer with him at an early date.

Cordially and sincerely yours,   Woodrow Wilson

TLS (SDR, RG 59, 811 G. 01/8½, DNA).

E N C L O S U R E

From William Joel Stone

Dear Mr. President: [Washington] January 2 1917.

I write you respecting the Danish West Indies Islands. As soon as there has been an exchange of the ratifications of the Treaty, and formal delivery of the Islands made to us, we must pass some law for the government of the Islands. Have you thought this out?

I suggest that probably the best thing we can do would be to pass a law authorizing the appointment by the President of a Governor and other necessary officials under the Governor to carry on the administration of the government of the Islands as may be required under their present laws and forms—at least in the main. We must keep in mind the character of the population of the Islands. I am inclined to the view that a very simple Act putting our officials there in control, without now undertaking to provide all the complicated machinery for a semi-territorial government, would be about the wisest thing we could do.

I wish you would think about this matter and at an early convenient time allow me to talk with you concerning it.

I have the honor to be,

Very sincerely yours,   Wm. J. Stone

TLS (SDR, RG 59, 811 G.01/8½, DNA).

To William Joel Stone

My dear Senator: [The White House] 3 January, 1917

Oddly enough, the Secretary of State and I had been consulting the very day you wrote your letter of January second about providing for the government of the Danish West Indies, and our own judgment had been very similar to yours.

I have asked the Secretary of State to consult with you about the matter, and I am sure he will do so at an early date. The next time we get together we can have a little talk about it.

In haste
                    Cordially and faithfully yours,   Woodrow Wilson

TLS (Letterpress Books, WP, DLC).

To John Franklin Shafroth

My dear Senator: [The White House] 3 January, 1917

Personally, I do not doubt our power to join in any arrangement with regard to the maintenance of the peace of the world in which the President and the Senate may unite, but I realize the interest and importance of resolutions such as you have introduced and am very glad indeed that the matter is to be thoroughly canvassed.[1] My own feeling is that the power of dealing with foreign affairs is given in as complete terms as necessary in the Constitution and I think the more the question is discussed, the more clear that will become.

                    Cordially and sincerely yours,   Woodrow Wilson[2]

TLS (Letterpress Books, WP, DLC).
  [1] Wilson was responding to J. F. Shafroth to WW Dec. 28, 1916, TLS (WP, DLC). Shafroth called attention to Senate Joint Resolution 131, which he had introduced on May 18, 1916. This resolution proposed the following amendment to the Constitution:
  "The President is authorized to negotiate and, after ratification by two-thirds of both Houses of Congress, to sign a treaty or treaties with all or a part of the other sovereign nations of the world, engaging the United States to submit for final determination all its international disputes threatening war to an international tribunal or tribunals, and also engaging the United States to assist in supplying funds for the support of said tribunal or tribunals and of any international civil and military establishment, to be controlled by an international authority, that may be required by the treaty or treaties as a sanction for the execution of the decrees and the fulfillment of the demands of the said international organisms when such decrees or demands are made in conformity with the agreements instituting said organisms, and engaging the United States to recognize the authority of said international organisms (or one or more of them) to make final interpretation of the powers conferred upon them."
  This proposed amendment was, at least in part, the work of Oscar Terry Crosby, long an advocate of a world court with power to enforce its decrees. See Warren F. Kuehl, *Seeking World Order: The United States and International Organization to 1920* (Nashville, Tenn., 1969), pp. 120-21, 149-50, 177-78, 228-29.
  In his letter to Wilson, cited above, Shafroth suggested that recent international events, as well as administration policy, justified serious consideration of constitutional limitations which might embarrass efforts to set up either an international tribunal with power to enforce its decrees or any other form of international organization capable of maintaining peace. In particular, he observed that only a constitutional amendment could deprive Congress of the sole power to make war. He also stated that he was "reliably informed" that the foreign press would soon point out the lack of power in the American government to conclude treaties for the enforcement or insurance of peace.

Shafroth also noted that the Senate Judiciary Committee was "about" to hold hearings on his resolution. If these hearings were in fact held, they were not made public.

2 Shafroth made public a summary of the contents of this letter on January 13, 1916. See the *New York Times*, Jan. 14, 1916.

To Harry Lane

My dear Senator: [The White House] 3 January, 1917

The Secretary of Commerce has informed me of your helpful suggestions in the matter of the Alaska fisheries bill, of which a draft, amended as you desired, has been sent you to be introduced in the Senate.

I believe that the measure is one which will do away with sad waste of valuable food fishes and will prevent monopolistic practices now existing on both of which matters you are fully informed.

I venture to express the hope, therefore, that your kind efforts toward its passage may be successful.

Cordially and sincerely yours,   Woodrow Wilson[1]

TLS (Letterpress Books, WP, DLC).

1 Wilson based this letter and the following letter upon the drafts by Redfield mentioned in W. C. Redfield to WW, Dec. 30, 1916.

To Joshua Willis Alexander

[The White House]
My dear Judge Alexander: 3 January, 1917

The Secretary of Commerce informs me that at a conference on the 28th of December with Senator Lane an understanding was reached respecting the Alaska fisheries bill that was satisfactory to the Senator, the Secretary of Commerce, and the Bureau of Fisheries. A copy of the measure, revised to include the suggestions made by Senator Lane, has been handed him, and he has agreed to introduce it in the Senate and to confer with you about it.

The Secretary of Commerce also informs me that he has placed in your hands a copy of the measure containing the changes proposed.

I venture to express the hope that the matter can be satisfactorily adjusted so that this important bill to prevent great waste of valuable foods and to stop serious monopolistic practices may become a law at the present session.

Cordially and sincerely yours,   Woodrow Wilson

TLS (Letterpress Books, WP, DLC).

From Robert Lansing, with Enclosures

PERSONAL AND PRIVATE:

My dear Mr. President: [Washington] January 3, 1917.

I am sending you a statement made by Mr. Arthur Page to Mr. Harrison, of this Department, and also confidential reports on the U-53 and the German submarine activities, which are furnished by the office of Naval Intelligence.

It will oblige me if you will return these to me after you have read them.   Faithfully yours,   Robert Lansing

TL (SDR, RG 59, 763.72/3105A, DNA).

ENCLOSURE I

Leland Harrison to Robert Lansing

Dear Mr. Secretary: [Washington] January 3, 1917.

Mr. Arthur Page of the World's Work, who recently returned from Europe, has told me that the peace proposal of December 12th last was not the first effort of Germany to make peace at this time. Mr. Page said that during November he had seen Mr. Hoover of the Belgium Relief Committee and that Mr. Hoover had told him that some time in October the Germans had asked him to present certain proposals of peace to the British Government, which he had refused to do. Mr. Page also said that during his visit to Paris he had heard from reliable sources that Germany had endeavored to sound out France as regards peace and had also approached Russia, which had caused considerable anxiety in French circles and which had no doubt led to the resignation of Sturmer.[1] Mr. Page spoke of the efforts made by Germany with Russia and France as a matter of general knowledge, but in the case of Great Britain his information was definite as it had come direct from Mr. Hoover.   L. Harrison

TLS (SDR, RG 59, 763.72119/408½, DNA).

[1] Emperor Nicholas II had dismissed Boris Vladimirovich Stürmer as Prime Minister and Minister of Foreign Affairs on November 22, 1916.

ENCLOSURE II

SECRET REPORT: The U-53.

It seems that the boat that accompanied the U-53 did not get close to American waters and that Commander Rose with his

53 sunk the ships off the Newfoundland Coast. The report of three submarines there was due to his painting out his number 53 and substituting other numbers. He did this on four separate occasions and finally came into Germany under the number 61.

Commander Rose's report of his adventures close to American waters filed with the German Admiralty teems with praise of the Americans. Their fairness and the sporting instinct of his American naval colleagues. His treatment by the authorities and the generous welcome extended him not only by German-Americans but ALL of Americans is the theme of his report. He has declared that the zone of his recent operations is a most lucrative one and suggests that more boats be sent and of larger tonnage and better carrying proportions to remain out longer under their own fuel.

SECRET REPORT: German U-boat activities.

Several U-boat commanders emphasize that if the "Marina" was shot at and sunk either by artillery fire or torpedo without warning the Commander violated his strict orders. They all deplore the fact that warning must be given for they declare that every third boat stopped is not only sailing under a false flag but has also masked batteries and that although keeping off the regulation 5,000 meters, they do, in hailing and stopping a ship risk the safety of their boat and the lives of the crew. They are most vehement in denunciation of this regulation and they are discussing the advisibility of petitioning the Kaiser to rescind this order.

One Commander said "They expect us to sink 40 or 50,000 enemy tonnage each time we go out and yet in rough weather when we cannot guarantee the safety of the passengers and crew of enemy vessels after they would take to the boats, we are, under existing orders, compelled to let the ships go by even [if] they are carrying the most deadly munitions." The same officer said that he had been close to British waters for 20 days at about the same time that the Marina was sunk and while he sighted 35 ships of the enemy, he was on account of the rough weather and high seas, forced to let them pass because no ships boat could live in such seas.

U-boat commanders emphatically declare that if Garrach[1] sunk the Marina he did so in absolute violation of his strict orders and will be punished therefor. At the same time they express their disgust at the existence of such orders and believe that the Admiralty in limiting their activities to meet the wishes of the United States is demonstrating a weakness that is most damaging to their cause. They similarly believe that this order will be rescinded and that in the very near future they will be given a free hand in the exercise of their own discretion as to what action to take against enemy's ships regardless of the nationality of the passengers and crew.

It is the general opinion among German Naval Officers that President Wilson will not break with Germany under any condition, being afraid of them. That the landing of the U-53 was an object lesson to him that he would speedily learn. Many of them are bitter enemies of America and pretend to believe that their submarines could cripple us. It is not known to what extent these wild expressions reflect the ideas of their superiors but the fact is that these young chaps are pretty cocky at present.

An Army officer of high rank said that a general U-boat warfare in opposition to the declared wishes of the United States must be inaugurated eventually to enable Germany to win the war. He too is of the opinion that high officers of the Army are ONE in that belief and that the Kaiser and his advisers must meet these wishes sooner or later for the Navy is also in harmony with extensive submarine warfare ideas. Another army officer of high rank is of the same belief.

The matter of a general U-boat warfare is now before the Kaiser and he is giving it his earnest attention. Great pressure is being brought upon him from all sides.

T MS (SDR, RG 59, 763.72/3105A, DNA).
    [1] Actually, one Commander Werner of the *U55* sank *Marina* on October 28. Werner mistook *Marina* for a British naval auxiliary ship. Arno Spindler, *Der Handelskrieg mit U-Booten* (3 vols., Berlin, 1932-34), III, 249-50.

From Franklin Knight Lane and Others, with Enclosures

To the President: [Philadelphia] January 3, 1917.

The Commissioners appointed by you on August thirty-first last to meet with the Commissioners appointed by the First Chief of the Constitutionalist Army, to consider and if possible arrive at a satisfactory solution of the controversies pending between the Government of the United States and the *de facto* Government of Mexico with reference to the withdrawal of American troops from Mexican soil, the protection of the international boundary, and such other questions as might be submitted by the respective governments, beg to present a report regarding the situation which now confronts them.

Your Commissioners have addressed themselves preferentially to the two questions above mentioned, namely, the withdrawal of troops and the safeguarding of the border. From the beginning of our negotiations we have impressed upon the Mexican Commissioners the importance of disposing of these two questions at the earliest possible moment, in order that the Commission might proceed to the consideration of a constructive program which would be helpful to Mexico and at the same time would satisfactorily settle those matters which are of vital concern to the United States and profoundly affect the amicable relations between the two countries. Of these, the most important is the protection of life and property of Americans and other foreigners who have taken up residence in Mexico.

After prolonged negotiations, which consumed far more time than we had anticipated, the Commission reached an agreement on November 24, 1916, with reference to the withdrawal of troops and the safeguarding of the international boundary. This agreement was signed by all the members of the American and Mexican delegations, and it was our earnest hope and expectation that we would proceed forthwith to the consideration of the other questions, which we regard as quite as vital to Mexico as to the United States. In this hope and expectation we have been disappointed. At the session of the Commission held in Philadelphia on December 18th we were informed that the First Chief had refused to ratify the Protocol for reasons set forth in a letter of the Mexican Commissioners dated December 18th, and which is appended hereto (Exhibit A).

At the session of December 19th the Mexican Commissioners submitted a series of amendments to the Protocol, which received the careful consideration of the American Commissioners, and were found to be unacceptable. Our conclusions were communicated to the Mexican Commissioners in a letter dated December 19th, a copy of which is submitted herewith (Exhibit B).[1]

We have now received from the Mexican Commissioners a written communication dated December 27th, in which the refusal of the First Chief to ratify the Protocol is confirmed (Exhibit C).

The sessions of the Commission held since the signing of the Atlantic City agreement, and the careful consideration given by your Commissioners to the amendments to the Protocol proposed by the Mexican Commissioners have forced us reluctantly to the decision that no agreement satisfactory to both parties with reference to the withdrawal of troops and border control can be reached by this Commission.

Because of the urgency of the other questions involved in our relations with Mexico, your Commissioners have reached the conclusion that the interests of both countries require that the question of the withdrawal of American troops be settled directly by the Government of the United States.

We remain firm in our conviction that the Protocol signed at Atlantic City on November 24, 1916, fully safeguards the interests of both countries. We, therefore, beg to suggest that it would be wise for the Government of the United States, voluntarily and of its own initiative, to put its provisions into effect, as far as practicable. This question once disposed of, it may be possible to press on, through direct diplomatic negotiations with the executive head of the *de facto* Government, to the grave and serious questions to which we believe that Government cannot refuse attention.

The careful study of the mass of information submitted to us through official and other channels, has created in our minds the deepest misgivings with reference to the course of events in Mexico. We have eagerly searched for indications that the revolutionary government was fulfilling the avowed purposes of its platform, but this has revealed to us most disquieting economic, financial, sanitary and social conditions, which involve untold misery and suffering for the masses of the people. Furthermore, the proceedings of the Constitutional Convention now in session at Queretaro indicate a fixed and settled purpose to place in the organic law of the republic provisions which tend to make the position of foreigners in Mexico intolerable, which open the door to confiscation of legally acquired property and which carry with them the germs of serious international friction.

It is this grave menace that creates in us the deepest anxiety and a desire no less insistent to have these matters taken up with the least possible delay.

We are deeply sensible, Mr. President, of the confidence which you have reposed in us, and sincerely trust that our prolonged conferences with the Mexican Commissioners may have served to clear the way for the carrying forward, through other and more direct channels, of the negotiations which have so closely occupied us in recent months.

We have the honor to be, with great respect,

Your obedient servants,   Franklin K. Lane
Geo. Gray
John R. Mott

TLS (WP, DLC).

[1] It is printed as an Enclosure with RL to WW, Dec. 20, 1916, and not reprinted here.

ENCLOSURE I

EXHIBIT A.

Communication of Mexican Commissioners to American Commissioners dated December 18th, 1916.

Gentlemen: Philadelphia, Pa., December 18, 1916.

Reducing to writing the subjects which were treated verbally during our session of today, we have the honor of informing you that the Citizen First Chief of the Constitutionalist Army has not ratified the protocol of agreement submitted to his consideration, for the reasons which we briefly give herewith:

The First Chief of the Constitutionalist Army considers that, as the presence of the American troops on our soil constitutes a violation of the sovereignty of Mexico, the acceptance of any agreement for the withdrawal of troops subject to conditions which later might justify a postponement in the withdrawal of said troops, would be interpreted as a tacit agreement on the part of the Mexican Government with the present occupation.

The Mexican Government does not wish to place itself in such a position, that owing to unforeseen circumstances which might later occur, it should seem to sanction a posteriori the presence of American troops on Mexican soil.

From this point of view, the Mexican Government would desire that the wording of the agreement should be sufficiently explicit, so as not to occasion future difficulties in its interpretation and execution.

The Mexican Government was likewise unable to approve the agreement after having been notified of the declared purpose of the American Government, of reserving to itself the faculty of sending into Mexican territory future expeditions in pursuit of outlaws. Under such conditions, the Mexican Government either could not have signed the agreement, because it would have been tantamount to agreeing tacitly to the policy announced by the American Government, or, in case of signing such an agreement, it would have been compelled to protest against new intentions of violating our territory, and this would lead to an unstable and perilous situation for the preservation of peace between both countries, which is precisely what the Mexican Government has tried to avoid by proposing that these conferences be held.

The Citizen First Chief believes that, the mutual respect for the sovereignty of both countries being the only solid basis for the preservation of peace and good relations between Mexico and the United States, the solution of our difficulties must be sought in the cooperation for the protection and vigilance of the border, thus precluding and avoiding causes of friction, instead of following a line of policy pointed out by the American Government, of sending into Mexico future military expeditions, which would only jeopardize said good relations.

As regards the discussion of the other subjects which the American Commission desire to submit to the Mexican delegates, the First Chief confirms the attitude taken by the latter, that such matters should be discussed after the withdrawal of the American troops will have taken place, if happily some conclusion respecting the vigilance and protection of the border be reached.

In brief, the Constitutionalist Government believes that any agreement regarding the withdrawal of American troops from Mexican soil which may be reached, must be effected without implying consent, either express or tacit, with the present occupation, without sanctioning in the future the said occupation, and without authorizing or tolerating in the future a new expedition of American forces into Mexican territory.

The Mexican delegates consider that it is possible to find a new formula which may fulfill the conditions suggested by the First Chief, in view of the good disposition which they do not doubt exists on the part of the American Commissioners to reach an agreement compatible with the respect for the sovereignty of our country.

With the assurance of our most distinguished consideration, we remain,   Very faithfully yours,   Luis Cabrera
Ygnacio Bonillas
Alberto J. Pani

TCL (WP, DLC).

ENCLOSURE II

EXHIBIT C.

New York
December twenty-seven
Gentlemen: Nineteen hundred and sixteen

We are in receipt of instructions from the First Chief of the Constitutionalist Army in charge of the Executive Power of the Mexican Republic, which enable us to reply to your letter of the 19th instant and confirm his former decision not to approve the Protocol ad referendum, dated November 24, 1916.

We deem it unnecessary in this letter to dwell upon the considerations which have led the Mexican Government to withhold its approval of the protocol, inasmuch as they have been clearly set forth in our letter of the 18th instant, and remain unchanged at the present time. The Mexican Government is not willing to agree to the withdrawal of the American troops under conditions which, because of subsequent and unexpected circumstances, might be interpreted as legalizing a posteriori the presence of American troops on Mexican soil.

Furthermore, the statement of the American Government reserving to itself the right to send further military expeditions into Mexico in pursuit of outlaws made it practically impossible for the Mexican Government to ratify the proposed protocol.

In our capacity as members of the Joint Commission, we consider it our duty to exert every effort to the end that the United States and Mexico may find a satisfactory solution of their present difficulties, and we are still confident that it will be possible to reach an understanding, upon the basis of the proposals made to the American Commissioners at the session of Tuesday morning, December 19th. We do not doubt that the American Commissioners will be actuated by the same spirit. In any event, we await their decision with regard to future labors of the Commission.

We fail to understand how, in spite of the express terms of the diplomatic correspondence, which led to these conferences, the American Commissioners consider that the functions of the Joint Commission come to an end because of the fact that the protocol is unsatisfactory to the Mexican Government, or because we are not disposed to discuss the other matters, which the American Commissioners wish to consider as long as the American forces have not left our territory, and no agreement has been reached concerning the protection and safeguarding of the border.

The Mexican-American Joint Commission was created for the purpose of studying and proposing to their respective Governments "an immediate solution to the two points which constitute the real cause of the controversy between the two countries, to wit, * * * the retirement of the American forces * * * and the protection of the frontier," (Notes of the Mexican Government of July 4, and August 2, 1916) and in case that "happily a solution satisfactory to both Governments of the questions set forth * * * may be reached, the Commission may also consider such other matters the friendly arrangement of which would tend to improve the relations of the two countries; it being understood that such recommendations as the Commission may make shall not be binding upon the respective Governments until formally accepted by them." (Note of the State Department of the 28th of July, 1916).

The Joint Commission after three months of labor was unable to reach any solution concerning the protection and safeguarding of the border, and the Mexican delegation had to confine itself to accepting an agreement concerning the withdrawal of American troops on the only terms to which the American delegation would agree. This does not mean that an agreement more satisfactory to both countries could not have been found but rather that the protocol was accepted with the idea of bringing the discussions to a conclusion and of formulating a concrete proposal for submission to our Government, since, as the American Commissioners may recall, we were not, as they were, in a position previously to consult our Government regarding each of the terms of the protocol. It was clearly understood, furthermore, that the above mentioned protocol was to be submitted to the judgment of the Mexican Government, which government reserved its freedom of action concerning the same. If, therefore, in conformity with the diplomatic correspondence which led to the appointment of the Commission, with the credentials of the Mexican Commissioners, with the tenor of the discussions of the Commission and with the wording of the protocol itself, this agreement was to be submitted to the approval of the First Chief, we fail to understand how the mere fact that it has not been ratified by him should be construed as a reason for bringing the conferences to an end. It would be incompatible with the above mentioned facts, to assume that the protocol must be ratified in the terms formulated by the Joint Commission. This would be equivalent to stating that the Mexican Government was deprived of its freedom of action; a conclusion contrary to diplomatic practice, even in negotiations between plenipotentiaries.

We also wish to call your attention to the fact, that according to the diplomatic correspondence, the functions of the Joint Commission cannot extend to questions other than those relating to the international boundary until a solution satisfactory to both countries had been reached with reference to this matter. Our Government believes that under present conditions, we should not discuss these other matters as long as American troops remain on Mexican soil. This does not mean a lack of confidence in the good faith of the United States, but is dictated by a proper regard for the dignity of our country. If, as was stated on several occasions during our recent sessions in Philadelphia, it is possible to affect the complete withdrawal of American forces in one week, the discussion of the other matters would not be deferred for any considerable period.

Awaiting your esteemed reply, we renew the assurance of our distinguished consideration.   Luis Cabrera
                                                      Ygnacio Bonillas
                                                      Alberto J. Pani.

TCL (SDR, RG 59, 812.00/20849, DNA).

Franklin Knight Lane and Others
to Luis Cabrera and Others

Gentlemen: [Philadelphia] January 3rd, 1917.

We are in receipt of your favor of December 27th, announcing that for the second time the First Chief of the Mexican Government has declined to agree to the Protocol submitted to him by both the Mexican and American Commissioners.

In your esteemed favor there are matters concerning which we think it timely that we should speak, lest there be misunderstanding. It is said, for instance, that the "Mexican Government is not willing to agree to the withdrawal of the American troops under conditions, which because of subsequent and unexpected circumstances, might be interpreted as legalizing a posteriori the presence of American troops on Mexican soil."

It may suffice as expressive of our view to quote from our letter to you of December 19th, in which this passage will be found: "We have not insisted nor urged that the Mexican Government recognize our right to occupy Mexican territory, even under such novel and necessitous conditions as have existed; and it will not be contrary to the spirit of our discussion for the approval of your Government to be given to this instrument with such expression of Mexican authority and right as to you may be desirable. Such expression could be spread upon the Minutes or could be added to the Protocol." It will be recalled also that during our conferences this preamble to any proposed protocol was tendered by us as expressive of our friendly attitude:

"WHEREAS, the so-called punitive expedition of the United States, under the command of General John Pershing, into the territory of Mexico, was undertaken for the sole purpose of pursuing and capturing, if possible, the bandit Francisco Villa and the band under his command, or of dispersing the same, and

"WHEREAS, the said expedition, from the necessity of the situation, was obliged to start with the utmost promptness, and acted under the tacit assumption of the acquiescence of the Mexican Government, after understood to be informally expressed, and

"WHEREAS, there is no longer necessity for the presence of American troops on Mexican territory, and

"WHEREAS, the American Government has no desire to continue that presence against the protest of the Mexican Government, or even to appear to violate the sovereignty of Mexico:

"IT IS THEREFORE AGREED * * * *"

Again, it is stated by you that "the statement of the American Government reserving to itself the right to send further military expeditions into Mexico in pursuit of outlaws made it practically impossible for the Mexican Government to ratify the proposed Protocol." We beg to call your attention to the fact that such statement was not included in the Protocol. It was made in the form of an announcement of the policy which this Government would be compelled to follow if, unhappily, raids such as the Columbus massacre were repeated. The language to which you refer was this:

"It is essential, as a matter of governmental policy, that the United States reserve the right to deal with any serious hostile incursion from Mexico into American territory as may be deemed advisable at the time, including the right to pursue marauders into Mexican territory when such pursuit is necessary to our own protection. Duly mindful of the obligations imposed upon us by international law, such pursuit will not be intended, and should not be considered an act hostile to the Constitutionalist Government of Mexico."

This was a frank declaration of what our Government considered its right of self-protection, and was worded so that any such action, if found later to be necessary, would be undertaken with due regard for the obligations imposed by international law, and should not be regarded as an act of hostility. So long as Mexico was not able to safeguard its side of the international boundary we did not wish to have a pursuit of our common enemy regarded as an act adverse to your interest, and we gave this notice as a word of caution against a wrong interpretation being placed upon our act either by your people or by our own.

With reference to your proposals of December 19th, we would respectfully represent that such proposals called for an unconditional withdrawal of our troops from Mexico, one that should begin immediately and be continuous hereafter, without stating any definite time when the withdrawal should be effected. The provision in the signed Protocol was that the American troops should withdraw within forty days after ratification of the agreement by both Governments, and this was inserted at your request and not at ours, it being your desire that a definite date should be fixed.

In the same proposals you omitted Article II. of the Protocol, which reads:

"The American commander shall determine the manner in which the withdrawal shall be effected, so as to ensure the safety of the territory affected by the withdrawal."

Why so reasonable a provision should be eliminated was not made apparent.

Under Article III. of the Protocol agreed to, it was provided that as our troops abandoned the territory now occupied, such territory should be occupied and held by your troops. This you omit from your proposals, although it was clearly intended to give to the *de facto* Government the territory abandoned and insure against its occupation by bandits who might threaten our border and harass your own people.

In Article IV. of the Protocol it had been agreed that:

"In case there are any further activities of the forces inimical to the Constitutionalist Government which threaten the safety of the international border along the northern section of Chihuahua, the withdrawal of American forces shall not be delayed beyond the period strictly necessary to overcome such activities."

This provision which was also omitted in your proposals was manifestly a limitation upon our right to delay our withdrawal for any period longer than necessary to overcome those forces inimical to your Government.

You state that one reason why the Mexican Commissioners have not been disposed to discuss other matters than the withdrawal of the troops and the protection of the border, is that "an arrangement has not been reached concerning protection and safeguarding of the border." Again you refer to this same point in the language: "The Joint Commission, after three months of labor, was unable to reach any solution concerning the protection and safeguarding of the border, etc." After repeated efforts to frame a system of cooperative border control, the Commission concluded that the wisest system that could be devised would be one made by the army officers of both Governments stationed at the border. The Protocol signed at Atlantic City recognizes the possibility of such cooperation and our promise was made that an effort in this direction would be seriously undertaken through the War Department.

While your letter and the proposals made suggest an unconditional withdrawal, it has certainly been our conception of the duty of this Commission that it was to find wise conditions upon which the withdrawal could be made; otherwise there would have been no purpose in the conference. The language of our respective letters of authority gives proof that it was contemplated by both Governments that there were matters of moment upon which agreement was necessary or advisable before withdrawal could reasonably be expected by you or effected by us. Indeed, we recall no proposal from you during the conference that did not contain conditions precedent to withdrawal.

In our communication of September 22nd this question was presented:

"Would this be a satisfactory program for the Joint Commission:

"That while the military details of a plan of border control formulated by us are under consideration at Washington, we pass to the consideration of three questions:

1. Protection to life and property of foreigners in Mexico
2. Establishment of a claims commission
3. Religious tolerance

"It being understood between us that our effort shall be to reach a tentative understanding upon those questions which the American Commissioners regard as of certainly no less importance than that of border control, and it being further understood that the border control matter shall not be made dependent in any way upon our agreement upon these above mentioned questions."

Under your interpretation of your authority, our conferences were limited to the question of withdrawal and border control, and we asked assurance that if the Protocol regarding withdrawal and border control was signed we could immediately pass to those other questions of vital importance to us. To allay all fear that the presence of American troops would be used to compel an agreement upon these matters that would not be entirely agreeable to you, the American Commissioners spread upon the minutes this statement:

"It shall be understood that if we meet for the discussion of other questions, the American Commissioners will not ask that any final agreement shall be reached as to any such questions while the American troops are in Mexico."

We have read with much interest the portion of your communication relating to the diplomatic correspondence leading up to the appointment of this Commission, and we desire to express our complete accord with the views you have expressed as to the reserved right of either government to withhold its approval of an agreement signed *ad referendum*. But the exhaustive discussions of the last three months have convinced us that the attitude of the *de facto* Government as to this Protocol, as well as the character of the amendments proposed by you at the sessions in Philadelphia, would make such further discussion fruitless and would only delay the solution of the questions now pending between the United States and Mexico.

We are sincerely reluctant to contemplate the closing of our conferences as a Commission. You may perhaps have been under embarrassment, as you suggest, because of your long distance from the seat of your Government. With this in mind we took frequent and sometimes extended adjournment, that full opportunity to consult your home officials might be given. It is not, however, in our mind that mutual effort in the direction of composing the differences between the two Governments should cease. We would suggest the advisability of all further negotiations being conducted under conditions which would make this embarrassment impossible. And we trust that you share with us the hope that the prolonged, thorough and intimate conferences that we have had during the recent months may not be without fruit.

We beg to remain,

Most respectfully yours   Franklin K. Lane
George Gray
John R. Mott.

TCL (WP, DLC).

From Newton Diehl Baker

MEMORANDUM for the President.

Dear Mr. President: [Washington] January 3, 1917.
FORM OF GOVERNMENT FOR THE DANISH WEST INDIES.

The question of the organization of the Danish West Indies after the exchange of ratifications between the two countries was casually referred to the other day. I have investigated the matter some and thought about it. It seems on all grounds that when the times comes, it would be wiser to allow the government to be carried on through the Bureau of Insular Affairs of the War Department. The alternatives to that course are, to organize the government through the Navy Department or the Department of the Interior. The following considerations, however, seem to point in favor of the advisability of the suggestion herein made:

1. The Bureau of Insular Affairs is an efficiently organized bureau specializing in the administration of insular government and already in charge of the administration of the Philippine Islands and Porto Rico.

2. The Danish West Indies, with Porto Rico and the Canal strip at Panama, really constitute a logical department of the Army. For some time it has been planned in the War Department to separate Porto Rico and the Panama Canal from the Department of the East and make an independent Department of them. Were the Danish West Indies added, the wisdom of the plan would become apparent.

3. Whatever form of government is ultimately organized for the Danish islands, the principal governmental operations there will be the installation of coast defenses, and there will have to be one or more coast artillery posts and a regular mobile army force on the islands. As these islands will never be able financially to support any expensive form of government, it would seem that the occupying military forces might well carry forward such civil administration as is necessary.

These considerations are merely submitted as a memorandum for your information.

Respectfully yours,   [Newton D. Baker]

CCL (N. D. Baker Papers, DLC).

From the Diary of Colonel House

The White House, Washington. January 3, 1917.

I took the 11.08 for Washington. As usual it was late and I did not arrive at the White House until just in time to dress for dinner. Dr. Grayson met me at the station. I was also met by Lincoln Colcord and Brougham of the Public Ledger. They had been unable to get in touch with the President. I promised to find out the trouble.

Grayson is exceedingly anxious to be appointed a rear admiral, but Daniels is halting his plans. I had, until now, thought of Grayson as among the few who were serving unselfishly.

The President, Mrs. Wilson, Margaret and I were the only ones at dinner. Immediately after dinner the President and I went to the upstairs sitting room and were in continuous session until half past ten.

We first took up the question of Federal Judges. Then the co-ordination of foreign relief societies, about which the President was averse to taking a leading part. He thought anything he might do would be misinterpreted by one side or the other of the belligerents. He was willing to help but he wanted the societies to take the lead. We threshed out what seemed to be a satisfactory plan and I am to explain it to those interested when I return to New York.

He read me the confidential despatch which Page had sent him with a notation at the top that it was to be decyphered by the President and not by the State Department.[1] He thought it a foolish proceeding since the despatch, from his viewpoint, was unimportant. Page began it "At Midnight." I suggested that perhaps we were to have a Sherlock Holmes recital, but it was merely telling the President of an interview with Lloyd George in which George expressed himself as being anxious to work in harmony with the United States. It was a long, rambling despatch, but of more importance I think than the President accorded it. It should be answered but I doubt whether he does so.

I asked what he had decided to do about Page. He replied that he inten[d]ed to accept his resignation. Mrs. Wilson asked if I would take his place. She thought I ought to do so during the war. The President also expressed a wish that I accept it. However, it did not take me three minutes to persuade him it would not be wise since it would confine my activities to Great Britain and I would not even be able to go to France in the event it were necessary for me to do so, much less to Germany.

The President said he was interested in Josiah Wedgwood's memorandum which I sent him and he wondered why I called it "fantastic." He asked whether it was because Wedgwood thought that he, the President, was the only one who could lay down the terms by which the war could be ended. I replied that I largely agreed with Wedgwood in that statement, but I considered his plan fantastic wherein this Government was to hold in trust, as it were, certain territory for the common use of other nations.

The President wished to know what I thought of his stating in some way what, in his opinion, the general terms of settlement should be, making the keystone of the settlement arch the future security of the world against wars, and letting territorial adjustments be subordinate to the main purpose. I was enthusiastic since it was the exact proposal I outlined to Bernstorff and wrote of to the President in my letter of December 27th. He had evidently forgotten where the thought came from, which is of no consequence if it is of value and I believe it is. This war and its consequences have become too great for any ordinary settlement, and the terms upon which it should be closed should be the fairest and best that the human mind can devise.

We went into a long discussion as to what terms he might properly lay down and how it could be done. I thought he should outline the terms in an address to Congress if he wished to make it impressive. If he desired not to attract marked attention at first, then it would be better to make it in an address before some society. He thought he might do it before the Senate, and that was the tentative arrangement when we finished our discussion. The time that it should be ready we left open, for it would be well to let the answers to his note come in and all discussion of them ended before he makes this other and more important move. We thought that the main principle he should lay down was the right of nations to determine under what government they should continue to live. This, of course, involves a wide range. We thought that since Germany and Russia had agreed to free Poland that should be put in. We naturally agreed upon Belgium and Serbia being restored. Alsace and Lorraine we were not quite certain of, but we agreed that Turkey should cease to exist. I urged in addition that something be put in regarding the right of Russia to have a warm seaport. If this were not done it would leave a sore which in time would bring about another war.

The question was raised as to what would happen to our Ambassador at Constantinople when this speech was made, and whether he would be promptly executed or be permitted to flee the country. The question of the American Colleges in Turkey was also thought of. It is my purpose when I return to New York to study this matter more closely and outline in some detail a plan which I think the President could follow, and bring it to him when I return next week.

I encouraged him in the thought of doing this great and dramatic thing. I said, "you are now playing with what the poker players term 'the blue chips' and there is no use sitting by and letting great events swamp you. It is better to take matters into your own hands and play the cards yourself."

I spoke to the President about the conversation I had with Joseph Willard just before he sailed and what he told me concerning the resentment which the King of Spain felt because he, the President, allowed three months to elapse before he answered his query.[2] The President looked embarrassed at this point and admitted that he should have replied sooner. I thought Spain's refusal to concur in his peace note was due to this. I also told him what Willard had said concerning Albert of Belgium.

We thought if he made his speech before the Senate, the occasion could be arranged in answer to a request from the Senate for information as to what America would demand if she consents to join a league to enforce peace. Whatever the President said in this way would be largely our own concern and could not be construed as meddling with the affairs of the belligerents. While it actually would be a proposal of peace terms, yet apparently, it would be a statement of the terms upon which we would be willing to join in a league to enforce peace.

I do not know whether the President will decide to discuss this matter with Lansing but I shall not mention it to anyone myself.

I got to bed at eleven o'clock. We agreed to meet for further talk just before lunch tomorrow. In the morning the President will play golf and in the afternoon he has many engagements.

[1] Page's No. 5390, Dec. 29, 1916.
[2] J. E. Willard to WW, May 11, 1916, Vol. 37, and RL to J. E. Willard, Aug. 23, 1916, Vol. 38.

To Robert Lansing

My dear Mr. Secretary,   The White House. 4 January, 1917.

Let me thank you for the enclosed, which I return for your files. The information about the U-boats makes painfully interesting reading.   Faithfully Yours,   W.W.

WWTLI (SDR, RG 59, 763.72/3106½, DNA).

Two Letters to Newton Diehl Baker

My dear Mr. Secretary,   The White House. 4 January, 1917.

I dare say you are right about the proper place to vest the administration of our new West Indian possessions. I have forwarded your memorandum to Senator Stone, the chairman of the Senate Committee on Foreign Relations, and shall discuss it with him late[r].[1]

Faithfully Yours,   Woodrow Wilson

WWTLS (N. D. Baker Papers, DLC).

[1] Henry D. Flood introduced on February 5, 1917, a bill (HR 20755) to carry out the treaty by which the United States had purchased the Danish West Indies. As finally enacted and signed by Wilson on March 4, the Act not only provided for the payment of $25,000,000 to Denmark but also for "a temporary government" for the islands. It stipulated that all military, civil, and judicial powers necessary to govern the islands were to be vested in "a governor and in such person or persons" as the President might appoint and should be exercised in such manner as the President should direct, until such time as Congress should make more permanent provision for the government of the new territories. It specifically authorized the President to select an army or navy officer as governor if he so desired; however, the governor was to be appointed with the advice and consent of the Senate. The Act further provided that, insofar as possible, until Congress should otherwise direct, the islands should be governed in accordance with the code of laws published by the Danish authorities in 1906. 39 *Statutes at Large* 1132.

As it turned out, Wilson decided to place the government of the islands under the Navy Department. Rear Admiral James Harrison Oliver became the first governor. The naval administration of the Virgin Islands continued until 1931.

My dear Mr. Secretary,   The White House, 4 January, 1917.

Thank you for letting me see this letter of Lippmann's.[1]

I cannot think that it would be wise for the Congress to take part in this, either by appropriation of money or otherwise. But I do see the pressing and immediate need for uniting private efforts under a single direction. There is a group of men in New York who are planning just such action and House has just been here to submit their plan to me. I shall take pleasure in making an opportunity to discuss it with you.

Cordially and faithfully Yours,   Woodrow Wilson

WWTLS (N. D. Baker Papers, DLC).
[1] It is missing in all collections.

Sir Cecil Arthur Spring Rice to the Foreign Office

Washington 4 Jan 1916 [1917].

House confirms story in World as to President's attitude. So does assistant editor of World.[1] That is President thinks war with Germany is possible or even probable and wishes to avoid it by every possible means. If war takes place he will have proved to Congress his desire to avoid it. ⟨Lodge tells me⟩ Temper in Congress is very pacific but not pro-German although there is strong pro German and Catholic and anti British influence and hostile language may be held. Supporters of President in Congress are mostly known pro-Germans. The West and Middle West are so indifferent that I greatly doubt whether peace pressure will not prove stronger than any other influence unless Germany forces the pace. It seems quite possible that S of S who was opposed to policy of the President's peace message, and is rather seriously ill, may resign. I cannot find proof of serious preparations against submarine warfare but House assures me President has warned Germany not to repeat attacks on commerce near U S ports. Private owners of small craft are on the watch but nothing suspicious has been found. Germans in N Y seem to anticipate possibility of war with U. S. within six months. I think it cannot be doubted that Catholics here are hostile mainly on account of Ireland and Russian Uniat[e]s.[2] They do not want mediation by President but peace with Pope as mediator.

Our friends here rather hope that allies answer will take the form of an appeal to American people as to common principles &c. Wall Street does not believe in possibility of any form of embargo direct or indirect.

Hw telegram (FO 115/2262, p. 351, PRO).

[1] The New York *World* does not seem to have had anyone with the title of assistant editor at this time. However, Spring Rice probably refers to Henry Noble Hall, the Anglo-American journalist, at this time on the editorial staff of the *World* and soon to become the Washington correspondent of the London *Times*. Hall wrote and signed the article, "Danger of U. S.-German Break Lies Behind the Peace Moves of the Kaiser and President," which appeared on the front page of the *World* on December 28, 1916. As the title suggests, the article was a detailed discussion of the circumstances which led to the German note of December 12 and the American note of December 18. Hall declared that the American note had not been conceived as a peace note: "It was conceived as a warning to the belligerents that the United States was in danger of being drawn into the war against its will and was entitled to know the aims and the terms of the belligerents." He asserted that Lansing's statement to the press on December 21 (about which see n. 1 to the Enclosure printed with JPT to WW, Dec. 21, 1916) was "a correct statement of the reasons that prompted President Wilson to address a note to all the belligerents" and quoted that statement in full.

[2] "Uniat[e]s" was the Russian term commonly applied to Catholics of the Greek rite living within the Russian Empire and in communion with Rome. Most of them resided in lands acquired during the three partitions of Poland in the eighteenth century. For over a century, the Imperial government had followed a policy of gradually forcing the Uniates into the Russian Orthodox Church by suppressing their own religious organizations. However, the edict of toleration of 1905 reversed this policy and permitted the adherents of the Eastern rite to form a Russian Catholic Church. Thus, up to the time of the Bolshevik revolution of 1917, the position of the Uniates, though hardly ideal, was improving. See James J. Zatko, *Descent into Darkness: The Destruction of the Roman Catholic Church in Russia, 1917-1923* (Notre Dame, Ind., 1965), pp. 2-28.

From the Diary of Colonel House

January 4, 1917.

I was with Lansing for more than an hour. His first concern was to put himself straight regarding the two statements he had made the morning the peace note was published. He has written a careful statement of his purposes and has made a good argument in favor of them.[1]

He is much concerned because the President fails to discuss international questions with him. He says he seldom sees him and that as far as he is concerned, the State Department is sailing without a chart. He said the President sees no one and that "his mind is a vacuum during your absences." Lansing does not know how constantly the President and I keep in touch and how, from day to day, I send him information concerning international affairs.

Lansing desires the President to press the submarine issue and to send Bernstorff home. He has written the President a note urging him to take a firm stand. He believes the President will not do this as the President told him the other day that he did not believe the people of the United States were willing to go to war because a few Americans had been killed.

From Lansing's rooms I went to see Phillips to talk of foreign appointments. Phillips expressed the hope that someone would take charge of this rather disagreeable and difficult task. I suggested that it be turned over to Vance McCormick under my supervision. In speaking to the President about it later he surprised me by saying that he did not intend to make a political appointment in the foreign service, at least, until the war was ended, and that he did not wish McCormick to have anything to do with it. I applauded this resolution for it is in line with what I have recommended from the beginning of his administration and many times since. Even the last time I talked with him he was inclined toward political appointment of some sort. I find he changes his views frequently. I noticed this change when we talked before luncheon about appointments in general. He declared he intended to pick out the best men regardless of factions. This, too, I applauded as it is in line with what I suggested at the beginning of his administration. . . .

I returned to the White House and had a few minutes talk with the President before luncheon. This discussion concerned departmental and routine affairs. There was no one at lunch excepting the President, Mrs. Wilson and myself.

The President made one remark which alarmed me. I told him, as I have many times before, how unprepared we were and that Jusserand had called my attention to it, expressing the hope that we would take some steps particularly if there was any chance of a break with Germany. Jusserand thought there would be from 20,000 to 40,000 Germans in the Eastern States who would for the moment have things their own way; blowing up bridges, powder magazines, munitions etc. He did not consider it improbable that they might capture Washington and the President himself. Neither the President nor I was disturbed at this thought, but I took the occasion to express the feeling that we should not be so totally unprepared in the event of war.

The President replied, "there will be no war. This country does not intend to become involved in this war. We are the only one of the great White nations that is free from war today, and it would be a crime against civilization for us to go in."

The President may change this view for, as I said before, he changes his views often. For instance, the last time I was here and suggested Cleveland H. Dodge for England, he thought it would not do. This time he suggested it himself.

¹ See WW to RL, Dec. 21, 1916, n. 1.

From Robert Lansing, with Enclosure

My dear Mr. President: Washington January 5, 1917.

I beg to enclose a flimsy of an important despatch just received from Mr. Hoover in London in reply to my request for information on the subject of the Belgian deportations. Mr. Hoover makes the suggestion that you send a personal and private message to the Emperor.

It has also occurred to me that we might attempt to secure an expression of opinion from the Latin American countries on this subject in order to present the picture of the Western Hemisphere protesting against such illegal methods.

I should be very glad for an expression of your views and wishes in respect to our further action in this important matter.

With assurances of respect, etc., I am, my dear Mr. President,
                    Faithfully yours,   Robert Lansing.

TLS (SDR, RG 59, 763.72115/3753a, DNA).

E N C L O S U R E

London. January 2, 1917.

5397. Hoover submits following statement:

"There has been no apparent change in German policy since the President's protest. Deportation continuing on a large scale, now apparently three to five thousand per week. Despite assertions made to the President no distinction is made as to whether deportatees are unemployed or not and in fact there seems a definite policy to secure all members of certain trades and the desire to secure these and other skilled labor leads press gangs to delegate choice of those in actual employment. Moreover, they have taken altogether up to December fifteenth over seven hundred persons employed by the commission despite the exhibit of credentials and their specific agreement with us to the contrary and against our protest. Furthermore, our American members have witnessed the taking of several thousands, particularly from Flanders, to northern France and together with local French people are now being forced to work for the German army in the preparation of timber and fascines for the trenches. Refusal to perform such labor has here been met with refusal of food and other brutal acts. It is also reported to us from what we believe to be reliable sources that Belgian and French civilians have been *reported* (deported?) to work on trench construction in northern France and certain deportees have been recently returned wounded by shell fire. Of the deportees to Germany some three hundred have been returned to Nainaut Province of whom a part were apparently returned because physically unable to work but the remainder maintain that they were returned because of their steadfast passive resistance to pressure although they were entirely refused food over a considerable period and were ultimately returned for their recalcitrancy, their appearance confirms this. Altogether the assurances given the President that only unemployed people were taken and that they are not being employed on military work or brutally treated are absolutely untrue not only before but since assurances were given. It does appear that the civil government in Brussels has made some efforts to prevent brutality in selection, to confine selections to unemployed and to protect the employees of the commission and they have even solicited complaints but they appear unable to control the military press gangs or effect any remedies. It does not appear to us, however, that protest from the President based on failure to carry out assurance given as to the method or purpose of these deportations is consonant with the attitude that the Americans should take for the real issue is the very act of forced deportation as being a violation of the most primary human liberty and international law. Any protest on method or purpose alone will be construed as a recognition by America of the right to force civilians from their homes and country. I am now convinced that the Entente Governments will take no action against the relief as a consequence of these deportations as they are convinced that stoppage of relief has been no remedy and they generally recognize would only accentuate the misery.

"The hourly witnessing of these outrages and the prayers to the Americans from a people now in a state of complete terror, since Americans have been so peculiarly their protectors during the past two years, make it difficult for us to control the natural feelings of our staff and we can only hope that no untoward incident may occur. My impression is that any further protest at the moment in the name of humanity and international law would have no other effect than to produce irritation and the usual denials although if other means fail a renewed protest should be delivered with the utmost vigor as a definition of America's attitude and as a deterrent to other outrages which may be contemplated.

"For immediate practical purposes in the hope of remedying or ameliorating this particular evil I would like to suggest a personal and private message from the President to the Emperor in the belief that the Emperor is intrinsically a humane man and generally desirous of promoting peace such message to take the general line that the constant filtration of reports of these deportations and their surrounding circumstances is today one of the strongest stimuli to resolution for continuance of the war amongst the population in the Entente countries and has afforded an unparalleled basis of anti-German propaganda among neutrals which no assertion of benevolent intentions can counteract for the fundamental basis of deportation and compulsion of the population to work against its will and conscience being wrong can only bring suffering and criticism; that if Germany is genuinely anxious for peace she can scarcely hope for sympathetic sentiment to grow abroad to that end coincident with these acts and that a total cessation of the deportations and forced labor and the return of the deported Belgians and French to their homes would be not only an act of great magnanimity but also of the greatest assistance in the promotion of peace sentiment. Hoover."   Page.

T telegram (SDR, RG 59, 763.72115/2728, DNA).

To Robert Lansing

My dear Mr. Secretary,   The White House. 5 January, 1917.

I shall of course ponder Mr. Hoover's suggestion, but my present judgment is that we have sufficiently made known our attitude to the German Government about the Belgian deportations, both in our formal and in our informal protests (for example, Gerard's recent conversation with Zimmerman)

Your own suggestion about intimations to the other American republics that they take such action as we have taken in the matter and make their feeling known at Berlin strikes me very favourably. I would discreetly sound them out, if I were you, and ascertain their disposition about it.

Faithfully Yours,   W.W.

WWTLI (SDR, RG 59, 763.72115/3754, DNA).

To Roland Cotton Smith

Personal

[The White House]

My dear Doctor Smith: 5 January, 1917

Your letter of January second reassures me. It shows that you understood me and I want you to know that I equally understand your own position and have no word of criticism to utter.

At the same time, I must frankly say in reply to your inquiry about Secretary Lane that I should personally prefer that no official member of the administration should appear upon the programme with the gentleman I have mentioned. Your kind and frank question makes this answer unavoidable if I am to be equally frank, and I am sure you will understand it.

Cordially and sincerely yours,   [Woodrow Wilson]

CCL (WP, DLC).

From Roy Wilson Howard

PERSONAL:

My dear Mr. President: New York City January 5, 1917.

I appreciate the kindly spirit prompting your note of January 2nd. You misunderstand me, however, if you feel that I entertain any idea of *personal* slight.

I thought it would have been good business for you to have aided us in our honest effort to avoid balling up your efforts through our being ignorant of your real objective. I should not have regarded your doing so as any personal favor to me, however, hence I cannot consistently regard your refusal to see me as any personal slight, can I?

Anyway, whatever your objective (we're still in the dark), we'll try and keep off the track until we can learn which direction the car is coming from.

Meanwhile, I am, with kindest, personal regards,

Faithfully yours,   Roy W. Howard

TLS (WP, DLC).

To Roy Wilson Howard

Personal.

My dear Howard: [The White House] 5 January, 1917

I certainly did not mean to leave you in the dark as to my objective. My state of mind is very simple indeed. I think the note really states its own purpose and spirit as well as I could state them, and that any explanation or addition at present would only darken the waters, and I am waiting with an absolutely open mind to see what the event will be.

In haste

Cordially and sincerely yours, Woodrow Wilson

TLS (Letterpress Books, WP, DLC).

From Edward Mandell House, with Enclosures

Dear Governor: New York. January 5, 1917.

Here is a copy of a letter which has just come from Buckler.

I am also sending you a memorandum from Gregory concerning the Trade Commission. I heartily concur with Gregory's conclusions and yet I was in hopes you could appoint Woolley on this commission. His mind runs in that direction and it is about the only place he wants. He would put more vigor in it than it has had and in the right direction.

Thank you and dear Mrs. Wilson for your kindness to me when I was in Washington.

Your affectionate, E. M. House

TLS (WP, DLC).

E N C L O S U R E I

William Hepburn Buckler to Edward Mandell House

Dear Col. House: London. December 22, 1916.

I am sending you copies of posters which summarize the unsympathetic attitude of the jingo press to the great new Note.

The Times of course regards it as "intervention," the Post as "amazing." But I do not believe this will represent the official attitude—judging from the few official persons whom I have seen and from the fact that the "Westminster" of this afternoon is so favorable. For a certain amount of annoyance one must be prepared. Northcliffe and Bryce are of course not likely to be enthusiastic. But the sense of weariness and of hopeless dead-lock has increased surprisingly since October 1st and among many Liberals the note is sure of a warm reception.

Buxton's speech last night on American support will I am sure interest you,[1] as also this copy of a confidential memorandum which he sent last Saturday to all the Cabinet. He got a favorable or appreciative reply from several Ministers, including even that sturdy anti-American Lord Curzon.[2]

So there is no doubt people here widely realize the importance of tenderly handling our peace sentiment. Lowry's articles in the "Times" (December 13-19)[3] on this subject have done much good in calling attention to this.

Yours sincerely,   W. H. Buckler.

P.S. I have seen Buxton who is of course delighted with the Note and thinks it most opportune.

TCL (WP, DLC).

[1] Noel Edward Noel-Buxton's speech in the House of Commons on December 21, 1916, printed in *Parliamentary Debates: Commons*, 5th Ser., LXXXVIII, cols. 1767-72. Buxton called attention to the ways in which the United States was in fact supporting Great Britain and her allies. America was providing Britain with supplies at the rate of £2,000,000 per day. Americans had raised huge sums for war relief work. The American government had done much to assist Allied prisoners of war. At least 30,000 Americans were serving in the armed forces of the British Empire. Buxton also asserted that the United States supported the British "in the main political aspects of the War." The United States deplored the invasion of Belgium, the German mode of submarine warfare, and other atrocities, especially Turkish atrocities in Armenia. Above all, Buxton argued, the United States was against militarism. "She is with us in demanding . . . restitution and security," he declared, "because in America those are regarded as the right ways to discredit militarism." Full restoration of Belgium and France would do far more to discredit militarism than a crushing defeat of Germany on the battlefield. Buxton also said that it would be a serious error for the Allies not to make known their precise terms for peace. He underlined once more the significance of the fact that the United States Government had expressed a willingness to guarantee the stability of a peace settlement. He concluded: "There is very intense sympathy across the water with our desire to continue the War until the sacrifices of those whom we have lost is rendered, as we think, profitable. . . . I think I am correct in saying that the view is taken that nothing will so fully do honour to or justify the sacrifices of those who have laid down their lives as the establishment of an international settlement based on the total defeat of aggression and the new international guarantees which would do what, at all events, is most possible to preclude war in the future and obviate the necessity that tragedies so deplorable should ever occur again."

[2] A handwritten note by Buckler at the top of this document, printed as Enclosure II, reads: "(Sent by N. Buxton on Sat. Dec 16, *confidentially* to all the Cabinet Ministers—acknowledged favorably by Curzon, B-Law & Ll. George)."

[3] Edward G. Lowry, "The States Revisited," London *Times*, Dec. 13, 14, 18, and 19, 1916. Lowry, an American journalist formerly associated with the Atlanta *Constitution* and the New York *Evening Post*, had recently returned to the United States after spending two years as a special agent of the State Department at the American embassy in London. In his articles, Lowry described for his British readers what he saw during a trip through the eastern, southern, and midwestern states, and especially the attitude of the people of those states toward the conflict in Europe. He found unprecedented prosperity in all the areas that he visited and no great enthusiasm for either Wilson or Hughes, but rather relief that the presidential election campaign was over. He found every-

where the same basic attitude toward the European war: "In effect: a strong desire for peace; no desire to fight unless and until actually attacked; no validity attached to the talk that 'the Allies are fighting our battles'; no understanding of the war or comprehension that the people of the United States have any share or interest in the present issues that are being decided by force of arms on the Continent of Europe. This latter is not only the majority of sentiment, I believe, but it is the virtually unanimous present belief." London *Times*, Dec. 18, 1916.

E N C L O S U R E   I I

A Memorandum by Noel Edward Noel-Buxton

NOTES ON AMERICAN OPINION REGARDING THE WAR.

American diplomats who have been in Berlin during the war are in agreement with the best pro-Ally opinion in America in regard to the much debated question of the right way to crush German militarism.

The desire to see German militarism destroyed is intense in America and is regarded as an American interest, but it is thought that for future security, reliance must rather be placed upon new international guarantees in which America would share, than upon extreme military humiliation.

Holding, as Americans do, that security for the future is best obtained by means of a negotiated settlement, there is naturally a tendency even in the most genuine pro-Ally circles in America, to feel that the attitude of the Entente has been too much inclined towards a blunt refusal to consider what are its aims in the form of terms, and it is seriously believed that favourable opportunities of negotiating have been missed. Opinion has certainly, in recent months, become less favourable to our cause for this reason. The party, tactical even if led to nothing, which favoured an embargo on the export of arms and which came fairly near to success in the early part of the war, has in some ways increased its strength through the Election, and the refusal of the Allies to consider terms would give its leaders new material, which they would readily make use of. Even if they should fail in regard to munitions, they would have a practical opportunity in regard to the limitation of the export of wheat, which has become a pressing question through the shortage of the crop. This danger would be met by a show of willingness to negotiate, even if the discussion ended in failure.

It is natural that sympathies should lean towards those who appear to aim at a settlement in harmony with American ideas. As to the nature of these ideas, one is strongly impressed by the fact that they are occupied in particular with guarantees of stability and facilities for economic development, and the defeat of aggression in such territorial terms as will show the German people that militarism and the desire for conquest have produced nothing but loss.

In some unofficial circles, the total military subjugation of Germany is desired, but the responsible view, based on knowledge of German conditions, is:

1. That military defeat (apart from the terms obtained) would, in Germany, be explained away, while the only lasting proof of failure to the German people will lie in the nature of the terms.

2. That the policy of aggression and the influence of the military leaders are discredited already.

3. That the renunciation of conquered lands by negotiation would be recognised in Germany as the complete failure of aggression.

4. That further humiliation would produce a degree of resentment and bitter feeling of revenge, which would obscure the unpopularity of the military school and revive aggressive policy.

5. That Germans see the reason why Bismarck's policy of negotiating with Austria in 1866 proved more successful than the policy of dictating to France in 1870.

6. That a Germany which had conquered the French army would have been a menace, and incapable of constitutional reform, but on the other hand a weak Germany must inevitably be the friend of Russia as against the Western Powers, for the Jingo Germany and the autocratic Russia would come to terms as the result of German exhaustion.

7. That the attempt forcibly to insist on a change in the German system of government would defeat itself.

8. That the internal development of Germany towards liberal institutions would not be hastened, but would be checked, by further exhaustion.

9. That the influential section led by Delbrueck, who is now in favour of constitutional reforms and international peace machinery, (although before the war he was an opponent of both), would inevitably induce the Government to desire moderate terms, and to adopt reform after the war, provided that the Allies do not adopt a policy of humiliation and subsequent strangulation.

10. That the Japanese, who are openly welcoming the exhaustion of Europe, will achieve a Russo-Japanese entente with Germany to dominate China in the future, if Germany is very weak.

T MS (WP, DLC).

ENCLOSURE III

P.S. Chairman Hurley of the Trade Commission has just been in and told me that he has handed in his resignation, to be effective in February. I doubt if you appreciate the possibilities of this situation. Hurley is away yonder the best man on this Commission, especially since Rublee left. If the two vacancies are not filled by first-class, A-1 men, who are quite generally well known and generally accepted as good men, the very life of the Commission is at stake. There are a good many men on the Hill who would like to abolish it any way.

I wish you would give this very serious thought. I am deeply interested in it myself, because the work of this Commission laps over on mine to some extent, and I have gotten along especially well with Hurley since he has been Chairman. One of the two men to be appointed will doubtless be a Democrat; the other will have to be a Progressive or a Republican. Both of them simply must be high class, and no politics whatever should be played in their selection.

The creation of this Commission is one of the great constructive measures of this administration and it must be made a success. The situation at present is, to my mind, extremely critical.

TWG

T MS (WP, DLC).

From Joshua Willis Alexander

My dear Mr. President: Washington, D. C. January 5, 1917.

In answer to your letter of the second instant, referring to the Alaska fisheries bills, beg to say that it will give me great pleasure to do everything in my power to secure the passage of this bill at the present session of Congress. The present outlook, however, is not at all favorable, for reasons you will readily understand.

The Committee on the Merchant Marine and Fisheries gave this proposed legislation very thorough consideration and the bill reported from the Committee is in all respects a good bill and would no doubt pass the House if it can again be reached on the calendar.

My hope is that the bill, modified to meet Senator Lane's views, will be introduced in the Senate and its consideration by the Senate Committee on Fisheries and the Senate will be hastened for the reason that if the members of the Committee on the

Merchant Marine and Fisheries have reasonable assurance that the bill will be passed by the Senate they will be justified in renewing their efforts to secure further consideration in the House.

At this time there is a general feeling that the appropriation bills should have the right of way. However, I shall not overlook any possible opportunity to secure the passage of the bill as I am very anxious that it should become a law at the present session.

I have the honor to remain,

Yours sincerely,   J. W. Alexander

TLS (WP, DLC).

From Gertrude Minturn Pinchot

New York, Jan. 5, 1917.

The Woman's Peace Party of New York sincerely hopes that the administration will withdraw our troops from Mexico and send Mr. Fletcher to Mexico City. We believe that these two measures will help to stabilize conditions and promote a lasting peace. We also desire to congratulate you most heartily upon your recent note to the belligerent powers, especially of the tends [tendency] to make the question of peace a popular one rather than to be decided solely by the executive[s] and diplomats of Europe. No wars are peoples wars, but you are helping to create a peoples peace.

The Woman's Peace Party of New York
Gertrude M. Pinchot, Vice Chairman.

T telegram (WP, DLC).

From the Diary of Colonel House

New York, January 5, 1917.

The usual accumulation of work awaited my return. Cleve Dodge, Jerome Green and Honnold[1] of the Belgian Commission came to hear what I had to tell concerning the President's decision regarding the plan to coordinate foreign relief societies.

The President is willing to help but not to take the lead, because he is afraid some criticism might arise on account of the critical condition of foreign affairs, all of which he wishes to avoid. I was amused to hear him say when I was in Washington, that if he took the lead in a general relief plan someone would be certain to say that he sympathized with one side or the other. I hope that feature of his last note has struck home.

¹ William Lincoln Honnold, mining engineer long active in South Africa, at this time the director in the United States of the Commission for Relief in Belgium.

From Robert Lansing

PERSONAL AND CONFIDENTIAL:

My dear Mr. President: [Washington] January 6, 1917.

I expect to go before the Rules Committee on the Wood Resolution concerning a "leak" Monday morning.

I realize they will ask me a number of embarrassing questions which may involve my first knowledge of a note to the belligerents and other matters of a like confidential nature. I think it would be advisable, therefore, if agreeable to you, that you should see me sometime before Monday morning, in order that I may get your exact views as to how far I should go in my statements.   Faithfully yours,   Robert Lansing

TLS (Lansing Letterpress Book, SDR, RG 59, DNA).

From Edward Nash Hurley

My dear Mr. President: Washington January 6, 1917.

On account of certain large plant improvements requiring personal attention to my business affairs, I respectfully tender you my resignation to take effect February first, nineteen hundred and seventeen.

With much helpful cooperative service in such an interesting American business era in prospect, I can assure you that I would not ask to be relieved of my work as Chairman of the Federal Trade Commission did I not feel that the helpful purposes of the Commission have been clearly demonstrated and the work will continue progressively without interruption.

I desire to take this opportunity to express to you my sincere appreciation of the hearty cooperative support you have given the Federal Trade Commission in its effort to solve the nation's industrial problems.

Your attitude toward business has been fair and just, and the accomplishments of the Commission in behalf of the small merchant and manufacturer, as well as the large business interests of the country, have had their inspiration in your constructive thoughts and wishes.

Respectfully yours,   Edward N. Hurley

TLS (WP, DLC).

From Benjamin Ryan Tillman

My dear Mr. President: Washington, D. C. January 6, 1917.

Secretary Daniels is urging the Naval Committee to preserve for the use of the Navy the oil reservations that have been set aside by your predecessors, Taft and Roosevelt. Upon investigation, I find this condition exists: Secretary Daniels and Secretary Lane differ in their views as to the policy which ought to be followed with regard to these oil reservations, and there is a prospect that both will be quoted in debate on the floor of the Senate in regard to this matter. Senator Phelan is pressing his bill in regard to these reservations, and the Naval Committee is hampered in preventing its being taken up by the fact that two members of your Cabinet are antagonistic to each other.

As Chairman of the Committee on Naval Affairs I naturally want to take care of the Navy oil reserves, for the fast destroyers and cruisers now in service, being built, and to be built, would be useless unless we have plenty of fuel oil for all time.

I make bold to suggest that you have your two Cabinet Officers lay all the facts before you and let the Cabinet determine just what policy ought to be followed. If you will make known what your own conclusions are after the Cabinet has discussed it, as to the equities in the matter which Secretary Lane urges with great force in his report, I believe a satisfactory decision can be reached. If the Navy has to pay millions for these equities it will be better than not to have a lasting supply of oil.

Anyhow, I beg you to take the matter up with these two Cabinet Officers and let me know as soon as practicable what conclusions you have reached.   Very respectfully,   B. R. Tillman

TLS (WP, DLC).

From Thomas W. Brahany[1]

The White House.

Memorandum for the President: January 6, 1917.

Miss Alice Paul has advised the office by telephone that there will be about 300 women in the party of suffragettes who are to see the President at the White House on Tuesday afternoon, January 9th, at 2:00 o'clock, to present the resolutions passed at different services over the country held in memory of Inez Milholland Boissevain. As the President knows, these women are the militant branch of the Suffrage women. Some of the newspapermen stationed at the White House inform me that they understand that it is the plan of leaders to have four or five of the women laud Mrs. Boissevain in presenting the resolutions. These newspapermen seem to think that if much encouragement is given Miss Paul and her associates, an effort will be made to have the presentation take on the form of a memorial service for Mrs. Boissevain, with the President as the central figure and the East Room as a setting.

Does the President wish any special instructions given to Miss Paul as to what he wishes the program to be on the occasion of the presentation of the resolutions?

TL (WP, DLC).
1 Chief Clerk of the White House staff.

A Report of a News Conference by Charles Merz[1]

January 8th [1917].

THE PRESIDENT'S CONFERENCE.
(A complete memorandum, set down in the order of the President's replies to questions.)

1. *Peace "Leak."* Asked if he had anything to say on this subject Mr. Wilson said: "I am not a critic of comedy." He refused to allow himself to be quoted as saying this.

2. *Mexico*: "There is nothing that can be said at the present time."

3. *Revenue.* The President said "It is not the duty of the executive to suggest the sources of revenue. I do not believe I shall have occasion to go before Congress before the appropriations are made." Asked if "the necessity of bond issues had been agreed upon," Mr. Wilson said: "It seems to have been agreed upon in the newspapers, but not elsewhere. I have held all along that each generation should pay for its own business."

4. *Adamson's new railway bill.*[2] The President said: "The general plan of the bill is along the lines I recommended to Congress. I was not privileged to go over the details of the plan, but I trust that no mention of this will be made, out of regard for Judge Adamson." (It seemed to me that the President felt more keenly about this than he admitted; possibly he had in

mind Mr. Adamson's earlier independence regarding the introduction of bills.)

5. *River and Harbor appropriations.* The President said any plan of a scientific commission administration would apply only to future bills, and that "no one can tell *how* future." Without using the words "executive budget" he said that this was the only means of curing "pork."

6. *Public buildings appropriations.* Mr. Wilson said that while a public buildings commission could have "a restraining influence," this was a different problem from the rivers and harbors situation. He said: "There is no way to systematize and coordinate public buildings." (His remarks here were confusing to me, and I felt that he was quoting McAdoo.)

7. *Railroad legislation.* Mr. Wilson said that the failure of the conference of railway executives and the Brotherhoods in New York[3] emphasized the need of his compulsory investigation legislation. (Whenever he spoke of this legislation the President seemed to me to be forcing his optimism; but I may be mistaken.)

8. *Possibility of a strike.* Mr. Wilson said that his only information on this point had come from the newspapers.

9. *Belgian deportations.* The President said there were no new dispatches or notes that he had seen.

10. *Veto of individual items.* Such a power, of course, would have to be granted by a constitutional amendment. The President seemed to be in favor of the theory of the idea.

11. *Tariff Commission.* The President announced that Professor Taussig had accepted a place on the board. Asked if this meant that he would be chairman, the President said "I declare I've forgotten whether the law gives me the power to delegate the chairman." The rest of the board would be announced in a few days, the President said. "I know who I want, but I do not know whether they want the jobs." Any revision of the tariff during the present session of Congress he regarded as premature.

12. *Porto Rico-Nicaraguan Treaty.* Nothing to be said.

13. *Peace.* The President seemed to feel very keenly about the rumors that have filled the press. He said: "It is useless to say anything about peace. We have explicitly denied that there will be another peace note, yet some newspapers have gone ahead and declared that there would be. They have, in other words, implied that we were liars. It is grievous the way these newspapers complicate the foreign situation. If it is done with deliberation it is worth [worse] than grievous.

I do not know where they get their information. Certainly it is not from official sources."

This ended the conference. I stayed behind and had about seven minutes with Tumulty and the President. During this time Tumulty railed against the "leak" inquiry, and the treatment that had been accorded him there. "Governor," he said, "they as much as called me a liar." Wilson said, "They won't get very far with such tactics."

After Tumulty left I had about five minutes with the President alone. He seemed to be really interested in what I told him about the organization of the next House, and asked several questions. At the end he said: "I wish you would write Mr. Croly and Mr. Lippmann and tell them that I appreciate the work they are doing and THAT I AM IN ENTIRE AGREEMENT WITH THEIR ARTICLES ON PEACE." I tried to get a more definite expression regarding a league to enforce peace, but did not have the right opportunity to hint at it nor the boldness to make a blunt inquiry.

T MS (W. Lippmann Papers, CtY).
1 Former managing editor of *Harper's Weekly*. He had just become the Washington correspondent of *The New Republic*.
2 After a conference with Wilson on January 3, Adamson announced that he would introduce new railroad labor legislation desired by the President without waiting for action by the Senate Commerce Committee on pending legislation. Adamson introduced his bill on January 6 as an amendment to the pending Newlands bill. The Adamson bill retained the Newlands bill's provision for investigation by a special board of inquiry—following the failure of the Board of Mediation and Conciliation—of controversies between railroads and employees. The Adamson bill also stipulated that there should be no strikes or lockouts during the period of investigation. The special board should submit, within at least three months after the reference of the controversy, a report to the President as to its findings of fact, etc., together with a recommendation for the settlement of the case. *New York Times*, Jan. 4 and 7, 1917. There are numerous documents in Volume 41 relating to Wilson's unsuccessful efforts to secure anti-strike legislation.
3 A conference of railway managers and the presidents of the brotherhoods had met in New York on December 28 and had utterly failed to come to any agreement that the railroads, which had instituted a test case of the Adamson Act, should agree to obey that Act forthwith. *Ibid.*, Dec. 29, 1916.

To Thomas W. Brahany

[The White House, c. Jan. 8, 1916]

Please say to Miss Paul that it is necessary for me to request that this presentation be made by a single person and as simply as possible. It will not otherwise be possible for me to give the time that would be needed. W.W.

WWTLI (WP, DLC).

From Franklin Knight Lane

Dear Mr. President: Washington January 8, 1917.

I have just learned in a confidential way that some of the Senators interested in the Shield's Bill are to see you on Wednesday.[1] My information is from the inside, and I want to give you the benefit of it. They are prepared to surrender as to the imposition of a tax, that is the point over which there is so much difference between the two Houses. They are also prepared to surrender if you insist upon the passage of the public lands bill, the Ferris Bill. I feel that the whole water power question can be put behind us at this Session, if you will insist that measures covering both navigable waters and public lands shall be passed; and it would be unfortunate from the standpoint of the West to have the navigable streams act alone passed.

I had a little conference with Senator Walsh, Senator Myers, Mr. Ferris and Mr. Lenroot on Saturday, regarding the bill which I sent to you sometime ago constituting a Water Powers Commission, and giving that Commission power to make rules and regulations.[2] I asked them if such a bill could be passed, and they said that while you doubtless would be able to do it if you insisted upon it, the Senate would not take kindly to such a delegation of power. I wonder, however, if it might not be practicable to have such a Commission of Cabinet officers as I suggested, who would make all leases; Congress to provide the terms upon which the leases would be made. It really would be better if there was but one act covering all streams and one administrative authority. This, however, is not vital, though I believe we will surely come to it eventually.

Cordially yours,   Franklin K. Lane

TLS (WP, DLC).
    [1] They were Senators Shields and Bankhead.
    [2] See FKL to WW, Dec. 9, 1916 (third letter of that date).

From William Joel Stone

Dear Mr. President: [Washington] January 8 1917.

I have your note of the 4th instant, enclosing me a memorandum made by Secretary Baker respecting the Danish West Indies recently acquired under our Treaty with Denmark. I think the suggestions of Secretary Baker are very well worth our most thoughtful consideration. Whenever the time comes for taking this matter up, I will be glad, as I am sure other Senators will, to confer more directly and definitely with you respecting the form of government to be established. I am confident there will be no trouble so far as the Senate is concerned touching the proper disposition of this matter.

I feel complimented that you took the trouble to send me your note in "your own hand writing," and I compliment you on your chirography. This note is not in my own hand writing. It is probable that I will not communicate with you in my own hand unless I have some design of leaving you in doubt as to what I meant. Very sincerely, Wm J Stone.

TLS (WP, DLC).

Robert Lansing to Breckinridge Long[1]

CONFIDENTIAL:

My dear Mr. Long: Washington January 8, 1917.

The President has determined, in accordance with his usual practice of advancing men in the service, to promote to the Assistant Secretaryship of State William Phillips, now Third Assistant Secretary. This promotion will leave the office of Third Assistant Secretary vacant and the President has authorized me to write to you, confidentially, and to ask you whether you would accept the office of Third Assistant Secretary if it should be tendered to you.

The position is, as you know, one of much responsibility and at the present time of absorbing interest. It is, in my opinion, a real opportunity for patriotic service. I trust, therefore, that you will be willing to meet the President's wishes and telegraph me that a tender of the office will be accepted.

Personally, I would be most gratified to receive a favorable response from you as I have very earnestly pressed your name on the President, and only your name.

With my very warm regards believe me—

Most cordially yours, Robert Lansing.

TLS (B. Long Papers, DLC).
[1] Princeton 1904, lawyer of St. Louis, who had made generous financial contributions to the Democratic campaign of 1916. He accepted the position on January 10.

A News Report

SUFFRAGISTS WILL PICKET WHITE HOUSE

[*Jan. 9, 1917*]

Washington, Jan. 9.—Women suffragists, representing all parts of the country, disappointed over the result of an appeal which they made this afternoon to President Wilson in the East Room of the White House, held an indignation meeting and decided to adopt a new plan of campaign. They intend to post women pickets hereafter about the White House grounds. Their purpose is to make it impossible for the President to enter or leave the White House without encountering a picket bearing some device pleading the suffrage cause. The pickets will be known as "silent sentinels."

Mrs. Harriot Stanton Blatch,[1] daughter of Elizabeth Cady Stanton, who presided over the indignation meeting, coined the title of "silent sentinels" for the White House pickets. These silent sentinels, all young women, commencing at 9 o'clock tomorrow morning will take up their stations near the entrances to the White House.

At the indignation meeting a subscription list was started to pay the cost of the silent sentinel campaign, to buy umbrellas to protect the sentinels from inclement weather, and pay other expenses. Miss Mary Burnham of Philadelphia started the subscription by giving $1,000. Mrs. Townsend Scott of Baltimore,[2] one of the group of six suffrage leaders who flung their banner from the gallery of the House of Representatives, gave $100. Mrs. William Kent,[3] wife of the independent member of Congress from California, subscribed $100 a month to the silent sentinel cause.

There were 300 suffragists in the delegation that went to the White House to present memorials on the death of Mrs. Inez Milholland Boissevain. The women were admitted by cards, which the White House sent to the headquarters of the Congressional Union yesterday. The delegation was headed by Sara Bard Field of San Francisco, who crossed the continent to present the Boissevain resolutions, which were adopted at a recent mass meeting in California.

Although the White House audience was arranged merely to present the Boissevain memorials, the women made it the occasion to renew their pleas that the President should support the Susan B. Anthony amendment. The President expressed his surprise, reminded the spokesmen of the party that he had not been apprised of their full purpose, and was not prepared to say any more than he had on previous occasions. His speech follows:

"I had not been apprised that you were coming here to make any representations that would issue an appeal to me. I had been told that you were coming to present memorial resolutions with regard to the very remarkable woman whom your cause has lost. I, therefore, am not prepared to say anything further than I have said on previous occasions of this sort. I don't need to tell you where my own convictions and my own personal purpose lie, and I need not tell you by what circumscriptions I am bound as the leader of a party.

"As the leader of a party, my commands come from the party and not from private personal convictions. My personal action as a citizen, of course, comes from no source but my own conviction, and, therefore, my position has been so frequently defined, and I hope so candidly defined, and, so, it is impossible for me, until the orders of my party are changed, to do anything other than I am doing; and, as a party leader, I think nothing else is necessary to be said.

"I do want to say this: I don't see how anybody can fail to observe, from the utterances of the last campaign, that the Democratic party is more inclined than the opposition party to assist in this great cause, and it has been a matter of surprise to me, and a matter of very great regret, that so many of those who were, heart and soul, for this cause seemed so greatly to misunderstand and misinterpret the attitude of the parties. Because in this country, as in every other self-governing country, it is only through the instrumentality of the parties that things can be accomplished. They are not accomplished by the individual voice, but by concerted action, and that action must come only so fast as you can concert it.

"I stand on my position. I have done my best and shall continue to do my best to concert it in the interest of a cause in which I personally believe."[4]

Printed in the *New York Times*, Jan. 10, 1917.
   [1] Harriot Eaton Stanton (Mrs. William Henry) Blatch.
   [2] Helen Evans Scott.
   [3] Elizabeth Thacher Kent.
   [4] Corrections and additions from the JRT transcript (WC, NjP) of the CLSsh notes (C. L. Swem Coll., NjP).

To Edward Nash Hurley

[The White House]

My dear Mr. Chairman: 10 January, 1917

It is with deepest and most genuine regret that I accept your resignation from the Federal Trade Commission, to take effect

February 1, 1917. I accept it only because I am convinced from what you tell me that you could not consistently with interests for which you must care continue the work you have been so admirably performing. I wish with all my heart that it might have been possible for you to stay, and I want you to know in what high esteem you have been held here by everyone who has had dealings with you and what a very high value I, in common with the public, have placed upon your work with the Commission.

Cordially and sincerely yours,   Woodrow Wilson

TLS (Letterpress Books, WP, DLC).

From Robert Lansing, with Enclosure

PERSONAL AND CONFIDENTIAL:

My dear Mr. President: Washington January 10, 1917.

I enclose a confidential report from Berlin—No. 4916, Dated December 21, 1916.

It is a most complete resumé of the entire negotiation relative to peace as conducted by Mr. Grew, our Chargé. I would call your special attention to the latter part of the report which I think is of very great importance.

It will oblige me if you will return the report to me at your convenience as it is the duplicate which belongs to the records of the Department.   Faithfully yours,   Robert Lansing.

TLS (R. Lansing Papers, NjP).

E N C L O S U R E

Joseph Clark Grew to Robert Lansing

Confidential.
No. 4916

Sir: Berlin, December 21, 1916.

I have the honor to make to the Department the following report on the development of the peace propaganda in Germany during the period in which I have been in charge of the Embassy.

On October 7th, in my telegram No. 4439, reporting the agreement which was said to have been reached between the Chancellor and his political opponents that the submarine issue should be dropped for the present, I informed the Department that this agreement appeared to be based upon the desire of the German

Government to avoid embarrassing the President should he desire to act on the matter dealt with in the Ambassador's highly confidential telegram No. 4375 of September 25th and to take steps looking towards peace. This information was received from a source which I regarded as trustworthy and well-informed, but I was not at that time able to confirm it.

On November 17th, in my telegram No. 4614, I directed the Department's attention to the importance of an interview with the Imperial Chancellor which Mr. William Bayard Hale, the Berlin correspondent of the Hearst newspapers, was about to cable to the New York American. . . .[1]

Meanwhile, on November 22nd, my first interview with the Chancellor regarding the Belgian deportations gave him an opportunity to turn to the subject of peace and to elaborate the theme at considerable length, knowing that what he said would be brought directly to the President's attention. I am not aware as to what he had previously said to Mr. Gerard and to Colonel House, but he approached the matter very directly and definitely and left no doubt as to his intentions in bringing up the subject. As soon as the Belgian matter had been discussed, the Chancellor settled back in his chair and began to speak slowly and distinctly in German giving me the impression that he had carefully considered his words in advance. He said that these difficulties in Belgium would never have arisen if his suggestions that Germany desired peace, which he had expressed in the Reichstag last December, almost a year ago, and subsequently to Mr. Gerard and to Colonel House and in other speeches and interviews, had been acted upon abroad. England and France, he said, had replied that this was no time to talk of peace. It had been said in those countries that he had made conditions, (Bedingungen); this was not true; he had made no conditions. If his intimations that Germany wanted peace should be continuously ignored, Germany would be forced in self-defense to adopt hard measures, but this would not be Germany's fault. Germany's readiness for peace absolved her from the guilt of this continued slaughter. It was utter craziness (Wannsinn) to continue this useless and futile taking of human life. This he repeated several times in different words. "What do these difficulties in Belgium matter," he said, "compared to the hecatomb of lives which have been lost on the Somme since last July?"

As I reported to the Department in my telegram No. 4636 of November 22, 10 p.m., the Chancellor gave an impression of great weariness and sadness and discouragement at the failure

[1] This telegram is printed as an Enclosure with WW to EMH, Nov. 21, 1916.

of his peace suggestions to bear fruit. His mood may to a certain extent have been influenced by the day, which was Busstag, the German day of penitence: he had lost his wife and son since the beginning of the war and his thoughts would naturally have turned to them on that particular day of the year. But, as I reported to the Department, the Chancellor, quite apart from any consideration of mood or manner, gave me the distinct impression, although not directly expressed, of his disappointment that the United States had not taken steps leading towards peace.

On December 1st, in my telegram No. 4671 I communicated to the Department my impressions of the general situation in Germany regarding the issue of peace. . . .[2]

On November 29th, in its telegram No. 3621 the Department directed me to obtain as soon as possible a further interview with the Chancellor and after making a textual protest against the Belgian deportations on behalf of the Government of the United States, to represent to the Chancellor in confidence and with great earnestness the very serious unfavorable reaction which the Belgian deportations were exerting upon public opinion in the United States at a time when that opinion was more nearly approaching a balance of judgment as to the issues of the war than ever before. I was also, and more particularly, to point out the great embarrassment which the President had been caused by that reaction in regard to taking steps looking towards peace. I was authorized to say that the whole situation was being watched by the President with the ultmost solicitude, as it was his wish and definite purpose to be of service at the earliest possible moment in that great aim and that it had repeatedly distressed him to find his hopes frustrated and his occasion destroyed by such unfortunate incidents as the Belgian deportations and the sinking of the MARINA and the ARABIA. Furthermore, authorization was given me to say that my report, in a recent despatch (telegram), of the evident distress and disappointment of the Chancellor that nothing had come of his intimations regarding peace had been noted by the President with the deepest interest and that what the President now earnestly desired was the creation of a favorable opportunity for some affirmative action by him in the interest of an early restoration of peace, this opportunity to be brought about through practical cooperation on the part of the German authorities. (paraphrase).

This telegram was not received at the Embassy until December 2nd. I immediately applied formally through the Foreign Office for an interview with the Chancellor and was received by

[2] This telegram is printed as an Enclosure with WW to EMH, Dec. 5, 1916.

him on the morning of December 5th after he had made two previous appointments with me for the day before and had been obliged to break them both, one on account of the funeral service for the Austrian Emperor and the other owing to an extended sitting with some committee. After making the formal representations with regard to the Belgian deportations and leaving a copy with the Chancellor in writing, I turned to the delivery of the President's communication.

The matter was one of some delicacy, owing to the fact, as I had reported to the Department, that the Chancellor had not directly expressed disappointment that the United States had taken no steps looking towards peace, but had given me that impression only by intimation. There was no question whatever as to his intention in having spoken to me as he did at my first interview, which was clearly indicated by his words, his manner and his allusion to what he had previously said to Mr. Gerard and to Colonel House, but I could not run the possible risk of first delivering the President's communication and then of having the Chancellor, owing to some alteration of circumstances in the meantime, say that I had not clearly understood him. Accordingly I began by repeating carefully word for word, so far as it was possible to remember it, the Chancellor's remarks to me at the previous interview and then inquired if I had understood him clearly. On his reply that I had made no mistake, I proceeded to make the representations stated above. The Chancellor listened with full respect to the President's communication, but made no comment and said that he would send for me in a few days after he had talked the matter over with Zimmermann.

In an informal talk with Zimmermann on December 6th, he expressed satisfaction at the President's communication and said that the Chancellor's reply would be "favorable and friendly." He also remarked that it was the desire of the German Government to smooth the President's way as much as possible in any steps which he might take looking towards peace.

On the following evening, December 7th, the Chancellor sent for me and said that while the answer of the German Government to our representations regarding the Belgian deportations would be communicated to me in due course by Zimmermann, he wished to reply immediately himself, before leaving for General Headquarters that night, to the statement regarding the President's attitude towards the question of taking steps looking towards peace, and he proceeded to make to me the following confidential oral communication:

"The German Government, desirous of maintaining amicable

relations with the United States, has given proof of its willingness to settle incidents arising between the two nations in a
friendly spirit by the replies recently transmitted to the American Government in the MARINA and ARABIA cases. It is with great
satisfaction that I have noted that the President of the United
States so earnestly tries to be of service in the restoration of peace.
Also my offers to open pourparlers for peace negotiations have so
far not met with a favorable response from the other side. I hope
the time will come when Germany's enemies will be more willing
to lend an ear to the voice of reason. I am extremely grateful to
see from the message you were good enough to deliver to me
that in this event I can count on the practical cooperation of the
President in the restoration of peace as much as the President
can count on the practical cooperation of the German authorities."

This statement and an account of my conversation with the
Chancellor were cabled to the Department in my No. 4700 of
December 7th.[3]

The following day, to my surprise, Mr. Conger,[4] the Associated
Press correspondent in Berlin, showed me a telegram which he
was about to send to the United States containing a more or less
complete account of my interview with the Chancellor both on
the subject of the Belgian deportations and on peace. The information, he said, had been given out to him by a certain official
in the Foreign Office with full permission to use it as news.

Endeavoring to look at the matter from every point of view,
I could not see that the publication of this interview, so far as
it related to peace, could do otherwise than embarrass the President. We did not know at that time that either the Chancellor or
the President would shortly come out with a public communication on the subject and it was my opinion, although no intimation
of the Department's attitude had been given me, that if the President were contemplating taking action, his way would be rendered more difficult by the unfavorable reaction which the publication of my confidential interview with the Chancellor would
have on public opinion in the countries of the Entente. Furthermore, if the President had no objection to the publication of the
interview, the Department would presumably not have characterized the communication to the Chancellor as confidential, which
was done in the Department's telegram No. 3621. It did not therefore lie with me to determine the advantages or disadvantages of
its publication and it was undoubtedly my duty to call the atten-

[3] J. C. Grew to RL, Dec. 7, 1916, FR-WWS 1916, pp. 81-82.
[4] Seymour Beach Conger.

tion of the Foreign Office to the fact that my communication to the Chancellor had been confidential, and that I had so stated when delivering it. This I did without delay. The Foreign Office averred that a mistake had been made, although I am now aware that the information had been given to Mr. Conger with the approval of a high official, and stated that they would suppress the telegram at the censor's office. This was done, for Mr. Conger came to me on the following day and said that to his suprise, his telegram had been badly cut up by the censor, all allusion to peace having been eliminated. I reported this incident to the Department in my telegram No. 4707 of December 8th.[5]

On December 10th, in my telegram No. 4712, I cabled the Department that the Reichstag had suddenly and unexpectedly been called to meet on December 12th and that it was generally believed that the subject of peace would be openly broached, possibly with a general statement of terms. During those few days, Berlin was full of the wildest rumors as to the meaning of the convocation of the Reichstag and it was not easy to sift the well founded rumors from mere gossip, so I telegraphed the Department with considerable reserve.

Immediately after the Chancellor had received me, I left the note at the Embassy to be translated and encoded and proceeded at once to the Reichstag, where the Chancellor spoke at 1:45 immediately after the meeting had been called to order. His remarks were cabled to the Department in my No. 4723 of December 12th. His speech, which was quietly delivered, called forth no great enthusiasm, although his remarks were frequently punctuated by "Bravos" from the house. Afterwards the leaders of the Central, Conservative and Socialist parties spoke, but at not great length. The representative of the Center Party moved to adjourn leaving it in the discretion of the President to fix the day of the next meeting. Herr Bassermann[6] of the National Liberal Party took the position that a measure of such moment as the peace proposal required dignified discussion by the Reichstag and moved that such discussion be entered upon immediately. Count Westarp,[7] of the Conservatives, and Herr Ledebour[8] of the Socialist Labor Wing supported Herr Bassermann's motion for open discussion by the Reichstag. Upon vote being taken the motion to adjourn was passed by a large majority.

On December 13th I cabled to the Department, in my Nos. 4728 and 4729, full comment and excerpts from the press.

[5] J. C. Grew to RL, Dec. 8, 1916, FR-WWS 1916, p. 82.
[6] Ernst Bassermann.
[7] Kuno Friedrich Viktor, Count von Westarp.
[8] Georg Ledebour.

In an informal conversation with me on December 19th, Zimmermann mentioned the subject of peace and said that while the Chancellor in his note of December 12th had clearly indicated that Germany, with her sincere desire for peace, would adopt no basis which it would be impossible for the Entente to accept, the German Government had particularly avoided giving any intimation as to what this basis would be, as this, among other reasons, might have demoralized the troops in the field who would have believed that there was no further purpose in fighting. This conversation was reported in my telegram No. 4753 of December 19th and was the first occasion on which the subject of peace had been commented upon at the Foreign Office since the Chancellor handed me his note on December 12th.

On the morning of December 21st I received the Department's circular telegram of December 18th, containing the President's communication for the Secretary of State for Foreign Affairs, which I read to Zimmermann at about 5 p.m., after the telegram had been decoded, the note prepared and an appointment made at the Foreign Office. I presented the matter with the utmost earnestness and clearly conveyed the impression, as directed, that it would be very hard for the Government of the United States to understand a negative reply. Zimmermann listened to the reading of the communication, a copy of which I left with him, with earnest attention and expressed great satisfaction at and appreciation of the President's "wise and highminded action." He said he would have to discuss the matter with the Emperor and the Chancellor before replying and that in any case he did not think that an answer could be given or action taken until the Entente Powers had replied to the Chancellor's note of December 12th. He said he was quite sure that Germany's peace terms were more moderate than those of the Entente, but that Germany could not be the first to divulge them, first because one party to a negotiation could not give its hand away at the start and second because of the unfavorable effect which this would have on the German public, part of whom would undoubtedly be dissatisfied with the terms offered by Germany. I remarked that if Germany could not be the first to divulge her terms and if, as was probable, the Entente Powers would be similarly reticent, the process of elimination would leave a mutual and simultaneous statement of terms as the only alternative, which he said might be considered. The word "soundings," he said, struck him as peculiarly appropriate and he believed that in any case the action of the President was a step nearer towards peace and that favorable results might possibly be expected.

I informed the Department of the receipt of the President's communication in my telegram No. 4760 of December 21st, 10 a.m., reporting at the same time that section 2 of the Department's circular for Vienna and Sofia had been sent to Berlin by an error of the telegraph authorities and that I had forwarded it immediately. My conversation with Zimmermann was reported in the Embassy's telegram No. 4784 of December 21st, 6 PM. I would add that in leaving with Zimmermann the President's communication in writing, I adopted the form of a note as had been done by the Ambassador in previous cases under identical instructions (vide the various LUSITANIA notes from the Embassy to the Foreign Office).

The Ambassador returned to Berlin at 10:30 p.m. on December 21st.

In summing up, I venture to remark that in my opinion this peace propaganda is a direct outcome of the food situation in Germany, which is steadily becoming more difficult. The German masses are suffering from undernourishment, which is already affecting adults but particularly young children, and there will probably be several months to come, before the next crops are ripe, when the supply of food available for rationing human beings and animals will be sensibly less than at present. If it becomes necessary to go through this period in a state of war, it may be expected that it can be done, though with great and widespread hardship. The fighting could then be prolonged for a considerable period, but under these circumstances, even if victorious in a military sense, Germany would probably be so far exhausted as to render a victory barren of results. It is, therefore, necessary for Germany to make great sacrifices at the present time in order to try to secure a peace. The attempts to detach Russia from the Alliance having proved abortive, the sacrifices to be offered appear at present, to be directed towards France and England.

As a basis for discussion, something of the following nature is talked about among well informed Germans: Belgium and Northern France to be given up; France to be compensated with a part of Alsace and Lorraine; England to be compensated with certain Colonial possessions. On the other hand, Germany to be allowed to follow her development of the Bagdad road and Mesopotamia; to have an influential position in the Balkans; and the independent kingdom of Poland to be continued as a buffer state. It is significant that in 1915 it would not have been possible to find a German voice to speak of the ceding of a square foot of Alsace-Lorraine.

The morale of the masses is low. The successes in Rumania

and the peace propaganda have given them new spirit for the moment and the Chancellor's action on December 12th was received with unconcealed joy. But this frame of mind cannot be expected to last if the peace offer fails.

The year 1916 has been a definite step in the growth of liberal ideas in Germany. The ideas so freely expressed by the ruling classes at the beginning of the war and throughout 1915, that Germany by virtue of her leadership in the arts of civilization and the moral superiority of her people must spread her power and methods throughout the world, are now generally relegated to obscurity.

Nevertheless the full regeneration of the country can only come from within. When it is brought home to the people that the building up of vast armaments for conquest and expansion and the fostering of that spirit of force which is militarism has led them to failure and suffering, the time will be ripe for new forms of government in Germany and for a stable condition in Europe.

It would appear from the statements made in the countries at war with Germany that they recognize this condition and are not prepared to accept terms unless they impose upon Germany definite losses and hardships which will bring home to her people the futility of future wars of expansion.

I have the honor to be, Sir,

Your obedient servant,   J. C. Grew.

CCL (R. Lansing Papers, NjP).

From Paul Samuel Reinsch

Personal & Confidential.

Dear Mr. President: Peking, January 10, 1917.

I have already expressed to you my conviction that the situation in the Far East, and especially in China, will be of cardinal importance in determining lasting conditions of world peace after the Great War. Should China be further divided, or become dependent upon an aggressive Power, causes of future wars would thereby be generated exceeding in scope the differences which have hitherto divided mankind. The peace and security of our own country is particularly affected by this, and it is evident that any exertions now made for maintaining the real independence of China will accomplish more as protective measures for the United States than could be achieved through any other method of defense.

The forces which attack the independence of China at present are most insidious, acting upon elements of weakness and disorganization which are found in the Chinese body politic. The Chinese are engaged in the enormous task of giving to their national life a free representative political organization. This goes to the root of their social existence and is, moreover, complicated by the fact that many qualities which were true virtues under the old régime are turned into weakness and vice under the new. Such a process—extremely arduous at any time—is in the case of China beset with dangers aggravated by the presence of outside influences eager to gain advantage from every defect in Chinese organization.

The only remedy lies in giving active assistance to the constructive elements in Chinese life. In fact through a relatively very small amount of cooperation an exceedingly great power for good can be exercised; and I do not believe that at any time could such moderate efforts as are here required, have brought results so decisive for the future good of China, of our own country, and of the world in general.

The opportunities to help China are restricted through the fact that certain lines of activity have been preempted by groups of Powers, who, though themselves unable to act at present, would oppose action undertaken by others. But the field of assistance in industrial and economic development is fortunately still open. At the present time the President[1] and the Cabinet of China are most anxious to have Americans share in the creation of a powerful industrial bank, through which the development of national resources, colonization, agriculture, and industrial enterprises may be facilitated. This method offers, undoubtedly, the best and surest way for helpfulness to China, through which her whole future development may be given a beneficent turn and her national independence may be preserved. I am enclosing herewith a copy of a brief report on this matter, made to the Department of State:[2] I do this because I consider the matter of sufficient importance to deserve your personal knowledge and attention. It is, to my mind, the best means available towards concrete and specific relief and encouragement of China.

In the matter of the international position of China, too, grave problems are at present being discussed; and, in order to lay the situation before you, I am likewise enclosing a copy of a despatch to the Department of even date.[3]

In this matter, too, it may be possible for the American Government to exercise a powerful influence towards assisting China to maintain her independence and her other national rights.

I have brought these matters to your personal attention because, in the past, you have expressed a desire to be informed of matters of real importance, and such I consider these to be— one for the internal development of China, upon which her national strength and stamina are dependent; the other for the maintenance of her international rights.

With the highest regard and sincere wishes for your continued well being, I remain,

Faithfully yours,　Paul S. Reinsch.

TLS (WP, DLC).

¹ That is, Li Yüan-Hung.
² It is missing in all repositories.
³ P. S. Reinsch to RL, Jan. 10, 1917, CC telegram (WP, DLC). It is printed in *FR 1917*, pp. 114-15.

From Newton Diehl Baker

Dear Mr. President:　　　　　　Washington. January 10, 1917

Representative David J. Lewis of Maryland has for many years been a student of telephone ownership and operation. He has introduced a bill into the House authorizing the Post Office Department to acquire and extend the telephone system of the District of Columbia, the purpose being to acquire complete Government control of the telephone, primarily for the safeguarding of its military and executive affairs, but undoubtedly a part of Mr. Lewis' impulse comes from the desire on his part ultimately to see the telegraph and telephone operation of the country a part of the Post Office Department. I have been working with Mr. Lewis for some years along this line, and he therefore asked me to call his bill to your attention in the hope that if any opportunity came to you to casually express your approval, you would feel disposed to do so.

I realize that this matter ought to be brought to your attention by the Postmaster General rather than by me, and I told Mr. Lewis that I would not be able to secure any statement from you for him, but would feel free merely to call your attention to the fact that his bill has been introduced.

Respectfully yours,　Newton D. Baker

TLS (WP, DLC).

William Graves Sharp to Robert Lansing

Paris, Jan. 10, 1917.

1806. Translation of French note as follows:[1]

"The Allied Governments have received the note which was delivered to them in the name of the Government of the United States on the nineteenth of December, 1916. They have studied it with the care imposed upon them both by the exact realization which they have of the gravity of the hour and by the sincere friendship which attaches them to the American people.

"In general way they wish to declare that they pay tribute to the elevation of the sentiment with which the American note is inspired and that they associate themselves with all their hopes with the project for the creation of a league of nations to insure peace and justice throughout the world. They recognize all the advantages for the cause of humanity and civilization which the institution of international agreements, destined to avoid violent conflicts between nations would present; agreements which must imply the sanctions necessary to insure their execution and thus to prevent an apparent security from only facilitating new aggressions. But a discussion of future arrangements destined to insure an enduring peace presupposes a satisfactory settlement of the actual conflict; the Allies have as profound a desire as the Government of the United States to terminate as soon as possible a war for which the Central Empires are responsible and which inflicts such cruel sufferings upon humanity. But they believe that it is impossible at the present moment to attain a peace which will assure them reparation, restitution and such guarantees to which they are entitled by the aggression for which the responsibility rests with the Central Powers and of which the principle itself tended to ruin the security of Europe; a peace which would on the other hand permit the establishment of the future of European nations on a solid basis. The Allied nations are conscious that they are not fighting for selfish interests, but above all to safeguard the independence of peoples, of right and of humanity.

"The Allies are fully aware of the losses and suffering which the war causes to neutrals as well as to belligerents and they deplore them; but they do not hold themselves responsible for them, having in no way either willed or provoked this war, and they strive to reduce these damages in the measure compatible with the inexorable exigencies of their defense against the violence and the wiles of the enemy.

"It is with satisfaction therefore that they take note of the declaration that the American communication is in no wise associated in its origin with that of the Central Powers transmitted on the *eighteenth* of December by the Government of the United States. They did not doubt moreover the resolution of that Government to avoid even the appearance of a support, even moral, of the authors responsible for the war.

"The Allied Governments believe that they must protest in the most friendly but in the most specific manner against the assimilation established in the American note between the two groups of belligerents; this assimilation, based upon public declarations by the Central Powers, is in direct opposition to the evidence, both as regards responsibility for the past and as concerns guarantees for the future; President Wilson in mentioning it certainly had no intention of associating himself with it.

"If there is an historical fact established at the present date, it is the willful aggression of Germany and Austria-Hungary to insure their hegemony over Europe and their economic domination over the world. Germany proved by her declaration of war, by the immediate violation of Belgium and Luxemburg and by her manner of conducting the war, her simulating contempt for all principles of humanity and all respect for small states; as the conflict developed the attitude of the Central Powers and their Allies has been a continual defiance of humanity and civilization. Is it necessary to recall the horrors which accompanied the invasion of Belgium and of Servia, the atrocious regime imposed upon the invaded countries, the massacre of hundreds of thousands of inoffensive Armenians, the barbarities perpetrated against the populations of Syria, the raids of Zeppelins on open towns, the destruction by submarines of passenger steamers and of merchantmen even under neutral flags, the cruel treatment inflicted upon prisoners of war, the juridical murders of Miss Cavel[l], of Captain Fryatt, the deportation and the reduction to slavery of civil populations, et cetera? The execution of such a series of crimes perpetrated without any regard for universal reprobation fully explains to President Wilson the protest of the Allies.

"They consider that the note which they sent to the United States in reply to the German note will be a response to the questions put by the American Government, and according to the exact words of the latter, constitute 'a public declaration as to the conditions upon which the war could be terminated.'

"President Wilson desires more: he desires that the belligerents powers openly affirm the objects which they seek by continuing the war; the Allies experience no difficulty in replying to this request. Their objects in the war are well known; they have been formulated on many occasions by the chiefs of their divers Governments. Their objects in the war will not be made known in detail with all the equitable compensations and indemnities for damages suffered until the hour of negotiations. But the civilized world knows that they imply in all necessity and in the first instance the restoration of Belgium, of Servia, and of Montenegro and the indemnities which are due them; the evacuation of the invaded territories of France, of Russia and of Roumania with just reparation; the reorganization of Europe guaranteed by a stable regime and founded as much upon respect of nationalities and full security and liberty [of] economic development, which all nations, great or small, possess, as upon territorial conventions and international agreements suitable to guarantee territorial and maritime frontiers against unjustified attacks; the restitution of provinces or territories wrested in the past from the Allies by force or against the will of their populations, the liberation of Italians, of Slavs, of Roumanians and of Tcheco Slovaques from foreign domination; the enfranchisement of populations subject to the bloody tyranny of the Turks; the expulsion from Europe of the Ottoman Empire decidedly # to western civilization. The intentions of His Majesty the Emperor of Russia regarding Poland have been clearly indicated in the proclamation which he has just addressed to his armies. It goes without saying that if the Allies wish to liberate Europe from the brutal convetousness [covetousness] of Prussian militarism, it never has been their design, as has been alleged, to encompass the extermination of the German peoples and their political disappearance. That which they desire above all is to insure a peace upon the principles of liberty and justice, upon the inviolable fidelity to international obligation with which the Government of the United States has never ceased to be inspired.

"United in the pursuits of this supreme object the Allies are determined, individually and collectively, to act with all their power and to consent to all sacrifices to bring to a victorious close a conflict upon which they are convinced not only their own safety and prosperity depends but also the future of civilization itself."   Sharp.

(#) apparent ommission.

T telegram (SDR, RG 59, 763.72119/370½, DNA).

[1] All apprehensions concerning Wilson's motives in his peace initiative had vanished on account of Lansing's and House's reassuring messages and explanations by the day, December 26, when an Anglo-French conference met at 10

Downing Street in London for the purpose, among others, to prepare a reply to Wilson's note of December 18.

There was considerable discussion about whether the Anglo-French reply should list Allied war aims in detail. Lord Robert Cecil insisted upon a detailed reply. Otherwise, he said, Americans would say that the Allies did not dare to avow their true objectives because they were bent upon the destruction of Germany. This would have serious repercussions both in the United States and in Germany. He had had a frank talk this morning with Ambassador Page, Cecil continued. Page had said that the United States had friendly feelings for the Allies, and it was very important that the Allies should regard the United States as a friend and speak to it freely. If the Allies did not respond fully, Cecil added, Americans would say that they had had an opportunity to say what they were fighting for and had not wished to do so. Phillipe Berthelot of the French Foreign Ministry said: "If the spirit of the American government and people is such as was revealed by the conversation of the Ambassador of the United States with Lord Robert Cecil, the terms suggested by Mr. Lansing, etc., we should, without doubt, try to give them satisfaction. . . . If anything in the way of terms had to be announced, it was preferable to do so in answer to Germany, rather than in answer to the United States. Mr. Lansing had given us to understand that the American Government knew what the Allies' aims were; what they wanted to know was what the German aims were. That situation should be maintained."

The discussion then turned to the question of whether the Anglo-French reply should be a formal diplomatic document or an appeal to the American people. Lloyd George said that it should be the latter. Balfour agreed and then went on with a long commentary on the dangerous fallacy of Wilson's note—that it would be possible to reconstruct the postwar international order so as to preserve peace and prevent aggression no matter on what terms the war was ended. It was necessary to make the American people see that an Allied victory was essential to a peaceful postwar world. Balfour, Berthelot, and Paul Cambon, French Ambassador to Great Britain, were then constituted a committee to draft the reply. The conferees discussed the draft on December 28 and asked Balfour and Cambon to prepare the final text. The conference approved their text that evening and voted to submit it to the other Allies for their approval. "CONFERENCE DU 26 DECEMBRE 1916 . . . " and "CONFERENCE DU 28 DECEMBRE 1916 . . . ," T MSS (Guerre, 1914-1918, Vol. 990, pp. 84-94, 132-39, FFM-Ar); and ANGLO-FRENCH CONFERENCE. *Minutes of a Meeting held at 10, Downing Street, S.W., on December 26, 1916,* and ANGLO-FRENCH CONFERENCE. *Minutes of a Meeting held at 10, Downing Street, S.W., on December 28, 1916,* in the Papers of Austen Chamberlain, University of Birmingham Library.

To Robert Lansing

My dear Mr. Secretary,   The White House. 11 January, 1917.

This is a most interesting report,[1] and the closing part is, indeed, as you say, most significant.

Faithfully Yours,   W..W.

WWTLI (R. Lansing Papers, NjP).
[1] That is, J. C. Grew to RL, Dec. 21, 1916, printed as an Enclosure with RL to WW, Jan. 10, 1917.

To Robert Lansing, with Enclosure

My dear Mr. Secretary,   The White House. 11 January, 1917.

Here is that message from Page which I forgot to show you.[1] It is in just the shape in which Sweet first deciphered it. Perhaps it would be just as well to keep it in your confidential file.

Will you not be kind enough to have a brief message sent to Page informing him of its safe arrival and saying that I would try to send him some comment on it very soon?

Faithfully Yours,   W.W.

WWTLI (R. Lansing Papers, NjP).
[1] That is, Page's No. 5391 of December 29, 1916.

To Josephus Daniels

CONFIDENTIAL.

My dear Mr. Secretary,   The White House. 11 January, 1917.

There are some aspects of the Grayson matter[1] (for example that the impression had gone abroad that he was to be appointed and our failure to do so would do him great harm professionally) that have come to my knowledge since I saw you, and I am anxious to have another talk with you about it. I hope it is not too late. I do not understand that those assignments have been made.

I am sending you this to head off further action until we can discuss these new phases of the case.

My congratulations to the Governor,[2] and my best wishes for a successful administration. Also my best wishes to Josephus in his new and highly responsible duties.[3]

In haste,   Faithfully Yours,   Woodrow Wilson

WWTLS (J. Daniels Papers, DLC).
[1] That is, Grayson's promotion to the rank of rear admiral.
[2] The new Governor of North Carolina, Thomas Walter Bickett, who was inaugurated on January 11.
[3] Josephus Daniels, Jr., had just been promoted to night city editor of the Raleigh *News and Observer*.

From Charles William Eliot

Dear Mr. President: Cambridge, Mass., 11 January 1917.

The new Institute for Government Research, incorporated in the District of Columbia,[1] has completed an excellent organization, and secured the money needed to pay its operating expenses for a term of years; and is now desiring to begin its helpful work in various Departments of the national Government in Washington.

Its researches are not to be of a critical character, directed to the discovery of errors or abuses, but on the contrary to be directed exclusively to the improvement of existing methods. To this end, its officers and agents will need aid and suggestion from the heads of Departments and Bureaus, and confidential knowledge of the existing structure and methods of the Departments themselves. The function of the Institute is to be a thoroughly friendly and helpful one; and it hopes to be able in time to make constructive suggestions which will prove welcome to all concerned. But before the Institute enters upon this cooperative service, it feels it necessary that the heads of the Departments in Washington should be made aware that you approve and support the intentions and objects of the Institute.

Here are some of the men who are serving as Trustees of the Institute: Presidents Lowell of Harvard, Hadley of Yale, Alderman of Virginia, Goodnow of Johns Hopkins, and Messrs. Martin Ryerson of Chicago,[2] Robert S. Brookings of St. Louis, Frederick Strauss,[3] R. Fulton Cutting, Theodore N. Vail of New York City, and Felix Frankfurter of the Harvard Law School. It is an admirable Board of Trustees.[4]

I am told that a committee from the Institute expects to be received by you next Monday; so I venture to tell you at once by letter what I know and believe about the purposes and hopes of the new Institute.

I am, with great regard,

Sincerely yours,   Charles W. Eliot

P.S. I hope that you will succeed in drawing a useful statement from the Entente Allies, and perhaps later from Germany also.

TLS (WP, DLC).
[1] After some two years of preliminary planning, the Institute for Government Research had been chartered by Congress on March 10, 1916. Forty-three private donors had pledged $160,000 to finance the organization for a five-year period. William Franklin Willoughby, Wilson's successor as McCormick Professor of Jurisprudence and Politics at Princeton University, had been appointed director of the Institute. Eliot well describes the organization's original research objectives and style. The Institute was merged in 1928 with two other organizations founded later by Robert S. Brookings—the Institute of Economics (1922) and the Robert Brookings Graduate School of Economics and Government (1924)—to form The Brookings Institution. See Charles B. Saunders, Jr., *The Brookings Institution: A Fifty-Year History* (Washington, 1966), pp. 12-40.
[2] Martin Antoine Ryerson, philanthropist of Chicago.
[3] Partner in the banking firm of J. & W. Seligman & Co. of New York.
[4] Eliot was himself a member of the board.

Robert Lansing to Walter Hines Page

Washington, January 11, 1917

Your 5391, December 29 midnight received and deciphered. The President will endeavor to send a comment on it very soon.

Lansing.

T telegram (R. Lansing Papers, NjP).

From the Diary of Colonel House

The White House, Washington. January 11, 1917.

We left for Washington this morning and, strangely enough, the train was on time. Grayson met us at the station.

Almost as soon as we arrived, the President and I went into executive session. The President closed his study door so as not to be interrupted and we were at it for about two hours, having more time than usual since the Lansing dinner to the President was not until eight o'clock, while the White House dinner is always at seven.

The President opened the discussion by reading me the "flimsy" containing the Allied response to his note. He then read the address which he had prepared in accordance with our understanding last week.[1] It is a noble document and one which I think will live.

As usual, he struck the wrong note in one instance which he seems unable to avoid. He said "this war was brought on by distrust of one another." I asked him to strike out this sentence, which he did. In another instance he said "both sides say they have no desire to humiliate or destroy the other." I asked him to strike out "humiliate" which he did.

I asked if he had shown the address to Lansing. He replied that he had shown it to no one but that he intended to read it to the Secretary and Senator Stone before cabling it. He thought Lansing was not in sympathy with his purpose to keep out of the war. This discussion came up when I mentioned the difficulty I was having with the Department in getting their permission to send Bernstorff's messages through to Berlin. I told him that Lansing disliked Bernstroff and Bernstorff disliked Lansing, but that the Secretary's grievance was perhaps more just since he thought he had evidence that Bernstorff was trying to have him removed from the State Department. I instanced the many rumors regarding Lansing's resignation appearing from time to time in papers. The President replied, "Bernstorff is not nearly so dangerous to Lansing as he is to himself, for I came very near to asking for his resignation when he gave out the statement regarding the last note."

We decided that his address should be delivered before the Senate and we then discussed how best to get the text of it to the peoples of the belligerent nations. The President is not so much concerned about reaching the governments as he is about reaching the people. He thought it would be best to cable it to Page and have him mail copies to all the other belligerent countries. This, I told him, was impracticable because of the time it would take. I suggested that it be cabled to London, Paris, Berlin and Petrograd letting Gerard give it to the Central Powers and Sharp to the Entente, other than Russia and England where it would be sent direct. This was tentatively agreed upon, although he rather hesitated on account of the cost.

It was also agreed that the Ambassadors should see that the address was published in full in the several belligerent countries. This is important as one can see by reading the text of the address.

When we had finished this subject, I read him some letters which I had just received from Lord Bryce,[2] Noel Buxton,[3] W. H. Buckler[4] etc. etc. He said he did not intend to allow Lansing to make any changes in the address since it was to be delivered before the Senate and was not a note to foreign governments.

When we parted to dress for the Lansing dinner, the President insisted upon my taking the address and reading it over more carefully and returning it to him when we meet tomorrow morning.

[1] Wilson, just this same morning, had completed all but the first page of his "Peace without Victory" speech to the Senate printed at January 22, 1917. Wilson made the deletions suggested by House on this copy. This WWT MS, with the composition date of Jan. 11, 1917, is in WP, DLC. It, in turn, was Wilson's transcript of an undated WWsh draft, entitled "Areopagitica," also in WP, DLC. The shorthand and typed drafts conform almost entirely. There is also a WWT outline of this address with the composition date of Jan. 5, 1917, and entitled "Americanism for the World," in WP, DLC.

[2] J. Bryce to EMH, Dec. 27, 1916, ALS (E. M. House Papers, CtY). Bryce commented on the attitude in England toward Wilson's peace note. He said that there was "some little annoyance" with Wilson's putting England and France "on a par with Germany." Many people were grateful for Wilson's lead toward a league of nations. However, even "peace lovers" like himself believed that this was not the time to open direct negotiations with Germany and Austria. Neither side seemed at all likely to offer terms which the other could accept. Germany, since she dominated Austria and Turkey, could easily state any peace terms that suited her, but the Allies would have difficulty coordinating their individual interests in a unified statement of terms. Germany's good faith was "utterly" distrusted: it was felt that she was simply buying time with talk of peace. However, if Germany really wanted peace, she should state her basis for negotiation, and there would be "no difficulty in conferring."

[3] N. E. Noel-Buxton to EMH, Dec. 28, 1916, ALS (E. M. House Papers, CtY). Buxton wrote that the "undercurrent" of British opinion on Wilson's peace note was "infinitely more friendly than appears in the press." Wilson's insistence that the belligerents state their terms was accepted by the governing classes, "not gladly, but with resignation, not unmixed with some sense of relief."

[4] W. H. Buckler to EMH, Dec. 27, 1916, TLS (E. M. House Papers, CtY). Buckler reported on a conversation that he had just had with James Ramsay MacDonald, former and future leader of the Labour party, and with other members of what Buckler called the "negotiation group" in Parliament. Buckler believed that this group, although it could muster only about forty votes in Parliament, carried weight "by their character." He wrote that they believed that the present was not a good time for Bryce or some other eminent man to go to Washington to discuss peace terms or, conversely, for a "missionary" to go from the United States to England to press for peace discussions. MacDonald,

usually a sworn foe of "secret diplomacy," favored it for discussion of peace terms in order to escape the wrath and extreme demands of the jingoes on both sides of the conflict. MacDonald and his friends believed, said Buckler, that both sides should state terms "frankly but confidentially" to the United States as the "honest broker," but also that "it would save time and misunderstanding if certain bedrock principles (e.g. evacuation of France and Belgium) could be fixed at the outset, no negotiations to begin until this minimum had been accepted by Germany." MacDonald and his friends admitted that the Italian demand for Dalmatia and the Russian demand for the Bosporus were large handicaps on the Entente side and that the services of an "honest broker" might be required to secure the abandonment of these demands. "These men," Buckler concluded, "think that the best way to settle the Balkan tangle would be to lay down certain general principles, racial or geographical, and refer the details to a neutral, preferably American, commission. They are of opinion that Great Britain would not seriously oppose the creation of Polish or Lithuanian States, but that she would strongly and rightly object to the permanent 'corridor' through Serbia eastward."

To Robert Lansing

My dear Mr. Secretary,   The White House. 12 January, 1917.

I saw Senator Stone this evening and he is generously ready to cooperate in our plan.

I am, therefore, sending you with this the address,[1] which I beg that you will set Mr. Sweet to put into code at once for transmission as we planned at the earliest possible hour.

I am sending the original because I do not want to take the time to make a copy and do not wish to have anyone else make one. I would be very much obliged if you would send it back to me when Mr. Sweet has finished putting it in code.

I will then myself make a copy to be sent later to the printer[2] for distribution to our press immediately after I shall have delivered it to the Senate.

Meanwhile I feel that *time is of the essence.*

Faithfully Yours,   W.W.

WWTLI (RSB Coll., DLC).
[1] That is, the WWT copy just referred to. It bears the encoder's marks.
[2] This copy is in WP, DLC.

From Robert Lansing, with Enclosures

PERSONAL AND CONFIDENTIAL:

My dear Mr. President: Washington January 12, 1917.

I enclose to you a copy of a letter from the German Ambassador dated January 10th, transmitting a memorandum upon the subject of armed merchant ships. His letter also requests an appointment to discuss the matter after I have had an opportunity to examine the memorandum.

I conceive that this memorandum is sent at the present time for the purpose of laying the groundwork for excuse in beginning a more drastic submarine campaign. Before seeing the Ambassador, therefore, I would like very much to have your views upon the memorandum, and the policy which should be taken in treating with him on the subject.

Faithfully yours,   Robert Lansing.

TLS (WP, DLC).

ENCLOSURE I

Count Johann Heinrich von Bernstorff to Robert Lansing

My dear Mr. Secretary: Washington, January 10, 1917.

Under instructions of my Government I beg to transmit to you the enclosed memorandum, concerning the new offensive armament of the merchant vessels of our enemies. I am further directed by my Government to discuss this matter with you and to add to the memorandum that it, of course, does not cancel the pledges given by my Government in the note of May 4th, 1916.

I should be very much obliged to you for an appointment as soon as you have been able to study a translation of the enclosed memorandum and are prepared to discuss it with me.

I further beg to enclose a cipher message for the Foreign Office in Berlin, which refers to the above-mentioned question and to your note of December 18th last concerning peace terms. I should be very grateful for kind transmission to Berlin.

With many thanks in advance, I remain,

my dear Mr. Lansing,

Yours very sincerely,   J. Bernstorff.

TCL (WP, DLC).

ENCLOSURE II

The German Government, in its memorandum of February 8, 1916, respecting the treatment of armed merchant ships, adduced a number of arguments for no longer considering merchantmen armed by enemy powers as peaceful vessels of commerce but regarding them as belligerents. Evidence in support of its position has largely increased since that time.

As may be seen from numerous press reports and parliamentary proceedings in enemy countries the number of merchant ships armed with heavy guns has grown considerably larger in the course of the year 1916. The limit of the evolution was placed by responsible statesmen of those countries such as Lord Crewe and Admiral Lacaze[1] at arming all merchant vessels. More particulars will be found in the enclosed resolutions of a conference held at London on December 10 by shipping interests with the assistance of Government representatives. Public opinion in enemy countries has long demanded that guns be mounted at the bow of merchant ships also, as a matter of fact, bow guns have already been found out by German naval craft in the Mediterranean.

That the armament of merchant vessels is not intended for defense only but for attack on the German submarines engaged in cruising warfare is shown by a number of established facts. The secret order of the British Government published with the German memorandum of February 8, 1916, may be here called to mind. In the meanwhile secret admiralty orders, which fully confirm their aggressive character, found on French and Italian merchant vessels, fell into the hands of the German naval forces that captured them. Thus were found on the French Merchant vessel MARIE THERESE on October 29th of this year, confidential instructions of the French Naval Staff, in which the following order is given, among others:

(In French) "Open fire as soon as the submarine is within range."

Like directions are given in the secret instructions found on the SS CITTA DI MESSINA on July 31 of last year.

(In Italian) If a vessel should spy a submarine forward and quite near, either below or in the act of coming to the surface, the best maneuver to make is resolutely to steer for it. By so doing it will either run into the submarine and sink it or at least, as has already happened, the impact will hurl the crew, or part of it, against the sides and disable them; or it will compel the submarine to submerge and come up abaft, which is a very advantageous position. From that moment close watch will have to be kept at the stern, and full speed put on to run away while trying to keep the submarine straight behind if the sea is smooth or not sufficiently rough to prevent the submarine firing to good effect, if taken in front.

In addition the British Government offered through Lord Crewe, on November 15, of last year, in the House of Lords the

---

[1] Marie Jean Lucien Lacaze, French Minister of Marine.

following explanation of the orders issued by it, which excludes every doubt.

(In English) "The German submarine is an enemy which it is permissible and proper to destroy, if you can, at sight." This aggressive intent of enemy merchant vessels has become clearly apparent to German naval warfare. Cases of merchant vessels which without even being attacked, assume an aggressive attitude toward German submarines, are increasing. Evidence of carrying out secret orders is brought forth in the very near past: Thus, the French steamer MISSISSIPPI on November 8 of this year opened artillery fire on a German submarine passing by a long way off that had made no preparation whatever for attack and even had never intended to stop her; likewise, on December 4 of this year, the armed English steamer CALEDONIA attempted to ram a German submarine although here again there had been no intention, let alone any preparation, to attack on the part of the Germans; again, in November, in the English Channel alone, there were recorded three attacks with artillery by unknown enemy steamers on German submarines which had not made the slightest move against the steamers, while six such occurrences took place in the Mediterranean in the past few months.

In this condition of things enemy merchant ships cannot in this particular claim the treatment provided by the rules of customary cruising warfare, they have rather assumed the character of belligerents under the principles announced by the Government of the United States in its memorandum of March 25, 1916,[2] concerning the status of armed merchant vessels.

The American Government starts from the principle that the vessel in neutral waters as well as on the high seas is to be regarded and treated as a warship when, among other things, it is under Commission or orders to engage in attacks. To be sure the American Government presupposes that the character of a belligerent on the high seas is not established on presumption alone but only on conclusive evidence; this conclusive evidence however is so abundant that it leaves no room for doubt. While the American memorandum lays stress on the point that the presence of armament on a merchant vessel does not by itself afford sufficient ground to presume her to be a war vessel, the German Government will point out that the belligerent character of the enemy merchant vessels now armed is denoted, besides the armament itself, by other weighty circumstances among which the above-cited instructions of the enemy Govern-

[2] Printed as an Enclosure with WW to RL, April 24, 1916, Vol. 36.

ments and the actual attacks unexpectedly delivered on German submarines stand foremost.

Further, the American memorandum will only consider Government commissions to attack as existing when they are attended with a threat to punish failure to attack or a grant of prize money when the attack is made. Here again the presumptions are proved to exist. For Captains who failed to carry out their orders to sink German U-boats, although opportunity offered to do so, are punished in England. The DAILY CHRONICLE reports, as early as the 8th of September 1915, that Ernest Alfred Sheldon, of the Royal Naval Reserve, Captain of an armed merchant ship, was dismissed from the Navy by a sentence of the court martial at Devonport for not attacking a German U-boat. It is further known, from the proceedings of the English Parliament, that for the sinking of or effort to sink German submarines not only have rewards been offered by the State but that claims for such rewards have been examined by Government organs and that the reward is given only when the said examination proves satisfactory to the Government. Rewards are granted in various shapes: They consist mainly of money, are equivalent to prize money, or again in awarding a gold watch or conferring distinction in the granting of a military officer's rank. To all this is added that the men detailed from the English Navy or Navy Reserve to man the guns on English merchant vessels on which they are now regularly, do not lose their military character or their being subject to the disciplinary or punitive power of the naval authorities though [to] the commander of the merchant vessel, and so they are, as they were before, part of the British naval forces. Ships so armed, manned and directed are no longer, as the American memorandum requires them to be in order to have their peaceful character recognized, simply armed for self-defense, they rather render, in the manner they are instructed to do, the same services against German submarines, as the war vessels intended to keep off U-Boats, and the circumstance that they are at the same time doing service in a commercial way does not make any difference as to their being treated like belligerents by German submarines.

Finally the American memorandum goes on to say that a warship may properly exercise force to compel a merchant vessel to surrender if the merchant vessel either offers resistance after a summons or, before the summons, uses its armament to keep the enemy at a distance. It then permits the merchant vessel to exercise the right to protect itself when certain of attack by an enemy war ship, as otherwise the exercise of the right would be so restricted as to be made ineffectual; exactly the same grounds support the theory that a war ship that is entitled to exercise the right of capture may use force when certain of attack by an armed enemy merchant vessel.

The German Government has drawn from the evidence hereinabove communicated the conclusion in accord with the American memorandum that armed merchant vessels of its adversaries in this war are to be treated as belligerents. In this it is fully convinced that it is moving on the same grounds as the American Government in Secretary Lansing's note of January 18, 1916, to the English Ambassador. In that note the American Government concurs in the view that at the present time of U-boat warfare any armament of a merchant ship appears to have the character of armament for aggression, for the mounting of large guns on merchant ships could only be explained by an intention to place the merchant vessel at an advantage over the U-boat and thereby prevent warning and searching by the latter.

T MS (WP, DLC).

ENCLOSURE III

(The Following was in English and appended to the above memorandum of Germany)

CONFERENCE

held at Foreign Office London on December 10th, in which Jellicoe, Balfour, Carson,[1] Maclay,[2] Cecil, Stanley[3] representatives of English, Scotch and Canadian shipowners as well as two representatives of France, Russia, Italy participated agreed that all merchant ships are to be armed as follows:

1) British steamers.

Up to 1200 tons and 1000 H.P. with two 2.24 Vickers Maxim guns; from 1200 to 5000 tons and 6000 H.P. two 4.0 Vickers guns, one 2.24 Vickers Maxim gun;

from 5000 to 10,000 tons and 15000 H.P. one 6.0 Armstrong and two 4.0 Vickers guns;

above 10,000 tons and 15000 H.P. two 6.0 Armstrong and two 4.0 Armstrong guns (figures in English inches).

Guns crews to consist of naval-artillery, men with one, two or three officers according to requirement.

2) French ships.

Up to 1200 tons and 1000 HP two 3.7 automatic Creuzot guns;

From 1200 to 5000 tons and 6000 HP two 4.7 and one 3.7 automatic creuzot guns;

from 5000 to 10000 tons and 15000 HP one 15.0 and two 4.7 Creuzot guns;

above 10000 tons two 15.0 and two 4.7 Creuzot guns (figures in centimeters).

3) Russian ships.

Up to 1200 tons and 1000 HP two 1.85 inch Vickers guns;

from 1200 to 5000 tons and 6000 HP two 7.5 centimeter and one 3.7 Creuzot guns;

Above 5000 tons two 15.0 and two 7.5 Creuzot guns.

4) Italian ships.

Up to 1200 tons and 1000 HP two 5.7 Terni guns;

From 1200 to 5000 tons and 6000 HP two 7.6 and one 5.7 Terni guns;

Above 5000 tons two 12.0 and two 7.6 Terny guns (figures in centimeters).

The same regulations for guns, crews and officers apply as for British ships.

T MS (WP, DLC).
[1] Edward Henry Carson, now First Lord of the Admiralty.
[2] Joseph Paton Maclay, shipping controller and head of the recently formed Ministry of Shipping.
[3] Albert Henry Stanley, President of the Board of Trade.

From Robert Lansing, with Enclosure

My dear Mr. President: Washington January 12, 1917.

I beg to enclose herewith a translation of a communication addressed to you by the King of Greece and communicated to the Department by the Greek Chargé d'Affaires, concerning the situation in Greece and commending your recent suggestion to the belligerent governments.

I am, my dear Mr. President,

Faithfully yours,   Robert Lansing

TLS (SDR, RG 59, 763.72119/366, DNA).

E N C L O S U R E

From Constantine

Mr. President: Athens, December 16/29, 1916.

I wish to express to you, Mr. President, my sentiments of sincere admiration for and lively sympathy with the generous initiative you have just taken with a view to trying whether this would not be the propitious time for a negotiation that might bring to an end the sanguinary strife that is raging on earth.

Coming from a Statesman who in so critical a period of human affairs is at the head of the great American republic, your humane efforts prompted by a spirit of high political wisdom and looking to a peace honorable for all, cannot but contribute in an eminent degree to expediting the restoration of normal life and securing in a stable poise of international relations the evolution of Man toward progress in which the United States of America has at all times taken a large part.

Greece, more than any other neutral country, has suffered from that worldwide crisis; she has, without being a belligerent, tasted the horrors of war. For a year and more, after the landing of the allied troops at Salonika, the soil of Macedonia was everywhere invaded from either side by the confronting armies which entered cities and fortresses, removed the authorities and even seized the war material found there. Much earlier, Greek islands and ports were occupied by foreign fleets and that desire of the Powers to insure the safety of the allied armies operating in Macedonia, which by the way nobody in Greece ever dreamed of disturbing, prompted the guarantees that were demanded and yielded, and even measures of violence and coercion after intermeddling with the internal life of the country and actually arresting the motion of constitutional machinery. Our fleet was impounded, our army reduced to a point where it was hardly equal to maintaining order, had further to scatter and withdraw to the South.

A misunderstanding, which we were the first to deplore and which degenerated into a sanguinary conflagration, at the time foreign battalions attempted to occupy heights overlooking the capital, even brought on a bombardment of an open city and of my palace.

At the present time, although the last ultimatum was accepted, a blockade, styled pacific, hems in the Greek islands and coasts, cutting off communication and trade even with neutral countries and exposing the whole population of the country to starvation.

We have proposed a joint commission of inquiry which would have determined the responsibilities and we accepted its verdict in advance. We never received an answer.

And as though all this were not enough, a violent revolt is being grafted on a movement which at the outset assumed the appearance of an intention to take part in the war with hopes to gain the upper hand in the Capital when the landed sailors marched on to Athens after spreading terror in our new provinces where action on our part had been made impossible. The revolt was easily put down thanks to the loyalty of nearly all the Greek people faithfully devoted to their institutions.

Those are the conditions in which your proposition finds my country. The brief and necessarily incomplete picture is not intended as a criticism of the cruel blows at her sovereignty and neutrality of which Greece was forced to bear the effects.

My only wish was to show you, Mr. President, how earnestly the soul of Greece now yearns for peace and how much she appreciates your proposition which comes at so important a stage in the ruin of the bloody worldwide tragedy we are now witnessing.   Constantin R.

T MS (SDR, RG 59, 763.72119/366, DNA).

Two Letters from Newton Diehl Baker

CONFIDENTIAL.

Dear Mr. President: Washington. January 12, 1917.

This morning Mr. William B. Howland called at my office and asked me to present to you the inclosed letter.[1] He has, I believe, presented to you in another connection the general proposition of the preparation of a history of the great war.[2] The particular part of this letter which he consulted me about is in the second paragraph and deals with a desire on his part to have Major General Leonard Wood granted leave of absence to visit certain European belligerent countries for the purpose of consulting with commanders and so to equip himself to act as the American military critic of the history in course of preparation.

I, personally, believe that no such leave of absence ought to be granted to General Wood and that he ought not to be authorized to visit any or all of the belligerent countries at this time.

So far as I could discover, Mr. Howland's purpose was to have General Wood go to England and France. Were he to do so, it seems to me that rumors and suspicions would at once be started to the effect that some sort of military cooperation between the United States and the countries visited by General Wood was secretly in prospect. In view of the fact that we have withdrawn Colonel Kuhn from Berlin, I think it would be unwise to ask the German Government to admit General Wood as a military observer into that country. In view of the fact that he is the senior Major-General of our Army, he could hardly go into Germany without our Government having first requested permission.

This forecast of possible embarrassments may be erroneous, but I confess I have some misgivings about the discretion with which General Wood might conduct himself, and his position in our Army is so high that a certain responsibility would attach to any utterance or action of his, even though his visit were purely for personal reasons and not as an accredited military observer.

If these views meet with your approval, I will write to Mr. Howland and tell him that I have determined against the advisability of any general officer of our Army visiting Europe at this time.

The latter part of Mr. Howland's letter deals with a suggestion to which, doubtless, he wished your personal attention drawn.[3]

Respectfully yours, Newton D. Baker

TLS (N. D. Baker Papers, DLC).

[1] W. B. Howland to WW, Jan. 12, 1917, TLS (N. D. Baker Papers, DLC). It discussed the proposed "History of the Great War, to be written by those participating in its various phases."

[2] See WW to EBG, Aug. 24, 1915 (first letter of that date), Vol. 34. In n. 3 to that letter, "Mr. Howland" is incorrectly identified as Harold Jacobs Howland. It was William Bailey Howland, the publisher of *The Independent*, who presented the project to Wilson.

[3] "A supremely important part of the History, if it is to be carried out in accordance with the broad plans now under consideration, would be a chapter or chapters by the President of the United States relating, as far as they may properly be related, the Steps toward Peace. Your own distinguished part in initiating these steps can only be clearly and fully understood when you are ready to give to the world an account of the events leading to your historic Note to the warring nations, and the results that have followed and will follow until all the nations lay down their arms. If while at the head of the nation it is impossible for you to do this, we may perhaps hope that you will co-operate with a writer of your own selection in giving so much of the story as may properly be told."

My dear Mr. President: Washington. January 12, 1917.

I inclose an Executive Order which, if it meets with your approval, will constitute the Secretary of War, the Secretary of the Interior and the Secretary of Agriculture a board to determine and recommend to you for designation a suitable site or sites for the production of hydroelectric power to carry out the provisions of Section 124 of the National Defense Act.[1]

In the preparation of this Order, I have limited the functions of the board to the selection and recommendation of a site or sites, feeling that you may desire to commit the actual construction of the dam to the control of one Department, and that it may even turn out to be wise to create another and different agency for the operation of the property when the dam is constructed. In other word[s], the power of the board now created will be exhausted when the site is located, and the question of the agency for the execution of the recommendation will remain undetermined.

I have not suggested the inclusion of the Secretary of Commerce on this board, for, while the Bureau of Standards of course contains many scientific men, I do not know of any especial consideration given to the subject of water powers by that Department. If there are reasons why the Secretary of Commerce ought to have been included, I will be very happy to have the Order redrawn. Respectfully yours, Newton D. Baker

TLS (WP, DLC).

[1] That is, to operate a plant or plants to produce nitrate.

From William Phillips

My dear Mr. President: Washington January 12, 1917.

The Secretary has given me the almost overwhelming news that you have decided to promote me to the office of Assistant Secretary of State, and I am at a loss to know how adequately to express my deep appreciation of this evidence of your confidence in me.

I am thoroughly aware of the fact that I do not in the lease [least] deserve the honor which you are conferring upon me; at the same time it is an intense gratification and an inspiration to me to feel that my labors during the last three years have met with your approval. In accepting the high responsibilities which you are entrusting to me, I assure you that I shall not fail to do my utmost to be of help to you and the Secretary in the years to come, which are sure to be full of strain and anxiety for you both.

I beg that you will accept, Mr. President, my heartfelt thanks. Faithfully yours, William Phillips

TLS (WP, DLC).

Paul Ritter to Arthur Hoffmann

111.4 Friede

Herr Bundesrat: Washington, D. C. den 12. Januar 1917.

Seit meiner Depesche vom 5. Januar[1] habe ich Ihnen am 6. dieses Monats gekabelt, dass der Senat, aus bisher nicht klar zu erkennenden Gründen, sich hinter den Praesidenten gestellt und dessen Ersuchen an die Kriegführenden, ihre Friedensbedingungen bekannt zu geben, untertützt hat. Die Resolution lautete:

"Beschlossen, dass der Senat das Ersuchen, welches der Praesident in den diplomatischen Noten vom 18. Dezember an die jetzt im Kriege begriffenen Nationen gerichtet hat, ihre Bedingungen kundzugeben, unter welchen die Friedensfrage erörtert werden könnte, billigt und nachdrücklich gutheisst."[2]

Die Republikaner hatten dieser konstitutionell nicht sanktionierten Haltung des Senats hauptsächlich mit der Begründung entgegenzutreten versucht, dass Wilsons Noten vom 18. Dezember—von welchen der Senat vorher nichts gewusst habe—eine neue auswärtige Politik der Vereinigten Staaten einleiten und die Monroedoktrin gefährden. Die Einmischung Amerikas in europäische Verhältnisse fordere eine Einmischung Europas in amerikanische Verhältnisse geradezu heraus. Von demokratischer Seite wurden diese Befürchtungen mit dem Hinweise darauf zurückgewiesen, dass diese Resolution des Senats nichts anderes bedeute als die Zustimmung in einem einzelnen gegebenen Punkte. Der übrige Inhalt der Wilson'schen Noten werde dadurch weder gebilligt noch missbilligt, auch sei darin keine Zustimmung für eine Abänderung der bisher befolgten Politik zu erblicken.

Am 9. Januar hat mich der Praesident empfangen. Wie Ihnen mein Kabel vom gleichen Tage zeigte, war Herr Wilson überaus liebenswürdig und herzlich, hat mir aber wenig Neues mitgeteilt. Für den Bundesrat sagte er: ["]please express my high appreciation to the Federal Council. His reply made me feel that we are seeking the same object." Von Spanien "das immer den Mund so voll genommen habe," sei er sehr enttäuscht, er hätte nicht erwartet, dass es, statt ihm zu folgen, eigene Wege gehen würde. (Spanien, in seiner Antwort, erwähnt 2 Noten die es von den Vereinigten Staaten erhalten habe, in Wirklichkeit aber war ihm, wie allen andern Staaten, nur eine einzige Note zugedacht, die andere "communication" scheint durch ein Missverständnis des amerik. Geschäftsträgers abgesandt worden zu sein, indem er die ihm zugegangenen Privatinstruktionen, statt sie zu behalten ebenfalls übermittelte).

Aus Berlin habe der Praesident seit der deutschen Note nichts neues mehr vernommen; es sei ihm unerklärlich wie die deutsche Presse Herrn Zimmermann die Worte in den Mund legen könne, dass Herr Wilson genau über die Friedensbedingungen Deutschlands unterrichtet sei. Er sei es nicht. Ebensowenig wisse er was in der längst erwarteten Alliirtennote stehen werde, "ich weiss darüber nicht mehr als jeder Mann auf Strasse" sagte er.

Dass Deutschland in seiner Antwort nicht weitergegangen sei, als bereit Bekanntes zu wiederholen, habe ihn enttäuscht (disappointed).–Ob Gerard wirklich am 7. Januar beim Bankette der amerik. Handelskammer in Berlin so auffallend herzliche Beziehungen zum Ausdruck gebracht habe, wisse er noch nicht. Man habe vom Botschafter soeben den Wortlaut seiner Rede eingefordert. (Dann gab Wilson einige Beispiele wie Citate aus seinen eigenen Reden, aus dem Zusammenhange herausgerissen, speziell in der englischen Presse, zum Hervorrufen falscher Meinungen benützt worden seien). Es kann nicht übersehen werden, fuhr er fort, dass seit den Friedensverhandlungen die oeffentliche Meinung in den Vereinigten Staaten weniger zu Gunsten der Alliirten ist als früher (less in sympathy with the Allies), besonders sei das hiesige Volk nun weniger England freundlich, während es mit dem grossen Frankreich, mit dem es so viele Bande verknüpfen, stets sympathisieren werde.

Als ich merkte, dass die Audienz ohne eine bestimmte Aeusserung seitens des Praesidenten für die Schweiz zu Ende gehen werde, gab ich Herrn Wilson nochmals vom Inhalte Ihres Kabels d.d. 18. Dez. Kenntnis.

Er antwortete, dass er mir nichts in dem von Ihnen gewünschten Sinne mitzuteilen habe (nothing to suggest). Er müsse die Ankunft der alliirten Note abwarten, um sich ein Situationsbild machen zu können. Die Pressgerüchte, dass er eine zweite Note plane ("ich wüsste zur Zeit nicht über was zu schreiben") oder die Entsendung von Colonel House nach Europa plane, bezeichnete er als unbegründet.

Gestützt auf das Vorstehende und unter Bezugnahme darauf, dass in Kongresskreisen gar viel Gewicht darauf gelegt wird, dass der Praesident allein vorgehen und sich nirgends binden möge, glaubte ich, um Ihnen freiere Hand zu geben, im Schlussatz des Kabels vom 9. Januar meinen persönlichen Eindruck, dass Wilson wohl allein zu handeln gedenke, Ausdruck verleihen zu sollen.

Die Congressuntersuchungen (Leak-Inquiry) darüber wessen Indiskretion die Börsenpanik in New-York hervorgerufen hat, gehen immer weiter und machen selbst in den Vereinigten Staaten einen sehr üblen Eindruck. Es sind in den letzten Tagen Staatssekretär Lansing, des Praesidenten Privatsekretär Tumulty, des Praesidenten Schwager Mr. Bolling (ein Börsenmakler)[3] und andere vor die 5 köpfige Untersuchungscommission citiert und erfolglos öffentlich verhört worden. (Beilagen Zeitungsausschnitte).

Die am 1. Januar hier durch die Associated Press veroeffentlichte "message of President Schulthess to the American People" ist sehr beachtet worden.[4] Ich habe darüber freudige Aeusserungen sogar von Schweizern im fernen Californien erhalten. Viel amerik. Blätter brachten das Bild unseres Praesidenten.

Gestern haben die N. Y. Zeitungen ein Interview General Wille's an den "Matin" d.d. Paris 9. Januar nachgedruckt, besagend, dass die Schweiz zum Kampf für die Neutralität bereit sei (Beilage).[5]

Das Vorstehende war bereits geschrieben, als die heutigen Blätter den Wortlaut der alliirten Antwort d.d. Paris 10. Januar brachten. Ich werweise auf die beiliegenden Ausschnitte.

Genehmigen Sie, Herr Bundesrat, die Versicherung meiner ausgezeichneten Hochachtung.[6]   P. Ritter

TLS (E2000 Washington, No. 34, Swiss Federal Archives).

[1] It stated that Wilson had ordered absolute silence on current negotiations and, more than ever, held policy in his own hands, primarily because of the leakage of secrets to the stock market. The dispatch mentioned tension between the White House and the State Department, conflicting news reports, replies or lack of replies from other neutral governments to Wilson's initiative, and possible sites (the Netherlands or Switzerland) for a peace conference. Ritter also reported that Tumulty had said that Wilson would see him "as soon as he had a minute's time." P. Ritter to A. Hoffmann, Jan. 5, 1917, TLS, E2300 Washington, No. 34, Swiss Federal Archives.

[2] On a motion by Senator Hitchcock, the Senate adopted this resolution on January 4 by a vote of forty-eight to seventeen. 64th Cong., 2d sess., *Senate Journal*, Jan. 4, 1917, p. 54.

[3] Richard Wilmer Bolling, of F. A. Connolly & Co. of Washington. Bolling retired from the company on February 14, 1917.

[4] In his message, Edmund Schulthess said: "The oldest democracy in the world sends fraternal wishes to her great sister republic, to the American people and to their illustrious President. Switzerland hopes to be able to salute with the United States the coming [of] peace in the year which commences." *New York Herald*, Jan. 1, 1917.

[5] The enclosure is missing. General Ulrich Wille's remarks are reported in the *New York Times*, Jan. 10, 1917.

[6] Ritter's telegraphic summary of the above dispatch is P. Ritter to the Swiss Foreign Ministry, Jan. 9, 1917, T telegram (E2300, No. 34, Swiss Federal Archives).

T R A N S L A T I O N

III.4 Peace

Mr. Federal Councilor: Washington, January 12, 1917.

Following my dispatch of January 5, I cabled you on January 6 that the Senate, for reasons not yet clear, placed itself behind the President and supported his efforts to get the belligerents to state their peace conditions. The resolution reads: "Resolved, That the Senate approves and strongly endorses the request by the President in the diplomatic notes of December 18 to the nations now engaged in war, that those nations state the terms upon which peace might be discussed."

The Republicans sought to oppose this position of the Senate, which has no constitutional sanction, mostly on the ground that Wilson's note of December 18—of which the Senate knew nothing in advance—introduced a new United States foreign policy and endangered the Monroe Doctrine. America's meddling in European relations would provoke Europe's meddling in American relations. These fears were rejected by the Democratic side with the comment that the Senate resolution meant no more than agreement on a single specific point. It neither approved nor disapproved of the remaining content of Wilson's note, and the resolution implied no agreement on changing the policy previously followed.

The President received me on January 9. As indicated in my cable of the same day, Mr. Wilson was very kind and cordial but told me little new. For the Federal Councilor he said: "Please express my high appreciation to the Federal Council. His reply made me feel that we are seeking the same object." Wilson was very disappointed with Spain, "which always talks so big." He had not expected that, instead of following him, it would go its own way. (Spain, in its reply, mentioned receiving two notes from the United States, but in fact only one note was sent to it, as to other states, and the other "communication" seems to have been delivered through a misunderstanding of the American Chargé d'Affaires, who sent along his accompanying private instructions.)

From Berlin, the President has received nothing new since the German note; he could not explain why Mr. Zimmermann had led the German press to say that Mr. Wilson was accurately informed of Germany's peace conditions. He was not. Just as little did he know what would be in the long-awaited Allied note. "I know no more about it," he said, "than any man in the street."

He was disappointed that Germany in its reply had gone no further than to report what was already known. He did not know whether Gerard on January 7 at the banquet of the American chamber of commerce in Berlin had actually spoken of such surprisingly cordial relations. The text of the Ambassador's speech had been requested right away. (Wilson then gave several examples of quotations from his own speeches, taken out of context, especially in the English press, that had been used to suggest false meanings.) We cannot overlook, he went on, that since the peace negotiations began, public opinion in the United States was less in sympathy with the Allies than before, and people here were less friendly toward England, whereas for the most part they remained sympathetic toward great France, with which there were so many ties.

When I perceived that the conversation would come to an end without any specific word from the President for Switzerland, I once again spoke to him about the content of your cable of December 18.

He replied that he had nothing to suggest along the lines you wished. He must await the arrival of the Allied note in order to form a view of the situation. He termed groundless the press rumors that he planned a second note ("at present I don't know what to write") or that he planned to send House to Europe.

On the basis of the foregoing and bearing in mind that congressional circles place very much stress on the fact that the President wishes to go alone and not commit himself anywhere, I thought, in order to give you a freer hand, I should, in the last sentence of my cable of January 9, express my personal impression that Wilson indeed plans to act alone.

The congressional investigation (leak-inquiry) to find out whose indiscretion led to the panic in the New York stock market still goes on and makes a very bad impression, even in the United States. In the last few days, Secretary of State Lansing, the President's private secretary Tumulty, the President's brother-in-law, Mr. Bolling (a stockbroker), and others have been called before the five-member investigating committee and have testified publicly without effect. (Newspaper clippings attached.)

The message of President Schulthess to the American people, published here on January 1 through the Associated Press, has been widely noted. I have received favorable comments even from Swiss people in far-off California. Many American papers printed the picture of our President.

Yesterday the New York papers reprinted from the Paris *Matin* of January 9 an interview with General Wille, which stated that Switzerland was ready to fight for its neutrality.

The above dispatch was already written when today's papers brought the text of the Allied reply, dated January 10 at Paris. I refer to the enclosed clippings.

Accept, Mr. Federal Councilor, the assurances of my highest respect.   P. Ritter

From the Diary of Colonel House

January 12, 1917.

I returned to the White House and found the President had been waiting for me. He had written another page to his address since last night. It is to be a prelude mentioning the receipt of the Allies' response to his last note. He has done it marvellously well and it tones in perfectly with the balance of the address.

He mentioned Page's resignation again and of his determination to accept it. He expressed the opinion that Page would come home disgruntled and would show his true state of mind through the pages of the World's Work. I did not believe he would do this as there would be no excuse for such action. The President had not made up his mind whom he would send in Page's place but I think he will offer it to Cleveland H. Dodge.

We discussed Gerard's latest indiscretion in his speech in Berlin.[1] At the time I talked to the President, they had not received a reply giving the text of Gerard's speech, but later, Lansing had it. In some ways it was as reported, in others, not.

Since we were going to lunch at the Wallace's I bade the President goodbye, for he has a Cabinet meeting at 2.30 which would be in session when I returned. He asked when I expected to come back, and if there was anything that would call me over again soon. I told him we expected to go to Texas for a week sometime this month. He hoped I would not go before he made his address and the echoes from it had come back. I promised not to do so.

In discussing foreign appointments he thought we ought to get the best man possible for Argentine since it was the only one of the A.B.C. Powers working cordially with us. . . .[2]

We returned to the White House where Mrs. Wilson was awaiting me. We had a long talk about affairs in general. She was disturbed about the Grayson-Daniels controversy. Daniels placed Grayson's appointment before the President in such a way that the President had to decline to advance him to the rank of Rear Admiral. Mrs. Wilson told me the entire story, how Grayson had been pushing for nearly two years to have this law passed in order to get the appointment. He enlisted her aid even before she had ever met the President. She feels, as we all do, that Grayson has been pushing his own fortunes in an indelicate and objectionable way. She said the President was so disturbed over it that he lay awake nearly all night. He feels that he should refuse Grayson this advancement.

I told Mrs. Wilson of my talks with Grayson and what I was doing to try to straighten the matter out. She said, since we last talked together, the President had told her about the Tumulty incident, and he thought Tumulty would resign on the fourth of March.[3] The little circle close to the President seems to have dwindled down to the two of us, Mrs. Wilson and myself.

¹ Gerard had spoken at a dinner given in his honor by the American Association of Commerce and Trade of Berlin on January 6. Acording to the report of his speech sent out by the Overseas News Agency, quoted in the *New York Times*, January 9, 1916, Gerard made the following remarks: "Never since the beginning of the war have the relations between Germany and the United States been as cordial as now. I have brought back an olive branch from the President—or don't you consider the President's message an olive branch? I personally am convinced that as long as Germany's fate is directed by such men as my friend, the Chancellor, and Dr. Hefferich and Dr. Wolf, by Admirals von Capelle, Haltzendorff, and von Mueller; by Generals von Hindenburg and Ludendorff, and last, but not least by my friend Zimmermann, the relations between the two countries are running no risk." "Dr. Hefferich" was Karl Helfferich, Imperial Secretary of the Treasury; "Dr. Wolf" was Wilhelm Solf, Colonial Secretary; and Admiral "Haltzendorff" was Henning von Holtzendorff, head of the Admiralty. All of these persons and the others mentioned in this report, except Helfferich, have been identified in this series.

These remarks stirred much comment in both the German and the Allied press and prompted the State Department to ask Gerard on January 8 to send a full text of his speech. According to a news report in the *New York Times*, Jan. 14, 1917, the full text sent to the State Department confirmed the accuracy of the press reports. The full text was not made public.

² As it turned out, Frederic Jesup Stimson remained as Ambassador to Argentina until the end of the Wilson administration.

³ See JPT to WW, Nov. 18, 1916, Vol. 38.

To Newton Diehl Baker

My dear Mr. Secretary,   The White House. 13 January, 1917.

I quite agree with your conclusions. Moreover, I think that it would be quite improper to cooperate in a publishing scheme by practically detailing a General of the army to go abroad in its behalf. It is a characteristic piece of impudence on Mr. Howland's part.

Personally I have no confidence either in General Wood's discretion or in his loyalty to his superiors.

Faithfully Yours,   Woodrow Wilson

WWTLS (N. D. Baker Papers, DLC).

From Edward Mandell House

Dear Governor: New York. January 13, 1917.

Sir William Wiseman was here today. He tells me that there is an insistent demand in England that some sort of propaganda be started in America to properly put their case before our people.

A committee has been tentatively formed, all of whom are more of [or] less antagonistic to you. I advised against the entire procedure and Wiseman personally agreed with me. He will discourage them, and if pressure is brought from England upon him to do this work it is his purpose to place it in the hands of people friendly to your administration.

He also proposed having a propaganda started in both England and France, under the auspices of the same committee, to present the American side.

Wiseman said if he could be told a few days in advance of any move you intended to make, he could arrange for the Foreign Office to call in the newspaper representatives and have them take a sympathetic attitude. He thought the papers would much more readily respond to a request from their own Foreign Office if done in this way than if the news came from This side suddenly and without explanation.

When he was speaking, it occurred to me that it might be well to tell him a day or two in advance of your next move and have him arrange as indicated. What do you think of this?

I am sending you a copy of a letter which comes to me from Robert Donald of the Chronicle.[1]

I am also sending a memorandum which Whitehouse has sent for your information.[2]

Your affectionate,   E. M. House

I never enjoyed a visit with you both more than the last one.

TLS (WP, DLC).

[1] R. Donald to EMH, Dec. 15, 1916, TCL (WP, DLC). Donald, editor of the London *Daily Chronicle*, wrote to introduce Frank Dilnot, who was the newly appointed chief correspondent of the newspaper in the United States. Donald had a general comment also: "I look forward to America playing a great part in world politics in the near future, and Mr. Wilson, whom, as you know, we have always supported, will, I believe, be the greatest President that America has ever had."

[2] J. H. Whitehouse, "Moderate Opinion in England," Jan. 12, 1917, TS MS (WP, DLC). Whitehouse described various expressions of sentiment in favor of a moderate, negotiated peace, many of them inspired by Wilson's peace note. He also listed newspapers and magazines which he considered "sound" on this question.

From Joseph Patrick Tumulty, with Enclosure

Dear Governor: The White House. January 13, 1917

I hope you will read every word of this letter. From my conversation with you the other evening, you will at once recognize its importance. From all I know of Mr. Easby-Smith, he is a thoroughly honorable man.   J.P.T.

Thank you very much for letting me see this.   W.W.

TL (WP, DLC).

ENCLOSURE

From James Stanislaus Easby-Smith

Sir: Washington, D. C. January 13, 1917.

I am constrained to protest to you, respectfully but most earnestly, against indignities and outrages, illegal if not indeed criminal in their nature, which have been and are being perpetrated against me and other honest and reputable citizens and lawyers of this community by employees of the Department of Justice and subordinates of the Attorney-General, who are habitually engaged in practices which are so iniquitous, so inquisitorial and so subversive of all the principles of justice that they would not be tolerated in any civilized country or community except this.

In order that you may understand the full measure of the indignity to which I am being subjected I state the following facts concerning myself:

I am a practising lawyer in this city. I have been a member of the bar for twenty-two years, and am now President of the Bar Association of the District of Columbia. I reside here with my wife and children. My personal and professional character and reputation are unassailable and above reproach. I have served the United States under Attorneys-General Olney, Harmon, Griggs and Knox[1] (all of whose warm friendship and esteem I enjoy) in various capacities; including Pardon Attorney in the Department of Justice, Assistant United States Attorney for the District of Columbia and Special Assistant to the Attorney-General.

My grandfather[2] was a resident of this city and held honorable positions by appointment of two of your predecessors. My father was a lawyer, a Congressman and a judge.[3]

I am a life-long democrat, was a delegate to the Baltimore and St. Louis conventions, and for more than twenty years I have, in every biennial national election contributed, to the extent of my ability, in money, time and services, to the success of the democratic party.

All these things are well known to many officials of the Department of Justice, but are particularly well known to one Bruce Bielaski, chief of the detective force of that Department.

Notwithstanding which Mr. Bielaski and his subordinates have tapped the telephone wires of myself and of other reputable lawyers and citizens; and his subordinate detectives have taken in shorthand and have transcribed for the records of the Department of Justice, telephone conversations thus overheard by them.

It seems sufficient only to call to your attention, without unnecessary comment, the important and confidential character of the communications which a lawyer has with his clients, his associates, and others; and the private nature of the conversations which he has with his social friends and the members of his family.

Upon learning that my telephone was tapped, having been assured by the Telephone Company that this was being done without its knowledge or consent, and having heard that the detectives of the Department of Justice had admitted tapping the wires of other lawyers, I immediately called upon Mr. Bielaski and demanded to know for what reason and by what right he committed this offense against me and my rights.

He denied that my telephone was or ever had been tapped; but at the same time admitted and boasted that he had tapped the telephones of other lawyers, that he did this without the knowledge or consent of the Telephone Company, and that he had experts with instruments by which this was easily done.

I thereupon demanded of the Telephone Company that it make an investigation, which it did; the result being that my "circuit," that is the two wires through which my telephone is served, was found to be tapped in or connected with other wires leading into buildings occupied by employees of the Department of Justice. This had been done surreptitiously and without the knowledge or consent of the Telephone Company, which says that it has no means of preventing this invasion of my rights.

My immediate intention was to resort to the courts, and by the process of injunction prevent this unwarranted invasion of my private rights and this indignity to myself; but have hesitated to do so in the fear that the resulting publicity might embarrass this administration, for which I entertain sincere loyalty, and in the hope that a report of the facts to you may bring about a redress of this evil.

I shall not complain to the Attorney-General because I cannot hope for redress from an official who permits his subordinates to commit these offenses.

If you desire the same I can furnish you with the facts and proof that this detective bureau of the Department of Justice is habitually engaged in the nefarious business of enticing men into the commission of crime, and that Mr. Bielaski (who is a republican holdover) and his subordinates very recently have attempted, with the use of $1500., to entice into crime one of your appointees and thereby discredit your administration. They have also tapped the wires of other prominent democrats who are holding office by your appointment.

The pernicious practices which I have mentioned were initiated under the administration of President Roosevelt, and unfortunately have continued and have grown in infamy since that time; and are now a stench in the nostrils of all those citizens who have knowledge of them.

I tender myself ready to furnish complete proof of all the statements I have made.

Respectfully yours,   James S. Easby-Smith[4]

TLS (WP, DLC).

[1] Richard Olney, Judson Harmon, John William Griggs, and Philander Chase Knox.

[2] William Easby.

[3] William Russell Smith.

[4] The Editors have found no evidence as to what, if anything, was done about this case. There were no further letters about this subject from Easby-Smith. However, he continued friendly correspondence with Wilson and Tumulty about other matters.

James Viscount Bryce to Edward Mandell House

Forrest Row, Sussex.

Dear Colonel House: January 14, 1917.

As I promised, I send you some further remarks on the situation. The President will I trust feel that the Allies response to his invitation to state terms has been met in a frank spirit and is a tribute to our conviction that his action was prompted by a large minded desire to clear the air and bring the possibilities of peace somewhat nearer.

It was not easy to state terms, because the German Government will doubtless use our statement to stiffen up their own people into more persistence and more ferocity. We may therefore suffer by encountering a fiercer resistance. But we have taken the risk, appreciating neutral feeling; and I think this action of the Allies will be appreciated in America.

As I wrote you before, there is no likelihood that the German Government will think of negotiating upon our basis. They know they cannot win, but they are too much afraid of their own Jingoes, and afraid of facing the disappointment of their own people whom they have deluded with hopes of victory. Our note may do something to dispel these illusions.

The Note expresses the practically unanimous sentiment of England. Out in Illinois and Nebraska, people dont seem to realize what we feel, what is the anger and horror with which the long series of German governmental aims has filled us. It is not the

German people that we regard as enemies but the German military caste and the abominable methods by which it has prosecuted the war, culminating in the Belgian Deportations and the Armenian Massacres.

These must be stamped with the brand of defeat. Nothing less will discredit them with the German people, and bring that people to a saner mind. When Prussian Militarism has been discredited at home, and Germany brought nearer to a democratic government, she can enter and ought to enter, with a League of Peace. Till this happens, she could not do so with any likelihood of her becoming a trustworthy member of it, prepared to abide by her engagements.

The President has rightly seen, and the Allied Note admits, that the highest ultimate aim for the belligerents and for all mankind, is to have a permanent security for peace after this war has ended: and he has rendered an inestimable service in leading the American people to the idea that they will serve the world, and incidentally their own security also by bringing about a general combination for peace, and by joining in it, though such a combination cannot be formed till after the war, because the conditions precedent to a permanent security will only then have been determined. The President's advocacy of it and the Allies response have now made it a practical suggestion, and we here can now proceed to familiarize our own people with the idea, and can consider what the main lines of such a scheme ought to be.

I am glad to hear this is being already done in America. It will of course take time to get your people to agree to renounce their isolation, but the popular response to the President's appeal seems to have been so far satisfactory; and I can hardly think that the Senate would refuse to follow his lead when they saw he had the people behind him. The more the object is studied, the greater will appear to be its value for mankind.

I am   Very sincerely yours,   James Bryce.

TCL (WP, DLC).

Sir Cecil Arthur Spring Rice to the Foreign Office

Washington Jan: 14th [1917].

No. 94. Well informed person[1] who has access to President tells me effect on public opinion of Allies' Note is decidedly good.

Following is result of conversations with President Wilson and represents view which it is desired should be conveyed to you. In at least two clear cases German pledges had been violated and there was prospect of further violations. Only course open to President was to ascertain whether objects of Allies were such as to justify United States Government in engaging in the war, should war become inevitable, on their side. If their objects are such as if attained to give assurance of permanent peace and not leave behind intolerable sense of wrong, then United States Government can with a clear conscience join in such a contest with such objects. If objects are aggressive then United States Government must keep out of the war at all costs.

He was convinced Germany could not state terms which would at once satisfy public opinion in Germany and here.

Terms of Allies on the whole seem to be reasonable.[2] Notice to Turkey to quit is certainly popular. Germany has failed to satisfy popular opinion.

Thus present reception is on the whole satisfactory but President's reserved character makes it impossible for him to speak his mind and as he is a good deal in advance of popular opinion reserve is imperative.

A personal message from State Department assures me that we have practically no open questions in dispute with United States now except a few shipping cases.

T telegram (FO 371/3075, No. 11062, pp. 413-14, PRO).
  [1] Colonel House. House left no record of this conversation.
  [2] Compare this statement with House's statement concerning Wilson's estimate of the Allied terms as reported in J. H. von Bernstorff to T. von Bethmann Hollweg, Jan. 27, 1917.

Remarks at a Press Conference

[Jan. 15, 1917]

Mr. President, is there anything you can tell us about peace today?

No, sir. I think you know as much as I do.

Mr. President, there seem to be different interpretations placed on your idea for a league to enforce peace. Are you free to discuss that at all in any way?

It is not in shape to be discussed. That would entirely depend upon the course of events and the terms of the peace by which the war was concluded.

It has been said that you would not favor a league that would enforce it through the use of the military and naval parts of it.

There are so many people speaking for me that I wouldn't like to be held responsible. I have stated often exactly what I believed. I haven't altered my opinion in the least.

Mr. President, the substance of a letter to Senator Shafroth written by yourself on the constitutionality of the thing has been
made public.[1] We have been wondering if we can get the text
of that letter upon the powers of the Senate in connection with
it?

> I haven't written any such letter.

Isn't that with reference to this plan of Oscar Crosby,[2] which
would deprive the Congress of the power of making war—the
Shafroth resolution?

> Well, I simply don't remember ever having expressed my
> opinion about it to anybody. There must be some mistake
> somewhere. Of course nobody can deprive the Congress of
> the right to declare war. Since the Constitution confers it,
> nobody can take it away.

It requires a constitutional amendment?

> Yes. I understood that he had submitted such an amend-
> ment. I don't remember expressing any opinion about it to
> anybody. There must be some mistake somewhere.

Mr. President, the resolution now in the Judiciary Committee
of the Senate, introduced by Senator Walsh, to have cloture in the
Senate—have you any opinion on that resolution?

> Well, I stand on the party platform which calls for a reason-
> able restriction of unlimited debate in the Senate.

Have you any opinion as to Senator Walsh's theory that the
Senate shall terminate a session on March 5 and is not a continuing body?

> No, that is a new idea to me. I am not ready to express an
> opinion about that, even if it were any business of mine.

Mr. President, I just want to ask for some information about the
use of the information that comes out here. I was absent the
first two conferences. I want to get it clearly in mind. Of course,
there are various ways by which it can be used, and direct quotation, I understand, has always been barred. And there is a way
of a direct description, that either the President said or the President told correspondents. There is also a way of saying the President's opinion is so and so. I just wonder which of those was the
proper way?

> I regard all those as quotations and as unjustified. I under-
> stand the object of this conference to be for you men to find
> out what I am thinking about and not make direct use of it.
> Of course, there are so many things you ask me that I would
> have to be extremely guarded about if I did not go on that
> theory. Because I think it is imperative, just at this critical
> period of our affairs, that I say, myself, anything I have to

say and don't say it through another medium. I am frankly astonished at the things I see in the papers every day—what I think and am going to do.

It is pretty important to have a definite understanding on that.

That is my understanding: No direct use is to be made of this. It is for the guidance of your own minds in making up your stories, and it is not legitimate to say that the "President thinks that," or that the "President intimated that," or the "President intends the other." I think that is quite a part of the understanding. . . .

Mr. President, take, for example, this matter that you spoke about a moment ago, of your attitude towards the cloture rule in the Senate. Now, in writing a story today on that subject, wouldn't we be permitted to say that the President regards this as a matter that comes within the scope of the party platform?

Well, now, you see, that is an excellent example to take, because it involves things that I have constantly in mind. When a matter comes up in the Senate, for example, like this, that concerns the Senate's own rules and the Senate's own business, senators rather resent gratuitous opinions from this end of the avenue. What I mean to say, they are often, they are generally kind enough to consult me and find out themselves what my attitude is. But until they do, for me to volunteer an opinion sometimes complicates matters and but irritates instead of assisting them. And my wish would be to exercise the most punctilious courtesy towards both the houses and not, for example, condemn anything they were doing and hold back opinion upon what some individual member had proposed until my cooperation had come about in a more regular way.

I think you see the delicate position I am placed in by things of that sort. Now, having said that; I am in favor of the position of the party platform. I think that can be taken for granted, that I feel bound by that. I am always in favor of that, and when that does not depend on my initiative, I have no initiative in the matter. I can only support it when my support is asked, or is of any use to anybody.

Mr. President, what I had in mind is different, that from the standpoint of the public or readers, whom we are trying to serve, there are certain matters which come up from time to time where the views of the President are very important. Now, we come to you and get your views. Now, to what extent, if any, can we make use of the information we get in that way?

Well, I admit that that is a difficult question. In ordinary times, when our affairs are domestic affairs, we could exercise a great deal of freedom about that, but just now such—let me say such excessive—importance is attached to the President's opinions that a thing offhand may have an effect that was not contemplated beforehand. I speak, of course, offhand here, without any calculation as to the general effects upon the opinion of the country, and I just don't know what answer to make to that.

I think, to go back to your other question, you could say this, that it can always be taken for granted that the President will support what is in the party platform. I think I have proved that that has been my bulwark in the matter of woman suffrage, because I have pointed out to the ladies that my personal opinion, and wish for, is in favor of suffrage soon, and is not a highly harming factor. Inasmuch as I am considered a party leader, I have got to take what my party says. I tried to get more than I did get in the St. Louis convention in the platform, and I have to be satisfied for the time being with what I got then. And I pointed out to them that there never has been a Wilson policy. All the policies I have urged upon Congress have been policies that were contained in the party platform, so that I could show chapter and verse for it, with one exception, and that was when I urged the repeal of the tolls exemption. And then I took the position, which I always take, that a treaty of the United States takes precedence in importance and authority over the party platform. When the country has given its solemn promise about anything, that concludes it until the promise is altered by a change in the treaty. But that was such plain sailing that I don't think it constitutes an exception. That was not a Wilson policy. That was the policy of the country embodied in a treaty which the Constitution itself says is part of the supreme law of the land. So there "ain't been no such animal" as a Wilson policy.

Are we to understand, Mr. President, that you don't want us to say that you said that?

Said what? What I have just said now? I don't care how you wish to call that general discourse. I have said that before, but don't apply it to woman suffrage. I am in trouble enough.

Mr. President, several weeks ago, you said that you were opposed to an issue of bonds except in cases of special emergency. Now, in using that, is it proper to say that the President is opposed to using the Wilson authority?

Well, that is another case of domestic etiquette, so to speak. The houses are in some trouble—very deep trouble, I believe—about making up a revenue bill. I mean, there is a great variety of opinion. The minute you tax any one thing, you affect one part of the country more than another, and the representatives of that part of the country aren't very happy about that suggestion. When you suggest something else, another part of the country may be hit harder, and the representatives of that part aren't very happy about it. So there is general anxiety. I say this with some hesitation, that there is a general disinclination to tax anything. They would rather find things for which it is appropriate to issue bonds and postpone the responsibility of imposing taxes. Now, I have taken the position, in private, when consulted by members of both houses, that I thought the only suitable objects for a bond issue were permanent improvements. One generation shouldn't be asked to pay for an unexpected emergency that rendered the expenditures asked for of long standing. For example, suppose it is something that calls for large expenditures at this moment and you put taxes on enough to pay for those, then, when the emergency is over you have got too many taxes. You have provided for the excise taxes, and the taxes are permanent while the expenses are temporary. Those are legitimate objects of a bond issue. But aside from those general principles, the best thing to do is to wait until you have got a bill and then comment on it. We haven't got a bill yet.

Mr. President, have you noticed anything that was disagreeable to you in the way of inferences? . . .

About those things such as you refer to, there is no trouble, and I haven't found anything by way of direct or indirect quotes of myself that has irritated me. What has irritated or has distressed me, as I have said several times, is this. For example, I read in one of the papers the other day, a very responsible paper, too, that the President, it was understood in high quarters—I am sure you know the phrases—that the President was looking around to see what should be his next move in regard to peace, and that he had summoned Colonel House from New York, which I did not. Colonel House came down to take dinner. He was summoned by a gastric summons and not by me. And that I had been consulting with the Secretary of State, and that there was a grand pow-wow as

to what would be our next step. All of that was pure fiction.
Nothing of the kind was happening. I haven't summoned
anybody, and I haven't consulted anybody since I last saw
you, for example, as to what our next step should be with
regard to a peace move. That does make me a little hot under
the collar, because it is really interfering with public affairs
by making the government seem mindless. You don't simply
cater to American audiences. These impressions get to other
parts of the water. But those impressions get abroad. They
are carried by the general press associations, and then the
foreigner says, "Well, what in thunder is this man going to
do next? Isn't he ever going to mind his own business?" I
am stating it from their point of view. "What monkey
wrench is he going to throw into the machinery next?"
That is the kind of irritation—and, if I were in their places,
I would be very much irritated. I would say, "Why doesn't
he mind his own business?" Now, I am trying to mind my
own business, and I haven't your cooperation. That is the
trouble. There wasn't any quotation from the President in
these things. There couldn't be. I hadn't said anything, for
the natural reason that there wasn't anything in my mind
to say. I try not to be the quicker one. James Russell Lowell
said, "If you haven't anything to say, then don't say it."
It is an admirable example to follow in public affairs.

Mr. President, here is another concrete case of confusion—the
Secretary of State's other statement, that our situation is critical,
that we are near the verge of war. Can you inform as to whether
you are initiating any measures for national defense?

No, I am not.

You wouldn't want us to say that you were?

You see, Senator Chamberlain has a bill,[3] for example,
which is very much discussed, and I am waiting for that
plan to be a discussable plan before forming an opinion
about it. But it didn't come on my initiative and, therefore,
I am not initiating anything new.

May I ask you, Mr. President, if you had given consideration any
time to a suggestion for a referendum in the District of Columbia
on matters of great importance here—on local matters? . . .

You see, there is no voting machinery in the District of
Columbia. It would have to be created. There are some practical difficulties about it. Of course, the District of Columbia
is an exceptional community, since so very large a proportion of the people here are governmental employees.

Can you say anything, Mr. President, about Mexico?

> No. The joint commission is, I believe, meeting today, or is to meet today. And I thought it was a week ago. And I was expecting to have their recommendation before now, but I will meet them, I understand, as soon as they meet.

Do you know, Mr. President, whether it is a fact that the War Department did instruct General Funston to pay over some money to the Carranza authorities to get the body of that soldier of the Fifth Infantry who was killed on the other side?

> I don't know. I doubt very much it is true.

Mr. President, have you selected a Tariff Commission?

> I have selected all but one man. I can't find him yet. He is in the woods yet.

You are not prepared to tell?

> I would rather tell as a whole. It is always a question of a combination, since I am definitely instructed that not more than three of them are to be of the same party.

Anything on the railroad situation, Mr. President?

> Nothing new, sir.

Mr. President, is the so-called compulsory investigation bill an essential part of the railroad program?

> Oh, yes.

Is the feature against strikes and lockouts pending investigation an essential feature of that bill?

> Yes. Of course, you understand this. I am always ready to accept anything better. There are imperfect remedies. If there are new railroad remedies, I am amenable to a partial plan rather than an entire remedy. But it is the best thing. I say I think I am from Missouri with regard to anything else.

Nothing better has been shown?

> Nothing better has been shown. I am perfectly willing to accept anything better.

You expect it to pass substantially in that form at this session?

> Yes.

Mr. President, the Federal Reserve Board has sent the Congress a series of proposed amendments to the Federal Reserve Act.[4] The most important of these deal with the supply of gold in the United States. Have you had an opportunity to study those amendments?

> No, I have not.

Mr. President, have you formed any opinion about the public buildings bill, the rivers and harbors bill?

No. Those are things that I always wait for until they get to me.

JRT transcript (WC, NjP) of CLSsh (C. L. Swem Coll., NjP).
  [1] WW to J. F. Shafroth, Jan. 3, 1917.
  [2] That is, Oscar Terry Crosby. See n. 1 to the letter just cited.
  [3] See n. 1 to the press conference printed at Dec. 18, 1916.
  [4] The Federal Reserve Board on January 13, 1917, transmitted to the chairmen of the House and Senate committees on banking and currency a number of proposed amendments to the Federal Reserve Act. They were inspired by the great changes in the financial conditions of the country brought about by the war and were intended primarily to increase the control of the board over the supply of gold in the United States. There is a detailed discussion of the proposals in the *New York Times*, January 14, 1917, sect. 7. The amendments failed to pass before the expiration of the Sixty-fourth Congress on March 3, 1917. *Ibid.*, March 5, 1917.

From Edward Mandell House

Dear Governor: New York. January 15, 1917.

In a conference with Bernstorff this morning he authorized me to say to you (1) His Government are willing to submit to ?1 *arbitration* as a means of peace.

(2) They are willing to enter a league of nations for the enforcement of peace and for the limitation of armaments both on land and sea.

? (3) They propose that you submit a *program* for a peace conference and they agree to give it their approval.

(4) To show their good will they are willing to sign the arbitration treaty immediately (that is the so called Bryan Treaty.)

In addition to this, the Chancellor told Bernstorff to say that Germany's terms are very moderate and they did not intend to take any part of Belgium.

This was the only definite statement as to actual terms made, but Bernstorff thought we could count upon their being willing to agree to the formation of an independent Poland and Lithuania. However, he believed they would insist upon the Bulgarian and Austrian frontiers touching. This would require a very small strip of territory, but is in line with what I thought they would demand—that is an uninterrupted route from Berlin to Constantinople.

Bernstorff said he believed if Lloyd George had stated that there should be *mutual*[2] restoration, reparation and indemnity, his Government would have agreed to enter negotiation on those terms.

He thought his Government would perhaps insist on a unity of Serbia and Montenegro under the Montenegrin dynasty. He said the Serbian dynasty had been so corrupt and was in such bad odor that something should be done to dispose of them.

To my mind, this is the most important communication we have had since the war began and gives a real basis for negotiations and for peace.

I am wondering what Lansing and Stone had to say in regard to your address. I am wondering, too, whether you have cabled it and when you will deliver it.

Affectionately yours,   E. M. House

I made notes of this conversation and read them to Bernstorff and he declared they were accurate.

TLS (WP, DLC).
 1 Wilson's emphases and question marks.
 2 House's emphasis.

From Robert Lansing

PERSONAL AND CONFIDENTIAL.

My dear Mr. President: Washington January 15, 1917.

I enclose for your information and consideration a revised list of the cases of sub-marine attack up to and including the twelfth of this month.[1]

Faithfully yours,   Robert Lansing.

TLS (WP, DLC).
 1 "List of December 8, 1916 amended to January 12, 1917," T MS (WP, DLC). The list covered all vessels with Americans on board sunk by submarines between October 12 and December 14, 1916. It gave brief accounts of the circumstances of each sinking; casualties, if any; diplomatic inquiries made, if any; and the responses, if any, by German and/or British authorities up to January 12, 1917. In many cases, there had been no response to American inquiries by the German government as of January 12.

Two Letters from Franklin Knight Lane and Others

Dear Mr. President: [New York] January 15, 1917.

Your Commission, appointed to act with a like body created by the Government of Mexico to compose the differences between the two Governments, begs to advise that the joint body has today adjourned after passing this resolution:

"WHEREAS, this Commission was created by the Governments of Mexico and the United States to promote a better understanding between the two peoples and thus bring about a relationship that would make for their mutual interest and the realization of their ideals as neighboring Republics, and

"WHEREAS, it is our hope that by the friendly and long continued consideration of those conditions along our common border and within Mexico, which have given rise to the present difficulties, a door has been opened to such a fuller understanding of the purposes and plans of both Mexico and the United States,

"IT IS HEREBY RESOLVED, That this Commission does now adjourn, recommending to both Governments the reestablishment of full diplomatic relations under which may be carried on directly the further negotiations necessary to secure these ends:

(1) The protection of the life, property and other rights of foreigners in Mexico.

(2) The establishment of an International Claims Commission.

(3) The elimination of the causes that may lead to further misunderstanding, friction or clash between Americans and Mexicans."

Having been unable to secure the approval of the Mexican Government to a protocol agreed upon by the Joint Commission as to the withdrawal of the American troops now in Mexico, we would respectfully suggest that the United States may now feel free to follow any course in the matter of such withdrawal which may seem consistent with the protection of our own territory and the friendly relations which it wishes to promote between the two republics.   Respectfully yours,   [Franklin K. Lane]
[Geo. Gray]
[John R. Mott]

CCL (CSmH).

To the President: [New York] January 15th, 1917.

Supplementing our communication of January 3rd, we beg to inform you that at the request of the Mexican Commissioners we held a final session of the Commission in New York City on Monday, January 15th.

We are still of the opinion, expressed to you in our communication of January 3rd, that the Protocol signed at Atlantic City, N. J. on November 24th last, providing for the withdrawal of troops and the protection of the international boundary, not only safeguards the interests of the United States but was framed with a view to assist the de facto Government in suppressing its enemies in Northern Chihuahua. Our further contact with the Mexican Commissioners has convinced us that however clear and definite this purpose may have been in the minds of the American Commissioners; the instrument was not interpreted in the same spirit in Mexico City. It is evident that the irritation caused by the continued presence of American troops on Mexican territory has reached a point which makes it quite impossible to secure the approval of the First Chief to any agreement, the terms of which might be interpreted by the Mexican people as sanctioning, or even giving tacit consent to the presence of American troops on Mexican soil. In view of this situation, therefore, it is evident that the only course open to the Government of the United States is to act on its own initiative without attempting to reach any agreement with the de facto Government concerning the conditions of withdrawal.

Our long continued contact with the Mexican Commissioners has impressed us more and more with the importance of effecting such withdrawal at the earliest possible date. All our efforts to convince them that unconditional withdrawal might work harm to the cause of the de facto Government have been unavailing. It has become increasingly evident to us that the withdrawal of these troops is the outstanding purpose of the de facto Government, and that in any negotiations with the United States all other considerations are subordinated to this purpose.

In view of the repeated refusal of the First Chief to accede even to those conditions of withdrawal which were framed for the protection of the de facto Government against its enemies, we have reached the conclusion that our relations with Mexico will best be subserved by an early and unconditional withdrawal of our troops. Such withdrawal will serve to clarify the situation by placing upon the de facto Government the responsibility for the protection of its side of the international boundary and for the full performance of its international obligations in the protection of the lives and property of foreigners resident in Mexico.

We are, furthermore, convinced that the withdrawal of American troops will pave the way for the consideration of the other questions, which we have constantly impressed upon the Mexican Commissioners as of vital importance to the United States, and of no less vital importance to the standing of Mexico amongst the nations. These questions are the protection of the lives and property of foreigners, adequate provision for an international claims commission and the establishment of conditions which will make possible the early resumption of industry.

Our experience during the months of exhaustive discussion of almost every phase of our relations with Mexico, has convinced us that the negotiations with reference to all of these questions can be conducted far more effectively in Mexico than in the

United States. It is necessary that our Government should know at first hand the mind of the First Chief, and we believe this can best be secured through direct negotiations with your personal representative in Mexico City. We would, therefore, strongly commend to your attention the desirability of sending your Ambassador to Mexico City at the earliest possible moment.

We have, with your authority, Mr. President, brought the sessions of the Commission to a close, fully convinced that the work of the Commission has paved the way for the amicable and effective settlement of the controversies now pending between the two countries. Our long contact and intimate association with the Mexican Commissioners enables us more fully to appreciate the point of view of the Mexican people. Our recommendations to you, therefore, are dictated not only by our desire to safeguard the interests of the United States, but also by the wish to further the purpose which you have so often expressed, to see a Mexico strong, prosperous and progressive.

We have the honor to be, with great respect,

Your obedient servants,   [Franklin K. Lane]
                          [Geo. Gray]
                          [John R. Mott]

TCL (CSmH).

From William Graves Sharp

CONFIDENTIAL

My dear Mr. President: Paris, January 15, 1917

Having in mind your request made at the time of our meeting just before my departure for France, that I write you, I feel that no more opportune time could present itself for carrying out my promise to do so than at the present moment. If, on account of the important nature of the subject about which I write, my letter seems a little long, I shall find some consolation in the fact that you ended your request by adding: "Even if I do not answer your letters." Fully appreciating the great demands made upon your time, I certainly shall expect none.

Without doubt the most important as well as most interesting event which has occurred since my assuming charge of this mission has been the sending of your recent communication to all the belligerent Powers. I was so impressed with the need of such an appeal at this time and with the clear insight of conditions which characterized your suggestions, that I briefly cabled you with the object of not only expressing my satisfaction over the action taken but to give it encouragement.[1] For I believe it is the greatest duty of the hour to find some way in which a further—and possibly a very long—continuance of this seemingly limitless destruction of life and property may be prevented.

In making this observation, I am only too well aware of the answer which is so persistently made that only that kind of termination of hostilities must be brought about as will ensure a permanent peace. In full sympathy with that position, I am yet constrained to ask "Will the still greater sacrifice of more millions of lives and untold billions of dollars of additional indebtedness bring the belligerent Powers any nearer to that universally desired end when there will be no more wars?"

I ask this question also fully aware of the terrible sacrifices that all the belligerent peoples have made—and particularly those of France who have suffered so much from the havoc wrought by the enemy in their country. The loss of more than one million of her soldiers, and nearly that many more seriously crippled, together with the fact that there are several hundred thousand more languishing in the prison camps of the enemy, all tend to cause great bitterness of feeling toward the Germans in particular. Then, too, among those who remember the days of 1870-1, there is an intense desire to redeem France from what they regard as her humiliation at the hands of the same enemy.

As far as the actual work of destruction to her towns and villages also is concerned, it is probably true that France has suffered the most in this war. A brief trip recently made to the cities of Rheims and Nancy,—near the latter of which are located a number of towns fairly typical, in their mass of ruins, of others all long the battle-front—revealed to me more than any written description could possibly do not only the completeness of the destruction wrought, but the sad plight of the inhabitants themselves, many of whom have been forced to abandon their homes entirely and seek shelter and employment elsewhere.

The occasion of this trip was the participation in ceremonies commemorating the beginning of the work of Americans who are helping in a most practical manner to re-build some of these destroyed homes. Incidentally, I may add that I forwarded to the State Department, in the pouch preceding this letter, a description of some of the conditions which I encountered, together with a book containing views showing what Rheims, with its famous old cathedral, and some of the other places visited by me look like at the present time after a bombardment of many

---

[1] It is missing.

months. This report may be of some interest to you if you have time to read it; if not, perhaps Mrs. Wilson herself will enjoy looking at the photographs, which, I think, have never appeared in any publication.

These very conditions, however, which find their duplicate in so many sections of Europe along the frontiers where bombardments have taken place, furnish, to my mind, all the stronger reason why an appeal for a return to reason and consequent cessation of hostilities should be heeded.

Sometimes, on account of the very proximity to these horrible scenes, it has seemed to me that I have been looking upon some great painting which, owing to the nearness of its location, I am only permitted to see in detail from a very small section of the canvas. The trunk of a tree or the banks of a stream near me alone stand out with any vividness, while it becomes impossible at such a short range of vision to grasp the whole conception of what the picture represents.

Applied to the war situation, the difficulty is even more complicated from receiving the divergent views of so many who, coming from various points in Europe, express widely different opinions born of their own particular environment. Often, when time would permit my seizing an opportunity during a quiet luncheon hour at my home, I have had occasion to discuss with many people, chiefly Americans, the conditions that they have found existing in the different capitals from which they come; yesterday perhaps a returning Special Agent from Constantinople; to-day a Secretary from Berlin; to-morrow an impartial observer from some other distant point, none of them so far removed, however, from the scenes of actual warfare but that they have formed most interesting and intimate impressions of the conditions about them.

But out of it all, if my judgment is good for aught, comes the settled conviction to me that the very inexorableness of the conditions existing in this war, demand—even if the questions affecting humanity itself be put aside—a most thoughtful consideration by all the Powers concerned of your suggestions.

That the answers now in from both sides do not give more hope that your efforts to bring about a cessation of hostilities may be successful will be a disappointment not only to the peoples of the neutral Powers but, I am forced to believe, also to many millions of those likewise of the belligerents, however much the trend of the public press may be otherwise.

Briefly stated,—and they do not need much elaboration for two years and a half of warfare ought to make quite plain the first one—there are two factors which tend to greatly prolong the duration of this war:

First, and above all other elements, aside from the remarkable equality in the strength and resourcefulness of the contending Powers, is that of the trench system of warfare. The results of a few days bombardment on the seemingly impregnable forts like Liège at the beginning of the war proved that no kind of man-made fortifications—if I may so describe them—could withstand the terrible impact of the ton weight shells hurled against them; neither could any force of men, infantry or cavalry, moving forward on a surface hope to withstand such fire either from the shells of those big guns or the rapid fusilade of bullets from the machine guns.

The retreat of the enemy forces for a distance of forty miles over the battlefields of the Marne, all accomplished within practically forty-eight hours after it began, shows how quickly one or the other of the contending forces may be compelled to retire when fighting above ground, but, given a breathing spell sufficient to burrow themselves under the earth in trenches which later were developed in security to a remarkable extent, and all was changed. The biggest shells but merely dent the surface of Mother Earth.

For more than two years the outer line of the German trenches stretching from the mountains of the Vosges in the south-east in an irregular line to the sea on the north-west have remained practically unbroken. Only at a few points has an advance been made —and in nearly all cases by the Allied forces—of more than a few miles at the most.

Mr. Hoover, Chairman of the Belgian Relief Commission, who, on account of his duties, frequently meets the German military officers during his visits to Belgium, told me many months ago that, for much of the time just preceding, the German forces on the west front were actually but one-third in numerical strength to those of the Allied forces, the larger guns in the rear, together with the protection of the trenches being sufficient for them to maintain their ground. This enabled them to send a large supply of their men to the south into Serbia, where rapid advances were then being made by them.

I have, indeed, every reason to believe that, more recently, the same tactics were followed in diverting their forces for the attack on Roumania. In that conversation Mr. Hoover also made the significant statement that, to use his exact words, "the Germans are in a panic for peace."

So confident was I of the strength of the impasse, particularly on the west front, created by this elaborate system of trenches, that I cabled the State Department soon after the commencement of the attack at Verdun, late in February, that from my information the Germans never would take that town, and in the early days of the engagement on the Somme in July I likewise cabled the Department that there would be no material advance for a long time to come.

The conditions that sustained my predictions then still exist and, notwithstanding the seeming new-born confidence of the Allies in their superior strength in men, guns and munitions, concerning which I cabled the Department on the 29th. ultimo, I believe it will be an exceedingly difficult, if not, indeed, impossible task for them to materially change the line of battle-front for many months ahead. It has developed not alone into a war of endurance and military prowess, but of resourcefulness in invention for, recognizing the tremendous sacrifice necessary in lives and munitions in carrying such trenches by storm, numerous devices have been invented to get across them—either by tunnelling underground, going on the surface in huge armored "tanks" or contemplated transportation of forces through the air. But with both sides equally alert and ingenious, it will furnish a case of the irresistible meeting the immovable.

With no surprise movements possible as in previous wars, because of a thousand aeroplanes overhead sending immediate warnings and taking photographs of every position, the difficulty of either side making any progress is greatly increased.

In these important respects, unlike any other war in history, one cannot judge by precedents, and this conflict which was predicted long ago would be but short on account of the very intensity of its destructiveness may still well continue for another year or two. In the absence of a successful intervention, only the inability to secure food for the people of Germany or Austria will end the war sooner if it is to be fought out to a conclusion by arms.

All this develops from what may be termed the more physical nature of the first of the two factors which I have mentioned.

The second is more of a political nature, and the causes for its existence ante-dates the war. What in times past has been considered an element making for stability in maintaining the balance of power in Europe—that of relationship of the Sovereigns resulting from the inter-marriage of the Royal families—has been a potent factor in not only fomenting but bitterly intensifying the hatreds between the two contending forces.

Some time ago Mr. Denys Cochin, a member of the present French Ministry,[2] sitting by my side at a dinner soon after his return from a special mission to Athens, told me that while a guest at the home of King Constantine, the Queen[3]—a sister, as you know, of Emperor William—said to him with great bitterness of feeling that the course pursued by her uncle, the late King Edward, was responsible more than anything else for this war.

Only the other day one of my colleagues told me during the course of a conversation I had with him at his Embassy, that no little difficulty was being experienced in meeting the situation in Greece on account of the peculiar claims upon or relations which that country had to one of the Allies. Indeed, it is no secret that, as naturally might be supposed, this is one of the problems which the Allied Governments have to meet to bring about a harmony of views as to methods used, though it is only fair to say that I do not believe there has been a lack of loyalty shown by any of them to the common cause.

Though it is a bridge still to be crossed, and far away I fear, yet if such differences of opinion exist at the present time among the Allied forces, what will be the problems of adjusting all these various differences when the final terms of settlement are to be arranged between the warring Powers? With assurances of divisions of territory and obligations of some of the most important nature outstanding, many of which it will be impossible from the very nature of the conditions to fulfil, I have likened such a situation to the task of untangling the many threads of a skein of silk with which children have been playing.

The most deplorable feature of the situation is that not alone does each day add to the bitterness of feeling but also to the complications which later on must be smoothed out and adjusted.

As a sample of the views which may be said to be fairly representative of the position of the Allies, I enclose a copy of a speech of Lloyd George delivered at a meeting in the Guildhall in London last Thursday afternoon and which, though you may have already seen in part in the American papers, may not have been sent over in full.[4] Its match in defiance and virulence may be

---

[2] Denys Pierre Augustin Marie Cochin was at this time Under Secretary of State in charge of the blockade of Germany.

[3] Sophie, formerly Princess of Prussia.

[4] Lloyd George had spoken at the Guildhall in London on January 11, on the occasion of the opening of a new war-loan campaign. His speech was rousingly patriotic and designed to stir enthusiasm for the loan. He declared that the Central Powers had presented, not a peace proposal, but "a trap baited with fine words." The Allies wanted peace, but a real peace. They believed that victory would be difficult but that defeat was impossible. With the financial backing provided by the new loan, the armies of the Entente would "cleave a road to

found in a speech delivered within the past few days by the Kaiser to his troops.[5]

Unfortunately, the pride and personal ambitions of men in authority have had much to do, not only with the very inception of the war itself, but with the course of it. To my mind it has always seemed such an absurd policy to seek to differentiate between the moral obligation of the State and that of the individuals who comprise it—just as though the State was something separate and apart from the men who direct its affairs.

It is indeed this false conception of the relation between the State and the individuals comprising it, as far as any moral obligation and accountability are concerned, that must have led Bernhardi, in his "Germany and the next War," to state, in speaking of the duty of the State,—

"But the acts of the State cannot be judged by the standard of individual morality. If the State wished to conform to this standard it would often find itself at variance with its own particular duties. The morality of the State must be developed out of its own peculiar essence, just as individual morality is rooted in the personality of the man and his duties toward Society. The morality of the State must be judged by the nature and the 'raison d'être' of the State and not of the individual citizen. But the end-all and be-all of the State is power * * * * "[6]

This same attitude prompted that author to boldly justify the State in reaching out and extending its domains by force, regardless of moral right, if extension for the State's activities should be needed. It is not surprising also to note that this writer further says:

"The lessons of history thus confirm the view that wars which have been deliberately provoked by far-seeing statesmen have had the happiest results."[7]

At the present moment, how delusive it would be to undertake to attribute the policies now being so vigorously advocated by Great Britain to something separate and apart and having no

---

victory" within the next few months. The full text of the speech appears in the *New York Times*, Jan. 12, 1917.

[5] Sharp referred to Emperor William's order to the German army and navy published on January 6. Since the Entente powers had rejected his peace offer, he declared, the war would continue. "With justified indignation at our enemies' arrogant crime and with determination to defend our holiest possessions and secure for the Fatherland a happy future, you will become as steel," he continued. "Our enemies did not want the understanding offered by me. With God's help our arms will enforce it." *New York Times*, Jan. 7, 1917.

[6] Friedrich Adam Julius von Bernhardi, *Germany and the Next War*, trans. Allen H. Powles, authorized edn. (New York, 1914), p. 45.

[7] *Ibid*.

relation to Lloyd George and his powerful backer, Lord North-cliffe. Only the most pronounced successes will save some men from a fall from high places.

I believe it all points unmistakably to the conclusion that the Allies, unwilling to let the verdict of the results of the war thus far go down into history as it is, and having a very great faith in their ability to win such victories over the Central Powers as either to crush them or cause them to at least offer very definite and liberal terms of peace, have irrevocably determined to push their offensive with renewed energy. To oppose them, the Central Powers will prosecute their side of the war with a fury and destructiveness both on land and sea such as have not character-ized their operations in the past.

Unquestionably, even more as an instrument for encompass-ing the defeat of the Central Powers than the greatly increased supply of guns and munitions, the Entente Powers consider the growing scarcity of food, both in Germany and Austria. While, undoubtedly, such scarcity acutely exists in many places in those countries, yet how far the radical steps taken to conserve the food supply may account for the rumors of this great need, I must confess I am in doubt.

The reply of the Allies to your communication just recently published has naturally caused a wave of hatred to pass over Germany, but I suppose it is out of the question to expect at this time such answers to be free from invectives and harshest criticisms.

Poor Dr. Littleton[8] of Eton College was, more than a year ago, anathematised by the public and even scorned by men of his own cloth, for raising his voice in favor of a more moderate attitude toward enemies with whom they must necessarily, in the future, be again compelled to associate.[9]

Such are the conditions, unhappily, which your message, inspired by such high purposes, must meet. Only can I with truth say at this moment that not only was it received with the greatest respect here in France, but its motives never questioned. It has most assuredly served the double purpose, at a time which, I must believe, is opportune, not only to acquaint the belligerent Powers with the fact that there is left open a door which may

[8] The Rev. Dr. Edward Lyttelton, Headmaster of Eton College, 1905-16.

[9] In a sermon delivered at St. Margaret's Church, Westminster, on March 25, 1915. A brief summary of his address appears in the London *Times*, March 27, 1915. See also his explanatory letter to the Editor in *ibid.*, March 29, 1915. Some historians believe that it was the public outcry caused by his sermon that led to his resignation from Eton College. See, for example, Christopher Hollis, *Eton: A History* (London, 1960), pp. 294-96.

lead to an honorable peace, but also to make manifest that questions affecting the war have suddenly taken on a civil rather than a military character. That is certainly something gained, and I hope for that kind of a continued discussion which may soon restore reason and justice to power.

In looking over these pages, I am afraid I have not accomplished much in acquainting you with those facts that you may desire most to know, but I trust I may have succeeded, nevertheless, in at least revealing to you the general nature of conditions over here such as to hearten you in the conviction that the strength and courage of someone high in authority could never be better used in the interest of humanity than now. I greatly wish that yours may be the voice to which heed may be given.

Wishing you, my dear Mr. President, abounding success and good health for the coming New Year,

I am, believe me,

Most sincerely yours,   Wm. G. Sharp.

TLS (WP, DLC).

From Charles Richard Crane

Dear Mr President   [Chicago] January 15 1917

I thought you might like to see the enclosed letter telling about Professor Merriam[1] and the difficulty he found in trying to accommodate his responsibilities so as to meet your wishes.[2] He is Chicago's most useful citizen.

The last Note carried, as I felt sure that it would, if they had a week to look at it. It is hard now-a-days to see the obvious and I have no doubt that Bryce is sorry he did not *see* the Note when he was *looking* at it. It is almost amusing that the Germans who immediately extolled the note are now having misgivings because it is now being treated sympathetically by the British. But the full weight of the Note will not be felt among the peoples for a time longer and will be pulling every day like gravity. It is certain to stand as one of your greatest services. I am very happy about it.

Mrs Crane and I send you and the White House family affectionate messages,

Always sincerely Yours   Charles R. Crane

ALS (WP, DLC).
[1] Charles Edward Merriam, Professor of Political Science at the University of Chicago.
[2] Wilson returned the letter to Crane. He had offered Merriam a place on the Tariff Commission. See Barry D. Karl, *Charles E. Merriam and the Study of Politics* (Chicago, 1974), p. 81.

From Samuel Huston Thompson, Jr.

Dear Mr. President: Washington Jan. 15. 1917.

Several weeks ago in your study where you gave me such a kindly hearing you asked me what character of position I had in mind in the event that I could make a change in the public service. I replied that I had thought of no particular place but outlined my idea in general and made some observations about my desire to do constructive work.

Since then a vacancy on the Federal Trade Commission has been created by Mr. Hurleys resignation.

If it met with your entire approval I would relish an opportunity for service in such a position. I will confess that the desire to dedicate my life to public service has been so quickened by four years under you that retreat to private practice looks very uninviting.

You expressed a fear at placing lawyers on the several Commissions because they as a rule immediately tie their hands or powers up in technical legal limitations. You may have no fears of me on this score.

I was never a lawyer of that kind and whatever good fortune I have had in the law was not attained through such processes.

It would ill become me to state my qualifications. As to my limitations—well, they are like my sins, perhaps you know them already—if not it would never do to reveal them.

You would be fortified politically for the results of the work I did last summer in Colorado attest that the forward thinking people did not take umbrage at your placing me in the government service in the first instance.

I may add that I have a very friendly acquaintanceship with all of the members of the Commission.

At our last meeting you asked me to come and see you again about the matter at hand. I feel however that I took too much of your valuable time so I am writing that I may thus save you that which you have always so generously placed at my disposal.

With my kindest regards to Mrs. Wilson.
                    Very sincerely yours   Huston Thompson.

ALS (WP, DLC).

From Josephus Daniels

Dear Mr. President: Washington. Jan. 16, 1917.

Admiral Dewey died at four minutes to six o'clock this afternoon. I thought you would like to give out a statement to the press about his life and service, for though he had not been privileged to know you well, his feeling toward you was one of unaffected admiration. He had been as generous and good to me as if he were of my own blood, and I am filled with sorrow at his death. Sincerely, Josephus Daniels

ALS (WP, DLC).

A Memorial Tribute

[*Jan. 16, 1917*]

The whole nation will mourn the loss of its most distinguished naval officer, a man who has been as faithful, as intelligent, and as successful in the performance of his responsible duties in time of peace as he was gallant and successful in time of war.

It is such men that give the service distinction, and the nation a just pride in those who serve it.

Printed in the *New York Times*, Jan. 17, 1917.

To Edward Mandell House

Dearest Friend, The White House. 16 January, 1917.

The thing is in course. Neither Lansing nor Stone is very *expressive*, but both have acqu[i]esced very generously (Stone, I thought, a little wonderingly, as if the idea stunned him a bit) and the cable went forward, for distribution as planned, yesterday. Poor Sweet worked all Saturday and Sunday and all of both nights getting it into code, poor fellow, so that as few should be in the secret as possible. We are now waiting to hear that the cables have reached the several embassies. So soon as we hear, I shall arrange to go before the Senate and telegraph the embassies to release at the same time we do here. Senator Stone generously gave up pressing business at home to stay over and be on hand to serve in the whole matter.

Your letter brought over by Mr. Auchincloss contains more than I have yet been able to digest. Do I understand you to mean that they are willing to submit the terms upon which the war is to be concluded to arbitration or only that they are willing to conclude a "Bryan treaty" with us?

In haste, Affectionately Yours, Woodrow Wilson

WWTLS (E. M. House Papers, CtY).

To Newton Diehl Baker

The White House

My dear Mr. Secretary: 16 January, 1917

Thank you for your letter of the tenth about Mr. David J. Lewis' bill for government ownership of the telephone system of the District. I have expressed to him my approval of the bill and have taken several occasions to speak of it to others. I shall welcome such occasions whenever they arise.

In haste

Cordially and faithfully yours,   Woodrow Wilson

TLS (N. D. Bakers Papers, DLC).

To Charles Richard Crane

My dear Friend: [The White House] 16 January, 1917

Thank you for having let me see the enclosed. I am heartily sorry that Merriam could not accept. I had quite set my heart on it, but he is moved by motives which I cannot challenge.

It makes my [me] very happy that you should think as you do of the last note. I hope with all my heart that it will work, as you anticipate, more and more upon the thoughts of the peoples concerned.

In haste

Cordially and faithfully yours,   Woodrow Wilson

TLS (Letterpress Books, WP, DLC).

To William Phillips

[The White House]

My dear Mr. Phillips: 16 January, 1917

Thank you sincerely for your letter of January twelfth. You may be sure that it gave me the greatest pleasure to show my appreciation of the services you have rendered. I only hope that no kind of bigotry in the Senate[1] will prevent the confirmation.

In haste, with the warmest regard,

Cordially and sincerely yours,   Woodrow Wilson

TLS (Letterpress Books, WP, DLC).

[1] Wilson probably feared opposition from Henry Cabot Lodge, whose approval was necessary for Phillips' confirmation by the Senate. Lodge had chided Phillips, a Republican, when he had accepted the third assistant secretaryship in 1914. See William Phillips, *Ventures in Diplomacy* (Boston, 1952), p. 62.

To Samuel Huston Thompson, Jr.

Personal.

My dear Thompson: The White House 16 January, 1917

I have your letter of yesterday and you may be sure will gladly consider its suggestion, though as a matter of fact I fear I must frankly say at the outset that I am particularly anxious, if possible, to get a well-known business man on the Commission. If you will recall the list, there is nobody in the Commission who has been identified with large business transactions, and in order to give the business men of the country the feeling that they are dealing with men who can understand their problems by personal experience, it is highly desirable that there should be some such person on the Commission. However, I may not find the man.

I am sure you know my cordial disposition to do anything that it is possible to do to show my warm feeling and admiration for you.

          Cordially and faithfully yours,   Woodrow Wilson

TLS (S. H. Thompson, Jr., Papers, DLC).

From Edward Mandell House, with Enclosures

Dear Governor: New York. January 16, 1917.

Here are some extracts from letters from Hapgood and a copy of one from Buckler which may be of interest.

Note what McKenna had to say about your power to "force the Allies to their knees."

It seems to me that with the German communication of yesterday you stand in a position to bring about peace much more quickly than I thought possible. They consent to almost everything that liberal opinion in democratic countries have demanded.

I think it is important that no move be made now without the most mature consideration. If a false step is not taken, the end seems in sight. The question is how to use the German communication to the best advantage. I am not clear upon this point. Are you?

I had a conference with Sir William Wiseman yesterday. He is the most sensible Englishman that has been connected with the Embassy here since the war began. He has intelligence enough to go with friends of the Administration rather than with its enemies. The opinion Spring-Rice hears from Roosevelt,

Lodge, Gardner and others may be pleasant, but it has no value to his Government. This opinion is governed by antagonism to you and not by any real sympathy with the Allies. Wiseman understand[s] this.

This morning I talked with the representative of the London Chronicle.[1] I think he will write sympathetically. He says it is not true that there is any considerable adverse feeling to America in England. Another Englishman tells me that most of the feeling in England against America has been created by Americans there and those visiting.

Your affectionate, E. M. House

TLS (WP, DLC).
[1] Sydney Brooks.

E N C L O S U R E   I

William Hepburn Buckler to Edward Mandell House

Dear Colonel House: London, January 5, 1917.

I enclose a note (with enclosure and copy) received from Buxton, and agree with what he says as to the "right of the United States to insist" on terms being declared. This right is admitted by every Englishman with whom I happen to have discussed it.

When one puts it up to them that according to McKenna's public statement about two million sterling *per diem* go into Uncle Sam's pocket,[1] they admit (so far as my experience goes) that Uncle Sam *has* a right to form and to express his own opinion as to whether and how long this process shall continue.

As to Buxton's views on the Bosphorus I don't entirely agree. The guarantees he proposes may be excellent, but I fail to see how in fairness *we* could propose that this trade-portal be kept open for Russia's benefit, unless the Suez-portal were at the same time neutralized and kept open for Germany's and Austria's benefit.

You will notice Buxton's letter in the "Morning Post" of January 2nd. If you are getting all this printed matter, etc. from other quarters, forgive my bothering you with it, but I feel you had better receive it twice than not at all.

"Common Sense" is a new review by Hirst, the ex-Editor of the "Economist." He shows pretty well how the Lincoln parallels (so called) are being overworked.

Yours sincerely, W. H. Buckler.

P.S. None of the Monthlies except the 19th Century have anything on the Note. I dont count the National Review, which is too cranky to cut any ice.

TCL (WP, DLC).

¹ Reginald McKenna, then Chancellor of the Exchequer, had made this statement in the House of Commons on October 19, 1916, in response to criticism of the high interest rates which the government was offering on its bonds. "We have to pay," he said, "at the present time a very considerable amount day by day in the United States. . . . At the present moment, I suppose, it would not be too much to say that we have to find £2,000,000 a day for every working day of the week. That means a prodigious amount of dollars to find every six days." *Parliamentary Debates: Commons*, 5th Ser., LXXXVI, col. 785.

ENCLOSURE II

Noel Edward Noel-Buxton
to William Hepburn Buckler

My dear Buckler,   [London] Jan. 4 [1917].

In case you are writing to Colonel House, here is a point which may interest him. The argument for negotiating with Germany now never appealed to more than a section. The argument for meeting Mr. Wilson's request for our terms appeals to liberals in general. This is evidenced by the Westminster—the most cautious of liberal papers. It is brought home to me still more by the adhesion of the Jingo press in my division, representing warlike opinion in *both* parties.

A point which I find much discussed is: Will the President let himself be put off with fair words which do not deal with the Constantinople question? The English officials are not set on helping Russia to get the Straits, far from it! But they would like Russia to come up against American objections rather than ours. I enclose a dictated note on this.

There is a feeling that Mr. Wilson will insist on having terms defined, if only because it would be humiliating for him to be ignored, and destructive of his future influence. There is no disposition to doubt his power of insisting or his right to insist.

                                        Yours,   N. Buxton.

"Enclosed dictated note" above mentioned:

                                                  [London] 4.1.17.

The Straits & America.

I can't help thinking that it might have immense value if the U. S. A. were at the right stage to put forward a fairly definite proposal for the administration of the Bosphorus and Dardanelles.

The diplomats mostly deprecate the idea because an international system gave them trouble in Egypt, but the experiment has never really been tried.

The Danube Commission was started by Treaty, and there are many precedents for international action involving joint contributions, such as the Hague Machinery. It is quite conceivable that the Treaty of Peace might include clauses laying down the outline of a System, and setting up a Commission which would elaborate the details.

From the point of view of Russia, the security against the closure of the Straits in time of war would be immensely increased by the participation of America. And if the riparian territory, within which fortifications and military establishments would be forbidden, is sufficiently wide, Russia would not be in danger of being forestalled at the Straits by a hostile movement from Bulgaria or from the State which occupied the adjoining territory in Asia Minor.

The idea would be that for practical purposes the Straits became as free, whether in peace or war, as the Straits of Gibraltar. And this idea would catch on psychologically.

In actual fact the Russians want security that in case of war they would "get there first," so as to prevent the enemy's approach (at one end of the Straits or the other).

If the "League of States" is attempted at all, international guarantees, which include America, will be far more weighty than any hitherto known, and they will preclude the violation of the international jurisdiction in the area actually guaranteed.

T MS (WP, DLC).

E N C L O S U R E   I I I

Extracts from letters of Norman Hapgood, December 30th and January 4th.

France is much more tired than England. I enclose a clipping you may or may not have seen about the French Socialists. Painlevé[1] may succeed Briand soon. He is a moderate. There is no such serious objection to war in England. There are a few pacifists, reasonless and advanced liberals, but no *mass* objection to the war. The people in the street, in restaurants etc. are amazingly cheerful. I hear they are even sadder in France than when I was there.

Of course with secret treaties containing promises to Italy, Roumania and Russia, a really definite answer to the President is almost impossible. Nobody expects any one of these countries to get all that has been promised, and to publish all these promises as conditions would make a bad impression, harden the situation, making negotiations more difficult.

That is the view of the ruling class, and there is little democracy here now.

There are two opinions on the spring offensive, some expecting little more than this Fall, others expecting a serious weakening. It seems to be true that the lack of fats and meat have begun to increase tuberculosis largely in Germany; and Germany is thinking of what will happen *after* this war.

The Asquith people are pretty bitter at Lloyd George, Northcliffe and the Times. Nobody seems to trust Lloyd George much, tho most think him the right man for an unremitting effort. His views may change absolutely at any moment, as there is no more complete opportunist.

Nearly all Liberals think the President's note a good one in its long distance results.

I spent an hour and a half with Mr. McKenna alone yesterday. He said the President could force the Allies to their knees any time in a moment. His remarks on Lloyd George, the Tories and Northcliffe were very bitter. There is no doubt that all the Asquith people look on Lloyd George as a traitor. McKenna says the Government will try to jolly the President along, long enough to let them have their "big push" in the Spring. He thinks that push will fail in a military sense (as to breaking through), tho it may be successful in attrition and wearing down if Germany is hungry enough.

T MS (WP, DLC).

[1] Paul Painlevé, mathematician; Minister of Education, October 1915 to December 1916; at this time out of office. He became Minister of War on March 20, 1917, and served briefly as Premier from September 12 to November 13, 1917.

From William Franklin Willoughby

My dear Mr. President:

Washington, D. C.
January 16, 1917.

In conformity with the wish expressed by you at the interview had with you yesterday by the Committee representing the Board of Trustees of the Institute for Government Research, I am writing to state that the Institute desires to undertake the work in respect to the three following matters:

1. The System of Financial Administration of the United States Government.

    2. The System of Public Works Administration of the United States Government.

    3. The Statistical Work of the United States Government.

I am indicating several studies as it is necessary that the Institute should have a number of inquiries under way at the same time in order to keep our staff fully employed.

This work will bring us into direct relations with officers of the Departments of the Treasury, Interior and Commerce. I may say that I have in the past had personal interviews with Secretary Lane of the Department of the Interior and Secretary Redfield of the Department of Commerce. Both of these gentlemen I think thoroughly understand the character and aims of the Institute, and both have expressed their entire willingness to cooperate with us provided your sanction is had. I have not had any personal interview with Secretary McAdoo of the Treasury but would like very much to have such an interview in order that I may personally inform him in respect to the character of study that we desire to make.

In respect to all three of the studies mentioned above, it is our intention that our work shall be primarily descriptive. If, as the result of our studies, we have any suggestions looking to the improvement of conditions, it is our plan to bring such suggestions directly to the attention of the officers concerned and will not give any publicity to them until the matter has been gone over thoroughly with them.

In addition to the foregoing, the Institute would like very much to be granted the permission to have access to the files of the late President's Commission on Economy and Efficiency.[1] Chairman Goodnow and myself were members of this Commission and we have thus knowledge of the fact that there exists in those files a great deal of material that would be of great value to the Institute and would save us a large expenditure of time and money if we could make copies of certain reports which were gotten into manuscript form but were never finally utilized. For example, a very detailed study was made of the accounting methods of the several services of the government, and it would be of great value to us to have copies of the reports that were made but which were never utilized by the Commission.

In conclusion, I wish again to state that the present program of the Institute is to emphasize its research function. For the present, at least, it wishes to concentrate its work upon the bringing into existence of information which it is believed will be of value to all persons concerned with the administration of public affairs, and also lay the basis for the subsequent preparation of critical and constructive reports. It is our desire to give publicity to the descriptive reports as fast as such reports are completed, but not to give any publicity to the critical and constructive reports until they have been submitted to officers of the government and an agreement if possible has been reached relative to the desirability of making such suggestions public with a view to securing the support of public opinion to the accomplishment of ends which administrative officers, as well as the officers of the Institute, believe would be desirable.

It is not our expectation that any burden of work will be thrown upon officers of the government. All that we desire is that we be not treated as intruders and will be given such information as it is proper should be given to an organization such as the Institute.

I remain,   Very respectfully,   W. F. Willoughby

TLS (WP, DLC).

¹ In June 1910, President Taft secured from Congress an appropriation of $100,000 for the purpose of conducting an inquiry into the organization and expenditures of the federal government with a view toward recommending changes to achieve greater efficiency and economy. In March 1911, Taft appointed a Commission on Efficiency and Economy to carry on this work. Frederick Albert Cleveland, the director of the Bureau of Municipal Research of New York, became chairman. On November 27, 1911, the commission submitted to the President a two-volume report on the organization of the national government as it existed on July 1 of that year (62d Cong., 2d sess., House Doc. 458). Taft transmitted the report to Congress on January 17, 1912, together with a request for an appropriation of $250,000 to continue the work of the commission. Congress appropriated only $75,000, thus compelling a drastic retrenchment of the commission's staff and work. However, during the remainder of Taft's administration, it did continue to produce detailed reports on various departments and agencies, as well as a pioneering volume, *The Need for a National Budget* (62d Cong., 2d Sess., House Doc. 854). For other reports of, and information about, the commission and its work, see 62d Cong., 2d sess., House Docs. 670 and 732, and 3d sess., House Docs. 1110 and 1252.

Sir Cecil Arthur Spring Rice
to the Department of State, with Enclosure

Handed me by British Amb.
Jany 16/17 RL.
Washington.

Mr. Balfour informs me that he will delay publication till morning of the 18th in order to learn the President's views. He hopes publication will be simultaneous in both countries.

Hw memorandum (SDR, RG 59, 763.72119/395, DNA).

E N C L O S U R E

Arthur James Balfour to Sir Cecil Arthur Spring Rice

Sir: London January 13th 1917.

In sending you a translation of the Allied Note I desire to make the following observations which you should bring to the notice of the United States Government.

I gather from the general tenour of the President's note that while he is animated by an intense desire that peace should come soon and that when it comes it should be lasting, he does not for the moment at least concern himself with the terms on which it should be arranged. His Majesty's Government entirely share the President's ideas; but they feel strongly that the durability of peace must largely depend on its character and that no stable system of international relations can be built on foundations which are essentially and hopelessly defective.

This becomes clearly apparent if we consider the main conditions which rendered possible the calamities from which the world is now suffering. These were the existence of Great Powers consumed with the lust of domination in the midst of a community of nations ill prepared for defence, plentifully supplied indeed with international laws, but with no machinery for enforcing them and weakened by the fact that neither the boundaries of the various States nor their internal constitution harmonised with the aspirations of their constituent races or secured to them just and equal treatment.

That this last evil would be greatly mitigated if the Allies secured the changes in the map of Europe outlined in their joint note is manifest, and I need not labour the point.

It has been argued indeed that the expulsion of the Turks from Europe forms no proper or logical part of this general scheme. The maintenance of the Turkish Empire was during many generations regarded by statesmen of world-wide authority as essential to the maintenance of European peace. Why, it is asked, should the cause of peace be now associated with a complete reversal of this traditional policy?

The answer is that circumstances have completely changed. It is unnecessary to consider now whether the creation of a reformed Turkey mediating between hostile races in the Near East was a scheme which, had the Sultan been sincere and the Powers united, could ever have been realised. It certainly cannot be realised now. The Turkey of "Union and Progress" is at least as barbarous and is far more aggressive than the Turkey of Sultan

Abdul Hamid.[1] In the hands of Germany it has ceased even in appearance to be a bulwark of peace and is openly used as an instrument of conquest. Under German officers Turkish soldiers are now fighting in lands from which they had long been expelled and a Turkish Government controlled, subsidized and supported by Germany has been guilty of massacres in Armenia and Syria more horrible than any recorded in the history even of those unhappy countries. Evidently the interests of peace and the claims of nationality alike require that Turkish rule over alien races shall if possible be brought to an end; and we may hope that the expulsion of Turkey from Europe will contribute as much to the cause of peace as the restoration of Alsace Lorraine to France, of Italia Irredenta to Italy, or any of the other territorial changes indicated in the Allied Note.

Evidently however such territorial re-arrangements, though they may diminish the occasions of war, provide no sufficient security against its recurrence. If Germany, or rather those in Germany who mould its opinions and control its destinies, again set out to domineer the world, they may find that by the new order of things the adventure is made more difficult, but hardly that it is made impossible. They may still have ready to their hand a political system organised through and through on a military basis; they may still accumulate vast stores of military equipment; they may still persist in their methods of attack, so that their more pacific neighbours will be struck down before they can prepare themselves for defence. If so, Europe when the war is over will be far poorer in men, in money and in mutual good will than it was when the war began, but it will not be safer; and the hopes for the future of the world entertained by the President will be as far as ever from fulfilment.

There are those who think that for this disease International Treaties and International Laws may provide a sufficient cure. But such persons have ill learned the lessons so clearly taught by recent history. While other nations, notably the United States of America and Britain, were striving by Treaties of Arbitration to make sure that no chance quarrel should mar the peace they desired to make perpetual, Germany stood aloof. Her historians and philosophers preached the splendours of war: power was proclaimed as the true end of the State; and the General Staff forged with untiring industry the weapons by which at the appointed moment power might be achieved. These facts proved clearly enough that Treaty arrangements for maintaining peace were not likely to find much favour at Berlin: they did not prove

[1] Born 1842, died 1918; ruled 1876-1909.

that such Treaties once made would be utterly ineffectual. This became evident only when war had broken out; though the demonstration, when it came, was overwhelming. So long as Germany remains the Germany which without a shadow of justification overran and barbarously ill-treated a country it was pledged to defend, no State can regard its rights as secure if they have no better protection than a solemn Treaty.

The case is made worse by the reflection that these methods of calculated brutality were designed by the Central Powers not merely to crush to the dust those with whom they were at war, but to intimidate those with whom they were still at peace. Belgium was not only a victim: it was an example. Neutrals were intended to note the outrages which accompanied its conquest, the reign of terror which followed on its occupation, the deportation of a portion of its population, the cruel oppression of the remainder. And lest the nations happily protected either by British Fleets or by their own from German Armies should suppose themselves safe from German methods, the submarine has (within its limits) assiduously imitated the barbarous practices of the sister service. The War Staffs of the Central Powers are well content to horrify the world if at the same time they can terrorize it.

If then the Central Powers succeed, it will be to methods like these that they will owe their success. How can any reform of International relations be based on a peace thus obtained? Such a peace would represent the triumph of all the forces which make war certain and make it brutal. It would advertise the futility of all the methods on which civilization relies to eliminate the occasions of International dispute and to mitigate their ferocity. Germany and Austria made the present war inevitable by attacking the rights of one small State, and they gained their initial triumphs by violating the Treaty guarantees of the territories of another. Are small States going to find in them their future protectors or in Treaties made by them a bulwark against aggression? Terrorism by land and sea will have proved itself the instrument of victory. Are the victors likely to abandon it on the appeal of neutrals? If existing Treaties are no more than scraps of paper, can fresh Treaties help us? If the violation of the most fundamental canons of International Law be crowned with success, will it not be in vain that the assembled nations labour to improve their code? None will profit by their rules but Powers who break them. It is those who keep them that will suffer.

Though therefore the people of this country share to the full the desire of the President for peace, they do not believe peace can be durable if it be not based on the success of the Allied cause. For a durable peace can hardly be expected unless three conditions are fulfilled. The first is that existing causes of International unrest should be as far as possible removed or weakened. The second is that the aggressive aims and the unscrupulous methods of the Central Powers should fall into disrepute among their own peoples. The third is that behind International law and behind all Treaty arrangements for preventing or limiting hostilities some form of International sanction should be devised which would give pause to the hardiest aggressor. These conditions may be difficult of fulfilment. But we believe them to be in general harmony with the President's ideas and we are confident that none of them can be satisfied, even imperfectly, unless peace be secured on the general lines indicated (so far as Europe is concerned) in the joint note. Therefore it is that this country has made, is making and is prepared to make sacrifices of blood and treasure unparalleled in its history. It bears these heavy burdens not merely that it may thus fulfil its Treaty obligations nor yet that it may secure a barren triumph of one group of nations over another. It bears them because it firmly believes that on the success of the Allies depend the prospects of peaceful civilization and of those International reforms which the best thinkers of the New World as of the Old dare to hope may follow on the cessation of our present calamities.

I am, etc.,   Arthur James Balfour.

TCL (SDR, RG 59, 763.72119/394, DNA).

Sir William George Eden Wiseman
to the Foreign Office

[New York] 16-1-17

Immediately after receipt of Allies reply, President summoned House for a conference. The President is well satisfied with the reply and believes his action is justified as having given to the Allies a splendid opportunity to state their position. He re-affirms statement that his idea was to obtain statement of objects by belligerents so that if the United States were drawn in they would know what they were aiming at. We must expect further notes and exchanges of views. We should emphasize continually that the Allies object is the liberation of Europe, and not war to crush the German people. President and advisers are particularly anxious about the Russian situation, fearing that power has gone back into the hands of the reactionaries. This impression has been strengthened by Jusserands indiscreet words to House to effect that he was much worried over Russian political situation. President says that Russia stands in the way of complete sympathy between United States and Allies. President Wilson believes that War has entered the final phase which may last three to twelve months, but peace discussion will go on from now to the end. His military advisers have told him not to expect any great military change as a result of next Spring's fighting.

TC telegram (W. Wiseman Papers, CtY).

Count Johann Heinrich von Bernstorff to Theobald von Bethmann Hollweg

Washington, den 16. Januar 1917.
Ankunft: den 21. Januar 1917.

Nr. 212. Antwort auf Telegramm Nr. 149 vom 7.1.[1]

Von Exzellenz Ermächtigung Mr. House gegenüber Gebrauch gemacht. Er sagte mir, Wilson betrachte diese Äußerung der Kaiserlichen Regierung als *höchst* wertvoll. Über den weiteren Verlauf der Wilson'schen Friedensaktion kann ich noch nichts Bestimmtes sagen. Nur soviel ist sicher, daß Präsident augenblicklich keinen anderen Gedanken hat als Frieden zu stiften und diese Absicht mit äußerster Energie und jeden möglichen Mitteln durchzuführen suchen wird. In allernächster Zeit ist eine weitere Erklärung Wilsons, vermutlich in Form einer Botschaft an den Kongreß zu erwarten. Anscheinend will er darin das amerikanische Volk auffordern, ihm zu helfen, den Frieden zu erzwingen; wenigstens lobt er und House jetzt die Hearstschen Zeitungsartikel, die in diesem Sinne geschrieben sind. Ob es wirklich zu einem Embargo auf *alle* Ausfuhr kommen wird, ist heute noch schwer zu sagen. Vielleicht wird auch die Drohung genügen, um unsere Feinde zu einer Konferenz zu zwingen.

Aus obigem geht hervor, daß wir mit den alten Unterseebootsfragen keine Schwierigkeiten haben dü[r]ften. Auch in der Frage bewaffneter Handelsschiffe hoffe ich auf modus vivendi. Nur müssen wir nicht allzubald und ohne weiteres vorgehen, damit nicht Konflikt eintritt, bevor Präsident fernere Schritte getan hat.

So merkwürdig dies Deutschen Ohren klingen mag, gilt Wilson jetzt hier allgemein als pro-deutsch. Seine Note wurde auf unseren Einfluß zurückgeführt und Gerards Rede verstärkt diesen Eindruck. Letztere Rede entspringt ja den Weisungen, die Herr Gerard hier erhalten. Unsere hiesigen Gegner sind förmlich tobsüchtig geworden und wenden jedes denkbare Mittel an, um Wilson Hindernisse in den Weg zu legen. Dadurch sind die Angriffe gegen Präsidenten zu erklären, sowie die Schmutzigen von Republikanern inszenierten Versuche, der [. . .] Börsenspekulationen vorzuwerfen, wobei auch mein Name (ohne jede Berechtigung natürlich) genannt wurde. Die deutsche Botschaft wird von unseren hiesigen Gegnern bekanntlich für alles verantwortlich gemacht. Fortsetzung folgt.[2]   Bernstorff.

T telegram (Der Weltkrieg, No. 23, geheim, Die Friedensaktion der Zentral-mächte, 4058/910584-5, GFO-Ar).

[1] In it Zimmermann informed Bernstorff that, for reasons of domestic public opinion, Germany did not desire American intervention in the actual peace negotiations. He instructed him to handle in a dilatory manner the question of disclosure of German peace conditions. On the other hand, Zimmermann author-ized Bernstorff to spell out Germany's willingness to cooperate in the part of the program in which Wilson was most interested, namely, arbitration of disputes, a league for peace, and discussion of the questions of disarmament and freedom of the seas. Further, Zimmermann continued, Germany agreed in principle to guarantees to be worked out in a general peace conference following a confer-ence of the belligerents to reach a preliminary peace. Also, as a sign of good faith in this direction, Germany in principle was ready to enter into negotiations immediately with the United States looking toward an arbitration treaty and a Bryan-type peace treaty. Bernstorff should inform Wilson of these points and ask him to perfect his program for a conference to secure world peace and to convey this program to the German government as soon as possible. In addi-tion, Bernstorff should impress upon House and Wilson that Germany's peace conditions were very moderate, particularly in the case of Belgium, and he should also state that Germany wanted a provision eliminating any question of a postwar boycott in communications and commercial relations. However, Ger-many would not discuss Alsace-Lorraine. Zimmermann concluded by asking Bernstorff's opinion as to how much pressure Wilson could exert on the Entente to accept peace negotiations and by asking for any suggestions as to how un-restricted submarine warfare could be undertaken without a break with America.

The German text of Zimmermann's telegram is printed in *L'Allemagne et les Problèmes de la Paix pendant la Première Guerre Mondiale: Documents extraits des archives de l'Office allemand des Affaires étrangères*, André Schérer and Jacques Grunewald, eds. (3 vols., Paris, 1962), I, 668-69. An English translation is printed in *Official German Documents relating to the World War, Translated under the supervision of the Carnegie Endowment for International Peace, Division of International Law* (2 vols., New York, 1923), I, 1012-13.

[2] The continuation, missing in the files of GFO-Ar, has never been found.

T R A N S L A T I O N

Washington, January 16, 1917.
Received: January 21, 1917.

Reply to telegram No. 149 of January 7.

The action authorized by Your Excellency has been taken in a meeting with Mr. House. He told me that Wilson considered this statement of the Imperial Government as of the *highest* value. On the further course of Wilson's peace action, I can still say nothing definite. Only this much is certain, that, at the moment, the President has no other idea but to promote peace, and toward this end he is striving with utmost energy and all possible means.

In the very near future we can expect a further declaration by Wilson, presumably in the form of a message to the Congress. Apparently in it he will call on the American people to help him force a peace; at least he and House now praise the articles to this effect in the Hearst newspapers. Whether it will really come to an embargo on *all* exports is today still hard to say. Perhaps even the threat will suffice to force our enemies to a conference.

From this it follows that we can allow no difficulties in the old question of submarines. Even in the question of armed merchant ships, I hope for a *modus vivendi*. We must just not move too hastily and abruptly, so that no conflict breaks out before the President has taken further steps.

Remarkable as this may sound to German ears, Wilson is generally regarded here as pro-German. His note is attributed to our influence, and Gerard's speech strengthens this impression. The latter's speech was, in fact, occasioned by instructions that Mr. Gerard received here. Our enemies in this country have gone stark raving mad and try in every conceivable way to put obstacles in Wilson's path. This explains the attacks on the President, as well as the attempts stirred up by the dregs of the Republicans to make accusations of stock market speculations, in which my name too (without any justification, naturally) has been mentioned. The German Embassy is, as you know, blamed for everything by our enemies here. Continuation follows.   Bernstorff.

To the Senate and House of Representatives:

The White House, January 17, 1917.

It is with the deepest regret that I announce to the Congress the death of Admiral George Dewey at 5:56 o'clock on the afternoon of yesterday, the sixteenth of January, at his residence in this city.

Admiral Dewey entered the naval service of the country as an acting midshipman from the first congressional district of Vermont on September 23, 1854; was graduated from the Naval Academy as Midshipman June 11, 1858; served with distinction throughout the war of 1861-1865; and thirty years later had risen to the rank of Commodore. It was as Commodore that he rendered the service in the action of Manila Bay which has given him a place forever memorable in the naval annals of the country. At the time of his death he held the exceptional rank of The Admiral of the Navy by special Act of Congress. During the later years of his life he was the honored President of the General Board of the Navy, to whose duties he gave the most assiduous attention and in which office he rendered a service to the Navy quite invaluable in its sincerity and quality of practical sagacity.

It is pleasant to recall what qualities gave him his well-deserved fame; his practical directness, his courage without self-consciousness, his efficient capacity in matters of administration, the readiness to fight without asking any questions or hesitating about any detail. It was by such qualities that he continued and added luster to the best traditions of our Navy. He had the stuff in him which all true men admire and upon which all statesmen must depend in hours of peril. The people and the Government of the United States will always rejoice to perpetuate his name in all honor and affection.   Woodrow Wilson.

Printed in *Cong. Record*, 64th Cong., 2d sess., p. 1578.

To Edward Mandell House

My dearest Friend,   The White House. 17 January, 1917.

Your letter containing extracts from letters from Hapgood and letters sent you by Buckler came to-day, and gives me much to think about.

Did Bernstorff, in his conversation with you the other day, touch at all upon the question what his government would be willing to do *during* the year of investigation provided for in a "Bryan treaty"? You no doubt see what I have in mind. Suppose such a treaty entered into between us, and suppose the subject of controversy which has exhausted the resources of ordinary diplomacy to be her use of submarines in the way we have objected to, would she, or would she not, feel herself obliged to discontinue such practices while the inquiry of the international commission into the merits of the case was in progress? That with me is the vital question. I do not want to walk into a trap and give them immunity for the next year.

A very interesting coincidence occurred to-day. Two men came in to see me, one of whom is, I believe, the permanent secretary or aide employed by Henry Ford in connection with his perpetual conference at the Hague,[1] and has been going about talking to the Foreign ministers here and there, like the other pacifists, and the other an English Jew[2] (with a very decided foreign twist to his tongue) who says he is on confidential terms with various men, his friends, attached to the British Foreign Office. His account of his arguments with these friends about my last note at least proved that he really knew the merits of the case and how to present the argument from our point of view. He said that the men in the British Foreign Office felt that if Germany would now offer to enter with us into a "Bryan treaty" they would begin to take notice and believe that she was in fact at last beginning to change her attitude towards international disputes, putting her aggressive principles behind her! What do you think of that?

I agree with you that it is most difficult to see now what our next move should be with regard to the German proposals,—how we should handle the changed case which Bernstorff has put in our hands. I hope that you are thinking about it more constantly and to better purpose than I have yet been able to do.

For one thing, it is hard to see how to guide Congress successfully.   Affectionately Yours,   Woodrow Wilson

WWTLS (E. M. House Papers, CtY).
¹ Louis Paul Lochner.
² Ferdinand Leipnik, actually Hungarian. Formerly a journalist in Budapest, he had more recently been living in England and the Netherlands.

From Edward Mandell House

Dear Governor: New York. January 17, 1917.

Your letter of yesterday comes this morning and fills me with enthusiasm. I shall look eagerly forward to the delivery of the speech and for its reception both here and abroad.

I am writing Bernstorff asking for confirmation of his statements to me, made as coming from his Government.

He said, and left the impression, that they were willing to submit to arbitration as a means of ending the war, and afterwards said that to show their good faith, they were willing to sign the Bryan Treaty now.

Phillips has just called me over the telephone to say that Bernstorff had asked them to transmit to his Government a very long code message (about 1000 groups) and Lansing wished to know whether there was a reason for its going through. I told him there was.

I cannot understand why he asks, for when I was in Washington I told him that the German Government was talking to you unofficially through me and that you approved the permitting Bernstorff to communicate with his government. I would suggest that you let Lansing see my last letter or tell him its contents.

If Bernstorff has correctly stated the position of his Government and they will stick to it, it seems to me certain that you will be able soon to do something of far-reaching importance.

Your affectionate,   E. M. House

I have concluded that it would be safer to inclose B.'s letter in this. Will you not have Phillips see that he gets it?

TLS (WP, DLC).

From Robert Lansing, with Enclosure

PERSONAL AND CONFIDENTIAL:

My dear Mr. President: [Washington] January 17, 1917.

I am sending you a confidential report from Ambassador Page at London (No. 5568, January 5, 1917) dealing with the question of armed merchant vessels, which I think that you will read with as much interest as I have, since it not only presents the British point of view but brings out very clearly the difficulties which enter into the problem.

I do not think that we can long delay determining upon a very definite policy in this matter, particularly in view of the fact that a renewal of submarine activities seems imminent. The trouble is there are reasonable arguments on both sides of the question which lead to conclusions utterly irreconcilable. I can see no common ground for compromise; in that lies the chief difficulty of our situation. It seems to me, however, that the position of this Government ought to be settled and a definite statement prepared which could be issued promptly at the proper time, as doubtless the question will soon become acute.

I enclose for your information in this connection our public statement of September, 1914, and March, 1916, dealing with this subject.[1]

As I am taking up the question from the politic as well as the legal point of view I would be greatly obliged for any comments on Mr. Page's report and also for any suggestions on the general subject. Faithfully yours, Robert Lansing

CCL (SDR, RG 59, 763.72111/4420, DNA).
[1] About these, see WW to RL, Sept. 17, 1914, n. 1, Vol. 31, and the Enclosure printed with WW to RL, April 24, 1916, Vol. 36.

ENCLOSURE

Walter Hines Page to Robert Lansing

No. 5568. CONFIDENTIAL.

Sir: London, January 5, 1917.

With reference to your telegram No. 4216 December 27, 1916, 4 p.m. and my No. 5416 of the 4th instant in reply, I have the honor to submit the following report. The difficulties in the way of obtaining any reliable information on this subject have been great, and I have not in fact succeeded in ascertaining anything worth mentioning in regard to the reported activities in developing railroad terminals and dock facilities at Halifax, North Sydney and St. Johns, nor on the point of the possible detail of disguised cruisers to protect the lines of trade, but I have gathered privately from an Admiralty source that though the British authorities do not appear to have taken any very definite steps as yet they are undoubtedly considering steps for the further protection of their merchant shipping to meet the increased dangers they apprehend.

The British Government does not appear to know exactly where they stand with our Government with regard to the arming of British merchantmen. In spite of our general pronouncement to the effect that merchantmen may properly be armed for defensive purposes they do not know how this would work out in practice or whether our authorities have laid down specific rules as to what constitutes defensive armament or what such rules might be. They understand in a general way that there is to be a limitation in number and in calibre of guns and that they should be mounted at the stern, failing which that ships might be classed as warships.

The British authorities look for a recrudescence of submarine activity off the American coast as soon as the Allies' reply to the President's note is made public, and they feel it their duty to see to it that their ships are adequately armed to meet this menace since from time immemorial it has been the undisputed right of merchantmen to arm for defence. In old times it was not thought unusual for a merchantman to be armed not merely with bow and stern chasers but with broadsides as well, and the necessity for this sort of armament is greater to-day than ever before, for, whereas in old times a hostile cruiser would be sighted on the horizon and the merchantman would take to flight using her stern chasers for defence, to-day a hostile submarine might suddenly appear on the surface a mile ahead of the merchant ship and if the latter mounted guns only at the stern she would be in no position to defend herself. So much for the number and position of guns.

With regard to the calibre, the Admiralty has knowledge that the new German submarines carry comparatively heavy guns with a range of something like eight thousand yards. A merchantman with guns of less range might just as well be totally unarmed.

A point which seems to me to be of some importance is that the British Admiralty holds that there is nothing in the question as to whether British merchantmen are armed for defence or offence. Whatever the armament might be a merchantman to-day could be armed only for defence, since there is nothing afloat against which she could take the offensive. She cannot be armed for the purpose of seeking out and destroying less heavily armed enemy merchant ships since none such is at present on the high seas, and it is not reasonable to suppose that a merchant ship, being without armour,—no matter how numerous or how heavy her guns might be—could possibly be so rash as to attack an enemy man-of-war, but a heavy and mobile armament obviously seems necessary for merchantmen to meet the present submarine menace, and, if there is any danger of British merchant ships being refused clearance papers in American ports because of this, they may have to give up using American ports whenever possible.

I do not know that any difficulties have lately arisen in American ports with regard to this matter, but the British disposition appears to be that they cannot afford to take the risk of arming their ships properly and then have three or four large ships libeled and interned at New York. This would be too expensive a way of ascertaining the attitude of our Government.

The foregoing should I think be considered in connection with the article I enclose on arming merchantmen from yesterday's MORNING POST and with the attached telegram in that newspaper from its Washington correspondent which states that the question of arming merchantmen is being reconsidered by the Neutrality Board, but that the President is opposed to permitting merchant ships to be more heavily armed than at present. This telegram also states that at present merchantmen are allowed two six-inch guns at the stern but no more.[1]

Another danger in New York harbor under present conditions is that the municipal regulations appear to make it necessary for all ships entering that port to take up a pilot, who is taken on board outside territorial waters. This compels ships to come practically to a dead stop outside the three-mile limit and would give a lurking hostile submarine an enormous advantage in attacking. The British Government, however, for obvious reasons have no desire at this time to make any efforts toward inducing neutrals to extend the limits of their territorial waters.

I have the honor to be, Sir,

Your obedient servant,   Walter Hines Page

TLS (SDR, RG 59, 763.72111/4420, DNA).
[1] Page summarizes these enclosures very well.

From Robert Lansing, with Enclosure

My dear Mr. President: [Washington] January 17, 1917.

The accompanying telegram[1] from Minister Reinsch indicates a crisis in Chinese-Japanese relations involving also American interests, and calls for a prompt determination of our policy in the Far East.

The Continental and Commercial Trust and Savings Bank of Chicago, as you will remember, made a loan of five million dollars to China with the approval of this Department. Reports having been received of opposition to the loan upon the part of the international group of bankers interested in the Reorganization Loan of 1913, the American Minister on December 5, 1916, was instructed, as you directed, to intimate to the representatives in Peking of the governments concerned that any strained construction of existing agreements between the Chinese Government and the Group Bankers or any attempt to exclude our bankers from a fair participation in Chinese affairs would meet with very decided resistance from this Government.

To this instruction Minister Reinsch replied on December 23d that the intimation had been received in a friendly manner by the representatives concerned who said there was no objection to the Chicago loan. All, however, expressed a desire for American cöoperation in a reorganization loan. In a mailed despatch received today Mr. Reinsch states that the representative in Peking of the French banks expressed himself:

> "as quite satisfied with the renewed activity of Americans in Chinese finance. He stated, 'Of course we had to object to the loan, but it is a good thing after all.' "

In the contract mentioned for the loan of five million dollars, it was provided that the Continental and Commercial Trust and Savings Bank should have an option on a further loan up to $25,-000,000, and it is understood that negotiations have already begun for such further loan.

The President of China and the Minister of Finance[2] suggested four days ago that the greater part of the funds be used for the organization of an American-Chinese industrial bank. This use of the funds would clearly exempt the loan from the objection made by the consortium banks to the five million dollar loan that funds were to be used for political purposes and that, therefore, the contract violated the agreement of 1913 with the consortium.

The use of the loan funds for the establishment of an industrial bank may prove to be a possible arrangement, but the Japanese Government has now served notice that the Chinese Government should not borrow except from the Group, and that while the British, French and Russian banks could not now do anything, the Japanese bank would advance ten million Yen ($5,-000,000) provided negotiations with American bankers were broken off. This sum is of course utterly inadequate for the purposes in view. The reply of the Chinese Minister[3] seems quite correct that so long as Germany is denied participation the consortium does not exist to which the option was given and that option cannot be exercised.

Japan evidently aims to take advantage of the preoccupation of her allies to obtain control of China. To do this she desires to prevent all assistance to China from the United States and to keep China weak and divided.

In this connection it should be mentioned that the statement published in American newspapers on Sunday last to the effect that Japan "will not countenance any financial negotiations which would give American capital or the capital of any other nation control of Chinese customs or enterprises" was given to the press by the Japanese Embassy here. This effort to intimidate American capital was possibly made in support of the representations being made in Peking.

Recently overtures were made by a Japanese concern to the American International Corporation for an interest in the project for the improvement of the Grand Canal. These overtures are being supported by the Japanese government. The Department has instructed Minister Reinsch to avoid interference, refusing either to approve or disapprove of such coöperation. The American International Corporation has been informed, however, that the Department looks upon that project as a part of the scheme for the amelioration of the Huai River as planned by the American Red Cross, and entitled, therefore, upon sentimental grounds to remain solely an American enterprise and, moreover, that an approval of the Japanese demand for an interest in the scheme would seem to acknowledge their possession of special rights in Shantung in succession to Germany, whereas the United States has never recognized that Germany had special rights there nor that German interests have been transferred to Japan.

I am disposed to believe that the more we yield to Japan the more we shall be asked to yield and that a firm stand upon our undoubted rights will compel a modification of Japanese demands upon China. But if we decide to insist upon our rights in this matter the Chinese Government will expect our assistance in case Japan should attempt to intimidate it.

I have the honor to be,

    My dear Mr. President,

Sincerely yours,   Robert Lansing

CCL (SDR, RG 59, 893.51/1746a, DNA).
  [1] He meant the letter printed as the Enclosure.
  [2] Ch'en Chin-t'ao, also serving at this time as interim Foreign Minister.
  [3] That is, Ch'en Chin-t'ao.

E N C L O S U R E

Paul Samuel Reinsch to Robert Lansing

No. 1311.

Sir: Peking, December 18, 1916.

I have the honor to report that, in compliance with the Department's telegraphic instructions of December 5, 4:00 p.m., relating to the American loan to China, I have called upon the Ministers of Russia and Japan, and the Chargés d'Affaires of Great Britain and France.[1]

In each case, I stated that the American Government had observed the political and financial situation in China and that it was not desirous of having the Chinese Government reduced to a situation where all kinds of desperate financial expedients would appear necessary to those in charge of China's affairs. Such a situation could benefit no one.

I further stated that in order to protect the right of American bankers to a fair participation in Chinese financial enterprise, the American Government would take a very decided stand against any strained construction of existing agreements made by the Chinese Government in matters of finance; particularly by expanding the scope of such agreements beyond the strict import of the language therein used. More particularly, I added that the American Government considered that the terms of the loan just negotiated with the Continental & Commercial Bank of Chicago did not conflict in any way with existing agreements.

On the basis of previous instructions and intimations which I have received from the Department, I felt justified in stating further that I did not believe that the American Government would countenance any loans not made upon sound principles with respect to the security thereof and the use of the funds provided; and that it did not favor loans carrying concessions or secret privileges.

In every instance, the respective representative with whom I was talking proceeded to ask me what would be the attitude of the American Government towards a re-entry of the American Group into cooperation with the Consortium. I reviewed the history of the attitude of the present administration on this question, and stated that the American Government could not do anything which would imply sanction to a monopolistic or exclusive domination of Chinese finance in general. If the cooperation of the American Group could be arranged, considering all the circumstances of the war and the limitation above set forth, I believed that the American Government would not withhold its approval. In every case, the representative with whom I was talking at the time expressed himself as greatly desirous that Americans should participate in the business of the Consortium. The Japanese Minister stated to me that, in his view, it would be better that the arrangements for the loan should be completed, in order to avoid delay and troublesome questions, and that then the American Group should be invited to participate. The French Chargé d'Affaires, on the other hand, stated that it was the preference of his Government and that of Great Britain that the American financiers should be consulted from the beginning of the negotiations, but that he was not informed as to the views of Russia and Japan.

As the German Minister[2] is at present sick, I have not had an opportunity of bringing to his attention the views of the American Government. He has, however, on other occasions, expressed to me his feeling that it is proper and desirable for American bankers and capitalists to take a part in Chinese affairs, and he has also expressed the readiness of German interests to cooperate with Americans in specific enterprises or undertakings.

In conclusion, I have the honor to report that during these conversations with the representatives of the Powers mentioned, none of them stated any objection to the loan of G$5,000,000.,[3] made by the Chicago bank, nor to the policy of the American Government with respect to the free participation of the American bankers in Chinese finance, as explained to them. On the contrary, they appear to consider such participation of Americans as quite natural and unobjectionable, provided existing agreements are not interfered with; the British and French Chargés d'Affaires were particularly friendly in their expressions concerning American enterprise in China.

I have the honor to be, Sir,

        Your obedient servant,   Paul S. Reinsch

TLS (SDR, RG 59, 893.51/1734, DNA).
[1] B. N. de Kroupensky, Baron Gonsuke Hayashi, Beilby Francis Alston, and Damien Joseph Alfred Charles, Viscount de Martel, respectively.
[2] Admiral Paul von Hintze.
[3] That is, a gold loan.

From Frank Oscar Hellier[1]

Dear Sir: Webster, Texas. Jan 17th, 1917

In a conversation yesterday with Mr. R. R. Dancey[2] of Houston, Texas, I learned that you were one of those who "Bought a Bale" to help the South 2 years ago and that said Bale is still in the warehouse in Houston.

The Webster church was damaged a year ago last Aug. in the Galveston Storm and is not yet repaired. Would you be willing to donate that Bale of Cotton to the Presbyterian Church of Webster to assist us in the repair. If you will grant this to the church perhaps you will send me an order for same to be presented to Mr. Dancey.   Respectfully yours   F. O. Hellier[3]

ALS (WP, DLC).
  [1] Stated Supply of the Webster, Texas, Presbyterian Church.
  [2] Robert R. Dancy, proprietor of a cotton ginning and warehouse company in Houston.
  [3] See F. O. Hellier to WW, March 14, 1917.

From Edward Mandell House

Dear Governor: New York. January 18, 1917.

Your letter of the 17th has just come. When I was in Germany before the war, the Kaiser told me that under no circumstances would they sign the "Bryan treaty." He said Germany was ready at a moment's notice to go to war and they did not intend to give their enemies a year in which to prepare.

When I went to Germany in the winter of 1914-15, I spoke of the reduction of armaments as a condition of peace, telling them that the Allies would never consent to conclude peace until some arrangement could be made in this direction. Again, they said it would be impossible because Germany could not permit herself to be placed at the mercy of her enemies.

The last time I was there, I spoke of a league to enforce peace and also reiterated the proposal for disarmament. They were less vehement in their attitude, but they did not look kindly upon either proposal.

Since then the Government is completely in the hands of the liberals and the war has cut so deeply into the very heart of the nation that their entire attitude seems changed, and today, if we are to believe Bernstorff, they are willing to reverse their former position and take a stand as advanced as any of the democracies.

It is a nice question to determine when it is best for peace to come. The Allies do not think that Germany is yet in a proper frame of mind, but is merely playing for position with the hope of getting off without further punishment, and being able to pursue at will her former purposes.

In my opinion, the best interests of the Allies and ourselves would be met by taking Germany at her word and concluding peace as speedily as possible. The fact that she does not always live up to her obligations ought not to deter us, for if we are unable to cope with her in conference, we ought to lose.

To go on much further, is to undertake a great gamble. There can be no question that Germany is badly pinched at present and that her rulers are greatly alarmed. The spring and summer campaign on land, augumented by an unbridled submarine warfare at sea, might change the entire situation leaving the Allies in the same position in which Germany finds herself today.

Would it not be well for me to send Balfour and Lloyd George a cable covering the points enumerated in this letter? To this might be added that the German Government had proposed an immediate signing of an arbitration treaty with us, and that they had proposed submitting the question of peace to arbitration, or, as an alternative, that you submit proposals yourself for a conference.

I wrote Bernstorff in detail and expect his confirmation or denial by tomorrow. There is no question that he accepted as correct the memorandum which I sent you in my letter of the 15th, for I read it to him and he acquiesced. The question is whether he will be willing to state it in writing. If he is, then I would suggest the cable to Lloyd George and Balfour.

If Bernstorff has stated his Government's proposals correctly, peace is in sight for you would be justified in forcing the Allies to consider it.

If it is decided to send this cable, and if a receptive answer comes back, I think you should then send me to England to press it in person.

As soon as I hear from Bernstorff I will send you a code message.   Your affectionate,   E. M. House

P.S. When I hear from Bernstorff I shall then draw from him an explanation of the doubt you have in mind regarding the proposed "Bryan Treaty."

TLS (WP, DLC).

From Robert Lansing, with Enclosure

My dear Mr. President: Washington January 18, 1917.

I enclose to you a draft of reply to the King of the Belgians' autograph letter of November 11, 1916. Might I suggest that, in view of the fact that the letter appears to be entirely in the Kings's own handwriting—(at least comparison of the signature with the body of the letter leads me to this belief) it would be a courtesy for you to write your own reply in longhand?

Faithfully yours, Robert Lansing.

TLS (WP, DLC).

E N C L O S U R E[1]

I ⟨duly⟩ *have* received Your Majesty's personal letter written at La Panne, November 11, 1916, in relation to the measures recently taken by the authorities now in occupation of part of the Belgian territory to effect forced labor on the part of the natives and to deport numbers of them into Germany.

Such measures ⟨, naturally,⟩ could not fail to affect the feelings and ⟨to⟩ arouse the sympathies of my countrymen ⟨, in whose⟩. *In their* name and as ⟨voicing⟩ *expressing what I knew to be* their sentiments, I ⟨forthwith⟩ *promptly* expressed to the Imperial German Government, in a message cabled to the American Ambassador November 29th last, the deep concern and regret with which the Government of the United States has learned of the policy of the German Government to deport from Belgium a portion of the civilian population for the purpose of constraining them to labor in Germany; *and* utter⟨ing⟩*ed*, in the most friendly spirit, a solemn protest against this action as being in contravention of all precedent and of those humane principles of international practice which have long been followed by civilized nations in their treatment of non combatants in conquered territory ⟨and⟩ *I* add⟨ing⟩*ed an* expression of the conviction of this Government that the effect of such a policy, if pursued, would in all probability be fatal to the Belgian Relief work, so humanely planned and so successfully carried out—a result which would be generally deplored.

I presume that, ⟨before now,⟩ *ere this* Your Majesty has become acquainted with the purport of that message as communicated to the Belgian Representative in this Capital on the 13th ultimo.

I ask Your Majesty to believe ⟨in the sincerity with which⟩ *that* I subscribe myself ⟨as⟩ *most sincerely*   Your friend

T MS (WP, DLC).
¹ Words in angle brackets deleted by Wilson; italicized words added by him.

From Robert Lansing

My dear Mr. President: Washington January 18, 1917.

I have the honor to enclose herewith translations of two notes, dated December 9 and December 28, 1916, from the French Ambassador here, relative to certain decrees that affect banking institutions in Mexico, and particularly the National Bank of Mexico, in which French citizens have invested a large amount of capital.¹

It appears from this correspondence that His Excellency the French Ambassador called upon you at Shadow Lawn, New Jersey, in October last, and that he discussed the matter with you, at that time. In view of this fact, I shall be pleased to receive from you such comment as you may wish to make on the Ambassador's communications.

In this connection, I may add that it has come to my notice that American citizens have large sums of money on deposit in some of the banking institutions affected by the decrees complained of by the Ambassador.

I have the honor to be, my dear Mr. President, with great respect,   Very sincerely yours,   Robert Lansing.

TLS (SDR, RG 59, 812.516/157, DNA).
¹ J. J. Jusserand to RL, Dec. 9, 1916, TCL, enclosing A. Briand to Sanchez Azcoña (Mexican Minister to France), Oct. 18, 1916, TCL; and J. J. Jusserand to RL, Dec. 28, 1916, TCL, all in SDR, RG 59, 812.516/157, DNA. All three documents are printed in *FR 1916*, pp. 645-50.

From Edward Nash Hurley

My dear Mr. President: Washington January 18, 1917.

Your letter of January tenth, enclosing letter to you from Congressman Kent, dated January ninth, regarding the proposed investigation by the Federal Trade Commission, of food, and especially of meat, and supplies, and their cost, has been received. The suggestion in Congressman Kent's letter that the Trade Commission proceed under paragraph (d) of Section 6, indicates that the investigation is aimed at present high prices and immediate relief therefrom. The Department of Justice is entrusted with the enforcement of the anti-trust laws and has existing facilities which it can presently use to determine whether or not there is a violation of these laws. If the purpose, then, is immediate relief, the Department of Justice is the proper body to make such an investigation.

If, on the other hand, the purpose of the proposed investigation into the cost of food products is to gather data and material which would be a basis for a complete economic study, then an investigation on a scale much larger than could be properly carried out by the Department of Justice seems obviously necessary. A general investigation, however, by any one administrative department of the Government along lines previously adopted seems to me at this time inadvisable. Probably two years, at least, will elapse before the investigating body could compile and publish such a comprehensive report. If abnormal war conditions prevailed during the entire course of such an investigation the cost figures and other facts gathered would have little value when applied to normal conditions. Furthermore, were the war to end after the investigating body had gathered half of its data, it seems unnecessary to say that the final compilation of cost figures and other facts, the first half based on abnormal war conditions and the second half based on conditions of a period of readjustment, would be absolutely valueless.

Artificial causes of high prices, such as the manipulation of cold storage plants, might be regulated by the national government in so far as interstate shipments are concerned, but a Federal law would not be as effective as individual action by the states.

The cost of practically all necessaries of life, such as coal and clothing, have been rising in cost proportionately with food products. A separate investigation of meat products would merely touch one factor in the high cost of food products, and an investigation of the high cost of food products, which in itself is a matter of great ramification and detail, would merely touch one factor in the high cost of living.

The appointment of an ordinary investigating committee, I fear, would not bring any real relief. It is so large a subject, involving all the fundamental principles of supply and demand as well as artificial manipulation, that I am convinced that the only kind of an inquiry that would be at all effective would be one made jointly by the heads of Government departments which would have the authority to adopt, and put into effect, any remedial suggestions that may result from the inquiry itself.

The trouble has been in the past that a voluminous report is invariably made at a time when public interest has subsided. The report is then submitted to the heads of departments, or to Congress, at a time when there is a decline of interest. Moreover, action is then asked from officials who have not the benefit of first-hand information and who do not care to wade through a report.

The Department of Agriculture deals more directly with the cattle raisers and the wholesale distribution of all food products than any other branch of the Government. The Department of Commerce has a direct relation with the middle man. The Department of the Interior has authority over such fundamental questions as the development of water power, which, I believe, would lead to a lowering of the cost of living, placing water power in competition with coal power, and thereby reducing the coal bill. All these departments have certain authority, which, if used to the fullest sense, even in an advisory capacity, might result in the adoption of fundamental improvements in our national system of costs.

The Federal Trade Commission is entrusted with the regulation of trade practices with the view to keeping competition free and open, so that competition may regulate prices; and the Department of Justice is the medium for the enforcement of the anti-trust laws.

My suggestion, therefore, is as follows: If you could see your way clear to appoint a departmental committee, which would invite various interests to appear in a friendly way and make their suggestions, such a committee might be constituted by the assistant secretaries or other representatives of the Department of Agriculture, Department of Commerce and Department of the Interior, with one member of the Federal Trade Commission, and an assistant attorney general.

The moral influence implied in the presence of the assistant attorney general doubtless would be helpful.

Whatever might be learned in this manner, and I believe a great deal could be learned by a small departmental committee of this kind, could be applied immediately.

It would not be necessary to ask Congress to give special powers to the committee. It has been my experience that most men asked to cooperate with the Government will do so without force, except in some rare instances.

Very respectfully,   Edward N. Hurley

TLS (WP, DLC).

From Newton Diehl Baker, with Enclosure

My dear Mr. President: Washington. January 18, 1917.

I inclose a copy of a dispatch which I have just sent to General Funston in code. It has seemed to me that in all likelihood we ought to have General Pershing's advice on at least some of the questions asked before making a public announcement of the intended withdrawal of his force.

Respectfully yours,   Newton D. Baker

TLS (WP, DLC).

ENCLOSURE

Washington. January 18, 1917.

TELEGRAM TO BE SENT IN CODE:

The Secretary War directs that you inform General Pershing in code that it is the intention of the Government to withdraw his command from Mexico at an early date. Direct him to keep this fact in strict confidence until he is authorized to announce it or until it is announced here after agreement with him as to date. Direct him to report as follows:

First: Shall the withdrawal be made by rail or marching, or both?

Second: What is the earliest date the movement should begin?

Third: Should residents in Mormon Colony be notified in advance of movement so that they can accommodate themselves to it as they may desire?

Fourth: Will his operations be embarrassed if announcement of withdrawal is made public before actual communication of the order to him?

He will report anything else important and pertinent to subject.

McCain.

T telegram (WP, DLC).

From Thomas James Walsh

My dear Mr. President: Washington. January 18, 1917.

As I told you yesterday, the water power bill, now the un-finished business of the Senate, is in peril. My colleague thinks it cannot pass, and this view is shared by some of our good friends. I am not hopeless, though a sanguine temperament may account for the view I take of the situation. However, the following Senators who ought to be with us are not; at least, not heartily.

Senator Husting, who thinks none of us are sufficiently radical with respect to water power legislation. Kirby,[1] who, without knowing much about the subject, has the impression that there is more or less rottenness in all pending legislation of this nature. Pomerene, who has heard and read much adverse criticism of the Shields bill, and is not sufficiently informed to differentiate between that measure and the one before us. Ashurst, much to my surprise, is reported as indifferent if not adverse. Martine is violently opposed to any legislation on the subject, insisting that the sites be held tied up until sentiment grows for their development by the Government itself. Bankhead, Underwood and Shields are altogether inhospitable in spirit toward the measure, but would vote for it if they were convinced that no progress will be made on their bill until both get into conference under a plan to bring out a conference report on both at the same time.

I thought you would be interested in knowing the attitude of those on our side in any degree unfriendly. I dare say a word from you to each of them individually would insure a practically solid support for the bill on our side, outside of Senators Thomas, Shafroth and Smith.   Very truly yours,   T. J. Walsh

P.S. Much to my surprise I learn that Senator Stone too, is not favorably disposed, just why I am unable to say.   T.J.W.

TLS (WP, DLC).
  [1] William Fosgate Kirby, Senator from Arkansas, elected to fill the vacancy created by the death of James Paul Clarke.

From Josephus Daniels

Dear Mr. President: Washington. Jan. 18. 1917.

I am enclosing the nominations for Rear Admirals in the staff corps.[1] It seemed best to me to make no announcements until the nominations reached the Senate. The examinations of Drs. Braisted[2] and Grayson were completed yesterday afternoon and they were recommended for promotion by the Board.

I suggest they be sent up to-day.
                              Sincerely   Josephus Daniels

ALS (WP, DLC).
  [1] The enclosure is missing.
  [2] William Clarence Braisted, M.D., Commander, U.S.N., surgeon general of the navy and chief of the Bureau of Medicine and Surgery.

To Edward Mandell House

Dear House,   The White House. 19 January, 1917.

There are two words in the German proposals, as you repeated them to me in the letter written just after you had seen Bernstorff, which I wish I had asked you to get him to define a little more fully: the word *arbitration* and the word *programme*. What did you understand him to mean by arbitration? Reference to a specially selected tribunal or the choice of an umpire to be added to representatives of the belligerents? It is hard, you see, to draw an exact line between arbitration and mediation.

He spoke of my originating a "programme" for a conference. I suppose he meant merely a plan. I take it for granted he did not mean that his government would like me to outline terms which might form a basis for discussion.

Your letter of yesterday certainly does set forth a very striking and significant change of attitude on the part of the German authorities since the old confident days before the war, and it is worth while to make the recital. It carries great encouragement with it.

Yes, I hope that you *will* prepare and code for prompt use a message to Balfour and Lloyd George, making a similar review in summary form and setting forth, as you get them in writing from Bernstorff, the terms and methods the Germans now indicate their willingness to accede to. But hold it until I can consult Lansing, and until the address I am about to make to the Congress has had time to sink in a little. You will then know what context to associate with your statement of fact and proposal and can complete the message, to be sent when we finally think it time to send it.

I am to address Congress on Monday (the text of the address could not sooner be got to the several capitals and decoded), I presume at one or two in the afternoon. Can't you come down and be present, staying with us, of course? Do, please.

I must have the address printed, but no advance copies will be given out, and the Senate itself will not be asked to give me the opportunity to address it until Monday forenoon, the whole affair being meanwhile locked up in the breasts of Stone, Lansing, and W.W. No "leak" will in such circumstances, I assume, be possible. I pray most earnestly that the effects will be what we hope for!

With affectionate messages from us all,

Affectionately Yours,   Woodrow Wilson

WWTLS (E. M. House Papers, CtY).

From Edward Mandell House, with Enclosure

Dear Governor: New York. January 19, 1917.

I herewith enclose you a copy of Bernstorff's reply to my letter of the 17th. It will have to be read in connection with my letter to you of January 15th.

I take it, they are merely willing to go to any length to insure peace in the future, and that is the only bearing it has upon the bringing about peace now.

Of course, it is a long way for them to go and puts both sets of belligerents in the same attitude regarding future guarantees, but it does not give you the opportunity to force peace now as my first interpretation of it would have done.

I am asking Bernstorff more particularly in regard to the "Bryan treaty," which they propose signing with us.

I think it would also be well for me to ask him to get his government to give you in confidence some idea of what their terms of peace would be. They are only definite as to the future, and it is the present you must know about before you can act.

Your affectionate,   E. M. House

TLS (WP, DLC).

E N C L O S U R E

Count Johann Heinrich von Bernstorff
to Edward Mandell House

Washington, D. C.

My dear Colonel House: January 18, 1917.

With many thanks for your favor of 17th instant I beg to give you the following further explanations, especially with regard to No. 1 and No. 3 of your letter.

The communication from my Government dealt with what we now always call the "guarantees for the future." The idea was, that by my Government agreeing beforehand to these guarantees, it might be possible to end the war by *a conference of the belligerents* which would lead to a preliminary treaty of peace.

Therefore, No. 1 of your letter means that, in future, arbitration should form a part of the stipulations contained in No. 2 of your letter.

With regard to No. 3, the idea of my Government was, that the President submit a program *for the general conference* concerning the guarantees for the future.

As you know, my Government thinks, that a conference of *the belligerents* about the terms of peace should precede the general conference about the guarantees. However, as it seemed impossible to have the first conference of belligerents without my Government agreeing beforehand in principle to the objects which the second general conference is to attain, I was authorized to make the communication to you which you have put down under Nos. 1 to 4.

I hope to have made the doubtful points quite clear, and I remain,   Yours very sincerely,   J. Bernstorff.

TCL (WP, DLC).

From William Kent

My dear Mr. President: [Washington] January 19, 1917.

I have been informed today that as a result of the passage and signature of the 640 acre homestead bill, that the land offices of the country have been jammed with business and that there is every indication that the filings are largely illicit.

No one can accuse me of having been an "I-told-you-so" Cassandra but in this case, I wish to make an exception to my record.

The fact that I am largely interested in the grazing business has been in a way an estoppal against me from making as vigorous a protest as I should have liked to have made against this particularly ill-timed attack upon control by the Federal Government of the greatest means of securing and perpetuating an adequate meat supply.   Yours truly,   [William Kent]

CCL (W. Kent Papers, CtY).

From Edward Mandell House, with Enclosure

Dear Governor: New York. January 20, 1917.

It is a great temptation to go over tonight and hear the address. I have thought of but little else for the past few days, but it seems to me that I ought to wait until later when it has been digested.

I am enclosing you a copy of a letter from Bernstorff which came this morning. They are slippery customers and it is difficult to pin them down to anything definite. With the English one knows where one is. They may be stubborn and they may be stupid but they are reliable.

The Germans are trying to manoeuvre themselves into a certain position, and just what is in the back of their minds is a matter for speculation.

I have a feeling that the Hohenzollerns are fearful for the Dynasty and they will do anything to maintain it. There is no doubt that the Russian bureaucracy and the German militarists have some understanding and will work together as far as the Russian and German people will permit.

The other Allies are thoroughly suspicious of Russian diplomacy and are watching them closely. Every move the reactionaries make in Russia, the other Allies try to expose so that the people may be aware of it. In this way they have held them in line up to now.

A member of the Russian staff in Washington is a German, and Germans permeate their official family everywhere. In consequence of this, the other Allies are not perfectly frank with the Russians, believing that the German Embassy gets information from that source.

German diplomacy is of the devious kind. For instance, Prince Lichnowski was sent as Ambassador to London. He was a genial, fair-minded, frankly pro-British gentleman. He lulled the British to sleep, and was honest in all he did and said. The real work in the Embassy there was done by two of the staff, one of whom was the head of the German Military Intelligence Office, who came to England and married a daughter of a man in high official position.

I have no doubt but that at the moment the liberal element have control of the German Government, but just how far the Kaiser is influencing the situation to hold himself secure is yet to be determined.

It is possible that they are manoeuvring for position in regard to the resumption of their unbridled submarine warfare. They would like to put the Allies wholly in the wrong, and justify Germany in the eyes of the neutrals in resorting to extreme measures.

This is the discouraging side, and I am glad that I have something brighter to tell.

I had a long talk today with Sir William Wiseman. Without telling him, of course, of your intended address I outlined some of the things which I thought you would stand for in a settlement, and I enumerated the points which you will make in your speech tomorrow. He acquiesced in them all, even to the freedom of the sea, but begged that the term be changed as he said it had become obnoxious to the British.

I told him that we thought England would be justified in demanding the freedom of the sea, as we interpreted it, as one of the conditions of peace. Wiseman thinks if we will stand for these things, that the only difficulty to be overcome will be the insistence that the German Government shall in the future be responsive to the people through the Reichstag.

Wiseman also suggested that it is possible that the other Allies will force Russia to a government responsive to the people, by with[h]olding, in the final settlement, some of the things which she so earnesltly desires—that is a warm sea outlet etc.

I urged upon him the advisability of his government going into a conference almost immediately, telling him that it need not necessarily stop the fighting. My argument was that it would leave Germany without an excuse to resume her frightfulness, particularly if they laid down the condition that they would be willing to continue negotiations until a settlement was reached, provided, pending the settlement, Germany would agree to observe international law.

Wiseman thinks this might be done, although he says the objection will probably be raised that if Germany once gets then [them] into a conference she will offer such terms to Russia, or perhaps to some one of the other allies, as would cause infinite trouble.

I have asked him to call tomorrow at 2.30. I shall then ask him to go to Washington at 3.30 so as to get from the Allied group a concensus of opinion regarding your speech and return here Tuesday morning. I will then report to you immediately.

If we can tie up Germany in a conference so that she cannot resume her unbridled submarine warfare, it will be a great point gained, and if a conference is once started it can never break up without peace.   Your affectionate,   E. M. House

TLS (WP, DLC).

E N C L O S U R E

Count Johann Heinrich von Bernstorff
to Edward Mandell House

Washington, D. C.

My dear Colonel House,   January 20, 1917.

Since telephoning to you yesterday I have changed my mind on second thought and do not think it necessary to trouble you Monday morning with a visit. All I have to say, I have told you over the phone, and I repeat it now, viz. that I am afraid, the situation in Berlin is getting out of our hands. The exorbitant demands of our enemies, and the insolent language of their note to the President seem to have infuriated public opinion in Germany to such an extent, that the result may be anything but favorable to our peace plans. For this reason I had hoped that some step, statement or note might be forthcoming right away, so that the whole world and especially our people would know that President Wilson's movement for peace is still going on. In Berlin they seem to believe, that the answer of our enemies to the President has finished the whole peace movement for a long time to come, and I am, therefore, afraid that my Government may be forced to act accordingly in a very short time.[1]

This morning I received your letter of 19th instant with many thanks. I am afraid that it will be very difficult to get any more peace terms from Berlin at this time for the reasons I mentioned above. However, I am very ready to try and to do my best in the matter.

With regard to the so-called Bryan treaty the submarine issue is, of course, the crux of the matter. If my Government is obliged to meet the British *illegal* starvation policy with the same kind of warfare by employing submarines, they would certainly not be ready to discontinue the practice during the investigation. At the present time, however, our submarines are not used in the way to which the American Government has objected, so that the question of principle is not involved and, therefore, every special case could be investigated according to the treaty. As far as I can see, every question leads us to the same problem, viz. which methods my Government will be obliged by public opinion to use against the English starvation policy,—a policy, by which all neutral countries in Europe are now suffering nearly as much as Germany.

Yours very sincerely,   J. Bernstorff.

P.S. In signing this letter I am reminded of the fact that all our troubles come from the same source namely that England has been permitted to terrorize the neutral nations. By *illegal* methods England destroyed the legal trade of the neutral countries among themselves.

TCL (WP, DLC).
  [1] Bernstorff's pessimism in this letter was due to the fact that he had, only the day before, received a telegram from Bethmann Hollweg informing him in strict confidence that German submarines would begin unrestricted warfare against all shipping in a broad zone surrounding Britain and France on February 1, and instructing him to take certain measures if the United States broke diplomatic relations. For a discussion of the German government's decision and its communication to Bernstorff, see Link, *Campaigns for Progressivism and Peace*, pp. 239-48, 260.

From Brand Whitlock

Dear Mr. President: [Brussels] 20 January 1917.

I am sending you by today's courier a medal presented to me by the gentlemen of the Belgian national relief committee. The medal has not been made public as yet, for reasons easily to be imagined, but I am privately, I had almost said secretly, giving them to a few intimate friends, and I should like you to be the first to have one. If my features are not distinctly numismatic, the fact that they are portrayed by the distinguished sculptor Godefroid De Vreese gives the medal a certain artistic interest. I am sending you too a photograph of a portrait painted at the instance of a number of Belgians by Van Holder.[1] Now that I come to write about [it] I feel an embarrassment in seeming to repeat a somewhat too personal note; I had no intention of overwhelming you with likenesses of myself, but perhaps they will have the effect of their intention and assure you that I think of you often and with affectionate sympathy and yet do not like to add to your burden by too frequently writing about it.

My cablegram of felicitation shortly after election[2] could not have expressed all the solemn joy I had in your triumph; no message could do that. Our first news was disappointing and we lived through days of such black despair as I had never known. With liberation everywhere in the world giving way before autocracy, it seemed too much that America should lower her ideal. Then came the good truth and I was ashamed of ever having doubted or despaired. Democracy justified itself as somehow it always does in great crises, and the result was the first ray of light in this long night of the world, reviving hope in every heart that loves liberty and respects mankind.

I should like to tell you too how beautiful in every way I think your note to the belligerant powers. Its lofty tone, its noble conceptions, its unselfish purpose, lift it high above those other notes that have sought to reply to it, with their punctilious points of "honour" and all that, differing only in form from the defiance that pugilists hurl at each other and little in expression from the discourtesies that [are] exchanged over back-yard fences in neighbourhood brawls. In comparison, how your note will shine in history! It marks the difference between the hopeful idealism of our young America and the weary cynicism of this old Europe. The two continents speak different languages but yours will be the felicity, I am sure, to express us, to reveal us, to make us understood as something far other than the types represented by Baudelaire and Dickens and the snobbish coterie of writers who could never apprehend the spiritual significance of America.

But it was not my intention to bore you with a long epistle. May the same God who said to the Pharoahs of old "Let my people go!" touch the hearts of the rulers of the world with something of that spirit which guides you in your high, lonely way!

I am, dear Mr. President, with the heartful wish that your next term may be less heavy in its burdens than this one has been, always with devotion,

Your humble servant   Brand Whitlock

ALS (WP, DLC).
1 Frans van Holder (1882-1919), Belgian portrait painter.
2 It is missing.

From John Lawson Burnett

Dear Mr. President: Washington, D. C. January 20, 1917.

In your veto of the Immigration Bill two years ago you laid stress on an objection which you had to the provision for excluding those who "advocate or teach the unlawful destruction of property."

I think we have fully met that objection by provision on page 11, which is as follows:

"Provided that nothing in this Act shall exclude, if otherwise admissible, persons convicted, or who admit the commission, or who teach or advocate the commission, of an offense purely political."

I do not desire to further discuss the bill, but call your attention to this provision which I was fearful you might overlook.

Very respectfully,   John L. Burnett

TLS (WP, DLC).

From Walter Hines Page

London, Jan. 20, 1917.

5514. The following is strictly confidential and of immediate importance to the President.

Since there has been an apparent delay in delivering your speech to the Senate I venture respectfully to offer a comment on the phraseology in the sentence about "Peace without victory" my experience of the state of mind in this country makes me fear that unless you define your use of the word "Victory" it will be misconstrued as an effort directly to influence the result of the present war, and even as an interference on behalf of Germany since you took no step while the Germans were gaining military advantages. Any phrase which now appears to the Allies to interfere just when they hope to gain a striking military advantage is enough [to] provoke a storm of criticism that may greatly lessen your influence hereafter. Nothing can now stop the war before the almost imminent great campaign in France for which every preparation has been made. There is a general expectation here that after that peace may soon come.

(If ?) instead of "Peace without victory" you should amplify your statement in some such manner as "Peace without conquest" or "People of either side" your speech will have the greatest good effect. Your words as they stand may be construed here as a sort of denial of Balfour's letter and possibly even as an unfriendly interference in the war at its most critical moment.

The sentiments you express are the noblest utterance since the war began, and with an explanatory modification of this passage the speech guaranteed greatly further the cause you plead, enhance your influence, and fix you at the front of the movement for securing permanent peace.   Page.

CC telegram (WP, DLC).

From William Graves Sharp

Paris, January 21 1917.

FOR THE PRESIDENT: CONFIDENTIAL.

During a half hour conversation last evening with Denys Cochin of the Foreign Office he expressed views of such a nature that I deem it highly important that you should know them as soon as possible. Greatly added weight must be attached to them because of his prominence in the Government and deserved confidence reposed by all classes in his integrity and judgment. The cordial relations existing between us since the early days of the war have always invited from him the greatest frankness. Referring to the recent reply of the Entente Powers to your communication, he said that he had understood that Zimmerman[n] had publicly stated that in behalf of the Central Powers he had confided to you in some form of statement the specific terms on which they would agree to peace. He said he greatly hoped this true and that they were of such a nature as could be accepted with honor so as to bring to a close a war which had been so terribly destructive. Declaring that an unprecedentedly vigorous attack by the Entente Powers was imminent, at the same time expressing his settled conviction that the enemy was feeling in its most drastic form results of the embargo shutting off food stuffs and also supplies much needed for explosives. He still earnestly deplored the fact that unless terms of peace could be quickly agreed upon the coming months would witness a terrible sacrifice of life on both sides. His clearly expressed lack of faith also in the efficacy of a subjugation of the enemy to guarantee in itself permanency of peace greatly impressed me. He has lost two most promising sons in this war.

While these statements can properly be said to only represent his personal views, yet coming from such a source I believe they are representative of a growing sentiment among many of the more thoughtful people. Confirmatory of this opinion, is the statement made to me a few days ago at my home by one of the most prominent senators in the French Parliament that most serious thought was being given by some of his colleagues to the discussion of the suggestions contained in your communication addressed to the belligerent Powers. He expressed to me the earnest hope that your efforts might bear fruit.

In view of what I must believe to be the encouraging symptoms of a more receptive public mind toward your recommendations than the various governments and the press reflect in their attitude, I am prompted to voice again my belief expressed to you in a former cablegram that the Central Powers ought to now come forward with definite and generous terms upon which peace may be secured. They should be free from arrogance, boasting, and recriminations.

It seems to me, on the eve of the delivering of your great message to the Senate which so effectively brushes aside the cobwebs of barbarous and old time doctrines and so clearly pioneers the way to a new international freedom and common brotherhood of nations, the time for setting forth these terms has been made psychological. Once the forces again grapple for supremacy with greatly intensified power to destroy, another million lives will have been given up before any pause can be made to heed a further call to peace. Your message is masterly.   Sharp

T telegram (SDR, RG 59, 763.72119/405, DNA).

An Address to the Senate

Gentlemen of the Senate: 22 January, 1917.

On the eighteenth of December last I addressed an identic note to the governments of the nations now at war requesting them to state, more definitely than they had yet been stated by either group of belligerents, the terms upon which they would deem it possible to make peace. I spoke on behalf of humanity and of the rights of all neutral nations like our own, many of whose most vital interests the war puts in constant jeopardy. The Central Powers united in a reply which stated merely that they were ready to meet their antagonists in conference to discuss terms of peace. The Entente Powers have replied much more definitely and have stated, in general terms, indeed, but with sufficient definiteness to imply details, the arrangements, guarantees, and acts of reparation which they deem to be the indispensable conditions of a satisfactory settlement. We are that much nearer a definite discussion of the peace which shall end the present war. We are that much nearer the discussion of the international concert which must thereafter hold the world at peace. In every discussion of the peace that must end this war it is taken for granted that that peace must be followed by some definite concert of power which will make it virtually impossible that any such catastrophe should ever overwhelm us again. Every lover of mankind, every sane and thoughtful man must take that for granted.

I have sought this opportunity to address you because I thought that I owed it to you, as the council associated with me in the final determination of our international obligations, to disclose to you without reserve the thought and purpose that have been taking form in my mind in regard to the duty of our Government in the days to come when it will be necessary to lay afresh and upon a new plan the foundations of peace among the nations.

It is inconceivable that the people of the United States should play no part in that great enterprise. To take part in such a service will be the opportunity for which they have sought to prepare themselves by the very principles and purposes of their polity and the approved practices of their Government ever since the days when they set up a new nation in the high and honourable hope that it might in all that it was and did show mankind the way to liberty. They cannot in honour withhold the service to which they are now about to be challenged. They do not wish to withhold it. But they owe it to themselves and to the other nations of the world to state the conditions under which they will feel free to render it.

That service is nothing less than this, to add their authority and their power to the authority and force of other nations to guarantee peace and justice throughout the world. Such a settlement cannot now be long postponed. It is right that before it comes this Government should frankly formulate the conditions upon which it would feel justified in asking our people to approve its formal and solemn adherence to a League for Peace. I am here to attempt to state those conditions.

The present war must first be ended; but we owe it to candour and to a just regard for the opinion of mankind to say that, so far as our participation in guarantees of future peace is concerned, it makes a great deal of difference in what way and upon what terms it is ended. The treaties and agreements which bring it to an end must embody terms which will create a peace that is worth guaranteeing and preserving, a peace that will win the approval of mankind, not merely a peace that will serve the several interests and immediate aims of the nations engaged. We shall have no voice in determining what those terms shall be, but we shall, I feel sure, have a voice in determining whether they shall be made lasting or not by the guarantees of a universal covenant; and our judgment upon what is fundamental and essential as a condition precedent to permanency should be spoken now, not afterwards when it may be too late.

No covenant of cooperative peace that does not include the peoples of the New World can suffice to keep the future safe against war; and yet there is only one sort of peace that the peoples of America could join in guaranteeing. The elements of that peace must be elements that engage the confidence and satisfy the principles of the American governments, elements consistent with their political faith and the practical convictions which the peoples of America have once for all embraced and undertaken to defend.

I do not mean to say that any American government would throw any obstacle in the way of any terms of peace the governments now at war might agree upon, or seek to upset them when made, whatever they might be. I only take it for granted that mere terms of peace between the belligerents will not satisfy even the belligerents themselves. Mere agreements may not make peace secure. It will be absolutely necessary that a force be created as a guarantor of the permanency of the settlement so much greater than the force of any nation now engaged or any alliance hitherto formed or projected that no nation, no probable combination of nations could face or withstand it. If the peace presently to be made is to endure, it must be a peace made secure by the organized major force of mankind.

The terms of the immediate peace agreed upon will determine whether it is a peace for which such a guarantee can be secured. The question upon which the whole future peace and policy of the world depends is this: Is the present war a struggle for a just and secure peace, or only for a new balance of power? If it be only a struggle for a new balance of power, who will guarantee, who can guarantee, the stable equilibrium of the new arrangement? Only a tranquil Europe can be a stable Europe. There must be, not a balance of power, but a community of power; not organized rivalries, but an organized common peace.

Fortunately we have received very explicit assurances on this point. The statesmen of both of the groups of nations now arrayed against one another have said, in terms that could not be misinterpreted, that it was no part of the purpose they had in mind to crush their antagonists. But the implications of these assurances may not be equally clear to all,—may not be the same on both sides of the water. I think it will be serviceable if I attempt to set forth what we understand them to be.

They imply, first of all, that it must be a peace without victory. It is not pleasant to say this. I beg that I may be permitted to put my own interpretation upon it and that it may be understood that no other interpretation was in my thought. I am seeking only to face realities and to face them without soft concealments. Victory would mean peace forced upon the loser, a victor's terms imposed upon the vanquished. It would be accepted in humiliation, under duress, at an intolerable sacrifice, and would leave a sting, a resentment, a bitter memory upon which terms of peace would rest, not permanently, but only as upon quicksand. Only a peace between equals can last. Only a peace the very principle of which is equality and a common participation in a common benefit. The right state of mind, the right feeling between nations, is as necessary for a lasting peace as is the just settlement of vexed questions of territory or of racial and national allegiance.

The equality of nations upon which peace must be founded if it is to last must be an equality of rights; the guarantees exchanged must neither recognize nor imply a difference between big nations and small, between those that are powerful and those that are weak. Right must be based upon the common strength, not upon the individual strength, of the nations upon whose concert peace will depend. Equality of territory or of resources there of course cannot be; nor any other sort of equality not gained in the ordinary peaceful and legitimate development of the peoples themselves. But no one asks or expects anything more than an equality of rights. Mankind is looking now for freedom of life, not for equipoises of power.

And there is a deeper thing involved than even equality of right among organized nations. No peace can last, or ought to last, which does not recognize and accept the principle that governments derive all their just powers from the consent of the governed, and that no right anywhere exists to hand peoples about from sovereignty to sovereignty as if they were property. I take it for granted, for instance, if I may venture upon a single example, that statesmen everywhere are agreed that there should be a united, independent, and autonomous Poland, and that henceforth inviolable security of life, of worship, and of industrial and social development should be guaranteed to all peoples who have lived hitherto under the power of governments devoted to a faith and purpose hostile to their own.

I speak of this, not because of any desire to exalt an abstract political principle which has always been held very dear by those who have sought to build up liberty in America, but for the same reason that I have spoken of the other conditions of peace which seem to me clearly indispensable,—because I wish frankly to uncover realities. Any peace which does not recognize and accept this principle will inevitably be upset. It will not rest upon the affections or the convictions of mankind. The ferment of spirit of whole populations will fight subtly and constantly against it, and all the world will sympathize. The world can be at peace only if its life is stable, and there can be no stability where the will is in rebellion, where there is not tranquillity of spirit and a sense of justice, of freedom, and of right.

So far as practicable, moreover, every great people now struggling towards a full development of its resources and of its powers should be assured a direct outlet to the great highways of the sea. Where this cannot be done by the cession of territory, it can no doubt be done by the neutralization of direct rights of way under the general guarantee which will assure the peace itself. With a right comity of arrangement no nation need be shut away from free access to the open paths of the world's commerce.

And the paths of the sea must alike in law and in fact be free. The freedom of the seas is the *sine qua non* of peace, equality, and cooperation. No doubt a somewhat radical reconsideration of many of the rules of international practice hitherto thought to be established may be necessary in order to make the seas indeed free and common in practically all circumstances for the use of mankind, but the motive for such changes is convincing and compelling. There can be no trust or intimacy between the peoples of the world without them. The free, constant, unthreatened intercourse of nations is an essential part of the process of peace and of development. It need not be difficult either to define or to secure the freedom of the seas if the governments of the world sincerely desire to come to an agreement concerning it.

It is a problem closely connected with the limitation of naval armaments and the cooperation of the navies of the world in keeping the seas at once free and safe. And the question of limiting naval armaments opens the wider and perhaps more difficult question of the limitation of armies and of all programmes of military preparation. Difficult and delicate as these questions are, they must be faced with the utmost candour and decided in a spirit of real accommodation if peace is to come with healing in its wings, and come to stay. Peace cannot be had without concession and sacrifice. There can be no sense of safety and equality among the nations if great preponderating armaments are henceforth to continue here and there to be built up and maintained. The statesmen of the world must plan for peace and nations must adjust and accommodate their policy to it as they have planned for war and made ready for pitiless contest and rivalry. The question of armaments, whether on land or sea, is the most immediately and intensely practical question connected with the future fortunes of nations and of mankind.

I have spoken upon these great matters without reserve and with the utmost explicitness because it has seemed to me to be necessary if the world's yearning desire for peace was anywhere to find free voice and utterance. Perhaps I am the only person in high authority amongst all the peoples of the world who is at liberty to speak and hold nothing back. I am speaking as an individual, and yet I am speaking also, of course, as the responsible head of a great government, and I feel confident that I have said what the people of the United States would wish me to say. May I not add that I hope and believe that I am in effect speaking for liberals and friends of humanity in every nation and of every programme of liberty? I would fain believe that I am speaking for the silent mass of mankind everywhere who have as yet had no place or opportunity to speak their real hearts out concerning the death and ruin they see to have come already upon the persons and the homes they hold most dear.

And in holding out the expectation that the people and Government of the United States will join the other civilized nations of the world in guaranteeing the permanence of peace upon such terms as I have named I speak with the greater boldness and confidence because it is clear to every man who can think that there is in this promise no breach in either our traditions or our policy as a nation, but a fulfillment, rather, of all that we have professed or striven for.

I am proposing, as it were, that the nations should with one accord adopt the doctrine of President Monroe as the doctrine of the world: that no nation should seek to extend its polity over any other nation or people, but that every people should be left free to determine its own polity, its own way of development, unhindered, unthreatened, unafraid, the little along with the great and powerful.

I am proposing that all nations henceforth avoid entangling alliances which would draw them into competitions of power, catch them in a net of intrigue and selfish rivalry, and disturb their own affairs with influences intruded from without. There is no entangling alliance in a concert of power. When all unite to act in the same sense and with the same purpose all act in the common interest and are free to live their own lives under a common protection.

I am proposing government by the consent of the governed; that freedom of the seas which in international conference after conference representatives of the United States have urged with the eloquence of those who are the convinced disciples of liberty; and that moderation of armaments which makes of armies and navies a power for order merely, not an instrument of aggression or of selfish violence.

These are American principles, American policies. We could stand for no others. And they are also the principles and policies of forward looking men and women everywhere, of every modern nation, of every enlightened community. They are the principles of mankind and must prevail.[1]

Printed reading copy (WP, DLC).
[1] The WWT copy of this address, which Wilson sent to the Public Printer, is in WP, DLC.

Two Letters from Edward Mandell House

Dear Governor: New York. January 22, 1917.

I am very very happy tonight. I have seen enough people to know that your address was all that I thought it was.

Lippman[n], Croly, Bainbridge Colby etc. etc. all characterize it in unmeasured terms of praise. Croly told me that he felt that it was the greatest event in his own life.

I feel that I have lost something that I can never recover by not being there, but something told me it was best not to go.

                    Your affectionate,   E. M. House

Dear Governor: New York. January 22, 1917.

Hoover of the Belgian Relief landed yesterday and he confirms what I wrote you in regard to the Russians.

He says that the only way Briand saved his government was to tell the House of Deputies in secret assembly that France and England were in no way responsible for the Roumanian fiasco, that it was done through the corruption of high Russian officials who permitted Germany to over-run that country by a preconcerted plan.

He tells me, too, that both France and England are greatly alarmed over the Russian situation. They believe if they can get them into a spring campaign they may hold them through the summer, but they consider that the time is critical between now and then.

He thinks if the Germans had answered your note by declaring they would evacuate both France and Belgium, and would agree to some sort of arrangement for reparation, that it would have been impossible to have held the English and French people to a continuation of the war.

Hoover is a man of good sense and has unusual facilities for obtaining information.

And this reminds me that he considers it almost imperative that this Government assume the expense of carrying on the Belgian Relief Commission. It does not amount to a great deal perhaps not more than $500,000. or a $1,000,000. a year which would be only a small part of the money France and England are voting to the relief of that country. They are giving now at the rate of nearly $200,000,000. a year.

Your affectionate,   E. M. House

TLS (WP, DLC).

From Charles Ferguson, with Enclosure

Dear Mr President: New York Jany 22 [1917]

I forward the enclosed letter to you—at the suggestion of the writer—George D. Herron[1]—a man of extraordinary faculty—most loyal to you—on the chance that he may possibly be of further use to the Administration in his present place—the meeting-place of so many currents of European opinion.

May I add to my telegram,[2] just sent, concerning the speech in the Senate today—my feeling that it erects "a standard to which the wise and honest can repair"—that it passes beyond prudence as it was fitting to do in so great a case—that it will be underwritten by the life, fortune & sacred honor of a sufficient number of men.   Yours always faithfully   Charles Ferguson

ALS (WP, DLC).

¹ George Davis Herron, born Montezuma, Ind., January 21, 1862. Largely self-taught, he entered the Congregational ministry in 1883 and held pastorates in Lake City, Minn., and Burlington, Ia. In Burlington, he came in contact with Mrs. E. D. Rand and her daughter, Carrie. Mrs. Rand endowed a professorship of "Applied Christianity" for Herron at Iowa (later Grinnell) College in 1893. There Herron attracted wide interest by his attempts to translate Christianity into social, economic, and political terms. His severe criticism of existing institutions ranged from marriage to capitalism, created much opposition, and led to his resignation of his professorship in 1899. He joined the Socialist party about this time in the hope of giving it a religious character.

In March 1901, his wife, Mary Everhard Herron, divorced him for desertion, and in May of that same year he and Carrie Rand were married in New York. He was soon deposed from the ministry and shortly thereafter took up residence with his new wife and mother-in-law near Fiesole, Italy. There he devoted himself to literary work and to intellectual discourse, both with a stream of visitors and through a large correspondence with persons in Europe and the United States. After the death of Carrie Rand Herron in 1914 and the outbreak of war, Herron abandoned his pacifism, became violently anti-German, and broke with the Socialist party.

For a sketch of Herron's early life and a detailed treatment of his later career, see Mitchell Pirie Briggs, *George D. Herron and the European Settlement* (Stanford, Cal., 1932).

² It is missing.

E N C L O S U R E

George Davis Herron to Charles Ferguson

Dear Ferguson: Geneva, Switzerland. Dec. 31, 1916.

By a curious and extraordinary chance, I find my being placed, all at once, in the position of Dr. Wilson's defender and interpreter, in this part of the world. As you may not know, I left Florence for Geneva, first, because my two boys are in school here and I did not want to be away from them, and, second, because I could not permit myself to go on amidst the old material surroundings, with the world lying in ruins. I decided upon a much simpler mode of life. Here, I had been a student years ago, and old friendships, among old Genevese families—and French also—remained. I found great misunderstanding of Wilson, and great hostility to him, and a preposterous idealization of Roosevelt. I undertook to explain Wilson to my friends. Then the editor of the old Genevese weekly—"Semaine Litteraire"—somewhat of the nature of a French New York "Nation"—asked me to write about Wilson, which I did, thinking it a very incidental matter, and never expecting to hear of it again. But, for some strange reason, the article attracted immediate and incredible attention all over Europe. It was republished from London to Moscow, from Paris to Vienna, from Berlin to Rome. It came to the attention of governments, and a messenger came from Paris to talk about it. I find myself in the astounding and terrifying position of being treated as an authority on Wilson—all over Europe. Heaven knows I never dreamed of such a situation. I have explained over and over again that I have not the slightest authority to interpret Wilson—that I never met him or spoke with him. I only meant, in a literary way, to present my view of him. If Wilson ever heard of me at all, it is probably only through the grotesque yellow reports of me in America; and, in any case, I am not at all the sort of interpreter he would choose.

I have only held fast, for years, to a certain ideal of him. I have trusted that it was he who would redeem democracy and organize freedom. And I undertook, when urged to do so, to set forth this ideal in French print. And now it has all been taken so wisely and authoritatively. It is one of those curious and fateful accidents— (are there any accidents?)—that happen to men and nations.

I am explaining it all to you in order that you, out of your chivalrous heart, may explain the matter to the President in case the matter perchance comes to his attention—you or his daughter Margeret.

I enclose a copy of the article that began the trouble,[1] and one (there have been several) in today's "Journal de Genève."[2]

Let me take this occasion, also, to thank you for your courtesy to Monsieur Guy of the French Foreign Office,[3] who came to you with a letter of introduction from me.

Did you receive my letter about your book?[4]

Faithfully Yours,   George D. Herron

P.S. Perhaps the best way, if perchance the matter should arise, would be to give Dr. Wilson this letter.

ALS (WP, DLC).
  [1] George D. Herron, "Le président Woodrow Wilson," *La Semaine Littéraire,* XXIV (Dec. 9, 1916), 589-92. It was printed in English translation as "The Man and the President" in George D. Herron, *Woodrow Wilson and the World's Peace* (New York, 1917), pp. 49-77. Herron, by this time strongly anti-German, portrayed Wilson as being on the side of the Allies, although American political realities forced him to pursue a policy of neutrality. Beyond that, however, Herron saw Wilson as a radical in both domestic and international affairs: "If we could look deep into this man's soul, I think we should find there the ideal of a world at last arriving at a universal communism of production and distribution, with a common and unfettered freedom as regards the right of each individual to choose the way in which he shall go, and grow, and give himself" (*ibid.,* p. 75).
  [2] This enclosure is missing, but the article appeared in English translation under the title of "His Initial Effort," *ibid.,* pp. 81-96. It was an interpretation of Wilson's peace note of December 18, 1916. Herron said that the note was, "in effect, nothing else than an ultimatum to Germany" (*ibid.,* p. 82). "Either Germany must place all her terms upon the table," he continued, "and prove them such as to satisfy the new international conscience Mr. Wilson has called into being, or she must add America to the number of her enemies. And it is

thus that the first point of our President's note is not peace but war" (*ibid.*, pp. 88-89).

³ Probably Jean Arthur Guy.

⁴ Ferguson's most recent book was *The Great News* (New York, 1915).

A Report of a Press Conference

January 23, 1917

Mr. President, can you tell us just what you are thinking about the Shields bill and the Myers bill and the Walsh bill?

> I would detain you too long if I told you what I was thinking about them. But my only relation to them at present is in trying to bring the different views together so as to get some action, and just what progress I am making in that, I don't know. I haven't heard the results yet. There were to be some conferences which I think have not yet taken place. I am sincerely interested in getting water-power legislation. I think it is of the utmost importance.

Mr. President, is it the barrier still?

> Yes, sir, simply because I don't know anything that is profitable to say.

Mr. President, there seems to be general disagreement as to what you mean by the force guaranteeing peace. Is that moral or economic or also military force? At one time, you spoke of co-operation of the nations.

> Well, I can't discuss that. That is a proper subject for the discussion of the conference and for submission to the league. This is not the time to discuss that.

If there were such a league to enforce peace, would it carry with it the possible abandonment of the Monroe Doctrine?

> I expressed my view about that yesterday.

You would be saying it was merely an extension of the Monroe Doctrine?

> Yes, sir, it is.

Mr. President, have your conferences in the Capitol evolved any possibility of an agreement with reference to the compulsory investigation bill?

> I think so. The thing is not as far advanced in committee action as I should like it to be, and therefore I can't answer that question with any degree of confidence. My impression is that it is possible.

That wouldn't carry with it any abandonment of the no-strike feature of the bill?

> Perhaps I didn't understand your first question. You meant whether there was any progress towards an agreement on

the process of delaying strikes until there has been an investigation. I think there has been progress in that direction. Because, of course, there is no proposal to prevent strikes.

It is merely to prohibit them while this inquiry is in progress, and, yes, that feature is not in danger?

So far as I can see, it is not. I again have to qualify that by saying I don't know of any.

You said a week ago, Mr. President, that you were of course not opposed to any better plan that may be suggested as a substitute for the present plan.

Yes.

Has there been any substitute considered by you?

No, sir. None has been proposed to me, as a matter of fact.

Mr. President, in the morning papers there are dispatches saying that two of our ambassadors abroad delivered copies of your statement to the governments.[1] How was that?

Merely for information. It was not official at all.

Any solution of the oil-leasing question, Mr. President?

I wish I could say "Yes." I don't see it yet. I conferred yesterday with a group of western senators about it, and I think they were in a very reasonable frame of mind about it, but just what can be generally agreed upon, I don't know.

Mr. President, can you say just when your address was cabled abroad to our ambassadors?

No, sir. That would be a leak. A sort of reverberatory leak.

Mr. President, can you tell us anything about the immigration bill? I believe it is before you now.

Yes, sir, it is technically before me, as a matter of fact. I haven't had time to tackle it. I have got a week or more on it. I am going to turn my attention to it very soon.

Is it your understanding of it, Mr. President, that it removes your objections on the score on which you vetoed it the last time?

Perhaps I had better say that later.

The tariff board ready, Mr. President?

No. The trouble there is that the men I have asked don't want to serve. There isn't any trouble about finding men. It's finding men who will take it when I find them. It is a big job to tackle, and very few men of the sort and size I want are able just to lay down their affairs and turn entirely to this matter. That is the real difficulty. It is not their lack of interest or unwillingness, but it is not feasible in many cases.

[1] Sharp in Paris and Francis in Petrograd. *New York Times*, Jan. 23, 1917.

Could you say, Mr. President, whether in your conferences at the Capitol you reached any understanding as to the character of the revenue legislation to be [considered?]

> I didn't have any conferences about the revenue legislation, for there were conferences about that precedent. I think things are going with a very considerable degree of unanimity about that.

Mr. President, do you know whether the plans for the establishment of a nitrate plant contemplate the establishment of one plant or more?

> That is an open question. I hope there will be more than one, if it is feasible to build them out of the appropriation. Of course, the site chosen will partly determine the amount of money that has to be spent. And I have appointed a committee from the cabinet to visit the proposed sites, the most feasible sites, in prospect, as an additional precaution to the reports we have had from engineers and others.

Can you say who is on that committee?

> I would, if I hadn't forgotten. The Secretary of War and the Secretary of Agriculture—of course the Secretary of the Interior.

Mr. President, would these all be water-power plants?

> That, you see, is part of the determination also. I would rather assume it will, but that is not finally determined. You see, there are four processes of production of nitrates, and three of the four are water-power processes, and the fourth is a steam process.

Mr. President, going back to the oil bill, our understanding is that the lands committee of the Senate is very anxious to effect a compromise. Do you expect to see Mr. Daniels in the hope of working out an agreement?

> I am going to see, rather, the Attorney General than Mr. Daniels, because of course I don't want to do anything that will prejudice the legal claims of the nation in the settlement effected. And I haven't yet had time, since yesterday, to confer with the Attorney General about that.

Mr. President, we have had intimations that the German government would submit its peace terms to you. Would you be willing to say whether you had any intimation about that?

> No, sir, I have not had any.

Any danger of an extra session, Mr. President?

> Why do you say "danger"? Why don't you say "promise"? I see no prospect of an extra session. I won't commit myself to the need.

Mr. President, can you tell us whether you are going to make a regular practice to go up to the Capitol?

> I am going there frequently for the present time only because it is a short session, and that is the rapid way to consult with the senators.

Well, are there any specific days that you are going? Is it going to be a regular thing?

> Well, I think it will be only when there is a clearance to effect, so that I can see a number of men within the shortest time.

The reason I asked that, Mr. President, is, we heard that you were going to take three days every week.

> I haven't anything so disproportionately arranged as that.

Are you going down there today?

> No. This is cabinet day.

Mr. President, could anything be said about Mexico now?

> A great deal could be said. No, there really isn't anything to say.

There are a lot of reports from the border, Mr. President, that the withdrawal of General Pershing's troops out has already been begun.

> He is withdrawing his troops from the outposts.

Can you say, Mr. President, whether there is any immediate intention of lifting the embargo on the border?

> No, there isn't any immediate intention, but, you know, that is a question that is very difficult to answer competently because it is very complicated, because we are willing to let them have arms any time we can be sure whose hands they are going into.

Mr. President, when you say that General Pershing is withdrawing his outposts, could it be said that he may now exercise his discretion as to further withdrawals?

> He will wait for orders.

No orders have been issued?

> I didn't say that. "Further, the deponent sayeth not."

Can you say how soon the ambassador will go to Mexico?

> No, I can't say.

Mr. President, a new code of maritime neutrality was taken up by the American Institute of Law.[2] Has that been placed before you?

> No, not in recent months. Not for a long time.

---

[2] "Havana, Cuba, Jan. 22.—A code of rules of maritime neutrality which should govern the relations between belligerents and neutrals, prepared at the suggestion of Secretary of State Robert Lansing of the United States, was submitted to the American Institute of International Law in annual session here today." *Ibid.*

I understood it was the result of a letter from Secretary Lansing to Mr. Scott.[3]

> I think it was at the time it was first taken up. The Secretary consulted me about it more recently.

Can you say, as it was in the form recently presented, whether it has the sanction of this government?

> I can't say. I have forgotten all about it, to tell the truth.

Mr. President, about a year or so ago—two years ago, I think it was —we asked you about the invitations for the next Hague peace conference, and the matter was dropped just about the time the war began, I think. Has any other step been taken since then about invoking another Hague conference?

> Not that I have heard of.

Could you tell us anything about the high cost of living inquiry, Mr. President? There has been a droop, apparently, so far as the public press has been concerned—there has been very little written about it.

> That is not our fault.

It has been forgotten?

> No, certainly not. It has been going on, as far as it can. It is going on, and thoroughly.

Can you tell us whether you have been considering legislation to bring in or submit before Congress adjourns?

> Not before the report. We wouldn't know what to suggest.

You haven't received any report from Mr. Gregory recently?

> No. I know he is hard at work on it. I saw him last night for a few minutes, but he hasn't made any report.

Mr. President, there are a number of bills which undertake to solve the high-cost-of-living situation now pending in Congress. Have you had an opportunity to study those?

> No, I haven't. I find there isn't room enough in my head for a daily study of all of them.

JRT transcript (WC, NjP) of CLSsh (C. L. Swem Coll., NjP).

[3] James Brown Scott, president of the American Institute of International Law. The *New York Times*, January 23, 1917, prints Lansing's letter, without date.

To Robert Lansing

[The White House]

My dear Mr. Secretary: 23 January, 1917

Will you not be kind enough to have the enclosed letter to the King of the Belgians sent forward by the proper pouch? I am very much obliged to you for having suggested a suitable answer. I have written the letter in my own hand.

> Cordially and faithfully yours,   Woodrow Wilson

TLS (Letterpress Books, WP, DLC).

To William Kent

My dear Mr. Kent: The White House 23 January, 1917

I am sincerely sorry that you feel as you do about the 640-acre homestead bill. I held a great many conferences about it and thought before I signed it that the most objectionable features had been removed or neutralized. I am sorry to hear that you think that illicit filings are going on. I shall call the attention of the department to it.

> Cordially and sincerely yours,   Woodrow Wilson

TLS (W. Kent Papers, CtY).

To Charles Richard Crane

My dear Friend: [The White House] 23 January, 1917

Before your interesting letter of January twentieth came about Reinsch,[1] I had already committed myself to the appointment of Breckinridge Long, of Missouri, to the Third Assistant Secretaryship of the Department of State.

Your suggestion about Reinsch interests me very much, and yet I should hesitate to remove him for the present from a post at which it would be so extremely difficult to find a substitute.

In haste, with the warmest regard from us all.

> Faithfully yours,   Woodrow Wilson

TLS (Letterpress Books, WP, DLC).
[1] C. R. Crane to WW, Jan. 20, 1917, ALS (WP, DLC).

To Anna Howard Shaw

My dear Doctor Shaw: [The White House] 23 January, 1917

May I not wish you for your seventieth birthday not only a return to strong health, but the happy anticipation of many more years of useful service? You certainly have many years of self-sacrificing work to look back upon with pride and satisfaction, and I want to join with your other friends in wishing you many returns of your birthday and an increasing happiness as they come.   Cordially and sincerely yours,   Woodrow Wilson

TLS (Letterpress Books, WP, DLC).

To Lynn Joseph Frazier[1]

[The White House]

My dear Governor Frazier: 23 January, 1917

May I not express through you my feeling of sincere gratification that the legislature of North Dakota should have passed a bill granting to the women of the state the same suffrage privileges that have been extended to them in Illinois?[2] My interest in the extension of the suffrage to the women is, as you know, very great and I feel that every step in this right direction should receive the most cordial endorsement and public recognition.   Cordially and sincerely yours,   Woodrow Wilson

TLS (Letterpress Books, WP, DLC).
  [1] Governor of North Dakota since January 3, 1917.
  [2] That is, the right to vote in presidential elections and for municipal officials.

To John Lawson Burnett

My dear Mr. Burnett: [The White House] 23 January, 1917

Thank you sincerely for your letter of January twenty-second[1] calling my attention to the new phraseology of the Immigration Bill with regard to those who teach or advocate the commission of political offenses.
                    Cordially and sincerely yours,   Woodrow Wilson

TLS (Letterpress Books, WP, DLC).
  [1] Sic in the Swem shorthand notebook.

To William Franklin Willoughby

[The White House]

My dear Professor Willoughby: 23 January, 1917

Thank you sincerely for your memorandum of January sixteenth, written in response to my request. I hope I shall be able to do something to further your work.
    In haste
            Cordially and sincerely yours,   Woodrow Wilson

TLS (Letterpress Books, WP, DLC).

To Robert Lansing, with Enclosure

[The White House]

My dear Mr. Secretary: 23 January, 1917

Here is an interesting suggestion from David Lawrence. I would be very much obliged if you would think it over and see whether there occurs to you any other method of using this leverage than another public address which at this time would seem to me unwise.

Cordially and faithfully yours,   Woodrow Wilson

TLS (Letterpress Books, WP, DLC).

ENCLOSURE

From David Lawrence

My dear Mr. President: [Washington] January 23, 1917.

Your peace message to the Senate has made such a favorable impression that I think you now have an opportunity to do another great service. Our own attitude toward the weaker nations has not been all that could be desired. We still neglect Colombia, whom we wronged. Would it not be opportune now to address the Senate in person on the matter of ratifying the Colombian treaty? All Latin-America would hail your effort with joy. It would mean that we were big enough to amend a wrong, that we were generous enough to give redress. We would make of our friendship with Latin-America not a mere theory but a concrete fact.

The present session of Congress must witness some effort on our part with reference to this Colombian matter or I fear that all Latin-America will think we are shirking again. You addressed the Congress with respect to the Hay-Pauncefote treaty, asking that an error in legislation be repealed. Would it not be everywhere applauded if, with your present moral power, you asked the Senate to correct the injustice we did Colombia in 1903 when we violated a solemn treaty and "took Panama"?

Very sincerely yours,   David Lawrence.

TCL (Lansing Letterpress Book, SDR, RG 59, DNA).

To David Lawrence

My dear Lawrence: [The White House] 23 January, 1917

Your suggestion about the Colombian treaty is a most interesting one and you may be sure will have my most serious consideration.

In haste   Faithfully yours,   Woodrow Wilson

TLS (Letterpress Books, WP, DLC).

To Newton Diehl Baker, with Enclosure

The White House

My dear Mr. Secretary: 23 January, 1917

The enclosed letter is from a young lady in Princeton who is a very close friend of one of my daughters and who is very anxious indeed to have her brother come down from West Point to attend her marriage, her other brother, who is already in the Army, being off on some distant service which prevents his attending. Do you think that this can be done without a serious departure from the rules of discipline at the Academy?

Cordially and faithfully yours,   Woodrow Wilson

TLS (N. D. Baker Papers, DLC).

E N C L O S U R E

From Ruth Preble Hall

My dear Mr Wilson,   [Princeton, N. J.] January 16th [1917]

I am sending you this note through Miss Benham, so that you will surely see it, and this is my reason.

I am going to be married on January 27th to Baldwin Smith[1] an instructor here. I am going to be married in New York so that I can have a very quiet wedding at my uncle's[2] and not get all tired out. Lacey[3] of course is in Mexico and, cannot be present, and so we arranged to have the wedding on Saturday, so Willard[4] could get away from West Point and give me away. It has always been the rule that a Cadet could get leave for his sisters wedding if he was her nearest male relation, and it never occurred to me that there would be any trouble. But now there is trouble, and Willard thinks he wont be allowed to leave. Of course I am horribly disappointed, and it just occurred to me that you might help me, so I am writing to you. I dont believe the Superentendant[5] can realize that Willard is to give me away, and so I am asking you to help me if you can. If you dont think it is right, I know you wont do it, so I feel perfectly easy about asking you.

I am writing this note in pencil, because I am sick in bed with a cold, and dont want to put off writing till I am up again.

I had a nice letter from Nell the other day, but do wish I could see her and her adorable baby.

Please forgive me for bothering you, and dont be cross with

Miss Benham for giving you this note, for she hasnt an idea what is in it.

Thanking you for your many kindnesses to me, I am,

Affectionately your friend,   Ruth Preble Hall.

ALS (WP, DLC).
    [1] Earl Baldwin Smith, Instructor in Art and Archeology at Princeton University.
    [2] Charles Merrill Hough, at this time United States district judge, Southern District of New York.
    [3] Her brother, Charles Lacey Hall, U. S. Military Academy 1908, a captain in the United States Army at this time.
    [4] Her brother, Willard Merrill Hall, a cadet at the Military Academy.
    [5] Col. John Biddle.

From Robert Lansing, with Enclosure

PERSONAL AND CONFIDENTIAL:

My dear Mr. President: [Washington] January 23, 1917

I call your special attention to this telegram received this morning from Berlin, which appears to me to create a very serious situation, if Mr. Gerard is accurate in his presumptions—which sound to me very reasonable.

Faithfully yours,   Robert Lansing

CCL (SDR, RG 59, 763. 72111/4441, DNA).

E N C L O S U R E

Berlin via Copenhagen, Jan. 21, 1916 [1917].

CONFIDENTIAL.

4912. At seven thirty yesterday evening Count Montgelas of the Foreign Office[1] called on me and said that the following note had been sent to the embassies and legations of several neutral nations, particularly Spain and Norway, but was not sent to the United States because that country did not seem to be arming its merchant vessels, that von Stumm,[2] Under Secretary of State, had asked him, Montgelas, to give me a copy. Montgelas further said that Germany had never receded from the position it took concerning armed merchant vessels in the German note of February, 1916.

The note verbale is as follows, and is in French. I send translation and will send original French tomorrow in open cable:

(Blue Code.)

"According to information worthy of belief which the Imperial Government has received from a neutral country, the British Government has endeavored quite recently to decide the neutral shipowners engaged in transportation on its order to arm their ships with cannons. Likewise the armament of these neutral ships has been called for in the most energetic manner by English public opinion.

"In view of these proceedings the German Government thinks it ought to call the attention of the neutrals to the fact that under existing conditions, neutral armed merchant ships run the risk of being taken for armed enemy merchant ships and of being in consequence attacked, these latter ships manoeuvering often under a neutral flag to lay trap for German submarines. Moreover neutral ships of commerce which may make use of their temporary armament will be treated as pirates by the German naval forces.

"The Imperial Department for Foreign Affairs leaves it to the (space for name of legation) to communicate the preceding to its government by telegraph. Berlin, the (blank), to the Legation of (blank)."

(Special Green.)

Many Germans have informed me lately that the public feeling for the resumption of reckless submarine warfare is so great that they do not see how any government can withstand it. I think myself in spite of assurances from all members of government that I have talked to that the course of the government will be to resume reckless submarine warfare by way of attacks without notice on armed merchant vessels, and that an endeavor is being made to place the United States in a position of tacitly or openly consenting to such attacks without notice on armed merchantmen. The above note verbale as I read it contains a plain intimation that armed enemy merchant vessels are subject to attack without notice, and if not answered by some declaration from the United States, may lay the way open to Germany to claim that the United States has consented to such attacks. I think the plan is to first compel all neutral governments except the United States to support the German position and thus leave the United States standing alone against all other neutrals. Note the fact of announcement that all recently captured crews taken on armed merchant vessels of enemies will be treated as prisoners of war. If this is accepted, then the ships from which they were taken are recognized as warships and therefore subject to attack without notice.

Gerard.

T telegram (SDR, RG 59, 763.72111/4441, DNA).
¹ That is, Count Adolf Montgelas, the head of the American section of the Foreign Office.
² Wilhelm von Stumm.

From Robert Lansing, with Enclosure

PERSONAL AND CONFIDENTIAL:

My dear Mr. President: [Washington] January 23, 1917.

I send you a confidential letter I have just received from Ambassador Gerard, which seems to me worthy of your attention.

Faithfully yours,   Robert Lansing

TLS (SDR, RG 59, 763.72/3107½, DNA).

E N C L O S U R E

James Watson Gerard to Robert Lansing

My dear Mr Secretary,   Berlin, January 3rd, 1916 [1917].

The weather is most depressing. Dark and rain every day. All hands seem cross. Zimmermann, I think finds it much more difficult to be the responsible first than the criticising second. It is not as easy as it looked to him.

The Kaiser, I hear *direct*, stated the other day that he did not expect peace now, that the English would try a great offensive in the Spring and would fail.

Hoover writes me that the Germans are violating all the pledges in Belgium. He expects a year of great difficulties

I hear this confirmed on the best authority and that even the German official who is supposed to see that food is not sent from Belgium to Germany, in violation of Germany's pledges, sends out butter to his family.

I hear on the best authority that there is an absolute reign of terror in Belgium. Sudden and arbitrary arrests etc. I think the Germans want to see all foreign diplomats out of Bucharest and Brussels and the charges against Vopicka¹ should be considered in this light.

Whitlock in Brussels is, I hear, sick mentally and physically and ought to have a rest in a sanitarium. He is writing a book.

Villalobar, the Spanish Minister, a cripple who literally comes apart, but a man of extra[or]dinary energy and force, has completely overshadowed Whitlock in Belgium.

The Embassy here seems in good condition.

The Ruddocks[2] are here on a visit from Belgium and Kirk and his mother[3] (he is a brother of Mrs Ruddock) have been in Belgium recently.

The greatest danger re submarine war is that unthinking persons in the United States may start a crusade against the President's policy, encourage the Germans in the belief that we are devided and lead them to resume reckless acts in that belief. The continuance of a strong front is the best way to keep the peace.

Both Zimmermann and the Chancellor asked me about Bernstorff and, returning good for evil, I said that he was O.K., on very good terms with the government, well liked, and that no one could do better. One of his kind friends sent Zimmermann the "Sketch" bathing picture.[4]

The Germans will do nothing about Belgium. The deportation was a military measure, demanded by Ludendorff, who constantly fears a British landing on the Belgian coast.

On fair authority—a man who called on von Tirpitz recently was told by von T that he, von T, was watched like a spy and all his letters opened. Von T said that Hindenburg was the real ruler of Germany, that anything Bethman[n] said was censored by H. and that H was now against reckless submarine war but that any substantial defeats in the field would make him change his mind. Von T said that the K was losing his mind and spent all his time praying and learning Hebrew.

The food situation grows worse. Potato cards must now be presented in restaurants and hotels. I doubt if the potatoes can last beyond April. There is food in Rumania but much will go to troops, Austrians and Turks, and railways are so used by troops etc. that it is doubtful if any food from there can reach Germany for months.

All apartment houses in Berlin are closed at nine and lights in halls extinguished. Theatres close at ten and cinos. There is want of coal due to lack of transportation.   Yours   J.W.G.

TLI (SDR, RG 59, 763.72/3107½, DNA).

[1] That is, Charles Joseph Vopicka, United States Minister to Rumania, Serbia, and Bulgaria. In early January 1917, the German government had requested his withdrawal from Bucharest. According to news reports published at that time, the German government had charged him with unneutral acts in that he had undertaken to protect subjects of Entente nations when the German army occupied Bucharest. On January 14, Zimmermann confirmed that Vopicka's withdrawal had been requested but denied that the reason was his alleged unneutrality. The request, he said, applied to all diplomatic representatives in Bucharest who had remained there instead of following the Rumanian court to its new seat of government in Jassy. However, the State Department announced on January 19 that it had given Germany a satisfactory explanation in response to its charges of unneutral conduct and that that government had therefore withdrawn them. Vopicka, it said, would probably take a leave of absence and then go to Jassy. *New York Times*, Jan. 6, 7, 16, and 20, 1916.

[2] Albert Billings Ruddock and Margaret Kirk Ruddock.

3 That is, Alexander Comstock Kirk and Clara Comstock (Mrs. James A.) Kirk.

4 A photographic illustration in the London *Sketch*, XCVI (Oct. 25, 1916), 73. It showed a smiling Bernstorff in beach attire with one arm around each of two attractive young women, also in bathing suits. The caption read in part: *"The Imperial German Ambassador at Washington on Holiday Bent: Count Bernstorff S'Amuse."*

From Robert Lansing, with Enclosure

PERSONAL AND PRIVATE:

My dear Mr. President: January 23, 1917.

I enclose to you a letter dated December 29th received from Mr. Page at Rome, which is of very real interest in connection with the situation in Italy.

Faithfully yours,   Robert Lansing

CCL (SDR, RG 59, 763.72119/307½, DNA).

E N C L O S U R E

Thomas Nelson Page to Robert Lansing

CONFIDENTIAL

My dear Mr. Secretary,   Rome December 29, 1916.

I telegraphed you two or three days ago of a curious report brought to me of the Vatican's suggestion about America's power to make peace.[1] I did not, however, telegraph the whole story, but I want you to have it just as I got it.

My informant is a man of high character and I feel sure that what was said to him was intended for my ears, even though he was not sent directly to me. He said that he had been sent for to go over there and on arrival was told by Cardinal Gasparri, the papal secretary of state, that America had it in her power to make peace within twenty-four hours if she wished to do so. He said: "How does Your Eminence mean?" And the cardinal said: "Simply by acting as a neutral in fact as well as in theory." He then went into a little discussion as to two kinds of neutrality, one a neutrality which followed the strict letter of the law, the other a neutrality which followed the spirit of the law. The first, he said, was the neutrality which America was following, but if instead of this she would follow the spirit of the law, as Spain had done and would stop all trading whatever with the Allies in as much as she could not trade with the Central Empires, the war would come to an immediate end and peace would be concluded. My informant suggested that for America to do this might be considered by the Allies at this stage as a hostile act. To this the cardinal replied substantially that governments could always find ways in which to meet such difficulties and that it would be easy for the United States, in as much as she was always having questions arise between her and Japan, to bring one of these questions to a point at which she might proclaim to the world that she could not longer send munitions and food supplies, etc., to foreign countries because she must reserve them for her own possible imperative use. Thus she would obviate the danger to which my informant alluded and at the same time need have no apprehension that Japan would wish to engage in war with her, and the question with Japan could be settled afterwards without serious trouble.

The story is so curious that I feel that the President and you will be interested to know it. I have no doubt, however, of the accuracy of the report made to me.

Believe me, my dear Mr. Secretary,

Faithfully yours,   Thos. Nelson Page

TLS (SDR, RG 59, 763.72119/307½, DNA).
¹ T. N. Page to RL, Dec. 26, 1916, T telegram (SDR, RG 59, 763. 72119/259, DNA). The relevant portion of this brief dispatch reads as follows: "Learn from Vatican sources Vatican says America can stop war in twenty-four hours if would act as it terms with absolute neutrality and stop all trading with Allies. This would confirm opinion frequently stated that Vatican's sympathies are with Central Empire."

From Robert Lansing

PERSONAL AND PRIVATE:

My dear Mr. President: Washington January 23, 1917.

You will recall I sent you, about the middle of December, this paper entitled AMERICANISM, stating that I had in mind using it for a public address. You replied advising me that you thought it would be unwise to deliver it at this particular time, and then suggested that it might be possible for me to maintain the general theory without making a specific application.

I hesitate to impose upon your time, when you are under such a great pressure, to ask you to look over the revision of the latter part of the paper, and yet, I feel that in view of your address yesterday, especially your remarks concerning the consent of the governed, that an utterance of this sort would not be untimely and would be very much in accord with your theory.

I am, therefore, taking the liberty of submitting the revision to you, which begins on page 6 of the paper, as, of course, I should not make a public declaration of this sort without your entire approval.[1]   Faithfully yours,   Robert Lansing.

TLS (WP, DLC).

[1] In revising his paper of December 5 (summarized in WW to RL, Dec. 19, 1916, n. 1), Lansing, removed references to the inherent defectiveness of a league open to all nations and to the desirability of setting qualifications based on democratic political institutions. However, he retained the view that all believers in democracy should "earnestly desire its universal acceptance by all nations" in order to "furnish a sure foundation for universal peace." TS MS, Dec. 5, 1916, revised Jan. 1917 (WP, DLC).

From Edward Mandell House

Dear Governor: New York. January 23, 1917.

The echoes of the speech sound increasingly good. The Manchester Guardian,[1] so far, has the best comment and warns the British Government in no uncertain terms.

Hoover was with me again today and I extracted this suggestion from him which seems well worth consideration. It is that the next move should be to ask each of the belligerent governments whether they agree to the principles laid down in your speech. If not, to what do they object. If they agree then it is well within your province to ask them to meet in conference.

Sir William Wiseman has not returned from Washington as he thought it best to remain there today in order to get the full opinion of the Allied group.

Whitehouse is tremendously pleased.

Your affectionate,   E. M. House

TLS (WP, DLC).

[1] In news dispatches printed on January 23, 1917, the New York *Evening Post* quoted extensively from editorial comment in British newspapers. Under a headline, "How Allied Capitals View Wilson's Address," it quoted the *Guardian* as follows:

"The speech in form was addressed to the Senate, but it equally concerns ourselves and our adversaries in the war. The President has no intention of taking any part in the actual negotiations of terms of peace; that he leaves wholly to the belligerents. He simply comes forward now to state in unmistakable terms, both for his own people and for the other people of the world, every one of whom is directly concerned, what kind of peace it is which he will consent to call upon his countrymen to approve and sustain.

"It is a splendid policy, nobly expressed. How will it be received? By the peoples everywhere we cannot doubt joyfully; by men of good-will and enlightenment everywhere not less joyfully and with a clear perception that this is no vision of Utopia, but a well thought-out and justly framed scheme of a man in a great position and versed in great affairs."

From Herbert David Croly

Dear Mr. President: New York City January 23, 1917

I should like to add one small word of congratulation to the many letters which you must be receiving about your recent address to the Senate in favor of the institution of peace. It seems to me that in that address you marshal with great lucidity and eloquence every important fact which has been brought up by the two and a half years of world warfare, and every important principle which the experience of that two and a half years has made authoritative and real. It is, I am sure, a document which will leave a permanent mark on the moral consciousness of, and I hope in the actual institution, of the American people, and which will reverberate throughout history.

May I make one suggestion? There seems to be a tendency among Republicans all over the country, but particularly in Congress, definitely to oppose the participation of the United States in a League of Nations under any conditions. They seem to have decided to try to make party capital out of it. Of course they are making a great mistake in doing this, but the fact that they have done it makes it very important for you to appeal to public opinion behind their backs and to make sure that you have it. Would it not be well after Congress adjourns to make a certain number of speeches throughout the country appealing directly to the people, as you did this time last year when the success of your preparedness programme seemed temporarily imperilled? I do not think your present programme is in any way endangered, but in such an important matter it is well to make assurance doubly sure, and it is almost necessary to weaken those Republicans in their own constituencies who are trying to obtain some partizan advantage from this important issue. From all I can make out, you will have little difficulty in securing almost unanimous popular endorsement throughout the Middle West, provided the matter is presented to them as effectively as it is in your power to do it. I hope you will give careful consideration to this idea.   Sincerely yours, Herbert Croly

TLS (WP, DLC).

From Charles Richard Crane

Boston, Mass., January 23, 1917.

Although Mr. Olney is at Brooks Hospital following operation Saturday he is very happy about the address yesterday and hopes to make an important comment on it tomorrow for world especially emphasizing the wisdom of having a peace not founded on victory. He says that you are the one world's statesman to strike this note and that it is vital. He sends you his congratulations and greetings, so do Mrs. Crane and I to the White House family.

                                                    Chas. R. Crane.

T telegram (WP, DLC).

From Andrew Carnegie

My dear Mr. President: New York January 23rd, 1917.

   Yesterday you told the whole world that peace must reign throughout that world, and we all know that the world will have to hearken to those words. This is the greatest service ever rendered by any President, and if your "Life of Washington" and "History of the American People" have not already made you immortal, your address to the Senate yesterday cannot fail to do so.

                        Yours ever,   Andrew Carnegie

TLS (WP, DLC).

From Harry Augustus Garfield

Dear Mr. President: Williamstown, Mass. Jan. 23/17.

   I rejoice in the noble message you have just given to the world. Let the ungenerous ones howl—those personally involved in the war on either side are forgivable—& the critics darken council with words; your message will be received.

                With affection & high regard,   H. A. Garfield.

ALS (WP, DLC).

From Franklin Knight Lane

My dear Mr. President: Washington January 23, 1917.

   I inclose you a memorandum as to the naval oil reserves, a copy of which I am also sending to Secretary Daniels and Mr. Gregory.[1]

   Commissioner Tallman informs me that the decision in the Honolulu case is not necessarily decisive as to any other claims within Naval Oil Reserve No. 2. That this is so is conclusively shown by the fact that the Land Office has filed charges and ordered proceedings against twenty out of the twenty-one remaining applications within Reserve No. 2, and that the twenty-first claim is involved in an adverse suit in the courts.[2]

Very truly yours,　Franklin K. Lane

TLS (WP, DLC).

[1] This unsigned and undated memorandum (T MS, WP, DLC), "Naval Oil Reserves and Pending Legislation," related primarily to Naval Petroleum Reserve No. 2, Buena Vista Hills, near Taft, Cal. An amendment proposed by Senator Phelan to the general leasing bill would permit various claimants to lease about 4,986 acres in Reserve No. 2, which, the memorandum stated, was "not a feasible reservoir" for the navy because of the "situation of patented lands" which had "producing oil wells and of the large number of wells upon the unpatented lands." The memorandum concluded as follows: "The need of the public for oil and gasoline and the prevention of monopoly in these necessities, as well as the very great present demand for phosphate and potash, call urgently for the enactment of this legislation." Wilson thanked Lane for the memorandum and commented: "I am glad to get all the light I can." WW to F. K. Lane, Jan. 25, 1917, TLS Letterpress Books, WP, DLC.

[2] For an account of the case arising from the claim of the Honolulu Consolidated Oil Co., see J. Leonard Bates, *The Origins of Teapot Dome: Progressives, Parties, and Petroleum, 1909-1921* (Urbana, Ill., 1963). Tallman had recommended to Lane in favor of the Honolulu Company's claim, but Daniels had objected and referred the matter to Wilson. Wilson met with Lane, Daniels, and Gregory on January 19, before the cabinet meeting, and went to the Capitol on January 22 to discuss the pending legislation with Senators Phelan, Pittman, Myers, Walsh, and Thomas. *New York Times*, Jan. 23, 1917.

From William Kent

Dear Mr. President:　　　　　[Washington] January 23, 1917.

Your message concerning peace and foreign relations is to my mind a noble statement of ideals and conditions, and I believe will do great good in this troubled world. You see clearly and clearly state the obvious fact that isolation is henceforth impossible for our country, and that if we are to live under reasonable terms in a world free from fear, we must take upon ourselves the burden of providing our share in international law-making and in the stern task of enforcing international law. As a citizen of a peaceful country and no mean country, I wish to thank you.

Yours truly,　[William Kent]

CCL (W. Kent Papers, CtY).

To William Kent

My dear Mr. Kent:　　　　　The White House 23 January, 1917

Your letter of today about my message yesterday has given me a great deal of pleasure of the deepest sort, and I want to thank you for it out of a very full heart.

Cordially and sincerely yours,　Woodrow Wilson

TLS (W. Kent Papers, CtY).

From Lloyd Walley Curtis[1]

Personal

Your Excellency: Great Lakes, Illinois, January 23, 1917.

As a Medical Officer of 35 years service in the Navy, which I believe I can claim, on the records, to have been respectable, I venture to address you, as Commander-in-Chief, with this petition for a reconsideration of your present purpose to promote over me a medical officer[2] who stands 128 numbers below me [on] the list of medical officers of the Navy.

My object in this plea is not with the view to any material benefit to myself; my aspiration for higher place in the service having vanished with my unsuccessful application for appointment as Surgeon General of the Navy, at the time the present incumbent of that office was appointed.

Sir, my only purpose, is to express the humiliation I should feel, in being subordinated to an officer so many years my junior in age and service.

I would say further in support perhaps of what may be regarded as a vain plea, that I too have done, or have thought to do you, sir, some personal service—not it is true in the way you so highly esteem, as performed by the officer you purpose to honor; in substantiation of which statement I beg to submit the enclosed copies of two letters to the public press.[3]

Very respectfully,
Your obedient servant,   L. W. Curtis

TLS (WP, DLC).
[1] Lloyd Walley Curtis, captain, Medical Corps, United States Navy, since August 7, 1912.
[2] That is, Grayson.
[3] Curtis had written two letters from Newport, R. I., to the Editor of the *New York Times*. In the first, dated September 21, 1916, and signed "L. W. Curtis," he praised Wilson's address on Lincoln of September 4, 1916. In the second, "A Diagnosis," which was not published, Curtis wrote sarcastically that Theodore Roosevelt's violent denunciations of Wilson indicated that Roosevelt was nervous and excited and was perhaps suffering from a "convulsive emission of mephitic vapors." The first letter was published by the *New York Times*, clipping (WP, DLC). The unpublished letter was M.D. to the Editor of the *New York Times*, Oct. 13, 1916, CCL (WP, DLC).

Robert Lansing to Joseph Patrick Tumulty, with Enclosure

Dear Mr. Tumulty: Washington January 23, 1917.

I enclose herewith, for the President's information, a copy of a despatch from the American Minister at Peking regarding his interview on the occasion of his presentation of the President's letter to the President of China.

The President's letter referred to was simply the usual formal acknowledgment of the announcement by the President of China of his assumption of the duties of his office.

I am, my dear Mr. Tumulty,

Very truly yours,   Robert Lansing

TLS (WP, DLC).

E N C L O S U R E

Paul Samuel Reinsch to Robert Lansing

No. 1294.

Sir: Peking, December 8, 1916.

I have the honor to report that, having received your instruction No. 517 of October 25th, enclosing a letter from the President of the United States to the President of China, I asked for a special appointment and presented the President's letter to His Excellency Li Yuan-hung today.

President Li expressed his high gratification at receiving the President's communication, the sentiments of which he fully reciprocated. In the course of the ensuing conversation, President Li expressed himself at some length concerning the American loan to China. He stated that China highly appreciated the benefits resulting from President Wilson's policy of refusing to countenance a fiscal monopoly in China in 1913, and thus delivering China from domination by a hard and fast combination of capital. As a complement to the President's action in 1913, the encouragement now given by the American Government to an independent American loan is also most highly appreciated. President Li stated that it was the firm purpose of his Government to use the proceeds of this loan exclusively for strengthening the credit of the Bank of China. He was determined not to allow any diversion of the funds for other purposes. Should the larger loan be concluded, it would probably be the policy of the Chinese Government to use the proceeds mainly for the establishment of a national industrial bank. The President agreed that the funds so employed should be administered with the greatest care, in order that real benefit should come through the encouragement of sound industrial enterprises. As to the security, the President stated that as the revenues from government sales of tobacco and spirits already amounted to $10,000,000. a year, it could be taken as certain that, with the reorganization of the system, which was now being undertaken, a revenue far in excess of the needs of the American loan service could be confidently expected.

President Li also expressed his highest appreciation of the personal attention which President Wilson has given to Chinese affairs during the last four years, and especially the fact that whenever agreements concerning China had been made, the American Government had taken steps to safeguard the rights of China and the principle of equal opportunity. In conclusion, he admitted that he realized that America could help China best in a measure as China helped herself through introducing efficiency into her administration.

I have the honor to be, Sir,

Your obedient servant,   Paul S. Reinsch.

CCL (WP, DLC).

ADDENDA

From Martha Berry[1]

Mount Berry, Georgia

My dear Mr. Wilson: November 19, 1914.

The girls in the Berry School wanted to decorate Mrs. Wilson's grave with flowers, so they walked in from the school to Myrtle Hill and each girl carried some flowers they had grown at Berry School to place on her grave. One of the members of the school made some pictures of the girls and they wanted you to have these pictures, so I am sending them to you under separate cover.

We wish very much to have a letter from you about our schools to frame with your photograph. We have a framed letter and photograph of Mr. Roosevelt, also one of Mr. Taft; and we are most anxious to have a letter from you to frame with your photograph.

We have a photograph of Edward Ax[s]on and one of Mrs. Wilson, which we greatly appreciate. Mrs. Wilson's endowing a scholarship in Berry School in memory of her brother has made her seem peculiarly near to us. We deeply appreciate this scholarship, which will help and bless poor boys so long as there is need of helping poor boys.

We hope that some day we may have the great privilege of having you visit our school.

Sincerely yours,   Martha Berry

TLS (WP, DLC).
[1] For Wilson's reply, see WW to Martha Berry, Nov. 21, 1914, Vol. 31.

From Anne Leddell Seward[1]

My dear President Wilson,   Boston July 2nd [1915]

As a niece of former Secretary of State, William H. Seward, I make bold to write you about a matter of doubtless no weight whatever, but of potential seriousness.

Last June in Germany I met socially a prominent Berlin banker. He is now here as (I am convinced) a secret but intimate emissary from the Kaiser. Whether his mission be friendly and his presence here harmless his utterances are distinctly offensive and his threats alarming. His national prominence in Germany and his high military rank coupled with his numerous aliases, his frequent changes of address give rise to uncomfortable suspicions. I have recently met him at dinners in New York three times and I feel increasing uneasiness from his sojourn here.

While seeking to do no injustice to a quasi-acquaintance and desiring above all to avoid publicity I nevertheless feel I cannot decently shrink from putting in your way means of probing a sinister situation or one which points to organized antagonism.

I prefer not to write the conversations which caused me to communicate with you but if I knew where to reach Mr. Axson, your brother-in-law, I could easily tell him. My address will be Kennebunkport Maine should you ever decide to notice the matter. Having freed my conscience by telling you I can only hope you will understand the spirit in which this is written and believe me

Sincerely at your service,   (Miss) Anne L. Seward

ALS (SDR, RG 59, Office of the Counselor—German Activities, DNA).
[1] This is the letter that is noted as missing in WW to Anne L. Seward, Vol. 33, p. 473.

Nine Letters from Ellen Axson Wilson to Jessie Woodrow Wilson (Sayre)

My precious little girl,   Princeton, Dec. 12, 1906

. . . Your father has just ridden off looking very fine indeed in his new riding togs; this is the first day he has worn them. They have a nice little ladies' horse now at the stable, and you and Margaret are to have a few rides,—at least enough to learn. Mr. McElroy[1] has offered to act as teacher. He goes every day and rides superbly. . . .

Your devoted Mother.

[1] Robert McElroy, Edwards Professor of American History at Princeton.

My darling,   Princeton, April 12 [1907].

. . . Your father was so wretchedly ill and so depressed all the week that I could hardly leave his side for a moment. But he is much better at last and has gone to New York to give his Columbia lecture today. I sadly fear it will bring on a relapse but the doctor consented he should take the risk. . . .

Your devoted Mother.

My darling, Princeton, Oct. 3 [Oct. 2, 1907].

I am sending off the books today,—the dictionary & the "State." The latest copy we have in the house is 1898 but your father has not revised it since then, so I suppose it is all right. Your father is out just now and so I am waiting until he comes in to ask if he has the other book. I am so sorry, dear, that I forgot to see about this sooner. We have all been under such a terrible strain for two weeks or so over the struggle in the faculty that I suppose it was inevitable that *something* should be forgotten! The insulting "counter-resolution" proposed last week in faculty, which was virtually a vote of want of confiidence in your father and a refusal to hear him explain his views and defend himself, was defeated on Monday by a vote of 81 to 23.[1] On Monday next they will proceed to discuss the whole case on its merits and your father will make his speech. His friends are very much pleased at the result of this "first round" and everyone is sure that the final result (in faculty) is now a foregone conclusion. Dr Van Dyke proposed the counter-resolution, reading it in a manner that was the most studied insult in itself, and then Mr. *Hibben seconded it*!! People could hardly believe either their eyes or their ears. Of course he has (being very slow and stupid) been made a tool of by those malignants, Van Dyke and West, and does not realize what he has done. But since our brains were given us to use that is no excuse. The veriest youngsters in the faculty who had been here but a year understood perfectly and were boiling with indignation—holding in fact "indignation meetings." The whole university was so tremendously aroused over it that the enemy took alarm—seeing that they had made a serious strategic blunder in showing their venom so plainly,—so at the Monday meeting they amended the wording of their resolution and made very specious and smooth speeches. But for that clever move of theirs they would have had a much smaller vote even than the 23. Mr. Hibben is called the "Brutus" of the conspiracy, and everyone says his influence and prestige in the faculty are gone forever.

The *committee* of the *trustees* meet on Friday and the trustees on the 17th., and then all will be over for good or ill. The trustees are certainly "weakening" terribly, but your father may be able to brace them up again. He has been so hurt by Mr. Hibben that he doesn't seem to care very much *how* it goes; and I am so anxious about his health that I will be almost glad to have it all end with his resignation. Not that he is at all ill now, but he is

not strong enough to be so racked by pain and heart-break
as he has been in the last two weeks. . . .

Your devoted Mother.

¹ See the extracts from the minutes of the Princeton faculty printed at Sept.
26 and Sept. 30, 1907, Vol. 17.

My darling,   Princeton, Oct. 19, 1907.

I think you have some idea of what a desperately strenuous
time it has been for the last two weeks and how impossible it has
been for me to write even to my dear girls. I simply *had* to
leave it to Margaret. Things were so tense with your father that
I had to be with him a large part of the time;—Aunt Saidie and
the Smiths¹ were here,—also Katie Murray.² Margaret's clothes
had to be planned, and bought, in Phila., and all the arrangements made, notes written, &c. &c. for the freshman reception,
the trustee luncheon and the visit of Ambassador Bryce on the
31st.³

Well, the trustee meeting is over at last and they did desert
your father according to prediction,—and yet somehow we are all
feeling better and more hopeful than we did before it. Margaret
wrote you that the Trustee committee,⁴ which met ten days or
more ago, found that the board were determined to beat a retreat
in the face of the storm in New York, and that Pyne & Dodge,⁵
members of the committee, were bowing their heads to the same
storm. And also that your father had told them (the committee)
that he would of course resign when the board met. For two
days we felt that it was all settled and it was a real relief to
have it so. But the storm of appeal and entreaty was so tremendous that finally your father was made to see that his resignation
at this time would mean utter ruin for the University, and that it
would in a way be dishonourable to desert the friends who have
stood by him so splendidly. Dodge & Pyne were the most frenzied
of all in their efforts to keep him. Dodge said he would never
have done anything much for Princeton but for his love for and
faith in Woodrow;—as it was he had really pledged his fortune
to it. Of course you can see how impossible it was after that for
Woodrow to leave his post. So at the trustee meeting they voted
to reconsider and withdraw the resolution of last June, and at the
same time they voted to request the president "to continue his
endeavors to convince the board and all others concerned"!⁶ Our
side is delighted with the motion because the trustees have made
themselves (by its form as well as its substance,) supremely
ridiculous, and have left your father with all the honours of the

field. They do not attempt to deny that in June they voted *for* the quads and to abolish the clubs;—they merely take it back now, and so while your father is for the time being defeated he has not been in the least insulted or humiliated. It is really *better* that things should go more slowly for a time so that the unwholesome excitement stirred up by the clique here may have a chance to subside. Everyone will begin to grow more reasonable about it now and we all feel pretty sure that your father will win in the end. Of course there was a row in the board after all! Dodge & Pyne thought they had got everything arranged beforehand, your father having promised to fall in with their wishes and make no speech. But a large and important minority proved unwilling to make themselves so absurd and both spoke and voted against the Dodge resolution. Dodge says that if Wilson had said a word all would have gone his way again and he (Dodge) can never thank him enough for keeping silent and not pushing his advantage. Of course your father did not *want* them to vote again under excitement. Dodge & Pyne *mean* well; the real reason they weakened is that the New York Alumni, headed by Ledyard Blair,[7] were withdrawing their annual subscriptions, so that if it had been forced now, the college would have been in a serious financial difficulty. And Dodge couldn't have made it all up because at present "copper" has dropped away down in price.

Well, dearest, it is late, *late* & I haven't a moment for any other subject at present. We are all well though tired. You will see the Smiths in a few days and hear all our news from them. May God bless you, my darling, and make you happy in welldoing. With love inexpressible, I am as ever

Your devoted Mother.

[1] Lucy Marshall Smith, Mary Randolph Smith, and Saidie Cooper (Mrs. Thomas Alexander) Hoyt.

[2] Unidentified.

[3] About this affair, see the news report printed at Nov. 1, 1907, Vol. 17.

[4] That is, the special Committee on the Supplementary Report of the President, about which see, e.g., n. 1 to the draft of an announcement printed at Oct. 4, 1907, *ibid.*

[5] Moses Taylor Pyne and Cleveland Hoadley Dodge.

[6] See the minutes of the Princeton board of trustees printed at Oct. 17, 1907, *ibid.*

[7] Clinton Ledyard Blair, Princeton 1890, banker and capitalist of New York.

My darling,   Princeton Dec. 14, 1907

Just a line to enclose the check—for $25.00. Your father is better than when I last wrote though still far from comfortable. A troublesome hacking cough disturbs him at night and makes him more tired in the day than he would otherwise be. But the inflammation in the arm is sufficiently relieved now for him to be massaged and that is a great comfort to him; he has it every day, and on that account will not think of leaving home before the holidays. . . .   Your devoted Mother.

My darling,   Princeton, Jan. 14, 1908.

Margaret, I am glad to say, has written all about the trustee meeting; for I think it would make me ill to have to go over it all again![1] It is all pretty bad, yet we must not exaggerate the troubles. The vote was only ten to nine against him, and I doubt whether all those ten would have voted so in a more clearly drawn issue. They probably did not all realize that it was "against *him*"! I think if we can be patient and get someone to offer *money* for it we will certainly win in the end. Those cowardly trustees are hardly responsible for what they do now, they are in such a panic over the money question. Your father is in the mood for a stern fight now, and has no idea of resigning under two years at any rate. He seems very well and even cheerful. He sails, you know, early Saturday morning. We will spend Friday night in New York and go to a play,—I don't know what.

There has been no news since Margaret wrote you except that our old house is sold to Mrs. Maitland,[2] Mrs McCosh's newly widowed daughter. It is an excellent thing, for she will be next her sister, and she is all alone, you know,— has no children. They will extend it at the back so as to make a larger dining-room and laundry. Margaret sang at the little musical club and made the most charming impression on everyone,—Mrs. Michaud,[3] Mrs. Wykoff,[4] Ann Armstrong[5] and various other really musical people who had never heard her before. They were *genuinely* charmed—and declare her voice *exquisite*! We are all *so* pleased! Next week they are to have a Grieg memorial meeting and she is learning two *lovely* Grieg songs.

I suppose you have heard from Nell.[6] She seemed very gay and happy when she wrote;—is especially overjoyed because her friend Helen has joined the fraternity after all. Stockton is still very unwell but is giving his lectures. Did the express package reach you safely? With haste and dearest love

                              Your devoted Mother.

[1] See the minutes of the Princeton board of trustees printed at Jan. 9, 1908, Vol. 17.
[2] Mary Jane (Mrs. Alexander) Maitland.
[3] Jennie W. (Mrs. Régis) Michaud.
[4] Leah Lucile Ehrich (Mrs. Walter Augustus) Wykoff.
[5] Anne Armstrong, about whom see WW to EAW, Jan. 26, 1907, Vol. 17.
[6] At this time, Eleanor was a student at St. Mary's School in Raleigh, N. C.

My darling,   Princeton, New Jersey May 8, 1910.

. . . We shall have visitors all the week, Mrs. Peck[1] tomorrow and next day, and some others Wednesday. Your father is in bed again today, but more as a precaution and to avoid talking all day to the minister (Dr. McIlvaine).[2] He (your father) spoke at the Bankers Ass. night before last[3] and his throat being still weak he renewed the trouble somewhat.

There is no news as to the situation but he gets numbers of fine letters from Alumni. There are many indications that they understand the game that New York is trying to work. Did I tell you about the "Princetonian" dinner and the perfectly *tremendous* ovation the boys gave him.[4] I must have done so. Everyone is saying that it was the most "*beautiful* speech" they ever heard him make. Mr. Spaeth (senior)[5] says "the most beautiful *anybody* ever made." He told his class that the greatest compliment they ever had was that Woodrow Wilson thought them *worthy* to be so spoken to. . . .   Your devoted Mother.

[1] Mary Allen Hulbert (Mrs. Thomas Dowse) Peck.
[2] The Rev. Dr. James Hall McIlvaine, Princeton 1866, rector of Calvary Episcopal Church in Pittsburgh. Dr. McIlvaine was preacher in the Marquand Chapel on May 8.
[3] Wilson's address to the New Jersey Bankers' Association is printed at May 6, 1910, Vol. 20.
[4] See the news report of this speech printed at April 30, 1910, *ibid.*
[5] John Duncan Spaeth, preceptor in the English Department at Princeton University.

My darling,   The White House Dec. 19, 1913

. . . Your father is, of course, better but still far from well. So it is settled that we must have three weeks holiday on his account and we are going to Pass Christian, Miss. We *hope* to get off on Tuesday, for they have actually decided to vote on the Currency Bill tonight. It seems too good to be true. I'll believe it when it happens.

There is no reason to be *anxious* about your father. He is quite well of the grip,—but needs now to be rested and built up. He is hard at work again, but the work brings on severe head-aches, showing a generally depressed condition. His heart, blood pressure, and all his organs are in perfectly good condition. . . .

Your tenderly devoted,   Mother.

My darling,   The White House Feb 20, 1914.

. . . And finally your father's indisposition of course took a good deal of my time. He had another heavy feverish cold and was in bed several days. It has almost gone now, but a rather sharp attack of indigestion followed it and he is still in rather bad shape—but nothing serious.

Feb. 23. . . . Your father is *quite* well again—and looks well. It is snowing hard and he has gone to an open air Washington's birthday affair, so I am rather anxious about him. But he is to be carefully protected, they say. . . .

Your devoted Mother.

ALS (received from Eleanor Axson Sayre).

Seven Letters from Helen Woodrow Bones to Jessie Woodrow Wilson Sayre

Dearest Jessierite,   The White House October 17, 1914

I was so perfectly delighted to get a letter from you! It certainly would be good to see you in your dear new home, but better even than seeing it myself would be to have your father go up for a few days' rest with you. If only you could beg him into it! He says he will *not* leave Washington and really he is very well; but he is very tired too, and it seems a crime for him to begin the winter's work tired out. This is one case where I believe it would be perfectly justifiable to play his love for you against his decision, which latter sounds reasonable enough. Can't you be a "little Ann"?

. . . It's hard on your father not to have a golf partner; but Mr. Brown[1] is to get here on Tuesday thank fortune, and he knows how to keep quiet when he should and speak (not about business) when he should. . . .

Lots of love to *all* of you from   Helen

PS Margaret, the Smiths, etc., are hanging on at C.,[2] hoping against hope that we can get your father to go.

[1] That is, Edward T. Brown.
[2] Cornish, N. H.

Dearest little Cousin,   The White House November 21, 1914

Of course you've seen in the papers that your father is to spend Thanksgiving with you, but unless Dr. G. has written you to the same effect you don't believe it. However, it is pretty nearly a sure thing—just think, he has actually promised to go "if . . . nothing unfor[e]seen happens," and he said to-night he thought nothing would! They (he and the doctor) expect to get to Williamstown Wednesday at four o'clock or thereabouts and they must start back Friday—that's what your father says now, but perhaps things will turn out differently.

The doctor says he means to stay at the hotel, so don't have him on your mind. Oh, I'm *so* glad your father is at last to see you in your dear little home! . . .

Margaret and I went for a long ride in the open car with your father this afternoon and almost froze to death. When we got home your father declared he had never suffered more keenly having pleasure! Now Maggie has gone out to a committee meeting and your father is reading and my puppy and I are writing letters. . . .   Lots of love to you *all* from   Helen

The White House

Dearest little Jessierite,   December sixth [1914]

. . . Your father came back from Williamstown looking so refreshed! Before he went his face looked so tired and drawn that it made my heart ache—for the effect of the little visit to New York soon wore off—and when he came home he seemed quite another man. He was so full of you and your little home and the pleasant time he'd had, with everybody so considerate of him! It was great to hear him tell about it and I've heard him talking to several people about his visit and how sweet your little house is.

It must have seemed queer to you that I didn't even let you know that I wasn't going up with your father. I thought that my saying your father and Dr. G. were to go would show M. & I were not—and never thought of explaining, because it seemed to me your fathers going was the all-important thing. . . . I did feel that a change of company would be better for your father than being surrounded with the circle he sees every day here. . . .

Your father and Margaret are out riding this afternoon. . . .

On Tuesday your father will greet Congress with one of his wonderful messages. I wish I thought a third of the men he will address were worth the time and breath the message will take— let alone the great thoughts in it! Pearls before swine!

With loads of love to the Sayre family,

Your loving   Helen

Darling Jessierite,   The White House April 12, 1915

. . . Your father will try to make up his mind about the visit to you at once. That is, to see his way fairly clear to it. He wants to know how much notice you ought to have, for you know he can't plan definitely twenty-four hours ahead. I told him I thought if you were expecting him within a certain number of days you wouldn't have to have any warning to speak of; isn't that true? I'll write you again as soon as he's "thot agin." . . .

Sister[1] stayed over a week. She had the time of her life playing golf with your father. Then in the evenings they and Margaret and Marion[2] would sing the old four-part songs your father and she used to sing when they were young. Margaret of course sang soprano and your father tenor; Sister sang alto and Marion *bass*! I think your father had a good time, but it was a little hard on Margaret. . . .

With loads of love, you dear child, to you and your blessed baby and your dear old goose of a Frank, from   Helen

[1] Jessie Bones Brower.
[2] Marion McGraw Bones Erskine.

Darling Jessie,   The White House May 29, 1915

. . . I rather think I'll go up the last of June,[1] taking with me Mrs. Galt, a Washington woman (a dear friend of Dr. Grayson's) who has become a great friend of all of us. She is to spend July with us. . . .

By the way, don't say anything to any one about Mrs. Galt. The Howes, I think, feel rather badly about not being invited for July and we (or I, for she is my friend, chiefly) don't want them to learn of Mrs. G's being asked until she is there and they *must* know it. I hope you will like her, Jessie: she is a dear person; I'll always be grateful for Dr. Grayson for having brought us together, for she has saved my life walking with me and seeing I get out a lot.

. . . Now have I given you any idea of our plans for the summer? You see, of course, that Hamlet is left out. I knew he would be; it can't be helped, I suppose. He means to try to get up for week-ends and we must all pray that he will be able to. Bless his heart!—he is so cheerful and so unconcerned about himself! He seems to be able to stand the strain simply by not considering himself at all. He really is well, though one of his bad headaches yesterday made him give up Cabinet meeting. To-day he seems quite himself. . . .

Loads of love, you darling, for all three of you from   Helen

[1] That is, to Cornish.

Sweetest little Girl   The White House March 8, 1916

. . . Honey, I'll ask your father point-blank, as soon as I can see him for more than a moment, just what he said about our Navy. I have wondered myself about it, but have never thought to ask him. He never by any chance discusses "affairs" in our—Margaret's and my—presence and we know no more about what is going on than any one else who can read the newspapers. The other day Nell let me read your last letter to her and in it you said that she was the only one who ever told you of what was going on. I stopped when I got to that and exclaimed, "Why, Nell, how can Margie and I tell her anything! Your father never says an interesting word in our presence!" Then we both shrieked, for it was quite a shocking thing to say, of course, and yet had come popping out so spontaneously that we were both startled. And really, when one is simply *aching* to know a *little* of what is really happening, small talk is perfectly maddening, and that's all we hear in the White House now—delightful small talk when it's from your father, of course, but really only small talk. It's *galling* (joke which should be appreciated by one Frank Sayre!)

I almost committed suicide when your father said he thought it might not look right for me to be in the Executive Gallery during the debates on the Armed Ship Resolutions—for that was one chance of hearing something interesting. He felt that some one might think he was "keeping tab" on the Senate and House if a member of the family were present. Of course I want to do anything in the world that will make him feel a little less worried, but my heart was quite broken. I did so long to be in the excitement. Marion and Bert[1] are here and Marion has been up there for a good many of the debates; and she was thrilled by it all, as it all came out right for Cousin Woodrow. Have you ever known anything so contemptible as the attitude of Congress? I'm *so* happy over the drubbing they've had! . . .

Lots of love to you and the Frances from   Helen

ALS (received from Eleanor Axson Sayre).
[1] Marion's husband, Robert Erskine.

Dearest little Mother: The White House July 9, 1916

. . . Your father was so interested in all I could tell him about the children. He is as sceptical as Frank, though, about Francis's conversation—it's meaning something, I mean. He approves very decidedly of spankings and says the trouble with children to-day is that they aren't *made* to do anything. When I told him of the change in Eleanor's disposition, or behavior, rather, he said to tell you not to worry, for you had the most violent temper when you were her age—that you howled till you were purple when you did not get what you wanted when you wanted it. So she can show a good deal more anger before you feel troubled.

He seems very well, though very tired. I hate the thought of New Jersey almost as much as Edith does, but I almost wish we were to go soon, if the air at that horrible place is at all bracing. I think he needs a change as much as a rest—some real air to breathe. It is absolutely true that there is none here: I don't mind it, except at night, but I feel a lot better for my two weeks at Williamstown.

Cousin Woodrow and Edith are leaving at six o'clock for Detroit, where your father is to make three speeches to-morrow. . . .   Your loving   Helen

TLS (received from Eleanor Axson Sayre).

INDEX

NOTE ON THE INDEX

THE alphabetically arranged analytical table of contents at the front of the volume eliminates duplication, in both contents and index, of references to certain documents, such as letters. Letters are listed in the contents alphabetically by name, and chronologically within each name by page. The subject matter of all letters is, of course, indexed. The Editorial Notes and Wilson's writings are listed in the contents chronologically by page. In addition, the subject matter of both categories is indexed. The index covers all references to books and articles mentioned in text or notes. Footnotes are indexed. Page references to footnotes which place a comma between the page number and "n" cite both text and footnote, thus: "624,n3." On the other hand, absence of the comma indicates reference to the footnote only, thus: "55n2"–the page number denoting where the footnote appears.

The index supplies the fullest known form of names and, for the Wilson and Axson families, relationships as far down as cousin. Persons referred to by nicknames or shortened forms of names can be identified by reference to entries for these forms of the names.

Two cumulative contents-index volumes are now in print: Volume 13, which covers Volumes 1-12, and Volume 26, which covers Volumes 14-25. Volume 39, which covers Volumes 27-38, is in preparation.

INDEX

WOODROW WILSON

APPOINTMENT SUGGESTIONS, APPOINTMENTS AND RESIGNATIONS